BLACKSTONE'S SALE AND SUPPLY OF GOODS AND SERVICES

For Ian Mackay,
Legal Accounts Manager
at the Temple Bar branch of the
National Westminster Bank plc
(and my overdraft therein)

BLACKSTONE'S SALE AND SUPPLY OF GOODS AND SERVICES

Richard Miles

BLACKSTONE
PRESS LIMITED

Published by
Blackstone Press Limited
Aldine Place
London W12 8AA
United Kingdom

Sales enquiries and orders
Telephone +44–(0)–20–8740–2277
Facsimile +44–(0)–20–8743–2292
e-mail: sales@blackstone.demon.co.uk
website: www.blackstonepress.com

ISBN 1–84174–120–5

First published 2001

British Library Cataloguing in Publication Data
A catalogue record for this book is available from the British Library

Typeset by Style Photosetting Ltd, Mayfield, East Sussex
Printed and bound in Great Britain by Antony Rowe Limited,
Chippenham and Reading

Contents

PART III: OWNERSHIP AND RISK

PART IV: TERMS IMPLIED IN FAVOUR OF THE BUYER

Preface

The law relating to the sale and supply of goods bridges the spectrum between complex commercial cases and the smallest small claims track cases. It affects businesses and consumers alike. Furthermore, since the litigation in *Dimond* v *Lovell* [1999] 3 All ER 1 many practitioners have taken the dramatic step of reading the Consumer Credit Act 1974 and litigation in this area has increased enormously, both in credit hire cases and general credit matters.

No one text can span this diverse field and satisfy both a commercial expert and a consumer one to the level which the more demanding of each expects. Accordingly, I have endeavoured to produce a comprehensive guide to the law surrounding these areas as it tends to arise from day to day in both commercial and consumer areas of general practice. I have tried to present the law as clearly as possible, avoiding the overly academic aspects where I can and concentrating upon the arguments which are likely to achieve success before a common law circuit judge.

Unlike most authors writing a preface such as this I have, unfortunately, received neither advice nor assistance from friends or colleagues in writing this text and accordingly (despite my best contortions of logic) it seems inescapable that the responsibility for any and all errors and failings rests entirely with myself. This being said, I must pass my thanks in advance to the proof-reading team at Blackstone Press who, from a brief reading of my draft, appear to have their work cut out! However, the errors were mine in the first place.

My thanks do, however, go to those solicitors and other friends who have been foolish enough to brief me in this area of the law over the past years, fuelling my enthusiasm for achieving windfall gains for insurance companies and bankrupting otherwise prosperous small businesses.

I make no apologies to any of those referred to in the model statements of case at Appendix A, none of whom is fictitious or dead, and none of whose inclusion was accidental. Their activities are, however, in most cases, out of character.

Finally, no preface from a barrister would be complete without a modicum of touting: if any of the areas covered by this text appear unclear in print, further advice is always available in chambers!

Richard Miles
The Chambers of Lord Campbell of Alloway QC,
2 King's Bench Walk, Temple,
London EC4Y 7DE
DX 477 Chancery Lane
Tel: 020 7353 9276
31 December 2000

Table of Cases

Table of Statutes

Table of Secondary Legislation

European secondary legislation

PART I
BACKGROUND

1 The contract of sale defined

1.1 THE STATUTORY DEFINITION

There are many types of contract under which the property in goods may pass, but this chapter is concerned with the contract of sale. Section 2 of the Sale of Goods Act 1979 (the '1979 Act') defines the contracts to which the Act applies:

> (1) A contract of sale of goods is a contract by which the seller transfers or agrees to transfer the property in goods to the buyer for a money consideration, called the price.
> (2) There may be a contract of sale between one part owner and another.
> (3) A contract of sale may be absolute or conditional.
> (4) Where under a contract of sale the property in the goods is transferred from the seller to the buyer the contract is called a sale.
> (5) Where under a contract of sale the transfer of the property in the goods is to take place at a future time or subject to some condition later to be fulfilled the contract is called an agreement to sell.
> (6) An agreement to sell becomes a sale when the time elapses or the conditions are fulfilled subject to which the property in the goods is to be transferred.

The section distinguishes the contract of sale from other contracts by which the property in goods is transferred. Since many of the 1979 Act's provisions are applied to similar contracts in identical terms under a series of 'sister Acts', such as the Supply of Goods Act 1982 and the Supply of Goods (Implied Terms) Act 1973, the distinction is of less practical importance in modern times than in the past.

The essence of the contract of sale is to transfer the property in the goods from the seller to the buyer. There are some points to note however. First, the contract of sale may be executed or executory, that is to say the contract may operate to immediately transfer the property in the goods under s. 18, rule 1 of the 1979 Act or it may operate to do so at a future date or upon fulfilment of specified conditions. An executed contract is known as a sale and an executory one an agreement to sell. Both forms of contract are 'contracts of sale' within the meaning of the 1979 Act by virtue of s. 61(1). Secondly, under s. 5 the goods in question may not exist or may not be owned by the seller at the time the contract is made; such goods yet to be acquired by the seller are known as 'future goods'. Where the seller purports to make an immediate sale of future goods the contract is not void but operates as an agreement to sell under s. 5(3).

The statutory definition may be broken down into several key elements: (a) a contract; (b) the subject matter of which is 'goods'; (c) that the contract operates to transfer the 'property' in those goods from the buyer to the seller; and (d) that the buyer provides a money consideration. It is these key elements which distinguish the contract of sale from other similar contracts which transfer the property in goods. This distinction is best explored by a comparison of similar contracts, but the individual components will be examined first.

1.2 A CONTRACT

The 1979 Act does not dictate any particular means by which a contract of sale may be made (s. 4 provides that it may be made in writing, or by word of mouth, or by a mixture of the two). This is governed by the ordinary rules of contract as to offer, acceptance and intention to create legal relations. It is the content of the contract that defines it as one of sale and not its form. There must, however, be a contract: a gift or deed will not suffice.

1.3 THE DEFINITION OF 'GOODS'

Section 61(1) of the 1979 Act defines 'goods' in the following terms:

> 'goods' includes[1] all personal chattels other than things in action and money, and in Scotland all corporeal moveables except money; and in particular 'goods' includes emblements, industrial growing crops, and things attached to or forming part of the land which are agreed to be severed before or under the contract of sale . . . .

In most cases there will be no difficulty in deciding whether the item or items in question are goods. The section defines goods as 'all personal chattels other than things in action and money'. The fact that the chattels in question must be personal distinguishes them from 'chattels real' which are associated with land, for example a lease. A personal chattel is any tangible item which is capable of possession and this extends to cars, boats, electrical items, animals, food, crops, building materials: the list is inexhaustive. A thing or chose in action is merely an intangible right which may be enforced by legal action to gain the benefit which is the subject matter of the right: this includes items such as debts, shares, copyrights and patents. Difficulties do arise, however, particularly where the transaction is governed by another Act. The following sections give a guide to the distinctions between goods and similar items listed below:

(a) Goods and land.
(b) Goods and money.

---

1. Note that the definition is not exclusive.

(c) Goods and animals.
(d) Goods and ships.
(e) Goods and the human body.
(f) Goods and electricity or other energy sources.
(g) Goods and computer software.

1.3.1 Goods and land

It may at first seem strange to consider land as the subject matter of a contract for the sale of goods. The definition does, however, state that 'emblements, industrial growing crops, and things attached to or forming part of the land which are agreed to be severed before or under the contract of sale' are within the definition of goods. Thus crops (see, e.g., *Scully* v *South* [1931] NZLR 1187), trees (*Kursell* v *Timber Operators and Contractors* [1927] 1 KB 298), fixtures, minerals (see section 1.3.3 below), clay or soil are all capable of being the subject matter of a contract of sale. Section 205(1)(x) of the Law of Property Act 1925 defines land as including:

> land of any tenure, and mines or minerals, whether or not held apart from the surface, buildings or parts of buildings (whether the division is horizontal, vertical or made in some other way) and other corporeal hereditaments; also a manor, an advowson, and a rent, and other incorporeal hereditaments and an easement, right, privilege, or benefit in, over or derived from land; but not an undivided share in land.

It is thus clear that the subject matter of certain transactions may be both 'goods' for the purposes of the Sale of Goods Act 1979 and 'land' for the purposes of the Law of Property Act 1925 and associated statutes. This was not so formerly.[2] The removal of this hard-and-fast distinction between goods and land has led to a great deal of confusion as to how and when the property in goods attached to land passes.

This text is concerned with contracts for the sale of goods. When therefore can the sale of matter forming part of the land be goods for the purposes of the 1979 Act? In all cases, except the sale of crops which are *fructus industriales*, the general rule is that the parties must have provided for the subject matter to be severed before or under the contract in order for it to be a contract for the sale of goods. Where the seller has extracted the subject matter from the land and offers it for sale severed from the land, or contracts to do so, no difficulty arises as the materials are clearly goods (*Anglo-Iranian Oil Co. Ltd* v *Jaffrante* [1953] 1 WLR 246 at 260). Where the parties have contracted to allow the buyer to enter the land and extract it difficulties arise as to whether the agreement is a sale of goods or a grant of a *profit à prendre*. There are two possible constructions of the agreement: one option is that the parties may have made a contract for the sale of goods coupled with a contractual licence to enter the land and extract the goods;[3] the other option is that the seller may have granted the buyer a *profit à prendre*. The

2. Under the Statute of Frauds 1677 'land' and 'goods' were construed independently.
3. The court will readily infer such a licence, see *Jones & Sons Ltd* v *Earl of Tankerville* [1909] 2 Ch 440.

distinction is not always easy to make in practice. The technical difference is that, in order for the contract to be one of sale, the buyer must be obliged to extract the goods, as opposed to merely having an option to do so (*Commissioner of Taxes* v *Kauri Timber Co.* (1989) 17 NZLR 696; *Egmont Box Co. Ltd* v *Registrar General of Lands* [1920] NZLR 741; *Waimiha Sawmilling Co.* v *Howe* [1920] NZLR 681; this is considered in more detail at section 1.3.4). The distinction is of importance as a *profit à prendre* is required to be made by deed (Law of Property Act 1925, s. 52), whereas a licence to enter land need only be in writing (Law of Property (Miscellaneous Provisions) Act 1989, s. 2).

The application of these principles is considered in more detail below in relation to crops, fixtures, and other matter forming part of the land.

1.3.2 Crops

It is first necessary to distinguish two forms of crops, *fructus naturales*[4] and *fructus industriales*.[5] Under the Statute of Frauds the former were considered part of the land (*Saunders* v *Pilcher* [1949] 2 All ER 1097), the latter as chattels independent from the land (*Evans* v *Roberts* (1826) 5 B & C 829; *English Hop Growers* v *Dering* [1928] 2 KB 174). This distinction has survived the repeal of the Statute of Frauds and the introduction of the Sale of Goods Act 1979 (*English Hop Growers* v *Dering*; *Saunders* v *Pilcher*). It is clear that the 1979 Act uses the term 'emblements' to mean '*fructus industriales*';[6] the term 'industrial growing crops' probably means the same under Scottish law.[7]

Some authors[8] have suggested that both *fructus industriales* and *fructus naturales* should be treated in the same way under the 1979 Act, i.e., that in both cases the parties must provide for their severance in order for them to be goods under the Act. It is submitted that this is not so. *Fructus industriales* are always goods for the purpose of the 1979 Act, *fructus naturales* are 'things attached to or forming part of the land' and the parties must agree their severance before they come within the Act. This follows from the definition 'emblements, . . . and things attached to or forming part of the land which are agreed to be severed before or under the contract of sale'. The term 'emblements' should be read disjunctively from the latter part of the definition. The requirement as to severance does not embrace emblements, and hence does not embrace *fructus industriales*. This is supported by the New Zealand case of *Waimiha Sawmilling Co.* v *Howe* [1920] NZLR 681 where Cooper J said (at p. 689):

> . . . 'goods' includes all things attached to or forming part of the land which are agreed to be severed before sale or under the contract of sale, and [this definition gives] a general rule for dealing with all things attached to land, other than emblements. . . .

The position is therefore that *fructus industriales* are always goods for the purpose of the 1979 Act; *fructus naturales* are only goods if the parties have provided for

4. The natural produce of the land such as trees, grass, timber or fruit from trees.
5. Crops produced from skill and labour such as corn, potatoes, wheat or barley.
6. *Benjamin: Sale of Goods*, 5th ed. (London: Sweet & Maxwell, 1997), para. 1-092; *Evans* v *Roberts*; *Scully* v *South* [1931] NZLR 1187 at 1190.
7. The term was added to the definition when the Act was extended to cover Scotland.
8. *Benjamin: Sale of Goods*, 5th ed., para. 1-092; Goode, R., *Commercial Law*, 2nd ed. (Penguin, 1995), p. 206.

their severance. In either case, if the buyer is to extract them then he must be under an obligation to do so otherwise the agreement will amount to a grant of a *profit à prendre*. Furthermore the agreement should be in writing (*Evans* v *Roberts* (1826) 5 B & C 829; *English Hop Growers* v *Dering* [1928] 2 KB 174).

A further consequence which arises from *fructus industriales* status as chattels distinct from the land is that where land is conveyed with crops still growing in the land then the conveyance will operate to transfer the crops only if they are *fructus naturales* (*Saunders* v *Pilcher* [1949] 2 All ER 1097). If the crops are *fructus industriales* then they will not automatically pass under the conveyance (*English Hop Growers* v *Dering* [1928] 2 KB 174). The parties could of course expressly agree that the property in the crops will pass on conveyance. A contract to convey land containing *fructus naturales* is incapable of being a severable contract part of which is to convey the land and part of which is to convey the crops. The contract will always be entire (*Saunders* v *Pilcher*).

1.3.3 Fixtures

Fixtures are chattels which have become permanently affixed to the land so as to be considered part of it. Clearly, of things forming part of the land they are the easiest to envisage as goods for the purposes of the 1979 Act. They lose their status as chattels when they are affixed to the land and become the property of the landowner. This is so even if this happens without the consent of the owner of the chattel. They regain their status as goods upon severance.

1.3.4 Minerals and the ground itself

Minerals, gravel and the soil itself clearly form 'part of the land' and are capable of being within the definition of goods. As with *fructus naturales*, there is no problem where the seller agrees to extract them and sell them severed from the land. However, in the situation where the buyer is to extract it is a highly difficult question to answer whether the seller has granted a *profit à prendre* or made a sale of goods.

The difficulty arises because the distinction between the sale of goods and dispositions of interests in land has never been effectively explored. It appears that the only English case to have considered the point is *Morgan* v *Russell & Sons* [1909] 1 KB 357. In that case the buyer was given a right to enter land and take slag which had become part of the land. The buyer was to pay a specified price per tonne. The argument that this was a sale of goods was rejected, but the reasoning in that case is rather thin. Lord Alverstone CJ rejected the argument on the grounds that the seller did not sell a 'definite quantity' and the slag was not a 'definite thing'. Walton J expressly stated that the sale of mining goods in the ground at the time of contract was capable of being a sale of goods, but that the particular contract in question was not because it was more akin to a mining lease.

One test as to the distinction which has been propounded is that if the parties intend the buyer to gain an interest in the materials *in situ* then the agreement is the grant of a *profit*.[9] However, since the holder of a *profit à prendre* gains no

9. Goode, R., *Commercial Law*, 2nd ed. (Penguin, 1995), p. 202.

interest in the materials *in situ* (*The Queen* v *Tenor* (1985) 17 DLR (4th) 1, at 17; Gray, K., *Elements of Land Law*, 2nd ed. (London: Butterworths), p. 1045) this test does not properly distinguish the two. The proper test to apply would appear to be that the buyer must be obliged to extract as opposed to hold a mere right to do so in order for the contract to be one of sale (*Ellison* v *Vukicevic* (1986) 7 NSWLR 104; Gray, K., *Elements of Land Law*, 2nd ed., p. 1045). There is no authority binding upon the English courts as to which test to adopt. However, the distinction between an obligation and a right does appear to distinguish a sale of goods from the grant of a *profit à prendre*.

1.3.5 Can the property in goods forming part of the land pass prior to severance?

Having established that things forming part of the land are capable of being goods, the question of whether the property in them may pass prior to extraction must be examined. Under the 1979 Act the only barrier to property passing is the requirement that the goods be ascertained. Other than this requirement the property will pass under s. 18, or in accordance with the parties' intentions. In the case of crops, soil, minerals or gravel it is difficult to conceive of a situation whereby the goods may become ascertained prior to severance. The property in such goods could thus only pass after severance. However, the same cannot be said of a chattel fixed to the land in such a way as to become a fixture. The good may be sufficiently identified by the parties to be a specific good. If it is in a deliverable state (*Underwood Ltd* v *Burgh Castle Brick and Cement Syndicate* [1922] 1 KB 343) the property in it will pass at the time the contract is made, or according to the parties' intentions. Hence the property may pass before it is severed. This situation raises many questions: Could the good trespass the land, or the land trespass the good? Would the buyer have an implied licence to enter the land?[10] Furthermore the idea that property can pass prior to severance is contrary to the established rule that a chattel becomes part of the land when affixed to it and only regains its status as a chattel when removed. This problem has arisen by virtue of the overlap between the Sale of Goods Act 1979 and the Law of Property Act 1925.

Clearly to hold that the property in goods can pass prior to extraction would be absurd. It would probably be better to hold that the concept of 'ascertainment' in s. 16 of the 1979 Act imports the concept that the goods must have obtained a status independent from the land before they are to be treated as goods. The property would not then pass prior to extraction.

1.3.6 Goods and money

The 1979 Act excludes money from the definition of 'goods' (s. 61). This is done so as to take outside the scope of the Act transactions such as currency trading or loans. It is possible, however, for legal tender to lose its status as money and be treated as a good. In *Moss* v *Hancock* [1899] 2 QB 111 a commemorative coin was treated as a good even though it was still legal tender because it was dealt with not as money but as an antique or collector's item.

10. The answer to this is probably in the affirmative, see *Jones & Sons Ltd* v *Earl of Tankerville* [1909] 2 Ch 440.

1.3.7 Goods and animals

Animals, whether dead or alive, are capable of being goods within the meaning of the 1979 Act. The only difficulty which may arise is in relation to wild animals; domestic or agricultural animals are clearly within the definition. A wild animal will become a good if it is captured or tamed so as to be under the owner's control (*Hamps* v *Darby* [1948] 2 KB 311). Animals will remain goods whilst in captivity or under the owner's supervision, or where they are going about their home in their usual manner[11] in obedience to their status as captive. They will lose their status as goods if they escape from captivity or fail to return to their home in obedience to their owner (*Hamps* v *Darby*).

1.3.8 Goods and ships

A ship is clearly capable of being a good within the meaning of the 1979 Act. The only respect in which ships differ from other goods is that the transfer of ownership of a registered ship is governed by the Merchant Shipping Acts. The other provisions of the 1979 Act will apply whether or not the ship is registered.

1.3.9 Goods and the human body

Whether parts of the human body may form goods within the meaning of the 1979 Act is of limited significance since commercial dealings in human organs are prohibited by the Human Organ Transplants Act 1989. Since the statute is penal, it would not necessarily prevent an illegal contract from coming within the scope of the 1979 Act. However, in any case, it has been held that there can be no property in a human corpse (*Williams* v *Williams* (1882) 2 Ch D 659). Arguably, however, parts of the human body are distinct from the whole of a human corpse itself and are hence capable of being goods.

1.3.10 Goods and electricity and other energy sources

Electricity itself clearly cannot be a good within the meaning of the 1979 Act. Equally clearly, if it is stored in some form such as a battery then the battery can be a good. Oil, gases or other fluids contained in the earth are treated in the same way as solid matter under the ground, as to which see section 1.3.4.

1.3.11 Goods and computer software

There is no doubt that computer hardware may be goods within the meaning of the 1979 Act. The position is much less clear in relation to software. There is at present no binding authority in England and Wales as to whether it is a good. The issue was considered by the Court of Appeal in *St. Albans City and District Council* v *International Computers Ltd* [1996] 4 All ER 481. Whilst the dicta in that case are *obiter*, the case does provide the only judicial guidance on the topic from an English court. The facts of the case, so far as relevant, were that the

11. For example, a homing or carrier pigeon not directly under its owner's supervision but following its usual route.

defendants had written a computer program which failed to work properly. The flaw was entirely in the program, not in the hardware or the physical storage disk. Sir Iain Glidewell adopted the following explanation of the workings of a computer system:

> By itself hardware can do nothing. The really important part of the system is the software. Programs are the instructions or commands that tell the hardware what to do. The program itself is an algorithm or formula. It is of necessity contained in a physical medium. A program in machine readable form must be contained on a machine readable medium, such as paper cards, magnetic cards, magnetic tapes, disks, drums or magnetic bubbles.

He then said:

> . . . it is necessary to distinguish between the program and the disk carrying the program. In both the Sale of Goods Act 1979, s. 61, and the Supply of Goods and Services Act 1982, s. 18, the definition of goods includes 'all personal chattels other than things in action and money'. Clearly, a disk is within this definition. Equally clearly, a program, of itself, is not.

He later posed the following problem:

> Suppose I buy an instruction manual on the maintenance and repair of a particular make of car. The instructions are wrong in an important respect. Anybody who follows them is likely to cause serious damage to the engine of his car. In my view, the instructions are an integral part of the manual. The manual including the instructions, whether in a book or a video cassette, would in my opinion be 'goods' within the meaning of the 1979 Act, and the defective instructions would result in a breach of the implied terms in s. 14. If this is correct,[12] I can see no logical reason why it should not also be correct in relation to a computer disk onto which a program designed and intended to instruct or enable a computer to achieve particular functions has been encoded. If the disk is sold or hired by the computer manufacturer, but the program is defective, in my opinion there would prima facie be a breach of the terms as to quality and fitness for purpose implied by the 1979 Act or the 1982 Act.

He then went on to hold that because in that case an employee of International Computers Ltd (ICL) had attended the premises and transferred the program on to the computer from a disk provided by ICL,[13] and since the program itself was not goods, the software supplied was not goods. This analysis assumes that an intangible item such as information or a computer program can become a good if it is an 'integral part' of a physical good.

It is clear that the difficulty is in the form of storage of the computer program. A computer program has no physical form. It exists on a storage device merely as a magnetic or optical pattern. A software licence agreement is therefore a right to

---

12. This is possibly incorrect. In another case publishers have been held not to be liable where information contained in a book is incorrect, see *Winter* v *G. P. Putnam's Sons* 938 F 2d 1033, 9th Cir. (1991); Atiyah, *The Sale of Goods*, 9th ed. (Pitman Publishing, 1995), p. 24, n. 82.

13. Meaning that the buyers only received the program, they were never supplied with the disk.

have the magnetic pattern on the buyer's storage device in the pattern that forms the program. In so far as this is so Sir Iain Glidewell's analysis is correct — the program in itself is not a good. The difficulty comes in asserting that the program can become a good simply by being placed on a disk or a CD-rom. This is a novel[14] suggestion and does not rest easily with the theory of the 1979 Act.

If the judgment is applied it would allow the purchaser of an 'off the peg' computer program *which runs directly from the disk or CD-rom*, or the purchaser of a computer with pre-loaded software,[15] to sue if the program is not of satisfactory quality. This is of substantial benefit as many computers are now supplied with the software pre-loaded by the vendor. Unfortunately, this is as far as the decision goes. Many, indeed most, modern computer programs are supplied on disk or CD-rom which are then 'installed' on to the computer system from the disk to the computer's internal hard disk. This is precisely what was done in *St. Albans City and District Council* v *International Computers Ltd* and Sir Iain Glidewell stated that the program was then not a good.[16] A further problem is that many computer programs are supplied or updated by way of the Internet whereby they never take any physical form. They are never goods under the judgment.

1.4 THE MEANING OF THE TERM 'PROPERTY IN GOODS'

The meaning of this phrase has been the matter of considerable academic debate since the decision in *Rowland* v *Divall* [1923] 2 KB 500. The prevailing view is that the case was incorrectly decided (see section 1.4.1 below), but it does represent the law.

The first point to note about the phrase is that it is the 'property *in* goods', connoting that the property is something other than the physical goods themselves. The 'property' is the proprietary interest held over the goods by the seller. It is this interest which s. 2(1) of the 1979 Act requires the seller to convey to the buyer in order for the contract to be one of sale. What then is this interest?

In *Rowland* v *Divall* the facts (abridged for the purpose of exposition) were that a third party had acquired a car in good faith from a thief. He sold the car to the seller who in turn sold it to the buyer. The buyer retained and used it for a considerable period. Subsequently the police took possession of the car as being stolen. The buyer then sued the seller for a total failure of consideration on the basis that good title to the car had not been transferred to him. In defence it was argued that since the buyer had retained the car for a considerable period, he should be deemed to have accepted it (under what is now s. 35(4) of the 1979 Act), and that consequently any breach on the part of the seller should be treated as a breach of warranty and not condition (under what is now s. 11(4) of the 1979 Act), disentitling the buyer to terminate the contract. It was held that the buyer was entitled to succeed on the basis of a total failure of consideration, and recover the

14. There is some dicta to this effect in *Wormell* v *R. H. M. Agriculture (East) Ltd* [1987] 3 All ER 75.
15. During the judgment in *St. Albans City & District Council* v *International Computers Ltd* the Australian case of *Toby Constructions Products Pty* v *Computa Bar Pty* [1983] 2 NSWLR 48 was approved. This case held that where software and hardware were supplied pre-loaded then the software was a good for the purpose of the Act.
16. Arguably, the position is different where the buyer installs the software himself since at the time the buyer receives the software it is a good and it only loses its status as such when installed on to the computer. At the time he receives it therefore it is governed by the Act.

entire price which he paid for the car with no reduction for the period when he had the use of the car. Lord Atkin said (at p. 506):

> . . . there can be no sale at all of goods which the seller has no right to sell. The whole object of a sale is to transfer the property from one person to another.

He then went on to hold that since good title had not been transferred, the buyer had not received *any* part of what he had bargained for, namely the property in goods, and could therefore claim that there had been a total failure of consideration. This reasoning assumes that 'the property' means 'good title' (otherwise why did the buyer succeed for a *total* failure of consideration?).

Whilst unsatisfactory, it is clear that the basis of the law is that the property in goods means a good title to those goods. Furthermore, the courts have given effect to this interpretation many times since (*Butterworth* v *Kingsway Motors* [1954] 1 WLR 1286; *Karflex* v *Poole* [1933] 2 KB 251; *Barber* v *NWS Bank plc* [1996] 1 WLR 641). Wherever a good title is not transferred the buyer may terminate the contract and sue for all monies paid under the contract as for a total failure of consideration.

1.4.1 The fallacy of *Rowland* v *Divall*

Whilst it has to be conceded that the law is as stated in *Rowland* v *Divall* [1923] 2 KB 500, the interpretation given in that case to the term 'property' is not in accordance with the 1979 Act. It follows from *Rowland* v *Divall* that wherever good title has not been transferred the buyer may claim that there has been a total failure of consideration, and he has no need to rely on the provisions of the Act. If this were correct why would the 1979 Act include an implied condition that the seller must transfer good title to the goods under s. 12? There would be no need for such a provision. Furthermore, s. 5(1) of the 1979 Act states that there may be a contract of sale of goods 'owned *or* possessed' by the seller. If the seller merely had a possessory title then, following *Rowland* v *Divall*, the buyer would be entitled to sue for a total failure of consideration. The Act, however, clearly states that there may be a contract for the sale of goods possessed by the seller.

It appears likely that this incongruity was reached by failing to consider the concept of relativity of title to personal goods. A proprietary interest in goods refers to two items. First, the interest held in those goods. Usually this will be an absolute interest, though a limited interest such as a bailment may be created. Secondly, the title to that interest. More than one title may be created to the same interest in goods, each relative in strength to each other. A person may hold a title to goods merely by having possession of them. His title, however, is liable to be defeated by someone having a better claim to those goods, such as a person holding an indefeasible title. What then is meant by the proprietary interest referred to by the term 'property in goods'? In order to answer this question both the interest in the goods and the title to that interest must be considered. As to the interest, s. 61(1) of the 1979 Act provides that the property means 'the general property in goods, and not merely a special property'. Thus, the interest to be transferred must be the absolute interest, and not merely a limited interest such as a bailment or life interest. As to the title, it has been seen that the Act clearly does not intend that the title to be transferred must be a good title. The title which must be transferred would appear to be *any* title to this interest. This accords with the Act in that if this is so then ss. 5 and 12, which imply the terms as to title and refer to goods possessed by the seller, have an application. The property in goods may therefore properly be defined as 'any title to the absolute legal interest in the goods' (*Battersby & Preston* [1972] MLR 268).

1.5 MONEY CONSIDERATION

The reference to a money consideration in s. 2 of the 1979 Act is used not to require that the buyer pays for the goods in cash, but to ensure that the consideration provided by the buyer is fixed by reference to a monetary sum and not 'moneysworth'. The buyer may therefore pay for the goods by cheque, credit or charge card, by way of finance transaction, by a bill of exchange or on credit terms provided by the seller. However, some difficulties arise where the parties agree that the buyer may tender other goods by way of trade-in or part exchange: this is discussed below at section 1.6.1.

1.6 THE CONTRACT OF SALE DISTINGUISHED FROM SIMILAR CONTRACTS

The foregoing discussion has defined the components of the contract of sale. It is the absence of any one of these components which distinguishes the contract of sale from other contracts. Frequently a contract may bear the hallmarks of one type of contract yet in fact be another. In many cases this will be of little practical importance as the same provisions may apply by virtue of another Act or by operation of the common law; in other cases the consequences may be quite different. The difficulty in distinguishing the contracts is usually one of construction, as Hilbery J said in *Dawson (Clapham) Ltd* v *Dutfield* [1936] 2 All ER 232 (at p. 232):

> This is a troublesome case; troublesome not because of difficulty in ascertaining the principles of law which are applicable, but because of the business relations between the parties. They left, to a great extent, the details of the transactions loosely expressed or not expressed at all, in the belief that they would have no difficulty in adjusting any difficulties which might arise. As it turned out they were unable to effect these adjustments. That is why these matters fall to be decided by the court.

The following sections are a guide to the boundaries between the contract of sale and similar transactions:

(a) A contract of exchange, trade-in or barter.
(b) A contract for the supply of a service or the supply of goods and services.
(c) A gift.
(d) A contract of bailment.
(e) Contracts involving the financing of the purchase of goods.
(f) A pledge, mortgage or similar loan on security.
(g) Goods provided under a public service or duty.

1.6.1 Contracts of exchange, trade-in or barter

It is the absence of a money consideration which frequently takes contracts of exchange, trade-in or barter outside the definition of a contract of sale. In order for the contract to be one for the sale of goods within the meaning of the 1979 Act there must be an element of total price discernible from the agreement between the parties. That is to say that the consideration to be provided by the buyer must be fixed by reference to a specified sum, and not by reference to the exchange of goods. Once this sum is established it is permissible for part of this debt to be discharged by provision of goods or by discharge of a debt owed from the seller to the buyer.

The principle that there must be an element of total price discernible is best brought out by the Irish case of *Flynn* v *Mackin* [1974] IR 101. In that case the supplier agreed to provide a new Vauxhall Viva car in exchange for the defendant's old Vauxhall Viva car together with £250. It was argued that this amounted not to a sale but to a barter. Walsh J said (at p. 111):

> In my view, this submission is correct. There is no evidence in the case of an agreement to buy the motor car for an agreed price. The question of the price of the motor car, if it arose, is not referred to at all in the evidence. The terms of the transaction, as given in evidence, are that the new motor car was to be obtained by [the defendant] in exchange for the motor car which he possessed plus a sum of £250. If the transaction had been that the new motor car was to be a particular price but that in lieu of part of that price the vendor would take an existing motor car and cash for the balance then, in my view, the contract would have been a contract for sale because it would have been an agreement to buy a new car for an agreed price. That is not the case here. Therefore, the provisions of ... the Act ... are not applicable to the transaction under review.

Conversely, in *Aldridge* v *Johnson* (1857) 7 E & B 885 the seller agreed to sell 32 bullocks at an agreed price, the price to be satisfied by the provision of 200 sacks of barley together with a cash balance. The point was not raised on appeal, but this would have amounted to a sale as the cash price for the goods (the bullocks) was fixed (see also *Dawson (Clapham) Ltd* v *Dutfield* [1936] 2 All ER 232 where the price for two lorries was fixed at £475, to be paid partly by the transfer of two other lorries). The effect of these cases is that a sale may be within the 1979 Act even if part of the money consideration is satisfied by the provision of other goods.

The question of whether there is an element of total price discernible may often be answered by the structure of the agreement between the parties. Both transactions of part exchange and trade-in may amount to sales within the meaning of the 1979 Act; a barter will almost always be outside the scope of the Act. The main difficulty which arises is in determining what the parties had intended.

An agreement of part exchange, as the phrase should be correctly understood, involves not one but two contracts. Under the agreement the seller of the goods being purchased contracts to sell them to the buyer for an agreed price. The seller of those goods also agrees, under a separate contract, to purchase the goods being exchanged. The seller further agrees that the price he owes under the contract for the sale of the exchanged goods may be set off against the money owed by the buyer under the contract for the sale of the new goods. There are therefore two contracts of sale, both of which are governed by the 1979 Act.

By contrast, a contract of trade-in involves only one contract.[17] The seller agrees to sell the goods at an agreed price, but that part of that agreed price may be satisfied by the provision of other goods.[18]

A contract of barter occurs where goods are merely traded for other goods, as in the case of *Flynn* v *Mackin* above. A difficult case in this regard is *Koppel* v *Koppel* [1966] 1 WLR 802 where it was held that a contract whereby one party transferred the entire contents of his house in order to 'compensate [his ex-wife] for giving up her own and daughter's home and for disposing of her furniture' was a contract to which the 1979 Act applied. Harman LJ distinguished the transaction only from a gift in that the transaction was for money or moneysworth. No reference was made to a money consideration. It is submitted that this case should be confined to its facts and not followed in future cases.

The distinction between sale and exchange is of relatively little importance since the introduction of the Supply of Goods and Services Act 1982 which applies to contracts of exchange.[19] The 1982 Act implies similar terms as to title, quality, description and fitness for purpose as the Sale of Goods Act 1979 does. However, the rules as to acceptance and rejection of the goods differ markedly between the two types of contract.

1.6.2 Contracts for the supply of a service or the supply of goods and services

The distinction between a contract for the sale of goods or the supply of work and materials is a matter which has caused great difficulty for a number of years. The Sale of Goods Act 1979 does not apply to contracts for work and materials. The distinction is of much less importance now since the decision in *Young & Marten Ltd* v *McManus Childs Ltd* [1969] 1 AC 454 and the introduction of the Supply of Goods and Services Act 1982: where goods are supplied under a contract of work and materials as opposed to sold under a contract of sale, similar terms are implied in respect of the goods as are implied by the Sale of Goods Act 1979. However, differences do remain between the different forms of contract which may be decisive in a given case. First, the property may pass to the purchaser at different times under the different forms of contract. Secondly, the remedies to which the parties are entitled may differ depending upon the form of the contract. Thirdly, the exceptions to the *nemo dat* rule contained in the 1979 Act do not apply. Fourthly, the Law Reform (Frustrated Contracts) Act 1943 does not apply to sales of goods. Finally, miscellaneous provisions within the 1979 Act such as ascertainment of the price, liens or subsales are not replicated within the Supply of Goods and Services Act 1982. However, the common law will frequently reach the same result.

The difficulty has largely arisen because where a service is provided it is judged by the standard of reasonable skill and care, as opposed to the stricter standard of fitness for purpose which is applied to goods.

17. In *Dawson (Clapham) Ltd* v *Dutfield* [1936] 2 All ER 232 Hilberry J said, 'I have no doubt that there were not two purchases but only one' (at p. 233).
18. *Dawson (Clapham) Ltd* v *Dutfield* and *Aldridge* v *Johnson* (1857) 7 E & B 885 are examples of this type of contract.
19. An exchange of goods would form a 'contract for the transfer of goods' within the meaning of the Supply of Goods and Services Act 1982, s. 1.

Were many items to be held to be goods as opposed to services injustice may result. For example, where a solicitor prepares a conveyancing document in no way negligently, but fails to effect the conveyance, if the document were held to be a good then it would be unfit for its purpose. But great difficulties arise where both goods and services have been provided and the goods but not the services prove to be defective. Should the goods be judged by the standard of reasonable skill and care or by the stricter standards implied by the 1979 Act? In *Young & Marten Ltd* v *McManus Childs Ltd* [1969] 1 AC 454 tiles were provided by a contractor to be fitted to a roof. Subsequently, it transpired that the tiles had a latent defect which could not have been discovered by reasonable skill and care. The tiles were not, however, fit for their purpose. It was argued that the contract was one of work and materials to which the appropriate standard was merely one of reasonable skill and care. The House of Lords rejected the argument and adopted the following statement (per du Parcq J in *G. H. Myers & Co.* v *Brent Cross Service Co.* [1934] 1 KB 46):

> a person contracting to do work and supply materials warrants that the materials which he uses will be of good quality and reasonably fit for the purpose for which he is using them, unless the circumstances of the contract are such as to exclude any such warranty.

The Supply of Goods and Services Act 1982 follows this rule. The supply of goods under the contract will form a 'transfer of goods' under s. 1 and the implied terms as to title, description, quality and transfer by sample will be implied into the contract. The service element of the contract will be governed by the standard of reasonable skill and care under s. 13. Therefore, as regards quality, title, description or transfer by sample little or no practical difference arises as to whether the contract is one of sale or work and materials; virtually the same terms will be implied into either contract.

As discussed above some important differences do remain between the two forms of contract and it is necessary to consider whether the contract is one of sale, governed by the Sale of Goods Act 1979, or one of work and materials, governed by the Supply of Goods and Services Act 1982 and the common law. The test once propounded was that if the parties contracted for the seller to produce a finished article to be sold to the buyer once complete then the contract was one of sale (*Lee* v *Griffin* (1861) 1 B & S 272). This appears to still be a consideration within the reasoning of some cases. However, since the decision in *Robinson* v *Graves* [1935] 1 KB 579[20] it would appear that the proper test is to consider whether the service or materials element forms the 'substance of the contract'. If it is the former then the contract is one of work and materials; if it is the latter then it is a sale of goods. In considering this test three situations must be considered.

1.6.2.1 Goods fitted to the buyer's land or another chattel belonging to the buyer Where goods are to be attached to the buyer's land or another chattel

20. Some authors argue that the law as stated in *Lee* v *Griffin* should be followed, indeed in Australia this has been done, see *Deta Nominees Pty Ltd* v *Viscount Plastic Products Pty Ltd* [1979] VR 167; *Benjamin: Sale of Goods*, 5th ed. (London: Sweet & Maxwell, 1997), para. 1-048, n. 85). However, it is submitted that since the test laid down in *Robinson* v *Graves* was added as 'a qualification' to the rule in *Lee* v *Griffin* the courts in England and Wales are bound by, and do follow, *Robinson* v *Graves*. Whilst this case is arguably unsatisfactory it does represent the law.

belonging to him the application of the test is fairly straightforward. The following have been held to be contracts predominantly for the sale of a chattel and hence held to be within the Sale of Goods Act 1979: the supply and fitting of a carpet (*Philip Head & Sons Ltd* v *Showfronts Ltd* [1970] 1 Lloyd's Rep 140), the fitting of special curtains (*Love* v *Norman Wright (Builders) Ltd* [1944] KB 484), and the delivery and erection of an agricultural feeding tank (*H Parsons (Livestock) Ltd* v *Utley Ingham & Co. Ltd* [1978] QB 791). By contrast the following have been held to be cases where the service element of the contract is more substantial than the supply of goods element and hence outside the scope of the 1979 Act: the fitting of connecting rods (*G. H. Myers & Co.* v *Brent Cross Service Co.* [1934] 1 KB 46) or brake pads (*Stewart* v *Reavell's Garage* [1952] 2 QB 545) to a car, the fitting of boilers to a ship (*Anglo-Egyptian Navigation Company* v *Rennie* (1875) LR 10 CP 271), and the supply and fitting of roofing tiles (*Young & Marten Ltd* v *McManus Childs Ltd* [1969] 1 AC 454).

1.6.2.2 Goods supplied by the buyer Where the purchaser supplies all the materials and the other party merely performs some service upon them this is clearly not a sale of goods unless the parties explicitly state that the materials are to be sold to the serviceman and then resold to the buyer after the work has been completed. Where each party provides part of the materials the issue becomes more vexed. In *Dixon* v *London Small Arms Co.* (1876) 1 App Cas 632 the buyer supplied gun barrels to which the defendants supplied the remaining parts and manufactured the rifles. It was held that the defendants had sold the completed rifles to the plaintiff under an ordinary contract for the sale of goods.

1.6.2.3 Goods supplied as an ancillary part of skilled services Whether a contract whereby the benefit of a skilled service is represented by a physical good is held to be a contract of sale appears to depend upon the degree of skill the courts credit the expertise with. Where a solicitor prepares a document, or an engineer or architect prepares plans, then the contract will be one for services (*Robinson* v *Graves* [1935] 1 KB 579; *Lee* v *Griffin* (1861) 1 B & S 272). Where a veterinary surgeon or private doctor advises, administers or supplies a drug then the situation will depend upon the amount of advice given. Where the advice is of a specialist nature or the practitioner administers the drug then the contract will be for services (*Dodd* v *Wilson McWilliam* [1946] 2 All ER 691). Where the advice is minimal, such as where a pharmacist recommends a particular cough medicine, then this would be a sale of goods. Artistic works are clearly goods if sold once completed, but where they are specifically commissioned this will form a contract for work and materials (*Lee* v *Griffin*; *Robinson* v *Graves*). Where a hairdresser uses dyes or lotions as part of the process then the materials will be supplied under a contract of work and materials and not under a contract of sale (*Watson* v *Buckley* [1940] 1 All ER 174). Similarly, a contract for a printer to print a work would be a contract for services (*Clay* v *Yates* 1 H & N 76; *Robinson* v *Graves*).[21] By contrast, where a dentist supplies false teeth, this is a sale of goods (*Lee* v *Griffin*; *Samuels* v *Davis* [1943] KB 526). If the dentist were to give a filling or perform dental hygiene tasks then this would be a contract for work and materials; any materials so used would be incidental to the service performed.

21. Contra *Benjamin: Sale of Goods*, 5th ed. (London: Sweet & Maxwell, 1997), para. 1-045.

1.6.3 Gifts and promotional gifts

Clearly a gift is only enforceable by the donee if it is made by deed. However, even where this is the case the agreement would not be governed by the 1979 Act as there would not be a money consideration. In the case of promotional gifts, the legal relations intended between the parties will in each case fall to be construed on the facts of the particular case. The House of Lords in *Esso Petroleum Co. Ltd* v *Customs and Excise Commissioners* [1976] 1 WLR 1 considered the common situation whereby a free gift (a commemorative coin) was supplied to a buyer for every four gallons of petrol which he purchased. Lord Simon, with whom Lord Wilberforce agreed, considered that the coin passed under a collateral contract, the consideration for which was the purchase of petrol, but that since the consideration was not a money consideration the contract was not one of sale. Viscount Dilhorne and Lord Russell considered that there was a lack of legal relations since the coin was of little intrinsic value. It is respectfully submitted that the approach taken by Lord Simon should be preferred. First, were the courts to assess the transaction on the basis of value a great deal of difficulty would arise as to where the dividing line should be drawn. Secondly, a customer may very well have made a purchase on the basis that he will thereby obtain an extra benefit. The gift forms part of the consideration which the buyer expects to receive and, despite the unlikelihood of his pursuing the matter in the courts, he should at least have the legal right to demand it. However, the consideration provided by the customer is his choice of the particular brand or product; it is not a money consideration. The collateral contract analysis therefore seems the best.[22] Another situation is where the gift is supplied within the package which the customer purchases. Here the gift would appear to be an integral part of what the customer purchases and would form part of the goods supplied under the contract of sale (*Wilson* v *Rickett Cockerell & Co. Ltd* [1954] 1 QB 598; *Taylor* v *Smetten* (1883) 11 QBD 207; *Scott & Co. Ltd* v *Solomon* [1905] 1 KB 577; see also the speech of Lord Fraser in *Esso Petroleum Co. Ltd* v *Customs and Excise Commissioners*).

1.6.4 Bailment

A contract of bailment exists where the possession of goods is transferred from one person to another for a limited purpose or period of time. The purpose may be that some process is performed on the good, that the good be delivered to another, or simply that the bailee has the enjoyment of the good for a certain period of time. The transaction is not one of sale since the general property in the goods is not transferred to the bailee.

1.6.5 Transactions involving the financing of the purchase of goods

Historically the various forms of financing the purchase of goods have evolved from an attempt by the financier to avoid the provisions of the 1979 Act and in particular to avoid the exceptions to the *nemo dat* rule, the latter being of importance because the buyer being in possession of the goods may easily dispose

22. Note that the transaction would form a 'transfer of goods' under the Supply of Goods and Services Act 1982.

of them to a third party, thus removing the seller's security. Since the introduction of the Supply of Goods (Implied Terms) Act 1973 the same terms as to title, quality, description and fitness for purpose will apply whether the contract is one of sale, conditional purchase or hire purchase. The issue is now not so much whether the terms are implied but which Act are they implied by.

Whether the Sale of Goods Act 1979 applies will depend upon whether the buyer has unequivocally agreed to take the property in goods, whether or not upon fulfilment of certain conditions. The Act will not apply if the buyer has merely an option to take the property exercisable at his discretion. The conditions to which the contract is subjected may be numerous or dependent upon the act of one of the parties, but, so long as the parties are bound to transfer the property upon their fulfilment, as opposed to merely having an option to do so, the contract is one of sale. This requirement deems conditional sale agreements to be governed by the 1979 Act, but hire purchase agreements to be outside its scope.

In *Helby* v *Matthews* [1895] AC 471 the House of Lords defined a hire purchase agreement as one whereby the hirer is given possession of the goods under a bailment coupled with an option to purchase the goods. Whilst embracing the common law definition the contract is now statutorily defined by both the Consumer Credit Act 1974, s. 189(1) and the Hire Purchase Act 1964, s. 29(1) as:

> an agreement, other than a conditional sale agreement, under which
> (a) goods are bailed in return for periodical payments by the person to whom they are bailed, and
> (b) the property in the goods will pass to that person if the terms of the agreement are complied with and one or more of the following occurs —
> (i) the exercise of an option to purchase by that person,
> (ii) the doing of any other specified act by any party to the agreement,
> (iii) the happening of any other specified event.

During the currency of the bailment the property in the goods remains in the seller, the buyer merely taking possession. Under the agreement the buyer has not agreed to take the property in the goods so it is not governed by the Sale of Goods Act 1979.[23] However, the Supply of Goods (Implied Terms) Act 1973 implies the same terms as to quality, description, title and fitness for purpose as the Sale of Goods Act 1979.

By contrast in *Lee* v *Butler* [1893] 2 QB 318 it was held that a conditional sale agreement was an agreement whereby the buyer agrees to purchase the goods, making payment by instalments. The buyer is *bound* to make the instalments and to take the property in the goods. The seller, however, need only convey the property in the goods if the condition that the instalments are paid is met. The agreement is now defined as:

> an agreement for the sale of goods or land under which the purchase price or part of it is payable by instalments, and the property in goods or land is to remain in the seller (notwithstanding that the buyer is to be in possession of the goods or land) until such conditions as to payment of instalments or otherwise as may be specified in the agreement are fulfilled.

23. Note also that the Supply of Goods and Services Act 1982 specifically excludes the contract from the definition of a transfer of goods.

The agreement is therefore one under which the buyer is bound to take the property in the goods and is hence governed by the Sale of Goods Act 1979.

Formerly, this distinction between conditional sales and hire purchase agreements led to the hire purchase contract being used as opposed to conditional sale agreements. Hire purchase agreements were not governed by the Factors Act 1889, s. 9 (*Helby* v *Matthews*), which allowed a buyer in possession to pass good title to a third party, whereas the conditional sale agreement was (*Lee* v *Butler*). The financier under a hire purchase agreement was therefore able to tender goods which were not protected by the Act and his security was maintained because the hirer could not pass good title to third parties. The position between the two forms of contract is now the same: the Supply of Goods (Implied Terms) Act 1973 implies similar terms as to quality, fitness for purpose, title and description as the Sale of Goods Act 1979; the buyer under a conditional sale agreement is deemed not to have 'bought or agreed to buy' any goods under the Sale of Goods Act 1979, s. 25 and cannot therefore pass good title to third parties; the Hire Purchase Act 1964, s. 26 which allows good title in cars to be passed to a third party applies to both hire purchase and conditional sale agreements; and hire purchase agreements have never been subject to the statutory doctrine of acceptance introduced under the Sale of Goods Act 1979. Under the Sale of Goods Act 1979, s. 11(4) the buyer may only treat a breach of a condition as a breach of a warranty if he has accepted the goods. The position is now the same for conditional sales by virtue of the Supply of Goods (Implied Terms) Act 1973, s. 14 which states that s. 11(4) does not apply to conditional sale agreements where the buyer deals as a consumer.

In modern times the situation is further complicated by the fact that in most cases the transaction will be funded by a specialist finance company, and not by the owner of the goods. The 'provider' will sell the goods to the finance company who will in turn make a hire purchase or conditional sale agreement with the 'purchaser'. Here there is a sale which is governed by the 1979 Act between the provider and the finance company, but the customer has no direct relationship with the provider. In many cases this will make little difference; where the goods are faulty the customer will benefit from the implied terms as to quality under the 1979, 1982 or 1973 Acts and may sue the finance company.

One final form of credit agreement which falls to be considered is the credit sale. This is defined by the Consumer Credit Act 1974, s. 189(1) as 'an agreement for the sale of goods, under which the purchase price or part of it is payable by instalments, but which is not a conditional sale agreement'. The property in the goods passes immediately to the buyer, and the seller is left merely with a debt owed from the buyer which has been agreed to be paid by instalments. The contract is clearly one of sale.

1.6.6 A pledge or mortgage

Goods are frequently used as security for a loan granted in favour of their owner. Where this is done the Sale of Goods Act 1979 will not normally apply. Three forms of transaction require consideration: the pledge, the mortgage, and 'refinancing' or 'sale and leaseback' transactions. Section 62(4) provides that 'the provisions of this Act . . . do not apply to a transaction in the form of a contract of sale which is intended to operate by way of mortgage, pledge, charge or other security'.

Furthermore, the transaction may very well be void for want of registration under the Bills of Sale Acts or the Companies Act.

The pledge is the form of security most commonly used by pawnbrokers. Under a pledge the owner of goods passes possession of the goods to the pledgee under a bailment in return for the pledgee granting a loan in favour of the owner. The pledgee has the right to maintain possession of the goods unless and until the loan is repaid. Whilst the pledgee does not automatically have the right to sell the goods if the loan is not repaid in a specified time (*Franklin* v *Neate* (1844) 13 M & W 481, at p. 484), such a right will frequently be expressly provided in the contract. Since the pledgor merely passes a special property in the goods, i.e., a bailment, and does not pass the general property the contract is not one of sale (see 1.4 above). In any event, s. 62(4) of the 1979 Act clearly excludes a pledge from the provisions of the Act. However, the pledgor does retain the general property in the goods, as qualified by the rights of the pledgee, and this may properly form the subject matter of a sale (*Franklin* v *Neate* (1844) 13 M & W 481). It is unlikely that such a sale would be caught by s. 62(4) since the transaction is not intended to operate as a grant of a security; it is a transfer of the ownership of the goods.

A mortgage arises where the owner of goods passes the absolute legal title to those goods to the mortgagee in return for the grant of a loan. The owner retains a right of redemption, that is to say a right to have the legal title passed back to him on repayment of the loan. Such a transaction is clearly excluded from the provisions of the 1979 Act by s. 62(4).

1.6.7 Goods supplied under a public service or duty

Where a person supplies goods under a public duty, such as the provision of drugs under the NHS, he does not do so under a contract and the supply is not one of sale (*Pfizer Corporation* v *Ministry of Health* [1965] AC 512). This is so even though the recipient of the goods may pay a fee in order to be entitled to the goods. Neither the Sale of Goods Act 1979 nor the Supply of Goods and Services Act 1982 will therefore apply since both require that there be a contract between the parties. The recipient's remedy for any defect in the goods supplied will lie in negligence.

2 *Hire purchase agreements and agreements for the transfer of goods*

2.1 INTRODUCTION

The emphasis on this text is upon contracts which are governed by the Sale of Goods Act 1979 (the '1979 Act'), but it is important to note that the law is almost identical wherever goods are transferred as between supplier and buyer. This is certainly the case in relation to the terms implied by the 1979 Act which are repeated in the Supply of Goods (Implied Terms) Act 1973 (the '1973 Act') and the Supply of Goods and Services Act 1982 (the '1982 Act') in relation to hire purchase agreements and agreements for the transfer of goods.

It is necessary, however, to properly identify the nature of the contract and the particular statutory provisions which apply to it as differences do exist. Perhaps the most fundamental difference is that the doctrine of 'acceptance' only applies in relation to contracts governed by the 1979 Act, and has no application to contracts governed by the common law or other statutory regimes. Similarly, it is only in the case of contracts of sale that the time at which the property is to pass is made subject to a statutory code; in other cases this will be governed by the common law. Accordingly, it may be permissible to devote a few pages to these particular contracts.

The definition and nature of the different contracts by which the ownership of goods pass was fully explored in chapter 1. Section 1.3 dealt with the definition of 'goods' which is used in the 1973 Act and the 1982 Act. Section 1.6 dealt with the distinction between contracts of sale and other contracts such as hire purchase and the provision of services. Reference should be made to those sections in order to identify the nature of the contract.

It should also be noted that, as with the 1979 Act, similar contracts are governed by the general law of contract. Thus the doctrines of frustration, mistake and misrepresentation apply just as much to hire purchase contracts or to the supply of services as they do to the sale of goods. These are dealt with in their respective chapters.

As was noted above, one of the key differences between sales of goods and other contracts by which goods are transferred is that the doctrine of acceptance does not apply to such contracts. However, by s. 14 of the 1973 Act the effects of acceptance (loss of right to reject and reduction of remedy to damages) do not apply to conditional sale agreements, which are ordinarily governed by the 1979 Act. Contracts other than sales are governed by the common law doctrine of affirmation, which is dealt with in section 4.7.3.

Another important distinction between contracts of sale and similar transactions is that many of the exceptions to the *nemo dat* rule enabling a non-owner to pass good title to the goods apply in relation to sales only. By contrast, of course, the exception contained in s. 26 of the Hire Purchase Act 1964 does not apply to sales. This is discussed in chapter 13.

One of the most important rules relating to the passing of property is that the risk passes with the property. This applies just as much at common law as with contracts for sale (see, for example, *Donaghy's Rope and Twine Co. Ltd* v *Wright, Stephenson & Co.* (1906) 25 NZLR 641; *Head* v *Tattersall* (1871) LR 7 Ex 7). The parties may, of course, expressly provide to the contrary. Accordingly, in all contracts for the transfer of goods the risk of accidental damage to the goods lies on the person who holds the property in the goods.

The remaining important difference between contracts of sale and other contracts therefore is the time at which the property is to pass. For the most part, this is dealt with by the terms of the contract, express or implied. The general rules are dealt with in relation to each type of contract in section 2.2 below. Where no particular rules apply to the situation then some of the general guidelines applied at common law are dealt with at section 2.3 below. It should be noted that specialist forms of contract such as building, shipbuilding or aircraft contracts have developed their own code. This is beyond the scope of this text and reference should be made to a specialist text.

2.2 ASPECTS OF CONTRACTS OF TRANSFER OTHER THAN SALE

The general rules in relation to the passing of property, together with the important rights and duties at common law or statute, will be considered in turn in relation to hire agreements, hire purchase contracts, conditional sale agreements, credit sale agreements and transfers of goods.

2.2.1 Hire agreements

Hire agreements are straightforward contracts for the bailment of goods. This means that the hirer takes a limited interest in the goods, namely a right to possession for the period of hire.

Like terms to those contained in the 1979 Act regarding the title to the goods, quality of them, description and correspondence with description are implied into contracts for the hire of goods by ss. 6 to 10A of the 1982 Act.

2.2.2 Hire purchase agreements

The key difference between a hire purchase agreement and a sale agreement is that in a hire purchase agreement the hirer takes only an option to purchase, whereas in a sale agreement or conditional sale agreement the buyer binds himself to take the property in goods. A fine distinction is to be drawn between hire purchase agreements and conditional sales because in each the property may pass upon payment of the final instalment. However, in the case of a hire purchase agreement the final payment is optional; the hirer may decline to make it and so not complete a sale. Ascertaining the nature of the contract requires an examination of its particular terms. This distinction is discussed at sections 1.6.5 and 7.2.1.

Hire purchase contracts benefit from exactly the same implied terms relating to sale by description, quality, fitness for purpose, hire purchase by sample and title as contracts for the sale of goods. However, these terms are implied by the 1973 Act.

In the case of hire purchase the law is governed by the general law of bailment. In order for there to be a bailment there must be a transfer of possession (*National Cash Register Co.* v *Stanley* [1921] 3 KB 292). During the period of the bailment the buyer has exclusive right of possession and may not be ousted by the owner of the goods unless there has been a breach of one of the terms of the contract.

During the period of the bailment the hirer is under a duty to take reasonable care of the goods, but the owner is under no duty to repair them (*Tilling* v *Balmain* (1892) 8 TLR 517). However, the hirer is not liable for loss caused otherwise than through his fault, nor for fair wear and tear (*Sanderson* v *Collins* [1904] 1 KB 628; *Blakemore* v *Bristol & Exeter Railway* (1858) 8 E & B 1035). Upon conclusion of the hire, the hirer may either exercise his option to purchase or hold the goods available for collection at his address (*Elsey & Co. Ltd* v *Hyde* (1926)).[1] If the hirer holds on to the goods at the end of the period of hire without exercising his option then he commits conversion.

By its very nature a hire purchase agreement supposes that the property in the goods remains with the owner until the hirer comes to exercise his option to purchase.

2.2.3 Conditional sale agreements

A conditional sale agreement is a contract of sale where there exists a condition precedent upon the passing of the property. Usually, the condition will be the payment of the final instalment of the sale price. This distinction is discussed at sections 1.6.5 and 7.2.1.

Conditional sale agreements are sales within the meaning of the 1979 Act and accordingly all the rules contained in that Act apply to such contracts. One exception exists to this, however — by s. 14 of the 1973 Act, s. 11(4) of the 1979 Act has no application (restriction upon right to reject where buyer has accepted the goods). Instead the buyer is deemed to have accepted the goods when he would have been deemed to have done so were the condition contained in a corresponding hire purchase agreement as a condition to be fulfilled by the creditor.

Because the agreement constitutes a 'sale', the various exceptions to the *nemo dat* rule which apply to sales apply to conditional sales.

By its very nature, the property in the goods remains with the seller under a conditional sale agreement until the condition precedent is fulfilled. Accordingly, the same rules as to the allocation of risk apply to conditional sale agreements as

1. See *Jones & Proudfoot's Notes on Hire Purchase Law*, 2nd ed., pp. 107–9; *Halsbury's Laws of England* (London: Butterworths), vol. 9(1), para. 27, n. 10.

apply to hire purchase agreements and the risk for damage is upon the seller for accidents which are not the fault of the buyer.

2.2.4 Credit sale agreements

As with hire purchase agreements and conditional sale agreements a credit sale agreement involves the buyer paying in instalments (Consumer Credit Act 1974, s. 189(1)). However, in the case of a credit sale agreement the property passes immediately to the buyer, with the consequent results relating to risk. A credit sale agreement is a 'sale' within the meaning of the 1979 Act and the usual rules relating to such contracts apply.

2.2.5 Transfers of goods

The concept of a 'transfer of goods' is something of a residual category created by the 1982 Act. By s. 1 it is defined as follows:

> (1) ... a 'contract for the transfer of goods' means a contract under which one person transfers or agrees to transfer to another the property in goods, other than an excepted contract.
>
> (2) For the purposes of this section an excepted contract means any of the following:—
>
> (a) a contract of sale of goods;
>
> (b) a hire purchase agreement;
>
> (c) a contract under which the property in goods is (or is to be) transferred in exchange for trading stamps on their redemption;
>
> (d) [a transfer supported only by deed];
>
> (e) a contract intended to operate by way of mortgage, pledge, charge or other security.
>
> (3) For the purposes of this Act ... a contract is a contract for the transfer of goods whether or not services are also provided or to be provided under the contract, and (subject to subsection (2) above) whatever is the nature of the consideration for the transfer or agreement to transfer.

Section 1(3) brings into the agreement contracts for work and materials. The seller cannot claim that the contract is entirely one for services, which is governed by s. 12 of the 1982 Act. Such contracts only require that *reasonable* skill and care is used in performing the service.

By s. 1 any goods supplied under the agreement will form a transfer of goods to which s. 1 applies. Thus where the seller agrees to supply and install a carpet the supply of the carpet will form a transfer of goods within the meaning of s. 1.

2.3 COMMON LAW RULES AS TO THE TRANSFER OF OWNERSHIP

The 'ownership' of goods connotes a bundle of rights held over the goods by the owner of them. For example, the owner of goods has the right to possess, enjoy, destroy, alienate or sell the goods in question. He may, however, divide his rights over the goods and pass some or all of those rights to another party. In modern times, the most common split of those rights occurs where the owner of them gives another party the right to possess them, whilst himself retaining the title to them. Commonly, this occurs where the owner hires the goods to another. Equally a contract may provide that another is to take possession of the goods prior to the property passing. This occurs in contracts of hire purchase, conditional sales, contracts for sale or return and where the seller of goods inserts a retention of title clause. Here the other party obtains a right to possess the goods even though he is not the owner of them. The owner has dispossessed himself of the right to possession and the retaking of that possession would form a breach of contract.

Some of the common law rules relating to the transfer of ownership are discussed below. It is possible that ownership can be obtained or transferred outside these rules, for example by their being lost and found by another person, but these circumstances are beyond the scope of this text (see, e.g., *Parker* v *British Airways Board* [1982] QB 1004).

2.3.1 Succession

Ownership may be transferred by succession where the goods are transferred by sale, gift, under a will or by any contract which expressly or by implication provides for the transfer of the property in the goods. Here the recipient only takes such title and interest as the previous owner had. In the case of contracts for the sale of goods this much is clear from s. 21(1) of the 1979 Act which provides that 'where goods are sold by a person who is not their owner, and who does not sell them under the authority or with the consent of the owner, the buyer acquires no better title to the goods than the seller had...'. This is, of course, subject to the *nemo dat* rules discussed in chapter 13. It is, however, possible for a person with a limited interest in goods to carve out a lesser interest in the goods than he himself has. For example, where a person has hired goods for a certain period he has acquired a right to possess them for that period. He could therefore validly subhire them to a third party for any period less than he has himself contracted to hire them. In modern times, however, this is likely to be in breach of an express or implied term of the contract.

2.3.2 Accession

Accession occurs whereby one good is attached to another so as to lose its separate identity and to become part of that other good. Accession requires that there is a principal and an accessory. The principal thing is that which forms the physical bulk or skeleton and not its financial value. Thus in *McKeown* v *Cavalier Yachts* (1988) 13 NSWLR 303 a yacht hull was fitted out with an extensive amount of equipment such as mast, sails, fittings, radar etc. All of this cost more than the original hull and was in practice as important as the hull, but it was still held that the hull formed the principal. The ordinary rule is that the property in the accessory passes to the principal (*Hendy Lennox (Industrial Engines) Ltd* v *Grahame Puttick Ltd* [1984] 1 WLR 485).

Whether or not there has been an accession depends upon the nature, degree and purpose of the annexation. This is a question of fact and degree in each case. For example in *Regina Chevrolet Sales Ltd* v *Riddell* [1942] 3 DLR 159 it was held that tyres had become part of a truck because:

> the tyres were ... practically available for the purpose for which they were manufactured, only as parts of a truck; it seems ... that the truck must be regarded not as a mere aggregation of separate parts, but as a working unit into which the several parts have been integrated and harmonised.

By contrast, in *Thomas* v *Robinson* [1977] 1 NZLR 385 it was held that an engine had not become part of another car because it could be easily removed.

It is submitted that the *dicta* in *Regina Chevrolet Sales Ltd* v *Riddell* should be preferred as this better reflects modern practice (see Guest, MLR (1964), p. 508). However, the point is far from certain and English authorities can easily be said to point in the opposite direction (*Hendy Lennox (Industrial Engines) Ltd* v *Grahame Puttick Ltd* [1984] 1 WLR 485; *Sandeman & Sons* v *Tyzack & Branfoot Steamship Company Ltd* [1913] AC 680).

2.3.3 Mixture

A mixture of goods occurs where fluids or granular substances are mixed so as to become one indistinguishable mass. The rule thus applies to goods such as oil, wine, corn, coal or any other such item. The general principles are set out in *Sandeman & Sons* v *Tyzack & Branfoot Steamship Company Ltd* [1913] AC 680:

> My Lords, if we proceed on the principles of English law, I do not think that it is a matter of difficulty to define the legal consequences of the goods of A becoming indistinguishably and inseparably mixed with the goods of B.
>
> If the mixing has arisen from the fault of B, A can claim the goods. He is guilty of no wrongful act and therefore the possession by him of his own goods cannot be interfered with, and if by the wrongful act of B that possession necessarily implies the possession of the intruding goods of B he is entitled to it.
>
> But if the mixing has taken place by accident or other cause, for which neither of the owners is responsible, a different state of things arises. Neither owner has done anything to forfeit his right to the possession of his own property, and if neither party is willing to abandon that right the only equitable solution of the difficulty, and the one accepted by the law, is that A and B become owners in common of the mixed property.

Whilst this case appears to suggest that where A's goods are mixed deliberately with those of B, A acquires the rights in the whole of the goods, more modern authorities suggest that A will only acquire a proportionate share (*Indian Oil Corporation Ltd* v *Greenstone Shipping SA (Panama)* [1988] QB 345). The law is not clear, but it is submitted that this latter case is more likely to be followed in the modern day.

Where there has been a diminution in quality of the goods by virtue of the mixture, and the culprit can be identified, then the injured party or parties may claim against that person for the loss suffered (*Indian Oil Corporation Ltd* v *Greenstone Shipping SA (Panama)* [1988] QB 345).

The rule stated in *Sandeman & Sons* v *Tyzack & Branfoot Steamship Company Ltd* sets out the common law doctrine of confusion as well as the situation where one of the parties has wrongfully mixed the goods of another with his own. It has been said that this doctrine only applies to fluids such as grain and liquids and not to distinct chattels such as cars (*Smith* v *Torr* (1862) 3 F & F 505; *Halsbury's Laws of England* (London: Butterworths), vol. 35, para. 1239). However, it is arguable that where goods have become annexed to another within the sense mentioned in the previous section, and neither owner is at fault, that the only fair solution would be the application of the doctrine of confusion as outlined in the *Sandeman & Sons* case. Certainly, there is no reason in principle that the rule should not apply to such cases (see Guest, MLR (1964), p. 508). The vital point remains, however, that the goods must have become annexed so as to be regarded as inseparable, and as was seen in the previous section, it seems that the English courts have taken a less relaxed attitude to this than other Commonwealth courts.

3 *Background to the law of contract*

3.1 INTRODUCTION

It must be remembered that contracts for the sale or supply of goods and services are simply contracts to which additional rights and duties attach. The general law of contract still applies, albeit modified in certain respects. It is beyond the scope of this text to explore the law of contract fully, but those aspects which arise frequently in practice need to be discussed. As regards the detail, the reader is respectfully referred to more specialist texts on the general law, *Chitty on Contracts* (London: Sweet & Maxwell) traditionally being regarded as the best.

However, the practitioner must be wary of relying upon too academic an analysis of the law. Contract is very much a common law area and individual cases are frequently no more than an application of the general principles to the facts of a particular case. Accordingly, broad statements which appear to cast a general rule of law should be considered with caution; the judgment should never be considered in isolation of its facts.

Furthermore, in practice, judges prove themselves to be masters at reaching the conclusion which they think *ought* to be reached, and a legally technical argument will not necessarily succeed where this does not lead to a result which appeals to the particular judge's sense of justice. Accordingly, it is always best to step back from the details of a case and consider its overall merits. This is particularly so when considering terms of the contract implied at common law, or deciding whether a representation is or is not a term or whether it is a condition or a warranty. The courts appear to decide this almost entirely without reference to principle, particularly so in the latter case where the courts appear to have simply reached the conclusion that a term is a condition when it ought to lead to the right to terminate the contract (which is entirely circular).

The points that will be dealt with here are those which arise more frequently in contracts for the sale of goods: formation of the contract — offer and acceptance, auction sales, determining whether a representation is a term of the contract, if so whether it is a condition, a warranty or an innominate term, the collateral contract mechanism and the parol evidence rule. Misrepresentation is dealt with in the next chapter.

3.2 FORMATION OF THE CONTRACT

The traditional formula for establishing whether or not a contract has arisen has been to see whether there is an offer and an acceptance coupled with an intention to create legal relations and supported on both sides by consideration. The latter two requirements will not be considered here as the circumstances where a case may come before the courts in the context of the sale or supply of goods where there is a dispute as to whether they were present are so rare as to be ignored. However, determining whether there is a contract or when it was formed is something which arises in commercial situations and will be explored.

Whilst this is the traditional formula for determining whether a contract exists, in modern times the courts have been quick to find that a contract exists where it is clear that the parties intended to be bound, although on a strict analysis the traditional formula has not been adhered to. The fundamental question is whether the parties intended to bind themselves to an agreement (*Pagnan SpA* v *Feed Products Ltd* [1987] 2 Lloyd's Rep 601). Thus there may be a contract even though the parties have not agreed on something as fundamental as the price (Sale of Goods Act 1979, s. 8(2); *Foley* v *Classique Coaches* [1934] 2 KB 1). Here the courts can imply a term that the parties intended that the buyer would pay a 'reasonable price'. But in some cases failure to agree on something so fundamental to the agreement as the price can be construed only as meaning that no concluded agreement was reached (*Courtney and Fairbairn Ltd* v *Tolaini Bros (Hotels) Ltd* [1975] 1 All ER 716).

Where the contract contains meaningless phrases then this does not detract from the fact that there may be a contract where those parts can be ignored without affecting the other parts. But where the ambiguity goes to the root of the contract then this cannot be done (*Scammel & Nephew Ltd* v *Ouston* [1941] 1 All ER 504).

It is quite possible that the parties may leave a fundamental matter to be determined by a third party, or even by one of the parties themselves during the currency of the contract and still form a binding agreement (*Lombard Tricity Finance Ltd* v *Paton* [1989] 1 All ER 918).

Where the parties have made their agreement but have stipulated that it should be written down in a formal document then it is a question of fact in each case as to whether they merely intended this to evidence their agreement (e.g., *Rossiter* v *Miller* (1878) 3 App Cas 1124) or whether they intended not to be bound until the agreement is so written, e.g., where it is expressed to be 'subject to contract' (*British Steel Corporation* v *Cleveland Bridge and Engineering Co. Ltd* [1984] 1 All ER 504; *Chillingworth* v *Esche* [1924] 1 Ch 97; *Alpenstow Ltd* v *Regalian Properties plc* [1985] 2 All ER 545). Where the parties have reached agreement concerning the broad heads of the agreement, but have left the detail to be dealt with in a formal written document, the issue is probably to be determined by reference to the importance of the terms left to the written document and whether the parties have acted on the broad heads pending the written document being drafted. Where the details are of minor importance then the courts can properly infer that there was an agreement and that in respect of any outstanding details the parties had agreed to perform the contract 'reasonably', i.e., reasonable delivery times, reasonable carriage charges, etc.

3.2.1 Offer distinguished from an invitation to treat

Advertisements frequently appear to form the basis of an offer at first glance, but it is settled law that they will rarely do so. Thus in *Partridge* v *Crittenden* [1968] 2 All ER 421 an advertisement offering birds for sale in a trade magazine did not amount to an offer in the legal sense. Similarly the display of goods in a shop window is merely an invitation to treat and not an offer (*Pharmaceutical Society of Great Britain* v *Boots Cash Chemists* [1953] 1 QB 401), and the display of the price of petrol at a filling station is not an offer (*Esso Petroleum Co. Ltd* v *Customs and Excise Commissioners* [1976] 1 WLR 1), nor is the attachment of a price in the advertising of a house for sale (*Gibson* v *Manchester City Council* [1979] 1 All ER 972). An advertisement will usually be treated merely as an invitation to treat, with the actual offer being made when the customer selects the goods and takes them to the payment counter or appropriates the petrol and does so.

An advertisement may amount to an offer where it is expressed with sufficient sincerity to be presumed by a customer that the business intends to be bound by the offer. Thus in the famous case of *Carlill* v *Carbolic Smoke Ball Co.* [1893] 1 QB 256 the Smoke Ball Company expressed their sincerity by depositing £1,000 with a bank. Similarly in *R* v *Warwickshire County Council, ex parte Johnson* [1993] AC 583 an electrical goods retailer had promised to beat any of his local competitors on price by a £20 reduction on the spot.

This distinction between offers and invitations to treat leads on to another point, that an offer may be distinguished from an invitation to treat where a reasonable person would infer from the way that the offer is expressed that the offeror intended that the words would constitute an offer. The test is objective; for example see *Moran* v *University of Salford (No. 2)* (1993) 4 ELR 187 where a university accidentally offered a place to a prospective student.

In the case of a contract 'going out to tender', the person requesting the tenders is usually construed as making an invitation to treat, with the person putting in the tender making an offer capable of acceptance. The person to whom the tender is made may, however, bind himself not necessarily to accept the offer, but at least to consider it (*Blackpool and Fylde Aero Club* v *Blackpool Borough Council* [1990] 3 All ER 25). The person inviting tenders may not therefore put others to the expense of preparing a formal tender merely to clothe himself with the appearance of having fairly allocated the contract. Similarly, an invitation to tender may be expressed in terms that the best tender will be accepted. Here that person may bind himself to accept the best tender (*Harvela Investments Ltd* v *Royal Trust of Canada (CI) Ltd* [1986] AC 207), but in many cases which tender is the 'best' tender will be a highly subjective matter and the invitation to tender cannot be construed as an offer. The general rule remains that a person who receives a tender is not bound to accept it, but may reject any or all tenders received (*William Lacey (Hownslow) Ltd* v *Davis* [1957] 1 WLR 932).

3.2.2 Acceptance and 'battle of the forms'

An acceptance may be made by words or conduct, but it must amount to an assent to all the terms of the offer. The acceptance must furthermore be communicated. Thus if the acceptance of the offer is drowned out by an airplane flying overhead then there is no contract (*Entores Ltd* v *Miles Far East Corporation* [1955] 2 QB 327). An exception to this general rule is where the offer, by its own terms, dispenses with communication of the acceptance. Thus, in the classic case of *Carlill* v *Carbolic Smoke Ball Co.* [1893] 1 QB 256 the acceptance was the mere use of the smoke ball. Similarly, when a person uses a credit card a contract arises between the retailer and the credit card company despite the fact that the retailer has not expressly contacted the card issuer (*First Sport Ltd* v *Barclays Bank plc* [1993] 3 All ER 789).

The general rule is that an acceptance is made when it is posted, and not when it is received (*Adams* v *Lindsell* (1818) 1 B & Ald 681; *Bruner* v *Moore* [1904] 1 Ch 305). However, the offeror may preclude this rule by dictating a particular method of acceptance (*Holwell Securities Ltd* v *Hughes* [1974] 1 All ER 161). But even where the offeror has prescribed a particular form of acceptance, an acceptance may still be made if the method chosen is more efficient than that prescribed by the offeror and does not prejudice him (*Manchester Diocesan Council for Education* v *Commercial and General Investments Ltd* [1970] 1 WLR 241; *Western Electric Ltd* v *Welsh Development Agency* [1983] QB 796). Similarly, the rule will not operate where it is unreasonable to use the post in order to accept the offer, for example where there is a postal strike at the time for acceptance or rejection of the offer where time is of the essence (*Henthorn* v *Fraser* [1892] 2 Ch 27; *Holwell Securities Ltd* v *Hughes* [1974] 1 All ER 161; *Brinkibon Ltd* v *Stahag Stahl und Stahlwarenhandelsgesellschaft mbH* [1983] 2 AC 34).

Where the general rule applies then the contract is deemed to have been concluded at the time it is posted (*Potter* v *Sanders* (1846) 6 Hare 1). This can lead to some harsh results. Once accepted the offer cannot be withdrawn, and this is so even where a retraction of the offer is posted after the acceptance, but received before its arrival (*Byrne & Co.* v *Leon Van Tienhoven* (1880) 5 CPD 344). Furthermore, there will be a concluded contract even where the acceptance is delayed in the post (*Dunlop* v *Higgins* (1848) 1 HL Cas 381), or even lost altogether (*Household Fire and Carriage Accident Insurance* v *Grant* (1879) 4 Ex D 216).

Silence will not generally amount to an acceptance (*Felthouse* v *Bindley* (1862) 11 CBNS 869). Thus, in the obvious example, A cannot write to B offering to buy his horse and stating that if he hears nothing within two weeks that there will be a contract. In exceptional circumstances, however, silence may amount to an acceptance where the circumstances are such that there was a duty upon that party to speak. This may be the case where one party has initiated and driven negotiations and has failed to respond to what appeared to be an acceptable counter offer (*Rust* v *Abbey life Assurance* [1979] 2 Lloyd's Rep 334; *The Leonidas D* [1985] 2 All ER 796; *Rafsanjan Pistachio Producers Co-operative* v *Bank Leumi (UK) plc* [1993] 1 Lloyd's Rep 513). Certainly the circumstances where such a 'duty to speak' may arise will be more often found in commercial situations rather than consumer ones. Of course, an offer may be accepted by conduct rather than words, as in the *Carbolic Smoke Ball* case.

Given that in order to amount to an acceptance the communication must form an assent to all the terms of the offer, any variation in what purports to be an acceptance will operate as a counter offer. Thus where A is offered 1,000 tonnes of coal at a certain price, there will be no contract where he purports to accept only 500 tonnes of it (*Tinn* v *Hoffman & Co.* (1873) 29 LT 271). However, very minor alterations may not prevent the acceptance being binding, as in the situation where the contract is amended to include terms that would in any event have been implied by statute (*Lark* v *Outhwaite* [1991] 2 Lloyd's Rep 132). However, such variations must be exceptionally trivial.

The effect of a counter offer is to reject the offer made and to make a fresh offer. This means that the counter offeror cannot subsequently accept the offer originally made to him. Where the parties use standard forms in the making of their contracts then a 'battle of the forms' situation arises. It is common practice for large firms to have 'purchase order' forms and 'sales order' forms. The standard terms and conditions are, naturally, drafted in terms of the particular party's interest so one party's 'purchase order' form will contain the implied terms inserted by the Sale of Goods Act 1979 (the '1979 Act') for the avoidance of doubt, whereas the other party's form will exclude them. In *British Road Services* v *A. V. Crutchley Ltd* [1968] 1 All ER 811 (see also *Butler Machine Tool Co. Ltd* v *Ex-cell-o Corporation (England) Ltd* [1979] 1 All ER 965) the buyer had purported to buy goods on his standard purchase form, which the seller had accepted by use of his standard sales form. At this stage there was no completed contract, simply a counter offer. But when the goods were delivered with the buyer having said nothing more then there was an acceptance of the seller's counter offer by conduct. The reverse result would have been reached had the buyer's form been the second in time.

3.2.3 Auction sales

Section 57 of the 1979 Act provides as follows:

> (1) Where goods are put up for sale by auction in lots, each lot is prima facie deemed to be the subject of a separate contract of sale.
>
> (2) A sale by auction is complete when the auctioneer announces its completion by the fall of the hammer, or in other customary manner; and until the announcement is made any bidder may retract his bid.
>
> (3) A sale by auction may be notified to be subject to a reserve or upset price, and a right to bid may also be reserved expressly by or on behalf of the seller.
>
> (4) Where a sale by auction is not notified to be subject to a right to bid by or on behalf of the seller, it is not lawful for the seller to bid himself or to employ any person to bid at the sale, or for the auctioneer knowingly to take any bid from the seller or any such person.
>
> (5) A sale contravening subsection (4) above may be treated as fraudulent by the buyer.
>
> (6) Where, in respect of a sale by auction, a right to bid is expressly reserved (but not otherwise) the seller or any one person on his behalf may bid at the auction.

In auction sales the bidder is the offeror under a contract of sale and not the auctioneer. It follows that the auctioneer may accept or reject any offer made (see *British Car Auctions* v *Wright* [1972] 3 All ER 462). However, arguably the auctioneer may not reject a bid for capricious reasons, and a duty to accept the highest bid could probably be implied by analogy with the duty to consider a tender (per *Warlow* v *Harrison* (1859) 1 E & B 309; *Blackpool and Fylde Aero Club* v *Blackpool Borough Council* [1990] 3 All ER 25). In any event, most auctions will be run according to expressed conditions of sale advertised at the auction (*Richards* v *Phillips* [1968] 2 All ER 859).

Where a lot has been notified as being subject to a reserve price then where a buyer's offer is mistakenly accepted by the auctioneer the buyer has no remedy (*McManus* v *Fortescue* [1907] 2 KB 1). However, if the reserve price is not advertised then the buyer could claim for non-delivery as the auctioneer would have been acting within the apparent authority of his principal under a contract of agency.

The remaining provisions of s. 57 of the 1979 Act are reasonably straightforward: the seller cannot secretly reserve a power to bid in the auction (hence driving up the price artificially). A corresponding prohibition exists in the Auctions (Bidding Agreement) Act 1969 against buyers running a 'bidding ring' whereby the buyers agree not to compete for certain goods and hence drive the price down.

3.3 THE TERMS OF THE CONTRACT

Many statements are made during negotiation of a contract or are contained in a written contract. The exact status of any such statement or phrase is a matter of great uncertainty. It is trite law to say that a pre-contract representation may be a 'mere puff', or a term of the contract or a representation which if wrong gives rise to the right to rescind the contract in an action for misrepresentation. Under a contract, whether written or oral, a term may be a warranty, the breach of which gives rise only to a claim for damages, a condition, the breach of which gives rise to a right to terminate the contract and seek damages or an innominate term, the rights under which depend upon the severity of the breach. Even if the representation is likely to form a term of the contract evidence may not be permitted of it under the parol evidence rule. To add to this minefield the courts have been reluctant to give guidance as to when the representation is a term, and if so whether it is a condition or a warranty. The position reached is somewhat circular: it is a term when it ought to be, and it is a condition when the injured party deserves to be entitled to repudiate the contract. Given this it is not surprising that the layman looks with horror at his solicitor or counsel when told that he has no remedy and says 'but it says here in black and white that . . .'. The law in this area is not satisfactory as it leaves too much open to doubt and the idiosyncrasy of an individual judge. Furthermore, where the law is so vague it is difficult for accurate legal advice to be given which in turn means that it is harder for cases to be settled out of court.

Such guidance as there is as to when a representation will be an express term is examined below in section 3.3.1. The distinction between conditions, warranties and innominate terms is examined in section 3.3.2. The circumstances when the courts would be prepared to imply a term are explored at 3.3.3, the collateral contract mechanism is examined at 3.3.4 and the parol evidence rule at 3.3.5 together with the effect of reducing a contract into written form. Misrepresentation is examined separately in the next chapter.

3.3.1 Express terms of the contract

Where a contract has been reduced to writing little difficulty arises as to whether something stated in the contract is a term — it will be unless one of the parties can show that it was included in the contract by mistake, or is excluded as an unfair contract term. The real difficulty lies in deciding whether an oral statement is a term or a 'mere' representation. The various cases are probably best discussed on this issue by Lord Denning in *Oscar Chess Ltd* v *Williams* [1957] 1 WLR 370. It is worth quoting extensively from that case (albeit with some extractions):

> The crucial question is: was it a binding promise or only an innocent misrepresentation? The technical distinction between a 'condition' and a 'warranty' is quite immaterial in this case, because it is far too late for the buyer to reject the car. He can at best only claim damages. The material distinction here is between a statement which is a term of the contract and a statement which is only an innocent misrepresentation. This distinction is best expressed by the ruling of Lord Holt: Was it intended as a warranty or not? Using the word warranty there in its ordinary English meaning: because it gives the exact shade of meaning that is required. It is something to which a man must be taken to bind himself.
>
> In applying Lord Holt's test, however, some misunderstanding has arisen by the use of the word 'intended'. It is sometimes supposed that the tribunal must look into the minds of the parties to see what they themselves intended. That is a mistake. Lord Moulton made it quite clear that 'The intention of the parties can only be deduced from the totality of the evidence'. The question whether a warranty was intended depends on the conduct of the parties, on their words and behaviour, rather than on their thoughts. If an intelligent bystander would reasonably infer that a warranty was intended, that will suffice. And this, when the facts are not in dispute, is a question of law. That is shown by *Heilbut, Symons & Co.* v *Buckleton* [1913] AC 30 itself, where the House of Lords upset the finding by a jury of a warranty.
>
> Turning now to the present case, much depends on the precise words that were used. If the seller says 'I believe it is a 1948 Morris. Here is the registration book to prove it', there is clearly no warranty. It is a statement of belief, not a contractual promise. But if the seller says 'I guarantee that it is a 1948 Morris. This is borne out by the registration book, but you need not rely solely on that. I give you my own guarantee that it is', there is clearly a warranty. The seller is making himself contractually responsible, even though the registration book is wrong.
>
> Once that fact is put on one side I ask myself: What is the proper inference from the known facts? It must have been obvious to both that the seller had himself no personal knowledge of the year when the car was made. He only became owner after a great number of changes. He must have been relying on the registration book. It is unlikely that such a person would warrant the year of manufacture. The most he would do would be to state his belief, and then produce the registration book in verification of it. In these circumstances the intelligent bystander would, I suggest, say that the seller did not intend to bind himself so as to warrant that it was a 1948 model. If the seller was asked to pledge himself to it, he would at once have said 'I cannot do that. I have only the log-book to go by, the same as you'.

> The judge seems to have thought that there was a difference between written contracts and oral contracts. He thought that the reason why the buyer failed in *Heilbut, Symons & Co.* v *Buckleton* and *Routledge* v *McKay* [1954] 1 WLR 615 was because the sales were afterwards recorded in writing, and the written contracts contained no reference to the representation. I agree that that was an important factor in those cases. If an oral representation is afterwards recorded in writing, it is good evidence that it was intended as a warranty. If it is not put into writing, it is evidence against a warranty being intended. But it is by no means decisive. There have been many cases where the courts have found an oral warranty collateral to a written contract such as *Birch* v *Paramount Estates*, 2 October 1956, unreported....

The first point to note from this case is that the issue of establishing what the terms of the contract are is not entirely, as is often broadly stated, a question of fact. Ascertaining the representation and the background circumstances is a question of fact, but deducing whether or not that they confirm whether those words were intended as a term is an application of law. Should a party wish to appeal a case this is an important distinction.

The second point to note is that the test is objective. The issue is not whether the person making the statement believed that it was intended to be a binding promise or indeed whether the person hearing it thought as much, but whether a reasonable man looking on at the parties would have believed that the statement was intended to be a binding promise.

Thirdly, it is important to note the distinction between determining whether the term is a condition or warranty, as determined by the importance attached to it, and simply whether it was a term at all, as determined by deciding whether it was intended as a binding promise.

Finally, it must be noted that there is a distinction between a representation which becomes a term because a reasonable person would have supposed that the party meant to be bound by the representation and an implied term. An implied term arises where nothing was said, but it is reasonable in the circumstances to suppose that had it been raised the parties would have said 'but of course'.

The test above is very broadly applied and is very much left to the discretion of the trial judge. Analysing the meaning of the words used and the background circumstances may be a question of law, but the Court of Appeal would in practice be loath to interfere with a judge's analysis of a case upon which he had heard live evidence.

That each individual case is very much at the mercy of a particular judge is shown by a brief comparison of some of the cases decided in this area. In *Dick Bentley (Productions) Ltd* v *Harold Smith (Motors) Ltd* [1965] 2 All ER 65 a car dealer represented that a car had done less than 20,000 miles. This was held to be a term of the contract. By contrast in *Oscar Chess Ltd* v *Williams* (above) a private seller had represented that the car was a 1948 model when it was not. This was held to be a mere representation. Similarly, in *Hopkins* v *Tanqueray* (1854) 15 CB 130 the seller represented that his horse was sound. This was held to be a mere representation. By contrast in *Couchman* v *Hill* [1947] KB 554 the seller had represented that a cow being put up for sale had not been 'served'. This was held to be a term of the contract.

Given these cases, a thorough analysis of all the cases decided would neither be useful nor within the scope of this text. In practice, the answer to whether a representation is a term or not is best answered by asking whether or not a party would be justified in complaining should the representation prove to be false. Note the distinction between this and deciding whether or not it would be fair to allow someone to terminate the contract should the representation prove untrue.

In the modern day, the answer to the question is likely to be decided more favourably to a consumer than a business man. For example, the sale in *Dick Bentley (Productions) Ltd* v *Harold Smith (Motors) Ltd* was by a dealer, whereas in *Oscar Chess Ltd* v *Williams* it was by a private individual. One could also cite as an example *Harlingdon & Leinster Enterprises Ltd* v *Christopher Hull Fine Art Ltd* [1991] 1 QB 564. In that case a representation was made that a painting was by a particular artist. Both parties were dealers in such art. It was no surprise that the court held that the representation was not a term. By contrast, if the buyer was an ordinary member of the public with no expertise, and the seller a high street shop, a court would almost certainly hold that a representation that a painting was an original was a term of the contract.

3.3.2 Conditions, warranties, innominate terms and fundamental terms

At the time that the Sale of Goods Act 1979 was passed it was assumed that contractual clauses fell into only two categories: conditions and warranties. This remains very much the case today. However, throughout the early twentieth century a further type of term came to be recognised; a fundamental term, a term where no other clause could exclude liability for its breach. An example of a fundamental term may be that the seller transfers the property in the goods to the buyer. This strain of authority did not survive, however. In *Suisse Atlantique Société d'Armement Maritime SA* v *NV Rotterdamsche Kolen Centrale* [1967] 1 AC 361 the House of Lords held that there was no separate category of term called a fundamental one. However, as a rule of construction exclusion clauses would be construed against the suggestion that they excluded liability for a fundamental breach of the contract. The whole doctrine, however, is of limited practical importance since the introduction of the Unfair Contract Terms Act 1977.[1] The phrase is, however, used in commercial contracts, probably to make it as clear as possible that the parties intend a term to operate as a condition.

The notion of an innominate or intermediate term was first accepted in *Hong Kong Fir Shipping Co. Ltd* v *Kawasaki Kisen Kaisha* [1962] 2 QB 26. An innominate term is one whereby the injured party is allowed to repudiate the contract depending upon the severity of the breach. Such a result seems sensible and in practice is what happens in any event — if the court thinks that an injured

1. See, however, Atiyah, *The Sale of Goods*, 9th ed. (Pitman Publishing, 1995), p. 55, where it is suggested that the doctrine of fundamental breach may operate to prevent a buyer from being deemed to have accepted goods where the seller has committed a fundamental breach. There is probably some merit in this argument, although it is not one currently recognised by the law. For example, in *Rowland* v *Divall* [1923] 2 KB 500 — 'But I think that the answer is that there can be no sale at all of goods which the seller has no right to sell. The whole object of a sale is to transfer property from one person to another.'; and in *Varley* v *Whipp* [1900] 1 QB 513 — 'If a man says that he will sell the black horse in the last stall in his stable, and the stall is empty, or there is no horse in it, but only a cow, no property could pass'; the example of the 'peas and beans' example in the *Suisse Atlantique* case also supports this.

party should be entitled to repudiate then it holds that the term was a condition; if it does not then it is held to be a warranty. Innominate terms are discussed in more detail below.

Section 11(3) of the Sale of Goods Act 1979 provides as follows:

> Whether a stipulation in a contract of sale is a condition, the breach of which may give rise to a right to treat the contract as repudiated, or a warranty, the breach of which may give rise to a claim for damages but not to reject the goods and treat the contract as repudiated, depends in each case on the construction of the contract; and a stipulation may be a condition, though called a warranty in the contract.

This provision aptly summarises the common law definition of conditions and warranties: a term is a condition when it gives rise to a right to terminate the contract. But this is circular: a party has a right to terminate the contract when it is a condition, as opposed to a warranty, that has been breached. When then does a party have a right to terminate a contract? The answer to this seems to be 'when they ought to'. All that is certain is that if not a condition or an innominate term, a term will be a 'mere' warranty.

The circumstances when a term will be a condition were discussed in *Schuler AG* v *Wickman Machine Tool Sales Ltd* [1974] AC 235. In this case Schuler sought to rely on a clause which was labelled within the contract to be a condition, though it was held to be only a warranty. Lord Reid said (at p. 251):

> Sometimes a breach of a term gives that option [to repudiate the contract] to the aggrieved party because it is of a fundamental character going to the root of the contract, sometimes it gives that option because the parties have chosen to stipulate that it shall have that effect. Blackburn J said in *Bettini* v *Gye* (1876) 1 QBD 183, 187: 'Parties may think some matter, apparently of very little importance, essential; and if they sufficiently express an intention to make the literal fulfilment of such a thing a condition precedent, it will be one; ...'.
>
> In the present case it is not contended that Wickman's failures to make visits amounted in themselves to fundamental breaches. What is contended is that the terms of clause 7 'sufficiently express an intention' to make any breach, however small, of the obligation to make visits a condition so that any breach shall entitle Schuler to rescind the whole contract if they so desire.
>
> Schuler maintains that the use of the word 'condition' is in itself enough to establish this intention. No doubt some words used by lawyers do have a rigid inflexible meaning. But we must remember that we are seeking to discover intention as disclosed by the contract as a whole. Use of the word 'condition' is an indication — even a strong indication — of such an intention but it is by no means conclusive.
>
> The fact that a particular construction leads to a very unreasonable result must be a relevant consideration. The more unreasonable the result the more unlikely it is that the parties can have intended it, and if they do intend it the more necessary it is that they shall make that intention abundantly clear.

The fundamental criterion which the courts must apply in determining whether a term is a condition or warranty is therefore the intention of the parties. In determining whether the parties did so intend, *factors* to be taken into account are whether they expressed the clause as a condition or a warranty, whether the term is one which goes to the 'root' of the contract and the disparity (or otherwise) between the breach and the result if the injured party were allowed to repudiate.

This loosely defined test creates a trade-off of certainty for justice. It was noted above that in professionally drafted contracts the phrase 'fundamental term' is used to express the term as a 'condition'. What the draftsmen are trying to say, in legalese, is 'we really really mean this clause to be a condition'. Likewise, great difficulties arise attempting to advise a client who complains of a breach of contract as such advice necessarily involves a subjective assessment of the severity of the breach compared with the overall contract. Any given lawyer's subjective opinion may differ greatly from any given judge's. This leads to great uncertainty within the law. By contrast, if the courts slavishly follow precedent or the contract great injustice can be caused.[2]

However, within the context of the sale of goods, s. 11(3) of the Sale of Goods Act 1979[3] does not provide that a condition can ever be a warranty. All the terms implied by that Act regarding quality, title, fitness for purpose, etc. are conditions and if there is a breach of them then the injured party has a right to repudiate the contract. There are only three circumstances where the 1979 Act deals with warranties: first, the implied terms under s. 12 (quiet possession, limited title, etc.) are warranties, secondly, where the buyer is deemed to have accepted the goods then he may only treat the implied conditions as warranties, finally, where the breach in relation to quality, correspondence with sample or condition is so slight that it would be unreasonable to reject the goods then the buyer is precluded from doing so and must treat the breach as a breach of warranty. This latter exception only applies to contracts where the buyer does not deal as a consumer.

The possibility of a term being an innominate term was first upheld in *Hong Kong Fir Shipping Co. Ltd* v *Kawasaki Kisen Kaisha* [1962] 2 QB 26. In that case there was a contract for a charterparty (hire of a ship). There was a term that the ship would be seaworthy. Seaworthiness is a matter capable of precise legal definition, such that any failure to comply could make the ship 'unseaworthy' in a strict legal sense. Whilst it is clear that if the ship were totally unsafe it would certainly form a breach going to the root of the contract, if there were only minor defects it could hardly be held that the injured party should be entitled to repudiate the entire contract. Accordingly, the term was innominate — whether it has been breached depended upon the severity of the breach. This necessarily involves an assessment of the situation after the breach, rather than examining the intention of the parties prior to or at the time of forming the contract. Subsequent cases have affirmed this decision. However, the rule does not apply to the terms implied into contracts for the sale or supply of goods (*Reardon Smith Line Ltd* v *Hansen-Tangen* [1976] 1 WLR 989; *Cehave NV* v *Bremer Handelsgesellschaft (The Hansa Nord)* [1976] QB 44). Furthermore, the construction of terms as being innominate has been urged upon the courts, as opposed to finding that the terms are conditions (*Bunge Corporation* v *Tradax Export SA* [1981] 2 All ER 513, at 541; *Tradax International SA* v *Goldschmidt SA* [1977] 2 Lloyd's Rep 604, at 612). Finally, it

2. On this point see Treitel, *An Outline of The Law of Contract*, 5th ed. (London: Butterworths, 1995), p. 315.
3. See also *Bunge Corporation* v *Tradax Export SA* [1981] 2 All ER 513, and *Tradax International SA* v *Goldschmidt SA* [1977] 2 Lloyd's Rep 604.

is worth noting that the courts lean in favour of construing clauses as innominate where they would otherwise be conditions as opposed to warranties. For example, in *The Hansa Nord* [1976] QB 44 the court managed to find that goods were merchantable (so as there was no breach of condition), yet also find that they were not in 'good condition' within the meaning of a term deemed to be innominate (yet in the circumstances there only being a breach of warranty).

3.3.3 Implied terms

An implied term is one which was not mentioned by the parties prior to or at the time of entering the contract but is written into the contract regardless. Whilst the factors taken into account may be similar, the test for implying a term is not to be confused with the tests for deciding whether a representation was a term, or whether such a term was a condition. Those tests deal with what *was* said by the parties, not what was *not*.

Terms may be implied by assessing the presumed intent of the parties, by operation of law or by trade custom. In the context of the sale or supply of goods and services the terms implied as to title, freedom from encumbrances, description, quality, fitness for purpose and correspondence with sample are dealt with in detail in their respective chapters.

The circumstances where a court will imply a term by virtue of custom are where that term is notorious and reasonable. Thus, for example, where standard terms have been negotiated between trade associations and it is the normal practice that those terms will be used, those terms can be implied into the contract even though no express provision has been made for their inclusion (*British Crane Hire Corporation Ltd* v *Ipswich Plant Hire Ltd* [1975] QB 303). Whether it is the trade or custom that particular transactions are conducted on certain terms is a question of fact, and the onus of proving it is upon the party asserting it. Trade customs arise in a variety of circumstances, and the list is unlimited: *Anderson* v *Commercial Union Insurance Company plc* (1998) SLT 826 (no implied term that building contracts are paid for by interim certificate); *Eastwood* v *Ryder*, *The Times*, 31 July 1990 (no custom in the magazine industry that X warrants his article is true where it is published in Y's magazine); *General Reinsurance Corp* v *Forsakringsaktiebolaget Fennia Patria* [1982] 2 WLR 518 (customs within the underwriting industry).

Whether to incorporate a term by reason of the presumed intention of the parties is judged by the officious bystander test: had a bystander listening to the parties suggested the inclusion of the term the parties would have replied 'but of course' (*Shirlaw* v *Southern Foundries Ltd* [1939] 2 KB 206). The test is sometimes suggested as being that the parties would have necessarily included the term so as to give the contract business efficacy (*Luxor (Eastbourne) Ltd* v *Cooper* [1941] AC 108; *Trollope & Colls Ltd* v *North West Metropolitan Hospital Board* [1973] 2 All ER 260). This latter expression of the test appears somewhat broader than the officious bystander test. However, it is to be remembered that the test relates to the presumed intention of the parties and it is not for the court to write the parties a better contract than they had done (*Ashmore* v *Corporation of Lloyds (No. 2)* [1992] 2 Lloyd's Rep 620; *Liverpool City Council* v *Irwin* [1977] AC 239).

It must also be noted that the courts will only imply a term into the contract where both parties would have agreed to its inclusion at the time of contracting, not simply one of them (*Spring* v *National Amalgamated Stevedores & Dockers Society* [1956] 2 All ER 221; *Shell (UK) Ltd* v *Lostock Garages Ltd* [1976] 1 WLR 1187). Nor is it sufficient that the parties agree that had they considered the matter at the time of contracting they would have agreed to some provision in respect of it, but that they each would have wanted a different provision (*Lister* v *Romford Ice and Cold Storage Co. Ltd* [1957] AC 555).

Whilst the test as defined appears quite strict, in practice the courts are willing to imply quite complicated terms into quite complicated contracts.

3.3.4 Collateral contracts

The collateral contract mechanism may be used to obviate the privity rule where that prevents a person who makes a misrepresentation from escaping liability. The first case which applied the mechanism was that of *Shanklin Pier Ltd* v *Detel Products Ltd* [1951] 2 KB 854. In that case the defendants were paint manufacturers who had visited the plaintiff's pier and represented that their paint would last for at least three years. The plaintiff accordingly instructed a third party contractor to paint the pier and stipulated that the defendant's paint should be used. The paint failed after only three months. It was held that there was a binding contract between the parties with the representation forming a term of it and that the plaintiff was entitled to recover damages in respect of its breach. This case has been followed in many others: *Wells (Merstham)* v *Buckland Sand and Silica Co.* [1964] 1 All ER 41; *Brown* v *Sheen and Richmond Car Sales* (1950) CLY 9203; *Andrews* v *Hopkinson* [1956] CLY 7947; *Yeoman Credit* v *Odgers* [1962] CLY 1392. The latter cases relate to hire purchase, where the supplier of goods makes a statement in respect of them and they are subsequently sold to the finance company and let to the hirer. These have been overtaken by s. 56 of the Consumer Credit Act 1974 as the supplier will usually be deemed to be an agent of the finance company. The buyer therefore has a direct remedy against the finance company in respect of anything said by the supplier.

However, it is not every statement by a manufacturer which will lead to a collateral contract. There must be an intention on the part of the maker for the statement to have binding force. In *Lexmead (Basingstoke) Ltd* v *Lewis* [1982] AC 225 it was argued in the Court of Appeal (but not the House of Lords) that advertising literature formed a collateral contract between the buyer and the manufacturer of a tow-bar which proved to be defective. The Court of Appeal dismissed this (essentially) because the statements were 'mere puffs' and the element of intention to be bound by the statement that was to be found in *Carlill* v *Carbolic Smoke Ball Co.* [1893] 1 QB 256 was missing. There was much discussion in that case as to the 'special relationship' required in tort to establish a duty of care between the consumer and the maker of a negligent misstatement (as in *Hedley Byrne & Co. Ltd* v *Heller & Partners Ltd* [1964] AC 465, *Caparro Industries plc* v *Dickman* [1990] 2 AC 605 and *Murphy* v *Brentwood District Council* [1990] 2 All ER 908). It is submitted that the element which distinguishes *Lexmead* from *Denham*, and (in a sense) forms the special relationship in the tort cases, is (in this context) to be found in the simple definition of a warranty that was put forward in *Oscar Chess Ltd* v *Williams* [1957] 1 WLR 370:

> The material distinction here is between a statement which is a term of the contract and a statement which is only an innocent misrepresentation. This distinction is best expressed by the ruling of Lord Holt: Was it intended as a warranty or not? Using the word warranty there in its ordinary English meaning: because it gives the exact shade of meaning that is required. It is something to which a man must be taken to bind himself.
>
> If an intelligent bystander would reasonably infer that a warranty was intended, that will suffice.

The law here is not substantially affected by the Contracts (Rights of Third Parties) Act 1999, as the Act will not generally provide a consumer of goods with a right to sue up the chain of sale, as to which see section 3.4.

3.3.5 Contracts reduced to writing and the parol evidence rule

Not unnaturally the law attributes weight to agreements where the terms are set out and signed by a contracting party. Accordingly, it remains the general rule that where a party has signed a document which purports to be the contract between the parties then he must be taken to have assented to all the terms contained therein (*L'Estrange* v *F. Graucob Ltd* [1934] 2 KB 394). This rule applies whether or not the signer understood the terms or indeed whether they were in his own language (*The Luna* [1922] P 22). Accordingly, most businesses employ standard contracts which they expect to be signed by their customer. This applies in both business situations and consumer ones.

However, where the contract incorporates an onerous or unusual term in circumstances where the buyer is not seriously expected to read the terms and conditions then it is open to the court to hold that that term did not become part of the contract unless it was sufficiently drawn to the buyer's attention (*Tilden Rent-a-Car* v *Clendenning* [1978] 83 DLR (3d) 400). Furthermore, if there was a misrepresentation relating to that term then the buyer may not be bound by the term, whether that misrepresentation was fraudulent or innocent (*Curtis* v *Chemical Cleaning and Dyeing Co.* [1951] 1 All ER 631).

It is quite possible for the parties to incorporate terms into the contract by reference to another document. Thus, for example, many contracts of sale are expressed to be 'subject to our standard terms and conditions as displayed [e.g., in the showroom]'. But the rule is not so limited: in one case a sale of securities was held to incorporate the company's prospectus as part of the contract between the parties (*Jacobs* v *Batavia & General Plantations Trust Ltd* [1924] 1 Ch 287).

In practice, most contracts are formed partly orally and partly in writing, whether or not they are then subsequently reduced to writing. Thus, it is normal for a car salesman to give his 'patter' to the buyer before the sale is completed, or for a salesman of a computer or engineering system to visit the potential buyers and explain the marvels that the technology will achieve. Such transactions are then usually put into a written contract, most likely on the seller's standard terms. The law somewhat hardens its face to these representations by use of the parol evidence rule: evidence may not be adduced at trial in order to add to, vary or contradict a written agreement (*Jacobs* v *Batavia & General Plantations Trust Ltd* [1924] 1 Ch 287; *Rabin* v *Gerson Berger Association* [1986] 1 All ER 374; *Orion*

Insurance Co. plc v *Sphere Drake Insurance plc* [1992] 1 Lloyd's Rep 239). This rule can operate harshly as most transactions are entered into as a result of promises made orally but not necessarily written out in the contract. It is generally only in detailed commercial agreements that the agreement contains all the terms intended to be included by the parties. Furthermore, in the consumer or small business field the buyer usually has limited bargaining power — an assistant in a large retail outlet would hardly be supposed to be authorised to renegotiate the firm's standard terms. He simply would not make the sale if the buyer wished to vary them. Accordingly, where the parol evidence rule operates, the buyer's only remedy in respect of representations which prove to be false lies in misrepresentation. It is not surprising therefore that the courts have developed a series of exceptions to the parol evidence rule and these are listed below. It will be noted that some of these are not true 'exceptions' to the rule, but rather situations where the rule does not apply. It is, however, helpful to list them as one.

3.3.5.1 Mere memorandum of sale Where the document does no more than record that an agreement has been reached, but makes no (or limited) further provision then the parol evidence rule will not operate to exclude further evidence. Thus, in one case the seller simply jotted down that a horse had been sold and the price and it was held that further evidence of an oral warranty was admissible (*Allen* v *Pink* (1838) 4 M & W 140). However, if the document forms a completed and detailed agreement then no further evidence is admissible (*Hutton* v *Watling* [1948] Ch 398). The test to distinguish between the two is objective: would a reasonable person regard the document as *looking* like a complete agreement (*Gillespie Bros & Co.* v *Cheney, Eggar & Co.* (1896) 2 QB 59; *Hutton* v *Watling* (above)). If this is the case then the document will be adhered to and further evidence will remain inadmissible.

3.3.5.2 Implied terms The rule only operates to exclude evidence supporting express terms of the contract, not implied ones. Evidence may therefore be adduced to show that the circumstances are such that a term ought to be implied, for example a representation that goods were fit for a particular purpose under s. 14(3) of the Sale of Goods Act 1979. However, this rule is of limited use at common law as, by definition, an implied term is one where the parties made no provision in respect of a certain eventuality. If there is express provision, orally or in the written contract, then there is limited scope to invoke an exception to the rule.

3.3.5.3 Sham In *AG Securities* v *Vaughan* [1990] 1 AC 417 it was held that an agreement was a mere sham to avoid the application of the Rent Acts (the agreement in fact created a tenancy as opposed to a mere licence and the Rent Acts applied). Although most of the cases decided upon this case relate to landlord and tenant law, the rule is of general application. The most common application of it is in relation to credit hire agreements where the court holds that no agreement was reached because the hirer had entered the transaction on the basis that he would never have to pay for the goods hired, yet the written agreement states that he does.

3.3.5.4 Variation Whilst oral evidence may not be admitted to show that the contract varies from that which is recorded in the written contract, evidence is admissible to show that the contract has been varied subsequent to the contract being entered into (*Morris* v *Barron & Co.* [1918] AC 1).

3.3.5.5 Explanation of the contract Evidence may be admitted which assists the court in interpreting the written terms. This tends to be the case where the written contract is very vague, for example in one case the document failed to identify who the buyer was and who the seller was (*Newall* v *Radford* (1867) LR 3 CP 52). Likewise there is often need of explanation of technical terms (*Bank of New Zealand* v *Simpson* [1900] AC 182). Furthermore, an explanation of the background during negotiations may be admissible in interpreting what the parties meant by the terms they used (*Prenn* v *Simmonds* [1971] 1 WLR 1381).

3.3.5.6 Custom Evidence may be given of the existence of a custom in order to imply a term to its effect (*Hutton* v *Warren* (1836) 1 M & W 466). However, if the document expressly provides to the contrary of the custom then the custom will have to accede to the superiority of the document (*Palgrave, Brown & Sons Ltd* v *SS Turid (Owners)* [1992] 1 AC 397).

3.3.5.7 Rectification Where the document mistakenly does not record that which was actually agreed then the aggrieved party may apply for an order that the agreement be rectified, that is to say altered so as to reflect the actual agreement (*Rabin* v *Gerson Berger Association* [1986] 1 All ER 374).

3.3.5.8 Collateral contract A party may rely upon oral evidence which supports the existence of a separate collateral contract, such independent contract being oral and hence not one to which the parol evidence rule applies (*Mann* v *Nunn* (1874) 30 LT 526). This is so even where the collateral contract directly conflicts with the main contract (*City and Westminster Properties (1934) Ltd* v *Mudd* [1959] Ch 129). However, if the term is one that would be expected to be found in the main contract and there was no intent to form a separate contract then the rule will not apply (*Mitchell* v *Lath* 160 NE 646 (1928); *Preece* v *Lewis* (1963) 186 Estates Gazette 113).

3.3.5.9 Equitable defence In one case a party was permitted to adduce oral evidence which ran contrary to the contract in order to raise an estoppel based upon those misrepresentations (*Wake* v *Hemp* (1861) 6 H & N 768).

3.4 THE CONTRACTS (RIGHTS OF THIRD PARTIES) ACT 1999

Partial reform of the privity of contract rule has been achieved through the introduction of the Contracts (Rights of Third Parties) Act 1999 ('the 1999 Act') which was enacted on 11 November 1999. By s. 10 of the 1999 Act, it applies only to contracts which are entered into six months or more after that date or where the parties have expressly stated that the contract shall be governed by it.

The key provisions of the 1999 Act are to be found in s. 1, which provides as follows:

(1) Subject to the provisions of this Act, a person who is not a party to a contract (a 'third party') may in his own right enforce a term of the contract if—

(a) the contract expressly provides that he may, or

(b) subject to subsection (2), the term purports to confer a benefit on him.

(2) Subsection (1)(b) does not apply if on a proper construction of the contract it appears that the parties did not intend the term to be enforceable by the third party.

(3) The third party must be expressly identified in the contract by name, as a member of a class or as answering a particular description but need not be in existence when the contract is entered into.

(4) This section does not confer a right on a third party to enforce a term of a contract otherwise than subject to and in accordance with any other relevant terms of the contract.

(5) For the purpose of exercising his right to enforce a term of the contract, there shall be available to the third party any remedy that would have been available to him in an action for breach of contract if he had been a party to the contract (and the rules relating to damages, injunctions, specific performance and other relief shall apply accordingly).

(6) Where a term of a contract excludes or limits liability in relation to any matter references in this Act to the third party enforcing the term shall be construed as references to his availing himself of the exclusion or limitation.

The general effect of the provisions is thus clear: by s. 1(5) and (6) the third party will have any remedy that would have been available to the contracting party or will be entitled to avail himself of any limitation or exclusion provisions.

The 1999 Act, however, achieves only partial reform of the law in that it only applies where the contract expressly provides that the third party may rely on the contract (s. 1(1)(a)), or where the contract purports to confer a benefit upon him (s. 1(1)(b)). The latter provision only applies where the circumstances are such that it is apparent that the contracting parties intended the third party to have the benefit of the contract (s. 1(2)). Even here, the third party must be identified or identifiable to at least a class of person. It is clear that the Law Commission intended the 1999 Act to allow a consumer to provide a friend or relative with the benefit of any statutory protection where he buys them a gift, although he must tell the shopkeeper that he is buying the item for someone else and sufficiently identify them. However, this was largely the case before the Act's introduction as the contracting party could always recover damages on behalf of a friend or relative in a consumer situation (*Jackson* v *Horizon Holidays Limited* [1975] 1 WLR 1468). Furthermore, the courts have strived to obviate the harshness of the rule in such situations, e.g., it was said in *Lockett* v *A M Charles Limited* [1938] 4 All ER 170 that both the husband and wife were in a contractual relationship with a hotel even though the husband was paying the bill, where the wife had been served contaminated food which poisoned her. All that is required under the 1999 Act is that the contracting party identify the recipient of the item in question and, it is submitted, the usual inference will be, in a consumer situation, that the parties intended that person to be entitled to the benefit of the contract where the item proves defective.

By contrast, it is clear that the Law Commission did not intend that a consumer would necessarily have the benefit of any warranties made by a supplier to a retailer in respect of goods being sold or that any such warranties would work their way up the chain of a contract (Law Commission's Report, *Privity of Contracts for the Benefit of Third Parties*, Law Com. No. 242, 1996, Cm 3329, para. 7.18(iii)). Here it would not normally be the case that the parties to the contract intended the consumer to have the benefit of the term and the proviso under s. 1(2) would not be made out, although the class of the third party would likely be (e.g., high-street consumers).

Outside of these common situations, the term of any contract will depend greatly upon the circumstances surrounding the contract and any inferences which can be drawn from them. This is supremely a question of fact in each case.

Section 2 makes rather complicated provision for amending a contract where it makes provision for a third party. Essentially, the section requires the third party to consent to the variation. Section 3 provides the promisor under such a contract with defences of set-off and counterclaim where an action is brought under the 1999 Act. Importantly, this includes set-offs which would have been available to him had the action been brought by the promisee who was a party to the contract. Sections 4 and 5 provide that the Act makes no alteration to the rights of the promisee who was an original contracting party to enforce the contract. However, where he does so, if he recovers any damages on behalf of the third party (e.g., as in *Jackson* v *Horizon Holidays Limited* (above), then in any proceedings brought by the third party the court may reduce the damages awarded to him to reflect the award to the original contracting party. Section 6 restricts the application of the Act. Importantly, contracts of employment and contracts for the carriage of goods are excluded from the benefit of the 1999 Act.

4 *Misrepresentation*

4.1 INTRODUCTION

The general rule is that a cause of action for misrepresentation arises where a person makes to another an unambiguous and material representation of fact which induces that other to enter into a contract. A defence exists to the representor that he had reasonable grounds to believe and did believe that the representation was true. The common law in this area has been modified by the Misrepresentation Act 1967 (the '1967 Act'). This Act does not, however, provide a cause of action in itself, or any general codification of the general law. The key amendment which the 1967 Act made was to bring about a cause of action for innocent as opposed to negligent or fraudulent misrepresentation. Where this has been the case then the injured party's remedy is rescission of the contract or damages (or both). Rescission means that the contract is treated as if it had never existed: it is rescinded *ab initio* (from the beginning).

Use of the word 'innocent' in this context causes confusion: at common law damages for misrepresentation used to be available in an action for fraud only and as such all other forms of misrepresentation, including negligent misstatements, became known as 'innocent misrepresentations'. However, in 1963 the House of Lords decided the case of *Hedley Byrne & Co. Ltd* v *Heller & Partners Ltd* [1964] AC 465, where it was held that there could be liability for negligent misstatement or, as it is often called, negligent misrepresentation. Then in 1967 the Misrepresentation Act was passed which created a right to damages in the absence of fraud, but with a defence based upon the representor's knowledge being based upon reasonable grounds. This defence is dealt with at section 4.6 below. Accordingly, a representation which although wrong was based upon reasonable grounds has become known as a 'wholly innocent' misrepresentation so as to (attempt) to avoid confusion between this and 'negligent misrepresentation' which was in older cases also known as 'innocent misrepresentation'!

The following issues are discussed here: factual representations distinguished from opinion; belief or representations as to law or the future; the circumstances when a failure to speak will amount to a representation; materiality; reliance upon the representation; and remedies.

4.2 FACTUAL REPRESENTATION

In order to bring about a cause of action in misrepresentation the representation must be one of fact and not opinion or belief. The distinction is a very fine one in some circumstances. For example, the fact that a representation is very vague may mean that it is not capable of being a representation of fact, e.g., a representation that a car is a 'good little runner'. Thus in *Dimmock* v *Hallett* (1866) 2 Ch App 21 the seller had represented that the land he was selling was 'fertile' but was not liable when this proved not to be the case.

Similarly, whilst a representation that a car was built in 1990 is clearly a representation of fact, a representation that the seller *thinks* the car was built in 1990 is a statement of belief and is not ordinarily actionable. However, this does not necessarily mean that the aggrieved party has no remedy. He may do if it was reasonable for him to rely not upon the mere fact stated in the representation but upon the representor's *belief*. As was said in *Edgington* v *Fitzmaurice* (1885) 29 Ch D 459:

> the state of a man's mind is as much a fact as the state of his digestion ... a misrepresentation as to the state of a man's mind is, therefore, a misstatement of fact.

Thus in *Jendwine* v *Slade* (1797) 2 Esp 572[1] an expert in art stated that he believed a picture to be an original. This proved not to be the case. Since the expert could not have held such a belief the statement became actionable, not because the painting was not a master but because the expert could not have *believed* it to have been. It was reasonable to rely on what the expert had said.

By contrast, in *Bisset* v *Wilkinson* [1927] AC 177 the seller had represented that a farm he was selling could support 2,000 sheep. However, he had no knowledge of the land and the buyer knew this. It was held that the representation had been no more that one of belief and as such was not actionable.

Just as representation of a belief in a statement is not normally actionable, neither is a statement of intention. However, if at the time the representor declared his intention he had no intention of doing as he had said then the statement will become actionable because he had misrepresented the state of his mind. By contrast, if he simply *changed* his mind after he had made the statement then no misrepresentation has been made.[2]

It is important therefore in cases where it is alleged that the statement of belief or intention was not actually held at the time it was made to establish as a matter of *fact* (and to plead) that the person in question did not hold the belief. Given that the matter involves reading into the mind of a person against whose interest it is

1. See also *Esso Petroleum Co. Ltd* v *Mardon* [1976] QB 801 where a statement that a garage would attract a certain level of customers and produce a certain revenue was actionable because, despite the statements necessarily being opinion as they relate to future predictions, the representor had expert knowledge of the facts which he stated and it was reasonable to rely upon the statements. See also *Smith* v *Land and House Property Corporation* (1884) 28 Ch D 7 where the seller of a freehold represented that the tenant currently in the property was desirable, when in fact he was grossly in arrears with his rent. The seller had this knowledge and it was reasonable for the buyer to believe him.
2. However, the circumstances of the case may give rise to a 'duty of disclosure' whereby the representor becomes bound to disclose his change of intention. This is discussed in the next section.

to admit the misrepresentation, it will only be cases where it is obvious that the person could not possibly have believed what he said that will succeed.

It is worth noting that a representation as to the law will not amount to an actionable misrepresentation. Thus, for example, a statement that the law presumes that the risk is on a particular party at a particular stage of a contract, inducing the other party to enter an insurance contract, will not amount to an actionable misrepresentation. However, such cases are very rare and this can (almost) be ignored in practice.

Finally, the representation must (obviously) be made to the person claiming misrepresentation, but it is sufficient that it is said to a person who can be expected to repeat it to the representee (*Pilmore* v *Hood* (1838) 5 Bing NC 97). Likewise, if the person claiming to have been misrepresented had not heard the representation at the time of the contract he cannot make out a claim (*Horsfall* v *Thomas* (1862) 1 H & C 90).

4.3 SILENCE AND 'HALF-TRUTHS' AS A REPRESENTATION

The general rule is that there is no duty upon a party to disclose any fact known to him. Each party is free to sit back and watch the other make a terrible bargain. However, in some circumstances a duty to disclose may arise. These exceptions are discussed below.

(a) *Half-truths* The first exception is not so much an exception, as a non-application of the rule. Where a person makes a statement which is worded to give one impression, but he technically does not actually make the statement implied then this will usually be held to amount to a representation (*Akerhielm* v *De Mare* [1959] AC 789; *The Sibeon and The Sibotre* [1976] 1 Lloyd's Rep 293). In *Nottingham Patent Brick and Tile Co.* v *Butler* (1886) 16 QBD 778 a solicitor acting for a vendor had said when asked that he did not know of any restrictive covenants affecting the land in question. However, the reason for his ignorance was that he had not read the papers supplied to him. Accordingly, he was held to have made a misrepresentation.

(b) *Change of circumstances* Where during negotiations prior to the making of a contract one of the parties makes a statement of his future intention or understanding then he will come under a duty to disclose if he changes it (*With* v *O'Flanagan* [1936] Ch 575; *Traill* v *Baring* (1864) 4 De GJ & Sm 318). However, in a family context (in *Wales* v *Wadham* [1977] 2 All ER 125 overruled on different grounds by *Jenkins* v *Livesy* [1985] 2 WLR 47) during negotiation of a divorce settlement the wife had said that she had no intention of remarrying and an offer of settlement was made on that basis. Later she changed her mind and decided to remarry and then accepted the offer. It was held that there was no duty of disclosure on her.

(c) *Contracts* uberrimae fidei A contract *uberrimae fidei* is a contract of the utmost good faith. The most common form of this type of contract is a contract of insurance. The insured must disclose everything which the insurer may take into account in determining whether to accept the risk, or what premium to offer (*St. Paul Fire & Marine Insurance Co. (UK) Ltd* v *McConnell Dowell Constructors Ltd* [1996] 1 All ER 96; *Pan Atlantic Insurance Co.* v *Pine Top Insurance Co.* [1993] CLY 3620). However, it is not every non-disclosure which will be actionable: the non-disclosure must be material to influencing the entry of the contract (*Babatsikos* v *Car Owners' Mutual Insurance Co.* [1970] 2 Lloyd's Rep 314). However, where there is a material non-disclosure then if the insurance broker knew of it then he too may be liable to the insurer (*Banque Keyser Ullmann SA* v *Skandia (UK) Insurance Co. Ltd* [1991] 2 AC 249). Additionally, some contracts, although not *uberrimae fidei*, require a certain level of disclosure. In contracts for a guarantee any unusual aspects of the contract which the guarantor is being asked to guarantee must be disclosed (*Cooper* v *National Provincial Bank* [1946] KB 1).

It is important to note that there is an exception between these types of non-disclosure. In *Banque Keyser Ullmann SA* v *Skandia (UK) Insurance Co. Ltd (No. 1)* [1989] 3 WLR 25 the Court of Appeal held that where there is non-disclosure under an insurance contract which is *uberrimae fidei* then there has been no disclosure 'made' by the 'representor' to which s. 2(1) of the 1967 Act applies. Accordingly, damages are not available for breach of such a contract. Rescission remains available, however, as s. 1 of the 1967 Act does not use the word 'made'.

However, in the context of the sale of goods, most non-disclosures will be of the 'half-truth' or 'change of circumstances' type. Here a representation has been 'made' and will, presumably, still attract the use of s. 2(1) of the 1967 Act and thus damages will be available.

4.4 MATERIALITY

In order to rely upon a representation it must be such that it would influence a reasonable person to enter into the contract. This does not mean that the representation must have been the predominant reason for having entered into the contract, but it must be a factor.

What is or is not material is a question of fact and degree in each case, but an example is to be found in *Museprime Properties Ltd* v *Adhill Properties Ltd* [1990] 2 Estates Gazette 196 where four properties had been sold at auction with a description which suggested that the rent in respect of the properties could still be negotiated. It had, however, been agreed at around £10,000 in respect of all four properties. The buyer felt that he might achieve higher rents than this, i.e., an increase of £4,000. It was accepted that the misrepresentation was material.

4.5 RELIANCE UPON THE REPRESENTATION

As discussed in the previous section, the representation must be material in that a reasonable person would have relied upon it. However, this is not of itself sufficient: the person to whom the representation is made must also (subjectively) rely upon the representation. This is supremely a question of fact, but there are certain situations which will strongly suggest that the representee did not in fact rely upon the representation, or where he may be deemed not to have done so:

(a) *Where the representee or his agent had actual knowledge contrary to the representation* In *Strover* v *Harrington* [1988] Ch 390 an estate agent's property details contained a representation that a house which they were selling had mains drainage. Despite it being pointed out to the buyer's solicitors on numerous occasions that this was wrong they failed to pass this on to him. It was held that his solicitor's knowledge was to be imputed (per *Thake* v *Maurice* [1986] CLY 422; *Wells* v *Smith* [1914] 3 KB 722) to him and accordingly he could not have relied upon the representation. Similarly, it was held in *Attwood* v *Small* (1838) 6 Cl & F 232 that where a buyer had, in fact, relied upon his own accountant's report and not that of the vendor of a business the buyer was not entitled to claim for misrepresentation.

More difficulty arises, however, in determining whether a person should be deemed to have knowledge where he has failed to take reasonable steps to discover the true facts, particularly where the means of discovery were at his disposal. Certainly there seems to be authority to the effect that the representee will not be deemed to have knowledge where the representation was fraudulent merely because he did not take steps to investigate the situation (*S. Pearson & Son Ltd* v *Dublin Corporation* [1907] AC 351). However, the position may be different where the representation was innocent or negligent. Certainly, there is authority which supports the view that it would not be sufficient (*Redgrave* v *Hurd* (1881) 20 Ch D 1). But it is noted in Treitel, *An Outline of the Law of Contract*,[3] that this case was decided when the law deemed all representations which were not fraudulent to be 'innocent' representations, so that it remains possible that a 'wholly innocent' representation, as opposed to a negligent one, may escape liability where the representee could have (perhaps easily) discovered the truth. It is argued that, in line with the tortious negligence cases such as *Smith* v *Eric S. Bush* [1990] 1 AC 831, the test should be whether in all the circumstances it was reasonable for the representee to rely on the representation. In the absence of clear authority, this seems a sensible argument.

(b) *Representation qualified by statement that it should not be relied upon* In *S. Pearson & Son Ltd* v *Dublin Corporation* (discussed above) the representation was qualified by a clause in the contract that any pre-contract representations should not be relied upon. However, that was a case on fraudulent misrepresentation and it will still be possible to argue that such clauses would be inoperative where the representation was merely innocent or negligent. That was the position in *Hummingbird Motors* v *Hobbs* [1986] RTR 276 where the mileage of a car was given as true to the best of the seller's knowledge and belief. The seller was not liable. However, s. 34 of the 1967 Act requires that, if made in a contract, such a clause must be reasonable within the meaning of s. 11(1) of the Unfair Contract Terms Act 1977 if it is to have any effect.

(c) *Representee would have entered into the contract on the same terms had he known of the falsity of the representation* In *JEB Fasteners Ltd* v *Marks Bloom & Co.* [1983] 1 All ER 583 (see also *The Lucy* v *Hallam* [1983] 1 Lloyd's Rep 188) accounts had been prepared by the defendants, which were taken into consideration by the plaintiffs in their decision to take over a company. The accounts proved to have been drawn up negligently and gave an inaccurate picture. However, on the facts the plaintiffs would have purchased the company even if they had known the true position and accordingly their action was dismissed.

3. 5th ed. (London: Butterworths, 1995), p. 143.

Whilst this is a case based upon tort, the same considerations would presumably apply here.

4.6 STATUTORY DEFENCE — REASONABLE GROUNDS IN BELIEF

It was noted at the start of this chapter that the Misrepresentation Act 1967 does not codify the law or create any cause of action. Accordingly, its provisions only apply to certain aspects of the common law. This is particularly so in relation to the right to claim damages. Section 2(1) of the 1967 Act provides that damages may be claimed for misrepresentation notwithstanding that the representation was not made fraudulently. This is akin to s. 1 of the 1967 Act which provides that rescission shall be available notwithstanding that the representation was not made fraudulently. However, s. 2(1) provides that that section will not apply where the person making the representation believed the representation and had reasonable grounds to do so. This defence is not made available to a claim for rescission. But by s. 2(2) of the Act the court, in its discretion, may award damages in lieu of rescission where this would be fair. Accordingly, it is no defence to a claim for rescission to state that the representor had reasonable grounds for his belief.

In *Howard Marine and Dredging Co. Ltd* v *A. Ogden & Sons (Excavations) Ltd* [1978] QB 574 the seller of two barges had misrepresented their deadweight capacity. In doing so he had relied upon the entry in the Lloyd's Register. However, he did have documents in his possession which indicated the true position and accordingly he was not entitled to rely on the defence. Whether it was reasonable for the representor to believe in his representation is a question of fact in each case. Certainly, where the representor relies upon an expert report it is likely that his belief will be reasonable, or depending upon the words used no more than a representation that an expert has made a representation.

It may be the case that the representor in fact knows that the representation was false, but has some supporting documents to corroborate his expressed belief. Whilst the representation would be fraudulent and the representor should have no defence fraud will be difficult to prove. Furthermore, even though the burden of proof is upon the representor to make out the defence under s. 2(1) of the 1967 Act, it will be difficult to show that he did not actually believe a representation made where he has evidence to support his view. In practice, therefore, such deceit may go without repercussion.

4.7 REMEDIES

In an action for misrepresentation an aggrieved party has two basic remedies: rescission of the contract and/or damages. Rescission is the termination of the agreement *ab initio* (from the start) and damages provide monetary compensation. Since rescission is an equitable remedy equitable defences will apply (such as affirmation) and the injured party may be prevented from claiming rescission and have his remedy 'reduced' to damages. A statutory power to do so also exists under the Misrepresentation Act 1967. Equally, it may be the case that the injured party wishes to continue with the contract in force. Since a contract entered into by virtue of a misrepresentation is *voidable* and not void, he may elect to do so, in which case his claim will be for damages only (*Lohnro plc* v *Fayed (No. 2)* [1991] 4 All ER 961).

Remedies for misrepresentation overlap with tortious remedies for negligent misstatement. However, cases where such a remedy is relied upon tend to relate to situations where there is no contract between the parties and a full discussion of this area is beyond the scope of this text. Equally, remedies for misrepresentation overlap with contractual remedies and this area needs to be discussed. This will be done prior to considering a claim for rescission, the bars to rescission and finally damages.

4.7.1 Relationship with contractual claims

A representation is capable of becoming a term of the contract and the circumstances where this will be the case were discussed in section 3.2. Where this is the case the measure of damages will usually be greater than that awarded for misrepresentation. This follows because the basic measure of damages for misrepresentation is the tortious measure (see e.g., *Cemp Properties (UK) Ltd* v *Dentsply Research & Development Corporation* [1991] 2 EGLR 197; *Downs* v *Chappell* [1997] 1 WLR 426; *Heinemann* v *Cooper* (1987) 19 HLR 262; *Andre & Cie SA* v *Ets Michel Blanc & Fils* [1977] 2 Lloyd's Rep 166), i.e., to put the buyer in the position that he would have been in had the representation not been made, whereas the contractual measure is the position that the representee would be in had the representation been true. For example, suppose that A agrees to sell B a car described as a 1995 model of a particular type of car for £10,000. B thinks that he has got a good bargain as 1995 models are generally worth about £15,000. In fact the car is a 1990 model worth only £5,000. Upon discovery of the misrepresentation B issues proceedings alleging breach of contract and alternatively misrepresentation. If successful in breach of contract B's measure of damages would be £10,000, being the difference in value between what he would have got had the representation been true (£15,000) and that which he has got (£5,000). However, suppose that B's only claim is for damages for misrepresentation, perhaps because the court found that the representation did not become a term of the contract. Here B would be entitled to only £5,000, being the difference between the position he would have been in had the misrepresentation not been made (£10,000 because he would never have bought the car) and the value that he has received (£5,000).

Accordingly, it is always best to bring an action framed in contract with misrepresentation framed as an alternative remedy.

4.7.2 Rescission

Rescission is available as a remedy wherever there has been a misrepresentation in accordance with the rules outlined above, be it fraudulent, negligent or 'wholly innocent'. At common law, damages for misrepresentation used to be available in an action for fraud only and as such all other forms of misrepresentation, including negligent misstatements, became known as 'innocent misrepresentations'. In *Hedley Byrne & Co. Ltd* v *Heller & Partners Ltd* [1964] AC 465, however, it was held that there could be liability for negligent misstatement. Then the Misrepresentation Act 1967 was passed which created a right to damages in the absence of fraud, with a defence based upon the representor's knowledge being based upon reasonable grounds (see section 4.6 above). Accordingly, a representation which although wrong but which was based upon reasonable grounds has become known as a 'wholly innocent' misrepresentation.

The position is somewhat amended by virtue of s. 2(2) of the 1967 Act which provides as follows:

> Where a person has entered into a contract after a misrepresentation has been made to him otherwise than fraudulently, and he would be entitled, by reason of the misrepresentation, to rescind the contract, then, if it is claimed, in any proceedings arising out of the contract, that the contract ought to be or has been rescinded, the court or arbitrator may declare the contract subsisting and award damages in lieu of rescission, if of the opinion that it would be equitable to do so having regard to the nature of the misrepresentation and the loss that would be caused by it if the contract were upheld, as well as to the loss that rescission would cause to the other party.

This section therefore provides that the court need not rescind the contract for a trifling 'wholly innocent' misrepresentation. Nor would such a person be *entitled* to claim damages as the representor could show that he had reasonable grounds for his belief. The only situation where there is no bar upon rescission is where the representation was made fraudulently. In the time honoured case of *Derry* v *Peek* (1889) 14 App Cas 337 this will be when it is made in the knowledge that it is false or made recklessly, without any care as to whether it is true or not.

Thus, for example, where the seller of a car 'wholly innocently' represents that it is capable of achieving 50 miles to the gallon, and it is in fact only capable of 45, perhaps because this was information he had read elsewhere, the buyer would have a right to rescind the contract. However, it is unlikely that the court would consider this a serious enough misrepresentation to warrant terminating the contract and could declare it subsisting and award damages in lieu of rescission. The buyer could not claim damages as of right since the seller had reasonable grounds for his belief.

By contrast, had the seller made the representation having failed to read the car's user manual that was in his possession and which told him that the car could achieve only 40 miles to the gallon, and had never read any article which said that it could achieve 50, it is likely that the court would find that the statement was made negligently and the seller could not rely on the statutory defence in s. 2(1) of the 1967 Act as he would not have reasonable grounds for his belief. Accordingly, the buyer could elect to claim damages under s. 2(1) and uphold the contract. If the buyer sought to rescind the contract it is likely, again, that the court would hold the contract as subsisting and award damages in lieu. However, if the seller had made the representation in the full knowledge that it was a lie, then there is no bar to rescission under s. 2(2) and the buyer may claim, and will be entitled to, rescission of the contract.

Rescission may be effected either by applying for a court order that the contract is rescinded or by any act indicating that the injured party has repudiated the contract. The rescission need not be communicated to the representor, it is sufficient that the injured party takes reasonable steps to bring it to the representor's attention (*Car and Universal Finance Co. Ltd* v *Caldwell* [1965] 1 QB 525). The exact date at which the contract is rescinded can have marked effects upon third parties' rights as, until the contract is rescinded, the buyer will have an ability to pass a good title under s. 23 of the Sale of Goods Act 1979. This is dealt with in more detail in sections 13.5.1 and 13.6.

Where the court does order rescission or finds that the contract has been rescinded it may order an 'indemnity'. This is an equitable remedy used to place the parties in the position which they would have been in had the misrepresentation not been made. Thus if a buyer rescinds a contract of sale the ordinary position is that he must return the goods and the court may order an indemnity to be given by the seller to the value of the goods together with any out-of-pocket expenses. However, an indemnity is not to be confused with damages. In *Whittington* v *Seale-Hayne* (1900) 16 TLR 181 the plaintiff had taken a lease of a farm from the defendant who had 'wholly innocently' represented that the farm was sanitary, which it was not. The plaintiff claimed, *inter alia*: (a) loss of profits; (b) loss of livestock; (c) rent; (d) rates; and (e) cost of repairs to the property which had been ordered by the council. The plaintiff was awarded items (c), (d) and (e) only as repayment of these sums would put him in the position he would have been in had the representation not been made. Items (a) and (b) were not awarded as the plaintiff was not obliged to run a business, but (c), (d) and (e) were obligations under the contract. As will be seen, the assessment of the indemnity does not differ markedly from the assessment of damages for misrepresentation.

4.7.3 Equitable defences — loss of the right to rescind

There are three principal bars to rescission: that a *restitution in integrum* is not possible, that the injured party has affirmed the contract or (possibly) that there has been a lapse of time.

Restitution in integrum refers to the possibility of restoring the parties to their pre-contract position. Where this is so then the court will not order rescission. An inability to restore the parties to their pre-contract position will ordinarily arise because either the goods are now in the hands of a third party purchaser for value or have deteriorated. Where the goods have been sold on to a third party then the transferee of the goods is no longer in a position to return them to the transferor and hence it is not possible to return the parties to their pre-contract position. Equity will not interfere with a third party's rights in these circumstances.

As regards deterioration, the court strives to achieve substantial justice between the parties. For example, if the 'deterioration' is simply due to a fall in the market price of the item this will not necessarily bar rescission (*Armstrong* v *Jackson* [1917] 2 KB 822). However, if the deterioration is due to the transferee's use of the goods or own destructive act then he may be barred from rescission (*Clarke* v *Dickson* (1858) EB & E 148), but the court will probably forgive minor deterioration through mild wear and tear (*Leaf* v *International Galleries Ltd* [1950] 2 KB 86; *Erlanger* v *New Sombrero Phosphate Co.* (1878) 3 App Cas 1218).

Affirmation occurs where the buyer has expressly elected to continue with the contract or acted in some way detrimentally to the party in breach despite the existence of the misrepresentation or breach of contract. A most important qualification of affirmation is that the injured party must have acted with full *knowledge of his right to rescind the contract*. Mere knowledge of the defect will not suffice (*Peyman* v *Lanjani* [1985] Ch 457).

Whether mere lapse of time will of itself act as a bar to rescission is not at all clear. In *Leaf* v *International Galleries Ltd* [1950] 2 KB 86 the plaintiff had purchased a painting which was innocently represented to be a Constable. He discovered after five years that it was not and took quick steps to rescind the contract. The Court of Appeal held that whether or not the representation had been a term of the contract the right to repudiate had been lost through lapse of time. The judge at first instance had found that there was no laches on the part of the buyer. The Court of Appeal did not base its decision on laches or as an adjunct of affirmation, simply stating that the law would be the same whether or not the representation was a term.

This causes difficulty as the loss of the right to reject under the Sale of Goods Act 1979 has traditionally been regarded as harsher than at common law. The common law doctrines apply to cases where misrepresentation has been alleged, where the contract is one for the transfer of goods under the Supply of Goods and Services Act 1982 or where the contract is a hire purchase agreement.

That a stricter rule is intended in the Sale of Goods Act 1979 can be seen from the case of *Peyman* v *Lanjani* [1985] Ch 457 where Stephenson LJ said:

> The Sale of Goods Act 1979 dispenses in some circumstances with any inquiry into the buyer's state of mind or knowledge by compelling him to treat a breach of condition as a breach of warranty and disentitling him from rejecting the goods and treating the contract as repudiated if he accepts the goods or part of them: ss. 11(4) and 53(1). So a buyer who accepts goods could not rescind the contract for, e.g., a breach of the condition implied by s. 12(1) that the seller has title to sell the goods.
>
> It would seem from those authorities to be the law that where a statute does not restrict a party's choice between alternative courses of action, as does the Sale of Goods Act 1979, but gives him a choice (called an option and not to be regarded as equivalent to an election in so far as that word imports a special connotation), . . . knowledge of the right to choose is essential to the loss of the right and the defendant who fails to prove that the plaintiff's knowledge goes that far has to rely on what he has done for the court to be able to decide that the right has been lost.

It is submitted that the application given in *Peyman* v *Lanjani* should be preferred: whilst the Sale of Goods Act 1979 creates a stricter rule, at common law a more relaxed approach is permitted. The decision in *Leaf* v *International Galleries* is best explained as an application of the doctrine of laches or that the Sale of Goods Act 1979 was applied. In *My Kinda Town* v *Lauren Sabin Soll and Grunts Investments* [1981] Com LR 194 the test for the doctrine of laches was stated as being whether in all the circumstances it has become unconscionable for the plaintiff to rely upon his legal rights (see also *Office Cleaning Services* v *Westminster Window and General Cleaners* (1946) 63 RPC 39 and *Shaw* v *Applegate* [1977] CLY 2485). Certainly, in the context of a sale of a work of art, it would be unconscionable to allow the buyer to reject after five years of opportunity to examine the picture, or have it examined by an expert.

A further problem is, however, caused by s. 1 of the 1967 Act which provides that an action will lie in misrepresentation notwithstanding that the representation has become a term of the contract. This must be contrasted with s. 11(4) of the Sale of Goods Act 1979 which provides that where the goods are deemed to have been accepted under (the more stringent) doctrine of acceptance contained in s. 35 of the Act that the buyer's remedy is reduced to damages. Thus where the buyer relies not upon an implied term (e.g., as to description), but upon misrepresentation he will not so readily be held to have lost his right to reject the goods as this will be governed by the doctrines of laches and affirmation, as opposed to the stricter doctrine of acceptance under the Sale of Goods Act 1979.

4.7.4 Damages for misrepresentation

A distinction must be drawn between cases where the injured party has a *right* to claim damages and where the court has a *discretion* to award damages in lieu of rescission under s. 2(2) of the 1967 Act. The circumstances where s. 2(2) applies were discussed above at 4.7.2. It was noted there that an injured party would have a *right* to claim damages only where the misrepresentation was made negligently or fraudulently. By contrast, where the misrepresentation was 'wholly innocent' the court may award damages only under s. 2(2) in its *discretion* where the injured party 'would be entitled to ... rescind the contract'. Section 2(2) appears to operate therefore only where the injured party has a subsisting right to rescind the contract. Where this right has been lost in accordance with one of the doctrines mentioned at 4.7.3 above this will not be so. Where the misrepresentation was made negligently then the injured party's right to damages subsists under s. 2(1) notwithstanding that he has lost the right to rescind (*Production Technology Consultants Ltd* v *Bartlett* [1988] EGLR 182).

Assuming that the right to reject has not been lost, what is the measure of damages? In *William Sindall plc* v *Cambridgeshire County Council* [1994] 1 WLR 1016 it was held that where damages are awarded in lieu of rescission then the appropriate measure of damages is different from that under s. 2(1) of the 1967 Act, being the difference in value between what the injured party was misled into thinking he was buying and the value of what he in fact received. Furthermore, damages under s. 2(2) of the Act should never exceed the sum which would have been payable had the representation been a warranty.

Where damages are awarded in respect of a fraudulent misrepresentation or a negligent one under s. 2(1) of the 1967 Act they are awarded on the tortious basis (*Sharneyford Supplies Ltd* v *Edge* [1986] Ch 128; *Royscott Trust Ltd* v *Rogerson* [1991] 2 QB 297). In the first place this means that the injured party will be entitled to claim the difference in actual value of the goods and their market value at the time of the contract, but not taking into consideration any fall in price through a drop in the market (*Naughton* v *O'Callaghan* [1990] 3 All ER 191). Whilst he will not be entitled to loss of profits from lost use of the goods, he will be entitled to the loss of the profits from goods which he would have acquired from another contract which he would have entered into but for the misrepresentation (*East* v *Maurer* [1991] 2 All ER 733). He may also be entitled to consequential costs incurred in entering into the contract (*Davis & Co. (Wines)* v *Afa-Minerva (EMI)* [1976] 2 Lloyd's Rep 27).

5 *Mistake*

5.1 GENERAL

Where one or more of the parties has entered into a contract under a mistaken belief then it is possible that such a contract may be rendered void by that circumstance. The grounds by which a contract may be rendered void by such a mistake fall under a variety of provisions of the Sale of Goods Act 1979 (the '1979 Act'), the common law and equity. The following shall be examined in turn before turning to the effects of mistake:

(a) Mistake under s. 6 of the 1979 Act (goods perishing).
(b) Mistake at common law:

 (i) as to the existence of the goods;
 (ii) as to identity;
 (iii) as to terms;
 (iv) as to quality;
 (v) as to documents signed.

(c) Mistake in equity.

5.2 MISTAKE UNDER SECTION 6 OF THE SALE OF GOODS ACT 1979

Section 6 of the 1979 Act provides as follows:

> Where there is a contract for the sale of specific goods, and the goods without the knowledge of the seller have perished at the time when a contract is made, the contract is void.

The definition of 'perished' is considered in section 6.2. The meaning of 'specific goods' is discussed in section 11.3.2. Apart from these two terms the effect of the 1979 Act is simple. However, it is worth noting that the effect of the s. 6 is to avoid the contract *ab initio* (from the beginning). Any monies paid pursuant to it may be recovered.

The 1979 Act is however ambiguous as to whether 'knowledge' means actual (subjective) knowledge or constructive (objective) knowledge. In other words, if the seller does not have knowledge, but ought to have done, can he rely on s. 6 as a defence to an action for non-delivery? There is no clear authority which answers this question, and the concepts of knowledge and notice are further discussed in this work at section 13.3.7. However, it seems that the answer is likely to be a sensible balance of the two. In *Feuer Leather Corpn* v *Frank Johnstone & Sons Ltd* [1981] Com LR 251 it was held that the doctrine of constructive notice should not be imported into commercial transactions, but that, when arriving at the conclusion as to whether a party had notice, an objective test should be applied. If clear notice had been given the absence of actual knowledge would be no defence.

An example of this would be where a seller walks out of his house and fails to notice that the car which he is about to sell has been reduced to a wreck following a fire yet goes on to sell it. It could not be said in these circumstances that he should be held to have no knowledge of its perishing. Accordingly, it is submitted that when assessing whether the seller had knowledge the court should ask itself whether the circumstances were such that a reasonable man would have had knowledge of its perishing (*Associated Japanese Bank (International)* v *Crédit du Nord SA* [1989] 1 WLR 255 at 269).

5.3 MISTAKE AT COMMON LAW

5.3.1 Mistake as to the existence of the goods

An interesting situation arises where there is a contract for the sale of goods which have never existed. This is highlighted by the peculiar case of *McRae* v *Commonwealth Disposals Commission* (1951) 84 CLR 377. In that case the Commission had sold to McRae a shipwrecked tanker which was lying off a specified reef. Bizarrely the tanker did not exist and indeed the reef did not either. McRae had spent a large amount of money in preparation for the salvage. It was held that there was an implied term that the tanker existed.

It is worth noting that the case would not come within s. 6 of the 1979 Act because goods which have never existed at all could not be said to have 'perished' within the meaning of that section.

A similar case is that of *Associated Japanese Bank* v *Crédit du Nord SA* [1989] 1 WLR 255. In that case J had entered into a sale and leaseback transaction with the bank. Such transactions are a form of arranging and guaranteeing finance, the goods are sold to the bank and then leased back to the user. The payments under the lease are, in effect, interest payments and the purchase price paid by the bank is again, in effect, the capital advanced by the bank. However, a sale does take place as between the bank and the 'borrower'. The machines in question were worth something in the order of £1 million. A guarantee had been provided by *Crédit du Nord*. It transpired that the machines had never existed and indeed the whole transaction was a fraud by J. J being a man of straw was not worth suing and the bank accordingly sued on the guarantee. It was held that the contract was void for mistake and/or that there was an implied term that the goods existed.

The existence of a term that the goods are in existence is something which must be inferred at common law from the particular facts of the case. Such a term can be implied into any contract where goods are sold or supplied and the situation is not restricted to contracts for the sale of goods but also applies to contracts for the hire or lease of them. Indeed, at common law the contract may be avoided where the goods have perished analogously with s. 6 of the 1979 Act (*Couturier* v *Hastie* (1856) 5 HLC 673).

Finally, an issue arises as to whether s. 6 of the 1979 Act overrides the express or implied intentions of the parties. Section 6 is phrased in absolute terms: where the goods have perished without the knowledge of the seller then the contract *is* void. What would be the position therefore if the seller had warranted that the goods were in existence, yet it later transpired that they had perished? Would the seller be able to raise s. 6 as a defence?[1]

It is submitted that such a result would be contrary to common sense and that it could be avoided by the use of s. 55 of the 1979 Act which states that where any right, liability or duty arises by implication of the Act then it may be varied by the parties.

5.3.2 Mistake as to identity

Where one of the parties is mistaken as to the person with whom he has contracted then it may be possible to avoid the contract for mistake. In order for a party to rely upon mistake as to identity he must be concerned with that person's identity and not his attributes in order to succeed. This brings about a very narrow distinction.

In *Cundy* v *Lindsay* (1878) 3 App Cas 459 the sellers received an order by post for goods from one Blenkarn who purported to trade from the same street as Blenkiron & Co., a well-known and respected company. He allowed the sellers to believe that he was in fact that firm. It was held on appeal that the sellers intended only to deal with Blenkiron & Co. and that the contract was void for mistake. By contrast in *King's Norton Metal Co. Ltd* v *Ederidge, Merrett & Co. Ltd* (1897) 14 TLR 98 an order was received by the sellers from a firm calling itself Hallam & Co. The notepaper represented that the company was of considerable substance and standing. The order was dispatched. On this occasion it was held that the sellers had intended to deal with the person placing the order, whoever he was, and not a particular individual. The cases are difficult to distinguish in principle because, presumably, the reason that the sellers in *Cundy* v *Lindsay* were prepared to deal with Blenkiron & Co. was because of their well-known creditworthiness.

The general presumption is that when the parties deal with one another face to face that they intend to deal with the person in front of them, and not a particular individual. In *Lewis* v *Avery* [1972] 1 QB 198 a man pretending to be a Mr Green, a well-known actor, purchased a car. It later transpired that he was not Mr Green the actor but a fraudster. It was held that the contract was not void for mistake. However, in *Ingram* v *Little* [1961] 1 QB 31 a man representing himself to be a Mr Hutchinson responded to an advertisement to purchase a car. At first the sellers refused to let him take the car away upon an uncleared cheque. However, when he gave them the address of a real Mr Hutchinson which could be checked in a telephone directory the sellers allowed him to take the car away. It was said that the identity of the buyer was raised to a matter of vital importance and that the

1. See Atiyah, *The Sale of Goods*, 9th ed. (Pitman Publishing, 1995), p. 70.

contract was thus void for mistake. Again, this distinction is very hard to apply in practice.

5.3.3 Mistake as to terms

Where the parties have ostensibly reached an agreement but the terms of the agreement are sufficiently vague for the parties to have reached their bargain at cross-purposes then the contract may be void for mistake. In *Raffles* v *Wichelhaus* (1864) 2 H & C 906 the contract was for a sale of goods to arrive '*ex Peerless* from Bombay'. In international sales this meant that the goods were being carried on a ship called the *Peerless* departing from Bombay. It transpired that there were in fact two sailings by a ship called the *Peerless* from Bombay at around the time of the contract, one two months after the other. The buyer had understood that the former was intended, the seller the latter. It was held that the contract was void. Similarly, in *Scriven Bros & Co.* v *Hindley & Co.* [1913] 3 KB 564 the sellers offered bales of hemp and tow for sale by auction. The auctioneers failed to properly distinguish the two lots and the buyer bid a price in the order of three times its value for the tow. It was held that the contract was void (see also *Hartog* v *Colin & Shields* [1939] 3 All ER 566).

5.3.4 Mistake as to quality

A unilateral mistake on the part of one party that the goods are of a particular quality will not avoid the contract. The maxim *caveat emptor* holds true. However, where one party is mistaken as to whether the other party is *warranting* that the goods are of a certain quality then the contract is capable of being void for mistake. This, however, is more akin to a mistake as to the terms of the contract and is very narrow in application.

Much ambiguity surrounds the law as to whether a common mistake on the part of both parties is sufficient to avoid the contract. In *Bell* v *Lever Bros Ltd* [1932] AC 161 the contract provided for a settlement to two employees being dismissed. Unknown to any of the parties the contracts could have been terminated in any event due to earlier breaches which the employees had committed, with no compensation being payable. It was held that the mistake was one as to quality and in this example this was insufficient to avoid the contract.

However, in *Associated Japanese Bank (International) Ltd* v *Crédit du Nord SA* [1989] 1 WLR 255 it was held that a contract was void for mistake where a lease for certain machines was held to be void when it transpired that the machines did not exist and were a mere fiction invented by a con-man. In that case it was said that before turning to the principles of mistake the court should first consider the question of risk and whether the contract provided, expressly or impliedly, for the event. When turning to the question of risk the contract could not only be held to be void where there was a mistake as to the existence of the subject matter but also where there was a common mistake which 'must render the subject matter of the contract essentially different from the subject matter which the parties believed to exist'. The court there relied upon *Bell* v *Lever Bros* in reaching this conclusion.

On this point, some cases have found that there has been a sufficiently fundamental mistake in order to avoid the contract. For example, in *Nicholson and Venn* v *Smith Marriott* [1947] 1 KB 557 tablecloths were believed to hold the crest of Charles I when in fact they were Georgian and of much less value. The contract was void for mistake. However, the bulk of the case law is much stricter. For example, in *Leaf* v *International Galleries Ltd* [1950] 2 KB 86 a painting was sold which was believed to be an original but was not in fact. The contract was not void for mistake (see also *Solle* v *Butcher* [1950] 1 KB 671; *F. E. Rose (London) Ltd* v *Wm. H. Pim Jnr. & Co.* [1953] 2 QB 450; *Harrison & Jones* v *Bunten & Lancaster Ltd* [1953] 1 QB 646; *Routledge* v *McKay* [1954] 1 WLR 615).

On the trend of authority it is best to assume that contracts will only very rarely be void for mistake as to the quality of the subject matter or where it is found that the goods have ceased to exist.[2]

5.3.5 Mistake as to documents signed

Where a party has signed a contract but that contract does not accord with his understanding of the agreement reached then in exceptional circumstances he may be able to avoid the contract by the special and limited plea of *non est factum*. The doctrine is narrow in application and the contract will generally be upheld as valid: only someone who has no real understanding of the document which he signed by reason of defective education, illness or inate incapacity can rely on the plea. The mistake must be fundamental. Finally, the plea cannot be relied upon where the document was signed carelessly (*Saunders* v *Anglia Building Society Ltd* [1971] AC 1004).

Where both parties have recorded their agreement in a document which does not accurately reflect the terms reached then an application may be made that the agreement be rectified, that is to say that a change to the wording be authorised by the court (*The Nile Rhapsody* [1994] 1 Lloyd's Rep 382). However, where only one party is mistaken then he would have to show that the other party knew of his mistake and took advantage of it (*Blay* v *Pallard & Morris* [1930] 1 KB 628).

5.4 MISTAKE IN EQUITY

Mistake in equity is largely redundant in contracts for the sale of goods. However, there is a strain of cases decided by Lord Denning which suggest that equitable relief by way of rescission may be available where the mistake is not sufficiently fundamental at law to avoid the contract (*F. E. Rose (London) Ltd* v *Wm. H. Pim Jnr. & Co. Ltd* [1953] 2 QB 450; *Oscar Chess Ltd* v *Williams* [1957] 1 WLR 370; *Magee* v *Pennine Insurance Co. Ltd* [1969] 2 QB 507). Given the court's analysis in *Associated Japanese Bank (International) Ltd* v *Crédit du Nord SA* [1989] 1 WLR 255, however, it is unlikely that these cases will be followed.

5.5 EFFECTS OF MISTAKE

The effect of a contract being found to have been entered into by mistake is that the contract is void. It is sometimes said that the contract is void *ab initio* (from the start). It is thus as if the contract had never come into existence at all. Any monies paid under the contract must be returned and any benefits received (or their value) must likewise be returned (*Griffith* v *Brymer* (1903) 19 TLR 434).

2. See *Cheshire, Fifoot & Furmston's Law of Contract*, 13th ed. (London: Butterworths, 1996), p. 208; Treitel, *An Outline of The Law of Contract*, 5th ed. (London: Butterworths, 1995), p. 266 *et seq.*

6 *Frustration*

6.1 GENERAL

Frustration occurs where circumstances have rendered it impossible to perform the contract or such that performance would yield a thing fundamentally different from that which was agreed upon. In relation to the sale of goods there are two legal bases by which a contract can be frustrated with two quite distinct results. The contract may be frustrated under s. 7 of the Sale of Goods Act 1979 (the '1979 Act') or under the rules of common law. Section 7 applies to sales of specific goods which have perished before the risk has passed to the buyer. The common law rules concern all other frustrating events. Different results are reached because the Law Reform (Frustrated Contracts) Act 1943 does not apply to contracts frustrated under s. 7 of the 1979 Act. The law which dictates the effect of frustration under s. 7 is therefore the old common law introduced prior to the Act of 1943. The key difference is that the old common law adopted an 'all or nothing' approach — the contract was avoided and in many circumstances the buyer could recover any monies which he had paid out under the contract. The seller bore the brunt of the frustrating event. The 1943 Act, however, introduced a power for the court to apportion the loss as between the seller and the buyer so as to achieve a fairer result. Quite why contracts frustrated under s. 7 were singled out not to receive the *reforms* introduced by the 1943 Act remains something of a mystery. Certainly, there seems no reason in principle why this should be the case.

The law and effects of frustration under s. 7 will be examined before turning to the same in relation to the common law.

6.2 FRUSTRATION UNDER SECTION 7 OF THE SALE OF GOODS ACT 1979

Section 7 of the 1979 Act states that:

> Where there is an agreement to sell specific goods and subsequently the goods, without any fault on the part of the seller or the buyer, perish before the risk passes to the buyer, the agreement is avoided.

In the first instance, s. 7 applies only to contracts for the sale of 'specific goods', the meaning of which is explored in section 11.3.2. Secondly, the goods must perish prior to the risk passing to the buyer. Given that the risk ordinarily passes with the property and the property will ordinarily pass at the time the contract of sale is made, s. 7 is limited to situations where the parties have either agreed for a delay in the transfer of property and/or risk or the contract falls under s. 18, rr. 2–4 of the 1979 Act (putting the goods in a deliverable state, weighing or measuring the goods or contracts of sale or return). Thirdly, s. 7 applies only once the contract is made; goods which perish prior to the contract being made are dealt with by s. 6 of the 1979 Act. Fourthly, neither party must be at fault for the goods perishing.

It can be seen, therefore, that the application of s. 7 is quite narrow. There remain two areas which need to be explored: the meaning of the word 'perish' and the effects of the contract being 'avoided'. The latter is discussed in the next section, the former below.

In *Horn* v *Minister of Food* [1948] 2 All ER 1036 it was held that potatoes which had deteriorated to the point that they were worthless had not 'perished' within the meaning of the 1979 Act because they were still potatoes. On this view only total destruction would suffice. It is submitted that a more commercial view should be taken toward the meaning of the phrase. Within the context of an insurance case, *Asfar & Co. Ltd* v *Blundell* [1896] 1 QB 123, Lord Esher MR stated:

> I am of opinion that this appeal should be dismissed. The first point taken on behalf of the defendants, the underwriters, is that there has been no total loss of the dates, and therefore no total loss of the freight on them. The ingenuity of the argument might commend itself to a body of chemists, but not to business men. We are dealing with dates as a subject matter of commerce; and it is contended that, although these dates were under water for two days, and when brought up were simply a mass of pulpy matter impregnated with sewage and in a state of fermentation, there had been no change in their nature, and they still were dates. There is a perfectly well known test which has for many years been applied to such cases as the present — that test is whether, as a matter of business, the nature of the thing has been altered. The nature of a thing is not necessarily altered because the thing itself has been damaged; wheat or rice may be damaged, but may still remain the things dealt with as wheat or rice in business. But if the nature of the thing is altered, and it becomes for business purposes something else, so that it is not dealt with by business people as the thing which it originally was, the question for determination is whether the thing insured, the original article of commerce, has become a total loss. If it is so changed in its nature by the perils of the sea as to become an unmerchantable thing, which no buyer would buy and no honest seller would sell, then there is a total loss. That test was applied in the present case by the learned judge in the court below, who decided as a fact that the dates had been so deteriorated that they had become something which was not merchantable as dates.

This approach was also used in the New Zealand case of *Turnbull* v *Rendell* (1908) 27 NZLR 1067. In that case there was a contract for the sale of 'table potatoes' which had deteriorated in quality but only such that they were of a substantially lower quality than had originally been bargained for — they could still be sold as a crop (as chipping potatoes perhaps). It was held that they had perished within the meaning of the relevant Act.

Another example of this commercial basis is *Barrow, Lane & Ballard Ltd* v *Phillip Phillips & Co. Ltd* [1929] 1 KB 574. In that case there was a contract for the sale of 600 bags of nuts lying in storage at a wharf. Around 100 bags of nuts were stolen. In the first part, it was never questioned that the theft of the nuts amounted to their 'perishing'. The nuts had not been destroyed but they were no doubt in the hands of a thieving worker. It was accepted, however, that this amounted to a perishing just as if they had been destroyed in a fire. The second point raised in this case was whether the loss of part of the bundle only rendered the goods 'perished'. It was held that it did. This is sound commercial logic as the effects of bulk buying are such that the price may radically vary were the buyer to have to obtain a mere 100 bags from a separate source — he may easily end up exceeding the contract price in order to obtain his required quotient.

6.3 THE EFFECTS OF FRUSTRATION UNDER SECTION 7 OF THE SALE OF GOODS ACT 1979

Section 7 of the 1979 Act merely states that the contract is 'thereby avoided', leaving it to the common law to sort out the effects of this. Moreover, s. 2(5)(c) of the Law Reform (Frustrated Contracts) Act 1943 states that, '[This Act shall not apply] to any contract to which [s. 7 of the Sale of Goods Act 1979] ... applies, or to any other contract for the sale, or for the sale and delivery, of specific goods, where the contract is frustrated by reason of the fact that the goods have perished.' The latter words rule out an argument that the contract is frustrated *at common law* by reason of the goods having perished and that the 1943 Act applies.

Two issues arise when a contract is frustrated under s. 7. First, whether the price remains payable or, if it has been paid, whether it becomes recoverable. Secondly, whether the seller may claim for any expenses incurred prior to the frustrating event or whether the buyer becomes liable for any benefits which he did receive. The first issue is discussed below at section 6.3.1, the second at section 6.3.2.

6.3.1 When does the price remain payable when a contract is frustrated under section 7 of the 1979 Act?

The effect of frustration under s. 7 of the 1979 Act is that the parties are relieved from any further obligations under the contract from the time that the goods perished. However, they are bound by any obligations that have accrued before that time. The seller will not be liable for non-delivery of the goods if that obligation has not accrued at that time. The buyer will only be able to recover the price, if paid, if he can show that there has been a total failure of consideration. Equally, if the time for delivery has arisen then the seller will be liable for failure to make it. In *Fibrosa Spolka Akeyjna* v *Fairbairn Lawson Combe Barbour Ltd* [1943] AC 32 Lord Atkin said:

> ... [when] a contract which is still executory on one or both sides is subject to frustration the law is that when the event happens the parties are excused from

further performance, but have to give effect to rights under the contract already accrued before the happening of the event. A sells a horse to B for £50, delivery to be made in a month, the price to be paid forthwith, but the property not to pass till delivery, and B to pay A each week an agreed sum for keep of the horse during the month. The horse dies in a fortnight. A is excused from delivery and B from taking delivery. B is bound to pay the sum due for the fortnight during which the horse was kept. But what is the position as to the £50, the price paid in advance? This is in simple terms the problem in the present case. The answer that I venture to think would occur to most people, whether laymen or lawyers, would be that the buyer ought to get his money back, having had nothing for it, and the lawyer would support the claim by saying that it is money had and received to the use of the buyer, being money paid on a consideration which has wholly failed.

In the context of a sale of goods there will be a total failure of consideration wherever the seller does not transfer the property in the goods to the buyer. However, where the property has been transferred the opposite will apply (see section 1.4).

6.3.2 Benefits received by the buyer and expenses incurred by the seller

It is possible that a situation may occur where part of the goods have been delivered to the buyer and the seller has incurred expenses in manufacturing or acquiring the goods and the contract is then frustrated under s. 7 of the 1979 Act. So far as expenses incurred by the seller are concerned it seems that he is not entitled to payment in respect of any expenses so incurred. This was the result in the *Fibrosa* case (see section 6.3.1 above).

Problems arise, however, in determining the parties' liabilities where only part of the goods have been delivered. For example, if B agrees to buy all 100 tonnes of wheat from a specific stock (a sale of specific goods) and after 10 tonnes have been delivered to him the remainder of the goods perish, an issue arises as to whether the buyer is liable for the price of the 10 tonnes and/or whether the seller may demand their return. The problem arises because here there has only been a partial failure of consideration and the principles enunciated in the *Fibrosa* case do not apply.

The problem is further complicated by the 'entire contracts' rule. The entire contracts rule arises where the parties have contracted to provide an indivisible thing. The rule there being that where the contract is frustrated then if there has been partial performance only the supplier can recover nothing. For example, in *Whincup* v *Hughes* (1871) LR 6 CP 78 the plaintiff contracted with H to provide his son with a six-year apprenticeship. After one year H died and the plaintiff sued his estate to recover the whole or part of the price paid. It was held that he was entitled to recover nothing.[1]

It was clearly said by Bovill CJ in *Whincup* v *Hughes* that there were exceptions to the rule: 'there may be cases of partial performance which form exceptions to this rule, as, for instance, if there were a contract to deliver ten sacks of wheat and

1. See also *Cutter* v *Powell* (1795) 6 TR 320; *Appleby* v *Myers* (1867) LR 2 CP 651; Atiyah, *The Sale of Goods*, 9th ed. (Pitman Publishing, 1995), p. 315 *et seq.*

six only were delivered. The price of the remaining might be recovered. But there the consideration is clearly severable'. The difficulty with this is in the last words — that the consideration is clearly severable. In many instances the parties will not have agreed a unit price so as to make the consideration severable. Furthermore, in modern times the unit price of a good would vary depending upon whether there were 10 or 100 tonnes being purchased. This is the effect of bulk buying.

Despite any theoretical barriers which the law presents it is submitted that the courts should follow the lead of *Whincup* v *Hughes*. A unit price is clearly ascertainable from the contract between the parties, even if this does not fully take account of business realities. Furthermore, there is no reason in principle why contracts of this nature frustrated under s. 7 should be singled out for unfair treatment.

It has also been argued that a restitutionary based claim could succeed in these instances.[2] In *Sumpter* v *Hedges* [1898] 1 QB 673 it was said that such a claim could succeed where it was possible to imply a fresh promise. This will depend much upon the facts of the case. But it is submitted that such a promise could usually be implied where the buyer has taken delivery of part of the contract goods.

6.4 FRUSTRATION AT COMMON LAW

Frustration at common law occurs where the contract has become physically or legally impossible to perform or where without default on either side the contract has become incapable of being performed because of circumstances which would render performance a radically different thing than envisaged by the contract.

The circumstances by which a contract may be frustrated at common law will be examined in this section and the effect of such frustration in the next section. The circumstances by which a contract may be frustrated at common law may be broken down into the following categories:

(a) Frustration of a contract for the sale of unascertained goods.
(b) Supervening illegality.
(c) Destruction.
(d) Unprofitability.
(e) *Force majeure* clauses.

6.4.1 Frustration of a contract for the sale of unascertained goods

As will be discussed in chapter 11, unascertained goods are goods to be manufactured or acquired by the seller. It is important to note that the seller is not obliged to provide them from any particular source. For example, a contract to sell a 'T registration Ford Mondeo' would allow the seller to obtain the car from any source he chooses. A contract to sell 'X's T registration Ford Mondeo' would make the goods in question identified and agreed upon by the parties and hence a contract for the sale of specific goods.

---

2. See Atiyah, note 1, above.

The difficulty here is that frequently the seller will have a particular source in mind and indeed the buyer may well know this. If that source dries up or is destroyed then the contract may become unprofitable or onerous for the seller to perform. However, he is at liberty within the terms of the contract to fulfil his obligations by using a different source. It is difficult to see how the contract has become impossible to perform and this has led to the courts leaning heavily against finding that such a contract has become incapable of performance. For example, in *Monckland* v *Jack Barclay Ltd* [1951] 3 KB 676 it was said that, using the example above:

> ... suppose, further, that the seller expects to acquire the goods from a particular source, which may, indeed, be the only source available, the bare fact, without more, that when the time for delivery comes, that source has dried up and that the seller cannot draw on it, does not absolve the seller. He is still, in the absence of some contractual term excusing him, liable for non-delivery.

And in *Blackburn Bobbin Co. Ltd* v *T. W. Allen & Sons Ltd* [1918] 1 KB 540:

> ... [a contract for the sale of unascertained goods] will not (unless most special facts compel an opposite implication) be dissolved by the principle, even though there has been so grave and unforeseen a change of circumstances as to render it impossible for the vendor to fulfil his bargain.

It would therefore seem that unless a source is identified by the parties then the inability of the seller to obtain the goods will not absolve him of liability, even if it is impossible to perform the contract.

6.4.2 Supervening illegality

Section 1(2) of the Trading with the Enemy Act 1939 makes it a criminal offence for a British subject to supply any goods to or for the benefit of an enemy or to obtain goods from an enemy. Thankfully, war is not commonplace in Britain and this is an area which need not be explored in depth. Suffice to say that upon a party being declared an enemy any contract between him and a British subject becomes frustrated.

Another common source of frustration by illegality is the passing of import or export prohibitions after the contract has been made.[3] However, it was held in *Andrew Millar & Co. Ltd* v *Taylor & Co. Ltd* [1916] 1 KB 402 that where the illegality is only temporary then the contract is not necessarily frustrated. This depends upon the circumstances of the contract and whether a temporary prohibition actually renders the contract incapable of performance. Furthermore, the party intending to declare an inability to perform should wait a reasonable time before doing so in order to see if the embargo will be permanent or merely temporary. Similarly, in *Regent Oil Co. Ltd* v *Aldon Motors Ltd* [1965] 1 WLR 956 it was said that if the event only goes to a subsidiary provision within the contract then it cannot be said that the entire contract is frustrated.

3. *Denny, Mott and Dickson Ltd* v *James B. Fraser & Co. Ltd* [1944] AC 265; *Nile Co. for the export of Agricultural Crops* v *H. & J. M. Bennet (Commodities) Ltd* [1986] 1 Lloyd's Rep 555; *Metropolitan Water Board* v *Dick Kerr & Co. Ltd* [1918] AC 119.

Where the contract is such that in order for a party to perform it he will require a licence then he is under an obligation to use reasonable endeavours to obtain one. If he fails to use such endeavours then he will not be permitted to rely upon this as a frustrating event unless he can show that any efforts which he did make would have been useless. However, if he has used all such efforts then his failure to obtain a licence may form the basis of a frustrating event.

6.4.3 Destruction

In the case of specific goods destroyed or 'perishing' then the contract may be frustrated under s. 7 of the 1979 Act. This is dealt with above (see section 6.2). Since the introduction of s. 20A of the 1979 Act the property in an undivided share of a bulk of goods may pass to the buyer and the process by which this happens is dealt with in chapter 11. Where this has happened and the goods are subsequently destroyed then the contract will not be frustrated as frustration occurs only prior to the property passing. This would therefore be dealt with as a question of risk.

However, where the goods in question are wholly unascertained goods then, as discussed above at section 6.4.1, destruction of a source which the seller intended but was not contractually bound to use will not frustrate the contract.

In *Howell* v *Coupland* [1876] 1 QBD 258 the parties had agreed that the seller would sell a specific quantity of potatoes to be grown on the seller's land. In the event the crop failed. It was held that this had frustrated the contract. Again, in *H. R. & S. Sainsbury* v *Street* [1972] 1 WLR 834 the seller agreed to sell 275 tonnes of barley to be produced from a specified crop. In the event the crop only produced 140 tonnes. Owing to the general crop failure, prices had in the meantime increased. The sellers took advantage of this and sold the 140 tonnes to a third party at a higher price. It seems following this case that the seller will be obliged to offer such crop as is produced to the buyer, but it does not appear that the buyer is bound to take it.

Difficulties arise, however, where from an identified source the seller has agreed to fulfil several contracts and subsequently part of the goods are destroyed. For example, S agrees to sell 100 tonnes of wheat to each of B1, B2 and B3 from an identified source of 300 tonnes of wheat, property to pass upon delivery. One hundred tonnes are subsequently destroyed. Here the seller cannot claim that any of the individual contracts are frustrated. In the event that any of the buyers were to sue him he could not claim that it was impossible for him to perform the contract, simply that he chose not to perform that contract.

This follows from the case of *J. Lauritzen A.S.* v *Wijsmuller B.V. (The Superservant Two)* [1990] 1 Lloyd's Rep 1. Whilst a case not directly on the sale of goods the principle is analogous. In that case the defendants were the owners of two ships capable of moving oil rigs — the *Superservant One* and the *Superservant Two*. By their contract they agreed to move the plaintiff's rig with the option of using either ship. Before the time for performance the *Superservant Two* sank and the defendants had already contracted to use the *Superservant One* for other contracts. They claimed that the contract was frustrated. Their claim failed and the court suggested that where a party was unable to fulfil all its contracts it could not claim that those which they could not fulfil were frustrated.[4]

4. See also *Maritime National Fish Ltd* v *Ocean Trawlers* [1935] AC 524; *Hong Guan & Co. Ltd* v *R. Jurnabhoy & Sons Ltd* [1960] AC 684; *Pancommerce S.A.* v *Veecheema BV* [1983] 2 Lloyd's Rep 645.

Where the contract is one for the supply of work and materials or goods to be manufactured and no particular source is mentioned then, if the goods are destroyed prior to the work being completed and the property passing, the loss falls upon the seller and the contract is not frustrated. The seller (or supplier) would be obliged to start work again. However, if the work is to be performed on a specified article or attached to it then the contract could be frustrated. In *Appleby* v *Myers* (1867) LR 2 CP 651, the plaintiffs contracted to install machinery on the defendant's premises. Through no fault of either party the premises together with the machinery were destroyed. The contract was held to be frustrated because it was with reference to the specified premises.

6.4.4 Unprofitability

The mere fact that a contract has ceased to be profitable for a seller to perform is insufficient to frustrate the contract (*Blackburn Bobbin Co. Ltd* v *T. W. Allen & Sons Ltd* [1918] 2 KB 467). This is so even where a large change in the value of money has radically altered the profit margin from that originally envisaged in an international sale.

Equally, the fact that the buyer no longer requires the goods in question will not frustrate the contract even though they are of no practical use to him. Rare exceptions to this do exist where it can be shown that the purpose for which the goods were bought formed the basis upon which the parties had contracted. This was so in *Krell* v *Henry* [1903] 2 KB 740 where rooms were hired to watch the coronation procession which in the event was cancelled. It was held that this was the basis for the contract and the contract was frustrated.

6.4.5 *Force majeure* clauses

The parties may provide expressly in the contract for particular events and as to what is to happen should those events occur. This is a matter of construction of the individual contract: the parties may provide for the suspension of the contract, that one party shall bear the risk of that event, for alternative performance, cancellation of the contract or for one party to have an option as to whether to continue the contract. The scope of such clauses will largely come down to the foresight of the parties when making the contract.

Where such a clause has been included in the contract then the court will not generally find that the contract has been frustrated. However, where on the proper construction of the clause it is found that full provision has not been made by it, then it is open for the court still to find the contract frustrated.

Where a party seeks to rely on such a clause in order to evade liability then the courts will construe the contract strictly against the party relying on the clause.

6.5 CONSEQUENCES OF FRUSTRATION AT COMMON LAW

Where the contract is frustrated at common law then the provisions of the Law Reform (Frustrated Contracts) Act 1943 (the '1943 Act') will apply. By s. 1(2) of that Act contracts frustrated under s. 7 of the Sale of Goods Act 1979 are not governed by the 1943 Act (specific goods which perish). Consequently, the 1943

Act will apply to contracts for the supply of goods and services under a contract of bailment or similar contract and contracts for the sale of unascertained goods. Indeed most contracts will be governed by the 1943 Act as it is fair to say that s. 7 of the 1979 Act has a limited scope.

The 1943 Act aims to achieve a greater fairness in apportioning the loss as between the seller and buyer than was achieved by the 'all or nothing' approach of the common law. It does this by allowing the seller to set off expenses incurred by him against the sale price and by allowing the court to make the buyer pay for any benefits received.

The parties are free to contract out of the 1943 Act if they choose to expressly make provision for certain events.

Finally, by s. 2(3) of the 1943 Act the court may, where part of the contract has been completed (except for payment) and may be properly severed from the remainder of the contract treat that part as a separate contract and apply the provisions of the Act to the remainder alone. This would be the case where goods are to be delivered and paid for in separate instalments.

6.5.1 Sums paid or payable pursuant to the contract

Section 1(2) of the 1943 Act provides as follows:

> All sums paid or payable to any party in pursuance of the contract before the time when the parties were [discharged by frustration] ('in this Act referred to as the time of discharge') shall, in the case of sums so paid, be recoverable from him as money received by him for the use of the party by whom the sums were paid, and, in the case of sums so payable, cease to be so payable.

The section is fairly self-explanatory. However, it is worth noting that it does not provide for repayment of sums paid after the frustrating event but in ignorance of it. It is likely that such sums would be recoverable by reason of mistake. This is dealt with in chapter 5. In any event, any sums payable after the frustrating event cease to be so payable at common law. Furthermore, the Act provides for *all* sums to be repayable or to cease to be payable. The buyer thus *prima facie* recovers his price in full (this is however subject to the next section).

6.5.2 Expenses incurred by the seller

Section 1(2) of the 1943 Act is followed by this proviso:

> Provided that, if the party to whom the sums were so paid or payable incurred expenses before the time of discharge in, or for the purpose of, the performance of the contract, the court may, if it considers it just to do so having regard to all the circumstances of the case, allow him to retain or, as the case may be, recover the whole or any part of the sums so paid or payable, not being an amount in excess of the expenses so incurred.

The first issue under this subsection is that there are two caps upon the amount of expenses which may be claimed. First, that the amount may not exceed those expenses actually incurred. This appears straightforward, but whilst it seems that the amount is intended to be pure expenses and not profits it also seems that a reasonable allowance may be made for the seller's overheads and time incurred by the seller or his staff following s. 1(4) of the 1943 Act. Secondly, any amounts recovered or set off by the seller are limited to the amounts paid or payable *at the date of discharge* by the buyer. This follows from the fact that the proviso talks of the seller retaining sums paid or recovering from the sums paid or payable by the buyer. This means that if the bulk of the price was payable at a later stage in the contract then there may be little against which the seller may set off his expenses.

Any assessment of the seller's loss is a matter of discretion for the trial judge and an appellate court will not interfere with his findings unless they are so obviously wrong as to be unjust. The court is required to take into account all the circumstances of the case. It would therefore consider whether any valuable benefit is retained by the seller. Furthermore, the court is under no obligation to apportion the loss evenly and it may even disallow the seller to set off anything. Finally, s. 1(5) of the 1943 Act requires the court to ignore any monies received by any party by way of insurance, unless the contract specifically takes account of this.

6.5.3 Valuable benefit obtained

Section 1(3) of the 1943 Act provides as follows:

> Where any party to the contract has, by reason of anything done by any other party thereto in, or for the purpose of, the performance of the contract, obtained a valuable benefit (other than a payment of money to which the last foregoing subsection applies) before the time of discharge there shall be recoverable from him by the said other party such sum (if any), not exceeding the value of the said benefit to the party obtaining it, as the court considers just, having regard to all the circumstances of the case, and in particular,—
>
> (a) the amount of any expenses incurred before the time of discharge by the benefited party in, or for the purpose of, the performance of the contract, including any sums paid or payable by him to any other party in pursuance of the contract and retained or recoverable by that party under the last foregoing subsection, and
>
> (b) the effect, in relation to the said benefit, of the circumstances giving rise to the frustration of the contract.

There are thus two stages to the assessment of the benefit. First, the value of that benefit *to the person receiving it*. This forms the upper limit of any award in respect of it. Secondly, the amount that the court will award in respect of it given the circumstances of the case and in particular the factors set out in s. 1(3)(a) and (b). Again, any valuation is to be made by the trial judge and will not be interfered with upon appeal unless clearly wrong.

In a contract for the sale of goods the benefit will usually be the value of the goods received. Where the buyer has performed some manufacturing process or otherwise improved the goods then the court must attribute that part which is fairly due to the seller as best it can. Where the contract is one for work and materials the court should also take into account the value of the part-completed work to the buyer. It may well be that a part-completed car, house or other item is of no value to the buyer.

The date for the valuation of the benefit is the date of discharge. Accordingly, if that part of the contract goods as are delivered to the buyer are destroyed by reason of the frustrating event then their value will be nil. It also appears that the buyer will have to account for the use of the goods prior to the frustrating event. Furthermore, the risk of depreciation between delivery and the time of discharge is upon the seller.

Finally, the court may, by virtue of s. 1(6) of the 1943 Act, treat a benefit obtained by a third party (e.g., a sub-buyer) as a benefit received by the party who assumes the obligations under the contract. In assessing the benefit, the court is required to ignore the consequences of either party benefiting by way of a policy of insurance.

PART II
ANCILLARY REGULATION

7 *Consumer credit agreements*

7.1 INTRODUCTION

Consumer credit agreements are regulated by the Consumer Credit Act 1974 (the '1974 Act'). To many practitioners this Act has been regarded as an impenetrable source of statutory gibberish which is best ignored. However, over the last five to ten years many have begun to realise that the 1974 Act can provide a good remedy to the purchaser of goods and litigation in this area has increased. This is ever more so in light of the litigation in *Dimond* v *Lovell* [1999] 3 All ER 1 in relation to credit hire agreements.

However, much of the 1974 Act relates to the regulation of very small purchases, upon which litigation or advice is rarely sought from the practising lawyers in private practice for whom this text is intended. For example, the use of credit cards and the purchases made with them are regulated by the Act. It would be beyond the scope of this work to attempt to explore such cases which rarely form the basis of litigation or advice.

Works covering this detail of the 1974 Act can easily extend to four loose-leaf volumes, the best of which is Goode, *Consumer Credit Law and Practice* (London: Butterworths, 1999). The reader is directed towards those works.

The points which are covered in this text are:

(a) the right to resile upon the agreement for failure to comply with the 1974 Act;

(b) the right of the purchaser to withdraw or cancel the agreement or a 'linked transaction' under a 'cooling off' period;

(c) the right of a purchaser to attach liability to the provider of credit for misrepresentations or breaches made by the supplier of the goods; and

(d) credit hire agreements.

The right to (a) resile from the agreement for failure to comply with the technicalities of the 1974 Act is relatively limited because most consumer credit contracts have been expertly drafted for the credit company and a technical deficiency is rare. The most likely breach is where the person supplying the goods introduces the buyer to the credit company and thus becomes an unlicensed credit broker, rendering the agreement unenforceable. Again the right to (b) withdraw or cancel an agreement is of limited use since it (generally) only applies to transactions which were concluded off business premises, which in the consumer field is rare.

However, the right to (c) attach liability to the credit company for breaches by the supplier is of enormous importance. Section 75 of the 1974 Act deems the supplier of the goods to be the agent of the credit company in many instances. Accordingly, the buyer has a direct remedy against the credit company. This can be of enormous practical use in litigation as it forms a useful bargaining tool to obtain a release from the finance agreement.

Finally, (d) credit hire transactions arise where a hire company allows a person to hire a vehicle following an accident with his own. The hire company then allows deferment of payment of the hire charges until settlement of the hirer's claim against the person who damaged his car. In reality, credit hire agreements do not form a separate category; it is simply that credit hire companies show a consummate disregard for compliance with the 1974 Act and the agreements become unenforceable for want of such compliance. These are the non-professionally drafted agreements referred to in (a) above. However, the area has become sufficiently specialised to warrant separate discussion of the topic.

Before these separate areas are examined the different forms of credit need to be considered. Also the terminology of the 1974 Act and the 'characters' that play a role in consumer credit transactions need to be examined as the terminology otherwise becomes somewhat confusing.

7.1.1 Terminology of the 1974 Act

7.1.1.1 'Debtor', 'creditor' and 'supplier' Agreements under the 1974 Act often involve three parties: a person who wishes to obtain finance, the person who provides that finance and the person from whom something will be supplied with the money advanced. Because of this the Act adopts the terminology of 'debtor', 'creditor' and 'supplier'. This avoids the difficulty that at some stages the 'debtor' may be a 'buyer', a 'hirer' or a 'transferee' for the purpose of the contract by which goods are supplied, depending upon the particular legal transaction by which the goods are provided, yet also be a 'debtor' for the purpose of the finance transaction. Likewise, the 'supplier' or 'creditor' may, depending upon the circumstances, be a 'seller', 'bailor' or 'transferor'. The 'supplier' always remains the person who physically provides the goods and only enters into the picture if this is someone other than the creditor by whom the debtor is supplied with the goods. Accordingly, it is best to use the language of the statute to avoid confusion.

7.1.1.2 Credit brokerage The 1974 Act also refers to 'credit-brokers'. The term credit-broker immediately conjures up the image of a dedicated or professional broker acting in the course of business arranging finance for those wishing to obtain it and charging a fee for his work. Whilst such a person is undoubtedly a credit-broker within the meaning of the Act, the Act widens the definition well beyond this. Section 145 defines 'credit brokerage' and 'credit-broker' in the following terms:

(2) ... credit brokerage is the effecting of introductions—

(a) of individuals desiring to obtain credit—

(i) to persons carrying on businesses to which this sub-paragraph applies, or

...

(b) of individuals desiring to obtain goods on hire to persons carrying on businesses to which this paragraph applies, or

(c) of individuals desiring to obtain credit, or to obtain goods on hire, to other credit-brokers.

(3) Subsection (2)(a)(i) applies to—

(a) a consumer credit business;

(b) a business which comprises or relates to consumer credit agreements being, otherwise than by virtue of subsection 16(5)(a), exempt agreements;

...

(4) Subsection 2(b) applies to—

(a) a consumer hire business;

...

For the purposes of this text, it is sufficient to note that credit brokerage is the effecting of introductions to either consumer credit businesses, consumer hire businesses or other credit-brokers. Accordingly, a shopkeeper will often be a credit-broker if he introduces a customer to a credit company or where he introduces the customer to a person who will introduce him to a credit company; an insurance broker will often be a credit-broker if he introduces a customer to a car hire company (for example, following a road traffic accident). It is worth setting out in full Example 2, sch. 2 to the 1974 Act:

Facts Representations are made about goods in a poster displayed by a shopkeeper near the goods, the goods being selected by a customer who has read the poster and then sold by the shopkeeper to a finance company introduced by him (with whom he has a business relationship). The goods are disposed of by the finance company to the customer under a regulated hire-purchase agreement.

Analysis The representations in the poster constitute antecedent negotiations falling within section 56(1)(b), the shopkeeper being the credit-broker and negotiator and the finance company being the creditor. The poster is an advertisement and the shopkeeper is the advertiser.

7.1.1.3 Antecedent negotiations Section 56 of the 1974 Act defines antecedent negotiations as follows:

(1) In this Act 'antecedent negotiations' means any negotiations with the debtor or hirer—

(a) conducted by the creditor or owner in relation to the making of any regulated agreement, or

(b) conducted by a credit-broker in relation to goods sold or proposed to be sold by the credit-broker to the creditor before forming the subject-matter of a debtor-creditor-supplier agreement within section 12(a), or

(c) conducted by the supplier in relation to a transaction financed or proposed to be financed by a debtor-creditor-supplier agreement within section 12(b) or (c),

and 'negotiator' means the person by whom negotiations are so conducted with the debtor or hirer.

7.1.1.4 Linked transactions Linked transactions are defined in s. 19 of the 1974 Act, which provides as follows:

> (1) A transaction entered into by the debtor or hirer, or a relative of his, with any other person ('the other party'), except one for the provision of a security, is a linked transaction in relation to an actual or prospective regulated agreement ('the principal agreement') of which it does not form part if—
>
> (a) the transaction is entered into in compliance with a term of the principal agreement; or
>
> (b) the principal agreement is a debtor-creditor-supplier agreement and the transaction is financed, or to be financed, by the principal agreement; or
>
> (c) the other party is a person mentioned in subsection (2), and a person so mentioned initiated the transaction by suggesting it to the debtor or hirer, or his relative, who enters into it—
>
> (i) to induce the creditor or owner to enter into the principal agreement, or
>
> (ii) for another purpose related to the principal agreement, or
>
> (iii) where the principal agreement is a restricted-use credit agreement, for a purpose related to a transaction financed, or to be financed, by the principal agreement.
>
> (2) The persons referred to in subsection (1)(c) are—
>
> (a) the creditor or owner, or his associate;
>
> (b) a person who, in the negotiation of the transaction, is represented by a credit-broker who is also a negotiator in antecedent negotiations for the principal agreement;
>
> (c) a person who, at the time the transaction is initiated, knows that the principal agreement has been made or contemplates that it might be made.
>
> (3) A linked transaction entered into before the making of the principal agreement has no effect until such time (if any) as that agreement is made.

In general, the purpose in making one transaction linked to another is to allow the debtor to withdraw or cancel the entire purchase which he intended to make if he chooses to do so. If the transactions were not linked in this way then even though the debtor might have a right to withdraw from the credit agreement he may still be bound by the contract to hire or purchase goods, making the option to withdraw or cancel the credit agreement meaningless in practice.

By s. 19(1)(b) the contract with the supplier to purchase goods under a debtor-creditor-supplier agreement will always be a linked transaction. However, other agreements peripheral to the main credit or supply agreements can also be linked transactions if they fall within s. 19(1)(c). Examples of such peripheral agreements are maintenance or service agreements, payment protection plans and extended warranties. In order to form a linked transaction they must have been initiated by the creditor or owner, a credit-broker in antecedent negotiations (usually the supplier) or a 'person who knows that the principal agreement has been made or might be made'. This latter part of the description is very wide. Likewise the transaction must have been entered into for a purpose mentioned in s. 19(1)(c)(i), (ii) or (iii). Again, these criteria are very wide: it may simply be 'another purpose related to the principal agreement' or related to the supply transaction under s. 19(1)(c)(iii).

7.2 CLASSIFICATION OF FINANCE TRANSACTIONS

Finance companies have become more and more adept at finding ever more ingenious methods of granting credit. There are usually three parties involved in the transaction: the purchaser, the supplier and a credit company. It is rare in the modern day to find that the finance is supplied directly by the supplier. If it is, the agreement will usually be assigned by the supplier to a factor who pays him a one-off fee and 'purchases' the debt, naturally at a value less than the aggregate of the future payments under the agreement. Whatever the nature of the agreement the result is invariably the same: goods or services are supplied by the supplier to the purchaser, the purchaser agrees to make periodical payments over a set future period and a credit company provides credit, taking the risk of default.

However, the formulation of the transaction will bring markedly different legal results. It may be that the credit company is a high street bank which makes a loan to the purchaser. Although the loan may be expressed to be in respect of the purchase of a car (for example), no particular car or supplier is mentioned and the money is provided direct to the purchaser. The buyer then purchases a car from his chosen source. Here there is no relationship between the credit company and the supplier. The buyer is liable to the credit company and has no recourse against them if the goods prove faulty. Likewise the supplier provides the car under a straightforward contract of sale and is liable to the purchaser if it is faulty. By contrast, in many cases the credit company actually purchases the good from the supplier and then provides it to the purchaser under a separate agreement for sale or hire purchase. There is no contract between the buyer and the supplier. However, as will be seen, the buyer will frequently have a remedy for any misrepresentations made by the supplier against the credit company.

On a practical level, the choice of legal mechanism by which credit is granted gives the creditor more or less security over the goods in the event of default over the loan element of the transaction. What dictates the choice of form of finance often relates to the utility of the goods if repossessed. In some cases the goods will retain value even if second-hand; in others they will be worthless or almost worthless. Accordingly, the creditor is more likely to choose a form of transaction whereby the property in the goods remains vested in the creditor where the goods retain some residual value. An example of this would be hire purchase of a car whereby the creditor may repossess the car in the event of default on the part of the debtor. By contrast, 'buy now pay later' schemes will be used where the goods have little residual value second-hand, for example a couch. The creditor has no desire to repossess the good and incur the expense of selling it, but would rather have a personal remedy against the purchaser. The value of the item in question also dictates the form of finance. The higher the value of the loan, the more security the creditor will want.

The different types of transactions are classified under Part II of the 1974 Act, the relevant parts of which provide as follows:

8.—(1) A personal credit agreement is an agreement between an individual[1] ('the debtor') and any other person ('the creditor') by which the creditor provides the debtor with credit of any amount.

(2) A consumer credit agreement is a personal credit agreement by which the creditor provides the debtor with credit not exceeding £25,000.

(3) A consumer credit agreement is a regulated agreement within the meaning of this Act if it is not an agreement (an 'exempt agreement') specified in or under section 16.[2]

9.—(1) In this Act 'credit' includes a cash loan, and any other form of financial accommodation.[3]

(2) ...

(3) Without prejudice to the generality of subsection (1), the person by whom goods are bailed ... to an individual under a hire purchase agreement shall be taken to provide him with fixed-sum credit to finance the transaction of an amount equal to the total price of the goods less the aggregate of the deposit (if any) and the total charge for credit.

11.—(1) A restricted-use credit agreement is a regulated consumer credit agreement—

(a) to finance a transaction between the debtor and the creditor, whether forming part of that agreement or not, or

(b) to finance a transaction between the debtor and a person (the 'supplier') other than the creditor, or

(c) to refinance any existing indebtedness of the debtor's, whether to the creditor or another person, and 'restricted-use credit' shall be construed accordingly.

(2) An unrestricted-use credit agreement is a regulated consumer credit agreement not falling within subsection (1), and 'unrestricted-use credit' shall be construed accordingly.

(3) An agreement does not fall within subsection (1) if the credit is in fact provided in such a way as to leave the debtor free to use it as he chooses, even though certain uses would contravene that or any other agreement.

(4) An agreement may fall within subsection (1)(b) although the identity of the supplier is unknown at the time the agreement is made.

12. A debtor-creditor-supplier agreement is a regulated consumer credit agreement being—

(a) a restricted-use credit agreement which falls within s. 11(1)(a), or

1. Defined by s. 189(1) of the 1974 Act as including a partnership or other unincorporated body of persons not consisting entirely of bodies corporate. A partnership between individuals as well as a company or companies would therefore be included. The only 'person' excluded is a pure company.
2. See section 7.6 in relation to credit hire for a discussion of exemption.
3. The deferment must probably be a contractual one, however see *Pearce* v *Duff* [1999] 8 CL 322; *Dimond* v *Lovell* [1999] 3 All ER 1.

(b) a restricted-use credit agreement which falls within s. 11(1)(b) and is made by the creditor under pre-existing arrangements, or in contemplation of future arrangements, between himself and the supplier, or

(c) an unrestricted-use credit agreement which is made by the creditor under pre-existing arrangements between himself and a person (the 'supplier') other than the debtor in the knowledge that the credit is to be used to finance a transaction between the debtor and the supplier.

13. A debtor-creditor agreement is a regulated consumer credit agreement being—

(a) a restricted-use credit agreement which falls within s. 11(1)(b) but is not made by the creditor under pre-existing arrangements, or in contemplation of future arrangements, between himself and the supplier, or

(b) a restricted-use credit agreement which falls within s. 11(1)(c), or

(c) an unrestricted-use credit agreement which is not made by the creditor under pre-existing arrangements between himself and a person (the 'supplier') other than the debtor in the knowledge that the credit is to be used to finance a transaction between the debtor and the supplier.

15.—(1) A consumer hire agreement is an agreement made by a person with an individual (the 'hirer') for the bailment . . . of goods to the hirer, being an agreement which—

(a) is not a hire purchase agreement, and
(b) is capable of subsisting for more than three months, and
(c) does not require the hirer to make payments exceeding £25,000.

Note that the 1974 Act uses a series of layers to arrive at the final two types of credit contracts: debtor-creditor agreements (DC agreements) and debtor-creditor-supplier agreements (DCS agreements). The importance of the distinction between these two types of agreement is brought about by ss. 56 and 75 of the 1974 Act: if the agreement is a DCS agreement within the meaning of s. 12(b) or (c) then the debtor can sue the creditor for misrepresentations or breaches of contract made by the supplier. Furthermore, if the agreement falls within s. 12 at all, any pre-contract negotiations made by the supplier or any credit-broker will be deemed to be made by him not only in his own capacity *but also as agent of the creditor*.

This does not mean that the other definitions are relevant only in deciding whether the agreement falls within s. 12. The various definitions are used throughout the 1974 Act. The most important phrase used in the above definitions is 'regulated agreement'. It is only if the agreement is a regulated one that the technical requirements of the Act apply (as will be seen in the next section, under a regulated agreement the agreement must be in a specified form, signed by the debtor or hirer and contain certain information). A regulated agreement arises either under s. 8 or s. 15 of the Act.

The different types of agreement broadly fall into the following categories: hire purchase agreements, conditional sale agreements, loans, loans linked to the purchase of goods or services, credit sale agreements, deferred payment agreements, running-account credit and consumer hire agreements. Each will be examined in turn.

7.2.1 Hire purchase agreements and conditional sale agreements

Hire purchase agreements are traditionally understood by laymen to be agreements whereby the 'buyer' takes the goods and pays by instalments over a period of time, and upon the last instalment owns the goods. However, both conditional sale agreements and hire purchase agreements can take this form and a distinction must be drawn between the two. A hire purchase agreement is defined in s. 189(1) of the 1974 Act as follows:

> ... an agreement, other than a conditional sale agreement, under which—
> (a) goods are bailed ... in return for periodical payments by the person to whom they are bailed ..., and
> (b) the property in the goods will pass to that person if the terms of the agreement are complied with and one or more of the following occurs—
> (i) the exercise of an option to purchase by that person,
> (ii) the doing of any other specified act by any party to the agreement,
> (iii) the happening of any other specified event ...

A conditional sale agreement, by contrast, is defined in the same section as being:

> ... an agreement for the sale of goods or land under which the purchase price or part of it is payable by instalments, and the property in the goods or land is to remain in the seller (notwithstanding that the buyer is to be in possession of the goods or land) until such conditions as to the payment of instalments or otherwise as may be specified in the agreement are fulfilled.

This distinction has already been examined in section 1.6.5 in relation to whether such agreements are 'sales' within the meaning of the Sale of Goods Act 1979. The old common law distinction was simply that in hire purchase agreements the property in the goods was to pass only upon exercise of an option on the part of the buyer by paying the last instalment. The hirer had not agreed unconditionally to take the property in the goods. By contrast, under a conditional sale agreement the buyer had agreed to take the property in the goods. The seller may have afforded him time to pay by instalments, but the buyer was obliged to make all of those instalments, upon payment of which the property was to pass to him. The key to the difference is that in a conditional sale agreement the requirements are obligations, conditions precedent to the passing of property, but in a hire purchase agreement they are options.

Some practical differences exist between the two types of contract. Conditional sale agreements are governed by the Sale of Goods Act 1979, whereas hire purchase agreements are governed by the Supply of Goods (Implied Terms) Act 1973. This means that identical conditions are implied into each contract regarding title, description, quality and fitness for purpose. However, a hire purchase agreement is not a 'sale or agreement to sell' for the purposes of the Factors Act 1889. This is discussed in section 1.6.5.

Both types of agreement are regulated by the 1974 Act. Hire purchase agreements are made subject to the Act by virtue of s. 9(3) which provides that a person who bails goods under a hire purchase agreement shall 'be taken to provide [the hirer] with fixed-sum credit'. The agreement is thus capable of being a regulated agreement under s. 8 so long as the hirer is an individual and the amount involved is under £25,000. It cannot be argued therefore that the contract is one of hire coupled with sale and that no 'credit' is being provided. The Act cuts through this legal illusion and deems hire purchase that which it is — credit.

By contrast, conditional sale agreements need no assistance to come within the definition of s. 8. Under a conditional sale agreement the seller allows the buyer time to pay for the goods. The seller is accordingly granting the buyer financial accommodation which comes within the meaning of 'credit' given in s. 9. Accordingly and again, so long as the sums involved are under £25,000 and the buyer is an individual then the agreement will fall within the definition of a consumer credit agreement in s. 8.

Hire purchase and conditional sale agreements are restricted-use credit agreements within the meaning of s. 11(1)(a) of the 1974 Act so long as they are regulated agreements within the meaning of s. 8. Section 11(1)(a) deems an agreement to be a restricted-use agreement where credit is granted 'to finance a transaction between the debtor and the creditor'. Hire purchase agreements fall squarely into this definition, as do conditional sales.

In turn, agreements falling within s. 11(1)(a) are DCS agreements within the meaning of s. 12(a). Such agreements are capable of coming within the ambit of s. 56 if the debtor is referred to the creditor by a 'credit-broker'. As was discussed in section 7.1.1.2 a supplier will become a 'credit-broker' if he introduces the debtor to the creditor and the creditor will be liable for statements made by him. There is no requirement that the supplier must act under 'pre-existing arrangements' with the creditor where the agreement is one of hire purchase, unlike the situation with personal loans to fund the purchase of goods. It is sufficient that the supplier acts as a 'credit-broker' within the meaning of s. 145 by effecting introductions of individuals to credit companies *or other credit-brokers* (such as a person who runs a business dedicated to assisting individuals obtain credit).

Thus, although in the situation referred to above, where the supplier sells the goods to the creditor who in turn lets them to the debtor on hire purchase or conditional sale, there is no contract between the debtor and the supplier, the debtor will have a remedy against the creditor for statements made by the supplier. The debtor will, of course, have a direct remedy against the creditor in respect of defects with the goods by virtue of the implied terms contained in the Sale of Goods Act 1979 in relation to conditional sales and those contained in the Supply of Goods (Implied Terms) Act 1973 in relation to hire purchase agreements.

7.2.2 Loans and loans linked with the supply of goods and services

Many high street banks and other financial institutions offer personal loans to the general public. Such loans are clearly a form of credit and, if under £25,000 and made to an individual, will form a regulated consumer credit agreement within the meaning of s. 8 of the 1974 Act. If they are over £25,000 then they will form a 'personal credit agreement' within the meaning of s. 8(1). Such regulated loans must comply with the technical requirements of the Act if they are to be enforceable against the debtor.

However, the purpose of this section is to examine the circumstances when these loans will become linked to the purchase of goods and give the debtor the rights derived under DCS and DC agreements. These rights include the right to claim against the creditor in respect of defect with the goods, even though the contract of sale was with the supplier. In order to make the creditor account for the actions of the supplier and for the quality of the goods the transaction must fall within either s. 12(b) or 12(c) of the 1974 Act. These will be examined in turn.

7.2.2.1 Section 12(b) The first stage of determining whether a loan agreement falls within s. 12(b) of the 1974 Act is to determine whether the agreement is a restricted-use credit agreement within the meaning of s. 11(1)(b). It will be if it is a regulated consumer credit agreement (i.e., under £25,000, etc.) and is made to 'finance a transaction between the debtor and a person (the supplier) other than the creditor'. Thus where a person arranges with a bank to borrow a sum in order to buy a car the agreement is capable of being a restricted-use credit agreement.

However, it must not be made such as to allow the debtor to spend the money as he chooses, whether or not that would contravene the loan agreement. The 1974 Act provides examples of transactions which fall within its definitions. Example 12 of sch. 2 states that the loan would only fall into s. 11(1)(b) if the advance was to be paid directly to the supplier. The mere fact that the creditor has knowledge of how the debtor intends to spend the money is not sufficient either. This much is clear from Example 8.[4] Furthermore, under s. 11(4) the particular person from whom the debtor plans to acquire the goods need not be identified at the time the contract is made, but presumably once he is identified the money must be advanced directly to him.

In order for the loan to fall within s. 12(b) it must not only fall into s. 11(1)(b) as described above, but must also be made 'under pre-existing arrangements, or in contemplation of future arrangements, between [the creditor] and the supplier'. 'Pre-existing arrangements' and 'future arrangements' are defined in s. 187 as follows:

> (1) A consumer credit agreement shall be treated as entered into under pre-existing arrangements between a creditor and supplier if it is entered into in accordance with, or in furtherance of, arrangements previously made between persons mentioned in subsection (4)(a), (b) or (c).
>
> (2) A consumer credit agreement shall be treated as entered into in contemplation of future arrangements between a creditor and supplier if it is entered into in the expectation that arrangements will subsequently be made between persons mentioned in subsection (4)(a), (b) or (c) for the supply of cash, goods, and services (or any of them) to be financed by the consumer credit agreement.
>
> (3) Arrangements shall be disregarded for the purposes of subsection (1) or (2) if—
>
> (a) they are arrangements for the making, in specified circumstances, of payments to the supplier by the creditor, and
>
> (b) the creditor holds himself out as willing to make, in such circumstances, payments of the kind to suppliers generally.

4. The transaction may however fall under s. 12(c).

(3A) [exclusion of use of debit cards for payment of goods coming within this section].

(4) The persons referred to in subsections (1) and (2) are—

(a) the creditor and the supplier;

(b) one of them and an associate of the other's;

(c) an associate of one and an associate of the other's.

(5) Where the creditor is an associate of the supplier's, the consumer credit agreement shall be treated, unless the contrary is proved, as entered into under pre-existing arrangements between the creditor and the supplier.

This definition is, of course, completely tortuous and circular. It is most interesting to note that even the draftsman of the 1974 Act could not bring himself to make an example of the application of this section in sch. 2. Indeed, he actually shies away from it in Example 8, simply stating that:

> ... Whether it is a debtor-creditor agreement (by section 13(c)) or a debtor-creditor-supplier agreement (by section 12(c)) depends on whether the previous dealings between U and W amount to 'pre-existing arrangements', that is whether the agreement can be taken to have been entered into 'in accordance with, or in furtherance of' arrangements previously made between U and W, as laid down in section 187(1).

A most unhelpful non-example!

The term 'associate' is defined in s. 184 as including partnerships, relatives and groups of companies. The purpose of this definition and inclusion in s. 187 appears to be to prevent the creditor and supplier attempting to evade liability by making the contract operate through the medium of an associate. Given that the definition contained in s. 184 is expansive, this does not appear to be something which credit companies have bothered attempting to do and the issue is a rare one. However, this still leaves the question as to when there will be pre-existing arrangements open.

In practice, many large retailers make arrangements with a finance company to provide credit for the purchase of their goods. Indeed, the credit element is specifically included in the 'package' offered to the customer and special credit application forms may be printed to allow for this. Cars and electrical goods in particular appear to be sold in this way. These would certainly seem to be pre-existing arrangements, or in the case of the first sale, future arrangements.

Likewise, the credit company may make arrangements for the retailer to carry a stock of its general application forms in his shop and give the retailer a reference code and set up a regular method of payment to the retailer. Again, this would appear to form a pre-existing arrangement.

However, where the retailer is simply supplied with the forms for display, the situation becomes a little unclear. It is submitted that in these circumstances even the simple act of the creditor sending out his application forms for display could only be interpreted as the parties contemplating their use for the granting of credit to buy the retailer's goods and, therefore, that the arrangement would be a pre-existing one. Certainly, the use of the word 'arrangement' implies that there need be no firm contract between the creditor and supplier. By contrast, if the retailer had obtained the forms from some other source (e.g., a retailers' association) then this would probably fall within s. 187(3) and would not form a pre-existing arrangement as the creditor holds himself out as being willing to provide credit generally.

7.2.2.2 Section 12(c) Section 12(c) of the 1974 Act is predominantly in place to catch transactions which fall within s. 12(b) of the Act in substance but not in form. It applies where the debtor is supplied with unrestricted-use credit but it is supplied pursuant to pre-existing arrangements between the creditor and supplier and in the knowledge that the credit will be used to make a purchase from the supplier. Therefore, if the contract purports to allow the debtor to spend the money as he wishes, but the funds are in fact transferred to the supplier, it would be extremely difficult for the creditor to say that he did not know that the funds were to be used to finance a transaction between supplier and debtor. Similarly, if the funds are supplied directly to the debtor, but the contract stipulates that the money must be applied for the purpose of purchasing goods from the supplier, the creditor could not say that he did have knowledge of how the money was to be spent. If the contract were silent on both of these points then it is a question of fact whether the creditor knew that the funds were to be applied for the purpose of a transaction between the creditor and supplier.

In any event the same considerations apply in relation to 'pre-existing arrangements' under s. 12(c) as apply in relation to s. 12(b). The section does not catch the ordinary high street bank which makes loans available to the public generally for such purposes as they wish, even though in applying for a loan the debtor makes known the purpose for which he requires credit.

7.2.3 Credit sale agreements and deferred payment agreements

The 1974 Act defines a credit sale agreement in s. 189(1) as being 'an agreement for the sale of goods, under which the purchase price or part of it is payable by instalments, but which is not a conditional sale agreement'. The fact that the definition excludes a conditional sale agreement must mean that a credit sale involves the immediate transfer of the property, but that the seller allows the buyer credit and the payment is made by instalments.

The 1974 Act does not specifically include deferred payment schemes in any particular definition, but 'buy now pay later' schemes appear to be becoming a major source of credit in the country at present and are hence worthy of inclusion. Such agreements are a straightforward sale coupled with credit and are regulated agreements if for less than £25,000 and made to an individual by virtue of s. 8.

Both types of agreement are potentially exempt from the Act by virtue of r. 3 of the Consumer Credit (Exempt Agreements) Order 1989, SI 1989/869, which provides as follows:

> (1) The Act shall not regulate a consumer credit agreement which is an agreement of one of the following descriptions, that is to say—
>
> (a) a debtor-creditor-supplier agreement being either—
>
> (i) an agreement for fixed-sum credit under which the total number of payments to be made by the debtor does not exceed four, and those payments

are to be made within a period not exceeding 12 months beginning with the date of the agreement; . . .

In order to come within this exception, however, these conditions must be spelled out: it cannot be assumed that the debtor will make payment in four instalments or less. If the contract is silent on this, the debtor could legitimately make payment in any number of instalments (*Majeed* v *Incentive Group* [1999] 8 CL 321).

7.2.4 Running-account credit

Running-account credit is a traditional form of credit frequently extended to small businesses and is often referred to as 'a line of credit'. It must be remembered that the 1974 Act applies to all credit contracts where the debtor is 'an individual' and accordingly sole traders and partnerships can come within this definition. The Act defines running-account credit in s. 10 as follows:

> (1) For the purposes of this Act—
>
> (a) running-account credit is a facility under a personal credit agreement whereby the debtor is enabled to receive from time to time (whether in his own person, or by another person) from the creditor or a third party cash, goods and services (or any of them) to an amount or value such that, taking into account payments made by or to the credit of the debtor, the credit limit (if any) is not at any time exceeded; and . . .
>
> (2) In relation to running-account credit, 'credit limit' means, as respects any period, the maximum debit balance which, under the credit agreement, is allowed to stand on the account during that period, disregarding any term of the agreement allowing that maximum to be exceeded merely temporarily.
>
> (3) For the purposes of section 8(2) running-account credit shall be taken not to exceed the amount specified in that subsection ('the specified amount') if—
>
> (a) the credit limit does not exceed the specified amount; or
>
> (b) whether or not there is a credit limit, and if there is, notwithstanding that it exceeds the specified amount,—
>
> (i) the debtor is not enabled to draw at any time an amount which, so far as (having regard to section 9(4)) it represents credit, exceeds the specified amount, or
>
> (ii) the agreement provides that, if the debit balance rises above a given amount (not exceeding the specified amount), the rate of the total charge for credit increases or any other condition favouring the creditor or his associate comes into operation, or
>
> (iii) at the time the agreement is made it is probable, having regard to the terms of the agreement and any other relevant considerations, that the debit balance will not at any time rise above the specified amount.

As can be seen, much of this definition relates to establishing the amount of credit which at any one time may be advanced to the debtor. In general, this is the 'credit limit' imposed by the creditor (s. 10(3)(a)). However, this need not always be so as s. 10(2) and (3) prescribe circumstances where a different credit limit will be used. Section 10(2) provides that allowance for temporarily exceeding the limit does not affect the credit limit. Section 10(3)(b) deals largely with preventing credit companies circumventing the Act by granting the debtor a credit limit above £25,000. Section 10(3)(b)(i) requires that any interest or profit element of the credit is not taken into account in establishing the credit limit. Section 10(3)(b)(ii) prevents the creditor from granting a high credit limit, but imposing a limit below £25,000 at which penalties would be imposed, making the 'real' credit limit below £25,000. Likewise s. 10(3)(b)(iii) allows an assessment to be made of how much credit the debtor is likely to actually use. Thus a creditor cannot grant a £50,000 credit limit to a small shop which never uses more than £3,000 worth of credit and expect to circumvent the Act.

Certain agreements for running-account credit may be exempt from the 1974 Act by reason of r. 3 of the Consumer Credit (Exempt Agreements) Order 1989, SI 1989/869, which provides as follows:

> (1) The Act shall not regulate a consumer credit agreement which is an agreement of one of the following descriptions, that is to say—
> (a) ...
> (i) [relates to fixed sum credit]
> (ii) an agreement for running-account credit which provides for the making of payments by the debtor in relation to specified periods and requires that the number of payments to be made by the debtor in repayment of the whole amount of the credit provided in each such period shall not exceed one;

The rule is a little ambiguous, but it is submitted that it exempts a situation where the agreement for credit provides that the debtor shall make periodical repayments (be they monthly, quarterly, annually or such other period as the parties specify) and agrees to make repayment of the whole amount outstanding in that period and does so by one payment.

7.2.5 Consumer hire agreements

Consumer hire agreements are not agreements which necessarily involve credit, although they may do. Section 15 of the 1974 Act defines them as follows:

> (1) A consumer hire agreement is an agreement made by a person with an individual (the 'hirer') for the bailment ... of goods to the hirer, being an agreement which—
> (a) is not a hire purchase agreement, and
> (b) is capable of subsisting for more than three months, and
> (c) does not require the hirer to make payments exceeding £25,000.

The wording of s. 15(1)(b) requires not that the hire actually subsists for a period exceeding three months, but that it is *capable* of doing so. If there is no maximum fixed period therefore, the agreement is capable of subsisting for greater than three months (*Golding* v *Mason* [1999] 12 CL 254).

Whilst such contracts are not consumer credit contracts, they are regulated agreements and the technicalities of the 1974 Act apply. For example, the owner of the vehicle must hold a licence to hire a vehicle under such an agreement and the agreement must be in writing signed by both parties.

7.3 COMPLIANCE WITH THE TECHNICALITIES OF THE CONSUMER CREDIT ACT 1974

The 1974 Act imposes strict requirements as to the form and content of consumer credit and consumer hire agreements (this is dealt with in detail below in section 7.3.1). However, it is sufficient to note here that in order to enforce the agreement the creditor or owner must hold a licence to carry on the relevant sort of business. Furthermore, the Act specifies that agreements must be in certain prescribed forms and contain certain prescribed information.

As was noted at the start of this chapter, most loan agreements have been expertly drafted and a standard form complying with the 1974 Act will have been produced for use in all that credit company's transactions. However, in many cases the parties have entered into a transaction which provides credit whilst being completely oblivious to the existence of the Act. Where this is the case, the agreement almost never complies with the Act and will generally be unenforceable against the debtor.

The sanctions for non-compliance are contained in ss. 40, 65 and 149 which provide as follows:

> 40—(1) A regulated agreement, other than a non-commercial agreement, if made when the creditor or owner was unlicensed, is enforceable against the debtor or hirer only where the Director has made an order under this section which applies to the agreement.

> 65—(1) An improperly-executed regulated agreement is enforceable against the debtor or hirer on an order of the court only.
>
> (2) A retaking of goods or land to which a regulated agreement relates is an enforcement of the agreement.

> 149—(1) A regulated agreement made by a debtor or hirer who, for the purpose of making that agreement, was introduced to the creditor or owner by an unlicensed credit-broker is enforceable against the debtor or hirer only where—
>
> (a) on the application of the credit-broker, the Director has made an order under section 148(2) in respect of a period including the time when the introduction was made, and the order does not (whether in general terms or specifically) exclude the application of this paragraph to the regulated agreement, or
>
> (b) the Director has made an order under subsection (2) which applies to the agreement.
>
> (2) Where during any period individuals were introduced to a person carrying on a consumer credit business or consumer hire business by an unlicensed credit-broker for the purpose of making regulated agreements with the person carrying on that business, that person or his successor in title may apply to the Director for an order that regulated agreements so made are to be treated as if the credit-broker had been licensed at the time of the introduction.

Note that the Act uses the phrases 'improperly executed' and 'enforceable'. The circumstances where an agreement will be 'improperly executed' are explored below in detail. The use of the word 'enforceable' as opposed to 'void' means that at common law the contract is still valid (see *R* v *Modupe* (1992) 11 Tr LR 59), but that the creditor is debarred from pursuing his claim through the courts without the appropriate permission from the court. The consequences of improper execution are therefore draconian: if the agreement does not comply with the Act and it is a regulated agreement (other than a non-commercial agreement), the creditor has no remedy and the buyer effectively takes the goods or cash for free.

This was the result in *Dimond* v *Lovell* [1999] 3 All ER 1, upheld by the House of Lords ([2000] 2 WLR 1121). That case involved 'credit hire', but the principles are relevant here. The claimant had hired a car on credit terms following a road traffic accident during the period when her car was out of use. In turn she claimed the cost of doing so from the defendant. It was held that the claimant was not entitled to recover in respect of those hire charges as she was not liable for them. It was conceded in that case that the agreement was improperly executed and, as such, unenforceable. However, no doubt appears to have been cast upon the correctness of that concession and it has been followed in many other cases since then.

The circumstances when the court may allow a party to enforce an improperly executed agreement are set out in s. 127 of the 1974 Act, which provides as follows:

> (1) In the case of an application for an enforcement order under—
>
> (a) section 65(1) (improperly executed agreements), or . . .
>
> the court shall dismiss the application if, but (subject to subsections (3) and (4)) only if, it considers it just to do so having regard to—
>
> (i) prejudice caused to any person by the contravention in question, and the degree of culpability for it; and
>
> (ii) the powers conferred on the court by subsection (2) and sections 135 and 136.
>
> (2) If it appears to the court just to do so, it may in an enforcement order reduce or discharge any sum payable by the debtor or hirer, or any surety, so as to compensate him for prejudice suffered as a result of the contravention in question.
>
> (3) The court shall not make an enforcement order under section 65(1) if section 61(1)(a) (signing of agreements) was not complied with unless a document (whether or not in the prescribed form and complying with regulations under section 60(1)) itself containing the prescribed terms of the agreement was signed by the debtor or hirer (whether or not in the prescribed manner).
>
> (4) The court shall not make an enforcement order under section 65(1) in the case of a cancellable agreement if—
>
> (a) a provision of section 62 or 63 was not complied with, and the creditor or owner did not give a copy of the executed agreement, and of any other document referred to in it, to the debtor or hirer before the commencement of the proceedings in which the order is sought, or
>
> (b) section 64(1) was not complied with.
>
> (5) Where an enforcement order is made in a case to which subsection (3) applies, the order may direct that the regulated agreement is to have effect as if

it did not include a term omitted from the document signed by the debtor or hirer.

Sections 135 and 136 of the 1974 Act, referred to in the above section, give the court a very wide power to impose conditions or suspend the agreement where it considers it just to do so, or even to vary the terms of the agreement. Furthermore, by s. 127(2) above, the court may reduce the amount payable if it thinks that this would produce a just result.

In *Nissan Finance UK* v *Lockhart* [1993] CCLR 39 the Court of Appeal stated that an order under s. 127 should be made unless there was evidence to show that the debtor's position would have been different if the document had been properly completed. Given that the main purpose of ss. 60 to 64 is to ensure that the debtor has been given full information about the agreement, it is likely that where important details such as the rate of interest are missing the court would be unwilling to make an enforcement order. In the context of credit hire agreements, it was said in *Smerdon* v *Ellis* [1997] 1 CLY 963[5] that no court would ever grant an order against the hirer where the hire company had represented to the hirer that the liability for the cost of the hire would be recovered from the other party's insurer.

In order for the court to have power to grant an enforcement order under s. 65 the agreement between the parties must (at least) have been reduced to writing and contain the terms of the agreement between them (s. 127(3)). It must also have been signed by the debtor or hirer, but not necessarily the creditor or owner.

Another argument which is sometimes raised in a consumer credit case when the agreement is improperly executed is that the debtor has consented to the agreement being enforced against him. However, it would be rare for the argument to be raised outside this area. Section 173(3) provides as follows:

> Notwithstanding subsection (1), a provision of this Act under which a thing may be done in relation to any person on an order of the court or the Director only shall not be taken to prevent its being done at any time with that person's consent given at that time, but the refusal of such consent shall not give rise to any liability.

In the context of credit hire agreements it is sometimes argued that the consent was given by the debtor on the basis that he instituted proceedings for recovery of the charges, thereby claiming liability. However, this argument was rejected in *Gibbons* v *Gibbons* [1998] CLY 2500 as consent had to be given at the time of enforcement. Furthermore, it was said in *Kemp* v *Ling* [1998] CLY 2502 that s. 173(3) did not make enforceable that which was not otherwise enforceable. Whilst only decisions of district judges, these decisions have been cited with approval in a Scottish case, *Bhoyrub* v *Cadzow* 1999 SCLR 539, and are probably correct. However, it is submitted that the better way to decide such a case would be to find that, as a matter of fact, consent was not given in respect of rights of which the claimant had no knowledge, it being rare in a credit hire case for the claimant to have any knowledge of the situation. Alternatively, that the issue of proceedings

5. See also *Re Dixon Vincent* [1997] 11 CL 114; *Rendle* v *Hicks* [1998] 2 CL 126; *Wotton* v *Flagg* [1997] CLY 959; *Rahman* v *Brassil* [1998] 8 CL 219; *Petrou* v *Kuti* [1997] CLY 1803; *Hunt* v *Severs* [1994] 2 AC 350; and *Pedelty* v *Jarvis* [1999] 6 CL 287, all of which appear to support this proposition.

was not an act which waived consent as it was never communicated to the creditor, nor in any event could it be construed as a waiver of the debtor's right to prevent the agreement being *enforced against him*, which is what is envisaged by the 1974 Act.

In the case of an agreement being entered into whilst either the creditor or credit-broker is unlicensed is slightly different than where the agreement is improperly executed. Here the creditor can make an application to the Director General of Fair Trading. There are no reported cases regarding when the Director General will give his permission, however the 1974 Act does set out in ss. 40 and 149 guidelines as to when permission should be granted. In particular these include the degree to which the debtor or hirer has been prejudiced and likelihood of a licence being granted if application had been made.

The buyer or hirer cannot therefore expect to take the goods for free where (for example) there has been a mere oversight on the part of the creditor in renewing the licence and the buyer or hirer has not suffered at all. However, where the value of the claim is relatively small then it will fall in the small claims limit and the claimant will not be entitled to recover his costs should he wish to pursue his claim. Tactically therefore, putting the creditor to the expense and inconvenience of making an application to the Director General may put him off pursuing his claim altogether.

It is not necessary to consider the criteria whereby the creditor or owner may acquire a licence. It is sufficient to note that s. 21 of the 1974 Act requires the creditor, or owner under a regulated hire agreement, to hold a licence where he carries on 'consumer credit business' or 'consumer hire business'. This will be the case wherever the parties enter into a regulated agreement. However, the creditor or owner is not precluded from enforcing the agreement where it is a 'non-commercial agreement', which is defined in s. 189(1) of the Act as being where the agreement is not made in the course of a business carried on by him. These words presumably bear the same meaning as they do in relation to s. 14 of the Sale of Goods Act 1979 and the fact that the credit or hire is incidental or collateral to the creditor's main business will not prevent it from being made 'in the course of a business'.

However, the fact that a potential debtor or hirer was introduced to the creditor or owner by a third party will often render that person a credit-broker within the meaning of the Act.[6] Where this is the case then, in accordance with s. 149, the agreement will be unenforceable. This is particularly likely to be so where the case is one for credit hire: people suffering from a road traffic accident are frequently referred to a credit hire firm by their solicitor, insurer, legal expense insurer, insurance broker or one of the new 'motor loss' recovery firms. If this person is unlicensed and a regulated agreement stems from the introduction, then the agreement will be unenforceable without leave of the Director General. As with creditors above, it may be a good tactic to take this point as it may prevent the creditor or owner from pursuing his claim.

7.3.1 Form and content of agreements

Sections 60 to 64 of the 1974 Act lay down the requirements as to form and content of regulated agreements. Note that some of the requirements apply to all regulated

6. As to when this will be the case, see section 7.1.1.2 above.

agreements, and some apply only to consumer credit agreements. This is simply because some matters, such as 'total charge for credit', have no application in relation to consumer hire agreements. The requirements fall into three categories: content and prescribed form, signing and supply of copies. Strict compliance is required. Each will be examined in turn.

Section 60 of the 1974 Act provides as follows:

> (1) The Secretary of State shall make regulations as to the form and content of documents embodying regulated agreements, and the regulations shall contain such provisions as appear to him appropriate with a view to ensuring that the debtor or hirer is made aware of—
>
> (a) the rights and duties conferred or imposed on him by the agreement,
>
> (b) the amount and rate of the total charge for credit (in the case of a consumer credit agreement),
>
> (c) the protection and remedies available to him under this Act, and
>
> (d) any other matters which, in the opinion of the Secretary of State, it is desirable for him to know about in connection with the agreement.
>
> (2) Regulations under subsection (1) may in particular—
>
> (a) require specified information to be included in the prescribed manner in documents, and other specified material to be excluded;
>
> (b) contain requirements to ensure that specified information is clearly brought to the attention of the debtor or hirer, and that one part of a document is not given insufficient or excessive prominence compared with another.

By s. 60(1), regulations are required to be made setting out the form and content of consumer credit agreements in detail. This is done by the Consumer Credit (Agreements) Regulations 1983, SI 1983/1553 as amended by SI 1984/1600, SI 1985/666 and SI 1988/2047. The Regulations are too detailed for a full analysis to be given here as they apply differently depending upon the nature of the agreement. However, the Regulations are contained in Appendix C. In practice, the agreement has either been professionally drafted and looks as such, or else no thought has been given to the 1974 Act and the agreement does not in any way comply with it. By s. 60(3) a creditor or owner may apply to have parts of the requirements varied due to the particular circumstances of his business.

Where the agreement is a credit hire agreement, compliance with the 1983 Regulations will be extremely difficult as the period of hire, and hence the total amount of credit,[7] will not be ascertainable until the end of the hire period. Whilst reg. 2(2) does allow an estimate in respect for the total charge for credit to be given, an estimate for the amount of credit cannot be used (*Constantinou* v *Ozcan* [1999] 12 CL 256).

Section 61 of the 1974 Act provides:

> (1) A regulated agreement is not properly executed unless—
>
> (a) a document in the prescribed form itself containing all the prescribed terms and conforming to regulations under section 60(1) is signed in the prescribed manner both by the debtor or hirer and by or on behalf of the creditor or owner, and

7. As opposed to 'total charge for credit'.

(b) the document embodies all the terms of the agreement, other than implied terms, and

(c) the document is, when presented or sent to the debtor or hirer for signature, in such a state that all its terms are readily legible.

Section 61 lays down the requirement that the agreement be signed by both debtor or hirer and by or on behalf of the creditor or owner. Again, strict compliance is required. 'Executed agreement' is defined in s. 189(1) of the Act as a 'document, signed by or on behalf of the parties, embodying the terms of a regulated agreement, or such of them as have been reduced to writing'. The effect, therefore, of signing is that the agreement becomes executed at the time the second signature is obtained. As is shown below, the creditor or owner comes under an obligation to supply a copy of the agreement upon execution.

A second requirement imposed by s. 61(1)(b) is that the document 'embodies all the terms of the agreement'. It is not, therefore, open to the creditor to insert terms by reference to another document. This is slightly at odds with the requirement in ss. 62(1) and 63(1) that a copy of 'any other document' referred to within the agreement be supplied to the debtor or hirer. However, it seems that whilst other documents may be referred to, nothing in them will form a term of the agreement unless set out in the principal document.

Section 62 of the 1974 Act provides as follows:

(1) If the unexecuted agreement is presented personally to the debtor or hirer for his signature, but on the occasion when he signs it the document does not become an executed agreement, a copy of it, and of any other document referred to in it, must be there and then delivered to him.

(2) If the unexecuted agreement is sent to the debtor or hirer for his signature, a copy of it, and of any other document referred to in it, must be sent to him at the same time.

(3) A regulated agreement is not properly executed if the requirements of this section are not observed.

Section 63 states:

(1) If the unexecuted agreement is presented personally to the debtor or hirer for his signature, and on the occasion when he signs it the document becomes an executed agreement, a copy of the executed agreement, and of any other document referred to in it, must be there and then delivered to him.

(2) A copy of the executed agreement, and of any other document referred to in it, must be given to the debtor or hirer within the seven days following the making of the agreement unless—

(a) subsection (1) applies, or

(b) the unexecuted agreement was sent to the debtor or hirer for his signature and, on the occasion of his signing it, the document became an executed agreement.

(3) In the case of a cancellable agreement, a copy under subsection (2) must be sent by post.

(4) ...

(5) A regulated agreement is not properly executed if the requirements of this section are not observed.

Whilst slightly confusing at first, ss. 62 and 63 ensure that the debtor or hirer is provided with a copy of the agreement bearing the signature of the creditor or owner and his own signature. These sections cater for the agreement being made by post and for the agreement being signed by the creditor or the debtor first.

If the agreement is given to the debtor or hirer to sign personally by the creditor or owner, and at the time he signs it the creditor has not signed it, the creditor is first obliged to give the debtor or hirer a copy then and there (s. 62(1)). Secondly, the creditor is then obliged to supply a copy of the executed agreement within seven days of its being signed by the creditor (s. 63(2)). If when the agreement is presented to the debtor for his signature it has already been signed by the creditor, the creditor must supply him with a copy then and there (s. 63(1)), but is not obliged to make any further copies (s. 63(2)(a)).

If the agreement is executed by post and if the agreement has not been signed by the creditor when it is sent to the debtor, a copy of it must be sent with the unexecuted agreement at the same time (s. 62(2)). Once this is returned and signed by the creditor, the creditor must supply a copy of the signed agreement within seven days (s. 63(2)). But if the agreement was sent to the debtor already signed by the creditor, the creditor is under no duty to copy it for him (s. 63(2)(b)).

Finally, s. 64 provides:

(1) In the case of a cancellable agreement, a notice in the prescribed form indicating the right of the debtor or hirer to cancel the agreement, how and when that right is exercisable, and the name and address of a person to whom notice of cancellation may be given,—

(a) must be included in every copy given to the debtor or hirer under section 62 or 63, and

(b) except where section 63(2) applied, must also be sent by post to the debtor or hirer within the seven days following the making of the agreement.

...

(5) A cancellable agreement is not properly executed if the requirements of this section are not observed.

Withdrawal and cancellation are dealt with in the next section, but it is sufficient to note here that the agreement must contain notice of the debtor's right to cancel. The prescribed form and content of the notice of cancellation rights is contained in the Consumer Credit (Cancellation Notices and Copies of Documents) Regulations 1983, SI 1983/1557.

7.4 WITHDRAWAL AND CANCELLATION

Withdrawal of an offer is the common law operation of withdrawing a prospective agreement before it is executed. Cancellation, however, is a special statutory right created under the 1974 Act to cancel a completed agreement within a 'cooling off' period. Both have the same effect under the Act, i.e., the debtor ceases to be bound by the credit agreement and any other 'linked transaction'. A linked transaction will often be the contract of sale which is to be financed by the credit transaction, and thus the debtor is not bound to buy the goods where he is not bound by the credit agreement.

The operation of withdrawal will be considered, then the operation of cancellation, before turning to the effects of both.

7.4.1 Withdrawal

In respect of withdrawal from a prospective loan agreement, the 1974 Act does not alter the debtor's right to withdraw at common law, but simply extends the mode of withdrawal and the range of people to whom the debtor may communicate it. It also extends the effect of such withdrawal to other 'linked transactions'.

7.4.1.1 Mode of withdrawal The general common law rule was expressed in *Financings Ltd* v *Stimson* [1962] 1 WLR 1184 that an offer may be withdrawn at any time prior to its acceptance. However, the 'postal rule' is slightly modified in relation to withdrawal of an offer where the offeror posts his withdrawal to the offeree, but before it reaches him the offeree has posted an acceptance. The offeree is then bound by the acceptance (*Byrne & Co.* v *Leon Van Tienhoven* (1880) 5 CPD 344). However, the withdrawal will be effective if it has been received by the offeree, notwithstanding that he has not read it (*The Brimnes* [1975] QB 929).

The rules as to supply of copies which were dealt with in the previous section are relevant in determining whether the debtor has an opportunity to withdraw from the prospective agreement. In many credit cases the debtor 'applies' for the loan from the creditor, who vets him by a process of credit scoring. This application will normally form the basis of an offer by the debtor to enter a consumer credit agreement. It will also normally be done by filling out the loan agreement which will become executed when the creditor signs the agreement and returns it to the debtor. Applying the common law rules above to this situation the debtor has any time until the creditor posts the signed agreement to communicate his withdrawal from it. This mode of forming the agreement is by far the most common. However, where the agreement is formed by the creditor sending the debtor a signed agreement for him to sign then the debtor has much more opportunity to withdraw as the time for acceptance is in his hands.

7.4.1.2 Agreement not to withdraw void The rationale behind the ability of a person to withdraw from a contract prior to its acceptance is that an offer is a promise unsupported by consideration. Thus at common law an offeror may bind himself to not withdraw from an offer or not to do so for a stated period by making the offer by deed or by supporting it with consideration. The 1974 Act modifies this rule in relation to regulated agreements by s. 59(1) which provides that 'an agreement is void if, and to the extent that, it purports to bind a person to enter as debtor or hirer into a prospective regulated agreement'. Accordingly, a debtor will never be bound not to withdraw his offer.

7.4.1.3 Persons to whom notice of withdrawal may be given The 1974 Act extends the mode of withdrawal from a prospective agreement by s. 57(2) which provides that withdrawal may be effected by giving 'written or oral notice which, however expressed, indicates the intention of the other party to withdraw from a prospective . . . agreement'.

The range of people to whom notice of withdrawal may be given is defined by s. 57(3) which provides as follows:

> Each of the following shall be deemed to be the agent of the creditor or owner for the purpose of receiving a notice under subsection (2)—
>
> (a) a credit-broker or supplier who is the negotiator in antecedent negotiations, and
>
> (b) any person who, in the course of a business carried on by him, acts on behalf of the debtor or hirer in any negotiations for the agreement.

The rule is quite harsh against the creditor in that it allows the debtor to effect notice not only by communicating it to the supplier of goods under a debtor-creditor or debtor-creditor-supplier agreement, but also to the buyer's own agent. The creditor may thus lose the benefit of the agreement even where it is the buyer's own agent who fails to pass on the notice of withdrawal. However, this is mitigated somewhat by s. 175 which deems any person to whom notice may be given to be under a contractual duty to transmit the notice forthwith. Withdrawal may also be effected by giving notice to a credit-broker where there is one. The meaning of the phrase 'credit-broker' was discussed in detail in section 7.1.1.2 above.

The effect of withdrawal from a prospective agreement is deemed by s. 57(1) to be the same as if it had been cancelled under s. 69. This is explored in detail in section 7.4.3 below, but it is sufficient to note here that upon withdrawal the debtor will be entitled to the return of any monies paid under the prospective agreement and to withdraw from any other 'linked transactions'.

7.4.2 Cancellation

The general effect of cancellation under the 1974 Act is to give the debtor an opportunity to withdraw from a transaction which he signed otherwise than at the creditor or supplier's premises within a specified cooling-off period. Section 67 defines when the agreement will be cancellable, s. 68 prescribes the cooling-off period during which notice of cancellation may be given and s. 69 prescribes the mode and effect of cancellation.

7.4.2.1 Cancellable agreement Section 67 of the 1974 Act provides as follows:

> A regulated agreement may be cancelled by the debtor or hirer in accordance with this Part if the antecedent negotiations included oral representations made when in the presence of the debtor or hirer by an individual acting as, or on behalf of, the negotiator, unless—
>
> (a) the agreement is secured on land or is a restricted-use credit agreement to finance the purchase of land or is an agreement for a bridging loan in connection with the purchase of land, or
>
> (b) the unexecuted agreement is signed by the debtor or hirer at premises at which any of the following is carrying on any business (whether on a permanent or temporary basis)—

(i) the creditor or owner;
(ii) any party to a linked transaction (other than the debtor or hirer or a relative of his);
(iii) the negotiator in any antecedent negotiations.

The exception provided by s. 67(a) is relatively self-explanatory. Further exceptions are provided by s. 74 and include overdrafts, non-commercial agreements and small agreements. These exceptions are, however, relatively rare within the context of a cancellable agreement.

This leaves four criteria which must be fulfilled in order for the debtor to rely on s. 67: he must have signed the agreement otherwise than at premises of the creditor or owner or those of a party to a linked transaction (usually the supplier); antecedent negotiations must have taken place; these must be in the presence of the debtor; and 'oral representations' must have been made during the course of those negotiations.

7.4.2.2 Signing of agreement away from business premises The premises to which s. 67(b) applies will usually be those of the creditor or supplier under a debtor-creditor-supplier agreement. It must be remembered that the requirement to sign the agreement otherwise than at the premises of the creditor or supplier does not mean to say that it must be signed at home, or that the negotiations take place at the debtor's home. If the agreement is posted to the debtor and he signs it at home then the subsection will apply.

7.4.2.3 Antecedent negotiations The meaning of the phrase 'antecedent negotiations' was discussed in section 7.1.1.3. The thrust of these provisions is to make all creditors or owners 'negotiators' within the meaning of the Act, together with most suppliers where the supplier introduces the debtor to the creditor. Whether the supplier under a hire purchase agreement comes within the ambit of s. 56 was discussed in section 7.2.1. Where the supplier supplies goods for which a loan is advanced by the creditor then, so long as the agreement is one to which s. 12(b) or (c) applies, the supplier will always be capable of coming within the definition given in s. 56(1)(c) and the supplier will be a negotiator.

7.4.2.4 Oral representations in the presence of the debtor or hirer Section 67 requires that the negotiations take place in the presence of the debtor. Accordingly, representations made over the telephone or by post do not bring the transaction within the ambit of s. 67. 'Negotiations' is not defined in the 1974 Act, but the phrase appears to cover all discussions relating to the sale of the goods or services.

Finally, in order to bring the agreement within s. 67, oral representations must have been made. Section 189(1) defines 'representation' as including 'any condition or warranty, and any other statement or undertaking, whether oral or in writing'.

7.4.2.5 Cooling-off period Section 68 of the 1974 Act provides as follows:

> The debtor or hirer may serve notice of cancellation of a cancellable agreement between his signing of the unexecuted agreement and—

(a) the end of the fifth day following the day on which he received a copy under section 63(2) or a notice under section 67(1)(b), ...

This provision is relatively straightforward: the cooling-off period is five days from the day upon which a copy of the executed agreement is supplied to the debtor, or five days from the day upon which notice of cancellation rights was served if this was not contained within the agreement in the first place. It is worth noting that the section is dependent upon the *actual* day of delivery, not the maximum period in which it could have been delivered or any deemed date of delivery.

7.4.2.6 Mode of cancellation Section 69 of the 1974 Act provides that a notice of cancellation may be served on any of the following:

(a) the creditor or owner, or
(b) the person specified in the notice under s. 64(1),[8] or
(c) a person who (whether by virtue of subsection (6) or otherwise) is the agent of the creditor or owner, which includes by subsection (6):
(i) a credit-broker or supplier who conducts antecedent negotiations;
(ii) any person who, in the course of a business carried on by him, acts on behalf of the debtor or hirer in any negotiations for the agreement.

Section 69(1) states that 'notice of cancellation' may be effected by a notice which however expressed indicates an intention of the debtor or hirer to withdraw from the agreement. Furthermore, and unlike withdrawal from the agreement, by s. 69(7) the notice is deemed to have been served when it is posted. Whilst not actually spelt out, the use of the phrase 'a notice' as opposed to simply 'notice' arguably requires that the notice is made in writing.

7.4.3 Effect of withdrawal or cancellation

Section 57(1) of the 1974 Act provides that the effect of withdrawal is the same as if the agreement had been cancelled under s. 69. Furthermore, this extends to linked transactions and 'any other thing done in anticipation of making the contract'. Section 69(1) provides that the effect of cancellation (and hence withdrawal) will be:

(a) to cancel the agreement, and any linked transaction, and
(b) to withdraw any offer by the debtor or hirer, or his relative, to enter into a linked transaction.

Once the agreement has been cancelled, by s. 69(4) it is to be treated as if it had never existed. Furthermore, any linked transaction is also so treated. Where there exists a prospective agreement in respect of a linked transaction (i.e., one where

8. Section 64(1) provides that the creditor must specify in the notice of cancellation rights the person to whom notice of cancellation may be given. It is thus open to the creditor to specify someone other than himself upon whom such notice may be given. This operates to extend the list of people to whom notice of cancellation may be given, but by s. 69(1)(a) the creditor or owner cannot remove himself from the list of people.

an offer has been issued but not yet accepted), by s. 69(1)(ii) the offer is to be treated as withdrawn.

The meaning of 'linked transaction' was fully explored in section 7.1.1.4 and it is sufficient to note here that where the agreement is a debtor-creditor-supplier agreement, upon cancellation of the principal credit agreement any contract for the sale or supply of goods or services (the goods to which the loan relates) will be a linked transaction, as will a contract for (e.g.) maintenance of the good being purchased. Accordingly, upon withdrawal or cancellation of the credit agreement the debtor is released from the sale agreement and is not further burdened with this as well.

However, the operation of this section is restricted in circumstances where it would be impracticable or impossible to return the goods to the creditor or supplier. This is done by s. 69(2), (3) and (5), which provide as follows:

> (2) In the case of a debtor-creditor-supplier agreement for restricted-use credit financing—
>
> (a) the doing of work or the supply of goods to meet an emergency, or
>
> (b) the supply of goods which, before service of the notice of cancellation, had by the act of the debtor or his relative become incorporated in any land or thing not comprised in the agreement or any linked transaction,
>
> subsection (1) shall apply with the substitution of the following for paragraph (i)—
>
> '(i) to cancel only such provisions of the agreement and any linked transaction as—
>
> (aa) relate to the provision of credit, or
>
> (bb) require the debtor to pay an item in the total charge for credit, or
>
> (cc) subject the debtor to any obligation other than to pay for the doing of the said work, or the supply of the said goods'.
>
> (3) Except so far as is otherwise provided, references in this Act to the cancellation of an agreement or transaction do not include a case within subsection (2).
>
> (4)...
>
> (5) Regulations may exclude linked transactions of the prescribed description from subsection (1)(i) or (ii).

The effect of s. 69(2) is to allow the debtor to withdraw from the credit element of the agreement(s) which he has entered into, but he is still obliged to pay for the goods or services supplied.

The cancellation of an unrestricted-use credit agreement does not require the debtor to make immediate repayment of any monies advanced; indeed the transaction continues much as before. By s. 71(1) the agreement is declared to continue in force as regards repayment of the credit and interest. This is so notwithstanding that any security (forming a linked transaction) is treated as if it had never existed. However, if the debtor repays the whole or a portion of the principal amount of credit within one month from the service of the notice of cancellation, or before the first instalment falls due, then no interest is payable on that amount. If the debtor chooses not to make a repayment of the capital, by s. 71(3) the creditor must send a written request setting out the repayments due as near as would be the case had the agreement subsisted. It is not until this has been done that any monies fall due.

As regards any amounts of money paid or payable by the debtor prior to cancellation in respect of the 'total charge for credit' (the interest element) this shall become repayable or cease to be payable under s. 70(1). Furthermore, the debtor shall have a lien over any goods supplied to him in respect of those sums and shall be entitled to recover them from any person to whom it was paid. Thus in *Colesworthy* v *Collmain Services* [1993] CCLR 4 monies had been paid by the debtor to an agent of the creditor in accordance with the agreement and were recoverable from that agent upon cancellation.

If the debtor has taken goods under a cancelled agreement, s. 72 requires him to return them to the person from whom he gained possession. Likewise s. 73 requires any goods given in part exchange to be returned to the debtor. The debtor's duty, however, is simply to hold the goods available for collection. He need not physically return them himself.

7.5 ATTACHING LIABILITY TO CREDITOR AND/OR SUPPLIER

Probably the most fundamental change to the law introduced by the 1974 Act was to bring about a general right of the debtor to affix liability to the creditor for defects in the goods. Without these provisions the debtor could find himself tied to a loan in respect of defective goods.

It must be remembered that in the typical debtor-creditor-supplier agreement the debtor will usually only have a contract with one party for the sale or supply of the goods. Under the privity of contract rule this person would be the only person against whom the buyer would have a remedy in respect of the defects in the goods. However, frequently (e.g., under a hire purchase or conditional sale agreement) the goods would for all commercial purposes have been sold by the supplier, not the creditor, yet the contract would be with the creditor. Certainly, any representations regarding the fitness for a particular purpose, description or quality of the goods would have come from the supplier and not the creditor. At common law,[9] the creditor could therefore legitimately defend any proceedings brought for misrepresentation or unfitness for a particular purpose as it was not him who made the representations. Equally, if the finance was provided by a loan (albeit a restricted purpose loan) and the goods proved defective, at common law the creditor could simply retort that it was not his problem and hold the debtor to the loan.

In one respect, the law need not address these problems as it is always open to the debtor to negotiate terms which suit him. However, the reality of the world is that the balance of power is firmly in the hands of the credit companies and not individual consumers. Furthermore, credit companies have much stronger resources at their fingertips and could easily circumvent the consumer's attempts to negotiate the situation with the use of small print. Accordingly ss. 56 and 75 were introduced into the 1974 Act which fundamentally reversed the position.

Section 56 provides as follows:

> (1) In this Act 'antecedent negotiations' means any negotiations with the debtor or hirer—

9. Some cases prior to the 1974 Act did hold the supplier liable under a collateral contract mechanism.

> (a) ...
> (b) conducted by a credit-broker in relation to goods sold or proposed to be sold by the credit-broker to the creditor before forming the subject-matter of a debtor-creditor-supplier agreement within section 12(a), or
> (c) conducted by the supplier in relation to a transaction financed or proposed to be financed by a debtor-creditor-supplier agreement within section 12(b) or (c), and 'negotiator' means the person by whom negotiations are so conducted with the debtor or hirer.
> (2) Negotiations with the debtor in a case falling within subsection (1)(b) or (c) shall be deemed to be conducted by the negotiator in the capacity of agent of the creditor as well as in his actual capacity.

The particular categorisation of the different types of credit agreement was dealt with in section 7.2 (categories of credit agreement). 'Credit broker' and 'antecedent negotiations' were defined in sections 7.1.1.2 and 7.1.1.3. However, it is sufficient to note that (in general) hire purchase and conditional sale agreements fall into s. 56(1)(b) where the supplier has become a credit-broker through introducing the debtor to the creditor and the supplier will generally be the negotiator under s. 56(1)(c) where he has introduced the debtor to the creditor and a restricted-use credit agreement has been formed for the purchase of the goods in accordance with pre-existing arrangements with the creditor. Accordingly, the supplier will be deemed to be the agent of the creditor for the purposes of any representations made by him. The privity rule is thus obviated. Furthermore, any term purporting to exclude the operation of s. 56 is void by s. 56(3).

Section 75 takes the situation further than s. 56 and provides the debtor with a like claim against the creditor for any misrepresentations or breaches of contract made by the supplier.

Section 75 of the 1974 Act provides as follows:

> (1) If the debtor under a debtor-creditor-supplier agreement falling within s. 12(b) or (c) has, in relation to a transaction financed by the agreement, any claim against the supplier in respect of a misrepresentation or breach of contract, he shall have a like claim against the creditor, who, with the supplier, shall accordingly be jointly and severally liable to the debtor.

Section 75 applies to loans advanced in favour of the buyer for the purpose of financing a transaction between the debtor and the supplier. It does not extend to hire purchase agreements. However, the debtor has no need to rely upon s. 75 where the agreement is one of hire purchase as his contract is with the creditor and, as regards remedies which depend upon statements made by the supplier, the supplier will be the creditor's deemed agent under s. 56. Whether or not an agreement falls within s. 12(b) or (c) was discussed in section 7.2.2.

It is clear that s. 75 gives the debtor a claim in damages against the creditor in respect of defects in the goods and in respect of any consequential losses. However, what is not clear is whether s. 75 is intended to give the debtor a right to rescind the credit agreement or whether he is bound by it. On the one hand, if the debtor has a claim to terminate the contract with the supplier, a 'like claim' against the creditor would include a claim to terminate that contract. On the other hand, a 'like claim' could simply refer to a like claim for damages or for the price for which the creditor is jointly and severally liable. It does not seem that the Crowther Committee intended the debtor to have a right to terminate the credit agreement, merely a right to set-off against any monies owing in respect of it.[10] However, there are a number of first instance decisions which have taken the other view, and seemingly none that have taken the view that the debtor cannot terminate the agreement: *United Dominions Trust* v *Taylor* 1980 SLT 28; *Forward Trust* v *Hornsby* [1996] CLLR 18; *Porter* v *General Guarantee Corpn.* [1982] RTR 384. However, the matter is not beyond doubt.[11] In any event, if the debtor's complaint is founded in misrepresentation then, as the supplier will be a deemed agent under s. 56, this ought to operate to rescind the credit agreement.

7.6 CREDIT HIRE AGREEMENTS

A credit hire agreement arises where a person who has been involved in a road traffic accident hires a vehicle from a specialist firm which is prepared to grant him credit so he may defer payment and recover the cost of hire from the driver who was at fault for the accident as part of a claim for damages. In short the agreement is one for the provision of credit so as to allow the driver to hire a vehicle. Where the agreement can be shown to be a regulated agreement which is unenforceable through non-compliance with the technicalities of the 1974 Act then the defendant to proceedings issued by the driver has a good defence to a claim for the cost of hire. This much is clear from the decision in *Dimond* v *Lovell* [1999] 3 All ER 1 (CA); [2000] 2 WLR 1121 (HL).

Credit hire agreements have become fiercely litigated by the insurance industry over the past few years. The essence of the problem is that the credit hire companies charge an enhanced rate over and above the normal rate of hire where no credit is advanced ('the spot rate'). This surplus accounts for the credit hire companies' profit element for their extra expense in granting credit and pursuing a claim on behalf of the hirer. The insurance industry is naturally reluctant to pay this element of the hire. However, since the House of Lords decision in *Dimond* v *Lovell* it will only be the hire element which will be recoverable. That proportion of the charge which relates to the provision of credit and the pursuit of the claim[12] will not be recoverable. Such matters are additional benefits, over and above the actual loss of use of the car, for which the claimant is not entitled to claim as against the defendant to road traffic accident proceedings. Put simply, the claimant would be put in a better position than if he had not been involved in the accident. Accordingly, most district judges can be expected to accept the rate from an equivalent (non-credit) hire firm in the same area as the claimant where credit is not provided as being the appropriate rate. Given that insurance companies cannot sensibly defend claims for the ordinary rate of hire it is likely that many claims of this kind will now settle.

There are three fundamental issues which arise in relation to credit hire agreements. Is the agreement regulated? If so, does it comply with the technicalities of the 1974 Act? If not, can it be enforced anyway?

---

10. Report of the Committee on Consumer Credit, Cmnd 4596 (London: HMSO), 1971, para. 6.6.26 *et seq.*
11. See *Chitty on Contracts* (London: Sweet & Maxwell), 38–264, n. 85.
12. So too any Collision Damage Waiver (CDW).

7.6.1 Regulated credit hire agreements

A credit hire agreement may become a 'regulated agreement' within the meaning of the 1974 Act if it is either a consumer credit agreement within the meaning of s. 8 or a consumer hire agreement within the meaning of s. 15. It is to be noted that the agreement may be regulated under either s. 8 or s. 15, the two regimes being independent. There is no need for credit to be provided in relation to regulation under s. 15. The circumstances when an agreement will be regulated under s. 15 will be considered before turning to s. 8.

7.6.1.1 Section 15 — consumer hire agreements Section 15 of the 1974 Act provides as follows:

> (1) A consumer hire agreement is an agreement made by a person with an individual (the 'hirer') for the bailment ... of goods to the hirer, being an agreement which—
> (a) is not a hire purchase agreement, and
> (b) is capable of subsisting for more than three months, and
> (c) does not require the hirer to make payments exceeding £25,000.

There is little doubt that a credit hire agreement is capable of coming within this definition. The key, however, is to show that the agreement is capable of subsisting for a period exceeding three months. To prevent agreements falling within this definition it is common practice to insert a clause in the agreement stating that the period of hire shall not exceed three months.

If the contract is silent on this point then it is arguable that the agreement is capable of subsisting for a period exceeding three months. It is not necessary to show that the agreement actually has, or is likely, to exceed three months, simply that it is capable of doing so (*Golding* v *Mason* [1999] 12 CL 254). It is usual in credit hire cases that, at the start of the hire, the length of the hire is unknown as it is dependent upon the length of time it will take to carry out the repairs to the hirer's vehicle. Accordingly, it is wise to adduce evidence to this effect from the claimant (if challenging the agreement). Given that the period of hire is then considered indeterminate, it can be said, notwithstanding the fact that it is unlikely to exceed three months, that it is quite capable of doing so.

Furthermore, there is some support for the view that a clause limiting the period of hire will not have the desired effect where the period of hire has actually exceeded the stated maximum period. In *Hoyle* v *Nutt*, 27 May 1999, unreported, the agreement contained such a clause but the period of hire actually continued for over three months. The hire company did not have any credible system in place for recalling the car after three months. It was held that, notwithstanding such a clause, the agreement was capable of subsisting for over three months and was unenforceable.

A further argument which can be made in relation to credit hire cases is that since the agreement provides credit for (say) 11 months, the fact that the period of hire may be restricted to (say) two months means that the *agreement* is capable of subsisting for a period exceeding three months. The only reported case where this seems to have been argued is *Bhoyrub* v *Cadzow* 1999 SCLR 539 but the report does not state whether the argument was accepted. Support for the argument can also be found in Lord Hoffman's speech in the House of Lords in *Dimond* v *Lovell* [2000] 2 WLR 1121 where he rejected any suggestion that a credit hire agreement was one of multiple obligations which were in any way severable — the agreement was one and was to be considered as such. However, it remains to be seen whether this argument will be accepted by the courts.

Assuming the agreement is regulated by s. 15, the 1974 Act imposes certain requirements upon it. It is important to note that these are not the same technical requirements imposed upon consumer credit agreements which are regulated by s. 8. However, the agreement must be signed by both creditor and owner under s. 61 and the owner is required to hold a licence to carry on consumer hire business under s. 21. If these requirements are not satisfied then the agreement is unenforceable and the claimant cannot claim in respect of the hire.

7.6.1.2 Section 8 — consumer credit agreements Section 8 of the 1974 Act defines a regulated consumer credit agreement as follows. It is a 'personal credit agreement' if credit is extended to an individual. Credit is the *contractual* deferral of payment for a service earlier rendered. A consumer credit agreement is a personal credit agreement where the sums involved are less than £25,000. The agreement becomes a 'regulated' agreement where it is not an 'exempt agreement'.

The first point to note from this is that the agreement must provide *contractually* for the deferral of payment. There are many situations where credit hire companies do not actually provide in the agreement for the deferral of payment, but simply do not enforce the agreement against the hirer. Where this is the case then prima facie credit is not being provided: the creditor is merely indulging the debtor. This makes little sense as credit would be being provided every time someone did not instantaneously sue for a debt (*Pearce* v *Duff* [1999] 8 CL 322; *Watson* v *James Robinson Fibres Ltd* [1999] 12 CL 263).

However, credit hire companies can be trusted to tell their clients that they will not have to pay until the claim is settled with the opponent insurance company. In line with *Oscar Chess Ltd* v *Williams* [1957] 1 WLR 370 this will amount to an express term of the contract if a reasonable person would have taken the parties to have meant as such. In a consumer field this will invariably be the case: one must consider the enforceability of the credit agreement as if it were the hire company suing the hirer. It is submitted that no court would uphold a claim where the hirer was told that he would not have to pay until his claim was settled but was subsequently sued. A court would undoubtedly find that this was a term of the agreement. It can then be said that credit is being *contractually* provided. However, this argument depends upon the claimant saying in evidence that he was told that he would not have to pay.

Most importantly, the agreement must not be an 'exempt agreement'. An exemption is provided by the Consumer Credit (Exempt Agreements) Order 1989 (r. 3) where the credit is to be repaid within one year and is to be made in less than four instalments. The relevant parts of the 1989 Order provide as follows:

> (1) The Act shall not regulate a consumer credit agreement which is an agreement of one of the following descriptions, that is to say—
>
> (a) a debtor-creditor-supplier agreement being either—

(i) an agreement for fixed-sum credit under which the total number of payments to be made by the debtor does not exceed four, and those payments are to be made within a period not exceeding 12 months beginning with the date of the agreement; . . .

Given this exemption, many credit hire companies insert a clause stating that in any event the credit period will expire within one year. There are many cases where such clauses will have the desired effect, for example, see *Feary* v *Buckingham* [1999] 7 CL 208; *Martin* v *Streamline Holdings Ltd* [1999] 12 CL 265; *Stratton* v *Browett* [1999] 12 CL 266; *Watson* v *James Robinson Fibres Ltd* [1999] 12 CL 263.

However, there are cases which look at these clauses and give them a restrictive construction. Indeed the points raised in this paragraph do not appear to have been argued in the cases in the previous paragraph where such clauses have been upheld. For example, in *Zoan* v *Rouamba*, *The Times*, 7 March 2000 (CA) it was said that a clause which required payment 'within 12 months' of the date of the agreement would come within this time period, whereas if payment was required 12 months 'after' or 'from' the date of the agreement this would not. Similarly, there are cases which say that a mere provision that the credit period will come to an end is not equivalent to a clause actually requiring payment and that this is what is required (*Cooper* v *Scammell* [1998] 10 CL 199; *Norman* v *Selvey* [1999] 7 CL 207). Again, the requirement to make payment in four instalments or less is something which must be spelled out. It will not be implied (*Radosavljevic* v *Rufus* [1999] 11 CL 276; *Majeed* v *Incentive Group* [1999] 8 CL 321; *Benson* v *Cummings* [1999] 12 CL 253). Accordingly, there are arguments which suggest that a clause attempting to bring the agreement outside the provisions of the 1974 Act must be tightly worded if it is to be operative.

Assuming the agreement is a regulated one, there are a variety of technical requirements imposed upon the agreement by the 1974 Act. For example, the agreement must be signed by both parties, notice of cancellation rights must be included and importantly a figure for the total amount of credit must be inserted.[13] Since at the time the agreement is made the period of hire is unknown and the amount of money being lent is similarly unknown, the requirement to include the total amount of credit cannot be complied with. It is sometimes argued that it is acceptable to include an estimate in respect of this and still comply with the Consumer Credit (Agreements) Regulations 1983, SI 1983/1553. However, this is not the case and decisions to this effect are incorrectly decided. It is only possible to include an estimate in respect of the total charge for credit, not the total amount of credit (*Constantinou* v *Ozcan* [1999] 12 CL 256).

Even if the agreement is regulated and complies with all the technicalities of the 1974 Act then it may still be unenforceable. For example, it is possible that the hire firm will enter the agreement initially for a week, with a fixed figure for the weekly rental,[14] all the other requirements of the Act being complied with. Any

13. It is rare to find an agreement which even attempts to comply with the 1974 Act given the technical stipulations laid down: e.g., under ss. 20 and 60 of the Act and the Consumer Credit (Agreements) Regulations 1983, SI 1983/1553, as amended by SI 1984/1600, SI 1985/666 and SI 1988/2047, the agreement is required to be in a particular form and contain certain information as to the amount of credit being advanced; under s. 21 of the Act the creditor and/or hirer is obliged to hold a licence to carry on consumer credit or consumer hire business.

14. And hence the total amount of credit being included.

further periods of rental are the subject of further contracts. However, where the driver was introduced to the credit hire firm by an unlicensed credit-broker then the agreement will still be unenforceable. Section 146(5) defines credit brokerage as the effecting of introductions of persons desiring to obtain credit or goods on hire to persons carrying out regulated consumer credit or consumer hire business. Often, the driver will be introduced to the hire company by another person, perhaps the garage repairing his car or his insurance broker who is assisting him with his insurance claim. If this person makes the introduction, he will be engaging in the ancillary credit business of credit-broking. Where this person does not hold a licence to do so, the agreement is unenforceable by s. 149.

Finally, in the ordinary course of events, a person entering into a credit hire agreement will often have been told that he will never have to pay for the car and accordingly the agreement can be struck out as a sham, resisted on the basis of an estoppel based upon this representation. Alternatively, it may be argued that there was no agreement in the first place on the basis of mistake as to terms of the contract (*Rahman* v *Brassil* [1998] 8 CL 219; *Rendle* v *Hicks* [1998] 2 CL 126; *Re Dixon Vincent* [1997] 11 CL 114; *Madhavji* v *Consort* [1999] 12 CL 145). This is something of a 'last ditch' attempt to resist the claim for hire charges and much depends upon what was actually said to the claimant.

In summary, the key issue in most credit hire cases is whether the clause in question brings the agreement within the 1989 Order. If it does the hire charges will generally be recoverable; if it does not then the hire charges will generally not be.

7.6.2 Recoverable notwithstanding non-compliance with the 1974 Act

There are two bases upon which a credit hire agreement may be recoverable notwithstanding that it is a regulated agreement and has not complied with the 1974 Act. First, an order may be made by the court under s. 127 that it may be enforced notwithstanding that it is improperly executed; secondly, it may be argued that as the hirer has brought proceedings for the recovery of the hire charges he has consented to the breaches. (The House of Lords in *Dimond* v *Lovell* [2000] 2 WLR 1121 has laid to rest any suggestion that the charges may be recoverable by way of implied trust or under the doctrine of *res inter alios acta*.)

As regards the first of these arguments it was said in *Smerdon* v *Ellis* [1997] 1 CLY 963[15] that no court would ever grant an order against the hirer where the hire company had represented to the hirer that he would not become liable for the cost of the hire but that it would be recovered from the other party's insurer. As this is frequently the case it is unlikely that there will be many credit hire cases where the court would find the case an appropriate one for the making of an enforcement order.

As regards the second argument, it is sometimes said in the context of credit hire agreements that the consent was given by the debtor under s. 173 on the basis that he instituted proceedings for recovery of the charges, thereby claiming liability. However, this argument was rejected in *Gibbons* v *Gibbons* [1998]

15. See also *Re Dixon Vincent* [1997] 11 CL 114; *Rendle* v *Hicks* [1998] 2 CL 126; *Wotton* v *Flagg* [1997] CLY 959; *Rahman* v *Brassil* [1998] 8 CL 219; *Petrou* v *Kuti* [1997] CLY 1803; *Hunt* v *Severs* [1994] 2 AC 350; and *Pedelty* v *Jarvis* [1999] 6 CL 287, all of which appear to support this proposition.

CLY 2500 as consent had to be given at the time of enforcement (see section 7.3). Furthermore, it was said in *Kemp* v *Ling* [1998] CLY 2502 that s. 173(3) did not make enforceable that which was not otherwise enforceable (see section 7.3).

Another argument would be that the claimant has failed to mitigate his loss reasonably by allowing the charges to be enforced against him. When could it ever be said to be reasonable to pay a bill for which there was no liability to pay and then claim it from the other side?

8 *Exclusion clauses and unfair contract terms*

8.1 INTRODUCTION

Clauses are frequently inserted in a contract which either limit or exclude altogether a party's liability in the event of breach by one or other of the parties. These clauses are usually found in standard form contracts used by one of the parties. Usually the clause will be in the seller or supplier's contract, but where the buyer uses purchase orders which contain his standard terms such clauses may be found in favour of the buyer.

In general there are two circumstances where such a clause will become incorporated into the contract: in a commercial contract following a 'battle of forms', or in a consumer or small business contract where the seller will usually have standard terms and conditions on its sales form. Where the latter is the case it is worth examining the time that the contract was concluded. In practice, many sellers simply take a phone order and dispatch the goods with an invoice which contains the exclusion clause. If this was the first time the parties did business it is highly unlikely that the clause became a term of the contract as it was not even mentioned before the conclusion of the contract. If the parties have previously done business then it may well have become incorporated through a course of dealing.

The common law deals with exclusion clauses in a threefold manner. First, it sets up barriers against the clauses becoming incorporated in the contract in the first place, secondly it gives a construction to the clause which operates against the party in whose favour the clause was drafted and finally, if the first two hurdles are overcome, it restricts the operation of the clause in certain circumstances (e.g., fraud). It is important to note that the first two hurdles stand in the path of a clause which is governed by the statutory controls as well as judicial ones. Put simply, the mere fact that a party's main argument is that the clause is unfair under the Unfair Contract Terms Act 1977 ('UCTA') does not prevent them from arguing that the clause never became part of the contract in the first place. Accordingly, the practitioner is well advised to consider this line of defence (or attack) before turning straight to the Unfair Contract Terms Act 1977 or the Unfair Terms in

Consumer Contracts Regulations 1999, SI 1999/2083. These aspects are however dealt with in the third section of this chapter — judicial control of exclusion clauses (see section 8.4). UCTA will be examined first.

For the most part the law sets its face against exclusion or limitation clauses — why should a party be permitted to exclude liability for his own non-performance? After all the whole point of a contract is to hold that party to account for his performance. However, in many contracts the exclusion or limitation of liability is simply an aspect of risk. The parties may know full well that performance is not going to be an easy task so accepting an element of risk of non-performance is a factor to be taken into account when negotiating the price. Looked at from this perspective the contract is really one for the seller or serviceman's best efforts, to a specified minimum standard.

In practice, in sale of goods cases the contract will tend to be 'all or nothing'; the parties anticipate and expect a good which conforms to certain standards. Furthermore, it will be rare that parties have genuinely negotiated the incorporation of an exclusion or limitation clause. It is much more likely that it will have become incorporated without the aggrieved party ever having read the contract terms, or where he mistakenly thinks that he won the 'battle of the forms'.

The law here applies equally to third persons relying on the benefit of an exclusion or limitation clause by virtue of the Contracts (Rights of Third Parties) Act 1999, as to which see section 3.4.

The law regulates exclusion clauses by four principal mechanisms: UCTA, the Misrepresentation Act 1967, the Unfair Terms in Consumer Contracts Regulations 1999[1] and finally the common law. Whilst similar sounding and certainly overlapping, UCTA and the Regulations provide two separate regimes and need to be examined separately; they are not in any way amalgamated. These will be examined first before considering the common law. The Misrepresentation Act 1967 contains provision against excluding liability for misrepresentations by a clause in the contract. However, it is subject to the overriding requirement of reasonableness as defined in the UCTA and will therefore be considered alongside that Act.

8.2 THE UNFAIR CONTRACT TERMS ACT 1977

The main provisions of UCTA which are of concern in relation to contracts for the sale or supply of goods and services are ss. 3, 6, 7, 11, 12 and 13. The general effect of these provisions is as follows. Section 3 provides the general rule that an exemption clause contained in a party's favour can only be relied upon by that party in so far as it is reasonable in the case of contracts concluded on that party's standard terms and conditions or where the other party deals as a consumer. Sections 6 and 7 cover between them almost all contracts whereby goods are supplied and provide that the appropriate implied term as to title (e.g., s. 12 of the Sale of Goods Act 1979) cannot be excluded at all. In respect of the implied terms as to quality, fitness and description these cannot be excluded against someone who deals as a consumer, but may be excluded against someone in other situations so long as the exclusion clause is reasonable. Section 12 defines when someone deals

1. Replacing the 1994 Regulations, SI 1994/3159.

as a consumer and s. 11, together with sch. 2 to the Act, defines the criteria to be used in deciding the reasonableness of the exclusion clause. Section 13 effectively extends the meaning of exclusion clause to terms which have the same effect but may not, technically, be exclusion clauses.

The clauses which UCTA regulates will be examined first, then the circumstances where one party 'deals as a consumer'. The overriding requirement of reasonableness will then be considered before turning to the limited circumstances where a party may still be able to evade the Act.

8.2.1 Clauses to which the Unfair Contract Terms Act 1977 or the Misrepresentation Act 1967 apply

Sections 3, 6 and 7 of UCTA provide as follows:

3.—(1) This section applies as between contracting parties where one of them deals as consumer or on the other's written standard terms of business.

(2) As against that party, the other cannot by reference to any contract term—

(a) when himself in breach of contract, exclude or restrict any liability of his in respect of the breach; or

(b) claim to be entitled—

(i) to render a contractual performance substantially different from that which was reasonably expected of him, or

(ii) in respect of the whole of any part of his contractual obligation, to render no performance at all,

except in so far as (in any of the cases mentioned above in this subsection) the contract term satisfies the requirement of reasonableness.

6.—(1) Liability for breach of the obligations arising from—

(a) [section 12 of the Sale of Goods Act 1979] (seller's implied undertakings as to title, etc.);

(b) section 8 of the Supply of Goods (Implied Terms) Act 1973 (the corresponding thing in relation to hire purchase),

cannot be excluded or restricted by reference to any contract term.

(2) As against a person dealing as consumer, liability for breach of the obligations arising from—

(a) [section 13, 14 or 15 of the 1979 Act] (seller's implied undertakings as to conformity of goods with description or sample, or as to their quality of fitness for a particular purpose);

(b) section 9, 10 or 11 of the 1973 Act (the corresponding things in relation to hire purchase),

cannot be excluded or restricted by reference to any contract term.

(3) As against a person dealing otherwise than as consumer, the liability specified in subsection (2) above can be excluded or restricted by reference to a contract term, but only in so far as the term satisfies the requirement of reasonableness.

(4) The liabilities referred to in this section are not only the business liabilities defined by section 1(3), but include those arising under any contract of sale of goods or hire purchase agreement.

7.—(1) Where the possession or ownership of goods passes under or in pursuance of a contract not governed by the law of sale of goods or hire purchase, subsections (2) to (4) below apply as regards the effect (if any) to be given to contract terms excluding or restricting liability for breach of obligation arising by implication of law from the nature of the contract.

(2) As against a person dealing as consumer, liability in respect of the goods' correspondence with description or sample, or their quality or fitness for any particular purpose, cannot be excluded or restricted by reference to any such term.

(3) As against a person dealing otherwise than as consumer, that liability can be excluded or restricted by reference to such a term, but only in so far as the term satisfies the requirement of reasonableness.

(3A) Liability for breach of the obligations arising under section 2 of the Supply of Goods and Services Act 1982 (implied terms about title etc. in certain contracts for the transfer of the property in goods) cannot be excluded or restricted by reference to any such term.

(4) Liability in respect of—

(a) the right to transfer ownership of the goods, or give possession; or

(b) the assurance of quiet possession to a person taking goods in pursuance of the contract,

cannot (in a case to which subsection (3A) above does not apply) be excluded or restricted by reference to any such term except in so far as the term satisfies the requirement of reasonableness.

(c) ...

Section 3 of the Misrepresentation Act 1967 provides as follows:

3. If a contract contains a term which would exclude or restrict—

(a) any liability to which a party to a contract may be subject by reason of any misrepresentation made by him before the contract was made; or

(b) any remedy available to another party to the contract by reason of such a misrepresentation,

that term shall be of no effect except in so far as it satisfies the requirement of reasonableness as stated in section 11(1) of the Unfair Contract Terms Act 1977; and it is for those claiming that the term satisfies that requirement to show that it does.

Section 3 of UCTA therefore creates a rule of general application to all contracts where one party 'deals as a consumer' or where he deals on the other's standard terms. 'Dealing as a consumer' is dealt with in the next section. It is important to note that s. 3 does not simply apply where a buyer deals on the seller's standard terms, but also where the seller deals on the buyer's. Accordingly, if it is the buyer who 'won' a 'battle of the forms' situation then a clause purporting to exclude or restrict liability on the part of the buyer would similarly be subject to s. 3. However, in contracts for the sale or supply of goods the buyer's duty is generally to pay only for the goods and to take delivery of them. Accordingly, it is unlikely that the buyer would seriously insert a clause exempting him from liability to pay. However, the buyer may insert a clause giving him an unreasonable time to pay and this may be subject to the Act.

A contract may be made on 'standard terms' even though some negotiation has taken place as to the exact terms. Indeed to insist upon one party entering *every* contract on precisely the same terms in order to come within UCTA would be placing an impossible construction on the Act as vital matters must invariably be left to negotiation in individual cases, for example the price and the goods to be sold (*St. Albans City and District Council* v *International Computers Ltd* [1996] 4 All ER 481). In *McCrone* v *Boots Farm Sales* [1981] CLY 2409 Lord Dunpark said of 'standard forms' that all that was required was that the contract contained 'a set of fixed terms which the [party] applies, without material variation, to contracts of the kind in question'. Furthermore, in *The Salvage Association* v *CAP Financial Services Ltd* [1995] FSR 654 guidelines were laid down for determining when the terms would be standard ones:

(a) the degree to which the standard terms were imposed upon the other party,
(b) the relative bargaining power of each party,
(c) the degree to which the party putting the terms forward is prepared to negotiate over them,
(d) the extent and nature of any alterations to the terms, and
(e) the length of the negotiations over the terms.

The list is not exhaustive. It is submitted that of these considerations (d) must carry the most weight as if the parties have actually substantially changed the terms they must be taken to no longer be 'standard' terms. By contrast, where one party has more or less refused to entertain negotiations over the terms and they are simply offered on a 'take it or leave it' basis then factors (b) and (c) apply and it is likely that the terms will be found to be standard (*Fillite (Runcorn) Ltd* v *APV Pasilac Ltd*, *The Buyer*, July 1995). Certainly where one party has had specific forms printed upon which he only enters contracts and there is no mechanism in place for amending the terms it is inevitable that they will held to be standard terms (*Oval Ltd* v *Aegon Insurance Co. (UK) Ltd*, *The Buyer*, August 1997).

Once one of the requirements of s. 3(1) has been met, s. 3(2)(a) then renders inoperative any clause which purports to exclude or restrict liability for any breach of contract by that person. Such clauses are relatively easy to identify since, by their very nature, they need to spell out that they are exclusion or limitation clauses. More problematical are clauses falling within s. 3(2)(b) which permit a party to render a performance which is 'substantially different than that which was reasonably expected of him'.

Whilst UCTA is a little ambiguous by bringing in the concept of reasonableness it is difficult to see what else could have been provided by the draftsman. In order to determine whether a clause permits a party to render performance substantially different from that which was reasonably expected it is necessary to examine the degree of non-performance against the whole contract. In *Zockoll Group Ltd* v *Mercury Communications*, 19 December 1997, unreported[2] (abridging the facts slightly for exposition) the defendant had provided 51 telephone numbers to the plaintiff, one of which was termed a 'golden number' because when dialled on an alpha-numeric keypad it spelled out the word 'Flights' (0500 354448), which was

2. See Lawson, R., *Exclusion Clauses and Unfair Contract Terms* 5th ed. (London: Sweet & Maxwell, 1995), p. 132.

of assistance to the plaintiff's business. The remaining 50 numbers were selected randomly. The contract contained a clause which permitted the defendant to change the numbers at any time in its sole discretion. When in due course the defendant allocated the number to a different client the plaintiff sued. It was found that the defendant had not rendered a performance substantially different from that reasonably expected, seemingly because the plaintiff had never informed the defendant of the reason they wanted the number 354448 and it appeared little more to the defendant than the other 50 random numbers (see also *Timeload Ltd* v *British Telecommunication plc*, *The Buyer*, September 1996).

Section 3 of the Misrepresentation Act 1967 is relatively straightforward. Since a representation is different in nature from a contract term, liability can only be excluded for its falsity by a direct term in the contract which expressly excludes or restricts liability for it. As with exemption clauses or limitation clauses, the clause will be readily identifiable as such. Unlike the corresponding provisions in UCTA, the Misrepresentation Act 1967 does not discriminate between people who deal as consumers or those who deal on standard terms. The provisions relate to all contracts.

Section 6 of UCTA needs only limited explanation as it is clear itself in its terms. It provides that as against any person liability cannot be restricted in respect of breach of the implied terms as to title in contracts for the sale of goods or hire purchase contracts. In respect of the conditions implied by ss. 13, 14 and 15 of the Sale of Goods Act 1979 and the corresponding provisions in relation to hire purchase under the Supply of Goods (Implied Terms) Act 1973 these may not be excluded in a case where the buyer or hirer deals as a consumer. However, where the buyer or hirer does not deal as a consumer the implied terms may be excluded so long as it is reasonable.

Section 7 of UCTA is something of a catch-all provision for all other cases where the property or possession of goods is transferred. Principally this relates to contracts for the transfer of goods under the Supply of Goods and Services Act 1982. However, s. 7 is wider than this and it captures all contracts where goods are supplied, although it is difficult to envisage circumstances where this will be so and none of the 1973, 1979 or 1982 Acts apply. As with s. 6, s. 7 prevents the exclusion or limitation of liability in respect of the breach of the implied terms as to quality (etc.) where the buyer deals as a consumer, but subjects it to the requirement of reasonableness where he does not.

Section 3 of UCTA deals with the more obvious cases where the seller attempts to exclude or restrict liability, not by directly accepting that a breach has occurred and excluding liability in respect of it, but by the use of small print which allows non-performance in the first place. Section 13 of the Act takes this further by preventing the seller using onerous terms to prevent the injured party from relying on his rights, it provides as follows:

> 13.—(1) To the extent that this Part of this Act prevents the exclusion or restriction of any liability it also prevents—
>
> (a) making the liability or its enforcement subject to restrictive or onerous conditions;
>
> (b) excluding or restricting any right or remedy in respect of the liability, or subjecting a person to any prejudice in consequence of his pursuing any such right or remedy;

(c) excluding or restricting rules of evidence or procedure;

and (to that extent) ss. 2 and 5 to 7 also prevent excluding or restricting liability by reference to terms and notices which exclude or restrict the relevant obligation or duty.

(2) But an agreement in writing to submit present or future differences to arbitration is not to be treated under this Part of this Act as excluding or restricting any liability.

Section 13 is very broad, s. 13(1)(b) in particular. A typical example of a clause attempting to circumvent the Act would be one which provided that in the event that the buyer wishes to reject the goods he must make a payment of 95 per cent of the contract price. This has exactly the same effect as an exclusion clause as for all practical purposes the buyer is prevented from asserting his rights. The clause would not be caught by the precise wording of s. 3, 6 or 7, but falls within the ambit of s. 13. That the section is very wide is shown by the bar against any terms which subject the injured party to 'any prejudice': s. 13(1)(b). A similar provision is contained in s. 10 which prevents the use of a second, tandem, contract which restricts or excludes liability.

Section 13 does not apply to clauses attempting to evade liability for misrepresentation, although no doubt the courts would rigorously apply the common law rules against such terms (*Cremdean Properties* v *Nash* (1977) 244 EG 547).

8.2.2 'Deals as a consumer'

Section 12 of UCTA provides as follows:

12.—(1) A party to contract 'deals as consumer' in relation to another party if—

(a) he neither makes the contract in the course of a business nor holds himself out as doing so; and

(b) the other party does make the contract in the course of a business; and

(c) in the case of a contract governed by the law of sale of goods or hire purchase, or by section 7 of this Act, the goods passing under or in pursuance of the contract are of a type ordinarily supplied for private use or consumption.

(2) But on a sale by auction or by competitive tender the buyer is not in any circumstances to be regarded as dealing as consumer.

(3) Subject to this, it is for those claiming that a party does not deal as consumer to show that he does not.

The definition uses the phrase 'makes the contract in the course of a business' which is used in the Sale of Goods Act 1979 in relation to s. 14 and is discussed in section 16.2. The same considerations apply here in relation to determining whether the seller or supplier was acting in the course of a business. Indeed, since *Stevenson* v *Rogers* [1999] QB 1028 those circumstances will be much wider than was previously supposed. Reference should be made to section 16.2 on this point.

As to the circumstances where the buyer will be acting in the course of a business, these too are wider than simply determining whether the buyer is running a business. Following the case of *R & B Customs Brokers Co. Ltd* v *United*

Dominions Trust Ltd [1988] 1 WLR 321 this is certainly not the only consideration. In that case the plaintiff bought a Range Rover vehicle on finance from the defendant, which it transpired was not of satisfactory quality. The contract contained a clause which excluded the implied terms as to quality in relation to business contracts. The car however was not bought for resale but for use as an ancillary part of the plaintiff's business, i.e., as a 'company car'. It was held that the plaintiff had not bought the car as an integral part of the business and that a degree of regularity would be required in order to show that he did. Clearly, had the car formed part of the plaintiff's 'stock in trade' the decision would have been different.

It is submitted that the decision in *R & B Customs Brokers Co. Ltd* v *United Dominions Trust Ltd* is unaffected by the decision in *Stevenson* v *Rogers*. In that case Potter LJ made the following observation about *R & B Customs Brokers*:

> Section 14(2) as amended by the Act of 1973 was itself a piece of consumer protection intended to afford wider protection to a buyer than that provided in the Act of 1893. Indeed, there is a sense in which the decision in the *R & B Customs* case can be said to be in harmony with that intention. It dealt with the position of consumer buyers and the effect of adopting the construction propounded in *Davies* v *Sumner* [1984] 1 WLR 1301 in relation to s. 12(1)(a) of the Act of 1977 was to further such buyers' protection. In the context of its statutory history, s. 14(2), as amended by the Act of 1973 and re-enacted in the Act of 1979, is the primary provision in the overall scheme of increased protection for buyers which the Act of 1973 initiated. To apply the reasoning in the *R & B Customs* case in the interests only of consistency, thereby undermining the wide protection for buyers which s. 14(2) was intended to introduce, would in my view be an unacceptable example of the tail wagging the dog.

It seems therefore that a wide interpretation should be given to the requirement that the seller deals in the course of a business, but a narrow construction to the requirement that the buyer does so. The effect of this is to widen the field of consumer protection to cover both consumers and small businesses. It is likely that the element of frequency of purchases of items ancillary to the business would render them to be purchases in the course of a business, and not merely incidental to it. Certainly it would be difficult to suppose that a large multinational company which purchased a fleet of cars on a specially negotiated contract could be said to be 'dealing as a consumer'.

The third requirement of 'dealing as a consumer' contained in s. 12(1)(c) is that the goods are of a type ordinarily supplied for private use or consumption. This phrase causes some difficulty as there are many goods which are usually supplied to businesses, but which a proportion are supplied to private individuals. The growth in home sales of computers has probably brought them into the field of a good ordinarily supplied for private use, despite the fact that they are more commonly supplied to businesses. However, transit vans and specialist tools are more frequently supplied to businesses, but are openly sold to the general public in lesser numbers. These appear to be outside the scope of s. 12(1)(c). It is difficult to see whether s. 12(1)(c) serves any useful purpose, and certainly seems contrary to the policy outlined in *Stevenson* v *Rogers*.

8.2.3 'Reasonableness'

Section 11 of UCTA provides as follows:

> 11.—(1) In relation to a contract term, the requirement of reasonableness for the purposes of this Part of this Act, section 3 of the Misrepresentation Act 1967 and section 3 of the Misrepresentation Act (Northern Ireland) 1967 is that the term shall have been a fair and reasonable one to be included having regard to the circumstances which were, or ought reasonably to have been, known to or in the contemplation of the parties when the contract was made.
>
> (2) In determining for the purposes of section 6 or 7 above whether a contract term satisfies the requirement of reasonableness, regard shall be had in particular to the matters specified in Schedule 2 to this Act; but this subsection does not prevent the court or arbitrator from holding, in accordance with any rule of law, that a term which purports to exclude or restrict any relevant liability is not a term of the contract.
>
> (3) . . .
>
> (4) Where by reference to a contract term or notice a person seeks to restrict liability to a specified sum of money, and the question arises (under this or any other Act) whether the term or notice satisfies the requirement of reasonableness, regard shall be had in particular (but without prejudice to subsection (2) above in the case of contract terms) to—
>
> (a) the resources which he could expect to be available to him for the purpose of meeting the liability should it arise; and
>
> (b) how far it was open to him to cover himself by insurance.
>
> (5) It is for those claiming that a contract term or notice satisfies the requirement of reasonableness to show that it does.

The criteria to be applied under s. 11(2) in relation to determining the question of reasonableness are set out below. It is odd that they are not deemed under the Act to be relevant in determining reasonableness under s. 11(1) in relation to cases under s. 3 of the 1967 Act. In any event the courts have held that they are factors which any court would take into account when considering reasonableness under s. 11(1) and may be applied there (*St. Albans City and District Council* v *International Computers Ltd* [1995] FSR 686; *Flamar Interocean Ltd* v *Denmac Ltd* [1990] 1 Lloyd's Rep 434; *The Salvage Association* v *CAP Financial Services Ltd* [1995] FSR 654). The list is not exhaustive. Schedule 2 lists the criteria as follows:

> (a) the strength of the bargaining position of the parties relative to each other, taking into account (among other things) alternative means by which the customer's requirements could have been met;
>
> (b) whether the customer received an inducement to agree to the term, or in accepting it had an opportunity of entering into a similar contract with other persons, but without having to accept a similar term;
>
> (c) whether the customer knew or ought reasonably to have known of the existence and extent of the term (having regard, among other things, to any custom of the trade and any previous course of dealing between the parties);

(d) where the term excludes or restricts any relevant liability if some condition is not complied with, whether it was reasonable at the time of the contract to expect that compliance with the condition would be practicable;

(e) whether the goods were manufactured, processed or adapted to the special order of the customer.

The test of reasonableness is therefore very broad, the general test set down in s. 11(1) is that the term be a 'fair and reasonable' one. It is important to note that the time to judge the parties is the time that the contract is made. This appears from the later words of s. 11(1), but it is no doubt a consideration in relation to cases where the implied terms are being excluded.

The first case to come before an appellate court on these provisions was *George Mitchell (Chesterhall) Ltd* v *Finney Lock Seeds Ltd* [1983] 2 AC 803.[3] In that case the buyers had agreed to buy 'late' cabbage seed but were supplied with a different seed. The contract included a clause restricting liability to the cost of the seed supplied. The buyers however had suffered something in the order of £60,000 losses. The House of Lords held the clause to be void. Of particular concern was the fact that settlements were often reached where such an error occurred. Given that all seed merchants conducted business on these terms this meant that not only did seed merchants recognise that this was bad practice, but the industry effectively ousted the courts and determined for themselves which claims would be paid. Furthermore, they could easily have obtained insurance against such matters, without significantly increasing their costs.

A similar case to *George Mitchell* is *R. W. Green Ltd* v *Cade Brothers Farm* [1978] 1 Lloyd's Rep 602. In that case it was seed potatoes which were sold and proved to be infected. The only difference between this case and *George Mitchell* is that in this case the potatoes were uncertified, but had certified potatoes been purchased they would have been checked and warranted as being of a certain standard. Naturally, uncertified potatoes were sold at a lower price. The contract, as with *George Mitchell*, limited liability in respect of consequential loss. This case was distinguished in the Court of Appeal in *George Mitchell*, but not dealt with by their Lordships in the House of Lords. Accordingly, its exact status remains in question. However, on its facts it certainly appears distinguishable from *George Mitchell* as the buyer is effectively being given an inducement to accept the clause. Likewise the buyer could have obtained goods from a different source and was not forced to take the particular batch he did.

A case perhaps at the limit of the provisions, or perhaps reflecting modern judicial interventionism, is that of *St. Albans City and District Council* v *International Computers Ltd* [1995] FSR 686. In that case the defendants had supplied a computer system to the plaintiffs which would be used in calculating the community charge. It got the calculation wrong, overestimating the area's population and hence reducing the amount needed to be charged by the council. The contract contained a clause (which was common in the industry) limiting liability to £100,000. This was held to be unreasonable, a significant factor being

3. This case was actually decided under the Sale of Goods Act 1979, but would now be governed by UCTA. The wording of the relevant sections is almost identical, the only difference being that the term is no longer void 'in so far as' it restricts liability, but void altogether (*Stewart Gill Ltd* v *Horatio Myer & Co. Ltd* [1992] 2 All ER 257).

that the loss would be borne by the residents of the district as opposed to an insurance company with whom the defendant had a policy.

The final point to be made was brought out by *Howard Marine & Dredging Co. Ltd* v *Ogden & Sons (Excavations) Ltd* [1978] QB 574. It was pointed out in that case by the majority of the court that the question of reasonableness was a question for the court of first instance. It is unlikely that an appeal would be successful on the point unless the judge had erred in principle, and given that the issue is so wide this would actually be an achievement on the part of the court.

8.3 THE UNFAIR TERMS IN CONSUMER CONTRACTS REGULATIONS 1999

As was noted above the Unfair Terms in Consumer Contracts Regulations 1999, SI 1999/2083[4] ('the 1999 Regulations') provide a separate, but parallel, regime to UCTA. This means that UCTA may apply and not the Regulations, or vice versa. Equally, both may apply to a given case.

The 1999 Regulations came into force on 1 October 1999. Contracts entered into before this date will be governed by the 1994 Regulations. There is no real change in substance in the 1999 Regulations and they were simply amended to bring them more into line with the requirements of the EC Directive which proposed them. Indeed, the only change is to remove any definition of 'requirement of good faith' and to marginally alter the manner in which the test is to be applied. Consequently, the only real change is to make the 1999 Regulations slightly more confusing, but this is probably what is meant by bringing the Regulations more into line with European law!

The most important provision of the 1999 Regulations is to render an unfair term unenforceable against a consumer. This is the primary concern in this text. Given that in many consumer situations the consumer is not in a position to litigate or properly know of his rights, the Regulations make provision for action to be taken by other bodies concerned with the regulation of consumer contracts. Most notably, the Consumers' Association is empowered to apply for an injunction preventing the continued use of an unfair term (regs 11, 12 and 13). Detailed analysis of such provisions is, however, beyond the scope of this text.

The 1999 Regulations are much broader than UCTA in that they apply to all terms; not simply those which seek to exclude or limit a party's liability. Six matters fall to be discussed in relation to the 1999 Regulations: terms to which the Regulations apply, the meaning of 'consumer', the consequences of inclusion of an unfair term, the definition of an unfair term, the requirement of good faith and factors indicative of unfairness. These will be discussed in turn.

8.3.1 Terms to which the 1999 Regulations apply

The terms to which the 1999 Regulations apply are defined by reg. 4, which provides as follows:

> (1) These Regulations apply in relation to unfair terms in contracts concluded between a seller or a supplier and a consumer.

4. Replacing the 1994 Regulations, SI 1994/3159.

> (2) These Regulations do not apply to contractual terms which reflect—
> (a) mandatory statutory or regulatory provisions (including such provisions under the law of any Member State or in Community legislation having effect in the United Kingdom without further enactment);
> (b) the provisions or principles of international conventions to which the Member States or the Community are party.

Regulation 5, which lays down the general test of fairness, only applies to terms which have not been individually negotiated. Whether a term is to be considered to have been individually negotiated is determined by reg. 5(2) to (4) which provide as follows:

> (2) A term shall always be regarded as not having been individually negotiated where it has been drafted in advance and the consumer has therefore not been able to influence the substance of the term.
> (3) Notwithstanding that a specific term or certain aspects of it in a contract has been individually negotiated, these Regulations shall apply to the rest of a contract if an overall assessment of it indicates that it is a pre-formulated standard contract.
> (4) It shall be for any seller or supplier who claims that a term was individually negotiated to show that it was.

These paragraphs were included together as reg. 4 of the 1994 Regulations. Given that the purpose of this section of this text is to identify which terms the test of fairness relates to, it is more helpful to consider them together. The thrust of the 1999 Regulations is to identify terms which are not individually negotiated. Regulation 5(2) provides that this will always be the case where the contract was drafted in advance. In the modern day it is the ordinary course of business that a contract is thrust in front of the consumer in 'small print' and the consumer has no choice but to accept the terms. Indeed it would be surprising if the sales assistant, or even the shop manager, had authority to alter the terms of the contract. Even where there is an element of negotiation between the parties, it must be such as to alter the 'substance' of the contract in order to contradict the presumption in reg. 5(2)

Regulation 5(2) brings in a similar requirement to that discussed in section 8.2.1[5] in relation to UCTA that even if there has been an element of individual negotiation over some terms the Regulations may still apply if an overall assessment of the contract shows that it is pre-formulated. However, the Regulations are wider in that they will apply to those parts of the contract which are pre-formulated, even though certain terms have been individually negotiated. The emphasis is on the term and not the contract as a whole.

Schedule 1 to the 1994 Regulations excluded from the application of the Regulations contracts of employment, succession rights, family matters, company matters and terms which are incorporated to adhere to UK or EC law. The 1999 Regulations do not exclude such contracts.

5. For example, cases such as *St. Albans City and District Council* v *International Computers Ltd* [1996] 4 All ER 481; *McCrone* v *Boots Farm Sales* [1981] CLY 2409; *The Salvage Association* v *CAP Financial Services Ltd* [1995] FSR 654.

The main criterion, however, is that the contract is made with a 'consumer' and this is discussed in the next section.

8.3.2 Definition of 'consumer'

Regulation 3(1) of the 1999 Regulations defines a consumer as follows:

> ... any natural person who, in contracts covered by these Regulations, is acting for purposes which are outside his trade, business or profession ...

This definition is narrower than that of 'deals as a consumer' which is contained in UCTA. In the first place the phrase 'purposes which are outside his business' would appear to exclude all contracts for business purposes, whether they are merely incidental to that business, regular or not. It follows that situations such as those in *R & B Customs Brokers Co. Ltd* v *United Dominions Trust Ltd* [1988] 1 WLR 321, discussed at section 8.2.2 above, would not be covered by the 1999 Regulations. Furthermore, the wide definition of business as including trade or profession would exclude partnerships and companies. The latter are also excluded by the phrase 'natural' person, but this also operates to exclude charitable companies. It seems therefore that the 1999 Regulations envisage a 'pure' consumer and this is in keeping with the wider protection which the Regulations afford.

8.3.3 Effect of inclusion of an unfair term

The effect of inclusion of an unfair term is prescribed by reg. 8 of the 1999 Regulations, which provides as follows:

> (1) An unfair term in a contract concluded with a consumer by a seller or supplier shall not be binding on the consumer.
> (2) The contract shall continue to bind the parties if it is capable of continuing in existence without the unfair term.

The effect of the regulation is self-explanatory: the term is not binding upon the consumer, but if the contract is capable of subsisting without the term the contract continues in force in accordance with those terms which are not unfair.

8.3.4 Unfair terms

The general test of fairness is defined in reg. 5 of the 1999 Regulations, which provides as follows:

> (1) A contractual term which has not been individually negotiated shall be regarded as unfair if, contrary to the requirement of good faith, it causes a significant imbalance in the parties' rights and obligations arising under the contract, to the detriment of the consumer.

. . .

> (5) Schedule 2 to these Regulations contains an indicative and non-exhaustive list of the terms which may be regarded as unfair.

Regulation 5(1) thus includes two fundamental tests. First, that the contract be made contrary to the requirement of good faith. This is discussed in the next section. Secondly, that the term causes a significant imbalance in the parties' rights and obligations to the detriment of the consumer. This is the fundamental test of fairness which is discussed fully in section 8.3.6 below. It is fundamentally assessed by the criteria outlined in sch. 2, referred to in reg. 5(5). It is clear however that the two tests are cumulative and both must be satisfied.

8.3.5 The requirement of good faith

The 1994 Regulations provided by sch. 2 a list of factors to be taken into account when determining whether the requirement of good faith had been complied with. Whilst the test for fairness still makes reference to the requirement of good faith, the 1999 Regulations have abandoned these criteria. Now, however, the criteria taken into account in determining whether the contract term is unfair are expressed as applying generally to the test of whether the term is unfair; there is no separate list of when the requirement of good faith is fulfilled.

8.3.6 Factors to be taken into account when assessing fairness

The general rule as to assessing fairness is set out in reg. 6 of the 1999 Regulations, which provides as follows:

> (1) Without prejudice to regulation 12, the unfairness of a contractual term shall be assessed, taking into account the nature of the goods or services for which the contract was concluded and by referring, at the time of conclusion of the contract, to all the circumstances attending the conclusion of the contract and to all the other terms of the contract or of another contract on which it is dependent.
>
> (2) In so far as it is in plain intelligible language, the assessment of fairness of a term shall not relate—
>
> (a) to the definition of the main subject matter of the contract, or
>
> (b) to the adequacy of the price or remuneration, as against the goods or services supplied in exchange.

The reference in reg. 6 to intelligible language requires reference to be made to reg. 7, which provides as follows:

> (1) A seller or supplier shall ensure that any written term of a contract is expressed in plain, intelligible language.
>
> (2) If there is doubt about the meaning of a written term, the interpretation which is most favourable to the consumer shall prevail but this rule shall not apply in proceedings brought under regulation 12.

Taken together, regs 6 and 7 prevent a court inquiring into the overall substance of a contract, i.e., regarding the price and the adequacy of that which is supplied under the agreement, unless the contract is not written in plain intelligible language. Accordingly, a supplier is prevented from stipulating in incomprehensible language that he may provide something radically different from that which a consumer reasonably envisages that he is purchasing. The circumstances where this will be relevant are, thankfully, relatively rare.

The time at which the term is to be assessed for its fairness is the time at which the contract is concluded. Subsequent events which make the term appear unfair should not be taken into account.

The main assistance for determining whether or not a term is fair is to be found in sch. 2 to the 1999 Regulations which sets out several criteria for determining what should be taken into account. Case law at present on the Regulations is thin. Furthermore, most cases on the Regulations will be decided at district judge level and are therefore of limited assistance as authority. Those advising on this area of law would be best advised to keep abreast of the law by reference to the *Current Law* case reports.

Whilst authority is thin, there are some cases which outline the areas where the court will be likely to grant relief. For example, in *Hartman* v *P & O Cruises Ltd* [1998] 7 CL 394, a clause limiting a customer's compensation to £40 in the event that he cancelled a cruise holiday was unfair, particularly in light of the degree of compensation offered if it were the cruise liner who cancelled. Similarly, a clause in a lease was unfair where it restricted activities on rented premises which were considered to be a nuisance within *the opinion* of the landlord (*Camden LBC* v *McBride* [1999] 1 CL 284). By contrast, in *Gosling* v *Burrard-Lucas* [1999] 1 CL 197, a clause in a contract to enter a public school was not unfair where it provided for the payment of one term's fees in the event of late cancellation of an accepted place at the school.

The criteria in sch. 2 are very wide and provide as follows:

1. Terms which have the object or effect of—

(a) excluding or limiting the legal liability of a seller or supplier in the event of the death of a consumer or personal injury to the latter resulting from an act or omission of that seller or supplier;

(b) inappropriately excluding or limiting the legal rights of the consumer vis-à-vis the seller or supplier or another party in the event of total or partial non-performance or inadequate performance by the seller or supplier of any of the contractual obligations, including the option of offsetting a debt owed to the seller or supplier against any claim which the consumer may have against him;

(c) making an agreement binding on the consumer whereas provision of services by the seller or supplier is subject to a condition whose realisation depends on his own will alone;

(d) permitting the seller or supplier to retain sums paid by the consumer where the latter decides not to conclude or perform the contract, without providing for the consumer to receive compensation of an equivalent amount from the seller or supplier where the latter is the party cancelling the contract;

(e) requiring any consumer who fails to fulfil his obligation to pay a disproportionately high sum in compensation;

(f) authorising the seller or supplier to dissolve the contract on a discretionary basis where the same facility is not granted to the consumer, or permitting the seller or supplier to retain the sums paid for services not yet supplied by him where it is the seller or supplier himself who dissolves the contract;

(g) enabling the seller or supplier to terminate a contract of indeterminate duration without reasonable notice except where there are serious grounds for doing so;

(h) automatically extending a contract of fixed duration where the consumer does not indicate otherwise, when the deadline fixed for the consumer to express his desire not to extend the contract is unreasonably early;

(i) irrevocably binding the consumer to terms with which he had no real opportunity of becoming acquainted before the conclusion of the contract;

(j) enabling the seller or supplier to alter the terms of the contract unilaterally without a valid reason which is specified in the contract;

(k) enabling the seller or supplier to alter unilaterally without a valid reason any characteristics of the product or service to be provided;

(l) providing for the price of goods to be determined at the time of delivery or allowing a seller of goods or supplier of services to increase their price without in both cases giving the consumer the corresponding right to cancel the contract if the final price is too high in relation to the price agreed when the contract was concluded;

(m) giving the seller or supplier the right to determine whether the goods or services supplied are in conformity with the contract, or giving him the exclusive right to interpret any term of the contract;

(n) limiting the seller's or supplier's obligation to respect commitments undertaken by his agents or making his commitments subject to compliance with a particular formality;

(o) obliging the consumer to fulfil all his obligations where the seller or supplier does not perform his;

(p) giving the seller or supplier the possibility of transferring his rights and obligations under the contract, where this may serve to reduce the guarantees for the consumer, without the latter's agreement;

(q) excluding or hindering the consumer's right to take legal action or exercise any other legal remedy, particularly by requiring the consumer to take disputes exclusively to arbitration not covered by legal provisions, unduly restricting the evidence available to him or imposing on him a burden of proof which, according to the applicable law, should lie with another party to the contract.

Paragraph 2 of sch. 2 excludes from the application of the criteria certain finance contracts. For example, the right to vary the interest rate on a loan. Provision is also made in ordinary contracts of supply or sale for the terms of the contract to be varied, on notice, where the contract is one of intermediate duration.

8.4 JUDICIAL CONTROL OF EXCLUSION CLAUSES

8.4.1 The process of judicial control

Judicial control over exclusion or limitation clauses takes a threefold process: first, hurdles are put up to prevent the clause having been incorporated into the contract in the first place. Here the ordinary rules of contract apply, but it is fair to say that they are more strictly applied where the clause in question is an exclusion clause. Secondly, the clauses are construed against the interests of the party in whose favour the clause purports to operate. These first two stages involve some straining of judicial logic as they usually involve the court saying that a clause does not say what it fairly clearly purports to. The third stage is only invoked where both of the first two stages have been overcome: that even if there is a clause which operates as it purports to that liability cannot be excluded or restricted for that type of breach, e.g., fraud. To some extent there is an overlap between the case of a person signing the document who is unable to understand or read the document — it will probably be binding only where reasonable steps are taken to draw the term to his attention (*Geir* v *Kujawa* [1970] 1 Lloyd's Rep 364).

Where the term has not been included in any written document signed by the other party, it may still be incorporated by reference to some other document or by a course of dealing between the parties. This is used in practice in many 'over the counter' sales where a notice states that the sale or order is 'subject to conditions displayed' or 'subject to our standard terms and conditions available upon request'. This is a perfectly proper method of incorporating terms (*Smith* v *South Wales Switchgear Ltd* [1978] 1 All ER 18). However, in order to incorporate the term reasonable steps must have been taken to bring it to the other party's attention (*Parker* v *South Eastern Railway* (1877) 2 CPD 416; *Interfoto Picture Library Ltd* v *Stiletto Visual Programmes Ltd* [1989] QB 433). The more onerous or unusual the term the greater the steps that must be taken to bring it to the other party's attention (*Thornton* v *Shoe Lane Parking Ltd* [1971] 2 QB 163). Once reasonable steps have been taken then the term will be incorporated notwithstanding that it has not actually come to the attention of the buyer (*Thompson* v *London Midland and Scottish Railway* [1930] 1 KB 41).

Where the parties have dealt over a period ostensibly on the same terms and conditions then those terms may become part of the contract notwithstanding that the formalities regarding signing or bringing the terms to the other party's attention have never formally been met. This may be the case, for example, where orders are placed by telephone and the invoice or sales voucher contains the terms. They would not be incorporated on the first occasion, but where the buyer continues to place orders with that firm he would appear to be placing the orders based upon those terms. In order to determine whether a course of dealing has arisen the whole course of dealing must be examined and not looked at in a 'battle of forms' manner (*J. Spurling Ltd* v *Bradshaw* [1956] 2 All ER 121). Once a course of dealing is established a party wishing to alter the terms comes under the same duty as the person originally putting forward the terms to bring the alteration to the notice of the other party (*Pancommerce SA* v *Veecheema BV* [1983] 2 Lloyd's Rep 304). Where the seller has used a variety of standard terms over the course of dealing then the terms will not have become incorporated; the other party will not be taken to have contracted from time to time upon the other party's standard terms as they may be from time to time (*McCutcheon* v *David MacBrayne Ltd* [1964] 1 All ER 430). Finally, a regular course of dealing must, of course, be established. A party cannot be taken to have bound himself to another's terms simply because he has used them half a dozen times over as many years (*Hollier* v *Rambler Motors Ltd* [1972] 2 QB 71).

8.4.2 Construction of exclusion and limitation clauses

The general rule when construing exclusion clauses is to construe them against the interests of the party in whose favour they operate. As is shown below, this has led to the judiciary straining the English language almost to breaking point in order to achieve this result. Before this is discussed, however, the doctrine of fundamental breach needs to be considered, and its relationship with the construction of exemption clauses.

At one stage the doctrine of fundamental breach was considered as a substantive rule of law — that a clause could not purport to exclude or restrict liability in respect of a breach of a term of the contract which was fundamental to the whole basis of the contract. The classic phrase used is the 'peas and beans' example: that if the contract stipulated for the sale of peas it could not by another clause permit the seller to deliver beans and exclude liability.

In *Suisse Atlantique Société d'Armement Maritime SA* v *Rotterdamsche Kolen Centrale NV* [1967] 1 AC 361 it was held by the House of Lords that the doctrine was not a rule of law but a rule of construction, so that liability for breach of a fundamental term may be excluded or restricted. This was confirmed in *Photo Production Ltd* v *Securicor Transport Ltd* [1980] AC 827. However, in order to do so the party must use very clear words.

A further qualification to this rule was then added by the House of Lords in *Ailsa Craig Fishing Company Ltd* v *Malvern Shipping Co. Ltd* [1983] 1 All ER 101 that a distinction was to be drawn between exclusion clauses (clauses which exclude liability for a breach altogether) and limitation clauses (which restrict the injured party's remedies to a particular amount or type of remedy). The latter are to be construed according to the plain and natural meaning of the words used, whereas the *contra proferentem* rule still applied to exclusion clauses.

This creates some difficulty in that a clause might be drafted so as to (in effect) exclude liability altogether, for example a multimillion pound contract which restricted liability to breach of a fundamental term to £1. Here the court could hold that the clause was a sham or possibly a penalty clause and that it was, in reality, an exclusion clause. In any event, UCTA now applies to all contracts not being individually drafted, or not substantially so (see section 8.2.1 above). Accordingly, it will be rare if some legal protection is not available in respect of the limitation clause, or if the contract has been individually drafted the circumstances are such that the disadvantaged party really ought to be taken to have agreed to the terms. Where such limitation clauses have been used so as to, in effect, exclude liability the courts have been seemingly happy to strike them down by the use of UCTA. For example, in *St. Albans City and District Council* v *International Computers Ltd* [1996] 4 All ER 481 a clause limiting liability to £100,000 was struck down where the real liability was vastly greater. Furthermore, the cases where a natural construction has been given to the words of an exclusion clause have generally been ones where UCTA has been available to come to the rescue of the disadvantaged party. For example, in *George Mitchell (Chesterhall) Ltd* v *Finney Lock Seeds* [1983] 2 AC 803 the court was in the position where it could use UCTA and could hence use plain language without being in fear of doing injustice to the parties.

Accordingly, it seems that the general rule is that an exclusion clause is to be construed strictly against the interests of the party in whose favour it purports to operate, whereas limitation clauses are to be given their plain and natural meaning. Once the terms are so construed, if they do validly exclude or restrict liability then there is no general rule of common law which will come to the assistance of a disadvantaged party and recourse will have to be made to statutory protection.

The only circumstances where the common law does come to the assistance of a disadvantaged party are limited and are set out in the next section. However, these circumstances do not involve an assessment of the substance of the term, but rely upon misrepresentation or fraud or something similar on the part of the person relying on the clause.

This leaves an important question so far unanswered: when will the courts construe an exemption clause as operating to exclude liability? As has been noted the courts have proved adept at stretching the language of the contract to breaking point and perhaps a few examples will suffice:

(a) In *Houghton* v *Trafalgar Insurance Company* [1954] 1 QB 247 an insurance policy stated that the policy did not provide cover where the driver carried *a load* in excess of a particular amount. It was held by the court that this did not cover the situation where the driver carried *passengers* taking the weight of the vehicle above this amount.

(b) In *Wallis, Son & Wells* v *Pratt* [1911] AC 394 (see also *Baldry* v *Marshall* [1925] 1 KB 260) a contract provided that it excluded liability in respect of all *warranties*. When seed was provided that did not match its contractual description, this was a breach of *condition* and hence not covered by the exclusion clause.

(c) In *Beck & Co. Ltd* v *Szymanowski & Co. Ltd* [1924] AC 43 cloth was ordered and to be delivered in rolls of 200 feet. The contract contained a clause stating that the goods would be deemed to be in accordance with the contract unless the seller was notified of any complaints within 14 days from delivery. It was not until 18 months had expired that the buyer noticed that the rolls were 188 feet long and not 200 feet. It was held that the clause did not operate as the buyer's claim was in respect of goods *not* delivered, not in respect of goods that were.

(d) Liability in respect of negligence is now entirely restricted in so far as it relates to death or personal injury, and in respects of other loss it must comply with the test of reasonableness (UCTA, s. 2). However, it is quite possible that such a clause will be construed as not covering loss caused by negligence and if it is to do so it must be in very clear words. For example, in *Rutter* v *Palmer* [1922] 2 KB 87 it was held that a clause which stated that a garage's staff drove the customers' cars and that this was at the customers' risk did operate to exclude liability. By contrast, in *Hollier* v *Rambler Motors (AMC) Ltd* [1972] 2 QB 71 a clause which stated that the risk of fire was on customers leaving their cars with the garage only covered the situation where the fire was not caused by the garage's negligence, not where it was.

(e) Where the contract excludes damages in respect of 'consequential loss' then this will be construed as meaning loss not arising directly and naturally from the breach of contract, and may be upheld as a limitation clause (*British Sugar plc* v *NEI Power Projects* (1998) 14 Const. LJ 365; 87 BLR 42).[6]

(f) A 'peas and beans' case is that of *Shepherd* v *Kain* (1821) 5 B & Ald 240 where a copper vessel was sold without allowance for any defects. This was held

6. See Lawson, R., *Exclusion Clauses and Unfair Contract Terms*, 5th ed., (London: Sweet & Maxwell, 1995), p. 51.

not to cover the situation where the seller delivered something which was not a copper vessel at all. Similarly, where a car is delivered which is so unsatisfactory as to render it useless for all practical purposes an exemption clause may be struck down (*Yeoman Credit Ltd* v *Apps* [1962] 2 QB 508; *Farnworth Finance Facilities Ltd* v *Attryde* [1970] 2 All ER 774; Treitel, *An Outline of the Law of Contract*, 5th ed., (London: Butterworths, 1995), pp. 86–87). These cases must be considered however at the absolute extreme of the construction rule put forward in relation to fundamental breach as no substantive explanation for the construction can be given, simply that the clause purports to exclude liability for all performance. They fall into the category of cases where manifest absurdity would be reached if the clause were upheld (*Suisse Atlantique Société d'Armament Maritime SA* v *Rotterdamsche Kolen Centrale NV* [1967] 1 AC 361, at 396).

8.4.3 Common law restrictions upon the operation of exclusion clauses

As was seen in the previous section, if a clause has become incorporated into the contract, and on its proper construction it does operate to exclude or restrict liability, then the courts will not assess the overall fairness of the term, regardless of whether it goes to a fundamental term of the contract. This much seems clear from *Suisse Atlantique Société d'Armement Maritime SA* v *Rotterdamsche Kolen Centrale NV* [1967] 1 AC 361, *Photo Production Ltd* v *Securicor Transport Ltd* [1980] AC 827, and *Ailsa Craig Fishing Company Ltd* v *Malvern Shipping Company Ltd* [1983] 1 All ER 101. The only residual area where such an argument could possibly survive is that which was mentioned in the previous paragraph: where placing a certain construction upon the clause would lead to manifest absurdity. However, it appears that this is still a rule of construction rather than a rule of substantive law.

Whilst there is no general rule that the court will assess the fairness of an exclusion clause, there are circumstances where the courts will deem it inequitable for a party to rely on an exclusion clause.

The first such situation is where the party purports to rely upon a clause to exclude or restrict liability for his own fraud. Here the courts will not let him do so (*Pearson & Son Ltd* v *Dublin Corporation* [1907] AC 351). Accordingly, if one party deliberately refused to perform his part of the contract he could not then rely on an exclusion clause.

A second situation is where the party attempting to rely on the exclusion clause has made a statement prior to the contract to the opposite effect than the exclusion clause. This may be by way of an oral representation (*Curtis* v *Chemical Cleaning and Dyeing Co. Ltd* [1951] 1 KB 805; *Couchman* v *Hill* [1947] KB 554), or by way of a 'memorandum of understanding' under which future (individual) contracts are made (*Gallagher* v *British Road Services Ltd* [1974] 2 Lloyd's Rep 440).

Finally, where a party employs independent contractors to fulfil his contractual obligations, an exclusion clause will not restrict that contractor's liability where this is owed directly to the other party unless it specifically purports to do so (*Scruttons Ltd* v *Midland Silicones Ltd* [1962] AC 446; *The Eurymedon* [1975] AC 154).

9 *Wrongful interference with goods*

9.1 INTRODUCTION

Wrongful interference with goods is a global phrase applied to a variety of different torts; conversion and trespass being the most common. They were brought together under this heading by the Torts (Interference with Goods) Act 1977 (the '1977 Act'). Conversion will frequently occur where one person buys goods which he knows were stolen. The owner has a direct remedy in conversion against the parties to that transaction. Similarly where a person has interfered with the claimant's possession of goods then an action will lie in trespass.

9.2 WRONGFUL INTERFERENCE WITH GOODS

Section 1 of the 1977 Act defines wrongful interference with goods as follows:

> In this Act 'wrongful interference', or 'wrongful interference with goods', means—
> (a) conversion of goods (also called trover),
> (b) trespass to goods,
> (c) negligence so far as it results in damage to goods or to an interest in goods,
> (d) subject to section 2 [abolition of the tort of detinue], any other tort so far as it results in damage to goods or to an interest in goods
> [and references in this Act (however worded) to proceedings for wrongful interference or to a claim or right to a claim for wrongful interference shall include references to proceedings by virtue of Part I of the Consumer Protection Act 1987 (product liability) in respect of any damage to goods and to the interest in goods or, as the case may be, to a claim or right to claim by virtue of that Part in respect of any such damage].

The Act does not therefore create a new tort of 'wrongful interference with goods', but introduces rules which cover existing torts. These rules are expanded upon below, but briefly, include such matters as accounting for improvements, abolition of the defence of *jus tertii*, torts between co-owners and sales and orders of the court. The two forms of wrongful interference with goods which are considered in this text, trespass and conversion, are dealt with in sections 9.3 and 9.4 below.

9.2.1 Form of judgment

Section 3 of the 1977 Act provides for the forms of order available to the court in an action for wrongful interference with goods. Of importance, the right to an order for delivery of the goods is not available as of right to the injured claimant, this remedy is discretionary.

Section 3 of the 1977 Act provides as follows:

> (1) In proceedings for wrongful interference against a person who is in possession or in control of the goods relief may be given in accordance with this section, so far as it is appropriate.
>
> (2) The relief is—
>
> (a) an order for delivery of the goods, and for payment of any consequential damages, or
>
> (b) an order for delivery of the goods, but giving the defendant the alternative of paying damages by reference to the value of the goods, together in either alternative with payment of any consequential damages, or
>
> (c) damages.
>
> (3) Subject to rules of court—
>
> (a) relief shall be given under only one of paragraphs (a), (b) and (c) of subsection (2),
>
> (b) relief under paragraph (a) of subsection (2) is at the discretion of the court, and the claimant may choose between the others.
>
> ...
>
> (6) An order for delivery of the goods under subsection (2)(a) or (b) may impose such conditions as may be determined by the court, or pursuant to rules of court, and in particular, where damages by reference to the value of the goods would not be the whole of the value of the goods, may require an allowance to be made by the claimant to reflect the difference.
>
> For example, a bailor's action against the bailee may be one in which the measure of damages is not the full value of the goods, and then the court may order delivery of the goods, but require the bailor to pay the bailee a sum reflecting the difference.
>
> (7) Where under subsection (1) or subsection (2) of section 6 an allowance is to be made in respect of an improvement of the goods, and an order is made under subsection (2)(a) or (b), the court may assess the allowance to be made in respect of the improvement, and by the order require, as a condition for delivery of the goods, that allowance to be made by the claimant.

. . .

The court is not obliged to order that the goods are delivered to their rightful owner — it may award damages where to do so would be unjust. However, the person in possession will never be unjustly enriched as he will always be made to pay over the value of the goods. Section 3(6) and (7) extend this rule in that if an order is made for delivery up of the goods the court may order that an allowance be made by the claimant to the defendant for any improvements or additions to the goods, and as a practical step (under s. 3(7)) that delivery be conditional upon this allowance. Thus, for example, where generic goods belonging to a bailor are mixed with other goods it would be inequitable simply to provide for delivery up of all those goods to the bailor as he would then have more goods. The court may make the claimant pay an allowance for the extra, or improved, goods he obtains by the order for delivery.

Where damages are paid in lieu of delivery of the goods, and the damages relate to the claimant's entire interest in the goods, then upon payment of those damages the claimant's title is extinguished by virtue of s. 5 of the 1977 Act.

9.2.2 Improvements to goods

Section 6 of the 1977 Act provides as follows:

> (1) If in proceedings for wrongful interference against a person ('the improver') who has improved goods, it is shown that the improver acted in the mistaken but honest belief that he had a good title to them, an allowance shall be made for the extent to which, at the time as at which the goods fall to be valued in assessing damages, the value of the goods is attributable to the improvement.
>
> (2) If, in proceedings for wrongful interference against a person ('the purchaser') who has purported to purchase the goods—
>
> (a) from the improver, or
>
> (b) where after such a purported sale the goods passed by a further purported sale on one or more occasions, on any such occasion,
>
> it is shown that the purchaser acted in good faith, an allowance shall be made on the principle set out in subsection (1).
>
> For example, where a person in good faith buys a stolen car from the improver and is sued in conversion by the true owner the damages may be reduced to reflect the improvement, but if the person who bought the stolen car from the improver sues the improver for failure of consideration, and the improver acted in good faith, subsection (3) below will ordinarily make a comparable reduction in the damages he recovers from the improver.
>
> (3) If in a case within subsection (2) the person purporting to sell the goods acted in good faith, then in proceedings by the purchaser for recovery of the purchase price because of failure of consideration, or in any other proceedings founded on that failure of consideration, an allowance shall, where appropriate, be made on the principle set out in subsection (1).
>
> (4) This section applies, with the necessary modifications, to a purported bailment or other disposition of goods as it applies to a purported sale of goods.

The operation of the section is fairly straightforward: where goods have been improved, in any claim for damages in respect of the conversion of the goods an allowance will be made for that improvement. However, the person claiming the allowance must have acted in good faith. For example, A's car is stolen by B, who resprays the car before selling it to C, an honest buyer acting in good faith. Upon a claim by A against C, C may claim an allowance for the improvements under s. 6(2). However, no allowance will be made in B's favour under s. 6(3) because he did not act in good faith. The same principle would be achieved regardless of the number of subsales.

9.2.3 Competing rights to goods

A person in possession of goods may not claim to be their owner, but may claim that the claimant of the goods is not their true owner, but another is. Where this was the case a rule, known as the *jus tertii* rule, operated to prevent the defendant setting up that third party's title as a defence to the claim. This rule is abolished by s. 8 of the 1977 Act.

Co-ownership is no defence to an action for conversion by a fellow co-owner where the offending co-owner acts to destroy the other co-owner's interest in the goods. This could be by way of destroying the goods or disposing of them in order to pass a good title to a third party (under the *nemo dat* rule).

9.2.4 Uncollected goods

Where a bailee is in possession of goods which have remained uncollected after their due time for collection then by s. 12 of the 1977 Act the bailee may in certain circumstances dispose of the goods and extinguish the title of the bailor. In order to validly do so the bailee must serve a notice which complies with Part II of sch. 1 of the Act (sending by recorded delivery, specifying date of disposal and sums due to the bailor, etc.). If the goods remain uncollected then the bailor may dispose of them. However, the bailor remains liable to account to the owner for any surplus between the value realised from the sale and the amount owing to the bailee. Furthermore, the bailee may only sell the goods if he is reasonably satisfied that the goods belong to the person to whom he sent the notice. If it subsequently transpires that they do not, and that the bailee had insufficient grounds for such belief, then the bailee will become liable to the true owner.

9.3 TRESPASS

Much academic debate surrounds what exactly is required to found a trespass. The general rule is that a direct interference with the claimant's possession of a chattel will suffice. However, the debate surrounds the issues of whether it is necessary that the action be 'direct', 'intentional' and whether proof of 'special damage' is required (actual pecuniary loss). For a thorough discussion of these issues see Chitty, *The Law of Contract*, (London: Sweet & Maxwell), p. 702 *et seq*.

In practice, the question is probably best answered by asking if the conduct has 'gone beyond generally acceptable standards of conduct' (*Collins* v *Wilcock* [1984] 1 WLR 1172). Thus, if the 1977 Act was intentional then there is probably no need for proof of special damage, for example where a pedestrian deliberately pulls off a car's wing mirror then the act may become actionable even though the mirror is easily reinstated. By contrast where the pedestrian merely accidentally knocks the mirror then he would probably escape liability (*Letang* v *Cooper* [1965] 1 QB 232; *National Coal Board* v *J. E. Evans & Co. (Cardiff)* [1951] 2 KB 861; *Wilson* v *Lombank Ltd* [1963] 1 WLR 1294).

An important distinction between trespass and conversion is that in order to sue in trespass the claimant must be in possession of the goods; a reversionary interest will not suffice (*Ward* v *Macauley* (1791) 4 TR 489). This is of limited practical importance since the holder of the reversionary interest will generally have an action in conversion where the goods are handled so as to destroy his title.

9.4 CONVERSION

Conversion is the most all-embracing cause of action whereby one person wrongfully interferes with another's goods. Indeed the acts capable of founding an action in conversion now overlap to such an extent with other torts that they have become somewhat obsolete by comparison.

It is almost impossible to state with any accuracy what exactly a conversion is, indeed even as far back as 1879 Bramwell LJ said 'I never did understand with precision what was a conversion' (*Hiort* v *L & NWR* (1879) 4 Ex D 188). The law has unfortunately not been greatly further refined since then. It is sufficient to say for present purposes that any deliberate act which deprives another of a right or rights which he holds over goods is capable of amounting to a conversion.

Two fundamental issues arise when considering whether an act is a conversion: whether the claimant is entitled to sue and whether the act is capable of being a conversion. The position of the defendant as a potential wrongdoer must also be considered, although in practice fewer issues generally arise in relation to this aspect of any potential claim. These issues will be considered in turn.

9.4.1 Entitlement to sue

In order to hold the right to sue in conversion a potential claimant must hold possession of the goods or the immediate right to possess the goods (*Wilbraham* v *Snow* (1669) 2 Wms Saund 47). The right must exist at the time of the conversion and not be a right which will come into existence in the future (*Pizza Express* [1993] 2 Lloyd's Rep 542), or will come into existence in the future conditionally upon some event (for example a person who holds the property in the goods following a sale but who has not yet obtained the right to delivery as he has not yet paid the price (*Lord* v *Price* (1873) LR 9 Ex 54)). To some extent, however, a right to sue in conversion is treated as a right *in rem* which passes with the goods. In *Bristol & West of England Bank* v *Midland Rly.* [1891] 2 QB 653 a conversion was committed to goods owned by A, but who went on to sell them to B. B was held entitled to sue on the conversion.

Two problems arise where it is contended that the claimant does not have the immediate right to possession: first, where the owner of the goods has bailed them or passed some other limited interest in them to a third party. Secondly, where the person wishing to sue has a mere possessory title. It must be noted that it is *possession* and not *ownership* which is essential.

9.4.1.1 Goods temporarily bailed Where the owner of goods has granted a third party a limited interest including exclusive possession of the goods then he has no right to sue in conversion. The exact nature of the interest passed to the third party must be examined. If the third party is a bailee at will then the owner would have the right to immediate possession since he could retake the goods (*Manders* v *Williams* (1849) 4 Ex 339).

A slight stretching of this rule has been achieved in the cases of *Fenn* v *Bittleston* (1851) 7 Ex 152 and *North Central Wagon & Finance Co.* v *Graham* [1950] 2 KB 7 (and see also *Union Transport Finance Ltd* v *British Car Auctions* [1978] 2 All ER 385). In each case goods were passed to a third party by way of a bailment and were sold contrary to the terms of the bailment. It was said that the act of selling the goods destroyed the bailment and that the property revested in the owner. In relation to pledging of goods the opposite has been held in a number of earlier authorities (see *Halliday* v *Holgate* (1868) LR 3 Ex 299; *Donald* v *Suckling* (1866) LR 1 QB 585). This is somewhat at odds with the principle that a contract remains alive until it is terminated (*Photo Production Ltd* v *Securicor Transport Ltd* [1980] AC 827) as until the contract is actually terminated the property should not revest in the owner and hence he would not hold a right to possession until the contract is actually terminated. However, these decisions remove an unnecessary technicality which merely complicates the law in an area which should be straightforward.

In any event, where the owner of goods merely has a reversionary interest in them (e.g., a bailor under a fixed-term contract of hire) then it is long established that a special cause of action for damage to that reversionary interest lies in his favour (*Mears* v *London & South Western Rly. Co.* (1862) 22 CB(NS) 850 and generally Tettenbourn, 'Reversionary Damage to Chattels' [1994] CLJ 326). The exact boundaries of the action are unclear, but it seems that so long as the act complained of would amount to a trespass, conversion or negligence but for the claimant's lack of title then this will suffice (*Mayfair Property Co.* v *Johnston* [1894] 1 Ch 508; *Tancred* v *Allgood* (1859) 4 H & N 438; *Mears* v *London & South Western Rly. Co.* (above)). In order to maintain the action, however, the claimant must prove that he has suffered damage to his *reversionary* interest. This may be by damage so that the goods are returned to him in a damaged state or by disposal in such a way as his title is extinguished (or possibly that the chances of his recovering the goods have been diminished by way of damages for loss of chance). However, where the goods are merely temporarily wrongfully interfered with so that they may be returned pursuant to the reversionary interest then the claimant has no loss for which he may sue (*Tancred* v *Allgood* (above); *Mukabi* v *Bhavsar* [1967] EA 473). This may be the case, for example, where a car is hired for a fixed period and is stolen but returned during the period of that hire, being returned undamaged. However, it seems that the owner may sue the wrongdoer in respect of damage even though he has a right to recover in respect of the damage from the bailee (*Dee Trading* v *Baldwin* [1938] VLR 173). Finally, there is some debate as to whether an action under this head falls within the provisions of the 1977 Act (see Tettenborn (above)). However, it is submitted that it does fall within the provisions of the Act being 'any other tort' within the meaning of s. 1(d) (see Bridge, *Personal Property Law*, 2nd ed. (London: Blackstone Press Ltd, 1996), p. 61).

9.4.1.2 Mere possessory title Turning to the second situation outlined above, that of whether a person who has possession is entitled to sue, it is clear that in many situations he is. It must be remembered that mere possession of goods is in itself a title to them, albeit subject to a superior title. For example, the finder of goods may acquire a title to them (*Parker* v *British Airways Board* [1982] QB 1004). So long as the claimant can show that he was once in possession of them then the onus switches to the defendant to plead *jus tertii* and show that another has better title to the goods (*Northam* v *Bowden* (1855) 11 Ex 70). This can lead to a curious situation whereby a thief may bring a cause of action in respect of goods which he has stolen. In such a situation the court does have power to prevent a thief from benefiting from the proceeds of crime (*Thackwell* v *Barclays Bank plc* [1986] 1 All ER 676). Whilst an action by a thief may be unmeritorious it could well be the case that a thief has sold the goods to an honest purchaser who holds the goods as a successor to the thief's possessory title. Assuming the owner remains untraced the onus would be on the defendant to show that a better title existed, and since there is no person to whom the defendant can point the claimant should succeed in this situation.

9.4.2 Acts capable of forming a conversion

Acts of conversion fall broadly into five categories: damaging or destroying goods and wrongfully taking, keeping, abandoning or receiving goods. Broadly speaking any act which is inconsistent with the rights of the owner may form a conversion so long as it is coupled with an intention to assert a right over the true owner's title and rights thereunder (*Lancashire Rly. Co.* v *MacNicholl* (1918) 88 LJKB 601; *Oakley* v *Lyster* [1931] 1 QB 148). Indeed it is extremely difficult to even attempt a clear definition of the operative principles since as soon as a satisfactory definition is set out which aptly covers one judicial decision, another (equally reasonable) decision appears to conflict with this. Given this, all that can be done is to consider the decided cases which give some guidance as to the factors which the courts will take into account in deciding whether an act constitutes a conversion. These cases will be considered in turn in relation to the various factual situations which arise.

9.4.3 Damage or destruction of goods

It is clear that altering the nature or constitution of goods may form a conversion, as where water is added to another's wine (*Penfolds Wines Pty Ltd* v *Elliot* (1946) 74 CLR 204; *Hollins* v *Fowler* (1875) LR 7 HL 757; *Lancashire Rly. Co.* v *MacNicholl* (1918) 88 LJKB 601). By contrast so long as the good remains in the same state as such then the action would lie solely in trespass, for example where a plank of wood is cut in two (*Simmons* v *Lillystone* (1853) 8 Ex 431).

As a general rule there is no liability in conversion for damage to goods caused by negligence (*Williams* v *Gesse* (1837) 3 Bing NC 849). Accordingly, where a manuscript was sent to a theatre company and was lost no liability attached in the case of *Howard* v *Harris* (1884) Cab & El 253 and in *Lethbridge* v *Phillips* (1819) 2 Stark 544 a lady left in charge of a painting was not liable when it was damaged due to exposure to heat. However, in *Moorgate Mercantile Credit* v *Finch* [1962] 1 QB 701 the defendant was presumed to have intended the natural and probable consequences of his act when he used a car for smuggling which gave rise to a likelihood that it would be impounded by Customs and Excise. It was held that this was a natural and probable consequence of the act of smuggling and he was liable. Furthermore, by s. 2(2) of the 1977 Act the tort of conversion is extended to cover breach of duty by a bailee as if it were the tort of detinue. Liability for negligence was always possible in an action for detinue. Seemingly therefore negligence may, in practice, suffice.

9.4.4 Abandoning goods

In *Fouldes* v *Willoughby* (1841) 8 M & W 540 the claimant's agent had taken two horses to a ferry for transportation across a river. Before the journey the agent became unruly and complaints were made to the defendant who was in charge of the ferry. The agent was asked to leave the ferry but refused. Accordingly, the defendant released the horses in the hope that the agent would follow them, he did not and the horses escaped. An action for conversion failed as there was no assertion of any right over the goods, or denial of the claimant's right, in the act of abandoning the horses.

9.4.5 Keeping goods

Of itself merely possessing goods belonging to another is not conversion (*Caxton Publishing Co.* v *Sutherland Publishing Co.* [1939] AC 178). For example, where a person acquires goods stored in premises which he takes possession of with no intention to deprive the owner of the goods (*Thorogood* v *Robinson* (1845) 6 QB 769).

However, where a demand is made to access the goods and this request is refused then a conversion will be committed (*Howard Perry & Co.* v *British Railways Board* [1980] 1 WLR 1375). Even where this is the case, the defendant is entitled to delay so as to make inquiries as to the ownership of the goods and need only hold them at the claimant's disposal; he is under no duty to deliver them (*Clayton* v *Le Roy* [1911] 2 KB 1031; *Capital Finance Co.* v *Bray* [1964] 1 WLR 323). This does not mean that as a pre-condition to liability a demand must be made. If the defendant knows full well that the goods are another's and keeps them for his own reasons then this may found liability without more (*London Jewellers* v *Sutton* (1934) 50 TLR 193; *Clayton* v *Le Roy* (above)).

9.4.6 Selling property

The circumstances whereby a buyer of goods may acquire a good title to them, despite the seller not being the true owner, are discussed at chapter 13 in relation to the *nemo dat* rule. Where the transferee acquires a good title to the property then no action for conversion will lie against him, but if he does not then such an action will (*Farrant* v *Thompson* (1822) 5 B & Ald 826).

The seller in such circumstances will inevitably be liable in conversion given that there can appear no greater assumption of the owner's rights than selling his goods.

9.4.7 Assistants

Despite conversion being theoretically a tort of strict liability and being founded irrespective of negligence it is almost impossible to escape the conclusion that it is precisely the issue of negligence which operates in the mind of the court when considering the position of those who, in some way, assist in the disposal of goods.

A third party who is neither the buyer nor seller (or equivalent) may assist in the disposal or alteration of goods which have been stolen or obtained by fraud in a number of ways, for example as broker, agent, auctioneer, repairer, employee, courier or warehouseman. In any of these situations the third party may well act innocently of any wrongdoing and may have little reason to doubt the honesty of the person then in possession of the goods who approaches him. It is difficult to decide in principle, therefore, where liability should be attached and where it should not.

In *Hollins* v *Fowler* (1875) LR 7 HL 757 a distinction was drawn between acts which would be within the scope of a finder of goods, or someone merely entrusted with their custody, and acts which would be within the scope of the owner. The third party, it was said, should judge the situation as if the transferor who has approached him were the finder of goods. It would be within the scope of the authority of the finder of goods to return the goods to the owner or store them pending the true owner's arrival. This would simply be in accordance with the finder's duty to return the goods. By contrast if the finder were to seek to sell the goods, this would be doubtless outside such authority.

Applying this distinction it is clear that third parties such as brokers or auctioneers will be liable; whereas couriers or warehousemen will not. Indeed precisely this distinction was drawn in *Barker* v *Furlong* [1891] 2 Ch 172 as brokers and the such like were those people who took some part in transferring the ownership of the goods whereas couriers merely moved them from one place to another.

At first glance this distinction appears a little hard and fast as it seems unfair to fix liability to one, yet let the other escape. There being little difference between the two in terms of their honesty or their ability to gauge the honesty of the transferor. Perhaps the best answer to this problem is given by Lord Denning in *R. H. Willis & Son* v *British Car Auctions* [1978] 1 WLR 438: auctioneers and brokers are able to insure more easily against such matters. In addition to this, however, a person who has obtained goods dishonestly is much more likely to wish to sell them than to ship or store them and accordingly the third party is already, to a certain extent, on notice as to a potential fraud.

Given this distinction it is no surprise that the general rule is that auctioneers are liable if they assist in the sale of stolen goods, indeed the only case where the contrary appears to have been found is that of *National Mercantile Bank* v *Rymill* (1881) 144 LT 767. However the decision in the *British Car Auctions* case, a more modern authority, appears to point firmly in the opposite direction.

9.4.8 Position of the defendant

It is ordinarily no answer for the defendant to show that he had no knowledge that the goods belonged to another; the defendant deals with the goods at his peril (*Hollins* v *Fowler* (1875) LR 7 HL 757). This applies just as much whether the defendant is the 'taker' of the goods, a bailee or a purchaser. Furthermore, the defendant need not have any reason to know of the transferor's lack of title (*M'Combie* v *Davies* (1805) 6 East 538). Indeed the defendant may be merely an employee acting under the instruction of his employer (*Stephens* v *Elwall* (1815) 4 M & S 259).

Seemingly one route whereby the honest defendant may escape liability is where he has become an involuntary bailee of the goods. In *Elvin & Powell* v *Plummer Roddis Ltd* (1933) 50 TLR 158 a rogue had ordered goods from the claimant and then contacted the defendant to explain that they had been sent in error and were shortly to be collected. The defendant assuming the rogue to be the owner duly handed them over. In these circumstances the defendant's actions were held to be reasonable and he was not held liable. By contrast, in *Hiort* v *Bott* (1874) LR 9 Ex 86, on similar facts, the goods themselves were not delivered to the defendant but a delivery note was. The defendant, at the rogue's request, endorsed the note in favour of the rogue. In this instance he was held liable as this had been an unnecessary assumption of control over the goods on his part — he had dealt with them at his peril. The same rule was applied where goods were delivered to a defendant who mistakenly thought they were his (*AUX Ltd* v *EGM Solders Ltd*, *The Times*, 7 July 1982).

10 Remedies in respect of damage caused by defective goods

10.1 INTRODUCTION — NEGLIGENCE AND THE CONSUMER PROTECTION ACT 1987 COMPARED

In general the buyer of goods will have a direct remedy against the seller in contract in respect of goods which have caused damage to himself or his property. It is highly unlikely that a court will find a good fit for its purpose or of satisfactory quality where it caused damage or injury accidentally. However, it may be the case that the damage was caused to a third party or his property and not to the buyer. Here the injured party's remedy will be in tort and not contract as a contractual claim is barred by virtue of the privity of contract rule.[1] This chapter is concerned with tortious claims and not contractual ones: the cases where a defect in a good has caused damage to a person entitled to sue under the contract are discussed in the relevant chapters on breach of the implied terms of the contract of sale.

In practice the Consumer Protection Act 1987 (the '1987 Act') adds little to the common law. One of the principal differences between the common law of negligence and the 1987 Act is that the common law requires proof of fault whereas liability under the Act is strict. Thus at common law the claimant must show that the damage was caused by a failure to take reasonable care in the design or manufacture of the product whereas under the 1987 Act liability is established simply by proving that the product was defective and that it caused damage or injury. Technically, this means that the claimant should be able to point to the problem with the good and how it came about and that it was reasonable for the defendant to know of the problem and take steps to prevent it. This may mean obtaining complicated evidence of the manufacturer's workplace and methods. However, in practice, the courts apply something of the doctrine *res ipsa loquitur* (the thing speaks for itself) and where a good is defective are quite prepared to infer negligence on the part of the defendant in the absence of a specific defence rebutting this inference (*Hill* v *James Crowe* [1978] 1 All ER 812). Furthermore,

1. Unless the injured party has the benefit of the contract by reason of the Contracts (Rights of Third Parties) Act 1999, as to which see section 3.4.

the claimant is not required to point to the exact person responsible (*Grant* v *Australian Knitting Mills Ltd* [1936] AC 85). Thus where a good is defective the onus shifts to the defendant to prove that there was no negligence in the manufacture of the good. There is little practical difference therefore between the strict liability of the 1987 Act and the common law of negligence.

Where this difference between the common law and the 1987 Act might have been important is (for example) where the state of scientific knowledge meant that it would have been unreasonable for the manufacturer to have discovered the defect at the time it was manufactured yet there existed a defect which caused injury. Here the Act would apply as the good was defective, but the common law would not as there would be no fault within the legal sense on the manufacturer. However Directive 85/374/EEC, pursuant to which the 1987 Act was implemented, made it optional for member States to include a defence based upon the defect not being discoverable due to the lack of scientific knowledge. This defence was adopted by the Act and accordingly the position is the same under the common law and the Act.

However, the 1987 Act does expand the range of people who may be liable to the claimant. This is of real practical importance when considering imported goods. It is of little practical use for an injured person to be told that he has a good remedy, but that the culprit is in China. The realities of litigation mean that this is no remedy at all. Whilst it was always possible to make a distributor liable in negligence at common law this has always depended upon it being practical for him to have examined the goods. If this was impractical, he is probably only under a duty at common law to purchase goods from a reputable supplier (*Watson* v *Buckley* [1940] 1 All ER 174), but this is a relatively low standard of care. The Act by contrast treats importers of goods from outside the EC in the same way as producers — if the goods are defective then they are liable. However, the Act is perhaps more lenient than the common law where the supplier has imported the goods from within the EC — here the supplier only becomes liable where he fails to identify the person who supplied the product to himself.

It seems, therefore, that the 1987 Act adds little to the common law of negligence and has really stated only that which Lord Atkin did in 1932 in the famous case of *Donoghue* v *Stevenson* [1932] AC 562. The practitioner may, however, be best advised to frame any claim under both the Act and the common law. Each of the two regimes is examined in more detail below.

10.2 NEGLIGENCE

The general rule that a manufacturer may be made accountable for defects in its products was first stated in *Donoghue* v *Stevenson* [1932] AC 562 by Lord Atkin as follows:

> A manufacturer of products which he sells in such form as to show that he intends them to reach the ultimate consumer in the form in which they left him with no reasonable possibility of intermediate examination, and with the knowledge that the absence of reasonable care in the preparation or putting up of the products will result in an injury to the consumer's life or property, owes a duty to the consumer to take reasonable care.

Six issues arise in relation to common law negligence which will be discussed in turn below: persons liable for a defective good; persons entitled to claim in respect of a defective good; proof of negligence; probability of intermediate examination of the goods; improper use of goods; and damage for which the producer is liable.

10.2.1 Persons liable in respect of defective goods

There is little doubt following *Donoghue* v *Stevenson* that manufacturers are liable for defects in goods created by them. Equally, designers, assemblers, installers and repairers will become liable where they negligently carry out their work (*Stennett* v *Hancock* [1939] 2 All ER 781; *Hartley* v *Moyah & Co.* [1953] 2 All ER 525; *Power* v *Bedford Motor Co. and Harris* [1959] IR 391). It is not only those who carry on a professional trade or calling who are liable; individuals may become liable for their own dubious DIY where the consequences of their actions are sufficiently obvious (*Sterna* v *Henkel Enterprises* (1972) 26 DLR 201).

The liability of distributors depends upon the degree to which they can be expected to inspect the goods prior to their distribution. In *Watson* v *Buckley* [1940] 1 All ER 174 hair dye had been distributed without prior inspection. The distributors became liable when the dye caused injury to a user. There are also dicta in that case which suggest that even where it is impractical to inspect the goods prior to their circulation, the distributor is under a duty to acquire the goods from a reputable dealer (at p. 181). However, where the goods are sold as seen with the time-honoured phrase 'with all faults' then this may denote that the user is under a duty to inspect the goods himself and ensure that they are safe for use (*Hurley* v *Dyke* [1979] RTR 265).

There is no reason in principle why a retailer stands in any different position than a wholesaler as regards liability (*Herschal* v *Stewart and Arden Ltd* [1940] 1 KB 155; *Andrews* v *Hopkinson* [1957] 1 QB 229; *Kubach* v *Hollands* [1937] 3 All ER 907). However, if the person injured is the buyer, he will have a more clear-cut action under the contract of sale. Even where it is a third party who is suing it is likely that he will be better off suing the wholesaler as the retailer is less likely to have funds or insurance to meet the claim. Furthermore, the courts are naturally sympathetic where the wholesaler or manufacturer is the real culprit.

10.2.2 Persons entitled to sue in respect of defective goods

There is little limit to the categories of people who may sue in respect of a defective good. The obvious person who is likely to sue is the user of the good itself, as was the case in *Donoghue* v *Stevenson*. However, bystanders and others likely to be injured by the defective good may also sue (*Stennett* v *Hancock* [1939] 2 All ER 578).

10.2.3 Proof of negligence

It has already been noted at the introduction to this chapter that the claimant must bring evidence to prove some negligent act, but that the law has mitigated this requirement to the extent that it has been suggested that the principle of *res ipsa loquitur* applies (per Lord Macmillan in *Donoghue* v *Stevenson* itself). Thus in *Hill* v *James Crowe* [1978] 1 All ER 812 a workman who was injured by a poorly-constructed packing case succeeded despite the fact that he had no evidence of how it had become so poorly constructed and the defendant gave evidence of its high standards of workmanship in general. The defect must have occurred as a matter of logic during construction by the defendant. Where the defect is not in the manufacture of the good, but in its design, the claimant will face a much harder struggle to show that the defendant was negligent. Where the good behaves in some unusual way, such as where a car violently swerves against the driver's control, then negligence within the design can probably be inferred. But where the defect is more subtle, cogent (probably expert) evidence will be required (*Rivtow Marine* v *Washington Iron Works* (1973) 40 DLR 530). Furthermore, the defendant may well have a defence that no amount of care could have foreseen the defect arising due to the state of scientific or technical knowledge existing at the time it left his hands (*Latimer* v *AEC* [1953] AC 643; *Roe* v *Ministry of Health* [1954] 2 QB 66). However, where this is the case the manufacturer will remain under a duty to inform users of his product where he subsequently acquires the necessary knowledge (*Hobbs (Farms) Ltd* v *Baxendale Chemicals Ltd* [1992] 1 Lloyd's Rep 54).

A failure on the part of the manufacturer to apply adequate warnings or instructions as to the use of the product may found an action in negligence (*Watson* v *Buckley* [1940] 1 All ER 174; *Vacwell Engineering Ltd* v *BDH* [1971] 1 QB 88). However, it is not every good which requires instructions as to its use. Where danger is obvious, such as in the use of a knife, liability will not attach (*Dehane* v *Deere & Co.* (1994) 106 DLR 385; *Thompson* v *Johnson & Johnson* [1991] 2 VR 449). In appropriate circumstances the duty may be discharged by giving the warning to retailers or professional users (*Homes* v *Ashford* [1950] 2 All ER 76) who then themselves come under a duty to warn the end user (*Clark* v *Army & Navy Co-Operative Society* [1903] 1 KB 155). Even where warnings have not been provided it remains incumbent upon the claimant to prove, as a matter of causation, that he would actually have heeded the warnings had they been given.

10.2.4 Probability of intermediate examination of the goods

It will be recalled that in *Donoghue* v *Stevenson* Lord Atkin defined the liability of a manufacturer as arising where:

> ... he intends them to reach the ultimate consumer in the form in which they left him with no reasonable possibility of intermediate examination.

However, in *Paine* v *Colne Valley Electricity Supply Co. Ltd* [1938] 4 All ER 803 the word 'probability' was substituted for the word 'possibility'. Certainly it seems rare that there will be no *possibility* of an intermediate examination, but in the modern manufacturing and distributing process an intermediate examination will be improbable in many circumstances (*Griffith* v *Arch Engineering Co. Ltd* [1968] 3 All ER 217). Furthermore, the test is objective: even if there has been an *actual* examination this will not necessarily absolve the manufacturer if, negligently, the defect is not discovered by that examination (*Clay* v *A. J. Crump & Sons Ltd* [1964] 1 QB 533).

10.2.5 Improper use of the goods

Where the user of goods uses them in the full knowledge of a defect then he may well be taken to have voluntarily assumed the risk of his injuries. Thus in *Gledhill* v *Liverpool Abattoir Ltd* [1957] 1 WLR 1028 a worker's action failed where he injured himself whilst using tools which were, to his knowledge, unsuitable.

Furthermore, the test is objective: it is possible to argue that the claimant *ought* to have known of the defect or misuse despite the fact that he did not (*Nitrigin Eireann Teoranta* v *Inco Alloys Ltd* [1992] 1 WLR 498). The user himself may also become liable to any third party who was injured where he continues using the goods in the knowledge of a defect (*Lambert* v *Lewis* [1979] RTR 61). However, if the user does not appreciate the entirety of the risk he is taking or that the consequences possibly to be caused by the defect were as serious as they in fact were then the manufacturer will not necessarily escape liability but may claim a contribution from the user (*Farr* v *Butter Bros* [1932] 2 KB 606).

10.2.6 Recoverable damages

Damages in respect of defective products are limited to damage to people and other property. By virtue of the economic loss rule damages in respect of the good itself are not covered (*Murphy* v *Brentwood District Council* [1990] 1 QB 373; *Nitrigin Eireann Teoranta* v *Inco Alloys* [1992] 1 WLR 498). The key difficulty is in determining whether one good can be considered as being a separate chattel where they are physically joined, for example where a defective gearbox causes damage to a car's engine or defective brake pads cause a car to crash. In the latter example, it is clear that where the goods were fitted to the claimant's existing good and they damage it, liability will attach (*Nitrigin Eireann Teoranta* v *Inco Alloys*). However, where the claimant has acquired the goods fitted with a defective part, liability will only attach where the defective element can be considered as a separate part of that which was acquired.

10.3 THE CONSUMER PROTECTION ACT 1987

The general rule as to liability under the 1987 Act is provided by s. 2(1):

> Subject to the following provisions of this Part, where any damage is caused wholly or partly by a defect in a product, every person to whom subsection (2) below applies shall be liable for the damage.

Despite its name the 1987 Act is not limited to consumers within the meaning attached to that phrase in other UK legislation. Any person who suffers damage caused by a defect in a product has a cause of action in respect of it. However, the types of loss for which a person may claim are limited to property of a kind used for (and intended to be used) privately. The Act likewise defines 'product' in broad terms as 'any goods' and includes 'a product which is comprised in another product' (s. 1(2)). 'Goods' are defined as including 'substances' by s. 45. The Act is therefore fairly clear as to its meaning, but certain issues remain which will be discussed in turn: those who may be sued under the Act; the meaning of 'a defect'; statutory defences; and recoverable damages.

10.3.1 Those who may be sued under the 1987 Act

Section 2 defines those who may be made liable under the 1987 Act in the following terms:

> (2) This subsection applies to—
> (a) the producer of the product;
> (b) any person who, by putting his name on the product or using a trade mark or other distinguishing mark in relation to the product, has held himself out to be the producer of the product;
> (c) any person who has imported the product into a member State from a place outside the member States in order, in the course of any business of his, to supply it to another.
> (3) Subject as aforesaid, where any damage is caused wholly or partly by a defect in a product, any person who supplied the product (whether to the person who suffered the damage, to the producer of any product in which the product in question is comprised or to any other person) shall be liable for the damage if—
> (a) the person who suffered the damage requests the supplier to identify one or more of the persons (whether still in existence or not) to whom subsection (2) above applies in relation to the product;
> (b) that request is made within a reasonable period after the damage occurs and at a time when it is not reasonably practical for the person making the request to identify all those persons; and
> (c) the supplier fails, within a reasonable period after receiving the request, either to comply with the request or to identify the person who supplied the product to him.

Potential defendants under the 1987 Act fall into four categories: producers, those who hold themselves out as producers, importers, and to a limited extent, suppliers. Producers are broadly defined by s. 1(2) as follows:

> 'producer' in relation to a product, means—
> (a) the person who manufactured it;
> (b) in the case of a substance which has not been manufactured but has been won or abstracted, the person who won or abstracted it;
> (c) in the case of a product which has not been manufactured, won or abstracted but essential characteristics of which are attributable to an industrial or other process having been carried out (for example, in relation to agricultural produce), the person who carried out that process . . .

The definition is, therefore, fairly straightforward. The only confusion which may arise is in relation to the third element of the definition which applies to products such as frozen peas which are difficult to describe as having been 'manufactured' but are nonetheless put through a process which may prove to be the source of the defect. There is no requirement that the product be supplied in the course of a business or for any consideration; nor is there any requirement that the producer be within the UK or the EC.

It is common practice for large producers to have their products manufactured according to their design or recipe by another firm who operates under licence for the main producer who attaches its brand to the product. Where this is the case, the person who attaches his name to the product is caught by s. 2(2)(b) and is treated in exactly the same way as the actual producer.

For the purposes of the 1987 Act an importer is a person who has brought the goods into the EEA from a producer outside it. The EEA is defined by the European Economic Area Act 1993 as encompassing members of the EU or the European Free Trade Area.

Suppliers are not liable under the 1987 Act simply by reason of their having supplied the goods in question. In order to become liable they must be unable, daliant or unwilling to supply the name of the producer (be he within the EEA or otherwise). This rule is subject to some further modification by the Act. First, those who do not supply in the course of a business are not deemed to be suppliers for the purposes of the Act by virtue of s. 4(1)(c). Secondly, s. 46 makes provision for goods supplied under a hire purchase agreement. Ordinarily the legal 'supplier' of such goods is the finance company and not the dealer, but the Act provides that the dealer shall be deemed to be the supplier for the purposes of the Act. Finally, and somewhat excessively, s. 46 provides that passengers on aircraft or ships shall not be deemed to have been supplied with the aircraft or ship.

10.3.2 The meaning of 'defective'

Section 3 of the 1987 Act defines a defect in the following terms:

> (1) Subject to the following provisions of this section, there is a defect in a product for the purposes of this Part if the safety of the product is not such as persons generally are entitled to expect; and for those purposes 'safety', in relation to a product, shall include safety with respect to products comprised in that product and safety in the context of death or personal injury.
>
> (2) In determining for the purposes of subsection (1) above what persons generally are entitled to expect in relation to a product all the circumstances shall be taken into account, including—
>
> (a) the manner in which, and purposes for which, the product has been marketed, its get-up, the use of any mark in relation to the product and any instructions for, or warnings with respect to, doing or refraining from doing anything with or in relation to the product;
>
> (b) what might reasonably be expected to be done with or in relation to the product; and
>
> (c) the time when the product was supplied by its producer to another;
>
> and nothing in this section shall require a defect to be inferred from the fact alone that the safety of a product which is supplied after that time is greater than the safety of the product in question.

Defining defectiveness in any all-embracing phrase is almost impossible given the variety of products on the marketplace. The Act gives the court a great deal of flexibility in determining whether or not a product is defective. In determining whether a good is defective the court may take into account the same factors as it does at common law: design defects, manufacturing defects, the warnings attached to goods and their instructions for use. Interestingly, the Act also permits the court to consider a good's marketing and 'get-up'. This could be used to suggest that a good is 'defective', for example, where a chain-saw is sold as a child's toy. The Act goes beyond the simple physical construction of the good and to this extent probably goes further than the common law.

10.3.3 Defences

Section 4 of the 1987 Act provides the following defences:

> (1) In any civil proceedings by virtue of this Part against any person ('the person proceeded against') in respect of a defect in a product it shall be a defence for him to show—
>
> (a) that the defect is attributable to compliance with any requirement imposed by or under any enactment or with any Community obligation; or
>
> (b) that the person proceeded against did not at any time supply the product to another; or
>
> (c) that the following conditions are satisfied, that is to say—
>
> (i) that the only supply of the product to another by the person proceeded against was otherwise than in the course of a business of that person's; and
>
> (ii) that section 2(2) above does not apply to that person or applies to him by virtue only of things done otherwise than with a view to profit; or
>
> (d) that the defect did not exist in the product at the relevant time; or
>
> (e) that the state of scientific and technical knowledge at the relevant time was not such that a producer of products of the same description as the product in question might be expected to have discovered the defect if it had existed in his products while they were under his control; or
>
> (f) that the defect—
>
> (i) constituted a defect in a product ('the subsequent product') in which the product in question had been comprised; and
>
> (ii) was wholly attributable to the design of the subsequent product or to compliance by the producer of the product in question with instructions given by the producer of the subsequent product.
>
> (2) In this section 'the relevant time', ... in relation to any other product, means—
>
> (a) if the person proceeded against is a person to whom subsection (2) of section 2 above applies [producers, those who hold themselves out as producers and importers], the time when he supplied the product to another;
>
> (b) if that subsection does not apply to that person in relation to the product, the time when the product was last supplied by a person to whom that subsection does apply in relation to the product.

Section 4 therefore creates six defences. The first, and most humorous, of these appears to display a lack of confidence in legislation and (understandably) EC regulation. It applies wherever the defect has arisen by virtue of *compliance* with legislation which was presumably enacted to ensure consumer safety in the first place. It appears that manufacturers of square bananas may therefore sleep in peace!

The second defence implemented by s. 4(1)(b) applies where the defendant did not put the product into circulation. Accordingly, where the goods are stolen or seized, the defendant will have a defence.

The third defence is split between producers and suppliers. Where a supplier supplies goods, even if he is unable to supply the name of his supplier, he may escape liability by showing that he did not act in the course of a business. The exception afforded to producers is, seemingly, somewhat narrower. Producers are exempt only if they did not act in any way for profit and in the course of a business. This exception appears only to cover someone who bakes a cake for a sick friend in hospital.

The fourth exception appears to cover the sensible situation where the defect arose after the goods had left the person's hands, for example where food becomes rancid through lack of refrigeration. It could not be supposed that a defect which manifests itself only after a period of time brings the producer within this exception, but was due to a design or manufacturing defect. In these circumstances the good would have been inherently defective at the time it was supplied.

The most controversial defence is the fifth defence, that of scientific knowledge. Here the defendant may show that a *producer of such products* (as opposed to any other category of person) would not have known of the defect at the time the goods were distributed. This brings an element of fault-based liability into the strict liability regime imposed by the 1987 Act as this is fundamentally the same rule as in common law negligence.

The sixth exception applies where a component has been produced and subsequently incorporated into another product. Here the defence is limited to defects which have been brought about through the design of the product in which they were incorporated or through the instructions supplied by the second producer. Seemingly, however, it is no defence to show that a manufacturing process (e.g., exposure to water or other chemicals) has brought about the defect, but such a situation would probably be covered by the fourth defence above.

10.3.4 Recoverable damages

The rules as to which damages are recoverable are essentially the same as those recoverable under common law negligence, but are proscribed by the 1987 Act under s. 5 which provides as follows:

> (1) Subject to the following provisions of this section, in this Part 'damages' means death or personal injury or any loss of or damage to any property (including land).
>
> (2) A person shall not be liable under section 2 above in respect of any defect in a product for the loss of or any damage to the product itself or for the loss of or any damage to the whole or any part of any product which has been supplied with the product in question comprised in it.
>
> (3) A person shall not be liable under section 2 above for any loss of or damage to any property which, at the time it is lost or damaged, is not—

(a) of a description of property ordinarily intended for private use, occupation or consumption, and

(b) intended by the person suffering the loss or damage mainly for his own private use, occupation or consumption.

(4) No damages shall be awarded to any person by virtue of this Part in respect of any loss of or damage to any property if the amount which would fall to be so awarded to that person, apart from this subsection and any liability for interest, does not exceed £275.

The overriding rule created by s. 5 is that damages may be awarded only in respect of personal injury or property damage. Any property damage must be to goods or land both ordinarily intended and actually intended for private use. A company which suffers loss to its premises and stock even if the premises were an ordinary house and the good a child's toy could not recover under the Act as despite the fact that they were of a *type* intended for private use they were not *actually* intended for such use.

The economic loss rules are proscribed by s. 5(2). No damages are recoverable in respect of damage to the product itself, and if the defective product is a component part of a composite good, any damage to the composite good (or another part of it) is not recoverable if it was supplied with the defective good. Thus if a car crashes because of defective brake pads supplied with it this would be irrecoverable. However, if the brake pads were fitted subsequently and proved defective they would not have been supplied as a component part of the whole and damage to the car and for any personal injury would be recoverable.

PART III
OWNERSHIP AND RISK

11 *The passing of property in goods*

11.1 INTRODUCTION

At the root of every contract of sale is the passing of property from the buyer to the seller. This is the conveyancing aspect involved in the contract of sale. The timing of the passing of the property has important ramifications in terms of risk, the right to sue in tort, the ability to pass a good title and the security of a party as against an insolvent other party.

One important preconception of which the newcomer to this area of law must divest himself is that the passing of property is related to the passing of possession or payment of the price; indeed in most cases the property in goods will pass before payment of the price or delivery.

The rules as to the transfer of the property in goods as between seller and buyer are contained in ss. 16 to 20B of the Sale of Goods Act 1979 (the '1979 Act'). Section 16 provides the general rule that the property in goods cannot pass unless and until the goods are ascertained. This is now subject to the recently introduced s. 20A which provides that the property in unascertained goods may pass where *inter alia* the price has been paid. Section 17 provides the general rule that the property is to pass at such time as the parties intend it to pass. The most important section is s. 18 which provides rules for the passing of property where the parties have not expressed an intention as to when the property shall pass.

11.2 FACTORS INDICATING A CONTRARY INTENTION

The general rule is that the property in the goods passes when it is intended to pass (1979 Act, s. 17(1)), and in ascertaining that intention regard is to be had to the terms of the contract, the conduct of the parties and the circumstances of the case (s. 17(2)). However s. 18 places a burden upon the party asserting a different intention owing to the opening words of the section: 'unless a different intention appears the following are rules for ascertaining the intention of the parties ...'. In many cases the parties have not addressed their minds to the question of when the property shall pass and it follows that s. 18 will apply. The best way of indicating a contrary intention is by express provision within the contract (*McEntire* v

Crossley Bros Ltd [1895] AC 457); this will be the case where there is a retention of title clause providing that the property will not pass until the price is paid.

In *Ward Ltd* v *Bignal* [1967] 1 QB 534 it was said that very little is needed in modern times to give rise to the inference that the property in specific goods is to pass only upon delivery or payment (per Diplock LJ). It is submitted that this cannot be correct in face of the plain words of s. 18, rule 1 that '. . . it is immaterial whether the time for payment or the time for delivery, or both, be postponed'.

Where the contract merely provides for deferment of payment of the price this will not ordinarily give rise to a contrary intention (*Dennant* v *Skinner & Collom* [1948] 2 KB 164; s. 18, rule 1). Whilst this is certainly the case in ordinary commercial transactions the courts have been willing, expressly or impliedly, to find a contrary intention where there is an element of fraud or criminal conduct. This has led to some inconsistency with the 1979 Act, for example in *Lacis* v *Cashmarts* [1969] 2 QB 400[1] Lord Parker CJ said:

> In my judgment when one is dealing with a case such as this, particularly a shop of the supermarket variety or the cash and carry variety, as this was, the intention of the parties quite clearly as it seems to me is that the property shall not pass until the price is paid. That as it seems to me is in accordance with the reality and in accordance with commercial practice.[2]

Another factor which has been argued to constitute a contrary intention is that the risk has passed to the buyer and therefore that the property has also passed. There is some support for this view (*The Parchim* [1918] AC 157; *Carlos Federspiel & Co. SA* v *Charles Twigg & Co. Ltd* [1957] 1 Lloyd's Rep 240) since in the ordinary course of events the risk passes with the property,[3] hence if the parties have stipulated that the risk is on the buyer it could be said that they have assumed in stating this that the property is also on the buyer. However, in *Re Anchor Line (Henderson Brothers) Ltd* [1937] Ch 1 the contrary reasoning was adopted. It was said that since the parties had stipulated that the risk was to pass to the buyer this indicated that the property had not passed because if it had such a stipulation would be unnecessary.

Some authors have suggested, in line with the New Zealand case of *Donaghy's Rope and Twine Co. Ltd* v *Wright, Stephenson & Co.* (1906) 25 NZLR 641, that where the seller merely advises the buyer to insure, this is an indication that the property has passed since the seller is reminding the buyer that the risk is on him. Whilst the reasoning here is attractive[4] this is not the *ratio* of the case, or indeed even suggested in the judgment.

Finally, any contrary intention should be expressed at the time the contract is made; the parties cannot provide for the property to pass at a different stage after

---

1. See also *Davies* v *Leighton* [1978] Crim LR 575; *R* v *Morris* [1984] AC 320; *Ingram* v *Little* [1961] 1 QB 31, at 49; *Phillips* v *Brooks* [1919] 2 KB 243; *Lake* v *Simmons* [1927] AC 487.
2. It should be noted that whilst this appears as a general statement of principle the buyer's conduct in this case was fraudulent.
3. However, there is no reason why the parties cannot agree that the risk and property shall pass independently under the agreement, or subsequent to the agreement by way of collateral contract, see *Donaghy's Rope and Twine Co. Ltd* v *Wright, Stephenson & Co.* (1906) 25 NZLR 641.
4. On the contrary view it should be noted that merely because the seller thinks that the risk is on the buyer, this does not necessarily indicate the *common* intention of the parties.

it has already done so. Thus in *Dennant* v *Skinner & Collom* [1948] 2 KB 164 the buyer purchased a car at an auction sale, the contract being made at the fall of the hammer. It was too late for the parties to negotiate a different stage for the property to pass, it having already done so under s. 18, rule 1.

11.3 SECTION 18, RULES 1, 2 AND 3

Section 18 of the 1979 Act, rules 1, 2 and 3 provide as follows:

> Rule 1.—Where there is an unconditional contract for the sale of specific goods in a deliverable state the property in the goods passes to the buyer when the contract is made, and it is immaterial whether the time of payment or the time of delivery, or both, be postponed.
>
> Rule 2.—Where there is a contract for the sale of specific goods and the seller is bound to do something to the goods for the purpose of putting them into a deliverable state, the property does not pass until the thing is done and the buyer has notice that it has been done.
>
> Rule 3.—Where there is a contract for the sale of specific goods in a deliverable state but the seller is bound to weigh, measure, test or do some other act or thing with reference to the goods for the purpose of ascertaining the price, the property does not pass until the act or thing is done and the buyer has notice that it has been done.

The general effect of the rules is largely self-explanatory; the property in specific goods in a deliverable state passes at the time the contract is made. If the goods are not in a deliverable state or some act has yet to be done to ascertain the price, the property does not pass until the goods are in a deliverable state or that act is done. Note that rules 2 and 3 do not prescribe that the property does pass when the act is done or the goods are in a deliverable state, only that the property does not pass until that is so. It is therefore possible for the property to pass some time after the goods are in a deliverable state or an act has been done to ascertain the price. However, in line with the general trend under the 1979 Act that the property passes to the buyer as soon as possible, the property would generally pass as soon as the act is done.

Each of the rules may be broken down into specified conditions. The phrase 'it is immaterial whether the time of payment or the time of delivery, or both, be postponed' has already been considered. The meaning of four other phrases must therefore be considered: 'an unconditional contract', 'specific goods', 'deliverable state', and 'bound to weigh, measure, test or do some other act or thing with reference to the goods for the purpose of ascertaining the price'.

11.3.1 'Unconditional contract'

It is submitted that the correct interpretation of the phrase 'unconditional contract' is a contract to which there are no conditions upon which the passing of the property depends. However, in *Varley* v *Whipp* [1900] 1 QB 513 it was held that a contract whereby there had been a breach of the condition implied by the 1979 Act, s. 13 (conformity with description) was not an 'unconditional contract for the sale of specific goods'. This leads to another interpretation of 'unconditional contract', i.e., a contract which contains no conditions unfulfilled by the seller which would give the buyer a right to reject. If this was the case, the property in goods would never pass where the buyer had a right to reject the goods. Such an interpretation does not rest easily with the structure of the 1979 Act and it is submitted that the former interpretation should be given (see too *Benjamin: Sale of Goods*, 5th ed. (London: Sweet & Maxwell, 1997), para. 5-020).

11.3.2 'Specific goods'

Section 61(1) of the 1979 Act defines specific goods as:

> ... goods identified and agreed on at the time a contract of sale is made; [and includes an undivided share, specified as a fraction or percentage, of goods identified and agreed on as aforesaid;] ...

The definition is targeted at individual goods, e.g., a car, a boat or a jumper However, it is quite possible to bring a bulk of generic goods (i.e., goods of the same type) within the description if they are sufficiently identified by the parties. In the Australian case of *Joseph Reid Pty Ltd* v *Schultz* (1949) 49 SR (NSW) 231 a sale of 'all the millable marketable hardwood timbers growing standing or being on the said land' was held to be a sale of specific goods. There is little doubt that if the parties agree to sell *all* the goods forming part of an identified bulk that that is a sale of specific goods, but where the parties add a subdefinition from within that bulk such as 'marketable' it becomes harder to decide whether the goods are sufficiently 'identified' by the parties to come within the definition. Where the goods are of a type such that an objective grade commonly used within the industry and readily understood between the parties is applied, there would be little difficulty. However, where a vague phrase such as 'marketable' is used it is submitted that this is too vague and *Joseph Reid Pty Ltd* v *Schultz* should not be followed. In *Kursell* v *Timber Operators and Contractors Ltd* [1927] 1 KB 298 it was held that a contract for the sale from a particular forest of such trees as became of a certain height over a 15-year period was not a contract for the sale of specific goods. The particular trees which would become the contract goods depended upon their rate of growth during the currency of the contract (15 years) and hence the goods were not identified. It had been argued during the case that the construction of the contract was such that the trees which passed under the contract were those trees which were of the particular height at the time the contract was made. Sargeant LJ considered that even if this was the case, the trees would not have been sufficiently identified, but merely identifiable.[5]

The latter part of the definition ('and includes an undivided share, specified as a fraction or percentage, of goods identified and agreed on as aforesaid') was introduced by the Sale of Goods (Amendment) Act 1995. It is important to note that the proprietary interest to which the definition applies is an *undivided* share;

5. Note that in *Lord Eldon* v *Hedley Bros* [1935] 2 KB 1 a sale of two stacks of hay was considered to be a sale of goods even though the contract provided that 'only good marketable hay, clear of mould' was to be delivered. This was construed as a contract for the sale of the hay with a right to reject those parts of the hay which were mouldy.

each shareholder owning part of the whole but no part individually. Furthermore, the definition only applies where the share is specified as a fraction or a percentage, not as a quantity from the bulk. If the share is described as a quantity from the bulk, even though the proportion of the share is readily ascertainable (e.g., 10 tonnes from a bulk of 100 is obviously 10 per cent), the definition does not apply and the goods would not be specific.

11.3.3 Deliverable state

Section 61(5) of the 1979 Act defines 'deliverable state' as follows:

> Goods are in a deliverable state within the meaning of this Act when they are in such a state that the buyer would under the contract be bound to take delivery of them.

In *Underwood Ltd* v *Burgh Castle Brick & Cement Syndicate* [1922] 1 KB 343 the sellers had contracted to buy a condensing machine which weighed several tonnes. The machine was still affixed to the floor of a factory and would take several days to detach and place on rail. It was held that the machine was not in a deliverable state even though it was complete in all its parts at the time the contract was made. Bankes LJ said, 'A "deliverable state" does not depend upon the mere completeness of the subject matter in all its parts. It depends on the actual state of the goods at the date of the contract and the state in which they are to be delivered by the terms of the contract.'

Problems arise under s. 18, rules 1 and 2 where the contract is arguably a contract for the supply of goods and services, or a contract for the sale of goods with a supplemental obligation on the seller to perform some act with or upon the goods (e.g., installing them). Where the contract is of the former type, the 1979 Act has no application; where the contract is of the latter type, the answer to whether the goods are in a deliverable state depends upon the importance of the supplemental obligation.

In *Head & Sons Ltd* v *Showfronts Ltd* [1970] 1 Lloyd's Rep 140 the sellers had agreed to sell and lay a large carpet to the buyers. The carpet was delivered to the buyers and was laying on the buyer's premises awaiting laying when it was stolen. It was held that the carpet was not in a deliverable state due to the importance of the last act to be performed by the sellers, namely to lay the carpet. Similarly in *Hendy Lennox (Industrial Engines) Ltd* v *Grahame Puttick Ltd* [1984] 1 WLR 485 the sellers had agreed to incorporate an engine into a generator system. The property in the engine was held not to have passed to the buyer until it had been incorporated into the generator. It should be noted that in *Head & Sons Ltd* v *Showfronts Ltd* the importance of the final stage was a large consideration. Had a large amount of work not been necessary, it is doubtful whether the laying of the carpet would have been sufficient a stage to justify delaying the passing of the property.[6]

One anomaly introduced by the Sale of Goods (Amendment) Act 1995 is that an undivided share in goods is defined as specific goods. It is difficult to see how

---

6. Although Mocatta J did state that the same result would have been achieved in the case of an ordinary household carpet being purchased; see also *Pritchett & Gold and Electrical Power Storage Company Limited* v *Currie* [1916] 2 Ch 515.

such a share could ever meet the requirement contained in s. 18, rules 1 to 3 that the goods be in a deliverable state. It seems that the Law Commission when making this provision envisaged that the property in such goods would pass in accordance with the intention of the parties, without meeting the criterion of being in a deliverable state (*Sale of Goods Forming Part of a Bulk*, Law Com. 215, para. 5.6).

11.3.4 'Bound to weigh, measure or test ... for the purpose of ascertaining the price'

This phrase forms the thrust of s. 18, rule 3. The first point to note about this rule is that it does not cover the situation where the seller is to weigh or measure a specified amount from a larger amount, e.g., three tonnes from a bulk of five tonnes. This relates to ascertaining the contract goods themselves, not ascertaining the price of the identified contract goods. Such a situation would be governed by s. 18, rule 5 and ss. 20A and 20B of the 1979 Act.

Weighing, measuring and testing the goods for the purpose of ascertaining the price must be distinguished from merely testing the goods to check that they are in conformity with the contract. In *Nanka-Bruce* v *Commonwealth Trust Ltd* [1922] AC 77 (abbreviating the facts for the purpose of exposition) the seller sold cocoa at an agreed price per bag. Each bag would be weighed at the buyer's premises upon delivery. The Privy Council held that the weighing was merely to check that the buyer had what he had bargained for; it did not suspend the passing of the property.

In *Tansley* v *Turner* (1835) 2 Bing 151 certain trees had been sold to the buyer at an agreed price per cubic foot. The trees had been measured but their size had not been calculated from those measurements. Tindal CJ said: 'I agree that if anything remained to be done by the seller, the property had not passed. But when I find that all that remained to be done was to ascertain the total number of cubic feet, ... the mere adding up of the whole is too trifling an incident to authorise us to say that the measurement was incomplete.' The case pre-dates the 1979 Act but clearly the principle in that case would still apply.

11.4 SECTION 18, RULE 4

Section 18, rule 4 provides as follows:

> When goods are delivered to the buyer on approval or on sale or return or other similar terms the property in the goods passes to the buyer:—
>
> (a) when he signifies his approval or acceptance to the seller or does any other act adopting the transaction;
>
> (b) if he does not signify his approval or acceptance to the seller but retains the goods without giving notice of rejection, then, if a time has been fixed for the return of the goods, on the expiration of that time, and, if no time has been fixed, on the expiration of a reasonable time.

The rule is largely self-explanatory. However, certain phrases must be discussed: 'on approval or on sale or return or other similar terms', 'when he signifies his approval or acceptance or does any other act adopting the transaction', and 'a reasonable time'.

11.4.1 'Sale on approval or sale or return or other similar terms'

At first glance a contract for sale on approval or sale or return would be thought to be easily distinguishable from other forms of contract. However, in practice such a contract may be very similar to a contract of sale subject to a condition subsequent that the buyer may return the goods or, more similarly, a contract of agency.

It is submitted that the only distinction which is of importance is the distinction between sale or return and agency. If the contract is one of agency then it is not a contract for the sale of goods at all since the agent never agrees to take the property in the goods (s. 2(1) of the 1979 Act), and the contract is not governed by the Act.

Some authors have suggested that a contract of sale subject to a condition subsequent (entitling him to return the goods) and a contract of sale or return or sale on approval should be treated as distinct forms of transaction with different consequences (*Benjamin: Sale of Goods*, 5th ed. (London: Sweet & Maxwell, 1997), para. 5-042). It is submitted that this is not so: the distinction between a contract of sale subject to a condition subsequent and a contract of sale or return is immaterial because either contract would be governed by s. 18, rule 4. This follows from the wording of rule 4 that it applies to a contract of sale 'on approval or on sale or return or *other similar terms*'. It is submitted that in practice a contract of sale or return and a contract of sale subject to a condition subsequent are so difficult to distinguish that the latter must fall within the phrase 'similar terms'. In practical terms, there is no difference between a contract whereby the buyer buys goods subject to a condition subsequent and a contract of sale or return. In either case the buyer takes the goods with an option to return them. In order to distinguish the two contracts a court would be required to look at whether the parties' course of dealing was such that an immediate sale had taken place, or whether the time of the sale was deferred until the buyer did an act adopting the transaction or a reasonable time passed.

Even if the courts did not follow this approach then at common law the same result may well be reached as far as risk is concerned, regardless of who holds the property at the time of the damage. In *Head* v *Tattersall* (1871) LR 7 Ex 7 the buyer purchased a horse which was warranted to have been hunted with the 'Bicester hounds', to be returned by a certain day if this proved to be false — 'otherwise the purchaser shall be obliged to keep the lot with all faults' (a contract of sale subject to a condition subsequent). The horse was injured through no fault of either party and then returned by the specified day. Cleasby B said:

> As a general rule, damage from the depreciation of a chattel ought to fall on the person who is the owner of it. Now here the effect of the contract was to vest the property in the buyer subject to a right of rescission in a particular event when it would revest in the seller. I think in such a case that the person who is eventually entitled to the property in the chattel ought to bear any loss arising from any depreciation in its value caused by an accident for which nobody is in

fault. Here the defendant is the person in whom the property is revested, and he must therefore bear the loss.

The distinction between sale or return and agency is capable of causing greater problems. In *Poole* v *Smith's Car Sales (Balham) Ltd* [1962] 1 WLR 744 the plaintiff, a car dealer, was short of storage space and so sent a car to the defendant, also a car dealer, on terms that if he sold it that he should pay a set sum for the car to the plaintiff. At first instance it was held that this was not a contract for sale or return. This was overturned on appeal, Ormerod LJ said:

> The judge held that this was not a transaction having the sharply defined qualities of a contract for sale or return as envisaged by the Sale of Goods Act, 1893. Mr Chedlow has raised the point that a contract for sale or return in the ordinary way is a contract where the person to whom the chattel is delivered is intending either to purchase the chattel or to send it back, whereas this was a contract where the defendants might expect to sell the car to one of their customers and if they could not sell it, then to return it, and, in those circumstances, it was not a contract for sale or return. So far as I am concerned, I am afraid I do not understand that distinction. I know of no authority for it, and in the absence of authority which is binding on this court, for my part, I would not make it.

With respect to his Lordship, there is a difference. In a contract of agency, the agent may hope to sell on the good to one of his customers but the parties never intend that the agent shall become the owner of the good. In a contract of sale or return, the buyer becomes the owner of the good, albeit only for an instant, between buying the good from the seller and becoming a seller himself. The difficulty is that in practice the transaction operates in the same way. Regardless of whether the 'middle man' is an agent or a buyer under a contract of sale or return, the good is passed to the end purchaser for a certain price and a certain price is paid to the seller (a lower price than paid by the end purchaser).

One cause of the difficulty in distinguishing the two types of transaction is that at first glance the perception of the transaction between the parties depends upon their expressed capacity. However, this is but one factor indicating the nature of the transaction. If the defendant in *Poole* v *Smith's Car Sales (Balham) Ltd* had been a yacht broker and the car a yacht the instant reaction would have been that the transaction was one of agency. Conversely, if the defendant had been a small shopkeeper and the good a sandwich, the immediate reaction would have been that the transaction was one of sale or return. However, where the transaction does not fit into these easily recognised situations, as it did not in *Poole* v *Smith's Car Sales (Balham) Ltd*, the picture becomes blurred. In any case, it is hard to see why the work title of the parties should affect the terms of the bargain struck by them.

One important aspect to be considered in determining the nature of the transaction is the freedom given to the buyer or agent to deal with the goods as he pleases. In *Re Nevill* (1870) LR 6 Ch App 397 the defendant was described as an agent of the plaintiff. He took cotton from the plaintiff on terms that he was not to pay for it unless he disposed of it, he returned an account at the end of each month and then paid a fixed price for the cotton used in that period. At all times the defendant treated the cotton as his own. It was held that he was not the agent of the plaintiff, but a buyer. Conversely, in *Weiner* v *Harris* [1910] 1 KB 285 jewellery was described as being sold on sale or return, but the buyer took the goods subject to the following conditions:

> The goods referred to in that book mentioned are your property, and to remain so until sold or paid for, they being only left with me for the purpose of sale or return, and not be kept as my own stock. The goods I receive from you are to be entered at cost price, and my remuneration for selling them is agreed at one half the profit ...

It was held that the contract was one of agency because there was no duty upon the middleman to buy the goods, merely to sell them; he was not to keep the goods as part of his own stock, he took his remuneration by way of a percentage and did not pay a fixed price. In all the circumstances he had agreed to perform a service for the seller and not to act as a buyer.

11.4.2 Approval, acceptance or an act adopting the transaction

Section 18, rule 4(a) provides that the property will pass when the buyer 'signifies his approval or acceptance to the seller or does any other act adopting the transaction'. There is relatively little difficulty about approval or acceptance, and seemingly no case law. It is worth noting, however, that approval must be signified to the seller — signifying approval to a third party would not satisfy the rule.

More difficulty is caused by the question of what constitutes 'any other act adopting the transaction'. It is quite clear that if the buyer sells the goods then this is an act adopting the transaction (*Genn* v *Winkel* (1912) 107 LT 434), indeed in a sale or return contract this is the whole object of the transaction. However, where the buyer pledges the goods more difficulty is caused. In *Kirkham* v *Attenborough* [1897] 1 QB 201 it was held that pledging goods is an act adopting the transaction because it was inconsistent with the buyer's free power to return the goods. In *Genn* v *Winkel* Buckley LJ said that if goods were given by A on 14 days sale or return to B and then B immediately passed them on to C on the same terms the buyer would be acting in accordance with his contract.[7] However, if B waited seven days and then passed the goods on to a C on 14 days sale or return that would be an act adopting the transaction because by doing so B had rendered himself unable to return the goods. This case is of some interest because Buckley LJ spoke in terms of the property passing immediately upon the contract between B and C, not upon the expiration of 14 days under the original contract of sale or return. It is possible that C may return the goods after just two days, allowing B to return them to A. However, according to Buckley LJ's analysis the property would have already passed to B. It would, therefore, seem that wherever the buyer performs an act which deprives him of his unconditional power to return the goods the property will pass to him. Arguably *Kirkham* v *Attenborough* goes further than this. In that case it was said that pledging of goods renders the buyer unable to return them 'without paying the pawnbroker' and hence that the pledging of goods

7. If C were to sell the goods this would operate to pass the property through B and B would be held to have bought the goods.

was an act adopting the transaction. It would seem, therefore, that if the buyer even conditionally parts with his power to return the goods he may be held to have adopted the transaction.

11.4.3 Lapse of time

Where a time has been fixed by the parties by which the goods must be returned if not sold or approved of, there is no difficulty — the property will pass when that time has expired. Where the parties have neglected to stipulate a particular time, the property will pass upon the expiration of a reasonable time. What constitutes a reasonable time is a question of fact for the court (1979 Act, s. 59). It is important, therefore, to adduce some evidence of what should be considered a reasonable time (*Poole* v *Smith's Car Sales (Balham) Ltd* [1962] 1 WLR 744). Furthermore, when determining a reasonable time the court may take into account the conduct of the parties (*Poole* v *Smith's Car Sales (Balham) Ltd*).

11.5 SECTION 18, RULE 5 AND SECTION 20A

Section 18, rule 5 provides as follows:

> (1) Where there is a contract for the sale of unascertained or future goods by description, and goods of that description and in a deliverable state are unconditionally appropriated to the contract, either by the seller with the assent of the buyer or by the buyer with the assent of the seller, the property in the goods then passes to the buyer; and the assent may be express or implied, and may be given either before or after the appropriation is made.
>
> (2) Where, in pursuance of the contract, the seller delivers the goods to the buyer or to a carrier or other bailee or custodier (whether named by the buyer or not) for the purpose of transmission to the buyer, and does not reserve the right of disposal, he is to be taken to have unconditionally appropriated the goods to the contract.
>
> (3) Where there is a contract for the sale of a specified quantity of unascertained goods in a deliverable state forming part of a bulk which is identified either in the contract or by subsequent agreement between the parties and the bulk is reduced to (or less than) that quantity, then, if the buyer under that contract is the only buyer to whom goods are then due out of the bulk—
>
> (a) the remaining goods are to be taken as appropriated to that contract at the time when the bulk is so reduced; and
>
> (b) the property in those goods then passes to that buyer.
>
> (4) Paragraph (3) above applies also (with the necessary modifications) where a bulk is reduced to (or to less than) the aggregate of the quantities due to a single buyer under separate contracts relating to that bulk and he is the only buyer to whom goods are then due out of that bulk.

Section 20A provides as follows:

> (1) This section applies to a contract for the sale of a specified quantity of unascertained goods if the following conditions are met—

(a) the goods or some of them form part of a bulk which is identified either in the contract or by subsequent agreement between the parties; and

(b) the buyer has paid the price for some or all of the goods which are the subject of the contract and which form part of the bulk.

(2) Where this section applies, then (unless the parties agree otherwise), as soon as the conditions specified in paragraphs (a) and (b) of subsection (1) are met or at such later time as the parties may agree—

(a) property in an undivided share in the bulk is transferred to the buyer; and

(b) the buyer becomes an owner in common of the bulk.

These provisions concern 'future goods by description', 'unascertained goods' and 'unascertained goods forming part of a bulk'. Future goods are defined in s. 61 of the 1979 Act as 'goods to be manufactured or acquired by the seller after the making of the contract of sale', thus a contract for the sale of 1,000 bicycles of description Y would fall within the definition.

'Unascertained goods' is not defined in the Act but includes generic goods such as 1,000 tonnes of wheat. The important point to note is that the seller is not bound to provide them from any particular source.

Finally, a bulk is defined as 'a mass or collection of goods of the same kind which — (a) is contained in a defined space or area; and (b) is such that any of the goods in the bulk are interchangeable with any other goods therein of the same number or quantity' (1979 Act, s. 61(1)).

In order to place the rule in context it is important to consider s. 16. Section 16 provides that, subject to s. 20A, no property may pass in unascertained goods until they are ascertained. Section 16 is worded in mandatory terms; it cannot be circumvented by agreement between the parties. Subject to this rule the parties may agree when the property is to pass.

Unless such a contrary intention appears, the 1979 Act prescribes three ways in which the property in unascertained goods may pass:

(a) The property in wholly unascertained goods, goods forming part of a bulk or future goods may pass by unconditional appropriation under rule 5(1).

(b) The property in unascertained goods forming part of a bulk may pass by exhaustion under rule 5(3).

(c) The property in unascertained goods forming part of a bulk may pass by payment of the price, or a part thereof, under s. 20A.

11.5.1 Unconditional appropriation under section 18, rule 5(1)

In order for the property to pass under s. 18, rule 5(1) certain conditions must be met:

(a) the goods must be in a deliverable state (as to which see section 11.3.3);

(b) the goods must be unconditionally appropriated to the contract;

(c) the buyer must assent to the seller's appropriation or *vice versa* and, in the case of future goods by description;

(d) the goods must conform to that description.

In addition an issue arises as to the possibility of the property in future goods passing prior to their completion where the parties express an intention contrary to rule 5(1).

11.5.1.1 Unconditional appropriation Put briefly unconditional appropriation is the setting aside of goods such that that particular batch becomes irrevocably attached to the contract. In order for there to be an unconditional appropriation there must be a physical separation of the contractual goods from any bulk of which they form part (*Healy* v *Howlett & Sons* [1917] 1 KB 337; *Laurie & Morewood* v *John Dudin & Sons* [1926] 1 KB 223; *Wardar's (Import & Export) Co. Ltd* v *W. Norwood & Sons Ltd* [1968] 2 QB 663). Arguably, however, there must be something more than this in order for the property to pass. In *Carlos Federspiel & Co. SA* v *Charles Twigg & Co. Ltd* [1957] 1 Lloyd's Rep 242 Pearson J said:

> I think that one can distinguish these principles:
>
> First, rule 5 of s. 18 of the Act is one of the rules for ascertaining the intention of the parties as to the time at which the property in the goods is to pass to the buyer unless a different intention appears. Therefore the element of common intention must always be borne in mind. A mere setting apart or selection of the seller of the goods which he expects to use in performance is not enough. If that is all he can change his mind and use those goods in performance of some other contract and use some other goods in performance of this contract. To constitute an appropriation of the goods to the contract the parties must have had, or be reasonably supposed to have had, an intention to attach the contract irrevocably to those goods, so that the goods and no others are the subject of the sale and become the property of the buyer.
>
> Secondly, it is by agreement of the parties that the appropriation, involving a change of ownership, is made, although in some cases the buyer's assent to an appropriation by the seller is conferred in advance by the contract itself or otherwise.
>
> Thirdly, an appropriation by the seller, with the assent of the buyer, may be said always to involve an actual or constructive delivery. If the seller retains possession he does so as bailee of the buyer. There is a passage in *Chalmers' Sale of Goods Act*, 12th edn, at p. 75, where it is said: 'In the second place, if the decisions be carefully examined, it will be found that in every case where the property has been held to pass, there has been an actual or constructive delivery of the goods to the buyer.' I think that is right, subject only to this possible qualification, that there may be after such constructive delivery an actual delivery still to be made by the seller under the contract. Of course that is quite possible, because delivery is the transfer of possession, whereas appropriation transfers ownership. So there may be first an appropriation, constructive delivery, whereby the seller becomes bailee for the buyer, and then a subsequent actual delivery involving actual possession, and when I say that I have in mind in particular the two cases cited, namely, *Aldridge* v *Johnson*, and *Langton* v *Higgins*.
>
> Fourthly, one has to remember s. 20 of the Sale of Goods Act, whereby the ownership and the risk are normally associated. Therefore as it appears that there

> is thinking that on the construction of the relevant documents, that the goods were, at all material times, still at the seller's risk, that is prima facie an indication that the property had not passed to the buyer.
>
> Fifthly, usually but not necessarily, the appropriating act is the last act to be performed by the seller. For instance, if delivery is to be taken by the buyer at the seller's premises and the seller has completed his part of the contract and has appropriated the goods when he has made the goods ready and has identified them and placed them in position to be taken by the buyer, and has so informed, and if the buyer agrees to come and take them, that is the assent to the appropriation. But if there is a further act, an important and decisive act to be done by the seller, then there is prima facie evidence that probably the property does not pass until the final Act is done.[8]

In that case the seller had agreed to manufacture bicycles and to ship them to the buyer. The bicycles had been made and placed in containers with the buyer's address on them ready for shipment. Before the goods were shipped the seller became insolvent. The buyers claimed that the property had passed to them. It was held that the property had not so passed seemingly because the fifth element mentioned above, that the seller was bound to ship the goods, had not been completed.

Conversely, where there remains little or nothing to be done under the contract it would seem that the property may pass simply by physical separation of the contract goods from the bulk. In *Aldridge* v *Johnson* (1857) 7 E & B 885 the buyer had agreed to buy a quantity of barley from a particular bulk held by the seller. The buyer attended the seller's premises and filled the barley into sacks. The seller later emptied those sacks. It was held that the property had passed to the buyer as soon as it was placed in the sacks. Similarly, in *Hendy Lennox Ltd* v *Grahame Puttick Ltd* [1984] 2 All ER 152 the seller had agreed to incorporate engines into generator systems and supply these to the buyer. The seller duly completed the generators and sent delivery notes to the buyer. It was held that the property passed when the generators were ready for delivery, despite the fact that they were lying in the seller's warehouse.

11.5.1.2 Assent Rule 5(1) provides that the goods may be unconditionally appropriated by the buyer with the assent of the seller or the seller with the assent of the buyer and that the assent may be express or implied. Most commonly the appropriation will be by the seller and the assent implied.

As a general rule, the courts are less stringent as regards the requirement of assent. In many cases the courts are willing to find an implied assent from the facts of the case or frequently the point is not even raised (see generally *Rhode* v *Thwaites* (1827) 6 B & C 388; *Pletts* v *Beattie* [1896] 1 QB 519; *Wardar's (Import & Export) Co. Ltd* v *W. Norwood & Sons Ltd* [1968] 2 QB 663; *Hendy Lennox (Industrial Engines) Ltd* v *Grahame Puttick Ltd* [1984] 1 WLR 485). In *Pignatoro* v *Gilroy* [1919] 1 KB 459 the seller, in accordance with the buyer's request, sent the buyer a delivery note together with a request that the buyer collect the goods

8. It is worth noting that Pearson J appears to express this part of the rule somewhat tentatively. In reaching this decision it would seem likely that the cases of *Langton* v *Higgins* (1859) 4 H & N 402 and *Pignatoro* v *Gilroy* [1919] 1 KB 459 were being considered.

as the seller was short of space. The buyer failed to collect the goods and they were stolen a month later. It was held that the buyer's assent could be inferred from a month's silence. Similarly, in *Aldridge* v *Johnson* (1857) 7 E & B 885 the buyer's assent was inferred from the fact that he inspected the goods in bulk and sent his agents to collect the goods.[9]

11.5.1.3 Conformity with description Rule 5(1) states that the property shall pass when 'goods of that description' are appropriated. The issue which this raises is whether the property in the goods shall pass only if the goods conform to their description within the meaning of s. 13 of the 1979 Act, or whether the property is to pass to the buyer subject to a right to reject the goods and revest the property in the seller. The issue is similar to that of the phrase 'unconditional contract' (see section 6.4.1) following the case of *Varley* v *Whipp* [1900] 1 QB 513. In that case it was held that if the seller said that he would sell a horse in his stable, and it transpired that it was not a horse but a cow then no property would pass (see also *Vigers* v *Sanderson* [1901] 1 KB 608). Clearly where this is the case it would seem strange if any property did pass to the buyer. However, where the goods merely fail to conform in some minor respect, it would be contrary to the scheme of the 1979 Act if no property were to pass to the buyer. In *Kwei Tek Chao* v *British Traders and Shippers Ltd* [1954] 2 QB 459 it was said that where the buyer has a right to reject, he takes a conditional property in the goods and if he chooses to reject them the property will revest in the seller.

The position is, therefore, somewhat unsatisfactory. If the goods do not meet their description in a fundamental aspect, the property will not pass. However, if the goods merely fail to answer their description in a minor aspect, it would appear that the property may pass to the buyer, subject to a right to reject them.

11.5.1.4 Appropriation by delivery Rule 5(2) provides that where goods are delivered to a bailee for the purpose of transmission to the buyer, this shall be deemed to be an unconditional appropriation of the goods. However, in order for the property to pass, the other stipulations of rule 5(1) regarding there being an unconditional contract, that the goods be in a deliverable state and that there be assent still apply. Furthermore, mere delivery to a carrier will not be sufficient to pass the property unless the goods have been ascertained in accordance with s. 16 of the 1979 Act. For example, if 100 boxes containing the same type of good are placed on a lorry for delivery to three separate buyers, none of the goods will have been ascertained and no property will pass to the buyers (*Healy* v *Howlett & Sons* [1917] 1 KB 337).

11.5.2 Ascertainment by exhaustion

Section 18, rule 5(3) and (4) provides as follows:

> (3) Where there is a contract for the sale of a specified quantity of unascertained goods in a deliverable state forming part of a bulk which is identified either in the contract or by subsequent agreement between the parties

9. In these circumstances, however, one would expect the assent to come from the seller and not the buyer.

> and the bulk is reduced to (or to less than) that quantity, then, if the buyer under that contract is the only buyer to whom goods are then due out of the bulk—
>
> (a) the remaining goods are to be taken as appropriated to that contract at the time when the bulk is so reduced; and
>
> (b) the property in those goods then passes to the buyer.
>
> (4) Paragraph (3) above applies also (with the necessary modifications) where a bulk is reduced to (or to less than) the aggregate of the quantities due to a single buyer under separate contracts relating to that bulk and he is the only buyer to whom goods are then due out of that bulk.

Rule 5(3) was introduced by the Sale of Goods (Amendment) Act 1995, s. 1(2). Its introduction was prompted by the decision in *Karlshamns Oliefabriker* v *Eastport Navigation Corpn (The Elafi)* [1981] 2 Lloyd's Rep 679, which acts as a good illustration of the rule. In *The Elafi* the buyers had contracted to buy 6,000 tonnes of copra from the sellers to be delivered to Hamburg. The sellers then shipped 16,000 tonnes first to Rotterdam and then to Hamburg. The 10,000 tonnes not purchased by the buyers was intended for other buyers to be delivered at Rotterdam. During the course of the journey the buyers purchased a further small quantity from one of these other buyers. The ship called at Rotterdam and discharged all the copra intended for the other buyers. It was held that at this stage the property passed to the buyers since all the cargo remaining on the ship was intended for them; it had been ascertained by exhaustion.

Rule 5(3) only applies where there is a contract for the sale of a specified *quantity* of unascertained goods forming part of a bulk. It does not apply where there is to be a sale of all the goods forming part of a bulk, such a contract would be for the sale of specific goods (see section 11.3.2). Similarly, where there is a sale of a *fraction or percentage* of the bulk then rule 5(3) would not apply, this again would be a contract for the sale of specific goods. Furthermore, if the buyer had paid the price, or part of it, then it is possible that the property would pass under s. 20A of the 1979 Act at the time the contract was made.

11.5.3 Passing of the property under section 20A

The Sale of Goods (Amendment) Act 1995 introduced a new provision whereby the property in goods forming part of a bulk could pass to the buyer before physical separation. Prior to this there is no doubt that physical separation was required in order for the goods to meet the requirement of s. 16 of the 1979 Act that they be ascertained. Section 16 is now expressed to be subject to s. 20A of the 1979 Act. Section 20A requires consideration of four fundamental issues: which contracts the section applies to, calculation of the size of the share, the nature of the proprietary interest, and dealings by the seller and other co-owners in the buyer's goods.

11.5.3.1 Contracts to which section 20A applies Section 20A(1) provides as follows:

> (1) This section applies to a contract for the sale of a specified quantity of unascertained goods if the following conditions are met—
>
> (a) the goods or some of them form part of a bulk which is identified either in the contract or by subsequent agreement between the parties; and

> (b) the buyer has paid the price for some or all of the goods which are the subject of the contract and which form part of the bulk.

The definition is largely self-explanatory. However, the phrase 'specified quantity of unascertained goods' requires some further explanation. First, the quantity must be specified as an amount, not a fraction or a percentage. For example, a contract for the sale of 10 tonnes from a bulk of 100 would be within the section; a contract for the sale of 10 per cent of 100 tonnes would not be. This seems at first to be a rather arbitrary distinction. However, the new definition of specific goods now includes a share specified as a fraction or percentage of a whole bulk. A sale of a percentage of an identified bulk would now be a sale of specific goods with the property passing in accordance with the parties' intentions. Likewise, if there was a sale of the whole of a bulk this too would be a sale of specific goods.

Although a sale of a share of a bulk specified as a fraction or a percentage would come within the definition of specific goods it seems unlikely that such a share would pass in accordance with s. 18, rule 1, 2 or 3 since many of the provisions of the 1979 Act would be inapplicable to such contracts. For example, rules 1, 2 and 3 require that the goods be in a 'deliverable state'. If there was a contract for the sale of 40 per cent of a racehorse it would be difficult to see how that share could be in a 'deliverable state' without physical separation from the remaining 60 per cent of the racehorse. In any case, given that this form of co-ownership is in an *undivided* share, the phrase seems totally inappropriate. Finally, under the 1979 Act physical delivery and payment are concurrent obligations and it is difficult to see how the Act would apply where no physical delivery is contemplated. It seems that the Law Commission when considering these matters decided to leave these questions to the intention of the parties (*Sale of Goods Forming Part of a Bulk*, Law Com. 215, para. 5.3 *et seq*). Given that the general trend under the Act is that the property shall pass as soon as possible it is submitted that the presumption in such situations is that the property in the undivided share shall pass at the time the contract is made unless the facts of the case indicate a different intention.

A further problem which arises is where the quantity is specified by an option on the part of one of the parties, for example where there is a sale of '100 gallons of oil, 2 per cent more or less'. Since s. 20A quantifies the share by being that amount paid for by the buyer, the size of the share would not be affected by such an agreement. This eliminates any practical difficulties and the only issue is whether the section applies at all. It is submitted that such a contract should come within the definition since the goods are sufficiently specified. Different considerations would apply where the amount was almost entirely unspecified, for example where there was a contract for 'such amount of oil as the seller can supply from [an identified bulk]'.

11.5.3.2 Calculation of shares Section 20A(3) to (6) provides as follows:

> (3) Subject to subsection (4) below, for the purposes of this section the undivided share of a buyer in a bulk at any time shall be such share as the quantity of goods paid for and due to the buyer out of the bulk bears to the quantity of goods in the bulk at that time.
>
> (4) Where the aggregate of the undivided shares of buyers in a bulk determined under subsection (3) above would at any time exceed the whole of the bulk at that time, the undivided share in the bulk of each buyer shall be

reduced proportionately so that the aggregate of the undivided shares is equal to the whole bulk.

(5) Where a buyer has paid the price for only some of the goods due to him out of a bulk, any delivery to the buyer out of the bulk shall, for the purposes of this section, be ascribed in the first place to the goods in respect of which payment has been made.

(6) For the purpose of this section payment of part of the price for any goods shall be treated as payment for a corresponding part of the goods.

The effect of these provisions is to make the buyer's share fluctuate in accordance with the amount he has paid at any time and the amount in the bulk. The general rule is contained in s. 20A(3) that the buyer's share is 'such share as the quantity of goods paid for and due to the buyer out of the bulk bears to the quantity of goods in the bulk at that time'.

Thus if there is a bulk of 1,000 tonnes and A contracts to buy and pays for 100 tonnes, B pays for 300 and C pays for 200, A holds a 10 per cent share, B holds 30 per cent and C holds 20 per cent. The seller (S) holds the remaining 40 per cent. If B had only paid for 15 tonnes of the 30 that he contracted for, his share would be 15 per cent and S's 55 per cent and so on. If B takes delivery of 200 tonnes, the bulk is reduced to 800 tonnes. A's share is reduced to 100/800 tonnes, i.e., an eighth; B's share is likewise reduced to 100/800 tonnes; C's share becomes 200/800 tonnes, i.e., a quarter; S's share increases to 400/800, i.e., a half. Note that the respective amounts in respect of A, C and S do not change but simply, as a mathematical process, the proportionate shares change.[10]

Despite the apparent ease of operation of the provisions there are some technicalities:

(a) *The seller bears the first part of any diminution in the bulk, the buyers then bear it proportionately* This follows because the shares are defined under s. 20A(3) in terms of the amount that the buyer[11] has paid in relation to the amount in the bulk at any time. Thus if A pays for 10 tonnes from a bulk of 30 tonnes and B pays for a further 10 tonnes then the shares are respectively one third to A, one third to B and one third to S. If the bulk is damaged such that 10 tonnes are destroyed then, in accordance with s. 20A(3), the amount that the buyers have paid for remains the same but the amount in the bulk *at that time* has reduced. A and B's shares thus increase to 50 per cent in accordance with s. 20A(3). As a process of mathematics, however, since the bulk is now smaller, the physical quantity of their shares remains the same. Section 20A(4) does not at this stage apply because the amount paid for does not exceed the bulk. If a further 10 tonnes are destroyed then, in accordance with s. 20A(4), A and B's shares shall be reduced proportionately. In effect the shares remain the same, i.e., 50 per cent each, but the amount that each share is worth is diminished. However, the effect of s. 20A(4) is that no particular buyer bears the loss.

(b) *The buyers and the seller bear the loss for any diminution in the quality of the goods proportionately* Section 20A only deals with the *quantity* in the bulk at any time, not its quality. However, if some of the wheat is destroyed such that

10. Note, however, that the rights held by each party relate to an undivided interest in the bulk; each owns the whole jointly, not a specified portion.

11 As opposed to a co-owner (which would include the seller).

it no longer forms part of the bulk then, as explained above, the seller bears the loss. This produces a peculiar anomaly.

(c) *The seller may replenish or add to the bulk at any time* Section 20A(3) simply states that the buyer's share relates to the amount of goods in the bulk *at that time*; there is no prohibition on the seller adding goods to the bulk and diminishing the buyer's proportionate share in relation to the whole. The position is more complex where goods are removed from the bulk by the seller or another co-owner, accordingly this is discussed in more detail in section 11.5.3.4.

No provision is made for the situation where the seller, by accident or design, adds to the bulk goods of a different quality (e.g., differing grades of wheat). Here great difficulty would be caused because 'bulk' is defined as a mass of goods which are interchangeable with one another — the bulk would no longer be a bulk within the meaning of the 1979 Act. It is submitted that the best solution to this problem is that this be treated as a diminution in the quality of the bulk as a whole. The buyer will then retain his proprietary interest in the goods (in a lesser proportion than before) and be left with a personal remedy against the seller as bailee for interference with those goods.

(d) *Payment by or delivery to the buyer shall in the first place be ascribed to the goods in the bulk* Part payment or part delivery are common practice in commerce. Section 20A(5) provides that any delivery to the buyer shall be ascribed to the goods in the bulk. Thus where the buyer contracts to buy 20 tonnes from a bulk of 100, pays for 10 and then takes delivery of 10 his share in the bulk shall cease. It is not open to the buyer to contend that the 10 tonnes delivered to him were the 10 tonnes not yet paid for. Likewise, subsection (6) provides that any payment of part of the price shall be treated as payment for a corresponding part of the goods. Any payment under the contract for the goods will, therefore, provide the buyer with a share in the bulk.

11.5.3.3 The proprietary interest The proprietary interest held by the buyer (and indeed the seller) is similar to a joint tenancy of land. Each buyer takes an undivided share in the bulk. Individually, the buyer cannot say that he owns any specific part of the whole, but together the buyers and the seller can say that they own the whole.

11.5.3.4 Dealings with the goods Section 20B provides as follows:

> (1) A person who has become an owner in common of a bulk by virtue of section 20A above shall be deemed to have consented to—
>
> (a) any delivery of goods out of the bulk to any other owner in common of the bulk, being goods which are due to him under his contract;
>
> (b) any removal, dealing with, delivery or disposal of goods in the bulk by any other person who is an owner in common of the bulk in so far as the goods fall within that co-owner's undivided share in the bulk at the time of the removal, dealing, delivery or disposal.
>
> (2) No cause of action shall accrue to anyone against a person by reason of that person having acted in accordance with paragraph (a) or (b) of subsection (1) above in reliance on any consent deemed to have been given under that subsection.
>
> (3) Nothing in this section or section 20A above shall—

(a) impose an obligation on a buyer of goods out of a bulk to compensate any other buyer of goods out of that bulk for any shortfall in the goods received by that other buyer;

(b) affects any contractual arrangement between buyers of goods out of a bulk for adjustments between themselves; or

(c) affect the rights of any buyer under his contract.

The purpose of s. 20B is to facilitate normal trading in goods by restricting the rights held by a buyer and by giving his deemed consent to normal trading. The difficulty created by conferring a proprietary right in the goods upon the buyer is that he potentially has a claim against the other buyer, the seller and third parties in conversion and or breach of a contract of bailment.

The key subsection is s. 20B(2) which provides that no cause of action shall accrue between co-owners where one has acted in reliance upon s. 20B(1).

Section 20B(1)(b) causes little difficulty. It permits a co-owner to deal with the goods so far as they fall within his share *at the time of the dealing*. One co-owner cannot thus deal with another co-owner's share under this subsection.

Of greater difficulty is s. 20B(1)(a). This deems consent to another co-owner taking delivery of goods due 'under his contract'. Clearly where there has been no loss or destruction to the goods this provision sensibly allows one co-owner to take delivery of the goods due to him without fear that he is dealing with another's share. But what is the position where part of the goods are destroyed?

The difficulty here is that the phrase 'goods due to him under his contract' are used in s. 20B(1)(a) as opposed to the words 'in so far as the goods fall within that co-owner's undivided share in the bulk at the time of the removal' used in s. 20B(1)(b). For example, A and B contract with S to buy 50 tonnes each of the 100 tonnes of wheat on S's ship. Fifty tonnes are destroyed by fire. The next day S's ship delivers B's 50 tonnes, i.e., all the remaining wheat. In this situation can B hold up the shield created by s. 20B(2) and say to A that he has no cause of action against him? B can rightly say that 50 tonnes are 'due to him under his contract' and that, in accordance with s. 20B(1)(a) A is deemed to have consented to his taking delivery of them. Further, that he, B, had acted in reliance upon this. A could argue that the goods were no longer *due* to B since he bore the risk of any destruction along with A under the normal *res perit domino* rule contained in s. 20. Clearly, at the time of the destruction the property was held by both A and B and under s. 20 they accordingly held the risk. Should B be protected by the blanket wording of s. 20B(2) that 'no cause of action shall lie'?

It may well be the case that A has an action against S as bailee, but this may be worthless through S's insolvency or S may not be liable as a bailee through taking due care. In any event such an action would be a personal one against S without the security that a proprietary right gives. Whilst the position remains unclear there seems no reason in principle why A should be in a worse position simply because B's was the first port of call.

11.6 RETENTION OF TITLE AND SIMILAR CLAUSES

It is common practice in commercial contracts for the sale of raw materials to include a clause entitling the seller to either: (a) retain title in the goods which he supplies or the manufactured product; or (b) to be entitled to the proceeds of sale. The purpose of such clauses is to protect the seller against the insolvency of the buyer in respect of sums outstanding by the buyer under the contract of sale.

The essence of the problem is that in the event that the buyer becomes insolvent, if the seller has his remedy only under the contract of sale, this is a personal remedy. If the buyer is insolvent then, by definition, he cannot meet all his debts. Under the insolvency rules a personal remedy ranks equally with all the other creditors who are owed money by the insolvent party. In practice, these debts will not be paid in full but only an equal proportion of all the debts will be paid to the creditors. If the seller has a proprietary right over the goods which he sold, or the manufactured goods or the proceeds of sale, this means that he still 'owns' them for the purposes of the law; the buyer only holding them as bailee or trustee in favour of the seller. Such items are not brought into account as being the assets of the insolvent buyer and the seller can recover in full.

Clauses protecting the seller in such cases have become known generally as *Romalpa* clauses following the case of *Aluminium Industrie Vaasen BV* v *Romalpa Aluminium Ltd* [1976] 1 WLR 676 (CA). However, the actual decision in that case is less one on retention of title than on a claim to the proceeds of sale. The leading case on retention of title is probably *Clough Mill Ltd* v *Martin* [1985] 1 WLR 111 (CA) together with *Re Bond Worth Ltd* [1980] Ch 228. In the *Romalpa* case a seller was held entitled to the proceeds of sale and in the *Clough Mill* case the seller was entitled to claim back goods which he had sold. As will be seen, however, the practical application of the law in these two cases has now been restricted so much as to be almost beyond use as a general rule. Much depends in any case upon its own facts. Additionally, it should be noted that the cases are exceedingly difficult to reconcile and the law is best described as a 'maze if not a minefield' (*Hendy Lennox Ltd* v *Grahame Puttick Engines Ltd* [1984] 1 WLR 485).

Clauses claiming title in the goods themselves or a finished product will be examined before turning to cases claiming a right to the proceeds of sale.

11.6.1 Pure retention of title clauses

In the *Clough Mill* case the seller's had sold yarn to the buyer who intended to make fabric from it. The contract of sale provided that the property in the yarn remained with the seller until paid for. The buyer was, however, permitted to use the yarn in its manufacturing process and the seller was accordingly to become the owner of any product made from yarn supplied by them.

When considering the *Clough Mill* case another case becomes important: *Re Bond Worth* (above). In this case it was held that any clause which creates an interest in property which was defeasible upon payment of a debt created a charge. A charge over a company's assets is required to be registered in order to be binding. Naturally, in practice, a charge created by a retention of title clause is rarely registered and it was not in *Re Bond Worth*.

Re Bond Worth was distinguished by the Court of Appeal in the *Clough Mill* case on the basis that it did not create a charge over the company's property since the property never passed to the buyer in the first place. Accordingly, it seems that on the bare face of it a clause providing that the property in goods shall not pass until payment of the price will be operative.

However, the operation of the rule in the *Clough Mill* case is restricted in practice because many raw materials supplied will lose their identity in the course of manufacture. It seems that here the seller's title can be extinguished. For example, in *Borden (UK) Ltd* v *Scottish Timber Products Ltd* [1981] Ch 25 resin was supplied to the manufacturer of chipboard. This was subsequently combined with wood chips to make the chipboard and it was held that pursuant to the intention of the parties the seller's title ceased once it was used in the manufacturing process. By contrast, in *Hendy Lennox (Industrial Engines) Ltd* v *Grahame Puttick Ltd* [1984] 1 WLR 485 engines were attached to generator units and whilst it took several hours to separate the two they were separately identifiable and hence the seller's title was not extinguished.

That each case is dependent upon its facts is clear from the case of *Re Peachdart Ltd* [1984] 1 Ch 131. In that case leather had been sold for the purpose of incorporation into handbags. A reservation of title clause provided not only that the seller retained title in the unworked material, but also in the finished or part-completed products. It was held, as with the *Borden* case, that the seller's title in the goods must cease once it had lost its characteristics as a separate item, and at that point it became a charge which was void for want of registration. It seems, therefore, that the effect of the clause depends not only upon its wording, but the stage of manufacture that has *actually* been reached.

11.6.2 Claims to the proceeds of sale

The origins to a claim to the proceeds of sale come from the *Romalpa* case itself. In that case aluminium foil had been sold subject to a clause which provided that the goods remained the property of the sellers until all sums due to them were discharged. It was anticipated that the foil would be used in the buyer's manufacturing process, but in fact they sold it on to a third party. It was conceded that the buyer must hold the foil as bailee of the seller and upon this the Court of Appeal held that a fiduciary relationship existed between the seller and buyer. On the basis of this relationship they were held entitled to trace into the proceeds of the sale and the buyer was obliged to account for it.

Since the *Romalpa* case there have been other cases which suggest that a fiduciary relationship will not so easily be inferred from the circumstances. Thus in *Re Andrebell* [1984] 3 All ER 407 the fact that the buyers were afforded a 'credit period' suggested that they were free to use the proceeds of sale as they chose, rather than keep them in a separate account. Furthermore, they were not required to keep the goods separate from their own goods. In the usual course of events, these would be required where a fiduciary relationship existed (see also *Hendy Lennox (Industrial Engines) Ltd* v *Grahame Puttick Ltd* [1984] 1 WLR 485). Certainly, in the ordinary course of events it is presumed that where a buyer sells goods which he has obtained under a contract of sale, that he does so on his own account and not on behalf of the seller (*E. Pfeiffer Weinkellerei-Weineinkauf* v *Arbuthnot Factors* [1988] 1 WLR 150).

Indeed it seems that the courts will be reluctant to find that such a fiduciary relationship exists merely from the terms of the contract. In *Compaq Computers Ltd* v *Abercorn Group Ltd* [1991] BCC 484 the contract provided that the buyer stored the goods as bailee, and that he must account for the proceeds of sale and keep such proceeds in a separate account. It was still held that no fiduciary relationship existed. If the parties cannot create such a relationship from the terms of a contract such as this, it seems difficult to see when they can do so.

It has yet to be held by the courts that even if a fiduciary relationship exists that this may nevertheless amount to a registrable charge. However, it was suggested that this could be the case in *Tatung (UK) Ltd* v *Galex Telesure Ltd* (1988) 5 BCC 325.

12 *Risk — res perit domino*

12.1 INTRODUCTION

'Risk', for the purposes of the sale of goods, may be defined as the possibility of the goods deteriorating or being lost, stolen or destroyed without fault on the part of either party.

The difficult words in this definition are 'without fault on either party' because this leaves the law in the unhappy position that it must decide (frequently by seemingly arbitrary methods) which of the parties is to bear the loss for something which neither has caused or indeed wished for. This is not to say that the law is necessarily unfair in doing this: who will bear the risk at any particular stage of the contract is something that can be predicted with reasonable certainty or determined by the parties, hence it is a factor which may have a bearing when the parties determine the price.

Prima facie the party in whom the property is vested at the time the loss is suffered is the party who will bear the loss. This was the position at common law prior to the introduction of the Sale of Goods Act 1979 (the '1979 Act') and was contained in the maxim '*res perit domino*'. This is now codified by s. 20(1) of the 1979 Act which provides as follows:

> Unless otherwise agreed, the goods remain at the seller's risk until the property in them is transferred to the buyer, but when the property in them is transferred to the buyer the goods are at the buyer's risk whether delivery has been made or not.

The starting point in determining who bears the risk is therefore to determine in whom the property is vested, as to which see chapter 6. To this there are seven potential exceptions:

(a) The contract is voidable for frustration.

(b) The contract is void for mistake (notably the mistake that the goods have deteriorated or perished, or indeed do not exist at the time the contract is made).

(c) One of the parties as bailee, or a third party, is at fault for the loss of or damage to the goods.

(d) The parties stipulated in the contract that one party shall bear the loss despite the property being vested in the other party at the time of the loss.

(e) The rule in *Sterns* v *Vickers* [1923] 1 KB 78 applies.

(f) The cause of the loss is due to delay on the part of one of the parties.

(g) The loss is occasioned by a risk necessarily incident in the course of transit.

Of these only (e) to (g) may properly be called exceptions to the *res perit domino* rule. Frustration and mistake are separate doctrines. If one party is at fault, the loss occasioned cannot be described as a 'risk' within the definition given above. Finally, where the parties have expressly provided that a party in whom the property does not vest takes the risk, this is not an exception to the rule but rather a direct application of the opening words of s. 20, i.e., 'unless otherwise agreed'.

However, it is convenient to ascertain the party in whom the property vests and apply these exceptions as a means of identifying the party who bears the loss. The passing of property is discussed in chapter 11. Mistake and frustration are discussed in chapters 5 and 6 respectively. The other 'exceptions' are discussed in turn below.

12.2 PARTY OR OTHER BAILEE AT FAULT

As was noted in chapter 11, the 1979 Act frequently provides for the passing of property prior to actual delivery taking place. It is a common mistake to believe that the property or risk is upon the seller until he has delivered the goods. The reverse will more often be true. Equally, there will be many situations where the buyer is responsible for transit of the goods, yet the property remains with the seller until appropriation or delivery. This means that under s. 20 of the 1979 Act the goods will often be at the risk of a party not having physical or constructive possession of them. Unfortunately, it is all too common that goods are damaged or destroyed through carelessness whilst in storage or transit. The seller may be responsible for this storage or transit or a third party courier or warehouseman. Equally, under a conditional sale, hire purchase agreement or contract of sale or return the buyer or hirer may well have possession of the goods yet the property remains in the seller. Simply through ordinary use of the goods accidents may occur.

Where the goods are damaged or destroyed by the carelessness of the custodian, this is not a loss through a 'risk'; there is a culprit to whom liability must attach. This liability is specifically preserved by s. 20(3) of the 1979 Act which provides that:

> Nothing in this section affects the duties or liabilities of either seller or buyer as a bailee or custodier of the goods of the other party.

This liability will invariably be tortious in nature — a form of negligence, be it through breach of a duty of care or through a contractual duty. The difficult issue where possession and property are moving independently of one another is who should sue whom and for what.

The nature of the liability here is that of a bailee; one in possession of goods belonging to another. There are three main principles which govern liability in these situations. First, where possession is transferred whilst the property in the goods is not, the person in possession becomes a bailee of the person holding the property, sometimes called an 'involuntary bailee'. Secondly, only a person holding the property in goods has the right to sue in tort for damage to those goods. Thirdly, there is the 'privity' rule in contract, that only a person who has a contractual relationship may sue the other party to that contract, and that in order to recover he must show loss. As will be seen, it is worth remembering these general principles when deciding who should sue whom.

There are three potential culprits: the seller, the buyer or a third party, be he a warehouseman or a courier. These will be discussed in turn before turning to the practical issues of the standard of care required of a bailee and upon the party upon whom the burden of proof rests in proving a breach of that duty.

12.2.1 Liability of the seller or buyer as bailee

Where the property in goods is transferred to the buyer under the contract of sale, yet possession remains with the seller, the seller becomes a bailee of the goods until the time for delivery (*Wiehe* v *Dennis Bros* (1913) 29 TLR 250). Once the time for delivery has passed, it would seem that the seller remains a bailee of the goods (*Demby Hamilton* v *Barden* [1949] 1 All ER 435) but is now entitled to charge a reasonable storage fee for holding the goods (*China Pacific SA* v *Food Corporation of India* [1982] AC 939). However, if loss is occasioned by delay on the part of the buyer, the buyer must bear such loss (as to which see section 12.5 below).

Where the buyer takes possession of the goods prior to the property passing (for example under a contract of sale or return), he will become a bailee of the goods and the same standard of care will apply to him as applies to the seller.

12.2.2 Liability of a warehouseman or courier

No real difficulty arises in establishing that a warehouseman or courier is a bailee; the problem arises in deciding who has the right to sue him and for what.

The root of the problem arises here because in the ordinary course of events the seller has arranged for the storage or transport of the goods and it is hence the seller who has contracted with the warehouseman or courier. Under the privity of contract rule, the buyer has no right to sue on the contract because it was not he who made the contract. The law here is substantially unaffected by the Contracts (Rights of Third Parties) Act 1999 as that Act excludes from its ambit most contracts for the carriage of goods. Storage contracts may be affected where the parties have identified the buyer and intend him to have the benefit of the contract (as to which see section 3.4). Here the buyer may be able to sue on the contract between the seller and warehouseman if there was an express or implied term that the goods would be stored with reasonable care (which there usually would be).

It was held in *The Aliakmon* [1986] AC 785 that in order to sue in tort a claimant must hold either the property in the goods or a possessory title (an immediate right to actual possession of the goods: *Margarine Union GmbH* v *Cambay Prince SS Co. (The Wear Breeze)* [1969] 1 QB 219). Formerly, this caused problems in relation to the transit of goods in bulk since the property in goods did not pass until physical separation. Hence the buyer had no right to sue. However, since the introduction of s. 20A of the 1979 Act the property may pass to the buyer upon payment of the price.

Even where the property has passed to the buyer, difficulties still arise. It was held in *Schiffert und Kohlen GmbH* v *Chelsea Maritime (The Irene's Success)* [1982] 1 All ER 218 that where a carrier was contracted by the seller to deliver goods under a CIF contract that there existed a sufficient relationship of proximity between the carrier and the buyer to impose a duty of care upon the carrier in favour of the buyer. The buyer thus had the right to sue the carrier in negligence. This can be extended by analogy to most carriers; it being perfectly obvious that the goods are being delivered to the buyer under a contract of sale.

The same cannot always be said of a warehouseman. Goods may be stored by a warehouseman under the seller's order. However, unless the warehouseman has some form of notice that the goods are being stored for the buyer, no such relationship of proximity can be said to exist. Here the buyer would have no right to sue as no duty would exist. The seller could sue in tort if he could show a possessory title or indeed under his contract with the bailee, but if the property in the goods has transferred to the buyer the seller could show no loss and any damages so obtained would be nominal only.

The net effect of this area of the law is that a negligent courier or warehouseman will be liable for his acts in the following circumstances:

(a) he will be liable to the seller under a contract of bailment if the property remains in the seller;

(b) if the property is no longer vested in the seller, the seller has no loss for which he could sue; and

(c) he will be liable to the buyer if he has notice that he carries or stores the goods on the buyer's behalf and the property has passed to the buyer or the buyer has a possessory title.

Many of the difficulties encountered where a third party causes damage to the goods can be mitigated, however, because a party who bears the risk of damage to goods has an 'insurable interest' in them (*Inglis* v *Stock* (1885) 10 App Cas 128); he can thus protect himself against the third party's fault by obtaining a suitable insurance policy.

12.2.3 The standard of care

The standard of care expected of a bailee is to take reasonable care in the particular circumstances. Obviously, what is required when storing or transporting eggs will not be the same when doing the same with bricks and accordingly no firm rules can be laid down. The only firm rule is that an involuntary bailee is only liable for acts of gross negligence (*Martin* v *LCC* [1947–51] CLY 2558), whereas a voluntary one will be liable for all such negligent acts. In general a buyer or seller in possession of the goods after the property has passed will be a voluntary bailee because the other party has consented to such possession. However, where the seller remains in possession of the goods after the date when the buyer was due to take delivery but has failed to do so, the seller will become an involuntary bailee.

A bailee may also become liable in the absence of negligence where he has deviated from the express terms of the bailment. In *England* v *Heimbucker* (1977) 78 DLR 117 the defendant, a watch repairer, had sent the plaintiff's watch to the manufacturer for their opinion as to how to repair it. It was broken in transit. The plaintiff stated that he had no knowledge of this and had not provided his consent. Whilst accepting that obtaining the manufacturer's opinion was a sensible act it fell outside the instructions of the bailment and the bailee was liable.

The following cases give a guide to the degree of care which the courts expect: *Blount* v *War Office* [1953] 1 WLR 736; *Houghland* v *RR Low (Livery Coaches) Ltd* [1962] 1 QB 694; *Morris* v *C.W. Martin & Sons Ltd* [1966] 1 QB 716 (liability for fraudulent acts of employees); *Mitchell* v *Ealing LBC* [1979] QB 1; *China Pacific SA* v *Food Corporation of India* [1982] AC 939; *British Road Services Ltd* v *A. V. Crutchley & Co. Ltd* [1968] 1 All ER 811 (vicarious liability for employees and agents).

12.2.4 Burden of proof

The ordinary rule is that when determining against which party the burden of proof lies, 'he who asserts must prove'. However, when asserting that a bailee is negligent the burden of proof lies against the bailee to prove that this was not so (*Spurling* v *Bradshaw* [1956] 2 All ER 121).

12.3 EXPRESS PROVISION THAT THE RISK IS ON A PARTY NOT HOLDING THE PROPERTY

That the parties may agree that the risk is to pass independently of the property is expressly preserved by the opening words of s. 20 of the 1979 Act: 'Unless otherwise agreed'. It is normal practice in international shipping matters that the parties agree upon who bears the risk for accidental damage at each stage of transportation. Unfortunately, it is not a matter which the parties regularly turn their minds to in simple domestic transactions. It can, however, be inferred from their course of dealing or negotiations (*Horn* v *Minister of Food* [1948] 2 All ER 1036; *Martineau* v *Kitching* (1872) LR 7 QB 436). Arguably, a statement by one party that the other ought to have the goods insured may amount to an understanding that the risk is on that party (*Donaghy's Rope and Twine Co. Ltd* v *Wright, Stephenson & Co.* (1906) 25 NZLR 641; see also section 11.2).

12.4 THE RULE IN *STERNS* v *VICKERS*

The facts of *Sterns* v *Vickers* [1923] 1 KB 78 were that the defendant sellers had sold to the plaintiff buyers 120,000 gallons of spirit forming part of a bulk of 200,000 gallons. The case was decided prior to the introduction of s. 20A of the 1979 Act and in the absence of ascertainment it was impossible for the property to pass. The spirit was of a particular specific gravity. The plaintiffs subsold the spirit and a delivery warrant was issued to the subpurchaser. He failed to take delivery and reached an agreement with the storage company that he would defer delivery and pay rent for storage. In the intervening period a different spirit was mixed with the bulk, altering (and deteriorating) its quality. As between the plaintiff and the defendant, therefore, the buyers had delayed in taking delivery yet a delivery warrant had been issued giving them a right to immediate possession of the spirit. It was held that the risk was on the buyers, although the reasoning has never been entirely understood. Bankes LJ said simply:

> The question is who are to bear the loss of that, the buyers or the sellers? It seems to me plain that, upon the facts quite apart from the question whether the property in the spirit had passed, the risk of deterioration rested upon the buyers, and they must bear the loss.

In *Comptoir d'Achat et de Vente du Boerenbond Belge SA* v *Luis de Ridder (The Julia)* [1949] AC 293 the House of Lords confined *Sterns* v *Vickers* to its facts. Lord Normand said:

> In those cases in which it has been held that the risk without the property has passed to the buyer it has been because the buyer rather than the seller was seen to have had an immediate and practical interest in the goods, as for instance when he has an immediate right under the storekeeper's delivery warrant ...

This, however, still leaves it open to the courts to find that the risk has passed without the property having done so. The vital factor appears to be that the buyer has 'an immediate and practical interest' in the goods. However, in *The Julia* the House of Lords held that the risk had not passed to the buyer where 500 tonnes of wheat in a larger bulk of the same had been sold to the buyer who had taken a delivery order. The position, therefore, remains unclear. However, given the comments of the House of Lords in *The Julia* it is safest to assume that the risk in goods will not ordinarily pass prior to the property. Certainly, there is no provision within the 1979 Act for its so doing.

In any event, the introduction of s. 20A has mitigated much of the confusion as it is now possible for the property to pass prior to ascertainment (the precise workings of s. 20A are explored in section 11.5.3). However, s. 20A only operates where the buyer has paid the price or part of the price. There will be many situations where the price has not been paid and the rule in *Sterns* v *Vickers* may arguably operate.

12.5 DELAY BY ONE OF THE PARTIES

Section 20(2) of the 1979 Act states that: '. . . where delivery has been delayed through the fault of either buyer or seller the goods are at the risk of the party at fault as regards any loss which might not have occurred but for such fault'. It is important to note that only the loss which might not have occurred but for the delay is at the risk of the party at fault. It is not sufficient that there has been a delay; the loss must be caused by the delay.

Demby Hamilton & Co. Ltd v *Barden* [1949] 1 All ER 435 is a good example of the operation of the rule. In that case the sellers had agreed to sell 30 tonnes of apple juice. The sellers prepared the juice and the buyers took delivery of part of the order but delayed taking delivery of the remainder as they were awaiting instructions from sub-buyers. In the intervening period the juice deteriorated because of the delay. It was held that the loss was at the buyer's risk.

12.6 LOSS OCCASIONED IN THE COURSE OF TRANSIT

Section 33 of the 1979 Act provides that 'where the seller of goods agrees to deliver them at his own risk at a place other than that where they were sold, the buyer must nevertheless (unless otherwise agreed) take any risk of deterioration in the goods necessarily incident to the course of transit'.

The precise application of this rule has never been expressly clarified by the court. As Professor Goode points out in *Commercial Law*, 2nd ed. (Penguin, 1995), when the Act was first drafted roads were little more than tracks and there were still highwaymen on them!

In the ordinary course of events the property will have passed to the buyer by the time that the goods are delivered to a carrier. The risk is, therefore, usually upon the buyer during transit and the seller's duties extend only so far as ensuring that the goods are in a deliverable condition at the time they are delivered to a carrier. This is provided by s. 32 of the 1979 Act. Section 32(1) deems delivery to the carrier as delivery to the buyer unless (under s. 32(2)) the seller has failed to make such arrangements with the carrier as is reasonable given the nature of the goods and that they consequently deteriorate *en route*. The seller's duties are to ensure only that the goods are in a condition in which they can endure the ordinary rigours of transportation (*Beer* v *Walker* (1877) 46 LJQB 677; *Mash & Murrell Ltd* v *Emmanuel Ltd* [1961] 1 WLR 862).

Section 33 applies only where the seller undertakes to deliver the goods; the ordinary place of delivery is deemed to be the seller's business premises. Furthermore, the seller must agree to take the risk of delivery. It is only then that s. 33 operates and its application is merely to pass back to the buyer risks 'necessarily incident in the course of transit'. The seller only accepts the risk of extraordinary risks. In order to pass the whole risk to the seller the seller must agree to accept the risk of transit *and* agree to accept the risks necessarily incident in such a course! The rule is, therefore, of limited application.

13 *Nemo dat quod non habet*

13.1 INTRODUCTION

In *Bishopsgate Finance Corporation Ltd* v *Transport Brakes Ltd* [1949] 1 KB 322 Lord Denning said:

> In the development of our law, two principles have striven for mastery. The first is for the protection of property: no one can give a better title than he himself possesses. The second is for the protection of commercial transactions: the person who takes in good faith and for value without notice should get a good title.

This statement aptly summarises the law in this area. The general rule is expressed in the maxim *nemo dat quod non habet* (no one can give what he does not have). This rule is now embodied in s. 21 of the Sale of Goods Act 1979 (the '1979 Act'). Thus if a person purports to sell or dispose of property to which he does not have title, the general rule is that the person who received it gains no title to it. To this general rule exceptions have been developed. In general, these rules operate to pass a good title to the buyer only where the owner of the goods has in some way put the buyer in the position where he could reasonably have supposed that the person selling the goods had authority to sell them. Thus it is still the general law that where goods are stolen from their owner, no matter what chain of events follows, title remains with the owner.

As will become apparent some of the exceptions to the *nemo dat* rule are replicated in the Sale of Goods Act 1979 from the Factors Act 1889. Since this text is intended to cover not only dispositions of goods by sale, the Factors Act and not the Sale of Goods Act will be referred to. The law is, however, the same.

To the *nemo dat* rule the law has developed exceptions within both the common law and, more frequently, under statute. Before turning to the remedies of the parties these exceptions will be discussed in turn:

(a) Sale in market overt.
(b) Sale by a mercantile agent.

(c) Sale by a seller in possession.
(d) Sale by a buyer in possession of the goods.
(e) Sale under a voidable title.
(f) Sale of cars subject to a hire purchase agreement.
(g) Estoppel.
(h) Miscellaneous exceptions by way of possession proceedings against goods.

13.2 SALE IN MARKET OVERT

This exception to the *nemo dat* rule is included only for historical purposes: it has been abolished. Formerly, sales of goods made in a recognised market or in a shop in the city of London were deemed to be an exception to the rule and the buyer would acquire a good title to them. However, the Sale of Goods (Amendment) Act 1995 abolished this rule in relation to any such sales made after the Act came into force (3 January 1995).

13.3 SALE BY A MERCANTILE AGENT

The common law of agency is preserved by the Factors Act 1889 and accordingly the acts of an agent acting within the course of his express, implied or ostensible authority are binding upon his principal. A detailed analysis of the law of agency is outside the scope of this text and the reader is directed to a general work on contract law.

Section 2 of the Factors Act 1889 (the '1889 Act') provides as follows:

> (1) Where a mercantile agent is, with the consent of the owner, in possession of goods or of the documents of title to goods, any sale, pledge, or other disposition of the goods, made by him when acting in the ordinary course of business of a mercantile agent, shall, subject to the provisions of this Act, be as valid as if he were expressly authorised by the owner of the goods to make the same; provided that the person taking under the disposition acts in good faith, and has not at the time of the disposition notice that the person making the disposition has not authority to make the same.

The general effect of s. 2(1) is clear: where a mercantile agent is given possession of goods by their owner, the agent may dispose of them as if he had authority to do so and the buyer will gain a good title. There are, however, a number of phrases within the subsection which must be discussed:

(a) Mercantile agent.
(b) Possession of the goods.
(c) Consent of the owner.
(d) Sale, pledge or other disposition.
(e) Ordinary course of business.
(f) Good faith and without notice.
(g) Valid as if expressly authorised.

13.3.1 Mercantile agent

Section 1(1) of the 1889 Act defines 'mercantile agent' as meaning:

> ... a mercantile agent having in the customary course of his business as such agent authority either to sell goods or to consign goods for the purpose of sale, or to buy goods, or to raise money on the security of goods.

The mere fact that a person is given possession of the goods will not be sufficient to make him an agent of the owner. Nor will he be an agent if he is given the goods for another purpose — for example as a warehouseman or courier (*Oppenheimer* v *Attenborough* [1908] 1 KB 221; *Lowther* v *Harris* [1927] 1 KB 393). He should, however, be given possession of the goods for the purpose of sale or 'other disposition in the customary course of business' if he is to be brought within the definition.

However, this does not mean that the agent must take the shape of a well-recognised form of such an agent, i.e., a factor or broker. In *Weiner* v *Harris* [1910] 1 KB 285 jewellery was sent to F who ran a jeweller's shop in Hatton Garden on the following terms:

> The goods referred to in that book mentioned are your property, and to remain so until sold or paid for, they being only left with me for the purpose of sale or return, and not be kept as my own stock. The goods I receive from you are to be entered at cost price, and my remuneration for selling them is agreed at one half the profit.

It was held that on its true construction F was a mercantile agent. Whilst F kept his own stock of jewellery it was clear that this stock was to be kept separate and the fact that he was to take his profit as a percentage, as opposed to a fixed purchase price together with the fact that he would never become owner of the property, pointed towards agency. This case also shows that a mercantile agent can be such even though he acts in another capacity (as seller of his own goods) as well.

The fact that the agent has never acted as such before does not prevent him being an agent (*Mortgage Loan & Finance Co. of Australia* v *Richards* (1932) SR (NSW) 50), nor does the fact that he has only one principal (*Lowther* v *Harris* [1927] 1 KB 393).

It therefore seems that the courts have given a liberal interpretation to the phrase. However, the goods must be entrusted to the agent for the purpose of disposition and not some unrelated purpose.

Finally, s. 6 of the 1889 Act states that where the sale or disposition is made by a clerk or employee of the agent who is authorised to make such transactions in the ordinary course of business, the disposition is deemed to have been made by the agent.

13.3.2 Possession of the goods

It seems that the agent must be in possession of the goods (or their documents of title) at the time of the sale in order for the buyer to rely on s. 2 of the 1889 Act.

In *Beverley Acceptances Ltd* v *Oakey* [1982] RTR 417, O had pledged two cars with F in return for a loan. The cars were parked in F's garage. O borrowed the keys from F by a deception and purported to sell them to B who was considering loaning O an advance against the cars. O returned the car and some days later was advanced some money by B. It was held that even if O could be called a mercantile agent, he was not in possession of the goods at the time of the disposition and accordingly B could not rely on s. 2.

13.3.3 Consent of the owner

Formerly there was much confusion as to whether the owner's consent was valid where the goods had been obtained by way of larceny by trick. However, this was said to be immaterial in *Pearson* v *Rose & Young* [1951] 1 KB 275 and this case was followed in *Du Jardin* v *Beadman* [1952] 2 QB 712. It therefore seems safe to assume that even where the owner's consent is obtained by fraud, the consent is valid nonetheless.

However, it was also said in *Pearson* v *Rose & Young* that the owner must give the agent possession as a mercantile agent, not in some other capacity. It need not necessarily be that the owner gives the agent the goods for the purpose of sale, it may be for display or to invite offers, but something more than mere possession must be given. In *Henderson* v *Prosser* [1982] CLY 21, O had left his car with S to be valeted, but it was in turn sold. O had no knowledge of S's car sale business and consequently could not have given his consent for this purpose and accordingly s. 2 did not apply.

Where there are two or more owners of the goods, further difficulties may arise. In *Lloyds Bank Ltd* v *Bank of America National Trust and Savings Association* [1938] 2 KB 147 S had obtained an advance from Lloyds Bank against a trust receipt over the documents of title to certain goods. The documents were returned to S for the purpose of sale and any monies so received were said to be held on trust in favour of the bank. Fraudulently, S pledged the documents with the Bank of America in return for a further advance and duly went into liquidation. The American bank claimed that they could rely on s. 2 and this was upheld. It was held that in the circumstances both S and Lloyds Bank were owners given the different rights they had over the documents of title. As they had returned the documents to S, the documents were in his possession with the consent of the owners. The position would presumably be different were there to be two owners and only one had passed possession to the mercantile agent and the other had not so given his consent.

Section 2(2) of the 1889 Act provides as follows:

> (2) Where a mercantile agent has, with the consent of the owner, been in possession of goods or of the documents of title to goods, any sale, pledge or other disposition, which would have been valid if the consent had continued, shall be valid notwithstanding the determination of the consent; provided that the person taking under the disposition has not at the time thereof notice that the consent has been determined.

This subsection is fairly straightforward in its application: once the owner has given his consent, an innocent buyer will take good title unless he has had notice of the withdrawal of consent.

Section 2(3) and (4) provides that:

> (3) Where a mercantile agent has obtained possession of any documents of title to goods by reason of his being or having been, with the consent of the owner, in possession of the goods represented thereby, or of any documents of title to the goods, his possession of the first-mentioned documents shall, for the purposes of this Act, be deemed to be with the consent of the owner.
> (4) For the purposes of this Act the consent of the owner shall be presumed in the absence of evidence to the contrary.

Again, these subsections are reasonably self-explanatory. It is worth noting, however, that s. 2(3) creates an absolute rule; s. 2(4) creates an evidential presumption which may be rebutted.

13.3.4 Sale, pledge or other disposition

Section 2 applies only to a 'sale, pledge or other disposition'. Whilst this is a broad category, some transactions fall outside its scope.

The meaning of 'sale' may be taken to be the meaning given to the word in the Sale of Goods Act 1979. 'Pledge' is defined by s. 1(5) of the 1889 Act as including 'any contract pledging, or giving a lien or security on, goods, whether in consideration of an original advance or of any further or continuing advance or of any pecuniary liability'. This would appear to cover most forms of security upon goods, e.g., a mortgage or charge.

By s. 5 of the 1889 Act in order for a sale, pledge or other disposition to be valid under the Act there must either be a payment in cash, delivery or transfer of other goods, a document of title to goods, a cheque or other valuable consideration. It follows that a gift is not within the definition.

If the agent has simply gained some form of financial advantage by use of the goods but by which the property in the goods has not been acquired by a third party, this will not be a disposition within the meaning of the Act (*Worcester Works Finance Ltd* v *Cooden Engineering Co. Ltd* [1972] 1 QB 210). For example, where goods were given to an auctioneer by an agent for the purposes of sale and the auctioneer gave an advance against the sale this in itself was held not to be a disposition (*Waddington & Sons* v *Neale & Sons* (1907) 96 LT 786). Equally, if the property in the goods must be transferred, this would appear to mean that a disposition by way of hire purchase does not fall within the meaning of 'disposition' as under such a contract the property is not transferred, merely agreed to be so optionally.

Finally, s. 4 of the 1889 Act provides that in order for the Act to apply any pledge of the goods must be for a further advance and not in respect of an existing debt between pledgor and pledgee.

13.3.5 Ordinary course of business

On the facts of any given case the question of whether the sale was in the ordinary course of business and whether the buyer acted in good faith are closely intermingled. Where the sale is not in the ordinary course of business the buyer will usually be, at least to some extent, on notice that the agent is acting without authority.

The 1889 Act is also somewhat ambiguous where a sale is made by a mercantile agent without the authority of the owner as in the plain wording of the section this is not 'in the ordinary course of business'. It is submitted that the phrase, therefore, refers to appearing to act in the ordinary course of business.

The leading authority on this phrase is *Oppenheimer* v *Attenborough* [1908] 1 KB 221. In that case it was said that there was a difference between the wording of s. 1(1) of the 1889 Act (definition of a mercantile agent) and s. 2(1) (disposition by a mercantile agent). Section 1(1) deals with the time when the agent comes into possession of the goods and s. 2(1) deals with the time when he disposes of them. It was said that when an agent disposes of the goods in order to be acting in the ordinary course of business he must do so 'within business hours, at a proper place of business, and in other respects in the ordinary way in which a mercantile agent would act, so that there is nothing to lead the pledgee to suppose that anything wrong is being done, or to give him notice that the disposition is one which the mercantile agent had no authority to make'. It was irrelevant that the disposition was not customary in the particular trade. Presumably, however, if the disposition was so unusual, the facts would suggest that the buyer was on notice of the agent's want of authority.

Following this decision, sales between dealers or where the terms are slightly unusual, where the price was not paid in cash or where the sale was to a finance company have all been held to be in the ordinary course of business (*Janisch* v *Attenborough & Son* (1910) 102 LT 605; *Stadium Finance Ltd* v *Robbins* [1962] 2 QB 664; *Tingey & Co.* v *John Chambers* [1967] NZLR 785; *Lowther* v *Harris* [1927] 1 KB 393). Equally, a sale where the price was to be paid direct to the agent's creditor has been held to be outside the ordinary course of business (*Biggs* v *Evans* [1894] 1 QB 88). Likewise a sale of the agent's entire stock (*Pacific Motor Auctions Pty Ltd* v *Motor Credits (Hire Finance) Ltd* [1965] AC 867 (note, however, that in this case the sale was also outside business hours)). In *Pearson* v *Rose & Young* [1951] 1 KB 275 and in *Stadium Finance Ltd* v *Robbins* [1962] 2 QB 664 it was held that the sale of a car without its registration book was outside the ordinary course of business.

13.3.6 Good faith and without notice

A party wishing to rely on s. 2 of the 1889 Act must prove that he acted in good faith and without knowledge of the agent's lack of authority; the burden of proof rests on him (*Heap* v *Motorists' Advisory Agency Ltd* [1923] 1 KB 557; *Stadium Finance Ltd* v *Robbins* [1962] 2 QB 664). It is submitted that this is sensible given that it is very difficult for a party to prove that the other party acted in bad faith.

There is no difficulty in establishing that actual knowledge of the agent's want of authority is sufficient to deprive the buyer of a defence under s. 2. However, even if the buyer did have this knowledge it is unlikely that he will admit it. It is submitted that the concept of 'notice' within the Act is broader than the concept of 'good faith'. A party may act in good faith, yet the circumstances are such that he ought to have had notice. Courts are generally reluctant to find that a party has acted dishonestly unless there is strong evidence that they did. It is likely, therefore, that an argument based upon the allegation that the defendant ought to have had notice will be better received than an allegation that he acted dishonestly. Knowledge and notice will be discussed in turn.

In order for the court to decide whether the buyer had knowledge of the agent's want of authority it must look at all the circumstances surrounding the sale. The court must look at those circumstances and decide that there is sufficient fact to infer that the defendant did have subjective knowledge of the agent's lack of authority.

Circumstances surrounding the sale such as a particularly low price may suggest that the buyer knew that the agent had no authority to sell (*Heap* v *Motorists' Advisory Agency Ltd* [1923] 1 KB 557). Likewise where a car is sold without its registration documents (*Pearson* v *Rose & Young* [1951] 1 KB 275). However, where it is a new car being sold it is likely that this will not be of assistance as the car will not have gone through the process of first registration (*Astley Industrial Trust Ltd* v *Miller* [1968] 2 All ER 36). In any case the court must look at all the surrounding facts in order to draw an inference of knowledge and no exclusive list can be drawn up.

When turning to notice great difficulty arises as to whether the court does or should use a concept of constructive notice in determining whether the buyer should be allowed to rely on s. 2. Within trust law there is a similar problem in that a great deal of confusion exists as to whether negligently failing to have knowledge of a fact which someone ought to have done is sufficient to impose a constructive trust. Whilst the cases there are not strictly in point, the issues as to knowledge are largely the same and the cases in that area of the law helpfully set out the issue here. In *Re Montague's Settlements* [1987] Ch 264, Megarry VC said:

> Now, until recently I do not think there had been any classification of 'knowledge' . . . However in the *Baden*[1] case the judgment sets out five categories of knowledge: (i) Actual knowledge; (ii) Wilfully shutting one's eyes to the obvious; (iii) Wilfully and recklessly failing to make such inquiries as an honest and reasonable man would make; (iv) Knowledge of circumstances which would indicate the facts to an honest and reasonable man; (v) Knowledge of circumstances that would put an honest and reasonable man on enquiry.
>
> These types of knowledge correspond to two types of notice: (i) corresponds to actual notice, (ii), (iii), (iv) and (v) correspond to constructive notice.

The difficulty arises in determining whether categories (iv) and (v) do or ought to constitute sufficient notice. The form of knowledge (or lack of it) here is pure negligence. There is little doubt that forms (i), (ii) and (iii) are sufficient: in *Jones* v *Gordon* (1877) 2 App Cas 616 it was said that where a person refrains from making enquiry because he thought that it may reveal a problem, he would therefore be taken to have knowledge. This is clearly category (iii) above. Equally, it has been said in the context of an earlier version of the Factors Act that a 'person may have knowledge of a fact either by direct communication, or by being aware of circumstances which must lead a reasonable man applying his mind to them, and judging from them, to the conclusion that the fact is so. Knowledge acquired

1. *Baden Delvaux & Lecuit* v *Société pour Favoriser le Developpement du Commerce et de l'industrie en France SA* [1992] 4 All ER 161.

in either of these ways is enough, I think, to exclude a party from the benefit of the provisions of this statute: a slight suspicion, I think, will not' (*Evans* v *Trueman* (1830) 1 Moody & R 10). This would appear to be category (iv) above.

Whilst it has been said that the doctrine of constructive notice should not be imported into commercial transactions (*Feuer Leather Corpn* v *Frank Johnstone & Sons Ltd* [1981] Com LR 251) it is interesting to note that in the constructive trust cases it appears that the courts are adopting category (iv) in commercial situations (*Agip (Africa) Ltd* v *Jackson* [1990] Ch 265; *El Ajou* v *Dollar Holdings plc* [1993] 3 All ER 717).

Within the context of the sale of goods the courts are adopting a peculiar definition of 'actual notice' by applying an objective test to it. As is pointed out by Megarry VC above, imputing knowledge to someone where he does not actually have knowledge of it is a form of constructive notice. It is submitted that it is illogical to describe someone as having actual notice when they have not *actually* had notice of it! It would be simpler if the courts were to describe the notice which is required as being constructive notice and not give an objective test to something which is inherently subjective.

The test to apply does, however, seem reasonably clear and was expounded in *Feuer Leather Corpn* v *Frank Johnstone & Sons Ltd* [1981] Com LR 251 and subsequently approved in *Forsythe International (UK) Ltd* v *Silver Shipping Co. Ltd* [1993] 2 Lloyd's Rep 268, at 279 (and also, apparently, in *By Appointment (Sales)* v *Harrods*, unreported[2]). The test is as follows:

> For this purpose the court is concerned with actual notice and not with constructive notice. . . .
>
> (1) In deciding whether a person in the position of the defendants had actual notice:
>
> (a) the court will apply an objective test and look at all the circumstances;
>
> (b) if by an objective test clear notice was given liability cannot be avoided by proof merely of the absence of actual knowledge;
>
> (c) a person will be deemed to have had notice of any fact to which it can be shown that he deliberately turned a 'blind eye' . . .;
>
> (d) on the other hand the court will not expect the recipient of goods to scrutinize commercial documents such as delivery notes with great care;
>
> (e) there is no general duty on a buyer of goods in an ordinary commercial transaction to make inquiries as to the right of the seller to dispose of the goods;
>
> (f) the question becomes: looking objectively at the circumstances which are alleged to constitute notice, do those circumstances constitute notice?
>
> This must be a matter of fact and degree to be determined in the particular circumstances of the case.

13.3.7 Valid as if expressly authorised

The 1889 Act states that a disposition falling within s. 2(1) of the Act shall be 'valid as if [the agent] were expressly authorised by the owner of the goods to

2. See *Forsythe International (UK) Ltd* v *Silver Shipping Co. Ltd* [1993] 2 Lloyd's Rep 268, at 279.

make the same . . .'. What is important to note is that the Act simply affects the relationship of agency; it does not automatically pass good title to the buyer. Thus, if the buyer has yet to pay the price to the agent, the owner may recover this against the buyer. If the goods are pledged to a third party then the owner acquires the right to reclaim the goods by repaying the amount against which the goods are secured. Equally, if pursuant to the pledge, the goods are sold, the owner is entitled to any monies left over after the amount advanced has been repaid.

The owner may, of course, sue the agent himself or where appropriate his trustee in bankruptcy. However, this option is generally useless given that the agent is usually impecunious or else, being a fraudster from the start, he will be untraceable.

13.4 SELLER IN POSSESSION OF THE GOODS

Where a seller has sold goods to one buyer but remains in possession of the goods following a subsequent sale to another buyer, it is possible that the second buyer may be able to rely on s. 8 of the Factors Act 1889 or s. 24 of the Sale of Goods Act 1979 and claim a good title to those goods. Section 8 of the 1889 Act states as follows:

> Where a person, having sold goods, continues, or is, in possession of the goods or of the documents of title to the goods, the delivery or transfer by that person, or by a mercantile agent acting for him, of the goods or documents of title under any sale, pledge, or other disposition thereof, or under any agreement for sale, pledge, or other disposition thereof, to any person receiving the same in good faith and without notice of the previous sale, shall have the same effect as if the person making the delivery or transfer were expressly authorised by the owner of the goods to make the same.

The section is repeated in s. 24 of the Sale of Goods Act 1979. However, in the 1979 Act the words 'or under any agreement for sale, pledge or other disposition thereof' are omitted. Why the words were omitted is seemingly unknown. The 1889 Act has never been repealed and would appear to be wider than the 1979 Act. It is assumed, therefore, that the wider definition in the 1889 Act is still good law.

The first point to note is that s. 8 applies only where in the transaction with the first buyer there has been a sale of the goods, not merely an agreement to sell. Accordingly, the property must have passed under s. 18 of the 1979 Act or under the contract between the parties.[3] If the property has not passed at the stage of the second transaction then there is no need for the second buyer to rely upon s. 8 of the 1889 Act; the property in the goods remained in the seller at the time of the disposition and he was capable of transferring it in any event. However, the seller would be liable to the first buyer for non-delivery of the goods.

The meaning of the phrases 'mercantile agent', 'sale, pledge or other disposition' and 'good faith and without notice' have been considered in the previous section in relation to s. 2 of the 1889 Act. The same meaning of these words applies in relation to s. 8. However, the meaning of the phrases 'continues, or is,

---

3. As to which see chapter 11.

in possession', 'delivery or transfer' and 'same effect as if the delivery or transfer were expressly authorised' need to be discussed.

13.4.1 Continues, or is, in possession

Until the case of *Pacific Motor Auctions Pty Ltd* v *Motor Credits (Hire Finance) Ltd* [1965] AC 867 it was thought that the seller had to be in possession of the goods 'as a seller' in order for s. 8 of the 1889 Act to apply. For example, in *Staffs Motor Guarantee Ltd* v *British Wagon Co. Ltd* [1934] 2 KB 305, S, a lorry dealer, sold a truck to BW who in turn let it back to him under a hire purchase agreement. He then sold it to SM under a further credit arrangement. It was held that BW were not entitled to rely on the section because S was in possession of the truck not as a seller but as a bailee.

In the *Pacific Motors* case this requirement was disapproved of. Whilst the case is one of the Privy Council and not strictly binding upon the English courts, it is of strong persuasive authority and has indeed been followed in *Worcester Works Finance Ltd* v *Cooden Engineering Co. Ltd* [1972] 1 QB 210. Accordingly, it should be followed.

The facts of *Pacific Motors* were that M, a car dealership, sold cars to Motor Credits on what was described as a 'display plan' or 'floor plan'. This provided that M bought cars on his own account as part of his stock. He then sold the cars to Motor Credits for 90 per cent of their value. He was given authority to deal with the cars as he wished and to sell them on his own account, subject of course to repaying Motor Credits the 90 per cent advanced by them. Motor Credits made their money by the provision of finance to M's customers: if M's customers took the cars on a hire purchase agreement provided by Motor Credits then no interest was payable on the 90 per cent advance; if M sold the cars for cash then interest was payable. M being in financial difficulties, Motor Credits withdrew M's authority to deal with the cars. That afternoon M sold them to Pacific Motors expressly stating that he had authority to sell them and that they were in fact his cars. It was held that Pacific Motors could rely on s. 8 of the 1889 Act.[4] There was no requirement that he remain in possession of the goods as a seller of them, so long as he continued in possession this was sufficient.

However, where there is a break in possession, the seller will have to take back the goods in the same capacity. This is clear from the New Zealand case of *Mitchell* v *Jones* (1905) 24 NZLR 932 which was approved by the Privy Council in *Pacific Motors*. In that case S had sold a horse to B1, but had later borrowed the horse giving an excuse as to why he wanted it. He later sold it to B2. Here the seller was merely a bailee of B1 and not a seller in possession; B2 could not rely on s. 8.

It is worth noting that the meaning of possession here has its commercial meaning, thus where the goods are not actually in the seller's possession but with a warehouseman at the seller's disposal, they are in the seller's possession for the purposes of the Act (*City Fur Co. Ltd* v *Fureenbond* [1937] 1 All ER 239).

It has been said that the added words 'or is in possession of the goods' can refer to a situation only where the seller was not in possession of the goods at the first sale but only came into possession of them afterwards (*Worcester Works Finance*

4. In fact it was an Australian equivalent, but the wording is identical.

Ltd v *Cooden Engineering Co. Ltd* [1972] 1 QB 210). Indeed it is difficult to see how the words would operate other than by this situation assuming the commercial meaning of possession.

Finally, the seller need not remain in possession of the goods with the consent of the owner. Indeed, the seller may wrongfully retain possession of them and the second buyer may still obtain the protection of the Act.

13.4.2 Delivery or transfer

In order to rely on s. 8 of the 1889 Act it must be shown that the seller has made a delivery or transfer of the goods or their documents of title under a disposition; it is not sufficient that he has simply contracted to transfer the property in the goods. The issue here is whether constructive delivery is sufficient to rely on the section, that is to say where the goods have physically remained in the same place but are now held at another's disposal. An example of this would be where goods are stored in a warehouse at the seller's disposal but upon the sale the warehouse warrant is transferred to the buyer and the goods are now held at the buyer's disposal.

It is submitted that delivery here may be constructive. This is so despite the case of *Nicholson* v *Harper* [1895] 2 Ch 415 where it was held that constructive delivery was insufficient. More modern authorities have held that constructive delivery will suffice. In *Forsythe International (UK) Ltd* v *Silver Shipping Co. Ltd* [1993] 2 Lloyd's Rep 268 Clarke J adopted the Australian case of *Gamer's Motor Centre (Newcastle) Pty Ltd* v *Natwest Wholesale Australia Pty Ltd* (1987) 163 CLR 236 holding that constructive delivery would suffice. Although the situation in both of these cases was that of a buyer and not a seller in possession of the goods, the words 'delivery or transfer' appear in the same context in both ss. 24 and 25 of the Sale of Goods Act 1979 and in ss. 8 and 9 of the Factors Act 1889. Accordingly, it is submitted that their meaning applies in relation to both sales of goods by sellers in possession and buyers in possession.

In order to make such a delivery it was said in the *Forsythe International* case that there must be a voluntary transfer of possession within the meaning of s. 61(1) of the Sale of Goods Act 1979. This meant that there must be something more than mere acquiescence on the part of the buyer or seller in possession. Examples of a voluntary act were to be found in the *Gamer's Motor* case and in *Worcester Works Finance Ltd* v *Cooden Engineering Co. Ltd* [1972] 1 QB 210. In the former case upon the disposition of the goods the buyer had handed over a receipt. In *Worcester Works Finance* the keys to a car being repossessed had been handed over. By contrast in the *Forsythe International* case a charterparty was brought to an end and the ship repossessed by its owners. The charterers had done nothing, they had simply stood by and allowed it to happen. This was mere acquiescence and was insufficient. It does not seem, however, that any formal attornment is required in order for there to be a delivery or transfer within the meaning of the sections.

13.4.3 Same effect as if expressly authorised

Section 8 of the 1889 Act states that a disposition by the seller in possession shall have the same effect as if expressly authorised by the *owner* of the goods. Upon first reading of the section therefore it might appear that, no matter what chain of events has led up to the disposition, the second buyer will take not only such title as the seller had, but a good title as against the owner. On this reasoning if S stole goods from O and then sold them to B1 whilst remaining in possession of them, a subsequent sale to B2 would have the effect of extinguishing O's title. However, in *National Employers' Mutual General Insurance Ltd* v *Jones* [1990] 1 AC 24 the House of Lords held that this was not so as it was manifestly against the policy of the Factors Act 1889 and all the Factors Acts prior to that. 'Owner' in s. 8 meant the first buyer or disponee referred to in that section. The effect of the section is, therefore, that the first disponee is bound by such disposition as is made to the second disponee. The true owner is not bound by the transaction if he is other than the first buyer.

The position becomes problematic where there has been not a sale but an agreement to sell the goods to the second disponee. On the plain wording of the section it would appear that the first disponee is bound by the contract to sell the goods with the result that the price becomes payable to him.

13.5 BUYER IN POSSESSION OF THE GOODS

Section 9 of the 1889 Act provides as follows:

> Where a person, having bought or agreed to buy goods, obtains with the consent of the seller possession of the goods or the documents of title to the goods, the delivery or transfer, by that person or by a mercantile agent acting for him, of the goods or documents of title under any sale, pledge, or other disposition thereof, or under any agreement for sale, pledge, or other disposition thereof, to any person receiving the same in good faith and without notice of any lien or other right of the original seller in respect of the goods, shall have the same effect as if the person making the delivery or transfer were a mercantile agent in possession of the goods or documents of title with the consent of the owner.

The section is repeated in s. 25 of the Sale of Goods Act 1979. However, as with s. 8 of the Factors Act 1889 and s. 24 of the Sale of Goods Act 1979, the words 'or under any agreement for the sale, pledge or other disposition thereof' are omitted in the 1979 Act. As with s. 8, there seems no reason why the wider meaning of s. 9 should not apply.

Again the meaning of many of the phrases have been discussed in the previous sections and the same meaning applies in relation to this section. However, the meaning of certain phrases fall to be discussed: 'bought or agreed to buy', 'possession of the goods', and 'same effect as if the person making the delivery or transfer were a mercantile agent in possession of the goods or documents of title with the consent of the owner'. These will be discussed in turn.

13.5.1 Bought or agreed to buy

The general effect of s. 9 is clear: where a buyer has obtained the possession of goods which he has agreed to buy he is in a position to pass good title. However, the section also applies where there has been a sale, as opposed to an agreement to sell, the goods. At first sight this seems unnecessary as a person who has bought goods may transfer title to the goods as he himself has such a title.

However, the section also operates where the buyer has obtained a voidable title which has been avoided, e.g., by obtaining the goods by fraud, and the original seller has avoided the title (as in *Car & Universal Finance* v *Caldwell* [1965] 1 QB 525 discussed in relation to s. 23 of the Sale of Goods Act 1979). Here the buyer cannot pass good title under s. 23 because the title is not voidable but void. However, s. 9 of the 1889 Act will apply as the buyer has bought the goods and obtained possession of them with the consent of the seller. It was held in *Newtons of Wembley Ltd* v *Williams* [1965] 1 QB 560 that notwithstanding that the seller had withdrawn his consent the first buyer had obtained the car with the consent of the seller and that this was sufficient. The section will also operate where the buyer has bought the goods but they are subject to a lien by the original seller.

The most important provision of the section, however, remains where the buyer has 'agreed to buy' the goods, but the contract has not yet passed the property to him. This does mean, however, that there must be a contract of sale within the meaning of the 1979 Act. In general there are four types of contracts which will not fall within this description within the context of the 1889 Act: contracts for the supply of goods, contracts which are void *ab initio*, contracts of sale or return and conditional sale agreements. Thus,

(a) A contract whereby goods are supplied under a contract for work and materials is not a sale of goods within the meaning of the 1979 Act; the distinction between such contracts has already been discussed in section 1.6.2.

(b) Where a contract has been entered into by mistake such that the contract is void *ab initio*, it is as if there has never been such a contract. Accordingly, the buyer cannot be taken to have bought or agreed to buy the goods in this situation. The situations where a contract is void for mistake are discussed in chapter 5.

(c) Where the contract is one of sale or return, the buyer has not bought or agreed to buy the goods and it does not therefore fall within the definition. However, this is of little practical importance as the sale under such a contract is an act affirming the contract and the buyer becomes owner of the goods at the same time as he sells them. The buyer therefore becomes an owner of the goods in the ordinary course of events.

(d) The distinction between a conditional sale agreement and a hire purchase agreement has already been discussed in section 1.6.5. Thus, a conditional sale agreement is a contract for the sale of goods which is governed by the 1979 Act. However, by s. 9(ii) of the 1889 Act and s. 25(2) of the 1979 Act, the buyer under a conditional sale agreement is not to be taken as a person who has bought or agreed to buy goods for the purposes of the 1889 Act or the corresponding provision of the 1979 Act. Conditional sale agreements are defined for the purposes of the sections as being a consumer credit agreement for the sale of goods under which:

> ... the purchase price or part of it is payable by instalments, and the property in the goods is to remain in the seller (notwithstanding that the buyer is to be in possession of the goods) until such conditions as to the payment of instalments or otherwise as may be specified in the agreement are fulfilled.

An agreement by which the price is not payable by instalments would not appear to come within the definition and is not therefore governed by the 1889 Act.

However, the definition would appear to cover a situation where the price is payable by instalments, but the property is conditionally transferred by reason of some other event. The provision is further restricted as it must be a consumer credit agreement within the meaning of the Consumer Credit Act 1974. By s. 8 of that Act this means that the agreement must be one by which credit of less than £25,000 is extended and the buyer is an individual (or partnership) and not a corporation.

13.5.2 Possession of the goods

The buyer must obtain possession of the goods with the consent of the seller in order to be in a position to pass good title to a third party. As with s. 8 of the 1889 Act, the buyer may obtain possession by a criminal offence or fraud and this will be immaterial (see sections 13.4.1 and 13.5). Likewise it seems that if the buyer is not in actual, but constructive, possession that will suffice.

In *Four Point Garage Ltd* v *Carter* [1985] 3 All ER 12 the seller had sold a car to B1 who in turn sub-sold it to B2. B1 asked that the car be delivered directly to B2. It was held that for the purposes of s. 25 of the 1979 Act B1 was in possession of the goods. Similarly in *Capital and Counties Bank Ltd* v *Wariner* (1896) 12 TLR 216 the seller had sold goods to B1 and had issued transfer notes to B1 which had been acknowledged by a warehouseman. B1 subsequently pledged the transfer notes with B2. It was held that B2 was entitled to the goods held under the transfer notes. The doctrine of constructive possession was also upheld in *Forsythe International (UK) Ltd* v *Silver Shipping Co. Ltd* [1993] 2 Lloyd's Rep 268.

13.5.3 The effect of the disposition

Section 9 of the 1889 Act ends with the words that the disposition 'shall have the same effect as if the person making the delivery or transfer were a mercantile agent in possession of the goods or documents of title with the consent of the owner'. These differ from the words at the end of s. 8 of the same Act; that the disposition 'shall have the same effect as if the person making the delivery or transfer were expressly authorised by the owner of the goods to make the same'.

The case of *National Employers' Mutual General Insurance Ltd* v *Jones* [1990] 1 AC 24 has already been discussed in section 13.4.3. It was said in that case that the 'owner' meant the first seller, and not the actual owner of the goods. Consequently, the second buyer only takes such title as the seller had, which is not necessarily an absolute title.

However, the difference in the wording of ss. 8 and 9 create a problem. It must be recalled that in order for a mercantile agent to pass a good title he must dispose of the goods in the ordinary course of business. If this requirement applies, unless the first buyer under s. 9 is in fact a mercantile agent, the sale will rarely be in the ordinary course of business of a mercantile agent.

It was held in *Newtons of Wembley Ltd* v *Williams* [1965] 1 QB 560 that the buyer in possession must be assumed to be a mercantile agent, but that the court must go on to consider whether the sale was in the ordinary course of business, e.g., within business hours (this requirement is more fully discussed in section 13.3.5). The result of this is to make it extremely difficult for the buyer to pass a good title unless he is in fact a mercantile agent.

13.6 SALE UNDER A VOIDABLE TITLE

Section 23 of the Sale of Goods Act 1979 provides as follows:

> When the seller of goods has a voidable title to them, but his title has not been avoided at the time of sale, the buyer acquires a good title to the goods, provided he buys them in good faith and without notice of the seller's defect of title.

Two issues arise under this section. First, whether the seller has a voidable title. Secondly, if so, has it been avoided. These will be discussed in turn below. It should be noted that there is no requirement under this section that the seller should be in possession of the goods. However, the section does appear to envisage a sale of the goods to the buyer and not merely an agreement to sell them.

It must also be remembered that even if s. 23 does not apply, it is likely that s. 25 (buyer in possession) will apply. Accordingly, even if the seller has avoided the contract, an innocent purchaser may still rely on s. 25 (see section 13.5.1).

13.6.1 Voidable title

A distinction must be drawn between a contract which is wholly void and one which is merely voidable. A contract may be void *ab initio* where, for example, there has been a mistake as to the identity of the parties or under s. 6 of the 1979 Act. Here s. 23 of the 1979 Act will not apply. A contract will become voidable if it has been entered into as the result of fraud at common law, misrepresentation, duress or undue influence or equitable mistake.

13.6.2 Avoidance of the contract

It was held in *Car & Universal Finance Ltd* v *Caldwell* [1965] 1 QB 525 that a person may avoid the contract by taking all possible steps to communicate such avoidance even though that is not communicated to the buyer (fraudster). Thus if a seller has entered into a contract as a result of fraud or misrepresentation by a rogue, his reporting the matter to the police will act as a rescission of the contract. The rogue's title will thus be avoided and he will no longer be able to pass a good title to a third party.

13.7 DISPOSITION OF A CAR SUBJECT TO A HIRE PURCHASE AGREEMENT

Section 27 of the Hire Purchase Act 1964 (the '1964 Act') provides as follows:

> (1) This section applies where a motor vehicle has been bailed ... under a hire purchase agreement, or has been agreed to be sold under a conditional sale agreement, and, before the property in the vehicle has become vested in the debtor, he disposes of the vehicle to another person.
>
> (2) Where the disposition referred to in subsection (1) above is to a private purchaser, and he is a purchaser of the motor vehicle in good faith without notice of the hire purchase or conditional sale agreement (the 'relevant agreement') that

disposition shall have effect as if the creditor's title to the vehicle has been vested in the debtor immediately before that disposition.

The general effect of these provisions is simple: where a car which is the subject of a hire purchase agreement is disposed of, that disposition is as if the title held by the credit company were vested in the seller — the buyer gets a good title. There are, however, a few complicating factors.

First, the buyer must be a 'private purchaser'. A private purchaser is defined by s. 29(2) of the 1964 Act as a person who is not a 'trade or finance purchaser'. In turn this is defined as a person whose business consists wholly or partly in purchasing vehicles for resale or providing finance by buying them and agreeing to hire or sell them under a hire purchase scheme. The rationale behind this is simple — within the industry there are databases of cars subject to hire purchase or other finance agreements (most notably HPI). Those in the trade have ready access to these and can therefore easily check to see if the car is subject to such an agreement. If they choose not to check, it is fair that the risk is upon them.

The provisions of the 1964 Act apply to a trade dealer even if he is buying the car for personal use (*Stevenson* v *Beverley Bentick Ltd* [1976] 2 All ER 606). However, the mere fact that the purchaser is a company does not mean that it does not benefit from the protection of the Act — it is only if the business is such that cars are purchased for resale that the Act deems them a trade purchaser.

Equally, much finance in modern times is provided not by hire purchase or conditional fee agreements but by a straightforward loan which is not secured upon the vehicle. This is so even if the finance is provided by a subsidiary company of the car manufacturer or under a specific deal offered for car purchase. Indeed hire purchase is now quite an old-fashioned form of finance. These forms of finance are not covered by the Act.

Secondly, and perhaps obviously, the 1964 Act only applies to motor vehicles, not other goods.

Thirdly, the 1964 Act will assist a private purchaser even though the car was first purchased from the original hirer by a trade or finance purchaser. Section 4 of the Act provides that the first disposition to a private purchaser shall be deemed to be such that the seller held the title of the creditor. However, any intermediate trade purchasers will not escape liability for conversion by virtue of this position (s. 27(6)).

Fourthly, the disposition referred to in the 1964 Act must either be a sale, conditional sale or hire purchase agreement. Pledges and other forms of disposition are not protected.

Finally, the purchaser must act in good faith and without notice. For this purpose the mere fact that the purchaser thinks that the car was once the subject of hire purchase but that this has since been paid off will not render him to have acted in bad faith if this proves to be wrong (*Barker* v *Bell* [1978] RTR 444).

13.8 ESTOPPEL

The general principle that the owner of goods will be estopped from denying the validity of a sale was laid down in *Lickbarrow* v *Mason* (1787) 2 TR 63 where it was said that 'wherever one of two innocent parties must suffer by the acts of a third, he who has enabled such third person to occasion the loss must sustain it'. It is generally accepted that this phrase is, however, much too wide to definitively state the law, just the general principle.

The principle is maintained by s. 21 of the 1979 Act which states that where goods are sold by someone other than the owner of them or his agent, good title shall not pass unless the owner is 'by his conduct precluded from denying the seller's authority to sell'.

Estoppel can occur where the owner of the goods has held out the seller to have the authority to sell by his words, conduct or negligent omission. This last phrase has led to the phrase 'estoppel by negligence'. Much academic debate has ensued as to whether this is an apt phrase. However, it is sufficient to note that estoppel can occur where the owner of goods has failed to act in circumstances where he should have done. Estoppel will be dealt with here in two categories: estoppel by words or conduct and estoppel by negligence.

13.8.1 Estoppel by words or conduct

The best example of an owner holding out another to have authority to sell the goods is contained in *Shaw* v *Commissioner of Metropolitan Police* [1987] 1 WLR 1332 (see also *Farquarson Bros* v *J. King & Co. Ltd* [1902] AC 325; *Eastern Distributors* v *Goldring* [1957] 1 QB 371). In that case O, a young foreign (and presumably rich) student, had purchased a Porsche motor car for £16,000. When the time came for him to return home he advertised the car for sale in a newspaper for £17,000. One L responded to the advert stating that he was a car dealer and that he had a buyer interested in the car. O gave L possession of the car together with a letter stating that he had sold the car to L. L then agreed to sell the car to B, who gave him a cheque by way of deposit which bounced. L then disappeared, the police took possession of the car and brought an application to determine its ownership. Noting that B had very little merit in their claim given that they had not paid a penny for the car, it was held that B had not obtained a good title to it. Whilst O's conduct in giving L possession together with the letter was clearly conduct precluding him denying L's authority to sell, there had been no actual sale, merely an agreement to sell, consequently neither s. 21 of the 1979 Act nor the common law applied. However, had there been a sale and an exchange of money, O would have been precluded from denying B's title.

Where the representation is by words as clear as those in *Shaw*, little difficulty arises as to whether the owner has held the seller out as having sufficient authority to sell. However, where the representation is by conduct, the picture is not so clear. In *Commonwealth Trust Ltd* v *Atokey* [1926] AC 72 O had agreed to sell cocoa to L, but there remained some haggling to be done over the price. L in turn sold the cocoa to B, who paid L the agreed price. Applying *Lickbarrow* v *Mason* (1787) 2 TR 63, it was held that this was sufficient for O to be estopped from denying the validity of the sale to B. It is important to note that all O had done here was to agree to sell goods on credit and give over possession of them. Given the courts' reaction after these cases *Lickbarrow* v *Mason* and *Commonwealth Trust Ltd* v *Atokey* can probably be considered a high water mark; more will generally be required in order for an estoppel to be established.

For example in *Mercantile Bank of India Ltd* v *Central Bank of India Ltd* [1938] AC 287, O had pledged railway receipts (documents of title) to the Central Bank in return for an advance. As was the practice, the receipts were returned to him in order to collect the goods. However, O then pledged the receipts with the Mercantile Bank in exchange for another advance. It was held that the returning of the receipts to O by the Central Bank was not sufficient to raise an estoppel no more than if *the property itself* had been returned to him.

Again, in *Central Newbury Car Auctions Ltd* v *Unity Finance Ltd* [1957] 1 QB 371, S entered into a hire purchase agreement with O for the purchase of a car and was duly given possession of it together with its registration book. In due course B sold the car to B2. The mere fact that B had possession of the car (and the log-book) was not a representation that he was owner of the car or that he had authority to sell it. O was not therefore estopped from denying its title.

It is clear enough therefore that where the owner of goods has made a clear representation to a third party or the world at large that another is entitled to sell the goods either as his agent or as an apparent principal, this will suffice to establish an estoppel. This much is clear from *Shaw* v *Commissioner of Metropolitan Police* [1987] 1 WLR 1332 and *Eastern Distributors* v *Goldring* [1957] 1 QB 371. However, merely giving another possession of them will not suffice (*Central Newbury Car Auctions Ltd* v *Unity Finance Ltd* [1957] 1 QB 371 and *Mercantile Bank of India Ltd* v *Central Bank of India Ltd* [1938] AC 287). However, where the owner has given another certain authority to deal with the goods it becomes a question of fact and degree whether this will be sufficient to invoke an estoppel where the agent exceeds his authority. The issue is whether the apparent clothing given to the agent is such as to make him appear to have authority to deal with the goods.

In *Farquarson Bros* v *J. King & Co. Ltd* [1902] AC 325, O had authorised their clerk to make transfers on their behalf. He was not entitled to enter into contracts on their behalf, but was authorised to complete the necessary paperwork to inform the warehousemen of the transfer of the property. The warehousemen were aware of this authority. Fraudulently, he instructed the warehousemen to transfer the property to one X, a fictitious person. Pretending to be X he then sold the goods to B, pocketing the money. The House of Lords held that O had done nothing to hold out the clerk as having authority to sell and were appalled that it could ever be suggested that an estoppel arose and seemingly amazed that the Court of Appeal had accepted such a suggestion. With respect to the House of Lords, it seems difficult to envisage what more apparent authority could be required other than the authority to complete the paperwork to make a sale. All cases of this nature are one of fact and degree and it is possible that a similar argument to that raised by the defendants in this case may well succeed in more modern times (as it did then before the Court of Appeal).

In *Lloyd's and Scottish Finance Ltd* v *Williamson* [1965] 1 WLR 404, O had entrusted his car with A with instructions to sell above a certain price. As a fact, it was found that he knew very well that A may sell as apparent principal and not merely as agent and had authorised him to do so. In fact, A sold above the price to B but the price was paid not in cash but set off against a debt owed by A to B. As such, the sale was considered outside the ordinary course of business but this was considered irrelevant. O had given A authority and he was bound by it.

In the absence of a clear representation by the owner that another has authority to deal with his goods it seems on the decided cases very difficult to predict when an agent has been given sufficient clothing of authority to bind the owner. Particularly in *Farquarson Bros* v *J. King & Co. Ltd* [1902] AC 325, it seems difficult to see what more clothing the clerk needed to commit his fraud. In reality, these are cases which are bordering upon estoppel by negligence — the owner has placed too much trust in their agent such that he is able to easily defraud them. However, as will be seen in the next section in relation to the cases where estoppel by negligent omission on the part of the owner has been overtly argued before the courts, the courts are staggeringly reluctant to impose any kind of duty upon the owner of goods to protect them.

13.8.2 Estoppel by negligence

It was noted at the start of this section that the broad principle in relation to estoppel was established in *Lickbarrow* v *Mason* (1787) 2 TR 63 that 'wherever one of two innocent parties must suffer by the acts of a third, he who has enabled such third person to occasion the loss must sustain it'. By their own carelessness the owner of goods may enable another to be in a position whereby they may deal with the owner's goods. The question therefore becomes when will the owner be sufficiently careless as to protecting his goods from the meddler for the courts to find that they should be bound by and suffer from this carelessness. As will be seen, the answer to this would seem to be very rarely.

Indeed, the only case where estoppel by negligence appears to have succeeded is *Coventry Shepherd & Co.* v *Great Eastern Railway Co.* (1883) 11 QBD 776. In that case the railway had accidentally issued two delivery orders in respect of the same goods to the same person. That person was therefore enabled to represent to the plaintiff that the goods were still at his disposal (when in fact he had otherwise disposed of them under the other delivery order) and accordingly pledge the goods with them. It was held that the railway company were estopped by their own negligence.

Coventry Shepherd & Co. v *Great Eastern Railway Co.* is however an old case. In *Mercantile Credit Co. Ltd* v *Hamblin* [1965] 2 QB 242, O wished to raise some money against the security of her car. Trusting A she signed some hire purchase forms in blank and allowed him to negotiate with the hire purchase company to see how much money he could raise against the car. In fact, he completed the forms representing that he sold the car to the company and that they bailed it back to O under a hire purchase agreement. The Court of Appeal held that whilst O did owe a duty of care to the hire purchase company that, in the particular circumstances of the case, she had not broken that duty in trusting A. It seems hard to imagine circumstances of greater carelessness than to trust another with forms signed in blank and to trust another to complete them.

A more interesting case is that of *Moorgate Mercantile Co. Ltd* v *Twitchings* [1977] AC 890. This case concerned the activities of an organisation known as HPI (Hire-Purchase Information). This organisation compiled a database of vehicles subject to hire purchase agreements, its members being most finance companies and most motor vehicle traders. In that case, A had let to X a car on hire purchase but had failed to register the agreement with HPI. X duly sold the car to Y, a dealer, who sold it on to a private purchaser (Y having checked with HPI and found that there was no record of a hire purchase agreement). A brought an action against Y in conversion (Y, of course was not entitled to the protection of the Hire Purchase Act 1964 as he was a dealer, whereas the private purchaser would be protected). Y defended the action claiming that A was estopped by his own negligent failure to register the hire purchase agreement with HPI. By a majority, the Court of Appeal held that there was no duty of care owed on the part of A and gave judgment for A (this case was followed on near identical facts in *Cadogan Finance Ltd* v *Keith Avery* (1982) Com LR 248).

In light of these cases it certainly appears to be the modern trend on the part of the courts to restrict the circumstances where a defence based upon estoppel will succeed, outside of a clear representation by the owner.

13.9 MISCELLANEOUS EXCEPTIONS

A series of statutory provisions allow one person to sell another's goods and pass good title in certain, limited, circumstances. In reality, these mainly arise where goods are being seized and sold to secure payment of a debt:

(a) Police (Property) Act 1897, s. 2 (as amended by the Police (Property) Act 1997) — power to sell unclaimed stolen property.

(b) Road Traffic Regulation Act 1988, s. 101 (as amended by the Road Traffic Act 1991); Removal and Disposal of Vehicles Regulations 1986, SI 1986/183 — abandoned vehicles.

(c) County Courts Act 1984 — execution against goods.

(d) Torts (Interference with Goods) Act 1977 — bailee of uncollected goods.

(e) Unpaid seller's lien — discussed in section 22.3.

Additionally, an executor or administrator of an estate may dispose of the goods of the estate. Likewise a liquidator, administrator or administrative receiver of a company in liquidation or administration, a trustee in bankruptcy or receiver of a bankrupt's estate. These however are not really exceptions to the *nemo dat* rule as, in most cases, the property in the goods is vested in the person selling them by virtue of his status.

13.10 REMEDIES

The *nemo dat* rule does not create any specific cause of action or remedy, it acts as a defence to another cause of action brought by one of the injured parties. The purpose of this section is therefore to direct the reader to the appropriate section in relation to each of the parties.

The owner of the goods may either bring an action against the person who has sold them in excess of authority, stolen them from him or who is now in possession of them. An action for conversion of the goods will lie against the thief, although in practice most thieves or fraudsters have no money and cannot be traced. Where the owner expects the buyer to have gained a good title to the goods he can either sue against the agent's contract of agency (if appropriate) or in conversion against the agent. If the owner does not believe that the buyer has obtained good title to the goods, he may bring an action requesting a declaration as to the ownership of the goods and possession of them. The buyer may defend such proceedings on the basis that he has a good title by virtue of an exception to the *nemo dat* rule. The owner of the goods may also directly retake the goods. However, if he does so and it transpires that the buyer has gained good title to the goods, the owner may find himself liable in conversion.

If a warehouseman is in possession of the goods to which two parties are arguing as to ownership, the appropriate action would be to commence interpleader proceedings in order to bring the parties to court and allow the court to determine the issue — the warehouseman will not thereby incur liability.

Where the buyer is deprived of his goods as he is not entitled to the benefit of an exception to the *nemo dat* rule, he may sue the person that sold them to him as a breach of s. 12 of the Sale of Goods Act 1979 (failure to pass a good title), or for a total failure of consideration (per *Rowland* v *Divall* [1923] 2 KB 500). If he is in possession of the goods, the layman's rule that 'possession is nine tenths of the law' tends to prevail — the buyer need take no action and may wait to be sued if the owner believes that he has a chance of success. Alternatively, the buyer may seek a declaration as to the ownership of the goods.

PART IV
TERMS IMPLIED IN FAVOUR OF THE BUYER

14 Duty to pass good title

14.1 INTRODUCTION

Section 12 of the Sale of Goods Act 1979 (the '1979 Act') provides as follows:

> (1) In a contract of sale, other than one to which subsection (3) below applies, there is an implied [condition][1] on the part of the seller that in the case of a sale he has a right to sell the goods, and in the case of an agreement to sell he will have such a right at the time the property is to pass.
>
> (2) In a contract of sale other than one to which subsection (3) below applies, there is also an implied [warranty][1] that—
>
> (a) the goods are free, and will remain free until the time when the property is to pass, from any charge or encumbrance not disclosed or known to the buyer before the contract is made, and
>
> (b) the buyer will enjoy quiet possession of the goods except so far as it may be disturbed by the owner or other person entitled to the benefit of any charge or encumbrance so disclosed or known.
>
> (3) This subsection applies to a contract of sale in the case of which there appears from the contract or is to be inferred from its circumstances an intention that the seller should transfer only such title as he or a third person may have.
>
> (4) In a contract to which subsection (3) above applies there is an implied [warranty][1] that all charges or encumbrances known to the seller and not known to the buyer have been disclosed to the buyer before the contract is made.
>
> (5) In a contract to which subsection (3) above applies there is also an implied [warranty][1] that none of the following will disturb the buyer's quiet possession of the goods, namely—
>
> (a) the seller;
>
> (b) in a case where the parties to the contract intend that the seller should transfer only such title as a third person may have, that person;

1. See s. 12(5A) of the 1979 Act.

(c) anyone claiming through or under the seller or that third person otherwise than under a charge or encumbrance disclosed or known to the buyer before the contract is made.

The section thus creates two distinct sets of rights: first, where the sale is such that the parties (ostensibly) intend that the buyer should obtain a good title and, secondly, where the parties intend that the seller should only transfer such title as he is able. The rights in respect of the latter are, naturally, much more limited. These are examined in section 14.5.

The meaning of 'right to sell' used in s. 12(1) will be examined first before turning to remedies under that subsection. The implied warranty of quiet enjoyment will then be examined and finally the more limited rights created by virtue of s. 12(3).

14.2 'RIGHT TO SELL'

The principal mischief which s. 12 is aimed at is that of a non-owner purporting to sell a good; indeed the section is headed 'Implied terms about title, etc.'. However, were the section merely to state that the seller warrants that he has good title to the goods then certain situations legitimately occurring under the Act would be caught by s. 12.

First, s. 12(1) of the 1979 Act must be considered. This states that there is a contract of sale where the seller transfers or agrees to transfer the property in the goods. It is quite possible, therefore, for there to be a contract whereby the seller agrees that another will transfer the property to the buyer within this definition (see *Karshalmns Oliefabriker* v *Eastport Navigation Corp.* [1982] 1 All ER 208, at 215). Neither is such a situation necessarily rare. For example, one company may agree that its wholly owned subsidiary will transfer the property to the buyer. Furthermore, a contract whereby the seller is to manufacture or acquire goods falls within the definition of a contract of sale. The seller would not hold good title in such goods at the stage the contract is made and hence if s. 12 required him to do so there would be a breach although the contract is within the contemplation of the parties and the Act. Accordingly, one element of what s. 12 requires is that at the time the seller is due to transfer the property he has the power to vest good title in the buyer.

However, the use of the word 'right' extends the ambit of s. 12 beyond merely requiring the seller to have the power to vest a good title in the buyer. If in conferring a good title the seller would be acting unlawfully, the transaction may still form a breach of s. 12(1). There are at least three situations where this may occur.

One such situation is where the seller did not own the goods at the time of the sale but was able to transfer a good title to the buyer by virtue of an exception to the *nemo dat* rule (discussed in chapter 13). Here the buyer acquires good title but the seller does not have the 'right' to sell the goods; they were not his to sell.

There seems to be no clear authority on the point, but it is submitted that in these circumstances there will be a breach of the condition implied by s. 12. This is submitted despite the words said *obiter* by Atkin LJ in *Niblett* v *Confectioners' Materials Co. Ltd* [1921] 3 KB 387, at p. 401, that 'It may be that the implied condition is not broken if the seller is able to pass to the purchaser a right to sell notwithstanding his own inability'. Presumably, it was this situation which he was contemplating when using these words as there seems no other situation in English law whereby the buyer will acquire the right to sell notwithstanding the seller's inability to do so. Furthermore, the Crowther Committee on Consumer Credit (Cmnd. 4596, para. 5.7.32) has said that in such situations the buyer would have sustained no loss and hence could not maintain an action against the seller.

However, Atiyah points out in his work on this subject (*The Sale of Goods*, 9th edn, (Pitman Publishing), pp. 78–79) that where the buyer buys a good where there is outstanding credit secured upon the good (normally by way of hire purchase) the buyer will in all probability have difficulty selling the good on himself. This would be particularly so in the case of motor vehicles, the credit upon which is registered with a credit reference agency. In these circumstances the buyer of such goods would undoubtedly have difficulty explaining to a potential sub-buyer that the goods were no longer bound by such credit: would the average motor dealer trust a person coming off the street and explaining to them that a hire purchase company's title had been extinguished by virtue of s. 23 of the Hire Purchase Act 1964 because he, the buyer, had bought the car in good faith and without notice of the agreement? It is submitted that he would not.

In these circumstances, notwithstanding that the buyer *has* acquired a good legal title to the goods, he would have a loss in the market-place as he may have to sell the goods at a discount to account for any fears potential buyers may have. Here the buyer would have an actual loss to sue for, contrary to that suggested by the Crowther Committee.

Furthermore, the plain wording of the 1979 Act states that the seller must have the 'right to sell' in order for him to comply with the condition. If he does not have title to the goods, or authority from the owner to sell them, he does not have such right.

Finally, the buyer of such goods may have no desire to become embroiled in litigation with the owner and may simply wish to reject the goods and demand the return of the price. Where the seller is solvent and traceable, this is an option which the buyer should have; he should not be forced to do battle with the owner of the goods if the culprit can more easily be brought to account.

Another situation where the seller did not have the 'right to sell' the goods but passed a good title is demonstrated by the case of *Niblett* v *Confectioners' Materials Co. Ltd* [1921] 3 KB 387 which was referred to above. In that case the seller had sold condensed milk to the buyer for the purpose of sub-sale which blatantly infringed another firm's trade mark. The seller could have been restrained by that firm from making the sale. Accordingly, it was held that the seller had no right to sell the goods despite the fact that he could confer good title upon the buyer. There may be many more similar situations where the seller could be so restrained from making the sale, for example through want of an appropriate licence.

Finally, the case of *Lloyd's & Scottish Finance Ltd* v *Modern Cars and Caravans (Kingston) Ltd* [1966] 1 QB 764 raises some interesting questions upon s. 12. In that case a writ of *fieri facias* (a writ of execution) had been passed to the sheriff's officer in respect of seizure of the goods of W. The sheriff's officer delivered the writ to W at his caravan. However, before the caravan and its contents were physically removed by the sheriff's officer, W sold the caravan to the defendants. A few days later they discovered that the writ had been issued and a few days after that sold the caravan to the plaintiff. On the particular facts of the case it was held that there had been a seizure of the goods by the sheriff when he delivered the writ to W.

Given this the effect of the sale was to transfer the property in the caravan, but subject to the rights of the sheriff. Accordingly, there was a breach of s. 12(2) of the Act (right to enjoy quiet possession), but the defendants had the right to sell the goods and arguably there would be no breach under s. 12(1). In any event, it is unlikely that such a case will come before the courts in modern times as this case hinged upon the fact that the sheriff's officer had seized the goods despite his not taking actual possession of them.

Finally, it is worth noting that s. 12(1) is not expressed to be subject to the parties' contrary intentions. Furthermore, the Unfair Contract Terms Act 1977 prevents this. However, s. 12(1) does not apply to contracts to which s. 12(3) applies. Thus where the parties agree that the seller is to transfer only such title as he or a third party may have, s. 12(1) does not apply. This still means that in cases such as *Niblett* v *Confectioners' Materials Co. Ltd* the parties could not contract out of s. 12(1). This may lead to some injustice as there may be cases where the parties have expressly provided that the risk of, for example, the goods infringing some patent or trademark will be on the buyer yet the buyer could still rely on s. 12(1). No doubt this is something which the courts would be reluctant to allow to happen, but as drafted and upon its current interpretation this remains a problem.

14.3 THE EFFECT OF BREACH OF SECTION 12(1)

The normal remedy for a breach of a condition implied into the contract of sale is to terminate the contract and sue for the price or to claim damages for the loss. However, where the buyer has not received the property in the goods then he need not turn to remedies under the 1979 Act but he may make a restitutionary claim for money had and received as for a total failure of consideration. Indeed, following the case of *Rowland* v *Divall* [1923] 2 KB 500 it seems that s. 12(1) of the 1979 Act is rendered defunct altogether and it is unlikely that the buyer need rely on the Act at all, even to prove the breach.

The buyer's usual remedies for a breach of a condition implied by the Act are fully discussed in chapters 19 and 20, but it is worth explaining a little about them here. In the ordinary course of events, a buyer will be entitled to reject the goods if there is a breach of a condition of the contract and sue for the price of the goods and any other consequential losses which were within the contemplation of the parties at the time the contract was made. However, if the buyer is deemed to have accepted the goods (for example by lapse of a reasonable time) then by s. 11(4) he will not be entitled to reject the goods and his only remedy will be to sue for damages. The usual measure of damages is the difference between the value of the goods with the defect and their market value without it. This doctrine of acceptance is confined to the 1979 Act and does not apply to other contracts (such as hire purchase contracts or contracts for the transfer of goods). In these contracts the similar, but less stringent, common law doctrine of affirmation applies.

The 1979 Act also preserves the ordinary common law remedies which may be applicable. Of these, the right to sue for all monies paid under a contract whereby there has been a total failure of consideration is relevant here. This right accrues where the buyer has received no part of what he bargained to receive. The action is a common law action for monies had and received.

In relation to contracts whereby it transpires that the seller was not the true owner of goods and no exception to the *nemo dat* rule applies, this latter claim for monies had and received becomes relevant. Here the buyer has not received title to the goods and is obliged to return them to their owner. Following the leading case of *Rowland* v *Divall* [1923] 2 KB 500 the buyer is entitled to sue as for a total failure of consideration and recover all monies paid under the contract. Furthermore, the doctrine of acceptance has no application.

In *Rowland* v *Divall* the seller had purchased a car for £330 and in turn resold it for £400 to the buyer. It then transpired some four months later that the person the seller had purchased the car from was not the owner of it and that the true owner was making a claim in respect of it. It was held that the buyer was entitled to the return of his £400 and the seller was not entitled to bring into account the four months' usage of the car that the buyer had had. Lord Atkin observed that: 'The buyer has not received any part of that which he contracted to receive — namely the property and right to possession — and, that being so, there has been a total failure of consideration'. It has already been noted in section 1.4.1 that this decision is incorrect but that it remains good law. Following this decision it becomes unnecessary for the buyer to rely on s. 12 at all and it was further held that s. 11(4) has no application to such a contract.

The benefits of this decision to the buyer of the goods are well demonstrated by the later decision in *Butterworth* v *Kingsway Motors Ltd* [1954] 1 WLR 1286. In that case A took a car on hire purchase from O, thinking she had the right to do so she purported to sell it to B, who in turn sold it to C, who sold it to the defendant who sold it to the plaintiff. In the meantime A kept up with the payments to O. However, some 11 months after the sale to the plaintiff the finance company discovered that the car had been subject to all the sales and claimed to recover it from the plaintiff. O had of course remained the owner of the car at all stages. The plaintiff demanded the return of the price from the defendant who had sold it to him. A week later A made the final payment under her hire purchase agreement.

It was held that the plaintiff was entitled to recover the price in full. This was so despite the fact that he had had the use of the car for 11 months and, as it transpired, the market value in second-hand cars had fallen over this period and the car was now only worth £800 as opposed to the £1,275 at which it had been sold to the plaintiff. Furthermore, the court held that the title of the various buyers had been 'fed' up the chain of sale. The defendant was therefore left with a car worth less than when he had sold it and the plaintiff had had the use of it for 11 months and got out of a bad bargain. This decision has been criticised as unjust, but the buyer's remedies do not stop at this. It seems that he may recover any expenses he has incurred, or improvements made to the goods (*Warman* v *Southern Counties Corpn. Ltd* [1949] 2 KB 576; *Butterworth* v *Kingsway Motors Ltd*, above).

One interesting case to contrast with these is that of *Karflex Ltd* v *Poole* [1933] 2 KB 251. That case was decided on the particular terms of the contract, but it does highlight an interesting difference between the cases above and those of hire purchase. In that case the defendant had taken a car on hire purchase from the plaintiff, paying an initial deposit of £95 and agreeing to pay monthly instalments thereafter. The deposit was expressed as being in consideration of the acquisition of the option to purchase the car by payment of all the instalments; not in consideration of any hire of the car. The defendant never paid any instalments under the agreement and the plaintiffs began proceedings against him. After these proceedings were begun it was discovered that the person the plaintiffs had purchased the car from was not the owner of it, hence neither were the plaintiffs. The defendant argued that there was an implied term, similar to that in s. 12, that the plaintiffs were the owners of the vehicle and that as this term had been breached he was entitled to rescind the contract and counterclaim for his deposit. This argument succeeded. However, the court was reluctant to allow him to counterclaim for his deposit and did so only as the contract was expressed to make the consideration for the deposit the acquisition of the option to purchase. It seems that had the clause been expressed to link that deposit with the hire element of the contract, the court would have held that the deposit was irrecoverable.

14.4 FREEDOM FROM CHARGES AND QUIET POSSESSION

Section 12(2) of the 1979 Act provides that goods are free from any 'charge or encumbrance' and will remain so until the time the property is to pass and that the buyer will enjoy 'quiet possession' of the goods. These obligations are warranties only and the buyer's remedy for breach of them would be damages only.

The application of s. 12(2) is limited because goods are not normally subject to charges or security in the modern day. Such a course of action is generally used only in the case of ships and aircraft and those industries have developed specialist contracts to deal with such matters. However, these contracts are beyond the scope of this text and a specialist text should be referred to.

The first issue to explore in relation to this subsection is the meaning of 'charge or encumbrance' and 'quiet possession'. The first thing to note is that the former probably only applies to proprietary or possessory rights held by a third party. In *The Baranbels* [1985] 1 Lloyd's Rep 528 a ship was sold subject to an express term that it should be free from all 'charges or maritime liens' and the judge defined this as being restricted to proprietary or possessory rights. Accordingly, where a third party creditor had a debt due from the seller and a foreign court had impounded the ship to secure payment of the debt this was not a proprietary right in the ship and the express clause did not cover it.

However, even this seems to be of limited application since there are few charges recognised at law or in equity which would be operative in such circumstances. In order for such charges to be operative the person must be in possession of the goods and if this were the case the seller would not be in a position to deliver the goods and would hence be liable for non-delivery. The buyer would therefore have no need to rely on s. 12.

One, obvious, point is that it seems that the seller will only be liable for lawful acts of third parties. Certainly, it would seem bizarre if the seller was liable for acts which were in themselves unlawful.

Turning to the meaning of 'quiet enjoyment', it seems possible that a disturbance which merely prevents the buyer from disposing of the goods may not be sufficient. This follows from the dictum of Atkin LJ in *Niblett* v *Confectioners' Materials Co. Ltd* [1921] 3 KB 387 where he said (at p. 403):

> It may be that possession would not be disturbed if the only cause of complaint was that the buyer could not dispose of the goods, and that the warranty is confined to disturbance of possession of the goods delivered under the contract of sale.

The obligation to ensure that the buyer enjoys quiet enjoyment is, however, a continuing one; it is not a one-off duty at the time of sale. This appeared from the case of *Microbeads AC* v *Vinhurst Road Markings Ltd* [1975] 1 All ER 529. In that case the buyers had bought a road marking machine which infringed a patent. Whilst the patent had been granted after the contract had been entered into it had been published prior to that date. Under English law the right to sue for an infringement of the patent only accrues at the date the patent is granted, but the rights accrue from the date of publication. It was held that the buyers were entitled to recover.

Finally, the mere fact that there has been a breach of s. 12(1) does not mean that the buyer must rely on that section and ignore s. 12(2); he may sue on both. Likewise, the mere fact that there has been a breach of condition does not prevent the buyer treating that as a breach of warranty and suing for damages (*Mason* v *Burningham* [1949] 2 KB 545).

14.5 TRANSFER OF SUCH TITLE AS THE SELLER OR A THIRD PERSON MAY HAVE

Section 12(3) of the 1979 Act applies to cases where the seller agrees to transfer such title as he or a third party may have. There do not appear to be any cases which define the circumstances when such an intention will be inferred, indeed such circumstances will be rare. It is submitted that in order for a court to invoke s. 12(3) there must be clear evidence that the buyer took the risk that the seller was not the owner of the goods.

It must be recalled that there may be many titles and interests to goods. Thus a person who finds goods may gain a possessory title but his title will be liable to be defeated by the owner of the goods who holds an absolute title. Thus it is quite possible for one person to be legitimately in possession of goods, yet hold a title which is liable to be defeated.

15 *Sale of goods by description*

15.1 GENERAL

Section 13 of the Sale of Goods Act 1979 (the '1979 Act')[1] provides as follows:

> (1) Where there is a contract for the of sale of goods by description, there is an implied [term] that the goods will correspond with the description.
> (1A) As regards England and Wales and Northern Ireland, the term implied by subsection (1) above is a condition.
> (2) If the sale is by sample as well as by description it is not sufficient that the bulk of the goods corresponds with the sample if the goods do not also correspond with the description.
> (3) A sale of goods is not prevented from being a sale by description by reason only that, being exposed for sale or hire, they are selected by the buyer.

Several matters fall to be discussed in relation to s. 13:

(a) The contractual status of the term implied by s. 13.
(b) When is a sale of goods *by* description?
(c) Which words are capable of being words of description?
(d) Failure to correspond with description.

15.2 THE CONTRACTUAL STATUS OF THE TERM IMPLIED BY SECTION 13

Under the general law of contract a distinction is to be drawn between words which are 'mere' representations and words which have effect as contractual terms, be they conditions of the contract (entitling an injured party to terminate the contract for their breach) or warranties (entitling the injured party to damages only for their

1. Identical corresponding terms are implied in relation to the transfer of goods by the Supply of Goods and Services Act 1982 and in relation to the bailment or hire of goods under the Supply of Goods (Implied Terms) Act 1973.

breach). Chapter 3 of this text deals with the requirements for deciding which category the words fall in.

In order to fall within s. 13 the words of description must have been incorporated into the contract as a contractual term as opposed to a 'mere' representation. This much is clear from cases such as *T. & J. Harrison* v *Knowles and Foster* [1918] 1 KB 608, *Taylor* v *Combined Buyers Ltd* [1924] NZLR 627 and most recently *Harlingdon & Leinster Enterprises Ltd* v *Christopher Hull Fine Art Ltd* [1991] 1 QB 564.

The difficulty which this raises is that if the words of description form in any event a term of the contract what is the point of having s. 13? The buyer would be entitled to sue for breach of an *express* term of the contract without having to rely on the term *implied* by s. 13.

It is submitted that the effect of s. 13, if any, is to raise the status of terms which have been incorporated into the contract as warranties to conditions. However, even this does not seem certain. In *Harlingdon & Leinster Enterprises Ltd* v *Christopher Hull Fine Art Ltd* Nourse LJ said: 'The description must have a sufficient influence in the sale to become an essential term of the contract . . .'. The use of the word *essential* seems to imply that the words must have gained the status of conditions.

In any event, as is noted in more detail in chapter 3, the courts appear to adopt the somewhat circular approach of determining whether a term is a condition or a warranty or a mere representation by looking at whether the injured part *ought* to be allowed to avoid the contract or seek damages for its breach. For example, in *Ashington Piggeries* v *Christopher Hill Ltd* [1972] AC 441 Lord Diplock said: 'It is open to the parties to use a description as broad or narrow as they choose. But ultimately the test is whether the buyer could fairly and reasonably refuse to accept the physical goods proffered to him on the ground that their failure to correspond with that part of what was said about them in the contract makes them goods of a different kind from those he had agreed to buy.' In practice, therefore, the exact status of s. 13 seems to fall into academic obscurity.

On this basis any distinction as to whether a statement is a warranty, condition or representation is really one of nomenclature and not substance (see also Lord Denning in *Oscar Chess Ltd* v *Williams* [1957] 1 WLR 370). The law becomes somewhat circular — a party is entitled to terminate the contract when he ought to be.

As will be seen below, the key to a claim based upon s. 13 is *reliance* upon the words used by the seller. Where the buyer reasonably relies on the words he may terminate the contract; where he does not then he cannot. There do not appear to be any cases where the courts have decided that the words have contractual effect but only such as to entitle the buyer to damages, i.e., the words have become a warranty and not a condition, or indeed an innominate term. Indeed, the courts seem to willingly ignore the possibility of an innominate term or warranty and adopt an all-or-nothing approach (for example, *Re Moore & Landauer & Co.* [1921] 2 KB 519). However, it still seems open to the courts to find that the words fall into any of these three categories — s. 13 does not appear to have destroyed this distinction (*Ashington Piggeries* v *Christopher Hill Ltd* [1972] AC 441; *Reardon Smith Line Ltd* v *Hansen-Tangen* [1976] 1 WLR 989). It would seem, therefore, that s. 13 operates as no more than a statement of the common law.

Whatever the status of s. 13, the circumstances where a buyer is entitled to terminate the contract for breach of a term of description will be concentrated upon below.

15.3 SALE BY DESCRIPTION

In order for there to be a sale by description there must be more than the mere use of descriptive words; the buyer must rely upon them in entering into the contract. This issue is a question of fact in each case; there is no firm rule of law on the point.

In the case of future goods the sale will almost always be by description — given that the goods are not yet in existence, or have yet to be acquired by the seller, the only reference made to what the buyer is buying is the description of the goods (*Varley* v *Whipp* [1900] 1 QB 513, at 516). Indeed, it is difficult to envisage a situation where the buyer under such a contract has bought the goods other than in reliance upon the description.

It may be assumed that where the buyer has examined the goods themselves, the contract is not one where the goods were sold by description. However this is not so. This is specifically declared by s. 13(3) of the 1979 Act, but it was always the case prior to this addition to the statute. In *Beale* v *Taylor* [1967] 1 WLR 1193 a car was advertised for sale as being a 'Herald Convertible, 1961'. In fact it was what is now known as a 'cut and shut' — one car made up from two. It transpired that part of the car was not manufactured in 1961. It was held that there could be a sale by description where the buyer had inspected the car so long as he had relied upon the descriptive words used. In this case he had and was accordingly held entitled to recover. The question of whether the buyer does so rely upon the description is a question of fact in each case. Accordingly, there is nothing which prevents a sale being by description simply because a buyer has examined the goods. However, evidentially, the buyer will find it harder to displace the inference that he bought what was in front of him and did not rely upon the description (see also *Oscar Chess Ltd* v *Williams* [1957] 1 WLR 370; *Grant* v *Australian Knitting Mills Ltd* [1936] AC 85).

Where a buyer has relied not upon the description of the goods but upon his own assessment of them, he will not be shown to have relied upon the description. In *Harlingdon & Leinster Enterprises Ltd* v *Christopher Hull Fine Art Ltd* [1991] 1 QB 564 a painting was advertised as being by a particular artist. The buyer was a specialist dealer and on the facts appeared to have relied upon his own judgment as opposed to the description. When the painting transpired to be a forgery he was not entitled to recover under s. 13.

15.4 WORDS CAPABLE OF BEING WORDS OF DESCRIPTION

The key to whether words fall within the meaning of 'description' in s. 13 of the 1979 Act is whether they *identify a substantial ingredient* of the goods and not the attributes of the goods. This much seems clear from the cases of *Couchman* v *Hill* [1947] KB 554, *Reardon Smith Line Ltd* v *Yngvar Hansen-Tangen* [1976] 1 WLR 989 and *Ashington Piggeries* v *Christopher Hill Ltd* [1972] AC 441 (at 503).

For example, suppose a car is advertised as being a '1995 Ford Sierra. Excellent condition'. If the latter words have any contractual effect at all (being possible 'mere puffs') then this is as a warranty as to quality, not as to the description of the goods. By contrast if the car sold turned out to be a Ford Escort, this would clearly relate to the identity of the goods and fall within s. 13.

Much here depends upon the context of the descriptive words. For example, were a shopper to purchase a shirt from a pile of shirts marked as '100 per cent wool' then there would clearly be a breach of s. 13 if the shirt proved to be a mix of wool and polyester (e.g., in *Tradax Export SA* v *European Grain & Shipping Ltd* [1983] 2 Lloyd's Rep 100 soyabean meal was described as being 'maximum 7.5 per cent fibre' — this formed part of the description of the goods). Whilst the words do not 'identify' the goods in the sense that the buyer knew perfectly well that the shirt he was buying was the one in his hand, they do identify a substantial ingredient of the shirt (*Beale* v *Taylor* [1967] 1 WLR 1193). By contrast, in *Reardon Smith Line Ltd* v *Yngvar Hansen-Tangen* [1976] 1 WLR 989 a ship was described as lying at 'Yard 354', when it was in fact being built at an associated yard of the manufacturer at 'Yard 4'. These words merely identified where the ship was and not any special ingredient of it.

Again, depending upon the context, even seemingly vague words may constitute 'descriptive' ones if the context permits. For example, in *Toepfer* v *Continental Grain Co.* [1974] 1 Lloyd's Rep 11 the word 'hard' in the context of 'hard wheat' was accepted as capable of being a descriptive word as it appeared to have a particular meaning within the industry. Likewise in *Toepfer* v *Warinco AG* [1978] 2 Lloyd's Rep 569 the words 'fine ground' were accepted as being descriptive in the context of soya meal. Phrases such as these are to be found in regular usage in particular industries and within such industries are understood to have an exact meaning.

Where the goods are future goods, the courts have been stringent as to the application of s. 13. In *Arcos Ltd* v *Ronaasen* [1933] AC 470 the buyers ordered staves from the sellers which were to be half an inch thick. Staves were delivered of which 5 per cent only conformed with this and the remainder did not, but only by about one sixteenth of an inch. It was held that they did not conform with their description, despite their being commercially within their specification and fit for their purpose. Similarly, in *Rapalli* v *K. L. Take* [1958] 2 Lloyd's Rep 469 onions did not conform with their description when they were 6 per cent too small. More stunningly, in *Re Moore & Co. Ltd and Landauer & Co. Ltd* [1921] 2 KB 519 tins of fruit were ordered which were to be delivered in packs of 24 tins. They were held to be outside their description when they were delivered in packs of 30.

These cases were decided before the section was given the lengthy analysis by the House of Lords in the *Ashington Piggeries* case and in *Reardon Smith Line Ltd* v *Yngvar Hansen-Tangen* (above) and criticism was made of the stringent application of the rule in the latter case. However, of these three cases only *Re Moore & Co. Ltd and Landauer & Co. Ltd* seems to be on the borderline — it is at least questionable whether the packaging of the tins was a 'substantial ingredient of the identity of the goods'. In the former cases the size of the thing ordered does seem to be a substantial ingredient of the good's identity.

15.5 CORRESPONDENCE WITH DESCRIPTION

Whilst the same principles apply to all goods it seems that the circumstances when a good will be held not to conform to its contract description will vary according to the nature of the good in question. These cases appear to fall into three categories: sales of future goods, admixtures and consumer or small business cases. The last of these shall be examined first.

Cases involving consumers and small businesses inevitably involve a much less detailed contract and the descriptive words are accordingly much more general. This is not to say that commercial cases cannot fall into this category, simply that the parties will generally have specified much more exactly what they have contracted to buy as the size of the contract and the parties' resources justifies them in taking more time over the formulation of the contract.

Where the words are more general, a much more serious discrepancy will normally be needed before a breach of s. 13 will be found. For example, in *Varley* v *Whipp* [1900] 1 QB 513 there was a contract for the sale of a reaper 'new the previous year', when in fact the machine was very old. This was held to be a breach of the condition of description. Likewise in *Andrews Bros Ltd* v *Singer & Co. Ltd* [1934] 1 KB 17 there was found to be a breach of the condition of description when a second-hand car was delivered in place of the new one ordered. Again, in the case of *Beale* v *Taylor* [1967] 1 WLR 1193 where a 'cut and shut' car (two cars welded into one) was delivered there was a breach of s. 13 where the parts of one of the cars were not those of a 1961 model as specified.

Turning to the second category of cases, admixtures, the courts seem to simply ask whether what was delivered can properly be described as being that which was contracted for. As will be seen finding any particular form of words to define when this will be so seems to have eluded the courts.

For example, in *Pinnock Bros* v *Lewis and Peat Ltd* [1923] 1 KB 690 copra cake was mixed with castor seed in such proportions as to be poisonous. It was held that the goods could not properly be described as copra cake at all.

In *Robert A. Munro & Co. Ltd* v *Meyer* [1930] 2 KB 312 Wright J said:

> I need not refer to authority, because it has been frequently laid down that a seller cannot justify delivering goods which to a substantial extent are of the contract description, but are mixed with other goods which do not answer the contract description.

He went on to hold that bone-meal mixed with between three to five per cent cocoa husk was a substantial amount and that the goods did not conform to their description within the meaning of s. 13. It must be noted that the addition of the husk meant that the resale by the buyers of the goods in their market-place of England and Germany was an offence.

A harder distinction to draw is where the goods have become contaminated during a manufacturing process, adding some further ingredient to the goods. In *Ashington Piggeries Ltd* v *Christopher Hill Ltd* [1972] AC 441 herring meal was sold which was preserved in sodium nitrate. When heated in a further process this caused a reaction which produced a poison known as DMNA which killed mink to which the end product was fed. It was contended that the goods sold did not match their description in that what was sold was not herring meal but herring meal plus DMNA and that *Pinnock Bros* v *Lewis* and *Munro* v *Meyer* applied. This argument was rejected by the majority of the House of Lords. Lord Wilberforce, whilst pointing out that the argument would appeal best to Aristotle, said that the test was whether an ordinary mercantile man would still describe the good as herring meal. In this case he thought that they would. However, the House of Lords did not dissaprove of *Pinnock Bros* v *Lewis* and *Munro* v *Meyer*, they simply distinguished the instant case from them. To define this difference with any degree of precision of words seemed however to elude the House, and indeed is probably best left to Aristotle.

Turning to the third type of good, future goods, it is clear from cases such as *Reardon Smith Line Ltd* v *Yngvar Hansen-Tangen* [1976] 1 WLR 989 (per Lord Wilberforce at p. 998) that sales of this type of good are treated differently than other goods. Reference was made in the previous section to the cases of *Arcos Ltd* v *Ronaasen* [1933] AC 470, *Rapalli* v *K. L. Take* [1958] 2 Lloyd's Rep 469 and *Re Moore & Co. Ltd and Landauer & Co. Ltd* [1921] 2 KB 519. Following these cases it seems that exact compliance with the contract description is required in cases of the sale of future goods. Following *Arcos Ltd* v *Ronaasen* it seems that this is required even where the goods are fit for their purpose. Whilst this remains good law today it was pointed out in the *Reardon Smith* case by Lord Wilberforce that these cases were excessively technical and were open to reconsideration by the House of Lords in an appropriate case. It may be that a more relaxed attitude to the law will be taken in the future. In any event the new s. 15A of the 1979 Act which was inserted by the Sale and Supply of Goods Act 1994 now provides that where the breach is slight the court may refuse to permit the buyer to reject in non-consumer cases.

16 *Implied terms as to quality, fitness for purpose and correspondence with sample*

16.1 GENERAL

Section 14 of the Sale of Goods Act 1979 (the '1979 Act') provides as follows:

> (1) Except as provided by this section and section 15 below and subject to any other enactment, there is no implied [condition or warranty] about the quality or fitness for any particular purpose of goods supplied under a contract of sale.
>
> (2) Where the seller sells goods in the course of a business, there is an implied term that the goods supplied under the contract are of satisfactory quality.
>
> (2A) For the purposes of this Act, goods are of satisfactory quality if they meet the standard that a reasonable person would regard as satisfactory, taking account of any description of the goods, the price (if relevant) and all the other relevant circumstances.
>
> (2B) For the purposes of this Act, the quality of goods includes their state and condition and the following (among others) are in appropriate cases aspects of the quality of goods—
>
> (a) fitness for all the purposes for which goods of the kind in question are commonly supplied,
>
> (b) appearance and finish,
>
> (c) freedom from minor defects,
>
> (d) safety, and
>
> (e) durability.
>
> (2C) The term implied by subsection (2) above does not extend to any matter making the quality of goods unsatisfactory—
>
> (a) which is specifically drawn to the buyer's attention before the contract is made,
>
> (b) where the buyer examines the goods before the contract is made, which that examination ought to reveal, or

(c) in the case of a contract for sale by sample, which would have been apparent on a reasonable examination of the sample.

(3) Where the seller sells goods in the course of a business and the buyer, expressly or by implication, makes known —

(a) to the seller, or

(b) where the purchase price or part of it is payable by instalments and the goods were previously sold by a credit-broker to the seller, to that credit-broker, any particular purpose for which the goods are being bought,

there is an implied term that the goods supplied under the contract are reasonably fit for that purpose, whether or not that is a purpose for which such goods are commonly supplied, except where the circumstances show that the buyer does not rely, or that it is unreasonable for him to rely, on the skill or judgment of the seller or credit-broker.

. . .

(4)

(5) The preceding provisions of this section apply to a sale by a person who in the course of a business is acting as agent for another as they apply to a sale by a principal in the course of a business, except where that other is not selling in the course of a business and either the buyer knows that fact or reasonable steps are taken to bring it to the notice of the buyer before the contract is made.

(6) As regards England and Wales and Northern Ireland, the terms implied by subsections (2) and (3) above are conditions.

Section 14 implies a condition into many contracts for the sale of goods that they must be of satisfactory quality and fit for the purpose for which they were bought. This probably represents the most important provision in the 1979 Act. It is also probably the piece of law best known to the layman. Prior to the 1994 amendments (see section 16.3 below) the term 'satisfactory quality' was known as 'merchantable quality', a phrase many shopkeepers came to fear.

Prior to the original Act of 1893 there was no general rule that goods must be of any particular quality; the maxim *caveat emptor* (buyer beware) prevailed. Indeed this general position is maintained by s. 14(1) — other than ss. 14 and 15 (and the corresponding provisions in relation to the supply of goods) there is no implied term that goods must be of any particular standard. The only other exception provided by the 1979 Act is that contained in s. 14(4) which maintains the old rule that any term implied by trade usage survives under the general law of contract.

Section 14 in fact imports two distinct terms: first, that the goods must be of 'satisfactory quality', and secondly, that they must be 'fit for their purpose'. These two terms are discussed separately below. Briefly, however, there are two differences in the tests: the term of satisfactory quality is more stringent than the term of fitness for purpose in that the former demands a higher standard of quality. Thus a carpet with a hole in it is fit for its purpose as a carpet because it covers a floor, but it is not of satisfactory quality due to the unsightly defect. However, the term as to fitness for purpose is wider than the term as to satisfactory quality in that the former applies to purposes of goods which are not necessarily the usual purposes of such goods but which are specifically made known to the seller. For this reason some lawyers refer to the test of satisfactory quality as being an objective test and the term as to fitness for purpose as being a subjective one.

The common stipulation in both s. 14(2) and (3) that the seller sells the goods in the course of a business will be examined before turning to the individual requirements of each section. Finally, contracts for sale by sample under s. 15 of the 1979 Act will be examined. A list of cases is provided at the end of the chapter, section 16.7, which may give guidance as to the application of the sections in specific case situations.

16.2 IN THE COURSE OF A BUSINESS

Until recently there has been much confusion as to the meaning of the phrase 'sells in the course of a business'. The confusion essentially arises because, on occasions, a business has need to sell a good but the sale of such goods is not the principal (or indeed any) part of its business. Similarly, a person may undertake a one-off venture in manufacturing or acquiring and then selling a good, although such sales are not undertaken on a regular basis. Likewise, there exists the situation where a business sells off part of its capital but this in no way forms part of the principal business of the firm. This would be the case where, for example, a car hire firm sells off some of its cars or where an accountants' firm sells off its old computers.

There is no doubt that a large retailer or manufacturer sells goods in the course of its business: it is the entire part of its business. However, it is sales at the margin which cause difficulty. In the now leading case of *Stevenson* v *Rogers* [1999] QB 1028 Potter LJ accepted that the following categories existed:

> ... in the field of consumer protection three broad categories have been developed to identify whether a sale is made 'in the course of a business', namely (a) a sale in a one-off venture in the nature of a trade carried through with a view to profit; (b) a sale which is an integral part of the business carried on; (c) a sale which is merely incidental to the business carried on but which is undertaken with a degree of regularity.
>
> In categories (a) and (b) the transaction is in the course of a business because it is the conduct of the very business itself. In (c) the transaction is in the course of such business because its regularity has made it so; see also *Devlin* v *Hall* [1990] RTR 320. It is not in dispute that we need not concern ourselves with (a) in this case.

To this there may be added the situations where the sale is (d) merely incidental to the business, but there is no regularity, and (e) a purely private sale of a chattel never used as part of a business.

There is no doubt following the above definitions that (a) and (b) are sales made in the course of a business. Likewise there is no doubt that (e) is not a sale made in the course of a business. The difficulty arises in deciding whether categories (c) and (d) are sales made in the course of a business. As will be seen, it seems, following *Stevenson* v *Rogers*, that both are.

Prior to the decision in *Stevenson* v *Rogers* there does not appear to have been a decision specifically on s. 14 of the 1979 Act and recourse had to be made to similar provisions in other statutes. For example, s. 1(1) of the Trade Descriptions Act 1968 makes provision in respect of sales 'in the course of a trade or business' and s. 12(1) of the Unfair Contract Terms Act 1977 refers to *purchases* made in the course of a business.

It seemed, following the decisions in *Davies* v *Sumner* [1984] 1 WLR 1301 and *Havering London Borough Council* v *Stevenson* [1970] 1 WLR 1375, that in order to constitute a sale in the course of business for category (c) above the sale must be made with a degree of regularity. In those cases the defendants were charged with selling goods under a misdescription 'in the course of a trade or business' under the Trade Descriptions Act 1968. In *Havering* the defendant ran a car hire firm and regularly sold off the cars once they were no longer usable for hire. This was held to be a sale in the course of a business. By contrast, in *Davies*, the defendant ran a courier firm and had sold his car after a specific period of time. No degree of regularity had however been established in the sale and it was held not to be in the course of a business. Accordingly, the distinction in category (c) that an incidental sale must possess a degree of regularity if it is to be in the course of business was recognised as being essential on the authorities before the court.

However, in *Stevenson* Potter LJ distinguished these authorities on the ground that they were criminal cases which necessarily enjoyed a more restrictive interpretation. Looking at the development of the 1979 Act a different parliamentary intent could be found. In *Stevenson* a fisherman had formed an intent to sell his boat and replace it with another. This he did and it was held that the sale was in the course of his business. After a careful analysis of the statutory development Potter LJ said:

> In my view, it is not necessary to do more than to turn to the statutory change of wording in s. 14(2) as between the Act of 1893 and s. 3 of the Act of 1973 (which s. 14(2) of the Act of 1979 simply re-enacted) to see that it was the intention of the Act of 1973 to widen the protection afforded to a purchaser by s. 14(2) from a situation where the seller was a dealer in the type of goods sold to one where he simply made a sale 'in the course of a business'; the requirement for regularity of dealing, or indeed any dealing, in the goods was removed. Given the removal of that requirement, there is on the face of it no reason or warrant (at any rate in a civil rather than a criminal context) to reintroduce some implied qualification, difficult to define, in order to narrow what appears to be the wide scope and apparent purpose of the words, which is to distinguish between a sale made in the course of a seller's business and a purely private sale of goods outside the confines of the business (if any) carried on by the seller.

Following this decision, it seems that any sale of a chattel owned and utilised by a business will be a sale 'in the course of a business'.

It must be noted as well that, by virtue of s. 14(5), a sale by a purely private seller can acquire the status of a sale in the course of a business if it is sold by an agent who is acting in the course of a business unless reasonable steps are taken to bring this to the notice of the purchaser. This applies whether or not the principal is disclosed or undisclosed (*Boyter* v *Thompson* [1995] 2 AC 629). What will form 'reasonable steps' does not appear to have been the subject of judicial consideration. This therefore seems to be a question of fact which is very much left open to the court of first instance.

16.3 SATISFACTORY QUALITY

The phrase 'satisfactory quality' was substituted for the phrase 'merchantable quality' by virtue of a House of Lords amendment to the Sale of Goods (Amendment) Bill 1994 which was put forward by the Law Commission in its report *Sale and Supply of Goods* (Law Com. 160). However, it does not appear that this amendment changed the intent of the Bill, the amendment was one of nomenclature and not substance. Likewise, some authors have suggested that the new definition means that the law starts with a clean sheet from the introduction of the amendments and that the old case law has no bearing on the meaning of 'satisfactory quality'. A short reading of the Law Commission report indicates that this was not the intent of the Commission. Indeed, in order to fully understand the law an analysis of the old law is essential. This, together with the analysis of the Law Commission, leads to the proper interpretation of the 1979 Act as it now reads.

Equally it must be remembered that the 1979 Act gives only a very broad definition of what forms 'satisfactory quality': it is what, in the time-honoured phrase, a reasonable man would consider satisfactory. Accordingly, the issue is very much left to the judge dealing with the case at first instance. This leads to the problem of consistency between courts. There exists a belief within the law that all courts will dish out justice fairly and in equal measure. However, a quick reading of *Bernstein* v *Pamson Motors (Golders Green) Ltd* [1987] 2 All ER 220 and *Rogers* v *Parish (Scarborough) Ltd* [1987] QB 933, which were decided in the same year, shows that this is not the case. Whether it is possible to give an all-embracing definition to a phrase which covers so broad a spectrum as 'goods' is clearly open to question. The guidance that has been given will be examined, but it should be borne in mind that the issue is always one of fact and degree upon which a different court may take a different view on the particular facts before it.

The 1979 Act adopts a two-stage test in determining quality. First, s. 14(2A) defines 'satisfactory quality' as being what a reasonable man would regard as satisfactory in all the circumstances. When will this be? Secondly, under s. 14(2B) various factors of quality are highlighted. The particular approach of the courts and the Law Commission to these aspects will be examined. Finally, the exceptions to s. 14 are also considered.

First, the goods to which s. 14 applies are considered. As will be seen, this is not restricted to the goods which are the subject of the contract.

16.3.1 Goods supplied under the contract

The goods supplied under the contract include all the goods supplied to the buyer, not merely the contract goods. For example, the packaging of the goods and items mixed into the goods by accident are supplied to the buyer, although they were not contracted for. A defect in such an 'extra' item can form the basis of a claim under s. 14.

Perhaps the most startling case on this point is that of *Wilson* v *Rickett, Cockerell & Co. Ltd* [1954] 1 QB 598. In that case an explosive had accidentally become mixed with a consignment of coalite. Unsurprisingly, when the coalite was being burned it exploded. It was held that the explosive formed part of the goods supplied under the contract of sale. Similarly, in *Geddling* v *Marsh* [1920] 1 KB 668 a defective bottle supplied with mineral water was held to form part of the goods supplied under the contract even though the bottle was due to be returned to the seller. Again, in *Chaproniere* v *Mason* (1905) 21 TLR 633 a stone in a bun which damaged the tooth of the person eating it was held to form part of the goods supplied under the contract.

Following these cases the section was amended to read 'goods supplied under the contract' in 1973 and this terminology has been retained following the 1994 amendments.

16.3.2 Standard that a reasonable man would regard as satisfactory

As was noted above, the statute now adopts a two-stage process: the overriding standard that the goods are of satisfactory quality and the second stage of looking at aspects of that quality. We are concerned here with the guidance given as to when the courts should hold that a reasonable man would or would not consider goods to be of satisfactory quality. We will consider first the general test to be applied before looking at specific considerations, 'aspects of quality', which must be taken into account when making this evaluation.

16.3.2.1 Development of the test for 'satisfactory quality': acceptability and fitness for purpose The law has developed in this area in a stage-by-stage fashion, adopting some tests put forward and rejecting others. Looking at those strands which have survived the various amendments and contrasting those which have not is therefore a good way of highlighting what the proper test is.

Two types of test have been predominantly used in assessing quality: fitness for purpose and acceptability. Whilst fitness for purpose remains an important consideration under the present law, it is the acceptability test which appears to have the greatest weight attached to it now.

The acceptability test was first formulated in *Bristol Tramways* v *Fiat Motors* [1910] 2 KB 831 where it was said that goods were of merchantable quality if they were of such quality 'that a reasonable man acting reasonably would after full examination accept [them] under the circumstances of the case in performance of his offer to buy [them]'.

The fitness for purpose test was put forward in *Cammell Laird & Co. Ltd* v *Manganese Bronze & Brass Ltd* [1934] AC 402. Here merchantable quality was defined as meaning that goods were not of that quality if goods that were 'in a form in which they were tendered were of no use for any purpose for which such goods would normally be used'.

Arguably the acceptability test is broader and more favourable to the buyer. It is also quite circular in that all it really says is that goods are of merchantable quality if a reasonable person would say that they are. The fitness for purpose test can also be said to be more strict because goods may be fit for *a* purpose for which goods are commonly bought but not fit for the particular purpose of which such goods are bought, albeit a common purpose.

Both of these cases came for consideration by the House of Lords in *Henry Kendall & Sons* v *William Lillico & Sons Ltd* [1969] 2 AC 31. In the first place the House of Lords preferred an Australian version of the acceptability test put forward in *Australian Cotton Mills Ltd* v *Grant* (1933) 50 CLR 387 that the goods were of merchantable quality where a buyer would buy them without asking for a reduction in the price of them. It also criticised the fitness for purpose test put forward in the *Cammell Laird* case on the basis that it would be better if it were to read that the goods were of 'no use for any purpose for which goods which complied with the description under which those goods were sold would normally be used'.

This resulted in the enactment of a definition of merchantable quality by the Supply of Goods (Implied Terms) Act 1973 as being: 'Goods of any kind are of merchantable quality . . . if they are as fit for the purpose or purposes for which goods of that kind are commonly bought as it is reasonable to expect having regard to any description applied to them, the price (if relevant) and all the other relevant circumstances.' A compromise was thus reached between the two tests.

The new test, however, did not spell out whether the goods had to be fit for *all* the purposes which goods of that kind were bought, or whether it was sufficient that they were fit for some of those purposes. This was somewhat resolved in *Aswan Engineering Establishment Co.* v *Lupdine Ltd* [1987] 1 WLR 1. In that case plastic pails had been purchased and were shipped to the Persian Gulf. They were then stacked six high in extreme temperatures — they melted. In finding that they were of merchantable quality it was said that goods need not be fit for all foreseeable uses in order to be merchantable. The old test propounded in the *Cammell Laird* case had survived.

Perhaps driven by an increase in the perception of what consumers were entitled to expect, the law moved away from the strict approach of the fitness for purpose test, and following the 1994 amendments it is no longer a principal consideration.

For example, in *Rogers* v *Parish (Scarborough) Ltd* [1987] QB 933 the Court of Appeal overturned a decision that a car was of merchantable quality because it was fit for the normal purposes for which a car was bought in that it was roadworthy and drivable. The car in question was a £16,000 Range Rover and the Court of Appeal held that the degree of comfort, ease of handling, reliability and pride in appearance were all 'purposes' of the purchase of such a car.

Following the 1994 amendments, the test is now whether a reasonable man would consider the goods to be satisfactory and the test for fitness for purpose is now relegated to one of the aspects of quality. The broad 'acceptability' test is to be used. Furthermore, when considering fitness for purpose as an aspect of quality the court must consider whether the goods were fit for *all* the common purposes which goods of that type are commonly used. It is clear that the Law Commission intended that the onus was to be on the seller to point out to the buyer that the goods are not fit for one of their common purposes if that is the case (Law Commission Final Report, *Sale and Supply of Goods*, para. 3.36).

This does not mean that fitness for purpose fails to be a relevant test, but it is no longer paramount. Goods may continue to be of satisfactory quality if they are only fit for some of their common purposes depending upon the circumstances of the case (for example an extremely low price). Nor does the new test necessarily mean that a different result would necessarily be reached in cases decided before the amendment. For example, in the *Aswan Engineering* case above it would be open to the court to find that stacking pails six high in excessive temperatures was not a common purpose for such goods and that in respect of their common purposes they were fit for those purposes. This would be a question of fact for the judge dealing with the case at first instance. Similarly, in *Sumner Permain & Co. Ltd* v *Webb & Co. Ltd* [1922] 1 KB 55 the seller had sold tonic water to the buyer which contained salicylic acid, such acid being legal in every country except the Argentine. The buyer unfortunately had purchased the tonic with a view to export to the Argentine. A claim based upon lack of merchantable quality failed. As with *Aswan Engineering* it would still be open to the court to find that such export was not a *common* purpose within the meaning of the current law.

The use of the word 'common' must be distinguished from 'possible' or even 'probable'. In order to comply with the statute the goods need to comply with all their 'common' purposes: the seller need not consider every conceivable use of the goods which he is selling.

16.3.2.2 The price Goods may be of satisfactory quality despite the fact that they are not fit for *any* of their common purposes. The court is allowed to take into account the price and other relevant considerations. Thus if a car is purchased for £50 from a scrap-yard and it breaks down as it leaves the gates of the yard it would probably not be considered fit for any of the purposes for which cars are commonly supplied. However, the price is a relevant factor and the court could still say that the car was of satisfactory quality.

However, using the price as a relevant consideration is a tricky issue. Section 14 is not in place to remedy a bad bargain on the part of the buyer. In *B. S. Brown & Son* v *Craiks Ltd* [1970] 1 WLR 750 Viscount Dilhorne said:

> ... surely it is not enough just to show that there is a difference between the contract price and that which the goods would fetch if sold for a different use. The buyer might have agreed to pay too high a price.

But went on to say:

> But if the contract price was so far above the price that the goods would have fetched if sold for another purpose as to indicate that goods for that other purpose were unsaleable at anything approaching the contract price, then it might be held that the goods were not of merchantable quality.
>
> If, for instance, the evidence in this case showed that the rayon cloth for which the appellants agreed to pay £36.25 a yard would only fetch 15 a yard for an industrial purpose, then it might be held that the abatement of price was such as to indicate that the cloth delivered at £36.25 a yard was not commercially saleable for any industrial use and so not of merchantable quality.

It must be borne in mind that this was said at a time when goods were considered of merchantable quality if they were fit for any of their common purposes. Accordingly, it is best to interpret the second part of the statement as an 'exception' to the old rule: proof that the goods were fit for any of their common purposes would not be sufficient if the goods could not be sold for that other purpose at anything approaching the contract price. Aside from *B. S. Brown & Son* v *Craiks Ltd* there do not appear to be any cases where it has seriously been argued that because the buyer paid a price above the market price that the goods were not of satisfactory or merchantable quality. Furthermore, the difference between the contract price and the price that they were resold at following discovery of the defect may be proof only of a drop in market value, and nothing to do with the quality of the goods (see generally *Cehave N.V.* v *Bremer Handelsgesellschaft (The Hansa Nord)* [1976] QB 44).

When considering the price of the goods as a factor, the background circumstances to the transaction become most relevant. For example, in *Rogers* v *Parish (Scarborough) Ltd* [1987] QB 933 the fact that the car in question cost £16,000 (a high price in 1987) certainly seemed to have a bearing on the court's mind: a person buying a luxury car and paying the price for it was entitled to expect high quality. By contrast, in *Harlingdon and Leinster Enterprises Ltd* v *Christopher Hull Fine Art Ltd* [1991] QB 564 the fact that a painting bought for £6,000 turned out to be a forgery and worth considerably less did not appear to influence the court: 'If the plaintiffs fail to establish a breach of contract through the front door of s. 13(1) [because they had relied upon their own judgment they could not claim a breach of a term of description], they cannot succeed through the back door of s. 14' (per Slade LJ at p. 586).

16.3.2.3 Second-hand goods Turning to 'other considerations' which are to be taken into account when determining the reasonable man's assessment of the quality of the goods, the courts have been quite favourable to the buyer of second-hand goods. These decisions would appear to be unaffected by the 1994 amendments.

An extreme example is to be found in the case of *Crowther* v *Shannon Motor Co.* [1975] 1 All ER 139. In that case the buyer had bought a second-hand Jaguar motor car for £390 which had been driven over 80,000 miles. Three hundred and ninety pounds was not a high price, even in 1975. The engine seized up after a further 2,000 miles. It was held that there had been a breach of s. 14. The buyer was awarded damages in the sum of £460, a decision which was upheld by the Court of Appeal.

In *Business Appliances Specialists Ltd* v *Nationwide Credit Corpn Ltd* [1988] RTR 332 the Court of Appeal said that more could be expected from the sale of a second-hand car than that it be safe and roadworthy (contrast *Bartlett* v *Sydney Marcus Ltd* [1965] 1 WLR 1013 and *Lutton* v *Saville Tractors (Belfast) Ltd* [1986] 12 NIJB 1): the principles enunciated in *Rogers* v *Parish (Scarborough) Ltd* [1987] QB 933 in relation to new cars should be applied. However, it is submitted that most courts would take the view that the reduction in price together with the age of the car would cause some reduction in the quality which a buyer would be entitled to expect. Indeed in the *Business Appliances* case a Mercedes car costing some £14,000 was bought second-hand after it had been driven over 35,000 miles. After it had been driven a further 800 miles it broke down suffering from excessive wear to the engine valves which cost £600 to be repaired. It was held to be of merchantable quality with the court saying that a second-hand car could be expected to suffer from some defects and it was a question of fact and degree as to whether it matched the reasonable expectations of the reasonable buyer.

Another startling case arose in *Shine* v *General Guarantee Corpn Ltd (Reeds Motor Co. (A Firm), third party)* [1988] 1 All ER 911. Where the Court of Appeal held that a car was unmerchantable because, although there were no specific defects with it, it transpired before its repair that it had been an insurance 'write-off' and had been submerged in a pond for 24 hours. This adversely affected the value of the car.

16.3.2.4 Description of the goods Section 14(2A) of the 1979 Act specifically includes 'any description of the goods' as being a consideration when determining whether a reasonable man would determine that the goods were of satisfactory quality. This can cause problems as many commodities are sold in a bracket of differing grades under the same general description. Such commodities can be of a 'low' grade without suffering from something which may be described as a 'defect', simply that (for example) the meat is more fatty than other meat or the oranges less juicy. In some cases the descriptions are very wide, e.g., 'hard wheat'. Often these terms have a specific meaning which is understood within the particular market-place and may form a breach of the implied term of correspondence with description if they do not match that description (see section 15.4). However, so long as the goods fall within that description it seems that the extent of the seller's duty is to supply the lowest quality of the good which meets that description (per *Henry Kendall & Sons* v *William Lillico & Sons Ltd* [1969] 2 AC 31, and in New Zealand and Australia, *Taylor* v *Combined Buyers Ltd* [1924] NZLR 627 and *George Wills & Co.* v *Davids Pty Ltd* (1956) 98 CLR 77).

It seems unlikely that the 1994 amendments will have any impact on this issue as to do so is likely to involve the court assessing whether the buyer obtained a good bargain. If the buyer wished to specify a particular quality it was open to him to do so.

16.3.3 Aspects of quality

There is no definitive list which may form all the aspects of quality, or lack of it, upon which a claim may be based under s. 14(2) of the 1979 Act. To this extent the inclusion of a list of potential aspects of quality within the section is superfluous. Furthermore, as the section is drafted it does not require that those aspects must be adhered to in order for the goods to be of satisfactory quality; they simply may be required to be adhered to depending upon the standard expected by the reasonable man in the circumstances of the case. However, it seems that the Law Commission by including a list wished to highlight points which should be taken into account and guide the courts as to those areas where a higher standard should be applied, hence the inclusion of 'freedom from minor defects' and 'durability'.

A balancing act is always required when considering whether there has been a breach of s. 14(2). The background to the case must be considered and weighed against the severity of the defect in the good.

The aspects of quality which will be examined here are as follows:

(a) Fitness for purpose.
(b) Freedom from minor defects.
(c) Non-functional aspects of quality.
(d) Safety.
(e) Warnings, instructions and action required before use of the goods.
(f) Packaging.
(g) Post-purchase maintenance.

(h) Hidden or latent defects.
(i) Durability.
(j) Goods manufactured at the buyer's request.

16.3.3.1 Fitness for purpose 'Fitness for purpose' is referred to in both s. 14(2) and (3) and, as noted above, has formed the central part of the definition of merchantable quality for the best part of the last century. It is therefore important to define what exactly is meant by the phrase.

The classic example of a good 'fit for its purpose' but not of 'satisfactory quality' is that of a new carpet with a hole in it. The fact that it has a hole in it does not mean that it is not capable of being used as a carpet, and hence not fit for its purpose. However, given that it is a new carpet and assuming that a fair price was paid for it, it is unlikely to be considered by the reasonable man to be of satisfactory quality. Fitness for purpose relates to functionality: is the good capable of doing the thing that it is meant for? However, the pre-1994 definition had always required that the goods be 'as fit for its purpose as it was reasonable to expect' accordingly there has always been room for the courts to bring non-functional aspects of quality into consideration.

The 1979 Act now stipulates that the court is to consider whether the goods are fit for *all* their common purposes. Perhaps a good example of a good with multiple purposes is that of an off-road vehicle. One only has to turn on the television to discover that there are cars available on the market-place which are not only capable of running the children to school but also capable of climbing mountains with apparent ease whilst towing trucks behind them. Such an old second-hand vehicle may still be capable of the former but may no longer be capable of the latter, does this mean that it is not of satisfactory quality? After all, it is no longer fit for *all* the purposes for which goods of that kind are commonly supplied. In answering this question the court would have to look at the background circumstances: the age of the car and the price paid for it. This is a question of fact and degree. However, the mere fact that the car is not capable of all of its purposes does not of itself render it of unsatisfactory quality.

One difficult case in point is that of *Rogers* v *Parish (Scarborough) Ltd* [1987] QB 933. In that case it was said by Mustill LJ (at p. 944) in the context of a new (luxury) car:

> Starting with the purpose for which 'goods of that kind' are commonly bought, one would include in respect of any passenger vehicle not merely the buyer's purpose of driving the car from one place to another but of doing so with the appropriate degree of comfort, ease of handling and reliability and, one might add, of pride in the vehicle's outward and interior appearance. What is the appropriate degree and what relative weight is to be attached to one characteristic of the car rather than another will depend on the market at which the car is aimed.

Whilst the conclusion in that case was undoubtedly right (the car suffered from a litany of minor defects and the buyer was entitled to reject) it does appear to be straining the language to describe 'degree of comfort' as a 'purpose'. This case was, however, decided when the definition of 'merchantable quality' necessarily involved an assessment of whether the goods were fit for their purpose. No such assessment is now necessary and the court can consider aspects of quality other than fitness for purpose. It may be hoped, therefore, that 'fitness for purpose' will be restricted to functionality and not extended to cover non-functional aspects of quality.

16.3.3.2 Freedom from minor defects The cases of *Rogers* v *Parish (Scarborough) Ltd* (above) together with *Bernstein* v *Pamson (Golders Green) Ltd* [1987] 2 All ER 220 probably reflect a change in the perception of consumers' rights at the end of the 1980s. In both those cases purchasers of cars with minor defects in their construction and appearance were held entitled to rely on s. 14(2).

Whilst the Law Commission did not comment on *Bernstein* as it was subject to an appeal at the time, it does seem that the approach taken in those cases was endorsed by the Commission and the Act now specifically states that 'freedom from minor defects' and 'appearance and finish' are aspects of the quality of goods.

In *Bernstein* Rougier J considered when a buyer was going to be entitled to reject on the basis of a series of minor defects. He noted in that case that defects come in forms which are either easily repairable or such that they are difficult to trace and rectify, repeatedly manifesting themselves and in the end destroying the use and enjoyment that the purchaser of a car is entitled to expect. He used the example of a loose battery lead. In such a state a car may be undrivable, but it would be difficult to say that the car is unmerchantable in light of a defect which takes less than a minute to cure. The question remained one of fact and degree to be decided in all the circumstances of the case.

In *Bernstein* the defect was easily locatable but took 20 hours to repair over a matter of days. There was also potential to believe that there could have been 'knock-on' damage to other parts of the car in light of the defect. The car was therefore held to be unmerchantable within the meaning of the definition then given to s. 14(2). Whilst this case has been criticised on other grounds it remains good law in relation to the meaning of satisfactory quality.

As will be noted in relation to acceptance, the right to reject goods has been lost in relation to non-consumer cases where the defect is so slight that it would be unreasonable to reject the goods. Accordingly, this may reduce the amount of litigation brought in respect of minor defects in commercial cases.

16.3.3.3 Non-functional aspects of quality As was noted above, it was accepted in *Rogers* v *Parish (Scarborough) Ltd* [1987] QB 933 that factors such as pride in appearance, comfort and safety were all to be taken into consideration when determining quality. Such factors are highly subjective.

A more extreme example is to be found in the case of *Shine* v *General Guarantee Corpn Ltd (Reeds Motor Co. (A Firm), third party)* [1988] 1 All ER 911. In that case a car had been submerged underwater in a pond for 24 hours and had been an insurance 'write-off'. There were no specific defects with the car, but it was accepted that by virtue of the car's history that it would be worth £1,000 less in the open market. It was held to be unmerchantable.

The decision in *Shine* is presumably based upon the 'lurking doubt' effect of buying a car which has been the subject of repair. Based upon no specific evidence the market-place tends to devalue such cars on the theory that something may later go wrong with them, but at the time it is impossible to identify why. Whilst there is no firm evidence to support the theory, it is clear that there will be a reduction in the perceived value of the car and indeed there was evidence to this effect in

Shine. A similar decision was reached in *Bernstein* v *Pamson (Golders Green) Ltd* [1987] 2 All ER 220. In that case Rougier J accepted that the car had been satisfactorily repaired but was influenced by the *potential damage* which may have been caused by the defect to other parts of the car, although there was no evidence that it had been so damaged.

As with minor defects, it may be that in commercial cases the courts will be reluctant to allow the parties to reject goods for perceived losses under the new s. 15A of the 1979 Act. This is discussed under acceptance.

16.3.3.4 Safety Whilst the 1979 Act has never specifically mentioned safety in relation to the quality of goods it has never seriously been doubted that goods which were unsafe would not be of merchantable or satisfactory quality. Indeed there are a number of cases where a dangerous defect is identified as a factor rendering a good unmerchantable, for example in *Bernstein* (above).

In some cases goods are unsafe unless a particular process is performed on them prior to use. For example, some foods need to be cooked prior to consumption. To some extent this overlaps with the obligation on the part of the seller to provide instructions and warnings with the goods which he sells and is accordingly discussed in the next section.

16.3.3.5 Warnings, instructions and action required before use of the goods Any warnings or instructions given on or with goods can be taken into consideration when determining whether those goods were of merchantable quality. In *Wormell* v *RHM Agriculture (East) Ltd* [1987] 1 WLR 1091 a farmer had purchased a herbicide spray. The spray contained instructions which, whilst somewhat ambiguous, did say that it should not be sprayed on oats after they had grown beyond a certain stage. Nonetheless, the farmer used the spray after this stage as he had not had an opportunity to do so before due to bad weather. The spray had no effect. It was held that the spray was not unfit for its purpose as had it been used in accordance with its instructions it would have had the desired effect.

In one case, *Heil* v *Hedges* [1951] 1 TLR 512, pork was held to be merchantable despite its being harmful upon consumption because had it been cooked properly prior to its being eaten it would have been safe. By contrast in *Grant* v *Australian Knitting Mills* [1936] AC 85 underpants which caused dermatitis were held to be unmerchantable, but would have been safe had they been washed prior to use. These cases highlight the need for warnings in certain circumstances.

In *Vacwell Engineering Co. Ltd* v *BDH Chemicals* [1969] 3 All ER 1681 the seller supplied a certain chemical which was liable to react violently if it came into contact with water. The chemical was perfectly fit for the buyer's purposes but the buyer was unaware of the need to avoid contact with water and no warning had been provided to them by the seller. The sellers were found liable under s. 14(3) as they ought to have foreseen that the chemical was liable to come into contact with water. Whilst this case was decided under s. 14(3), there is no reason to suppose that the result would be any different under s. 14(2) so long as the goods were being used for one of their common purposes.

But in the case of some goods it is questionable whether such warnings need reasonably be provided. Many frozen goods require thorough reheating prior to consumption to kill off bacteria. Likewise, many products now come labelled 'suitable for home freezing'. Where the goods are, as in *Heil* v *Hedges*, unsafe at the time of purchase but can easily be rendered safe it becomes a question of how reasonable it is to expect the buyer to know of the action required to be taken. This is a question of fact and degree in each individual case.

16.3.3.6 Packaging The packaging of goods can, in appropriate circumstances, form a breach of the condition implied by s. 14(2). In *Niblett* v *Confectioners' Materials Co. Ltd* [1921] 3 KB 387 milk was supplied in tins, the label upon which infringed another firm's trademark and the buyer could potentially have been subject to an injunction by that other firm. The Court of Appeal held that the label formed part of the goods' 'state or condition' and rendered the goods unmerchantable, although the milk itself was perfectly satisfactory.

16.3.3.7 Post-purchase maintenance In the modern day the continuing supply of spare parts and post-purchase maintenance support is an important factor in deciding which product to purchase in both commercial and consumer sales. The lack of availability of a spare part may render an entire machine or vehicle completely redundant. In *L. Gent & Sons* v *Eastman Machine Co. Ltd* (unreported, per Law Commission, Final Report, *Sale and Supply of Goods*, para. 3.66) it was argued that the lack of provision of such post-purchase support rendered the goods unmerchantable. The argument failed and the Court of Appeal found that there was no such continuing duty upon a manufacturer and that the goods were not unmerchantable by virtue of such failure of support.

The Law Commission decided that the issue was too complex to be dealt with by way of legislation and that individual codes of practice should be established by the Office of Fair Trading.

16.3.3.8 Hidden or latent defects The extremely vexed question of latent defects was explored in *Henry Kendall & Sons* v *William Lillico & Sons Ltd* [1969] 2 AC 31. In that case a ground nut mixture had been sold by the sellers to the buyers who incorporated it into poultry feed. The mixture contained a substance which was poisonous to poultry. Some years after the sale, but before trial, it was discovered that the mixture could be used in cattle feed in quantities of up to 5 per cent, but not poultry feed. This was not, however, known at the time of the sale or delivery. There was evidence that purchases of the feed would continue without requesting a reduction in price even once this fact was known. The House of Lords held that the mixture was not unmerchantable. The reasoning of the majority of the House appears to be as follows (per Lord Reid at p. 75 *et seq* and Lord Guest p. 108 *et seq*): the test to be applied is that of whether, upon knowledge of the defect being discovered, would the buyer demand a reduction in price. In the instant case the answer was no because the defect could be cured in respect of one of the goods' uses by inclusion in foodstuff at a lower rate. The goods were not therefore unmerchantable.

Three issues arise from this case: What is a latent defect? When will such a latent defect form a breach of s. 14(2) under the above test? Has the above test survived the 1994 amendments?

Lord Reid defined a latent defect as follows: 'By definition a latent defect is something that could not have been discovered at the time by any examination which in light of then existing knowledge it was reasonable to make.' Regardless of subsequently acquired knowledge it seems that under this test a latent defect is something not discoverable upon a reasonable examination.

In relation to the second issue, on the above test it would seem that a breach of s. 14(2) would be founded where there was no cure to be found for the defect or where as a result of the defect the buyer would request an abatement of the price.

Finally, it is submitted that the above test has not necessarily survived the 1994 amendments, at least in any strict application. It would certainly be open to the courts to reach a different conclusion on the same facts without recourse to the House of Lords. The test seemingly applied by the House in that case was whether the goods could be rendered fit for any one of their common purposes. If so, they would be merchantable. The 1979 Act is no longer so strict. Fitness for purpose is now only one aspect of quality. Furthermore, it is fitness for *all* purposes which must be considered. The courts may now take a much broader view of satisfactory quality; the question is whether a reasonable man would consider the goods satisfactory. A seller cannot escape liability simply because he can show that his goods are fit for any one of their common purposes.

This still leaves the problem of subsequently acquired knowledge. Should the reasonable man referred to in s. 14(2) be deemed to be making his decision on the basis of knowledge which existed at the time of the delivery or in light of knowledge which existed only at trial? It would seem in light of *Henry Kendall & Sons* v *William Lillico & Sons Ltd* that he may still be attributed with the after-acquired knowledge. This seems harsh, particularly in light of the fact that the time that the goods are to be of satisfactory quality is the time of delivery.

The main problem with hidden or latent defects is that by their very nature they rarely become discoverable in a short space of time. As with durability discussed below, this will often mean that the buyer will be deemed to have accepted the goods before he discovers the defects. The Law Commission report did not recommend any alteration of the law in this respect.

16.3.3.9 Durability One aspect of the quality of goods is that they are capable of adequately performing their function for a reasonable period of time after their delivery. This appeared to be a requirement of the 1979 Act prior to the 1994 amendments, but one which was highlighted by the Law Commission.

In the case of goods to be shipped or transported, the duty is to ensure that they are in a fit state to endure transit and a reasonable period thereafter (per *Lambert* v *Lewis* [1982] AC 225).

The difficulty with durability is that the lack of it usually becomes apparent only after some significant usage of the goods. Of course, where a buyer has retained the goods for a reasonable period of time after their delivery, he will be bound to have accepted them and his remedy will be reduced to damages. His right to reject will be lost. The Law Commission considered the implementation of a long-term right to reject but declined to grant such a right (Final Report, *Sale and Supply of Goods*, para. 5.6 *et seq*).

16.3.3.10 Goods manufactured at the buyer's request Where the seller makes up goods to the buyer's specification, a problem arises in that upon a strict interpretation of s. 14(2) the seller may become liable if the goods are subsequently found to be defective. Where the defect arises through parts of the components selected and supplied by the seller it seems reasonable to hold him liable. But where the defect arises either through the design supplied by the buyer or where the buyer has identified the components which he wishes the seller to use it seems unreasonable that the buyer should be entitled to reject the goods for a breach of s. 14(2).

It is unlikely that such an unmeritorious claim would actually be brought before the courts but should it be it may be possible for the court to hold that s. 14(2) was excluded by implication or that the reasonable man referred to in s. 14 considered that the goods were as satisfactory as could be expected in relation to 'all the relevant considerations'.

16.4 EXEMPTION OF LIABILITY — EXAMINATION OF THE GOODS

By s. 14(2C) of the 1979 Act the buyer does not gain any protection under s. 14(2) in respect of defects which were drawn to his attention prior to entering into the contract or, where the buyer examined the goods prior to making the contract, defects which that examination ought to have revealed. No substantial change was made to the law by the 1994 amendments.

The first point to note is that in either case the exemption only applies in respect of an examination which takes place before the contract is entered into. It is no defence for the seller to say that the goods were examined after the contract was made.

In the case of defects specifically drawn to the buyer's attention, there is nothing in the wording of the 1979 Act which requires the seller to be the person who does this. Accordingly, it would seem that where a bystander or an agent on the part of the seller draws the buyer's attention to the defect this will suffice.

As regards defects discovered or discoverable after an examination, the exception applies only to defects which *that* examination ought to have revealed. Accordingly, in *Wren* v *Holt* [1903] 1 KB 610 beer barrels were examined from the outside and there was no defence in respect of arsenic later discovered in the beer. Likewise in *Godley* v *Perry* [1960] 1 WLR 9 a toy catapult suffered from an internal weakness which was not visible from the exterior of the toy. It was held that there was no exemption in respect of the defect.

There is probably no merit in the argument that a buyer would not be bound by the exemption where he has undertaken a cursory examination of the goods, which would not ordinarily have disclosed a defect, yet he had in fact noticed the defect. It is unlikely that the courts would accept such a proposition where the buyer has continued with the transaction with full knowledge of the defect.

By contrast, there may be some merit in the argument that where the buyer has been given a full opportunity to examine the goods yet has declined, he may be bound by such defects as a reasonable examination would have revealed. In *Thornett and Fehr* v *Beers & Sons* [1919] 1 KB 486 the buyers had arranged a time to examine barrels of glue which they were considering purchasing. The sellers' foreman had been instructed to give them every opportunity to do so. However, due to lack of time, they merely looked at the outside of the barrels. They were deemed to have examined the barrels and that since any examination of the glue would have revealed its defects they were bound by the proviso.

It is pointed out in *Benjamin: Sale of Goods*, 5th ed. (London: Sweet & Maxwell, 1997), para. 11-054 that the wording of the statute has changed since the decision in *Thornett and Fehr* from 'defects which such examination ought to have revealed' to 'defects which that examination ought to have revealed'. This may have a bearing on whether the decision in that case should be followed or it may simply be a modernisation of the statutory language. In any event, the decision is not binding on any court and it does seem to be contrary to the plain language of the 1979 Act that the proviso applies only 'where the buyer has examined the goods'. Certainly, overseas decisions have taken the view that the proviso operates only in respect of the limited defects which a cursory examination ought to have revealed (see *Frank* v *Grosvenor Motor Auctions Ltd* [1960] VR 607).

Where the seller includes a term within the contract to the effect that the buyer acknowledges that he has examined the goods, the buyer will not necessarily be bound by such a term. In order for the seller to rely on the term he must believe it to be true and have entered the contract in reliance upon it (*Lowe* v *Lombank* [1960] 1 All ER 611).

16.5 FITNESS FOR A PARTICULAR PURPOSE MADE KNOWN TO THE SELLER

Section 14(3) of the 1979 Act provides as follows:

> Where the seller sells goods in the course of a business and the buyer, expressly or by implication, makes known—
>
> (a) to the seller, or
>
> (b) where the purchase price or part of it is payable by instalments and the goods were previously sold by a credit-broker to the seller, to that credit-broker, any particular purpose for which the goods are being bought,
>
> there is an implied term that the goods supplied under the contract are reasonably fit for that purpose, whether or not that is a purpose for which goods are commonly supplied, except where the circumstances show that the buyer does not rely, or that it is unreasonable for him to rely, on the skill or judgment of the seller or credit-broker.

The provision is an extension of the requirement under s. 14(2) in that s. 14(3) applies to unusual purposes which goods are used for. The primary test differs somewhat, in that s. 14(3) requires that the goods be 'reasonably fit for their purpose' whereas under s. 14(2) the fundamental test is whether the goods are of satisfactory quality, and 'fitness for all the purposes for which goods of that kind are commonly supplied' is merely an aspect of that quality. The test under s. 14(3) is therefore wider in that it applies to unusual purposes, but narrower in that it does not necessarily take account of the good's overall quality, including its finish and appearance or minor defects, although such factors may be relevant in deciding whether the good is fit for its expressed purpose. In addition, s. 14(3) requires communication of an unusual purpose and reliance upon the seller as to the suitability of the good for that purpose. Both s. 14(2) and (3) require the seller to sell the goods in the course of a business. The meaning in either case is identical and is discussed above in section 16.2. Accordingly, there are three issues which fall to be discussed: the meaning of 'reasonably fit for that purpose', communication of purpose to the seller and reliance upon the seller. First, however, the reference to a credit-broker is examined.

16.5.1 Credit-broker

As is discussed in more detail in chapter 7, goods may be supplied directly to the customer by a shopkeeper or similar supplier. However, due to the mechanisms of credit the transaction actually takes place by the shopkeeper selling the goods to a finance company who gives them back to the 'buyer' under a conditional sale or hire purchase agreement. In these circumstances the shopkeeper is for all intents and purposes the 'seller', yet legally it is the credit company who supplies the goods to the 'buyer'. Under the ordinary common law the credit company would not be liable for any representations made by the shopkeeper to the seller, nor would the shopkeeper be liable to the credit company. However, where the shopkeeper has introduced the buyer to the credit company, the Consumer Credit Act 1974 renders the credit company liable for any representations made by him. This is discussed in detail in chapter 7, however for the purposes of s. 14(3) of the 1979 Act it is sufficient to note that the credit-broker is treated as the seller for the purposes of s. 14(3) and the same considerations apply to credit-brokers as apply to sellers under an ordinary sale.

16.5.2 Reasonably fit for their purpose

The first point to note about the standard required under s. 14(3) is that it is not dependent upon the degree of care taken by the seller. In *Henry Kendall & Sons* v *William Lillico & Sons Ltd* [1969] 2 AC 31 Lord Reid said (at p. 84) 'the goods will be reasonably fit for his purpose and that covers not only defects which the seller ought to have detected but also defects which are latent in the sense that even the utmost skill and judgment on the part of the seller would not have detected them' (see also *Frost* v *Aylesbury Dairy Co. Ltd* [1905] 1 KB 608). It is accordingly no defence for the seller to say that he could not have discovered the defect if the good is not fit for its purpose. Liability is strict.

The second point relating to the test of fitness for purpose is that it is essentially one of functionality; questions of quality are best left to s. 14(2)[1]. If the good is capable of performing its function then it will generally be fit for its purpose. For example, in *Kendall* v *Lillico*, cited above, Lord Pearce said:

> I would expect a tribunal of fact to decide that a car sold in this country was reasonably fit for touring even though it was not well adapted for conditions in a heat wave; but not, if it could not cope adequately with rain. If, however, it

1. However, in some cases aspects of quality are brought into account when considering fitness for purpose. For example, in *Rogers* v *Parish (Scarborough) Ltd* [1987] QB 933 'ease of handling' and 'comfort' were considered 'purposes' of a luxury car. These cases were decided when the test of merchantable quality required the courts to consider whether the goods were 'as fit for their purpose' as was reasonable given the price and other factors. However, the test no longer depends upon fitness as an essential test. Accordingly, there is no need to stretch the statutory language and quality can be considered independently of fitness for purpose. It is submitted that the latter test should remain primarily one of functionality.

> developed some lethal or dangerous trick in very hot weather, I would expect it to be found unfit. In deciding the question of fact the rarity of the unsuitability would be weighed against the gravity of its consequences. Again, if food was merely unpalatable or useless on rare occasions, it might well be reasonably suitable for food. But I should certainly not expect it to be held reasonably suitable if even on very rare occasions it killed the consumer.

This excerpt also brings out a third point about the test of fitness for purpose — the seriousness of the consequences are to be brought into account in measuring the unfitness of the good. As is explained by Lord Pearce, a seemingly small defect (for example a weak nut) can have severe consequences. It is not simply the size of the defect which matters, it is the impact which the defect has upon the proper functioning of the good. For example, in *Parsons (Livestock) Ltd* v *Uttley Ingham & Co.* [1978] QB 791 food hoppers were supplied to a farmer which had ventilators. The ventilators were left open and the animal food became contaminated resulting in a loss of much of the farmer's livestock. Although the problem could be easily remedied, liability was still founded.

Finally, it must be remembered that the test under s. 14(3) is subjective; it depends upon the specified purpose. For example, in the leading case of *Bristol Tramways Carriage Co. Ltd* v *Fiat Motors Ltd* [1910] 2 KB 831 the buyers made known that they wanted buses which were suitable for carrying a large number of passengers around a known hilly area. The buses were not up to the job and were not fit for their purpose. That the buses may have been suitable for work around most, flat, areas is irrelevant: the buses were not suitable for the specified purpose. Equally, if the buyer has an unusual purpose or is unusually sensitive and this not known or communicated to the seller, liability cannot be founded under s. 14(3). Thus in *Griffiths* v *Peter Conway Ltd* [1939] 1 All ER 685 the buyer of a tweed coat could not found a claim under s. 14(3) when she contracted dermatitis from the coat because she had unusually sensitive skin.

Examples of breaches of s. 14(3) are as numerous as they are diverse. A list of examples is provided in section 16.7.

16.5.3 Communication of purpose

Section 14(3) requires that the buyer 'expressly or by implication makes known to the seller [or his credit-broker] any particular purpose for which the goods are being bought'.

Where the goods have one purpose only it will be assumed that they were being bought for that purpose, but if the good has a multitude of common purposes the buyer will need to make known the purpose for which he is buying the goods. This follows from the case of *Priest* v *Last* [1903] 2 KB 148 where, in the context of a hot-water bottle, Collins MR said:

> There are many goods which have in themselves no special or peculiar efficacy for any one particular purpose, but are capable of general use for a multitude of purposes. In the case of a purchase of goods of that kind, in order to give rise to the implication of a warranty, it is necessary to shew that, though the article sold was capable of general use for many purposes, in the particular case it was

> sold with reference to a particular purpose. But in a case where the discussion begins with the fact that the description of the goods, by which they were sold, points to one particular purpose only, it seems to me that the first requirement of the subsection is satisfied, namely, that the particular purpose for which the goods are required should be made known to the seller. The fact that, by the very terms of the sale itself, the article sold purports to be for use for a particular purpose cannot possibly exclude the case from the rule that, where goods are sold for a particular purpose, there is an implied warranty that they are reasonably fit for that purpose.

Where there are a range of purposes to which a good might be put, if the good proves unsuitable for a specific purpose within that range, liability will rest upon the specificity used by the buyer and the foreseeability of the particular purpose. If the particular use was a foreseeable one within that range, the seller may be held liable. For example, in *Ashington Piggeries Ltd* v *Christopher Hill Ltd* [1932] AC 441 herring meal was purchased for inclusion into animal food. The herring meal proved unsuitable for feeding to mink. It was held that it was sufficient that the buyer had made known to the seller that he intended to use the herring meal in animal food. It was foreseeable that this might include mink and the seller was liable. Likewise, in *Henry Kendall & Sons* v *William Lillico & Sons Ltd* [1969] 2 AC 31 it was foreseeable that meat may be included in either cattle or poultry food and should be suitable for either, and in turn it was foreseeable that 'poultry' might specifically include 'pheasants'. By contrast, in *Aswan Engineering Establishment Co.* v *Lupdine Ltd* [1987] 1 WLR 1 the buyers had only indicated that they required plastic buckets 'for export'. Thus when they were stacked six high in the soaring temperatures of Kuwait, this was not a sufficiently specific purpose for the buyers to rely upon a breach of s. 14(3) (per Nicholls LJ).

To a great extent these cases are no longer of vital importance since the amendment to s. 14(2) that the goods must be fit for *all* their common purposes. In most instances s. 14(2) will apply and there will be no need for recourse to s. 14(3). The relevance of s. 14(3) will now be much more upon the extended definition contained in that section: the goods must be fit for a particular purpose made known to the seller whether or not that is a common purpose of such goods. However, where that unusual purpose is expressed to the seller in (relatively) general terms, the cases above will still be relevant in determining whether that purpose has been expressed with sufficient specificity.

Where the seller includes a term in his conditions of sale to the effect that the buyer has not communicated any purpose to the seller this does not necessarily have any effect. Section 14(3) applies where the buyer has communicated a purpose; he cannot be deemed not to have done merely by a statement to that effect within the contract. In *Lowe* v *Lombank* [1960] 1 All ER 611 such a term was included in a contract of hire purchase but it was held that the seller could not rely on it unless he believed the statement to be true and had entered into the contract in reliance upon it.

16.5.4 Reliance upon the seller

Prior to the 1973 amendments brought about by the Supply of Goods (Implied Terms) Act 1973 it was necessary for the buyer to prove that he had shown reliance upon the seller's judgment in order to invoke s. 14(3). However, a trend of presuming this developed within the case law, as was noted by Lord Pearce in *Hardwick Game Farm* v *Suffolk Agricultural Poultry Producers Association* [1969] 2 AC 31 where he said (at p. 115): 'The whole trend of authority has inclined towards an assumption of reliance wherever the seller knows the particular purpose.' Following the amendments, reliance is presumed and so long as the purpose has been communicated to the seller reliance will be presumed unless 'the circumstances show that the buyer does not rely, or that it is unreasonable for him to rely, on the seller's skill or judgment'.

Whether there is such reliance is supremely a question of fact for the court of first instance. For example, in *Teheran-Europe Co. Ltd* v *S. T. Belton (Tractors) Ltd* [1968] 2 QB 545 air compressors were bought for export to Iraq. The sellers knew that they were to be exported to Iraq but on the facts it was shown that the buyers had not relied upon the seller's judgment in respect of Iraqi import requirements.

Where the seller has only one source from which to supply the buyer, this will be a factor in deciding whether the buyer actually relied upon the seller's skill or judgment or whether he simply took those goods which were offered to him. Thus in *Wren* v *Holt* [1903] 1 KB 610 the fact that a buyer bought beer from a tied public house (i.e., it could only sell beer from one brewery) was a fact from which the jury could draw an inference that the buyer had not relied upon the skill and judgment of the seller. However, a buyer in such circumstances could now rely on s. 14(2). Furthermore, there is no rule of law on this point. In *Manchester Liners Ltd* v *Rea* [1922] AC 74 the buyers bought coal for a ship from the sellers who had supplied the only coal they had following a rail strike. The coal proved unsuitable for the particular ship. The sellers were held liable on the grounds that they had warranted that their coal would be suitable for the particular ship.

Where goods are made up to the buyer's order, he will not normally be held to have relied upon the seller's skill or judgment. However, where he leaves part of the design or formula at the seller's discretion he may, and often will, be deemed to have relied upon the seller in respect of that part. Thus, if it is that part made up at the seller's discretion which proves unfit, liability may be attached to the seller. For example, in *Cammell Laird & Co. Ltd* v *Manganese Bronze and Brass Ltd* [1934] AC 402 the buyers ordered a propeller which was to be made up according to a blueprint supplied by them. However, the exact thickness of the propeller was left at the discretion of the seller. When the propeller proved unfit for its purpose it was held that the seller was liable as the defect occurred in that part of the design left to their discretion. Similarly, in *Ashington Piggeries Ltd* v *Christopher Hill Ltd* [1972] AC 441 animal food was made up according to the buyer's formula. However, he had relied upon the seller as to obtaining suitable ingredients and the seller was liable when those ingredients proved unsatisfactory.

The mere fact that the buyer intends to inspect the goods *after* delivery will not be sufficient to rebut the inference that he relied upon the seller's judgment *prior* to the sale taking place (per Lord Morris in *Henry Kendall & Sons* v *William Lillico & Sons Ltd* [1969] 2 AC 31). However, where the buyer relies upon a third party's inspection prior to the sale, it is possible that the court would find that he relied upon this and not the seller's skill or judgment. For example, in *Phoenix Distributors Ltd* v *L. B. Clarke Ltd* [1967] 1 Lloyd's Rep 518 it was held that the buyers had relied not upon the seller's skill or judgment but upon a certificate issued by the Northern Ireland Department of Agriculture where such a certificate was required to export potatoes from Northern Ireland to Poland. It seems, however, that the buyer's purpose may be made known and reliance inferred from the actions of an agent acting on behalf of the buyer. Thus in *Ashford Shire Council* v *Dependable Motors Pty Ltd* [1961] AC 336 the council buyers had sent their employee to inspect a tractor which they wished to purchase from the seller. The employee had made the purpose for which it was required known to the sellers and they were liable when it proved unfit for that purpose.

Finally, one difficult case to explain is that of *Lambert* v *Lewis* [1982] AC 225. In that case the buyer had bought a towing coupling which was to be suitable for towing a trailer on his farm and on the roads. Through a design fault the coupling proved unsatisfactory, resulting in the coupling becoming detached and the trailer crashing and injuring several people. However, the farmer had noticed the defect some time before the accident occurred. Lord Diplock gave the judgment of the House of Lords and held that whilst the duty under s. 14 was a continuing one, it could not continue in circumstances where the buyer knew of the fault yet ignored it. No particular reason was given by his Lordship however.

16.6 SALE BY SAMPLE

Section 15 of the 1979 Act provides as follows:

> (1) A contract of sale is a contract for sale by sample where there is an express or implied term to that effect in the contract.
>
> (2) In the case of a contract for sale by sample there is an implied [condition]—
>
> (a) that the bulk will correspond with the sample in quality;
>
> (b) [repealed by the Sale and Supply of Goods Act 1994];
>
> (c) that the goods will be free from any defect, making their quality unsatisfactory, which would not be apparent on reasonable examination of the sample.

Several issues fall to be discussed in relation to s. 15:

(a) When is a contract one for sale by sample?
(b) Correspondence with the sample.
(c) Exemption: defects apparent upon examination.

16.6.1 When is a contract for sale by sample?

The mere fact that a sample was shown to the buyer does not make the contract one for sale by sample, it follows from the plain wording of s. 15(1) that there must be an express or implied term to that effect. Where there is an express term there is no difficulty in identifying the contract as one to which s. 15 applies (for an example see *Re Walkers, Winser and Hamm and Shaw, Son & Co.* [1904] 2 KB 152).

Some difficulty is caused as there are cases which suggest that where the contract has been reduced to written form then, by way of the parol evidence rule, evidence may not be adduced to show that it was intended that the sale be one by way of sample (*Tye* v *Fynmore* (1813) 3 Camp 462; *Meyer* v *Everth* (1814) 4

Camp 22; *Gardner* v *Gray* (1815) 4 Camp 144). However, arguably evidence is admissible to show not what the express terms of the agreement are, but that a term ought to be *implied* that the contract be one of sale by sample (see Treitel, *An Outline of the Law of Contract*, 5th ed., (London: Butterworths, 1995), pp. 73 and 74). Alternatively, evidence may be admissible to show that there was a collateral contract which contained a warranty that the goods were to match the sample (*L. G. Thorne & Co. Pty Ltd* v *Thomas Borthwick & Son Ltd* [1956] SR (NSW) 81). However, upon a strict application of the law of evidence, if evidence is not admissible to prove that there was an implied term that the sale be one by way of sample, or such evidence is admissible for another purpose only, there would be insufficient evidence to hold that the contract was one for sale by sample. In any event, it is submitted that in the modern day a court would be reluctant to hold inadmissible evidence which suggests that the contract was one for sale by sample. Certainly, the point does not seem to have been raised in more modern cases (see, for example, *Godley* v *Perry* [1960] 1 WLR 9 — although in that case it does not seem clear whether the contract between the wholesaler and the retailer was in written form or not). Hopefully, in a consumer context, most such contracts will be oral in any event. Furthermore, an argument could be made that the contract was not one for sale by sample, but sale by description (as to which see chapter 15).

16.6.2 Correspondence with the sample

Section 15(2)(a) of the 1979 Act does not actually spell out that the goods supplied must correspond with the sample in specification, only in quality. Neither does s. 13(2) of that Act actually state that the goods must correspond with the sample in specification, merely that such compliance would be insufficient if the goods do not also correspond with any description given to them.

However, even if not expressly spelt out in the Act, it would seem that there is a requirement that the goods must match the sample in specification as well as quality (*Champanhac & Co.* v *Waller & Co.* [1948] 2 All ER 724). A claim could also be framed under s. 13 for failure to comply with description. Indeed where the complaint is that the goods do not comply with the specification this may be the better basis of such a claim (*Boshali* v *Allied Commercial Exporters*, *The Guardian*, 15 November 1961; *John Bowram & Son* v *Rodema Canned Food* [1967] 1 Lloyd's Rep 183). The 'description' of the goods under such a claim is, naturally, that they are identical to the sample.

A further problem with s. 15, as the Act is currently drafted, lies with the definition of 'bulk' in the revised s. 61. It is clear that the word 'bulk' in s. 15 was used in the sense of the 'goods to be delivered under the contract'. However, s. 61 was amended by the Sale of Goods (Amendment) Act 1995 to define 'bulk' by reference to a defined space. This was done for the purposes of the amendments to s. 20 (sale of goods forming part of a bulk). However, the definition as it stands seems inappropriate for the purposes of s. 15, which could involve an instalment sale by which the goods would never be in a 'bulk'. It is submitted that within the meaning of s. 15 the phrase 'bulk' should simply be construed as meaning 'the contract goods'.

When considering whether the goods do correspond with the sample, the background circumstances must be considered. In some cases seemingly trivial non-conformity with description can form the basis of a breach of the implied condition. For example, in *E. and S. Ruben Ltd* v *Faire Bros & Co. Ltd* [1949] 1 KB 254 the sellers had agreed to supply rolls of rubber which, when delivered, were crinkled and in such state unusable, but they could have been cured by a relatively simple process of 'ironing'. However, the mere fact that the non-compliance could easily be cured would afford no defence. By contrast, in *Steels and Busks Ltd* v *Bleecker Bik & Co. Ltd* [1956] 1 Lloyd's Rep 228 it was suggested that mere non-compliance with a sample clause would not in itself entitle the buyer to reject the goods if the discrepancy did not render the goods unsatisfactory (see also *F. E. Hookway & Co. Ltd* v *Alfred Isaacs & Son* [1954] 1 Lloyd's Rep 491). This was particularly so where the custom within the trade was to use a visual examination only; the mere fact that on microscopic examination there was a discrepancy would not avail the buyer.

16.6.3 Exemption: defects apparent upon examination of the sample

Section 15 of the 1979 Act does not apply in respect of defects which would be discoverable upon a reasonable examination of the sample. Unlike s. 14(2) of that Act, there is a supposition that an examination will be made. The buyer cannot escape responsibility for the defects by making no examination or a cursory one only as he can under s. 14. Under s. 15 the seller is exempt from responsibility for such defects as would be discovered upon a reasonable examination had one been carried out, regardless of whether an examination was carried out or whether the examination was reasonable.

The exemption only extends in so far as the defect is discoverable; the buyer is not forced to undertake a thorough analysis of the good. Thus in *Godley* v *Perry* [1960] 1 WLR 9 a defect within the structure of a toy catapult was not discoverable from the simple test of pulling back the elastic and hence the seller could not escape liability in respect of it.

16.7 EXAMPLE CASES

The following may provide assistance as to the application of the principles of ss. 13, 14 and 15 of the 1979 Act:

Section 13

(1) *Gill & Duffus SA* v *Berger & Co. Inc.* [1983] 1 Lloyd's Rep 622: beans; correspondence with description; declaration in certificate conclusive.

(2) *Beale* v *Taylor* [1967] 3 All ER 253: mere fact that the buyer has inspected goods does not mean that there cannot be a sale by description.

(3) *Amstrad plc* v *Seagate Technology Inc.* [1998] Masons CLR 1: computer hardware; correspondence with description; whether of merchantable quality.

(4) *Joseph Travers* v *Longel* [1947–51] CLY 9252: distinction between sale by description and sale by sample; reliance upon descriptive words.

(5) *Nicholson and Venn* v *Smith Marriott* [1947–51] CLY 1786: questions of description going to quality; tablecloths bearing crest of Charles I; failure to correspond with description.

(6) *Harlingdon and Leinster Enterprises Ltd* v *Christopher Hull Fine Art Ltd* [1990] 3 WLR 13: works of art; name of artist as description of goods; reliance by the buyer.

Section 14

(1) *Amstrad plc* v *Seagate Technology Inc.* [1998] Masons CLR 1: computer hardware; correspondence with description; whether of merchantable quality.

(2) *Chartered Trust plc* v *Kervill* [1998] 4 CL 291: mobile homes; merchantable quality; goods supplied under the contract of sale; conditional sale agreements.

(3) *Burnley Engineering Products Ltd* v *Cambridge Vacuum Engineering Ltd* (1994) 50 Con LR 10: precision welding machines; merchantability.

(4) *Rotherham MBC* v *Frank Haslam Milan & Co. Ltd* [1996] EGCS 59: merchantability of materials used in construction under a contract for work and materials.

(5) *US Leasing Ltd* v *Streathers* [1996] 6 CL 124: photocopiers; evidence required in order to hold whether merchantable or not.

(6) *University of Warwick* v *Sir Robert McAlpine* (1988) 42 BLR 1: merchantability of materials used in a contract for work and materials; construction contract.

(7) *Turnock* v *Fortune* 1989 SLT (Sh. Ct.) 32: defects brought to the buyer's attention; whether defects sufficiently brought to the buyer's attention.

(8) *Business Application Specialists Ltd* v *Nationwide Credit Corp Ltd*, *The Times*, 27 April 1988: cars; merchantability; *Rogers* v *Parish (Scarborough) Ltd* [1987] QB 933 applied (CA); in order for cars to be fit for their purpose they must be more than roadworthy.

(9) *Shine* v *General Guarantee Corp Ltd (Reeds Motor Co. (A Firm), third party)* [1988] 1 All ER 911: merchantability; car submerged under water; second-hand cars; non-functional defects.

(10) *Wormell* v *RHM Agriculture (East) Ltd* [1987] 1 WLR 1091: merchantability; fertiliser; need for instructions.

(11) *Rogers* v *Parish (Scarborough) Ltd* [1987] QB 933: cars; merchantability; luxury cars; general requirements of fitness for purpose.

(12) *Aswan Engineering Establishment Co.* v *Lupdine Ltd* [1987] 1 WLR 1: merchantability; buckets; fitness for particular purpose.

(13) *Lutton* v *Saville Tractors (Belfast)* [1986] 12 NIJB 1: merchantability; second-hand cars; rescission of contract; affirmation.

(14) *Kurkjian (SN) (Commodity Brokers)* v *Marketing Exchange for Africa (Formerly Motiram (TM) (UK) (No. 1))* [1986] 2 Lloyd's Rep 614: merchantability; cocoa butter; inspection of goods; compliance with description.

(15) *Bernstein* v *Pamson Motors (Golders Green)* [1987] 2 All ER 220: merchantability; new cars; perceived or potential defects; acceptance through lapse of a reasonable time.

(16) *Laurelgates* v *Lombard North Central* (1983) 133 NLJ 720: merchantability; car; timeliness of rejection under hire purchase contract.

(17) *Jackson* v *Chrysler Acceptances* [1978] RTR 474: merchantability; car; quantum of damages for breach of s. 14.

(18) *Sir Robert McAlpine & Sons* v *Minimax* [1970] 1 Lloyd's Rep 397: merchantability of fire extinguishers.

(19) *Lowe* v *Lombank* [1960] 1 All ER 611: examination of goods; communication to vendor of purpose goods to be used for; estoppel; insufficient that document signed purports that the buyer has examined the goods — reliance by the seller must be shown.

(20) *Godley* v *Perry* [1960] 1 WLR 9: merchantability; catapult (child's toy); defects not discoverable upon a reasonable examination.

(21) *Rapalli* v *K. L. Take* [1959] 2 Lloyd's Rep 469: merchantability; onions; *de minimis* principle.

(22) *Wilson* v *Rickett, Cockerell & Co.* [1954] 1 QB 598: goods supplied under the contract; explosive contained within consignment of coal.

(23) *Heil* v *Hedges* [1951] 1 TLR 512: merchantability of food; claim cannot be founded where food not properly prepared prior to consumption.

(24) *Horn* v *Minister of Food* [1948] 2 All ER 1036: exclusion of term of merchantability by contrary intent.

(25) *Decca Radar* v *Caserite* [1961] 2 Lloyd's Rep 301: fitness for purpose of packing cases; communication to seller of purpose.

(26) *McAllister* v *Crowe*, *The Times*, 25 June 1955: sale of greyhound; unfit for the purpose of racing due to tendency to fight.

(27) *Shields* v *Honeywill & Stein* [1953] 1 Lloyd's Rep 357: alcohol purchased for use in manufacturing process; latent defect; reasonableness of seller's knowledge of defect and particular purpose of purchase of goods.

(28) *NV Devos Gebroeder* v *Sunderland Sportswear Ltd* 1987 SLT 331: fitness for purpose of material purchased for golfing rainproof clothing; fitness for purpose requires that the goods be fit not only for manufacture but for use thereafter.

Section 15

(1) *R. W. Green* v *Cade Bros Farms* [1978] 1 Lloyd's Rep 602: whether previous goods supplied by the same seller to the same buyer can form a 'sample'.

(2) *Steels & Busks* v *Bleecker Bik & Co.* [1956] 1 Lloyd's Rep 228: defects which a reasonable examination of the sample ought to reveal; reasonableness of examination; visual examination required only.

17 Duty to supply goods in the right quantity

17.1 INTRODUCTION

The general rule is that the buyer is entitled to receive the contract goods, no more and no less. Furthermore, he is entitled to expect them to be delivered in one instalment unless the contract provides to the contrary. This much is fairly self-evident and the purpose of this chapter is, therefore, to examine the parties' rights upon delivery of the wrong quantity of the contract goods. Three situations fall to be explored:

(a) Delivery by instalments.
(b) Delivery of more or less of goods conforming with the contract.
(c) Delivery of the contract goods together with goods of another description.

17.2 DELIVERY BY INSTALMENTS

The general position regarding delivery by instalments is governed by s. 31 of the Sale of Goods Act 1979 (the '1979 Act'), which provides as follows:

> (1) Unless otherwise agreed, the buyer of goods is not bound to accept delivery of them by instalments.

The application of the rule is fairly straightforward: the buyer is entitled to reject goods where the seller attempts to deliver them in instalments. For example, in *Behrend & Co. Ltd* v *Produce Brokers Co. Ltd* [1920] 3 KB 530 the sellers delivered a small proportion of the contract goods two weeks before delivering the remainder. It was held that the buyers were entitled to accept the first instalment and reject the remainder.

It will be appreciated that the buyer will often be relying on his right to reject goods by reason of delivery by instalments not because it actually causes him any great difficulty, but because he simply wants to get out of a bad bargain. Here the right to cure may be relevant — if the seller can retender the goods in one instalment within the contractual time for delivery, the buyer will not be able to escape the contract. The right to cure is discussed in section 18.5.

The circumstances of the case may indicate that delivery by instalments was envisaged between the parties. Where this is the case, the buyer will not be entitled to rely on s. 31(1). For example, where the contract is for a large quantity of goods it may be the case that the parties must have envisaged the use of separate vessels to ship them, from that it can also be inferred that they intended (or at least permitted) delivery by instalments (*Pagnan & Fratelli* v *Tradax Overseas SA* [1980] 1 Lloyd's Rep 665).

Where the contract is one for delivery by instalments, whether a shortfall in delivery amounts to a breach going to the root of the contract entitling the buyer to terminate the whole contract is a question of fact and degree in each case (see, for example, *Regent OHG Aisenstadt* v *Francesco of Jermyn Street* [1981] 3 All ER 327 — discrepancy of one suit from 62 not *de minimis* but buyer not entitled to terminate the whole contract). This aspect of delivery and rejection is discussed in section 19.3.

17.3 DELIVERY OF WRONG QUANTITY

The general rules regarding delivery of the wrong quantity are contained in s. 30 of the 1979 Act, which provides as follows:

> (1) Where the seller delivers to the buyer a quantity of goods less than he contracted to sell, the buyer may reject them, but if the buyer accepts the goods so delivered he must pay for them at the contract rate.
>
> (2) Where the seller delivers to the buyer a quantity of goods larger than he contracted to sell, the buyer may accept the goods included in the contract and reject the rest, or he may reject the whole.
>
> (2A) A buyer who does not deal as a consumer may not—
>
> (a) where the seller delivers a quantity of goods less than he contracted to sell, reject the goods under subsection (1) above, or
>
> (b) where the seller delivers a quantity of goods larger than he contracted to sell, reject the whole under subsection (2) above,
>
> if the shortfall or, as the case may be, excess is so slight that it would be unreasonable for him to do so.
>
> (2B) It is for the seller to show that a shortfall or excess fell within subsection (2A) above.
>
> . . .
>
> (3) Where the seller delivers to the buyer a quantity of goods larger than he contracted to sell and the buyer accepts the whole of the goods so delivered he must pay for them at the contract rate.

Where the wrong delivery is delivered to the buyer, the prima facie rule is that he is entitled to reject the whole delivery. Alternatively, he may choose to accept all the goods delivered to him and pay for them at the contract rate. There is good reason for this rule — delivery of a shortfall may mean that the buyer has to go to the market and obtain the rest of the goods that he requires. Given the nature of bulk buying, this may mean that he pays in excess of the contract price in order to do so.

This rule is subject to the *de minimis* rules contained in s. 30(2A). These rules apply only where the buyer deals otherwise than as a consumer. 'Consumer' in this context bears the same meaning as in the Unfair Contract Terms Act 1977. The meaning of this phrase is discussed in section 8.2.2.

There are yet to be any cases detailing when an excess or shortfall is likely to be so slight as to render it unreasonable to reject the goods. Given that the provisions relate only to non-consumer agreements, it can be expected that the courts will look at the commercial reality of the situation. Where a shortfall is delivered, the buyer may recover the proportionate excess that he has paid in the price by way of money had and received on a total failure of consideration (*Ebrahim Dawood* v *Heath* [1961] 2 Lloyd's Rep 512). The buyer may also refuse to pay that part of the price which relates to the shortfall where the price remains payable. Where there is an excess that is delivered, the buyer is entitled to reject the excess; he is not forced to buy goods which he has not ordered (s. 30(2A)(b)). Accordingly, it is likely that only where the buyer has been put at a real commercial disadvantage will the courts allow a non-consumer to reject the whole of the goods for delivery of a shortfall or excess (see for a common law example *Re Shipton Anderson & Co. Ltd* v *Weil Brothers & Co. Ltd* [1912] 1 KB 574).

17.4 DELIVERY OF THE CONTRACT GOODS TOGETHER WITH OTHER GOODS

Where the seller delivered the contract goods, or part of them, together with other goods of another description the position was formerly governed by s. 30(4) of the 1979 Act. This is now repealed, but an examination of it is necessary to understand the new provisions. Section 30(4) remained in force until January 1995 and provided as follows:

> Where the seller delivers to the buyer the goods he contracted to sell mixed with other goods of a different description not included in the contract, the buyer may accept the goods which are in accordance with the contract and reject the rest, or he may reject the whole.

The important point to note is that s. 30(4) related to goods of a different description only. Whether the difference between the goods is one of description or quality is often little more than nomenclature. For example, in *Toepfer* v *Continental Grain Co.* [1974] 1 Lloyd's Rep 11 the word 'hard' in the context of 'hard wheat' was accepted as capable of being a descriptive word as it appeared to have a particular meaning within the industry. Likewise, in *Toepfer* v *Warinco AG* [1978] 2 Lloyd's Rep 569 the words 'fine ground' were accepted as being descriptive in the context of soya meal. The reality is often that 'fine ground' soya is simply a better quality product. Accordingly, the Law Commission did not remove the right to reject part of the goods where goods of another description are supplied, but extended it to cover all situations where non-conforming goods were supplied with the contract goods. This is provided by s. 35A, which provides as follows:

(1) If the buyer—

(a) has the right to reject the goods by reason of a breach on the part of the seller that affects some or all of them, but

(b) accepts some of the goods, including, where there are any goods unaffected by the breach, all such goods,

he does not by accepting them lose his right to reject the rest.

(2) In the case of a buyer having the right to reject an instalment of goods, subsection (1) above applies as if references to the goods were references to the goods comprised in the instalment.

(3) For the purposes of subsection (1) above, goods are affected by a breach if by reason of the breach they are not in conformity with the contract.

Section 35A is in fact more of a right of partial acceptance than a right of partial rejection. Prior to the introduction of s. 35A it was assumed that under a non-severable contract a buyer could only accept or reject the entire contract goods and could not accept part of the goods (Law Commission Report, *Sale and Supply of Goods*, para. 6.6). There does not appear to be a case where this was actually challenged. However, there are many where it was assumed to be the case (see *Wilensko Slaski Towarzystwo Drewno* v *Fenwick & Co. Ltd* [1938] 3 All ER 429; *Regent OHG Aisenstadt* v *Francesco of Jermyn Street* [1981] 3 All ER 327; *Re Shipton Anderson & Co. Ltd* v *Weil Brothers & Co. Ltd* [1912] 1 KB 574). This also proves the premiss that the buyer is entitled to reject *all* the goods where part of them do not conform with the contract. This position is probably no longer the case. Section 15A of the 1979 Act provides that a non-consumer may be debarred from rejecting goods which do not conform with the Act's implied terms. It may be said to be unreasonable to reject the whole where only part does not comply.

Where goods are supplied with other goods but mixed in such a way as to become inseparable (for example liquids mixed together in this way), this is probably a diminution in the quality of the overall product and not the supply of goods mixed with others.

PART V
PERFORMANCE AND BREACH

18 *Payment and delivery*

18.1 INTRODUCTION

The basic premiss of a contract of sale is that the seller delivers goods and the buyer pays for them. Whilst this seems straightforward enough, it can give rise to a number of problems. Usually, this occurs where there has been a breakdown of trust and confidence between the parties, each being wary of performing their obligations until they are sure that the other party will perform theirs. Accordingly, a number of questions have to be determined by the Sale of Goods Act 1979 (the '1979 Act'): When and where must the goods be delivered? When must the buyer pay for them? What happens if the seller refuses to deliver the goods, or the buyer refuses to accept them?

In general the 1979 Act provides a clear answer to most of these questions: the general rule is that whilst the seller has to 'deliver' the goods, the place of delivery is prima facie at the seller's place of business. Unless stipulated otherwise the time of delivery is not of the essence under a contract of sale and the seller must deliver within a 'reasonable time'. Payment and delivery are concurrent obligations and each party must be 'ready and willing' to perform before the duty for the other party arises. Delivery can be made constructively so that goods are not delivered to the buyer, but are delivered to a third party to the order of the buyer. It must always be remembered that delivery of the goods is an independent concept from the passing of the property in the goods. Ownership does not pass with delivery. Each of these duties will be examined in turn.

18.2 THE DUTY TO DELIVER THE GOODS

The general duty upon the seller to deliver the goods is contained in s. 27 of the 1979 Act, which provides as follows:

> It is the duty of the seller to deliver the goods, and of the buyer to accept and pay for them, in accordance with the terms of the contract of sale.

The first point to note is that the section simply requires the seller to deliver 'the goods . . . in accordance with the terms of the contract'. Which particular goods must be delivered is therefore dependent upon the nature of the contract. If it is a contract for the sale of specific goods, the seller has no choice; he must deliver the specific article ordered. If he has sold goods as a sale of a quantity from an ascertained bulk, e.g., wheat, he would have to fulfil the order from stocks from the bulk, he could not fulfil the contract from another source (even superior quality wheat). However, if he has merely agreed to sell generic goods, he is free to substitute the goods which he intended to use to fulfil the contract with others from another source at any time until delivery. The buyer cannot complain that goods other than those that he was expecting were delivered (*Carlos Federspiel & Co. SA* v *Charles Twigg & Co. Ltd* [1957] 1 Lloyd's Rep 240).

18.2.1 The meaning of 'delivery'

'Delivery' is defined in s. 61(1) of the 1979 Act as meaning:

> [the] voluntary transfer of possession from one person to another; except that in relation to sections 20A and 20B above it includes such appropriation of goods to the contract as results in property in the goods being transferred to the buyer . . .

This definition extends the notion of delivery beyond the traditional image of the seller arriving at the buyer's premises and unloading the goods. However, such a delivery is undoubtedly within the meaning of the definition. Delivery can occur in any of the methods outlined below. However, goods must be delivered 'in accordance with the contract' in order for there to be a delivery within the meaning of s. 27. Accordingly, it is not open to the seller to use whichever method he chooses. For example, goods may be delivered by handing to the buyer the means of control of the goods. Thus, should a buyer order a radio from a shop to be delivered one week later, it would hardly be supposed that delivery could be effected the next week by the seller handing the buyer the keys to a warehouse 30 miles away. There would undoubtedly be an implied term that the parties envisaged that the mode of delivery would be by physical transfer of possession and such delivery would not then be in accordance with the contract.

18.2.1.1 Delivery by transfer of physical possession No authority is needed to suggest that where the seller physically hands over the goods to the buyer that this constitutes delivery.

18.2.1.2 Delivery of the means of control It is settled law that delivery of the means of control of the goods is an adequate method of delivery. The most common example of this is where the seller gives the buyer the keys to a warehouse where the goods are stored (*Hilton* v *Tucker* (1888) 39 Ch D 669). However, the means of access must be absolute. Thus where there are two keys, both keys would need to be handed to the buyer in order to effect delivery (*Dublin City Distillery Ltd* v *Doherty* [1914] AC 823). Furthermore, it seems from *Wrightson* v *Macarthur* [1921] 2 KB 807 that if the buyer were given only a limited right of entry to collect the goods this may not suffice.

18.2.1.3 Attornment A process of delivery by documents which give the buyer the means of control is provided by s. 29(4) of the 1979 Act:

> Where the goods at the time of sale are in the possession of a third person, there is no delivery by seller to buyer unless and until the third person acknowledges to the buyer that he holds the goods on his behalf; but nothing in this section affects the operation of the issue or transfer of any document of title to the goods.

Where the goods are in the custody of a warehouseman or courier, it is usual that he holds the goods pursuant to a delivery order. The delivery order will be made out to the person who holds the right to collect the goods or have them delivered to him. Assuming that this person is the owner of the goods, when he sells them he communicates to the warehouseman or courier that he now wishes the goods to be held at the disposal of the buyer. However, the attornment is not complete until the warehouseman or courier acknowledges to the buyer that he now holds the goods to his order; until this time delivery is ineffectual (*Laurie & Morewood* v *John Dudin & Sons* [1926] 1 KB 223).

18.2.1.4 Delivery of documents of title Certain documents amount to a document proving ownership and are tantamount to the goods themselves. Possession of a document of title places the goods at the disposal of the holder of the document (*Biddel Bros Ltd* v *E. Clements Horst & Co. Ltd* [1911] 1 KB 934). The definition of a document of title is given in s. 1(4) of the Factors Act 1889, which provides as follows:

> The expression 'document of title' shall include any bill of lading, dock warrant, warehouse-keeper's certificate, and warrant or order for the delivery of goods, and any other document used in the ordinary course of business as proof of the possession or control of goods, or authorising or purporting to authorise, either by endorsement or by delivery, the possessor of the document to transfer or receive goods thereby represented.

The commonest form of document of title is a bill of lading — a document representing goods in transit, or to be transmitted, by ship. However, international sales are beyond the scope of this text. Other forms of document of title are rarely used in practice. However, there is nothing preventing an ordinary warehouse-keeper's certificate or a delivery order being a document of title, but it should state on its face that it may be transferred by delivery or endorsement by a third party (*Jurgens Margarinefabrieken* v *Louis Dreyfus & Co. Ltd* [1914] 3 KB 40; see also *Official Assignee of Madras* v *Mercantile Bank of India* [1935] AC 53). It is probably because warehouses face the possibility of becoming embroiled in litigation if they accept a forged or stolen delivery order that this method is not commonly used.

18.2.1.5 Delivery to agent Whilst there seems no authority directly in point, there seems no reason in principle why delivery to the buyer's nominated agent should not be an acceptable method of delivery.

18.2.1.6 Delivery to carrier Section 32(1) of the 1979 Act provides that delivery to a carrier is deemed to be delivery to the buyer. The carrier need not be nominated by the buyer, but s. 32(2) requires that the seller must take reasonable steps to ensure that the goods are properly transported and if he fails to do so the buyer may decline to treat delivery to the carrier as delivery to himself. The net effect of this is that the seller is under a duty to ensure that the goods are placed with a reputable carrier.

18.2.1.7 Sale under sections 20A and 20B The new definition of delivery contained in s. 61(1) means that when the property is transferred to the buyer in accordance with ss. 20A and 20B delivery is deemed to have taken place. This causes little difficulty as in order for the property to be transferred the buyer must have paid the price or part of it. The concurrent obligations of payment of the price and delivery are thus not affected.

18.2.1.8 Constructive delivery It is possible that in rare circumstances delivery may be deemed to have taken place even though the goods remain in the possession of the seller as a bailee of the goods. Such a situation is likely to arise in relation to a sale and leaseback transaction whereby the 'seller' of the goods is for all practical purposes the owner of them and he sells the goods to a bank or other financial institution which leases them back to him under a form of hire purchase agreement. This is simply a method of arranging finance against the security of goods. Such transactions used to be more common in the consumer field where a person needed to raise finance, but are not so common now. Here a form of constructive delivery will likely be deemed to have taken place, see section 13.4.2.

18.2.2 The place of delivery

The place of delivery is defined by s. 29 of the 1979 Act:

> (1) Whether it is for the buyer to take possession of the goods or for the seller to send them to the buyer is a question depending in each case on the contract, express or implied, between the parties.
> (2) Apart from any such contract, express or implied, the place of delivery is the seller's place of business if he has one, and if not, his residence; except that, if the contract is for the sale of specific goods, which to the knowledge of the parties when the contract is made are in some other place, then that place is the place of delivery.

The 1979 Act creates a presumption that the ordinary place of delivery is the seller's premises, unless the parties have expressly or impliedly contracted to the contrary. However, in the modern day this presumption will easily be displaced in the case of consumer or small business sales made by telephone (*Wiskin* v *Terdich Bros Pty Ltd* [1928] Arg LR 242). It would certainly be open to a court to find an implied term that the parties intended the seller to physically deliver the goods at the buyer's premises. It is likely, however, that the buyer will be expected to pay for such delivery as s. 32 appears to consider that any arrangements made by the seller are made 'on behalf of the buyer'. The cost of packaging and similar matters is clearly on the seller as s. 29(6) provides that 'the expenses of and incidental to putting the goods into a deliverable state must be borne by the seller'. Where the seller does agree to deliver the goods, it has been held that he may do so by delivering them to a respectable looking person at the buyer's premises (*Galbraith & Grant Ltd* v *Block* [1922] 2 KB 155). However, this decision must be open to question in modern consumer cases.

18.2.3 The time of delivery

The prima facie rule that time is not of the essence is laid down by s. 10(1) of the 1979 Act; that the parties may provide otherwise by the terms of the contract is provided by s. 10(2).

However, it is long established that in contracts for the sale of goods the timing of delivery is of the essence in commercial contracts (*Hartley* v *Hymans* [1920] 3 KB 475; *Bunge Corpn* v *Tradax SA* [1981] 1 WLR 711; *Gill & Duffus SA* v *Société Pour l'Exportation des Sucres* [1986] 1 Lloyd's Rep 322).

Where the parties have made no stipulations as to time, s. 29(3) provides as follows:

> Where under the contract of sale the seller is bound to send the goods to the buyer, but no time for sending them is fixed, the seller is bound to send them within a reasonable time.

This provision is somewhat curious because it applies where the seller is bound to 'send' the goods; it does not apply where the seller is bound to 'deliver' them. Given that the presumed place of delivery is the seller's place of business it would seem odd if a different rule applied where the buyer is to collect the goods. Certainly the courts would readily imply a term to this effect. The reason why the word 'send' is used and not 'delivery' is seemingly unknown, but it is out of place in an Act normally so tightly drafted.

Whilst delivery is required only to be made within a reasonable time, failure to make the delivery within such time will usually be treated as a breach of condition of the contract (*Thomas Borthwick (Glasgow) Ltd* v *Bunge & Co. Ltd* [1969] 1 Lloyd's Rep 17; *Bowes* v *Shand* (1877) 2 App Cas 455). If the seller merely agrees to try to deliver by a certain date, but does not actually set a date, the usual rule that he is obliged to deliver within a reasonable time will apply (*McDougall* v *Aeromarine of Emsworth Ltd* [1958] 1 WLR 1126).

In commercial contracts, or indeed in some consumer ones, the seller will frequently be unable to deliver in time, yet the buyer affords him some more time to make delivery before finally terminating the contract (or purporting to). Here difficulties arise because the buyer will usually have been ambiguous as to his waiver in respect of the delivery time. It is not unusual in such litigation for the seller to claim the price of the goods and/or damages claiming that the buyer has waived his right to strict performance in respect of the delivery date. The buyer counters this by saying that he did not waive his rights as he did not know what they were at the time and in any event no further consideration was provided to support the waiver. Unfortunately, the law is not at all clear as to the position here. However, it is submitted that if there is a 'golden thread' between the cases that it is a distinction between the buyer waiving his rights in totality, and merely waiving the right to rescind the contract for the breach (see Treitel, *An Outline of the Law of Contract*, 5th ed. (London: Butterworths, 1995), p. 321; *The Athos* [1983] 2 Lloyd's Rep 127).

In order to make a valid waiver, consideration will usually be required to support it (*Hartley* v *Hymans* [1920] 3 KB 475; *Foakes* v *Beer* (1884) 9 App Cas 605). Where no such consideration can be found (as there rarely will where the seller simply makes late delivery) there is nothing to support the waiver and the buyer is not bound by it. An alternative legal theory has been that a promissory estoppel operates to bar the buyer from resiling from his statement (*Charles Rickards Ltd* v *Oppenheim* [1950] 1 KB 616) and that this estoppel acts as a form of substitute for consideration. In any case it seems clear that the buyer must act with the knowledge that he has the right to rescind (*Peyman* v *Lanjani* [1985] Ch 457).

Accordingly, it is submitted that in order to validly waive his right to rescind the buyer must have had full knowledge of his right to do so within the meaning given in *Peyman* v *Lanjani*. Furthermore, he must have made an unequivocal statement that he intended to waive his right to rescind (*The Mihalios Xilas* [1979] 2 All ER 1044). If this is the case, the buyer will not be entitled to subsequently rescind the contract when the goods are delivered late. He may, however, claim damages.

Certainly it seems that the buyer will be permitted to bring an action for late delivery, or raise it as a defence, even though he did not do so at the time of the breach (*Fercometal SARL* v *Mediterranean Shipping Co. SA* [1989] AC 788).

Finally, it is worth noting that delivery may be treated as ineffectual by the buyer if it is made at an unreasonable time. What is or is not reasonable is a question of fact in each case, but in most instances if the delivery is made outside of business hours it will be so.

18.3 PAYMENT OF THE PRICE

Payment of the price is a fundamental aspect of a contract for the sale of goods. No great practical problems are raised by this aspect of the contract; the only difficulties which do arise relate to the method of payment.

When the 1979 Act was drafted the only forms of payment commonly in use were cash and cheques. Where the seller accepts a cheque, then in the event it is dishonoured the seller has two remedies: he may sue on the cheque, under what is known as the 'cheque rule' or he may sue for the price under the contract of sale. The cheque rule is invariably the better route as the action is simply for payment under a promissory note; the buyer cannot set up defences based upon a breach of contract by the buyer unless they amount to a set-off (*Jade International Steel Stahl und Eisen GmbH & Co. KG* v *Robert Nicholas (Steels) Ltd* [1978] QB 917).

Where the method of payment is by credit card a tripartite agreement will usually be formed consisting of a contract of sale between the buyer and the seller, a contract for the credit card company to pay the seller on the buyer's behalf and between the credit card company and the buyer to reimburse the credit card company (together with interest). Accordingly, if the credit card company defaults on payment the seller's remedy is against them, not the buyer (*Re Charge Card Services Ltd* [1988] 3 All ER 702).

As with delivery, the timing of payment is not of the essence (1979 Act, s. 10). However, given that payment and delivery are concurrent obligations, the seller need not deliver the goods unless the buyer is ready and willing to make payment. Notwithstanding this, if the contract is one for the buyer to collect and pay for the goods, and the buyer does not collect and pay for the goods on the date of delivery, the seller may not terminate the contract and sell the goods elsewhere (*Payzu Ltd* v *Saunders* [1919] 2 KB 581); the seller must afford the buyer a reasonable time to pay. Similarly, if the agreement is one whereby payment falls due upon request (e.g., where the buyer holds an account or running credit with the seller), the seller must afford the buyer a reasonable time to pay after the request (*Brightey* v *Norman* (1862) 3 B & S 305). Finally, it is worth noting that where the seller has suffered losses for any delay in payment he may claim damages for breach of the condition so long as that loss falls within the ordinary rules as to damages (*Wadworth* v *Lydall* [1981] 1 WLR 598).

18.4 THE DUTY TO TAKE DELIVERY

Section 27 of the 1979 Act provides that it is the buyer's duty to 'accept' the goods. Of course, this does not mean that the buyer is obliged to accept goods which are not in conformity with the contract.

As has been seen, the usual place of delivery is the seller's place of business. Where the buyer delays in collecting the goods this does not automatically mean that the seller may terminate the contract and resell the goods. He must afford the buyer a reasonable time to collect them (*Woolfe* v *Horn* (1877) 2 QBD 355; *Payzu Ltd* v *Saunders* [1919] 2 KB 581). This follows from the corollary of the rule that the time of delivery is not of the essence. However, if the goods are perishable and the opposite applies and time is of the essence, the seller may terminate the contract and resell the goods (*Sharp* v *Christmas* (1892) 8 TLR 687).

As with delivery, if the buyer agrees to take the goods as quickly as he can, but no particular date is actually set, the ordinary rule that taking delivery is not of the essence applies. The buyer has a reasonable time in which to collect the goods (*Penarth Dock Engineering Co. Ltd* v *Pounds* [1963] 1 Lloyd's Rep 359; *Maple Flock Co. Ltd* v *Universal Furniture Products (Wembley) Ltd* [1934] 1 KB 148).

18.5 THE RIGHT TO CURE

The rules as to delivery and payment give rise to an opportunity on the part of the seller to cure any defects in the goods as delivered. Given that time is not of the essence in a contract of sale it will quite often be the case that the seller delivers the goods before this time, or if a date for delivery is set and is of the essence before that time. Given that the seller's duty is to tender goods conforming to the contract within *that* time, if upon early delivery the buyer points out certain defects, the seller has until the time for delivery to retender goods which conform with the contract (*Borrowman Phillips & Co.* v *Free & Hollis* (1878) 4 QBD 500; *E. E. & Brian Smith (1928) Ltd* v *Wheatsheaf Mills Ltd* [1939] 2 KB 302; *The Kanchenjunga* [1990] 1 Lloyd's Rep 391).

18.6 PAYMENT AND DELIVERY ARE CONCURRENT OBLIGATIONS

Section 28 of the 1979 Act provides as follows:

> Unless otherwise agreed, delivery of the goods and payment of the price are concurrent conditions, that is to say, the seller must be ready and willing to give possession of the goods to the buyer in exchange for the price and the buyer must be ready and willing to pay the price in exchange for possession of the goods.

The section thus provides for a simultaneous exchange of payment and goods. Each party must at the time of delivery be 'ready and willing' to perform. In practice, difficulties often arise because the parties reach a 'stand off', each refusing to perform until the other agrees to, which is inherently circular. Quite often this has been brought about by late performance in the past under other contracts. Ambiguity in the law was previously caused by the cases of *Gill & Duffus SA* v *Berger & Co. Inc.* [1984] AC 382 and *Braithwaite* v *Foreign Hardwood* [1905] 2 KB 543. However, this appears to have been resolved by the House of Lords in *Fercometal SARL* v *Mediterranean Shipping Co. SA* [1989] AC 788. In that latter case A had agreed to charter a ship from B but it became clear from B's communications that the ship would never be ready to load on time and A purported to cancel the charter. At this stage B changed his position and stated that the ship would in fact be ready to load on time, A refused to accept this and continued to refuse to load or make payment. The ship in fact did arrive late. B then sued A for the price of the charterparty, to which A replied that B would never have been able to perform. It was held that an anticipatory breach must either be accepted or rejected, there was no half-way house whereby one party could refuse to accept the breach yet decline to perform himself. Accordingly, B had kept the contract alive by refusing to accept the anticipatory breach and was required to perform. Because they had not done so A had justifiably terminated the contract. Whilst this is not a case on the sale of goods it is clearly directly analogous with s. 28 and there is no doubt that it applies to contracts for the sale of goods.

The *Braithwaite* case was also explained and clarified by the House of Lords in the *Fercometal* case. In *Braithwaite* the sellers had agreed to sell 100 tonnes of timber to be shipped in two instalments. The buyer refused to accept delivery and the seller sold elsewhere. Later, the buyer discovered that the timber would not have conformed with the contract in any event and set this up as a defence when sued by the sellers for non-acceptance of the goods. The House of Lords in *Fercometal* explained that this defence was not available because the sellers had accepted the buyer's wrongful repudiation of the contract before the time for delivery arose. This termination prior to that time meant that the duty to deliver conforming goods never arose and the defence was not therefore available.

19 Rejection

19.1 REJECTION OF THE GOODS

A right to reject the goods arises where there has been a breach of a condition of the contract, or a serious breach of an innominate term giving rise to a right to reject. The most important conditions, and those most frequently relied upon, are those implied by the Sale of Goods Act 1979 (the '1979 Act') relating to title, description, fitness for purpose and correspondence with sample. However, a right to reject also arises in relation to other conditions of the contract, be they express or implied. The circumstances when a term will be a condition and where a right to repudiate arises from breach of an innominate term were examined in chapter 3.

In order to exercise a right to reject the rejection must be stated in unequivocal terms. Thus in *Lee* v *York Coach and Marine* [1977] RTR 35 the fact that the buyer's solicitor had demanded that the goods be repaired was not sufficient to amount to a rejection of them. Likewise, the buyer cannot reject the goods whilst at the same time acting in a manner quite inconsistent with his having elected to reject them (*Vargus Pena Apezteguia y Cia Saic* v *Peter Cremer GmbH* [1987] 1 Lloyd's Rep 394). Furthermore, it is not open to one party to purport to reject whilst still expecting the other side to perform, this was discussed in chapter 18.

Where the buyer has purported to reject the goods, it may be the case that the seller has a right to tender goods which do conform with the contract so long as doing so would not take him outside the contract time for delivery (see section 18.5 under the heading 'the right to cure').

The consequences of rejection are discussed at the end of this chapter. The bulk of this chapter is devoted to the circumstances where the buyer will have lost his right to reject them and his claim reduced to damages. Equally, there are circumstances where the buyer may wish to reject only part of the goods and keep the rest. The law formerly made this difficult, but it is now quite possible. Furthermore, an issue arises as to whether the contract is severable or not. This is an important issue as the buyer may or may not be entitled to reject the whole of the goods. Finally, the 1979 Act now restricts the right to reject in certain commercial contracts where it would be unreasonable to do so. Each of these issues will be discussed in turn.

19.2 ACCEPTANCE

Section 35 of the 1979 Act provides as follows:

> (1) The buyer is deemed to have accepted the goods subject to subsection (2) below—
>
> (a) when he intimates to the seller that he has accepted them, or
>
> (b) when the goods have been delivered to him and he does any act in relation to them which is inconsistent with the ownership of the seller.
>
> (2) Where goods are delivered to the buyer, and he has not previously examined them, he is not deemed to have accepted them under subsection (1) above until he has had a reasonable opportunity of examining them for the purpose—
>
> (a) of ascertaining whether they are in conformity with the contract, and
>
> (b) in the case of a contract for sale by sample, of comparing the bulk with the sample.
>
> (3) Where the buyer deals as a consumer . . ., the buyer cannot lose his right to rely on subsection (2) above by agreement, waiver or otherwise.
>
> (4) The buyer is also deemed to have accepted the goods when after the lapse of a reasonable time he retains the goods without intimating to the seller that he has rejected them.
>
> (5) The questions that are material in determining for the purposes of subsection (4) above whether a reasonable time has elapsed include whether the buyer has had a reasonable opportunity of examining the goods for the purpose mentioned in subsection (2) above.
>
> (6) The buyer is not by virtue of this section deemed to have accepted the goods merely because—
>
> (a) he asks for, or agrees to, their repair by or under an arrangement with the seller, or
>
> (b) the goods are delivered to another under a sub-sale or other disposition.

The effect of a buyer being deemed to have accepted the goods is laid down by s. 11(4) of the 1979 Act:

> Subject to s. 35A below, where a contract of sale is not severable and the buyer has accepted the goods or part of them, the breach of a condition to be fulfilled by the seller can only be treated as a breach of a warranty, and not as a ground for rejecting the goods and treating the contract as repudiated, unless there is an express or implied term of the contract to that effect.

The effect of accepting the goods is therefore to reduce the buyer's remedy to one for damages. The measure of damages is discussed later in this chapter. One important 'exception' to this rule exists however. Following the decision in *Rowland* v *Divall* [1923] 2 KB 500 where the seller does not hold the property in goods at the time he sold them the buyer need not treat this as a breach of s. 12, but as a total failure of consideration. The rules relating to acceptance and rejection have no application to such situations. Furthermore, the concept of acceptance differs from the common law doctrine of affirmation. The circumstances where a person will be deemed to have affirmed the contract were discussed in section 4.7.3. It must be noted that acceptance is a much stricter doctrine as a buyer may be deemed to have accepted goods even though he did not know of the fault or his right to reject, whereas under affirmation both of these must be present (*Peyman* v *Lanjani* [1985] Ch 457).

Section 35 creates three circumstances where the buyer will be deemed to have accepted the goods: where he 'intimates to the seller that he has accepted them', does an act 'inconsistent with the ownership of the seller', or where there has been a lapse of a reasonable time without the buyer intimating that he does not accept them. These three circumstances will be discussed in turn.

19.2.1 Intimation of acceptance

The notion of intimation of acceptance appears to be clear enough. However, difficulties may arise in that goods may be delivered and a signature on the delivery note requested. That delivery note may well contain a clause or statement to the effect that the buyer has accepted the goods. It may also often be the case that the delivery note is signed by a consumer or junior employee who does not read the note or does not understand it. It was for this reason that the Law Commission recommended that this method of deemed acceptance was made subject to an opportunity of examining the goods (Law Commission Report, *Sale and Supply of Goods*, para. 5.20 *et seq*). Consequently the 1979 Act, as amended, makes this method of acceptance subject to s. 35(2). Accordingly, the buyer will not ordinarily be deemed to have accepted the goods by express intimation until he has had a reasonable opportunity of examining them. When such an opportunity will have been had is discussed in section 19.2.3 below.

Section 35(2) does not however mean that a buyer will always be able to escape the consequences of a statement contained in a delivery note, or the consequences of his own gratuitous statement. In the first place, it is only as against a consumer that s. 35(3) provides that the operation of s. 35(2) cannot be excluded or waived. It is therefore open for this right to be waived by a business. Secondly, where the buyer has previously examined the goods, s. 35(2) does not apply. The Act does not concern itself with whether the buyer gave the goods a reasonable examination or whether that examination was sufficient to reveal the defect (as it does with ss. 14 and 34); it is sufficient that the buyer has actually examined the goods at all.

19.2.2 Act inconsistent with the seller's ownership

Three situations must be explored in relation to acts considered inconsistent with the seller's ownership: sub-sales, goods bought for use and documentary sales. Before examining these, however, it is necessary to consider the meaning of the phrase 'inconsistent with the ownership of the seller'.

In the first place the phrase is somewhat confusing as it will normally be the case that when the goods have been physically delivered to the buyer, so that he is in a position to do something to them, the property will have passed to him and the buyer will be the owner. This phrase was explained in *Kwei Tek Chao* v *British Traders and Shippers Ltd* [1954] 2 QB 459 on the basis of conditional ownership.

Thus the act should be considered inconsistent against the possibility of the property revesting in the seller. The phrase should therefore be read as an act 'which would be considered inconsistent with the goods being owned by the seller'. Whilst other legislative amendments have taken place this phrase remains in use.

19.2.2.1 Sub-sales In order to properly understand that provisions in the 1979 Act for loss of the right to reject by performing an act inconsistent with the seller's ownership it is necessary to look at the legislative history.

The concept of acceptance not being possible prior to an examination of the goods was governed by s. 34(1) of the 1979 Act prior to the 1994 amendments. Section 34(1) provided that the buyer was not to be deemed as having accepted the goods until he had had a reasonable opportunity of examining them. However, as drafted this appeared inconsistent with s. 35 which provided that the buyer was to be deemed to have accepted the goods after having performed an act inconsistent with the seller's ownership. The act of a buyer reselling the goods to a third party was considered an act inconsistent with the ownership of the seller, quite often this would occur without the buyer having examined the goods (indeed they may be delivered direct to the sub-buyer). Accordingly, where this happened ss. 34 and 35 were in direct conflict.

Exactly this situation arose in *Hardy & Co. Ltd* v *Hillerns & Fowler* [1923] 2 KB 490 and it was held that s. 35 prevailed. The buyer was deemed to have accepted the goods because he had delivered them to the sub-buyer. However, in 1967 the Misrepresentation Act was enacted which amended the Sale of Goods Act 1979 to read that s. 35 was subject to s. 34.

However, it is probable that the 1967 amendments did not go far enough and this is illustrated by the case of *E. & S. Ruben Ltd* v *Faire Bros & Co. Ltd* [1949] 1 KB 254. In that case goods had been delivered directly to carriers for delivery to the third party sub-buyer. It was noted that in order for the buyer to have lost his right to reject the goods under s. 35, they must have been delivered to the buyer and for him to have performed an act inconsistent with the ownership of the seller. However, it was held that a form of.constructive delivery had taken place to the buyers before delivery to the sub-buyers, consequently the subsale was an act inconsistent with the ownership of the seller after delivery and the buyer had lost his right to reject. Since there was nothing in the 1967 amendments which provided against the operation of this rule, it is likely that this case would have been decided in the same way following the 1967 amendments.

The difficulty which this rule creates is that it is quite possible that the buyer will be in a position to restore the faulty goods to the seller notwithstanding the sub-sale. In the situation where the goods have been examined not by the buyer but by the sub-buyer it will often be the case that the sub-buyer has rejected them (legitimately) under his contract of sale with the buyer. Whilst the sub-buyer is only obliged to hold them available for collection by the buyer (1979 Act, s. 36) there is nothing preventing the buyer collecting the goods at his own expense and holding them available for collection by the seller in accordance with his obligation (which is exactly what happened in *Molling & Co.* v *Dean & Son* (1901) 18 TLR 217). In this situation there is no reason why the buyer should be prevented from rejecting the goods. This was the view taken by the Law Commission (Law

Commission Report, *Sale and Supply of Goods*, para. 5.38) and accordingly the Act was amended. Section 35(6)(b) now provides that the buyer shall not be deemed to have accepted the goods merely because he delivers them to a buyer under a sub-sale or other disposition.

However, this does not mean that in all cases of sub-sale the buyer will not be held to have accepted the goods. Section 35(6)(b) provides only that the buyer will not be deemed to have accepted the goods *merely* because he has sub-sold them. Other circumstances may therefore dictate that the buyer is to be deemed to have accepted the goods. In particular, if the buyer is not able to restore the goods to the seller, he will be deemed to have accepted them. Thus if the sub-buyer does not reject the goods but instead seeks damages, the buyer could not restore the goods to the seller. This could be the case, for example, where the subbuyer has used the goods in some manufacturing process. There seems to be no express authority for this proposition, but it certainly seems to be the underlying theme of the Act (see Law Commission Report, *Sale and Supply of Goods*, para. 2.47).

A further problem arises as to whether the buyer will be deemed to have accepted the goods because they are being held at the disposal of the seller at some foreign place. For example, where the buyer sub-sells the goods to a foreign buyer and the foreign buyer then rejects them. Here the foreign buyer is obliged only to hold the goods available for collection by the buyer (s. 36). In this situation an issue therefore arises as to whether a communication by the buyer to the seller that the goods were rejected would be operative. It is submitted that the answer lies in determining whether the seller knew that the goods were being bought for resale in foreign parts.

In *Molling & Co.* v *Dean & Son* (1901) 18 TLR 217 the sellers had sold books to the buyers knowing that they were to be exported to America and there bought by a sub-buyer. The books even contained the details of the sub-buyer in the print. They were legitimately rejected by the sub-buyer, and in turn rejected by the buyer who paid for their transport back to the United Kingdom. It was held that they were entitled to reject the goods and to the cost of their transport back to the United Kingdom. The reasoning for this was that the proper place of examination was at the sub-buyer's address. The same result would probably be achieved under the current legislation on these facts as, in the first place, the buyer would not be deemed to have accepted them until he had had a reasonable opportunity to examine them, and secondly the cost of transport would be recoverable as damages as the cost would surely have been within the contemplation of the parties.

If the seller was unaware that the goods were to be resold, the situation may be different. For example, where the buyer buys goods and immediately resells them to a sub-buyer, but without communicating this to the seller. In such a case it is likely that the place of examination will be the place of delivery to the buyer (*Perkins* v *Bell* [1893] 1 QB 193) and accordingly the buyer is likely to be deemed to have had a reasonable opportunity to examine them, even though he has not taken advantage of this. Secondly, if the sub-buyer rejects the goods he is merely obliged to hold them available for collection by the buyer. In turn the buyer is obliged to hold them available at the place of delivery for collection by the seller. There seems no reason why the buyer should recover the cost of such transport as it would be outside the contemplation of the parties. The fact that the buyer cannot immediately hold the goods available for collection would probably not of itself mean that he cannot reject them. However, if the nature of the goods indicates that time is of the essence (e.g., if the goods are perishable), the buyer may be deemed to have accepted them because he is unable to restore them to the seller in substantially the same condition as they were sold to him. If the commodity were not perishable, the buyer would probably be able to do so.

19.2.2.2 Goods bought for use or consumption It is only with sub-sales that significant difficulties with the law are created. Where the goods are bought for use it seems that the buyer will be held only to have accepted them where he has done something to them so as to render himself unable to return them in substantially the same condition that they were in when sold to him. Thus where goods are incorporated into property so that they cannot be easily removed, the buyer may well be deemed to have accepted them (*Mechan & Sons* v *Bow, McLachlan & Co. Ltd* (1910) SC 758). This would also be the case where the buyer has used more of the goods than was necessary for the purpose of testing them (*Hanor* v *Groves* (1855) 15 CB 667). In New Zealand it has been held that registering a car in the name of the buyer amounted to an act inconsistent with the seller's ownership (*Armaghdown Motors* v *Gray* [1963] NZLR 5). However, it is submitted that such a case would not be followed in this country, not only because registration has no effect on ownership in English law, but also because for all practical purposes the buyer would be deemed to have done an act necessarily taking place before an opportunity to examine has been given. Likewise the making of an insurance claim in respect of the goods has been held not to amount to an inconsistent act (*J. & S. Robertson (Aust) Pty Ltd* v *Martin* (1955–56) 94 CLR 30).

19.2.2.3 Documentary sales Some difficulties are created by the case of *Kwei Tek Chao* v *British Traders & Shippers Ltd* [1954] 2 QB 459. The explanation given in that case as to the effect of rejection is explored in section 19.4. Briefly, however, Devlin J found in that case that where the goods are sold subject to a right to reject for breach, the buyer takes a conditional property in the goods. Any dealing with the goods by their documents of title is a dealing with that conditional property and does not amount to a dealing with the goods themselves. Hence the sub-sale by way of documents did not amount to an act inconsistent with the seller's ownership. This was to be contrasted with a physical dealing with the goods which could do so. Indeed a physical dealing with the goods could amount to an inconsistent act even where the goods are delivered prior to the documents of title. The buyer would have no separate remedy by purporting to reject the documents (*Tradax International SA* v *Goldschmidt SA* [1977] 2 Lloyd's Rep 604).

19.2.3 Acceptance through lapse of a reasonable time

Section 35(4) declares that a buyer is to be deemed to have accepted the goods if after the lapse of a reasonable time he does not indicate to the seller that he rejects them. By s. 35(5) the court must take into account the opportunity that the buyer has had of examining the goods to see if they are in conformity with the contract or whether they correspond with any sample of them.

Much difficulty has been caused in this area by the case of *Bernstein* v *Pamson Motors (Golders Green) Ltd* [1987] 2 All ER 220. In that case the buyer had bought a car which proved defective. At the time the car broke down (with major defects) it had been in the buyer's possession for only four weeks and had been driven only 140 miles. The buyer had been ill for one week of this time and this was taken out of consideration. It was held that the buyer had lost the right to reject for lapse of a reasonable time, after only three weeks! Rougier J held that a buyer was entitled to give the car a general trial, not a thorough examination. He also noted that the time span for rejection depended upon the complexity of the goods in question — 'what would be a reasonable time in relation to a bicycle would hardly suffice for a nuclear submarine'. The judgment in this case seems particularly hard within a consumer context and it is submitted that it would not, or need not, be followed in other cases.

In the first place it can be argued that *Bernstein* is no longer good law by virtue of the statutory amendments made in 1994 — this seems to be the view taken by some academic writers: see *Benjamin: Sale of Goods*, 5th ed. (London: Sweet & Maxwell, 1997), para. 12–054; Goode, *Commercial Law*, 2nd ed. (Penguin, 1995), p. 378. Prior to the 1994 amendments, the Act had not specifically provided that loss of the right to reject by lapse of time was subject to a right on the part of the buyer to examine the goods. Section 35(1) could be read as imposing this requirement only upon loss of the right through an inconsistent act (see *Benjamin: Sale of Goods*, para. 12–053). The Act now stipulates by s. 35(5) that in determining a reasonable time regard should be had to this. Given that the Act now brings concepts such as 'durability' and 'freedom from minor defects' into account in determining satisfactory quality, it can be argued that a longer time should be afforded. The Law Commission declined to comment on *Bernstein* as at the time of its report an appeal was pending in the case (which was subsequently abandoned).

Secondly, what is or is not a reasonable time is a question of fact, not law (1979 Act, s. 59). No court is therefore bound by *Bernstein* but can take a view of the particular case before it. Other courts have generally taken a more lenient approach than that in *Bernstein*. For example, in *Lutton* v *Saville Tractors (Belfast)* [1986] 12 NIJB 1 a car was returned after two months and the buyer was not denied his right to reject the car. Similarly, in the unreported case of *M & T Hurst Ltd* v *Grange Motors (Brentwood) Ltd* (see Reynolds, (1988) 104 LQR 17) the buyer who bought a car in early October was held still entitled to reject the following February (see also *Porter* v *General Guarantee Corpn* [1982] RTR 384). In *Rogers* v *Parish (Scarborough) Ltd* [1987] QB 933 the buyer rejected a car some six months and 5,500 miles after it was purchased. It was not argued in that case that the buyer had accepted the car. However, the sellers sought to raise the argument in the Court of Appeal, but leave was declined. One would have thought that if the Court of Appeal had considered this case a travesty of justice that leave would have been given, albeit subject to compensation by way of costs. Furthermore, cases on hire purchase (to which the doctrine of affirmation applies) have been much more favourable to the buyer or hirer. For example, in *Laurelgates* v *Lombard North Central* (1983) 133 NLJ 720 a car was bought in October and not rejected until June of the next year and it was held the buyer was held entitled to reject (see also *Farnworth Finance Facilities* v *Attryde* [1970] 2 All ER 774).

One theme which runs through many of these cases is that the buyer has repeatedly returned to the seller demanding that the goods be repaired. First, where this is the case the buyer will not be deemed to have accepted the goods merely because he asks for or allows them to be repaired (1979 Act, s. 35(6)). Secondly, it is clear that a court may take time spent repairing the vehicle into account. Indeed the Law Commission thought it so unlikely that a court would 'leave the clock running' whilst repairs were carried out that it was not worthy of separate inclusion within the Act (Law Commission Final Report, *Sale and Supply of Goods*, para. 5.31).

19.3 INSTALMENT SALES, SEVERABLE CONTRACTS, PARTIAL REJECTION AND LOSS OF THE RIGHT TO REJECT FOR MINOR BREACHES

There are many contracts whereby a mass of goods are delivered and part only are defective in some way. Whether the buyer is entitled to repudiate the entire contract, reject one instalment only or reject part of an instalment depends upon whether the contract is severable and whether the buyer is a consumer or not.

It is quite clear that where the contract is non-severable then, if part of the goods are defective, the buyer becomes entitled to reject all of them (*Gill & Duffus SA* v *Berger & Co. Inc.* [1984] AC 382; *Jackson* v *Rotax Motor & Cycle Co. Ltd* [1910] 2 KB 937; *Re Moore & Co. Ltd and Landauer & Co. Ltd* [1921] 2 KB 519). Equally, where the contract is severable the buyer will be entitled to reject the whole of an instalment if part of it proves defective. This together with the circumstances when the buyer is entitled to repudiate the whole of a severable contract, is discussed in section 19.3.1 below.

Formerly, the law provided that the buyer could *only* reject the whole of the goods, or accept the whole. There was no option for him to accept the part of the goods which conformed with the contract and reject that which did not. This is not the situation now. In so far as the buyer may reject for delivery of goods which do not conform with the contract the law is now contained in the following provisions below. The law relating to delivery and rejection of the wrong *quantity* of goods is discussed in chapter 17.

Section 31 of the 1979 Act, relating to instalment deliveries, provides as follows:

> (1) Unless otherwise agreed, the buyer of goods is not bound to accept delivery of them by instalments.
>
> (2) Where there is a contract for the sale of goods to be delivered by stated instalments, which are to be separately paid for, and the seller makes defective deliveries in respect of one or more instalments, or the buyer neglects or refuses to take delivery of or pay for one or more instalments, it is a question in each case depending on the terms of the contract and the circumstances of the case whether the breach of contract is a repudiation of the whole contract or whether it is a severable breach giving rise to a claim for compensation but not to a right to treat the whole contract as repudiated.

Section 35(7) of the 1979 Act provides as follows:

> Where the contract is for the sale of goods making one or more commercial units, a buyer accepting any goods included in a unit is deemed to have accepted all the goods making the unit; and in this subsection 'commercial unit' means a unit division of which would materially impair the value of the goods or the character of the unit.

Section 35A(1)–(3) of the 1979 Act states in relation to the right of partial rejection:

> (1) If the buyer—
> (a) has the right to reject the goods by reason of a breach on the part of the seller that affects some or all of them, but
> (b) accepts some of the goods, including, where there are any goods unaffected by the breach, all such goods,
> he does not by accepting them lose his right to reject the rest.
> (2) In the case of a buyer having the right to reject an instalment of goods, subsection (1) above applies as if references to the goods were references to the goods comprised in the instalment.
> (3) For the purposes of subsection (1) above, goods are affected by a breach if by reason of the breach they are not in conformity with the contract.

In addition to these sections, the new s. 15A provides that where a buyer deals otherwise than as a consumer that if the breach is so minor as to be unreasonable to reject that he may not do so, but may only claim damages instead. Section 15A, however, applies only to the terms implied by ss. 13, 14 and 15 of the Act. The examples given by the Law Commission (para. 6.16) in relation to these provisions is helpful and worth setting out in full:

> (a) If the buyer is a non-consumer and orders 100 objects, of which only 1 is defective (the breach being 'slight' or 'non-material'), he may not reject any but he may claim damages.[1] If the buyer were a consumer,[2] he could keep them all, reject them all, or keep 99 and reject 1[3] (and in all cases claim damages).
> (b) If the buyer orders 100 objects of which 50 are defective, he may reject 100, keep 100, or keep the 50 conforming objects and reject any or all of the 50 defective objects (and in all cases claim damages).[4]
> (c) If the buyer orders 100 objects and all are defective, he may reject all or any of them and claim damages.
> (d) If the 100 objects in the previous examples comprised an instalment of a larger order, the result would be exactly the same as regards *that* instalment;[5] the partial acceptance rules do not affect any rights the buyer may have as regards other instalments.[6]

These rules make a substantial improvement on the law prior to the 1994 amendments. Under the old law the buyer could only accept or reject the whole, he could not accept part of the goods and reject the rest. The only qualification to this was provided by s. 30(4) (now repealed) which provided that where goods of a different description were supplied with the contract goods, those goods could be rejected and the remainder accepted (see *Aitken Campbell & Co. Ltd* v *Boullen and*

1. Section 15A operates to restrict the right in this example.
2. Section 15A does not operate against a consumer. 'Consumer' here has the same definition as in the Unfair Contract Terms Act 1977, as to which see section 8.2.2.
3. Section 35A(1). This was not the case formerly, see below.
4. Since 50 per cent do not conform this cannot be considered a minor breach and s. 15A does not apply. Effectively the rule is the same as the consumer in (a).
5. Per s. 35A(2).
6. This is dealt with by the common law, see section 19.3.1 below.

Getenby 1908 SC 490; *W. Barker & Co. Ltd* v *E. T. Agius* (1927) 33 Com Cas 120; Atiyah, *The Sale of Goods*, 9th ed. (Pitman, 1995), p. 473 *et seq*).

There do not as yet appear to be any cases decided on s. 15A, but it appears that the thrust of the provisions is aimed at cases such as *Rapalli* v *K. L. Take* [1958] 2 Lloyd's Rep 469 and *Arcos Ltd* v *Ronaasen & Son* [1933] AC 470. In the latter case staves were delivered which were one eighth of an inch outside their contract description, but were commercially merchantable. It was held that they were delivered in breach of the implied condition as to description. It is these cases where the buyer is, in reality, simply trying to get out of a bad bargain by relying on technicalities which the new section is aimed at. Where the breach actually gives rise to real problems, it is likely that the provisions would not apply. For example, with machine-tooled components it is often vital that they are of the exact description as they are otherwise useless. It seems, however, that other factors such as the number of non-conforming goods should also be taken into account. The Law Commission in its examples above used the word 'defective' in example (a), accordingly it seems that it is s. 15A which is being invoked in that example and not s. 30(2A) which relates to delivery of the wrong quantity.

It is to be noted that s. 35A(1) allows the buyer to accept some part of the non-conforming goods and reject others. Why the buyer would wish to do so is not clear, but should he wish to do so he may. He is not obliged to accept only the conforming goods and to reject the rest, he may pick and choose.

The right to reject part of the goods is restricted to rejecting 'commercial units' in their entirety. A commercial unit is something such as a pair of shoes, the value of the unit being markedly affected if one shoe only were rejected. The buyer cannot therefore reject one shoe only, he must reject both.

19.3.1 Severable contracts

It seems that where part of an instalment is defective the buyer becomes entitled to reject all of that instalment. Certainly, the buyer is entitled under the rules of partial rejection to reject part of the goods and to keep the rest of the instalment (s. 35A(2)), and where (as will be seen in the next section) the breach is such as to go to the root of the contract, the buyer may repudiate the whole contract. However, is the buyer entitled to reject the whole of an instalment where he is bound by the contract as a whole?

On this issue the Law Commission declined to make any provision, leaving the matter to the common law. Unfortunately, the Law Commission (at para. 6.15) were unable to define exactly where the law stood on this issue commenting '*whatever* the exact extent of the buyer's right to reject under the existing law' and simply directing the reader to P. S. Atiyah's (albeit excellent) *The Sale of Goods* (see now the 9th ed., p. 454).

Atiyah argues that such a right would exist, noting that s. 31(2) appears to envisage that the buyer may either repudiate the whole contract or reject only an instalment, leaving no third option[7] that the buyer must accept those goods which conform with the contract, and reject only that part of the instalment which does

7. See also the case of *Regent OHG Aisenstadt* v *Francesco of Jermyn Street* [1981] 3 All ER 327 where the possibility of rejecting an instalment, but not repudiating the whole contract, seems to have been overlooked.

not. This is probably correct, whilst a contract may be severable as between instalments each instalment must be considered entire. Accordingly, a breach regarding one part of one instalment should be considered a breach of the whole of that instalment (see, by analogy, *Boston Deep Sea Fishing & Ice Co.* v *Ansell* (1888) 39 Ch D 339).

Where the contract is severable, whether a breach gives rise to a right to repudiate the whole contract (including future instalments), or whether it merely gives rise to a right to reject one instalment depends upon the proportion of non-conforming goods delivered and the likelihood of future breaches (*Maple Flock Co. Ltd* v *Universal Furniture Products (Wembley) Ltd* [1934] 1 KB 148). Some examples illustrate the application of the rule:

(a) In the *Maple Flock* case 100 tons of rag were agreed to be sold by instalments of one and a half tonnes. The first 15 instalments were satisfactory, but the sixteenth was not. By the time that the buyers had established this they had already taken delivery of four more instalments all of which were satisfactory. At this stage the buyers purported to terminate the contract. They were held not to have been entitled to do so.

(b) In *Munro & Co. Ltd* v *Meyer* [1930] 2 KB 312 the buyer had agreed to buy 1,500 tonnes of meat to be delivered in instalments of 125 tonnes. After over 750 tonnes had been delivered it was discovered to be defective. It was held that they were entitled to repudiate.

(c) In *Regent OHG Aisenstadt* v *Francesco of Jermyn Street* [1981] 3 All ER 327 the buyer had agreed to buy around six dozen suits to be delivered in five instalments. The fourth instalment was one suit short. It was held that he was not entitled to terminate the entire contract.

These cases appear to be fairly drastic examples of the application of the rule, in each case the result is obviously right. In cases on the borderline it is likely that the court would take strongly into account the second criterion put forward in the *Maple Flock* case: the likelihood of a future breach or breaches.

One difficulty is raised by these cases, namely where the buyer has accepted and utilised several instalments, how can he then be said to repudiate the *entire* contract. It is likely in these circumstances that the correct analysis would be that the buyer has accepted the earlier instalments, but has given notice of an acceptance of an anticipatory breach in respect of future ones.

19.4 THE EFFECT OF REJECTION

A rather elaborate explanation of the effect of rejection was given by Devlin J in *Kwei Tek Chao* v *British Traders & Shippers Ltd* [1954] 2 QB 459. In that case it was said that, where the seller supplies goods in respect of which there is a breach giving rise to a right to terminate, the buyer takes a conditional property in the goods. The condition being a condition subsequent, conditional upon acceptance of the goods. This is a rather convoluted way of stating that the property in the goods revests in the seller upon rejection of them.

Upon rejecting the goods, s. 36 of the 1979 Act provides that the buyer is not obliged to return them to the seller. It is sufficient that he holds them at the seller's disposal.

20 *The buyer's monetary claims*

20.1 INTRODUCTION

Provision is made in the Sale of Goods Act 1979 (the '1979 Act') for the buyer's recovery of damages, but this provision is little more than a statement of the common law. The ordinary rules of common law regarding remoteness, causation and mitigation apply to contracts of sale and supply just as they apply to any other contract.

This chapter is entitled 'the buyer's monetary claims' as opposed to 'damages' because a distinction can be drawn between claims for damages, which are strictly speaking claims for breach of a term of a contract, and restitutionary remedies, which are strictly made to return to the injured party any benefit which he has passed to the other party to the contract. This distinction is largely one of nomenclature and in practice the court will award the appropriate amount of money to properly compensate the injured party, mixing the remedies as seems just in any individual case. However, some understanding of the differing nature of the remedies is necessary and this will be examined before turning to the measure of damages in contracts of sale.

A buyer may recover in respect of three types of loss: expectation, reliance and restitution. He may choose between any of these, and may combine them to achieve the best result. This is subject only to the rule against double recovery.

Expectation loss This is strictly speaking a claim for damages. The object of the award is to put the claimant in the position that he would have been in had the contract been performed. This is different to the tortious measure which is to place the injured party in the position he would have been in had the tort never been committed. A good example of an expectation loss is where S agrees to sell B a car for £5,000. B knows at the time he made the contract that the car is in fact worth £7,500 and so happily hands over the £5,000. B can sue for his expectation loss where S refuses to deliver and claim the £7,500 not the £5,000 which he paid. Had B never in fact paid S he could still claim £2,500 as his expectation loss. Supposing the car was in fact a taxi, then subject to the rules relating to causation, remoteness and mitigation, the buyer could also claim the profits he expected to make from the use of the car as well.

In contracts of sale an action for damages exceeding the price where the goods have been delivered but rejected is probably the same as an action for non-delivery under s. 51 of the 1979 Act. Here the seller has not delivered goods which conform with the contract and has, in a sense, not made delivery at all. Alternatively, the claim is for breach of a term of the contract which the buyer is entitled to treat as a breach of a warranty and sue for damages under s. 53 of the Act (*Mason* v *Burningham* [1949] 2 KB 545).

Reliance loss This is probably a claim in damages and is not a restitutionary remedy. Here the purpose of the award is to allow the injured party to recover money which it has paid out in reliance upon the contract being performed. So, for example, where a firm buys a computer system and sends its staff on training courses to enable them to know how to operate it, the cost of this training would be recoverable where the system proved defective. It has even been held in one case that expenses paid out prior to the contract being formed are recoverable (*Anglia Television* v *Reed* [1972] 1 QB 60).

Restitutionary claim A restitutionary claim is one to recover a benefit that the injured party has conferred on the other party. Within the context of sale and supply of goods this will usually be an action for money had and received or for the price following a total failure of consideration. The money had and received being the price of the goods paid over to the seller. Accordingly, where S agrees to sell B a car for £5,000 cunningly knowing that it is in fact worth only £3,000 B may sue S for £5,000 upon a valid rejection of it.

It is important to appreciate that the injured party may pick and choose between the different types of remedy available to obtain his best remedy. There are, however, some limits upon this which are explained below. Taking the facts of *Millar's Machinery Co. Ltd* v *David Way & Son* (1935) 40 Com Cas 204 (and twisting them slightly) serves as a useful example. In that case B bought from S a machine for £10,000. He spent £5,000 in installing it. In the event the machine proved defective and was validly rejected. In the (reasonable) time it took him to replace it B expected to make £15,000 profit. The cost of the replacement machine was £10,000. The nature of the machine dictated that it was in the contemplation of the parties that it was to be used as a profit-making chattel and the damages were not too remote. B succeeded in recovering £30,000. The £10,000 was a restitutionary claim in respect of the price of the goods sold, the £5,000 a reliance claim, and the £15,000 an expectation one.

Supposing that B had only agreed to pay £5,000 for the machine in the first place (but it was in fact worth £10,000 on the open market), he would still be able to claim £10,000 in respect of it. However, this would be an expectation claim based on damages, and not a restitutionary one. The law places the buyer in the position he would have been in had the contract been performed. Supposing the machine had been worth £5,000 on the open market, but B had agreed to pay the £10,000 used in the first example, B could claim the £10,000 as money had and received on a restitutionary basis.

There are limits upon the various claims however. In the first place the buyer cannot have double recovery. Sticking to the facts put forward above in relation to the *Millar's Machinery* case, B could not claim both the price of the defective machine (£10,000) and the cost of replacing it (£10,000) as this would give him a machine for nothing and at the seller's expense. Similarly he could not recover the loss of profits, together with his expenses in making them, i.e., his gross receipts. This would put B in a better position than if the contract had been properly performed (*Cullinae* v *British Rema Manufacturing Co.* [1954] 1 QB 292).

Secondly, the injured party will not be able to recover where this would place him in a better position than had the contract been performed. Supposing that B buys a machine for £10,000, spends £10,000 in installing it, but expects to make only £15,000. Here B could claim only the £15,000 as otherwise he would be better off than had the bargain been performed (*C & P Haulage* v *Middleton* [1983] 3 All ER 94). However, in seeking to restrict the damages from reliance to expectation loss in these circumstances the burden of proof rests on the seller (or party in breach). The party claiming his reliance loss need not put forward evidence of his expectation loss and in such circumstances there is no evidence from which the court may infer that the damages should be reduced (*CCC Films (London) Ltd* v *Impact Quadrant Films Ltd* [1985] QB 16). Equally, where the expectation losses are so speculative that they are beyond proper measurement by the court, the injured party may be restricted to his reliance loss (*McRae* v *Commonwealth Disposals Commission* (1950) 84 CLR 377).

Thirdly, a restitutionary claim is available only where there has been a total failure of consideration. In contracts for the sale of goods where the buyer validly rejects the goods he has not gained any part of that which he has bargained for and may claim the entire contract price. Accordingly, the failure of consideration is total (*Rowland* v *Divall* [1923] 2 KB 500). Any period of actual use that the buyer has had is not taken into account (*Butterworth* v *Kingsway Motors* [1954] 2 All ER 694). The position is different with hire purchase claims however. Here the contract is for hire of the goods coupled with an option to purchase. Accordingly, where the hire is wrongfully brought to an end, or the car validly rejected as defective, then the hirer cannot claim the instalments paid upon a total failure of consideration, his claim is for damages only (*Yeoman Credit Ltd* v *Apps* [1962] 2 QB 508). However, it is common practice for the courts to measure damages in such a situation by reference to the cost of the instalments (*Guarantee Trust of Jersey* v *Gardner* (1973) 117 SJ 564), but a deduction should be made for the use of the car (*Charterhouse Credit Co. Ltd* v *Tolley* [1963] 2 QB 683). This being said the courts have striven to offset this use element, for example, in *Farnworth Finance Facilities* v *Attryde* [1970] 2 All ER 774 it was offset against the inconvenience the hirer had been put to by the defective car.

20.2 DAMAGES FOR NON-DELIVERY

Damages for non-delivery are to be assessed in accordance with s. 51 of the 1979 Act which provides as follows:

> (1) Where the seller wrongfully neglects or refuses to deliver the goods to the buyer, the buyer may maintain an action against the seller for damages for non-delivery.
>
> (2) The measure of damages is the estimated loss directly and naturally resulting, in the ordinary course of events, from the seller's breach of contract.

(3) Where there is an available market for the goods in question the measure of damages is prima facie to be ascertained by the difference between the contract price and the market or current price of the goods at the time or times when they ought to have been delivered or (if no time was fixed) at the time of the refusal to deliver.

This rule largely states the common law and raises two issues. First, assessment of the market price, in particular the date at which the prices are to be assessed. Secondly, those cases where the market price rule is displaced as an inadequate measure of loss, the market price rule only being a prima facie measure of damages. These will be discussed in turn below.

These provisions mirror those of the seller's claim for damages for non-acceptance by the buyer. These provisions are discussed in section 23.4. Cases on either set of provisions are relevant in respect of the other.

20.2.1 Assessment of the market price

Cases of refusal to deliver generally take one of three forms: first where the seller is struggling to make delivery and the buyer initially affords him a little extra time but eventually acts on the late delivery and terminates the contract. Secondly, where the buyer legitimately expects the seller to be unable to deliver and terminates the contract as for anticipatory breach. Thirdly, where the seller openly states that he cannot or will not deliver. It must be recalled that the buyer can either hold the contract open and continue to demand delivery, or he may terminate (*Fercometal SARL* v *Mediterranean Shipping Co. SA* [1989] AC 788; *White & Carter (Councils) Ltd* v *McGregor* [1962] AC 413). Where the buyer agrees to waive the strict delivery date for a certain period but, delivery not being made upon such further period, terminates, the date of delivery is probably unchanged. However, if the buyer agrees to take late delivery and accepts some further consideration (such as a drop in price) for it, there is probably an amendment to the contract changing the date of delivery.

Regardless of the actual date of termination the correct date at which the market price is to be assessed is the actual date for delivery (*Melanchrino* v *Nickoll and Knight* [1920] 1 KB 693; *Millett* v *Van Heeck* [1921] 2 KB 369). However, the date of termination is extremely relevant because as soon as the buyer terminates the contract he comes under a duty to mitigate. The effect of this is that the date for assessment of the market price becomes the date at which the buyer could reasonably have mitigated his loss. Where there is an available commodity market (e.g., oil) this date will occur very quickly in commercial situations, even the next day (*Kaines (UK) Ltd* v *Osterreichische Warrenhandelgesellschaft* [1993] 2 Lloyd's Rep 1). By contrast, the circumstances may be such that effecting a quick sale where the market is not so rapid may form a failure to mitigate in itself (*Blythswood Motors* v *Raeside* 1966 SLT (Sh. Ct.) 13).

It must be said that this places the risk of the market almost entirely on the buyer. However, by promptly mitigating his loss in a commercial situation the buyer cannot be criticised and can always sue for his actual loss. For example:

On 1 October 1999 B agrees to buy 1,000 gallons of oil at £15 per barrel, to be delivered on 1 January 2000.

(a) On 1 November 1999, S intimates that he will not deliver. B accepts this and terminates the contract. On 1 November the market price is £17 per barrel. On 1 January 2000 it is £20. Prima facie the measure of damages is £5,000, being 1,000 barrels x (£20–£15). However, B has failed to mitigate his loss to the sum of 1,000 barrels x (£20–£17), being £3,000. B can therefore only recover £2,000 (*Kaines (UK) Ltd* v *Osterreichische Warrenhandelgesellschaft*, above).

(b) On 1 November 1999, S intimates that he will not deliver. B does not accept this and holds him to delivery but, upon delivery not being made, terminates on 1 January 2000. B buys his 1,000 barrels on that date at £20 per barrel. He is entitled to £5,000 damages and cannot be criticised for failure to mitigate (*Melanchrino* v *Nickoll and Knight* [1920] 1 KB 693).

(c) On 1 January 2000, S requests and B permits one month extra for delivery. By 1 February 2000, S has still not delivered and by this stage the market price is £12 per barrel. B buys his 1,000 barrels thus saving himself £3,000. He can sue only for nominal damages as he has suffered no actual loss (*Lazenby Garages* v *Wright* [1976] 1 WLR 459).

Where no delivery date is set the appropriate date is the date at which the seller refused to deliver (see however *Tai Hing Cotton Mill Ltd* v *Kamsing Knitting Factory* [1979] AC 91, which is not strictly binding on the English courts).

20.2.2 Other methods of assessment

The first situation where a different rule will be applied is where there is no available market for goods of the kind in question. For example, there is apparently no market for cars in the United Kingdom, new or second-hand (*W. L. Thompson* v *Robinson (Gunmakers)* [1955] 1 All ER 154; *J. H. Sparshatt & Sons* v *Regan*, *The Times*, 18 December 1959; *Lazenby Garages* v *Wright* [1976] 1 WLR 459).

Where trading has ceased on a recognised exchange due to problems prevailing at the time there is a market when there are sufficient traders in touch with each other to evidence a market (*Shearson Lehman Hutton Inc.* v *MacLaine Watson & Co. Ltd (No. 2)* [1990] 1 Lloyd's Rep 441).

The mere fact that a buyer cannot replace the goods from one order does not of itself mean that there is no available market (*Garnac Grain Co. Inc.* v *H. M. F. Faure & Fairclough Ltd* [1968] AC 1130).

It is quite clear that the market price rule may be displaced where it does not provide an adequate remedy (*W. L. Thompson* v *Robinson (Gunmakers)* [1955] 1 All ER 154) and one point which is frequently argued is that a different rule should be applied because the buyer would have sub-sold the goods at a higher price, meaning that he has lost profit by reason of the seller's failure to deliver. The general rule is that this has no effect on the buyer's measure of damages, he should have purchased the goods in the open market (even at a loss) to fulfil his orders (*Williams* v *Agis* [1914] AC 510). However, where there is no available market, profits on the sub-sale may be recoverable (*Blythswood Motors* v *Raeside* 1966 SLT (Sh. Ct.) 13).

However, the buyer can probably recover loss of profits where the goods are a unique item and the seller knew that the buyer bought the goods for the purpose of sub-sale. Whilst not entirely clear it seems that this was the basis of the decision in *Re R. & H. Hall Ltd & W. H. Pim (Junior) & Co.'s Arbitration* (1928) 139 LT 50. In that case the buyer had sub-sold a cargo of corn at a higher price than the purchase price. There were two features of this case which brought it outside an ordinary commodity sale. In the first place the sub-sale related to specific goods. The cargo had been identified as existing in a particular ship and a particular load. Where the goods are unique in nature, it would be just for the rule to be displaced. Indeed where the goods sold under the sub-sale are specific within the meaning of the 1979 Act, it is not open to the buyer to obtain other goods in place of those which he has contracted to sell. This is the position where, for example, a particular painting is sold. Support for this can be found in the case of *Lazenby Garages* v *Wright* [1976] 1 WLR 459 where it was said that a second-hand car was a unique article. It may be that the rationale behind these cases is that there is no available market for the particular goods because of their very nature as specific items.

Secondly, in *Re R. & H. Hall Ltd & W. H. Pim (Junior) & Co.'s Arbitration* (1928) 139 LT 50 the sub-sale had been specifically dealt with in the original contract of sale. This is not a usual feature of such a sale and it is this element which is missing in other cases. Notably in *The Arpad* [1934] P 189 it was said that, even where the vendor might expect that the goods were to be resold, 'something more' was required in order for the buyer to recover in respect of his loss of profits.

20.3 DAMAGES FOR BREACH OF CONDITION OR WARRANTY

Where the seller has delivered the goods, but the buyer has another complaint regarding the seller's performance, the position is governed by s. 53 of the 1979 Act which provides as follows:

> (1) Where there is a breach of warranty by the seller, or where the buyer elects (or is compelled) to treat any breach of a condition on the part of the seller as a breach of warranty, the buyer is not by reason only of such breach of warranty entitled to reject the goods, but he may—
>
> (a) set up against the seller the breach of warranty in diminution or extinction of the price, or
>
> (b) maintain an action against the seller for damages for the breach of warranty.
>
> (2) The measure of damages for the breach of warranty is the estimated loss directly and naturally resulting, in the ordinary course of events, from the breach of warranty.
>
> (3) In the case of breach of warranty of quality such loss is prima facie the difference between the value of the goods at the time of delivery to the buyer and the value they would have had if they had fulfilled the warranty.
>
> (4) The fact that the buyer has set up the breach of warranty in diminution or extinction of the price does not prevent him from maintaining an action for the same breach of warranty if he has suffered further damage.

The first point to note about s. 53 is a practical one: s. 53 allows the buyer to set off a claim for breach of a warranty against a claim for the price.

Not all counterclaims amount to set offs. Where a counterclaim does amount to a set off, it will amount to a defence to a claim. The practical importance of this is that where a counterclaim does not amount to a defence by virtue of being a set off the party making the claim would be entitled to summary judgment in respect of his claim, whilst the injured party has to wait until trial in respect of a counterclaim which may have a greater financial value. In some cases, payment on the claim may bankrupt the injured party before he is able to bring his case to trial. This problem does not arise in sale of goods cases by reason of the right of set off. Furthermore, s. 53(4) provides that the buyer may make a claim over and above any amount that he wishes to set off.

Section 53(1) provides that the buyer is not bound to treat a breach of condition as giving rise to a right to reject but may if he chooses simply claim damages in respect of the breach (*Mason* v *Burningham* [1949] 2 KB 545). The nomenclature of s. 53(2) and (3) tends to suggest that a condition 'becomes' a warranty where the buyer loses his right to reject or where he elects not to do so. This is not the case however, the condition is simply treated as a warranty in that only damages are claimed (*Wallis, Son & Wells* v *Pratt & Haynes* [1911] AC 394).

Section 53(3) lays down the prima facie measure of damages: the difference in value of the goods with the defect and the value without. The time for assessing the difference being the time of delivery. However, in practice, in consumer cases at any rate, the court readily accepts that the cost of repairing the defect is representative of the difference in value. Indeed, in such cases it is difficult to measure the difference in value otherwise than by reference to the cost of cure. Certainly, in such cases it will rarely be financially worth the buyer engaging the services of an expert.[1] An interesting case on this issue is that of *Ruxley Electronics and Construction Ltd* v *Forsyth* [1995] 3 WLR 118. In that case the buyer had a swimming-pool built to specification in his back garden. As built it was seven inches too shallow in parts. It was found that this did not affect its value at all. The cost of rebuilding it to specification was £21,000. The Court of Appeal allowed the buyer to claim the cost of the repair, but the House of Lords overturned this. The appropriate measure of damages was the difference in value, nil. Whilst not a case on sale of goods the principles are of course relevant — where to allow the cost of cure would be unreasonable, the difference in value method is appropriate (see also *Channel Island Ferries Ltd* v *Cenargo Navigation Ltd (The Rozel)* [1994] 2 Lloyd's Rep 161).

A buyer in a consumer case can probably recover in respect of loss of enjoyment where the goods were ones which he bought for his use and enjoyment (*Jackson* v *Horizon Holidays* [1975] 1 WLR 1468). Certainly the niceties of privity of contract would not be strictly observed in the county court.

20.4 CONSEQUENTIAL LOSS

Broadly speaking consequential losses fall into four categories:

(a) damage or injury caused by chattels to other things (often people) around them;
(b) loss of enjoyment or inconvenience caused by a defective chattel;
(c) loss of profits where a profit-making chattel breaks down; and
(d) loss of profits on chattels bought for resale.

1. However, the new Civil Procedure Rules permit the cost of an expert even under the small claims track 'no-costs' regime to a maximum of £200 (Practice Direction 27, para. 7.3(2)).

It is worth bearing these different types of cases in mind when considering consequential losses as the courts' approach to consequential losses differs between these categories. This is not to say that the principles actually change, but the application of them certainly seems to.

The first rule regarding damages is that the loss must actually be caused by the breach. There is no remedy in respect of a loss simply because there was a breach of the contract. This being said the breach need not be the sole cause of the loss, so long as it is a seriously operative one. Where this is the case, the buyer may yet recover all his losses (*Heskell* v *Continental Express Ltd* [1950] 1 All ER 1033). But, for example, where a ship was already late but was then struck by a typhoon this would not be a real connection with the delay (*Monarch SS Co. Ltd* v *Karshamns Oliefabrieker* [1949] AC 196). Whether a particular loss has been caused by a breach in the case of a sale of goods will usually be self-evident from the facts of the case.

So long as the loss was caused by the breach, the two limbs of the rule in the famous case of *Hadley* v *Baxendale* (1854) 9 Exch 341 are relevant:

(a) That the loss arises according to the ordinary course of things from the breach. This much of the rule is set out in s. 53(2) of the 1979 Act.

(b) That the loss was of a kind which may reasonably be supposed to have been in the minds of both the parties at the time they contracted as a probable result of the breach.

The application of these criteria are looked at in relation to the different types of loss outlined above. It should be noted that the first two types of case tend to be concerned with consumers and the last two with businesses.

20.4.1 Damage to other things

It is clear that damage to other goods and people can form the basis of a claim for damages for breach of the contract of sale. In *Lambert* v *Lewis* [1982] AC 225 the buyer of a vehicle claimed an indemnity from the seller where a towing coupling had broken, causing the trailer behind the vehicle to hit another vehicle and kill and injure its occupants. But for the fact that the buyer had continued to use the coupling after he had noticed the defect there is no doubt that the court would have imposed the indemnity. An indemnity in this situation is different from direct liability and is more akin to the buyer himself being injured. Similarly in *Godley* v *Perry* [1960] 1 WLR 9 a young boy was injured where a catapult broke and he was entitled to claim damages for personal injury. Also in *Grant* v *Australian Knitting Mills* [1936] AC 85 the buyer of a pair of pants was entitled to make a claim where he contracted a form of dermatitis from them.

There seems no doubt that the courts are prepared to impose liability in respect of this kind of damage. These cases do bring out one aspect of the test in *Hadley* v *Baxendale* however — that the breach and its consequences need not *actually* be in the mind of the parties but need only be reasonable deductions in the event that the breach actually occurred. There is no doubt that the manufacturers or sellers in the above cases did not actually envisage the problems with their products.

20.4.2 Loss of enjoyment or inconvenience

The Court of Appeal has stated in *Bliss* v *South East Thames Regional Health Authority* [1987] ICR 700 that damages can never be awarded in respect of 'distress' in a contractual claim: see also *Dimond* v *Lovell* [2000] 2 WLR 1121 (HL). The practice in the county courts is therefore to claim in respect of 'inconvenience' which is frequently awarded (see, for example, *Robotics* v *First Co-Operative Finance* (1983) CLR 3329; *Lawson* v *Supasink* (1984) TrL 37; *Gascoigne* v *British Credit Trust* (1978) CLR 711; *McAuslan* v *Jack* (1956) 107 LJ 124; see also the case of *Bernstein* below).

In *Jackson* v *Chrysler Acceptances Ltd* [1978] RTR 474 the buyer had informed the salesman when he purchased a new car that he wanted it to use on a forthcoming holiday. Accordingly, it was in the contemplation of the parties that the buyer's holiday would be ruined if the car broke down and the buyer was entitled to recover in respect of this when it did so. Similarly in *Bernstein* v *Pamson Motors (Golders Green) Ltd* [1987] 2 All ER 220 the buyer of a car was entitled to claim in respect of a ruined day's shopping following the breakdown of his car.

20.4.3 Profit-making chattels

The principal question in relation to profit-earning chattels is whether the type of loss was one which was reasonably in the minds of the parties at the time the contract of sale was made. Thus, where a car is sold, for example, it would not ordinarily be used for profit and hence profits could not be claimed were it not to be available for use because of such defects. However, if the car in question was a taxi then (obviously) the parties would envisage that it would be used for profit and profits would be recoverable.

The leading case on loss of profits of this kind is *Parsons (Livestock) Ltd* v *Uttley Ingham & Co. Ltd* [1978] QB 791. In that case food hoppers had been sold to the buyers for feeding their pigs. The hoppers contained a vent which if not opened would cause the foodstuff to rot. The sellers neither told the buyers of this nor was the vent easily visible. The vent was not opened, the foodstuff rotted, pigs died and the buyer lost profit. It was held that the death of the pigs was a loss of a *kind* which was *foreseeable* and therefore this type of loss was within the contemplation of the parties.

The first point to note about the case is that the tortious method of looking at the loss was engaged to a certain extent; the court asked whether the loss was of a kind that was foreseeable. However, whether something is 'foreseeable' or whether it is 'in the contemplation' of a person is very much the same thing. Secondly, it was the 'kind' of loss which must be foreseeable. On this basis it was foreseeable that pigs might die, but not that profits may be lost. This is most unsatisfactory as it seems to assume that the buyers were pig farming for the sheer fun of it, which is extremely unlikely. Accordingly it is difficult to predict with certainty when the courts will uphold a claim for loss of profits.

One case which may show the current judicial attitude is *St. Albans City and District Council* v *International Computers Ltd* [1996] 4 All ER 481. In that case the sellers had supplied a computer system for the plaintiffs which had failed to properly calculate the plaintiff's rate charge which it needed to apply and accordingly the plaintiff made a loss. The loss was considered recoverable, although most of the argument was on an exemption clause. This case also highlights another practical point — many standard form sales contracts contain a clause excluding or limiting liability for consequential losses. Assuming it can be struck down as an unfair term, there is a strong argument that the seller had contemplated consequential loss (something he usually denies) as otherwise there would be no need for its inclusion in the contract.

Another case involving the sale of goods which is relevant is that of *R. W. Green* v *Cade Bros Farms* [1978] 1 Lloyd's Rep 602. In that case seed had been sold which proved defective. The buyers claimed loss of profits. Although the central issue in the case was an exclusion clause no doubt was cast that profits would be recoverable (see also *George Mitchell (Chesterhall) Ltd* v *Finney Lock Seeds Ltd* [1983] 2 AC 803).

Whilst the decision in *Parsons (Livestock) Ltd* v *Uttley Ingham & Co. Ltd* remains somewhat difficult to properly explain, it is clear enough that where the good is directly used in the profit-making process (e.g., seed) the loss of profits may be recoverable, but where it simply damages another item in the profit-making process it will not be.

20.4.4 Loss of profit on sub-sale

The position regarding loss of profit on a resale has already been examined in relation to non-delivery cases in section 20.2.2. It was seen there that the general rule was that such losses were not ordinarily recoverable.

Applying the test in *Hadley* v *Baxendale* where the case is one on sub-sale of defective goods it does not seem to be required, as it is with cases on non-delivery (per *The Arpad* [1934] P 189), that the seller be fixed with some kind of special knowledge that the sub-sale exists. All that *Hadley* v *Baxendale* requires is that a sub sale is reasonably foreseeable. In most cases of the sale of a commodity such as crops, produce or packaged goods this will be the case. However, it is submitted that if there is an available market from which the buyer can quickly and easily fulfil his obligations, and the buyer knows of the defect, he may well be held to have failed to mitigate if his loss (*Molling & Co.* v *Dean & Son Ltd* [1920] 2 KB 11; *Blythswood Motors* v *Raeside* 1966 SLT (Sh. Ct.) 13; *Kaines (UK) Ltd* v *Osterreichische Warrenhandelgesellschaft* [1993] 2 Lloyd's Rep 1).

For the most part the seller will be liable where it was reasonable to contemplate that the goods would be resold. Taking the situation where S sells to B1 who sub-sells to B2 in a situation where S knows that B1 intends to resell, it certainly seems that B1's claim against S will be of the same value as B2's claim against B1 where B1 has sold to B2 on the same terms (*Kasler and Cohen* v *Slavouski* [1928] 1 KB 78). It has also been held in one case that loss of business from his customers following the sale from B1 to B2 of faulty goods was something reasonably in the contemplation of S and hence recoverable (*GKN Centrax Gears Ltd* v *Matbro Ltd* [1976] 2 Lloyd's Rep 555).

21 *Specific performance*

An action for specific performance lies in respect of the buyer; that is to say an order that the seller completes the agreement and sells and delivers the goods to the buyer. The seller has no specific right to specific performance, but he may bring an action for the price of the goods. Given that in the ordinary course of events the only thing which the seller is to receive under a contract for the sale of goods is the price, this is for all practical purposes an order for specific performance. Where the seller's claim is for the price, to a certain extent the seller is in a better position than the buyer as he may bring his action as of right and not within the discretionary powers of the court.

In contracts other than those for the sale of goods, i.e., hire purchase agreements and agreements for the transfer of goods (etc.), the buyer's remedy is derived from the court's equitable jurisdiction. In the case of contracts for the sale of goods, the position is governed by s. 52 of the Sale of Goods Act 1979 (the '1979 Act'). Section 52 applies in respect of contracts relating to specific or ascertained goods only, and not in respect of unascertained goods (*Re London Wine (Shippers) Co. Ltd* 1986 PCC 121).

Section 52 provides as follows:

> (1) In any action for breach of contract to deliver specific or ascertained goods the court may, if it thinks fit, on the plaintiff's application, by its judgment or decree direct that the contract shall be performed specifically, without giving the defendant the option of retaining the goods on payment of damages.
>
> (2) The plaintiff's application may be made at any time before judgment or decree.
>
> (3) The judgment or decree may be unconditional, or on such terms and conditions as to damages, payment of the price and otherwise as seem just to the court.

In addition to these provisions the buyer may claim an order for delivery of the goods under the Torts (Interference with Goods) Act 1977 (the '1977 Act'). Such a remedy lies upon an action for wrongful interference[1] with the goods where the

1. Within the definition given in s. 1 of the Torts (Interference with Goods) Act 1977 this includes conversion or trespass to the goods.

property has passed to the buyer and he is therefore the owner of them. Given that payment and delivery are concurrent obligations it would not seem that such an action arises where the buyer has not yet paid for the goods, but instead he should rely on s. 52 above where the seller is refusing to accept payment and perform his obligations under the contract (i.e., delivery).

The order for delivery of the goods upon a claim for wrongful interference is regulated by s. 3 of the 1977 Act, which provides as follows:

> (1) In proceedings for wrongful interference against a person who is in possession or in control of the goods relief may be given in accordance with this section so far as appropriate.
>
> (2) The relief is—
>
> (a) an order for delivery of goods, and for payment of any consequential damages, or
>
> (b) an order for delivery of the goods, but giving the defendant the alternative of paying damages by reference to the value of the goods, together in either alternative with payment of consequential damages, or
>
> (c) damages.
>
> (3) Subject to rules of court—
>
> (a) relief shall be given under only one of paragraphs (a), (b) and (c) of subsection (2),
>
> (b) relief under paragraph (a) of subsection (2) is at the discretion of the court, and the claimant may choose between the others.
>
> (4) [provision where order for delivery not complied with]
>
> (5) Where an order is made under subsection (2)(b) the defendant may satisfy the order by returning the goods at any time before execution of judgment, but without prejudice to liability to pay any consequential damages.
>
> (6) An order for delivery of the goods under subsection (2)(a) or (b) may impose such conditions as may be determined by the court, or pursuant to rules of court, and, in particular, where damages by reference to the value of the goods would not be the whole of the value of the goods, may require an allowance to be made by the claimant to reflect the difference.
>
> For example, a bailor's action against the bailee may be one in which the measure of damages is not the full value of the goods, and then the court may order delivery of the goods, but require the bailor to pay the bailee a sum reflecting the difference.

Section 3(2) and (3) still leave the question of whether or not to make an order for delivery of goods at the discretion of the court. However, the 1977 Act is slightly more favourable than s. 52 of the 1979 Act in that if the court declines to make the order, the buyer may choose between s. 3(2)(b) and (c) at his election. The buyer can therefore at least achieve an order for the delivery of the goods, albeit that the defendant may satisfy the order by taking the option to pay damages in lieu.

Both s. 52 of the 1979 Act and s. 3 of the 1977 Act leave the decision as to whether to make an order at the discretion of the court. However, the considerations as to when to make an order will differ slightly between the two powers. For example, an action under the 1977 Act may be in respect of stolen goods, in which case the court would be reluctant not to make an order for delivery up. This text is primarily concerned with contracts of sale and supply, however, and cases in this context will be explored.

The first point to note about orders for delivery or specific performance is that the courts are extremely reluctant to grant them. This seems somewhat odd as an order for specific performance is the purest form of enforcing a bargain between the parties. Given that the object of damages is to put the injured party in the same financial position that he would have been in had the contract been performed, it is strange that the courts are slow to use a remedy that puts him in the *actual* position that he would have been in had the contract been performed.

It may well be the case that district judges and circuit judges of the county courts are quicker to use these powers than judges in the High Court dealing with complex commercial cases, but county court cases are less likely to find themselves in the law reports. In any event it may well be that the proactive approach dictated by the Woolf reforms may incline judges in favour of using the powers of specific performance and delivery in place of damages.

This reluctance on the part of the courts can be seen from examination of a few cases on the area. For example, in *Société des Industries Metallurgiques SA* v *Bronx Engineering Co. Ltd* [1975] 1 Lloyd's Rep 465 an order for specific performance over a contract of sale was refused even though the goods in question were specialist in nature and would take a year to obtain from any other source on the open market. However, where the property has passed, the court may be more willing to intervene. In *Redler Grain Silos Ltd* v *BICC Ltd* [1982] 1 Lloyd's Rep 435 an injunction was granted to prevent the seller reneging on his contract with the buyers and fulfilling other orders where the property had already passed to the buyers, even though the sellers were prepared to pay damages in lieu of performance (see also in a consumer context *Clarke* v *Reilly* (1962) 96 ILTR 96 where specific performance was ordered in respect of a car). By contrast, the courts will be reluctant to make an order for specific performance where this may interfere with a lien held by the seller (*Langen & Wind* v *Bell* [1972] 1 All ER 296).

22 *The seller's remedies against the goods*

22.1 INTRODUCTION

Where the seller of goods remains unpaid, he naturally has an action against the buyer for the price of the goods. However, this is a personal remedy only and in practice the buyer may be insolvent or sometimes untraceable. Furthermore, the seller is unlikely to wish to go through the tedious process of litigation in order to recoup his loss. Accordingly, a right to retain and resell the goods is of much greater practical advantage than the right to sue for the loss. The Sale of Goods Act 1979 (the '1979 Act') lays down the circumstances where the seller may exercise a lien over the goods and thus retain them as a physical security against payment.

Whilst there is some confusion upon the issue, it seems that the seller's rights depend not so much upon the passing of property but upon whether the seller retains physical control over the goods. It is, however, clear that the seller's right to exercise a lien does not amount to a termination of the contract. Accordingly, the mere fact that the seller has a right to detain the goods does not of itself mean that he has a right to resell them. When considering the seller's remedies over the goods it is helpful to take a four-stage approach:

(a) Is the seller an 'unpaid seller'? It is only if the seller is an unpaid seller within the meaning of the 1979 Act that he has any right to detain the goods.

(b) Assuming that the seller is unpaid, his rights over the goods need to be explored. Section 39 of the 1979 Act provides the circumstances where the seller may detain the goods so as to exercise a physical security against payment of the price. These rights accrue where the seller has physical control over the goods. The Act also stipulates situations where the seller will lose his right to detain the goods.

(c) Assuming that the seller has retained possession of the goods and has resold them, the third party buyer will almost certainly gain a good title to the goods. However, whether the seller is liable to the buyer in respect of the resale, or the buyer liable to the seller, depends upon whether the seller validly terminated the contract.

(i) If the seller validly terminated the contract for anticipatory breach (non-payment), the buyer will be liable for any extra expenses which the seller incurred.

(ii) If the seller simply resold the goods to another, but the contract was not terminated, the buyer will have a claim against the seller. Where the property in the goods has passed to the buyer, he may claim in conversion as well as on the contract of sale.

(d) If the goods have been delivered to the buyer, but the seller remains unpaid, he may either wish to make a claim for the return of the goods or (exceptionally) purport to resell them. In practice this will only be the case where the seller has utilised a valid retention of title clause. Retention of title clauses were discussed in section 11.6.

These four stages are examined in turn.

22.2 THE UNPAID SELLER

The unpaid seller is defined by s. 38 of the 1979 Act, which provides as follows:

> (1) The seller of goods is an unpaid seller within the meaning of this Act—
> (a) when the whole of the price has not been paid or tendered;
> (b) when a bill of exchange or other negotiable instrument has been received as conditional payment, and the condition on which it was received has not been fulfilled by reason of the dishonour of the instrument or otherwise.
> (2) In this Part of this Act 'seller' includes any person who is in the position of a seller, as, for instance, an agent of the seller to whom the bill of lading has been indorsed, or a consignor or agent who has himself paid (or is directly responsible for) the price.

The definition is fairly straightforward. A seller is an unpaid seller when he has not been paid *in full* or where a cheque has been tendered but has subsequently 'bounced'.

22.3 THE UNPAID SELLER'S LIEN AND RIGHT OF STOPPAGE IN TRANSIT

The unpaid seller's rights to physical control over the goods are set out in s. 39 of the 1979 Act, which provides as follows:

> (1) Subject to this and any other Act, notwithstanding that the property in the goods may have passed to the buyer, the unpaid seller of goods, as such, has by implication of law—
> (a) a lien on the goods or right to retain them for the price while he is in possession of them;
> (b) in the case of the insolvency of the buyer, a right of stopping the goods in transit after he has parted with the possession of them;
> (c) a right of resale as limited by this Act.
> (2) Where the property in goods has not passed to the buyer, the unpaid seller has (in addition to his other remedies) a right of withholding delivery similar to and coextensive with his rights of lien or retention and stoppage in transit where the property has passed to the buyer.

The first issue that this section raises is whether there is any difference between the rights afforded to the seller where the property has passed to the buyer or where it remains in the seller. It is submitted that there is not, and that the effect of s. 39 is merely to state that the unpaid seller's rights conferred by the Act exist over and above any rights which exist by virtue of the property being in a particular party. For example, where the property has passed to the buyer and the seller refuses to deliver, the buyer would have an action for wrongful interference with his goods and could seek an order for delivery of them. The effect of s. 39 is to prioritise the seller's lien over such a claim, i.e., 'notwithstanding that the property in the goods may have passed to the buyer'. Similarly, where the property remains in the seller, his rights exist in addition to any others he may hold over the goods. If this is not the proper construction, there appears little purpose in s. 39 as it merely repeats that which is already contained in ss. 41 to 48, and there is no purpose in the distinction between the property being in the seller and the property being in the buyer.

The seller's lien together with the circumstances when it is extinguished will be considered before turning to the right of stoppage in transit. The right to resell the goods is considered in section 22.4.

22.3.1 The seller's lien

Sections 41, 42 and 61(4) of the 1979 Act provide as follows:

> 41.—(1) Subject to this Act, the unpaid seller of goods who is in possession of them is entitled to retain possession of them until payment or tender of the price in the following cases:—
> (a) where the goods have been sold without any stipulation as to credit;
> (b) where the goods have been sold on credit but the term of credit has expired;
> (c) where the buyer becomes insolvent.
> (2) The seller may exercise his lien or right of retention notwithstanding that he is in possession of the goods as agent or bailee or custodier for the buyer.
>
> 42. Where an unpaid seller has made part delivery of the goods, he may exercise his lien or right of retention on the remainder, unless such part delivery has been made under such circumstances as to show an agreement to waive the lien or right of retention.
>
> 61. ...
> (4) A person is deemed to be insolvent within the meaning of this Act if he has either ceased to pay his debts in the ordinary course of business or he cannot pay his debts as they become due.

The seller's lien comes into operation only where he is already in possession of the goods; he cannot retake possession pursuant to the lien. The lien does not give the seller any property in the goods, although the right is a 'real' one over the goods and is not a purely personal remedy (*Lord's Trustee* v *Great Eastern Railway* [1909] AC 109).

Where the contract is one for instalment sales it seems that s. 42 of the Act will apply and the seller may withhold future instalments pursuant to the lien (*Longbottom & Co. Ltd* v *Bass Walker & Co. Ltd* [1922] WN 245). However, the seller cannot claim to withhold goods to be supplied under one contract through non-payment in respect of another.

22.3.2 Termination of the seller's lien

Section 43 of the 1979 Act provides as follows:

> (1) The unpaid seller of goods loses his lien or right of retention in respect of them—
>
> (a) when he delivers the goods to a carrier or other bailee or custodier for the purpose of transmission to the buyer without reserving the right of disposal of the goods;
>
> (b) when the buyer or his agent lawfully obtains possession of the goods;
>
> (c) by waiver of the lien or right of retention.
>
> (2) An unpaid seller of goods who has a lien or right of retention in respect of them does not lose his lien or right of retention by reason only that he has obtained judgment or decree for the price of the goods.

The general effect of these provisions is to deprive the seller of his lien when he lawfully gives up possession of the goods. Possession here probably means 'constructive possession', so that the goods being stored in a warehouse to the order of the seller will suffice to maintain the seller's lien.

The first, and probably most important, provision for the termination of the lien is made by s. 43(1)(a), being when the goods are delivered to a carrier for transmission to the buyer. It is at this stage that the lien ceases and the right of stoppage starts. The lien does not cease, however, if the seller retains constructive possession by retaining the right of disposal.

Once lost the seller cannot regain his lien by retaking possession (*Pennington* v *Motor Reliance Works* [1923] 1 KB 127). However, where the seller exercises his right of stoppage in transit this amounts to the same thing.

22.3.3 Stoppage in transit

Sections 44, 45 and 46 of the 1979 Act provide as follows:

> 44. Subject to this Act, when the buyer of goods becomes insolvent the unpaid seller who has parted with the possession of the goods has the right of stopping them in transit, that is to say, he may resume possession of the goods as long as they are in course of transit, and may retain them until payment or tender of the price.
>
> 45.—(1) Goods are deemed to be in course of transit from the time when they are delivered to a carrier or other bailee or custodier for the purpose of transmission to the buyer, until the buyer or his agent in that behalf takes delivery of them from the carrier or other bailee or custodier.

(2) If the buyer or his agent in that behalf obtains delivery of the goods before their arrival at the appointed destination, the transit is at an end.

(3) If, after the arrival of the goods at the appointed destination, the carrier or other bailee or custodier acknowledges to the buyer or his agent that he holds the goods on his behalf and continues in possession of them as bailee or custodier for the buyer or his agent, the transit is at an end, and it is immaterial that a further destination for the goods may have been indicated by the buyer.

(4) If the goods are rejected by the buyer, and the carrier or other bailee or custodier continues in possession of them, the transit is not deemed to be at an end, even if the seller has refused to receive them back.

(5) When goods are delivered to a ship chartered by the buyer it is a question depending on the circumstances of the particular case whether they are in the possession of the master as a carrier or as agent to the buyer.

(6) Where the carrier or other bailee or custodier wrongfully refuses to deliver the goods to the buyer or his agent in that behalf, the transit is deemed to be at an end.

(7) Where part delivery of the goods has been made to the buyer or his agent in that behalf, the remainder of the goods may be stopped in transit, unless such part delivery has been made under such circumstances as to show an agreement to give up possession of the whole of the goods.

46.—(1) The unpaid seller may exercise his right of stoppage in transit either by taking actual possession of the goods or by giving notice of his claim to the carrier or other bailee or custodier in whose possession the goods are.

(2) The notice may be given either to the person in actual possession of the goods or to his principal.

(3) If given to the principal, the notice is ineffective unless given at such time and under such circumstances that the principal, by the exercise of reasonable diligence, may communicate it to his servant or agent in time to prevent a delivery to the buyer.

(4) When notice of stoppage in transit is given by the seller to the carrier or other bailee or custodier in possession of the goods, he must redeliver the goods to, or according to the directions of, the seller; and the expenses of the redelivery must be borne by the seller.

Much of these provisions relate to international sales, with which this text is not concerned. The general rule is that transit starts upon delivery to the carrier and ends with delivery to the buyer. The right to stop the goods in transit noticeably arises only upon the insolvency of the buyer. Given this, the circumstances in modern domestic sales where the insolvency will come to the attention of the buyer whilst the goods are in transit, so as he is able to effect a lien on them, will be exceedingly rare.

22.4 RIGHT OF RESALE

The right of resale is governed by s. 48 of the 1979 Act, which provides as follows:

(1) Subject to this section, a contract of sale is not rescinded by the mere exercise by an unpaid seller of his right of lien or retention or stoppage in transit.

(2) Where an unpaid seller who has exercised his right of lien or retention or stoppage in transit resells the goods, the buyer acquires a good title to them as against the original buyer.

(3) Where the goods are of a perishable nature, or where the unpaid seller gives notice to the buyer of his intention to resell, and the buyer does not within a reasonable time pay or tender the price, the unpaid seller may resell the goods and recover from the original buyer damages for any loss occasioned by his breach of contract.

(4) Where the seller expressly reserves the right of resale in case the buyer should make default, and on the buyer making default resells the goods, the original contract of sale is rescinded but without prejudice to any claim the seller may have for damages.

The general rules regarding resale are contained in s. 48(1) and (2). However it is worth considering the limited rights of resale contained in s. 48(3) and (4) before considering the general rule.

Section 48(3) applies where the goods are of a perishable nature and the seller gives notice of his intention to resell. Given that the goods are of a perishable nature the 'reasonable time' afforded to the buyer to respond will necessarily be short, indeed time may be said to be of the essence in any contract of sale once notice of resale has been given (*R. V. Ward Ltd* v *Bignall* [1967] 1 QB 534). When the buyer fails to respond to this notice, the resale will act as a termination of the contract.

Section 48(4) provides itself for an 'automatic' form of rescission of the contract. Hence where specific provision is made in the contract for the buyer defaulting the seller may resell and this will act as a termination of the contract without more.

Turning to the general law, it is clear from s. 48(1) that the mere exercise of a lien does not terminate the contract. In order for the seller to lawfully sell the contract goods he must have terminated the contract. Here a distinction must be drawn between the seller having the *power* to sell and the *right* to do so.

A seller will invariably have the *power* to sell the goods (in other words the ability to confer good title) whilst they are in his possession either under s. 8 of the Factors Act 1889 or by s. 24 of the 1979 Act. These situations were discussed in chapter 13. In these circumstances there will be an exception to the *nemo dat* rule and he will be able to pass a good title to a third party. Section 48(2) goes beyond this, however, and confers a power of resale even where the goods are not in the seller's possession, but where the goods are in transit subject to the seller's right of stoppage. Here the third party buyer takes good title. Furthermore, this will be the case under s. 47(1) even where the buyer has subsold the goods to another buyer.

The situation in the previous paragraph must, however, be distinguished from the *right* of the seller to sell the goods. The mere fact that the seller has exercised his lien does not mean that the contract has been terminated. Furthermore, unless payment is of the essence under a contract of sale, late payment will not necessarily amount to a repudiation of the contract. If the property in the goods has passed, the seller will be selling the buyer's goods and will be liable in conversion for doing so. Even if the property has not passed, if the contract is for specific or ascertained goods, the seller is obliged to deliver *those* goods to the buyer. Failure to do so will be a breach of the contract. It is only if the goods are unascertained and the seller may fulfil the order with other goods that the seller is entitled to sell them. Where the seller has sold the goods in breach of these obligations, the buyer may maintain an action for non-delivery. This is discussed in chapter 23.

However, if the buyer has clearly indicated that he cannot or will not pay for the goods, this will entitle the seller to terminate the contract as for anticipatory breach. It seems likely that the courts will treat the resale by the seller as a termination of the contract (*R. V. Ward Ltd* v *Bignall* [1967] 1 QB 534). Upon termination the property in the goods will revest in the seller (if it had passed) and the seller's obligation to deliver any particular goods will have ceased. Accordingly, the seller has both the power and the right to resell the goods. Where this is the case, the seller may claim for his expenses of the resale and any loss he made (s. 37).

23 The seller's monetary claims

23.1 INTRODUCTION

The seller will have an action against the buyer where he refuses to accept or pay for the goods. The buyer must, of course, wrongfully refuse to accept the goods. If he has a legitimate claim that the goods did not conform with the contract, he is under no duty to accept them. Furthermore, the buyer may be able to set up this defence even though it was not known to exist at the time he refused to accept the goods. Whether or not he is able to do so will depend upon the timing of the buyer's repudiation and the seller's acceptance (or otherwise) of it.

If the buyer intimates that he will refuse to accept the goods before the time of delivery and the seller accepts this and terminates the contract, the buyer will be debarred from raising the defence when he later discovers it (*Braithwaite* v *Foreign Hardwood* [1905] 2 KB 543 as explained in *Fercometal SARL* v *Mediterranean Shipping Co. SA* [1989] AC 788). However, if the seller refuses to accept the repudiation and presses for delivery and payment, he will be keeping the contract alive and must be ready and willing to perform his obligations if he is to maintain an action for non-acceptance (*Fercometal SARL* v *Mediterranean Shipping Co. SA* [1989] AC 788). This was discussed in section 18.6.

When assessing the nature of the seller's claim, a vital distinction must be drawn between the circumstances when the seller may sue for the price and where his action is merely for damages for non-acceptance.

Where the seller is reduced to an action for damages, he will be under a duty to attempt to mitigate his loss, and where there is an available market for the goods he must go to the market and sell them. He will, of course, recover the difference in the contract price and the market price, but this measure of damages will invariably be less than the price of the goods. In either event, the seller should be placed in the position he would have been in had the goods been accepted by the buyer.

However, a claim for the price is a much simpler, more straightforward, action. The seller is not bound to mitigate his loss and the action is akin to one for specific performance of the contract. The seller will not be subject to criticisms of the time or place he sold the goods and he is therefore more assured of being placed in the position he would have been in had the contract been performed.

The seller cannot of course sell the goods to a third party buyer and also claim the price from the buyer as this would amount to double recovery (*R. V. Ward* v *Bignall* [1967] 1 QB 534).

The distinction between an action for the price and damages for non-delivery depends (subject to s. 49(2) of the 1979 Act) upon whether the property has passed to the buyer or not. It does not depend upon whether the goods have been delivered or not. As was seen in chapter 11 the property in the goods frequently passes before delivery of them. The position is governed by ss. 49 and 50 of the 1979 Act, which provide as follows:

> 49.—(1) Where, under a contract of sale, the property in the goods has passed to the buyer and he wrongfully neglects or refuses to pay for the goods according to the terms of the contract, the seller may maintain an action against him for the price of the goods.
>
> (2) Where, under a contract of sale, the price is payable on a day certain irrespective of delivery and the buyer wrongfully neglects or refuses to pay such price, the seller may maintain an action for the price, although the property in goods has not passed and the goods have not been appropriated to the contract.
>
> 50.—(1) Where the buyer wrongfully neglects or refuses to accept and pay for the goods, the seller may maintain an action against him for damages for non-acceptance.
>
> (2) The measure of damages is the estimated loss directly and naturally resulting in the ordinary course of events, from the buyer's breach of contract.
>
> (3) Where there is an available market for the goods in question the measure of damages is prima facie to be ascertained by the difference between the contract price and the market or current price at the time or times when the goods ought to have been accepted or (if no time was fixed for acceptance) at the time of the refusal to accept.

The vital question is therefore whether the property in the goods has passed. If so, the seller may maintain an action for the price. However, this does not mean he has to. If the property has passed before delivery, and the buyer refuses to accept the goods before delivery, the seller may treat the contract as repudiated, sell the goods on the open market and claim the difference in value. The seller has an option in this situation as to whether he brings a claim under s. 49(1) or under s. 50. There is nothing in principle preventing the seller from reselling the goods where the goods have been delivered to the buyer and are lying at the buyer's premises. However, the seller is naturally going to have greater difficulty selling goods which are not in his possession. Furthermore, the seller in this situation is trading a certain remedy of the price for a less certain one for damages. Whilst this may be the case from a strict legal analysis, in practice the seller may need to sell the goods for cash-flow reasons and cannot wait for the outcome of a legal action.

Where the seller does take this route, he would be well advised to obtain evidence of the state or condition of the goods to defend any suggestion later raised by the buyer that he legitimately rejected them. If the seller has sold them on, he may not be able to refute the suggestion as he will no longer have access to the goods. Furthermore, the seller will need to ensure that the buyer will cooperate with the sale otherwise the seller will find himself liable for non-delivery on the second sale.

Five situations are therefore created which need to be explored. The seller's claim for damages in situations (c) and (d) below will be considered together as the principles are the same.

(a) The property in the goods has passed to the buyer. The seller sues for the price under s. 49(1).

(b) The property in the goods has not passed but the price is payable on a day certain and the seller nevertheless sues for the price under s. 49(2).

(c) The property in the goods has passed but the goods have not yet been delivered when the buyer intimates that he will not accept them. The seller opts to treat the contract as repudiated and sell the goods on the open market and claim damages for non-delivery under s. 50.

(d) The property in the goods has not passed at the time the buyer intimates that he refuses to accept the goods. The seller is forced to sell them on the open market and make a claim for damages for non-acceptance under s. 50.

(e) Whether the property has passed or not the seller incurs further expenses in storing or reselling the goods and wishes to claim these. This may be done under either s. 37 of the 1979 Act or under the general law preserved by s. 54.

23.2 ACTION FOR THE PRICE UNDER SECTION 49(1)

Where the property in the goods has passed to the buyer, the seller may bring an action for the price. This much has been explored in the previous section. Where the goods have not been delivered to the buyer, if the seller is to maintain an action for the price, he is obliged to store the goods. If he resells them, he will have rescinded the contract and his action will be reduced to one for non-acceptance (*R. V. Ward* v *Bignall* [1967] 1 QB 534). He is, however, entitled to claim his expenses of storing the goods and this is discussed in section 23.4 below.

Where the contract is for the sale of goods to be delivered by instalments, whether or not the seller is entitled to sue for the price will probably be answered by the time the property is to pass. Thus where the seller agrees to sell 1,000 tonnes of coal in separate deliveries of 100 tonnes, the property in the coal will pass to the buyer at the time it is appropriated to the contract and the seller will be entitled to sue for the respective price of each instalment as this occurs. His remedy in respect of instalments yet to be appropriated to the contract will lie in damages for non-acceptance. Where the contract is for the sale of the whole of a bulk of (for example) coal to be delivered in instalments, this would be a contract for the sale of specific goods and the entire property would pass at the time the contract is made. The seller could therefore sue for the entire contract price.

Some difficulties are created by the analysis put forward in the previous paragraph by the case of *Hyundai Heavy Industries Co. Ltd* v *Papadopoulos* [1980] 1 WLR 1129.[1] However, it is submitted that in practice a court would undoubtedly reach the conclusions put forward here.

1. For a full analysis of these problems see Atiyah, *The Sale of Goods*, 9th ed., (Pitman Publishing, 1995), pp. 433 and 434 *et seq.*

23.3 PRICE PAYABLE ON A 'DAY CERTAIN'

Where the price has been specified as being payable upon a 'day certain', the seller may claim the price of the goods under s. 49(2) of the 1979 Act notwithstanding that the property has not passed to the buyer. This will generally only be the case where the goods have not been delivered, as the circumstances where the buyer will be in possession of the goods yet not hold the property in them will be rare.

Certainly a specified date such as '14 July' will be a day certain. However, difficulty is caused where the date of payment is merely ascertainable by reference to the actions of the parties. Two cases on the meaning of a 'day certain' are seemingly irreconcilable. The first is that of *Henderson and Keay Ltd* v *A. M. Carmichael Ltd* 1956 SLT 58. In that case payment was required upon presentation of the seller's invoice. This was held not to be a day certain. By contrast in *Workman Clark & Co. Ltd* v *Lloyd Brazileno* [1908] 1 KB 968 payment was to be made upon completion of certain stages being reached in the construction of a ship. These payments were held to be payable on a 'day certain' notwithstanding that the date would fluctuate depending upon the speed with which the seller completed his task. In both of these cases the date fluctuated according to the unilateral action of the seller and it is difficult to see how this can be a 'day certain'.

However, of the two cases *Henderson and Keay* would appear to be more authoritative, but it must be realised that in that case the seller would have received nothing had he not succeeded in his action for the price as he had no claim for damages. Policy considerations may have applied in the mind of the court and a different case may obtain a different result.

23.4 DAMAGES FOR NON-ACCEPTANCE

A buyer may refuse to accept goods either at the time they are delivered or he may intimate before delivery that he will not accept tender of them. Where the buyer takes the latter course, the seller may accept the buyer's anticipatory breach. A buyer need not expressly intimate that he will refuse to accept, but it is sufficient that he acts in such a way as would lead a reasonable man to conclude that he will refuse to accept the goods. The time at which this is to be assessed is the time at which the seller accepts the breach (*The Hermosa* [1982] 1 Lloyd's Rep 570).

Where the buyer refuses to accept the goods, the provisions of the 1979 Act mirror those of the buyer's remedy for non-delivery, i.e., the measure of damages is the difference between the contract and the market price where there is an available market and the seller comes under a duty to mitigate his loss. These principles were set out in section 20.2 and are not repeated at length here.

Prima facie the market price is to be assessed at the date of the delivery. If the goods are sold in a rapid market at the time of delivery, this will provide strong evidence of what the market price actually was (*Shearson Lehman Hutton Inc.* v *Maclaine Watson & Co. Ltd (No. 2)* [1990] 1 Lloyd's Rep 441).

Whilst this is the general rule, the duty to mitigate can almost override the delivery date rule and where the market for the type of goods in question is a ready and fast one the seller may be well advised simply to sell the next day (*Kaines (UK) Ltd* v *Osterreichische Warrenhandelgesellschaft* [1993] 2 Lloyd's Rep 1). To do otherwise may be construed as playing the markets on his own account for his own profit. Where the seller does take this course of action, if there is a discrepancy in the price he may claim for it.

The reverse of this situation is that if the seller does play the markets for his own account he is entitled to profit from it, and the buyer cannot offset this against his loss. In *Campbell Mostyn (Provisions)* v *Barnett Trading Co.* [1954] 1 Lloyd's Rep 65 the sellers had agreed to sell 500 tonnes of tinned ham. At the date of the buyer's non-acceptance the market price was below the contract price, yet the sellers later sold at a higher price. They were held entitled to the difference of the price at the date of delivery and the contract price notwithstanding the profit.

Had the market price in the *Campbell Mostyn* case in fact fallen the seller would be unable to claim the additional loss between the market price and the lower price he later chose to sell at as this would form a failure to mitigate (*Kaines (UK) Ltd* v *Osterreichische Warrenhandelgesellschaft*). Where, however, the market is not so rapid, simply disposing of the stock on the day may amount to a failure to mitigate in itself (*Blythswood Motors* v *Raeside* 1966 SLT (Sh. Ct.) 13).

The market price rule is only a *prima facie* rule and can be displaced. Where the seller sells the contract goods to another buyer this does not necessarily mean that he cannot claim his loss of profits. If he can show that he would have been able to fulfil both orders, his resale of the goods at a comparable price may not be construed as a mitigation of his loss and he may go on to claim his lost profits on the contract (*Re Vic Mill* [1913] 1 Ch 465). The seller will, however, need to lead evidence of his ability to perform both contracts, but this can be rebutted by the buyer leading evidence to the contrary (*Hill & Sons* v *Edwin Showell & Sons* (1918) 87 LJKB 1106).

23.5 ADDITIONAL EXPENSES

The seller's right to claim a charge for storage is maintained by s. 37 of the 1979 Act, which provides as follows:

> (1) When the seller is ready and willing to deliver the goods, and requests the buyer to take delivery, and the buyer does not within a reasonable time after such request take delivery of the goods, he is liable to the seller for any loss occasioned by his neglect or refusal to take delivery, and also for a reasonable charge for the care and custody of the goods.
>
> (2) Nothing in this section affects the rights of the seller where the neglect or refusal of the buyer to take delivery amounts to a repudiation of the contract.

Section 37 creates a right to claim for loss where the buyer not only refuses to take delivery but also where he delays in doing so. The last sentence of s. 37(1) relates to the seller acting as bailee of the goods where the property has passed to the buyer. However, it extends the common law and also covers the situation where the property has not passed to the buyer, but the property in the goods is held by the seller. In any event, such a right would presumably cease upon the seller accepting the buyer's repudiation as at this stage the property revests in the seller (if it has passed) and he handles the goods on his own account. There no longer exists a duty to store the goods.

There is some overlap between ss. 37 and 54, which preserves the seller's right to claim special damages for non-delivery. Accordingly, the cost of storing the goods, reselling them or converting them for sale on the open market are probably recoverable under either section.

Appendix A
Model statements of case

A. SALE OF GOODS — ACTION INITIATED BY THE SELLER

1. Claim for the price of goods sold.
2. Claim for the price of goods sold — contract of sale or return.
3. Claim for damages for non-acceptance.

Defences to seller's claim

1. Defence to (1) above — denial of contract.
2. Defence to (1) above — misrepresentation.
3. Defence to (2) above — goods damages without fault on either party — goods at seller's risk.
4. Defence to (3) above — breach of implied term as to fitness for purpose.

Seller's reply

1. Reply to (2) above — representation did not influence sale.
2. Reply to (4) above — buyer did not make unusual purpose known to seller.

B. SALE OF GOODS — ACTION INITIATED BY THE BUYER

1. Claim for the price — failure to correspond with implied term as to fitness and quality.
2. Claim for the price — defective title.
3. Claim for specific performance — failure to deliver goods.
4. Claim for damages for non-delivery of goods.
5. Claim for damages for breach of implied term as to quality and fitness.

Defences to buyer's claim

1. Defence to (1) above — buyer having accepted goods — denial of entitlement to price.
2. Defence to (5) above — incorporation of exclusion clause — denial of liability for breach of the implied terms as to fitness and quality.
3. Defence to (5) above — inspection of the goods.

Reply to seller's defence

1. Reply to (2) above — exclusion clause ineffective under UCTA — buyer not a consumer but clause unreasonable.

C. CONTRACTS FOR SERVICES

Claims by provider of service

1. Claim by builder for the price under a contract of work and materials.
2. Claim for price of repairs to car.
3. Claim for storage charges by warehouseman.

Defence by customer under contract for services

1. Defence to (1) above — lack of reasonable skill and care.
2. Defence and counterclaim to (2) above — lack of reasonable skill and care and damages for personal injury.
3. Defence to (3) above — negligent damage to goods.

D. CONSUMER CREDIT ACT CASES — CLAIMS BY THE DEBTOR

1. Breach of implied terms as to quality and fitness and misrepresentation — claim against seller and creditor under a debtor-creditor-supplier agreement.
2. Credit hire — defence to action for hire charges.

E. CLAIMS AGAINST THIRD PARTIES — WRONGFUL INTERFERENCE WITH GOODS

Claim by the owner of goods

1. Claim by the owner of goods — refusal to deliver up.
2. Claim by the owner of goods — conversion by repairer and claim for delivery up against third party.

Defences — third party

1. Defence to (2) above — acquisition of good title by virtue of an exception to the *nemo dat* rule — mercantile agent.

F. CLAIMS AGAINST THE MANUFACTURER OR SUPPLIER OF GOODS

Claims by the injured party

1. Claim under the Consumer Protection Act for supply of a defective product.
2. Claim under the Consumer Protection Act for the manufacture of a defective product.
3. Claim under the Consumer Protection Act against a person holding themselves out as the manufacturer of a defective product.

Defences

1. Defence to (2) above — counterfeit product.
2. Defence to (3) above — denial that defendant was held out as a producer.

A. SALE OF GOODS — ACTION INITIATED BY THE SELLER

1. Claim for the price of the goods sold

IN THE CENTRAL LONDON COUNTY COURT Claim number

BETWEEN:

TAKE 'EM OR ELSE COMPUTERS LIMITED Claimant

and

RENE WONG Defendant

PARTICULARS OF CLAIM

(1) The Claimant is a computer equipment dealer and the Defendant is a customer of the Claimant.
(2) On the 23rd May 2000 by its servant or agent, Robert Ruegg, the Claimant orally agreed to sell a Turbo Office Computer system and the Defendant orally agreed to pay the Claimant £3,000.
(3) Pursuant to the agreement on the 24th May 2000 the Claimant delivered to the Defendant's house the computer system and furnished the Defendant with an invoice in the sum of £3,000.
(4) In breach of the agreement the Defendant has wrongfully failed or refused to pay the sum of £3,000 or any part thereof.
(5) In the premises the Claimant claims that the sum of £3,000 is still due and payable to the Claimant and demands payment of it.
(6) Further, the Claimant claims interest pursuant to Section 69 of the County Courts Act 1984 at the rate of 8% upon the sum of £3,000 amounting to £xyz to date and continuing at the rate of £abc per day.
(7) Alternatively, the Claimant claims interest at such rate and upon such amounts as the Court deems fit.

AND the Claimant claims:

(1) The sum of £3,000;
(2) Alternatively damages;
(3) The interest set out above pursuant to Section 69 of the County Court Act 1984.

Richard Miles.
The Chambers of Lord Campbell
Of Alloway QC.
2, King's Bench Walk,
Temple,
London.
EC4Y 7DE
DX 477 Chancery Lane
020 7353 9276

The Claimant/Defendant believes that the facts stated above are true.
(Delete as applicable)

Signed:.. Dated:...........................

(The Claimant/Defendant/For and on behalf of the Claimant/Defendant being duly authorised to sign this statement of truth on behalf of the Claimant/Defendant (delete as appropriate))

Name of Person Signing[1] ....

Capacity in which Signed ....

XYZ Solicitors
12, High Street,
Tunbridge Wells,

Solicitors for the Claimant

2. Claim for the price of goods sold — contract of sale or return

IN THE CENTRAL LONDON COUNTY COURT Claim number

BETWEEN:

BULK FLOOR PLAN LIMITED Claimant

and

GREENWICH ELECTRICAL SALES Defendant

PARTICULARS OF CLAIM

(1) At all material times the Claimant was an electrical goods wholesaler and the Defendant was an electrical goods retailer. The Defendant was a customer of the Claimant.
(2) By a written agreement dated the 1st January 2000 the Claimant agreed to deliver to the Defendant such electrical goods from the Claimant's product catalogue as he may require from time to time upon sale or return and the Defendant agreed to pay for the goods at the rate prescribed in the Claimant's price list as prevailing at the time of the order.
(3) It was an express term of the agreement that in the absence of the Defendant intimating that he did not accept the goods that the Defendant would pay for such goods as were delivered within a reasonable time, or if he sooner sold them at the time of sale.
(4) Pursuant to the agreement on the 10th January 2000 the Claimant delivered to the Defendant 50 toasters then priced at £10 each.
(5) On the 10th March 2000 the Defendant's premises were burgled and the toasters were stolen.
(6) In the premises and pursuant to Section 18, rule 4 of the Sale of Goods Act 1979 the property in the toasters passed to the Defendant after a reasonable time from their delivery.
(7) In the electrical goods industry it is a trade custom that a reasonable time for the buyer to accept, sell or reject goods is one month.
(8) In the premises the property in the goods had passed to the Defendant at the time they were stolen. The risk of any accidental loss or damage to the goods was upon the Defendant.
(9) Further, in the premises the price of the goods, being £500, had become due and payable by the Defendant and the Claimant claims this.
(10) Further, the Claimant claims interest pursuant to Section 69 of the County Courts Act 1984 at the rate of 8% upon the sum of £500 amounting to £xyz to date and continuing at the rate of £abc per day.
(11) Alternatively, the Claimant claims interest at such rate and upon such amounts as the Court deems fit.

1. If not the Claimant or Defendant.

AND the Claimant claims:

(1) The sum of £500;
(2) Alternatively damages;
(3) The interest set out above pursuant to Section 69 of the County Court Act 1984.

[Signed by counsel/draftsmen; statement of truth as with statement of case 1]

3. Claim for damages for non-acceptance

IN THE CENTRAL LONDON COUNTY COURT Claim number

BETWEEN:

BIG CHEMICAL COMPANY LIMITED Claimant

and

LITTLE BOAT MANUFACTURER LIMITED Defendant

PARTICULARS OF CLAIM

(1) The Claimant is a manufacturer and supplier of industrial chemicals and liquids. The Defendant was a customer of the Claimant.
(2) By an oral agreement made on the 1st January 2000, as evidenced by the Defendant's purchase order and the Claimant's invoice attached and annexed hereto, the Claimant agreed to manufacture and deliver 10 tonnes of fibreglass resin ('the goods')
(3) The following were *inter alia* express terms of the agreement:
(a) The price of the goods was £10,000.
(b) The goods would be delivered on the 1st February 2000 at the Defendant's premises.
(4) Pursuant to the agreement the Claimant attempted to deliver the goods to the Defendant's premises on the 1st February.
(5) Wrongfully and in breach of the agreement the Defendant, by its servant or agent one Lee Freeman, refused to accept the goods.
(6) In the premises the Defendant repudiated the agreement and the Claimant, by its servant or agent one George Papageorgis, orally accepted the repudiation on the 1st February 2000 at the Defendant's premises.
(7) Given the perishable nature of fibreglass resin the Claimant was forced to dispose of the goods as rapidly as possible. It did this by placing an advertisement in 'Resin Monthly', a trade circular, and disposed of the resin to a company known as Household Goods Manufacturer Limited on the 10th February 2000. As evidenced by the Claimant's invoice attached and annexed hereto the price paid by Household Goods Manufacturer Limited was £5,000.
(8) By reason of the Defendant's breach of contract the Claimant has suffered loss and damage.

PARTICULARS

Contract price of the goods	£10,000
Price obtained on forced sale	£5,000
Damages claimed	£5,000

(9) Further, the Claimant claims interest pursuant to Section 69 of the County Courts Act 1984 at the rate of 8% upon:—

- The sum of £10,000 from the 1st February 2000 to the 9th February 2000 amounting to £xyz;
- The sum of £5,000 from the 10th February 2000 to date of judgment or sooner amounting to £abc to date and continuing at the rate of £def per day.

(10) Alternatively, the Claimant claims interest at such rate and upon such amounts as the Court deems fit.

AND the Claimant claims:

(1) The sum of £500;
(2) Alternatively damages;
(3) The interest set out above pursuant to Section 69 of the County Courts Act 1984.

[Signed by counsel/draftsmen; statement of truth as with statement of case 1]

Defences to seller's claim

1. Defence to (1) above — denial of contract

IN THE CENTRAL LONDON COUNTY COURT   Claim number

BETWEEN:

TAKE 'EM OR ELSE COMPUTERS LIMITED   Claimant

and

RENE WONG   Defendant

DEFENCE

1. Paragraph 1 of the Particulars of Claim are denied. At no stage was the Defendant a customer of the Claimant.
2. Paragraph 2 of the Particulars of Claim is denied. It is admitted that on the 23rd May 2000 the Claimant's servant or agent, Robert Ruegg, attended the Defendant's premises for the purpose of giving a demonstration of a Turbo Office Computer system. However the Defendant at no stage agreed to buy it. Robert Ruegg refused to leave the Defendant's premises for over two hours stating that unless he got a sale that week that he would be fired. The Defendant told Robert Ruegg that he could call the next day simply so as he would leave.
3. It is admitted that on the 24th May 2000 the Claimant delivered a Turbo Office Computer system and furnished the Defendant with an invoice. It is denied that this was pursuant to any contract as alleged in the Particulars of Claim or at all. Paragraph 3 of the Particulars of Claim is accordingly denied.
4. On the 24th May 2000 the Defendant telephoned the Claimant's offices and spoke with a servant or agent of the Claimant, one Janice Johnson, and informed her that he had not ordered the computer system and demanded that it be collected. To date the Claimant has failed or refused to collect the computer system.
5. Otherwise paragraphs 1, 2, 3, 4, 5, 6 and 7 of the Particulars of Claim are denied. In the premises the Claimant is not entitled to any relief as claimed or at all.

[Signed by counsel/draftsmen; statement of truth as with statement of case 1]

2. Defence to (1) above — misrepresentation

IN THE CENTRAL LONDON COUNTY COURT Claim number

BETWEEN:

TAKE 'EM OR ELSE COMPUTERS LIMITED Claimant

and

RENE WONG Defendant

DEFENCE

1. Paragraphs 1, 2 and 3 of the Particulars of Claim are admitted.
2. On the 23rd May 2000 the Claimant's servant or agent, Robert Ruegg, attended the Defendant's premises for the purpose of a demonstration of a Turbo Office Computer system ('the computer system'). During the demonstration Robert Ruegg told the Defendant that the computer system would be capable of running the Defendant's computer software 'Chambers Management' ('the representation').[2]
3. In reliance upon the representation and induced by that the Defendant entered the contract as stated in paragraph 2 of the Particulars of Claim ('the contract').
4. Further, the representation was an express and/or implied term of the contract.
5. Contrary to the representation and/or in breach of the term of the contract stated in paragraph 4 above the computer system is incapable of running the Defendant's computer software 'Chambers Management' as the software is based upon an Apple Macintosh operating system whereas the computer system is based upon an IBM compatible operating system.
6. On the 25th May 2000 the Defendant telephoned the Claimant's offices and spoke with a servant or agent of the Claimant, one Fiona Randell, and informed her that he considered the contract terminated and demanded that the Claimant collect the computer system. To date the Claimant has failed to collect the computer system.
7. It is admitted that the Defendant has refused to pay the sum of £3,000 as stated in paragraph 4 of the Particulars of Claim. It is denied that such refusal is wrongful or in breach of contract.
8. Paragraphs 5, 6 and 7 of the Particulars of Claim are denied. In the premises it is denied that the Claimant is entitled to any relief as claimed or at all.

[Signed by counsel/draftsmen; statement of truth as with statement of case 1]

3. Defence to (2) above — goods damage without fault on either party

IN THE CENTRAL LONDON COUNTY COURT Claim number

BETWEEN:

BULK FLOOR PLAN LIMITED Claimant

and

GREENWICH ELECTRICAL SALES Defendant

DEFENCE

1. Paragraphs 1, 2, 3, 4, 5 and 6 of the Particulars of Claim are admitted.
2. Paragraph 7 of the Particulars of Claim is denied and the Claimant is put to strict proof of it. There is no trade custom within the electrical goods industry accounting for any time for the buyer under a contract of sale or return to accept, reject or sell any goods so delivered.

2. If there are multiple representations set them out in a sub-paragraph numbered a, b, c, etc.

3. It was the practice of the parties that the Claimant would invoice the Defendant for any goods not rejected by the Defendant three months after their delivery.
4. In the premises a reasonable time for the Defendant to accept, sell or reject the goods was three months.
5. Paragraph 8 of the Particulars of Claim is denied. In the premises the property in the goods had not passed to the Defendant at the time the goods were stolen but remained vested in the seller. The risk of any accidental loss or destruction was upon the Claimant at the time of the theft.
6. Paragraphs 9, 10 and 11 are denied.
7. In the premises the Claimant is not entitled to any relief as claimed or at all.

[Signed by counsel/draftsmen; statement of truth as with statement of case 1]

4. Defence to (3) above — breach of implied term as to fitness for purpose

IN THE CENTRAL LONDON COUNTY COURT Claim number

BETWEEN:

BIG CHEMICAL COMPANY LIMITED Claimant

and

LITTLE BOAT MANUFACTURER LIMITED Defendant

DEFENCE

1. Paragraphs 1, 2, 3 and 4 of the Particulars of Claim are admitted.
2. At all material times the Claimant acted in the course of a business.
3. At the time of entering the contract of the 1st January 2000 the Defendant, by its servant or agent Lee Freeman made known to the Claimant, by its servant or agent, George Papageorgis that the Defendant required the fibreglass resin to be suitable for use in the construction of marine craft.
4. In the premises it was an implied term of the agreement that the resin would be fit for the purpose of constructing marine craft.
5. In breach of the term stated in paragraph 4 above the resin was not fit for use in constructing marine vessels.

PARTICULARS

As appears in the report of Mr Jolly Clever attached and annexed hereto the resin was of a kind not suitable for use in the construction of marine vessels.

(a) The resin was of inadequate consistency being of only 80% specific gravity, whereas 90% specific gravity or more is needed in marine construction.

(b) etc.
(c) etc.
(d) etc.

6. It is admitted that the Defendant by its servant or agent Lee Freeman refused to accept the goods, but it is denied that such refusal was wrongful or in breach of contract as alleged in paragraph 5 of the Particulars of Claim or at all.
7. Paragraphs 6 and 7 of the Particulars of Claim are admitted.
8. Paragraphs 8, 9 and 10 of the Particulars of Claim are denied.
9. In the premises it is denied that the Claimant is entitled to any relief whereas claimed or at all.

[Signed by counsel/draftsmen; statement of truth as with statement of case 1]

Seller's reply

1. Reply to (2) above — representation did not influence sale

IN THE CENTRAL LONDON COUNTY COURT Claim number

BETWEEN:

TAKE 'EM OR ELSE COMPUTERS LIMITED Claimant

and

RENE WONG Defendant

REPLY

1. Paragraphs 2 and 3 of the Defence are admitted.
2. Paragraphs 4, 5, 6, 7 and 8 of the Defence are denied.
3. It is denied that the Defendant at any stage relied upon the representation made by the Claimant's servant or agent Robert Ruegg. During the course of the demonstration Robert Ruegg demonstrated 18 different computer programs including 4 business management programs. It was only as the Defendant was leaving the Claimant's premises that he asked whether the system would be capable of running the program 'Chambers Management' adding simply that this 'might also be useful'. During the course of the demonstration the Defendant had stated that he predominantly wanted the computer for playing games and 'surfing the internet'.

[Signed by counsel/draftsmen; statement of truth as with statement of case 1]

2. Reply to (4) above — buyer did not make unusual purpose known to seller

IN THE CENTRAL LONDON COUNTY COURT Claim number

BETWEEN:

BIG CHEMICAL COMPANY LIMITED Claimant

and

LITTLE BOAT MANUFACTURER LIMITED Defendant

REPLY

1. Paragraph 2 of the Defence is admitted.
2. Paragraph 3 of the Defence is denied. At no time did the Defendant's servant or agent Lee Freeman make known that the Defendant required the fibreglass resin for the purpose of the construction of marine craft and the Defendant is put to strict proof of the same. When placing the order Lee Freeman stated only that the resin was required as soon as possible.
3. Paragraph 4 of the Defence is denied.
4. Paragraph 5 of the Defence is denied. If, which is denied, it was a term of the agreement that the resin would be fit for the purpose of constructing marine craft then it is averred that the resin supplied was in any event fit for such purpose.

[Signed by counsel/draftsmen; statement of truth as with statement of case 1]

B. SALE OF GOODS — ACTION INITIATED BY THE BUYER

1. Claim for the price — failure to correspond with implied term as to fitness and quality

IN THE CENTRAL LONDON COUNTY COURT Claim number

BETWEEN:

JAMES CARTWRIGHT Claimant

and

MICHAEL HALL Defendant

PARTICULARS OF CLAIM

1. The Defendant is and at all material times acted in the course of a business as the retailer of cars. The Claimant was a customer of the Defendant.
2. On the 10th February 2000 the Claimant attended the Defendant's premises and viewed a Ford Fiesta 1.0 LX motor vehicle ('the vehicle'). The vehicle was brand new.
3. The Claimant agreed to purchase the vehicle and paid the sum of £12,000 in cash to the Defendant.
4. In the premises it was an implied term of the agreement that the vehicle would be of satisfactory quality.
5. In breach of the agreement the car was not of satisfactory quality.

PARTICULARS

As appears in the report of Andy Fryman of the Automobile Association dated the 12th June 2000 the vehicle suffered from the following defects:

(a) the windscreen leaked water into the interior of the vehicle during periods of rain;
(b) paint flaked off the car's bodywork;
(c) etc;
(d) etc.

7. On the 12th June 2000 the Claimant telephoned the Defendant and told him that he refused to accept the car and that he was holding it for the Defendant to collect.
8. The Defendant has wrongfully and in breach of the agreement refused to take back the goods and to return the contract price of £12,000 or any part of it.
9. Further, the Claimant claims interest pursuant to Section 69 of the County Courts Act 1984 at the rate of 8% upon the sum of £12,000 amounting to £xyz to date and continuing at the rate of £abc per day.
10. Alternatively, the Claimant claims interest at such rate and upon such amounts as the Court deems fit.

AND the Claimant claims:

(a) The sum of £12,000;
(b) Alternatively, damages;
(c) The interest set out above pursuant to Section 69 of the County Courts Act 1984.

[Signed by counsel/draftsmen; statement of truth as with statement of case 1]

2. Claim for the price — defective title

IN THE CENTRAL LONDON COUNTY COURT Claim number

BETWEEN:

BRIAN KENNEDY Claimant

and

MICHAEL CLARKE Defendant

PARTICULARS OF CLAIM

1. On the 12th March 1999 the Defendant sold to the Claimant a Ford Mondeo motor vehicle registration number M440 EESN for a price of £15,000. The Claimant paid the Defendant in cash.
2. It was an implied term of the agreement that the Defendant had the right to sell the vehicle.
3. In breach of the agreement the Defendant had no such right as the vehicle was owned by Screw 'Em then Sue 'Em Finance Limited who had let the car to the Defendant under a Hire Purchase agreement.
4. On the 10th February 2000 the Claimant was obliged to and did allow Screw 'Em then Sue 'Em Finance Limited to re-take possession of the vehicle.
5. In the premises the consideration for the Claimant's payment of £15,000 has wholly failed and the Claimant demands the return of the same.
6. Further, the Claimant claims interest pursuant to Section 69 of the County Courts Act 1984 at the rate of 8% upon the sum of £15,000 amounting to £xyz to date and continuing at the rate of £abc per day.
7. Alternatively, the Claimant claims interest at such rate and upon such amounts as the Court deems fit.

AND the Claimant claims:

(a) The sum of £15,000;
(b) Alternatively, damages;[3]
(c) The interest set out above pursuant to Section 69 of the County Courts Act 1984.

[Signed by counsel/draftsmen; statement of truth as with statement of case 1]

3. Claim for specific performance — failure to deliver goods

IN THE CENTRAL LONDON COUNTY COURT Claim number

BETWEEN:

BRIAN NEWTON Claimant

and

MATTHEW WADHAMS Defendant

PARTICULARS OF CLAIM

1. The Defendant is a dealer in fine art and the Claimant is a customer of the Defendant.

---

3. In accordance with *Rowland* v *Divall* [1923] 2 KB 500 a failure to pass the property in goods will amount to more than a breach of contract but also a failure of consideration. However, it is proper to plead a contractual claim for damages in addition to a restitutionary claim for money had and received, as the buyer may also have a claim for damages.

2. On the 10th May 2000 the Defendant agreed to sell an original painting by an artist known as Jack Vettriano entitled 'Mad Dogs' for a price of £80,000. The Claimant agreed to buy the painting.
3. Pursuant to the agreement the Claimant paid to the Defendant the sum of £40,000 with the remainder becoming payable upon delivery.
4. The Defendant has wrongfully and in breach of contract refused to deliver the painting and continues to so refuse to date.
5. In the premises the Claimant is entitled to and seeks an order that the Defendant performs the agreement and delivers up to the Claimant the painting.
6. Alternatively, by reason of the Defendant's failure to deliver the good and perform the contract the Claimant has suffered loss and damage.

PARTICULARS

Contract Price of the Painting	£80,000
Price achievable upon auction sale in accordance with the report of Melissa Young attached and annexed hereto	£120,000

7. Further, the Claimant claims interest pursuant to Section 69 of the County Courts Act 1984 at the rate of 8% upon such amounts as the Court deems fit.

AND the Claimant claims:

(a) Specific performance of the agreement and delivery up of the painting;
(b) Alternatively, damages;
(c) The interest set out above pursuant to Section 69 of the County Courts Act 1984.

[Signed by counsel/draftsmen; statement of truth as with statement of case 1]

4. Claim for damages for non-delivery of goods

IN THE CENTRAL LONDON COUNTY COURT Claim number

BETWEEN:

PHILIPPA DANIELS Claimant

and

ABIGAIL DEAN Defendant

PARTICULARS OF CLAIM

1. The Claimant is a manufacturer of soups and other foodstuffs and the Defendant is a wholesaler of vegetables.
2. By a written contract made on the 12th April 2000 the Claimant agreed to buy 10 tonnes of peas at a price of £2,000 per tonne.
3. It was a term of the agreement that the peas would be delivered at the Claimant's premises on the 22nd April 2000.
4. On the 21st April 2000 at the Defendant's request the Claimant agreed to extend the time for delivery until the 25th April 2000.
5. On the 25th April 2000 the Defendant informed the Claimant that she would be unable to make delivery in accordance with the contract and the Claimant informed the Defendant that she considered the contract thereby terminated.

6. On the 25th April 2000 the Claimant attended the Spitalfields fruit and vegetable market and purchased 10,000 tonnes of peas at a price of £2,500 per tonne.
7. By reason of the Defendant's breach of contract the Claimant has suffered loss and damage.

PARTICULARS

Contract price of the goods	£20,000
Market price as at the 25th April 2000	£25,000
Loss	£5,000

8. Further, the Claimant claims interest pursuant to Section 69 of the County Courts Act 1984 at the rate of 8% upon the sum of £5,000 from the 25th April 2000 amounting to £xyz to date and continuing at the rate of £abc per day.
9. Alternatively, the Claimant claims interest at such rate and upon such amounts as the Court deems fit.

AND the Claimant claims:

(a) Damages;
(b) The interest set out above pursuant to Section 69 of the County Courts Act.

[Signed by counsel/draftsmen; statement of truth as with statement of case 1]

5. Claim for damages for breach of implied term as to quality and fitness

IN THE CENTRAL LONDON COUNTY COURT Claim number

BETWEEN:

CHARLES NEWMAN Claimant

and

BLACK CAB COMPANY LIMITED Defendant

PARTICULARS OF CLAIM

1. The Defendant is and at all material times was acting in the course of a business as a retailer of motor cars, more particularly hackney carriages. The Claimant was a customer of the Defendant.
2. By a written agreement dated the 20th January 2000 ('the agreement') the Defendant agreed to sell a 'Turbo-Cab' hackney carriage ('the taxi') to the Claimant for a price of £27,000. The Claimant agreed to buy the taxi and to pay the sum of £27,000.
3. It was an implied condition of the agreement that the taxi would be fit for its purpose as a hackney carriage.
4. Further or alternatively it was an implied condition of the agreement that the taxi would be of satisfactory quality.
5. Pursuant to the agreement the Claimant paid to the Defendant the sum of £27,000 on the 28th January 2000.
6. Pursuant to the agreement on the 12th March 1999 the Defendant delivered to the Claimant the taxi.
7. In breach of the agreement the taxi was not of satisfactory quality.

PARTICULARS

(a) The paintwork is chipped and faulty;
(b) the driver's door is stiff and difficult to open;

(c) the rear passenger seat is torn;
(d) the rear wheel arch is rusty on the underside;
(e) etc;
(f) etc.

8. By reason of the breaches the Claimant became entitled to and did reject the vehicle by facsimile on the 5th April 1999.
9. The Defendant has wrongfully refused to re-take the taxi or to return any amount of the purchase price.
10. At the time the contract was made it was within the contemplation of the parties that the Claimant would use the taxi for the purpose of carrying passengers for reward. Further, that in the event that the taxi was unusable that the Claimant would suffer a loss of earnings and/or profits.
11. Further and alternatively, by reason of the breaches the Claimant has suffered loss and damage.

PARTICULARS

Expected weekly profits from the use of the use of the taxi	£200
Loss of profits from 5th April 2000 to date	£3,000

12. Further, the Claimant claims interest pursuant to Section 69 of the County Courts Act 1984 at 8% or such rate as the court thinks fit upon:

- The sum of £27,000 from the 5th April or for such period as the Court deems fit, amounting to £xyz to date accruing at the rate of £abc per day.
- On such sums as are found to be due to the Claimant by way of unliquidated damages for such period as the court thinks fit.

AND the Claimant claims:

(1) Return of the purchase price of £27,000;
(2) Further or alternatively damages;
(3) The interest set out above pursuant to Section 69 of the County Courts Act 1984.

[Signed by counsel/draftsmen; statement of truth as with statement of case 1]

Defences to buyer's claim

1. Defence to (1) above — buyer having accepted goods — denial of entitlement to price

IN THE CENTRAL LONDON COUNTY COURT Claim number

BETWEEN:

JAMES CARTWRIGHT Claimant

and

MICHAEL HALL Defendant

DEFENCE

1. Paragraphs 1 to 7 of the Particulars of Claim are admitted.
2. On the 11th June the Claimant attended the Defendant's premises and the Defendant examined the vehicle. The Defendant agreed that the vehicle suffered from a series of minor defects and agreed to rectify them. A schedule of the defects was prepared and is annexed

hereto in the Defendant's standard repair estimate form. An estimate in respect of the repairs was prepared and totals £1,500.
3. Pursuant to Sections 35 and 11(4) of the Sale of Goods Act 1979 the Claimant was deemed to have accepted the goods after a reasonable time had elapsed and the Claimant had failed to notify the Defendant of his intention to reject the goods. Further, that upon such lapse of time that any claim the buyer has would be in damages only.
4. In the premises a reasonable time to have notified the Defendant of any defects in the vehicle would have been one month from delivery of the vehicle.
5. In the premises the Claimant is and was not entitled to purport to reject the vehicle and any remedy he may have is one for damages and not the price of the goods.
6. The Defendant admits the extent of the claim in the sum of £1,500 in accordance with the Defendant's repair estimate attached and annexed hereto.
7. It is admitted that the Defendant has refused to take back the vehicle or to return the price, but it is denied that this was wrongful as alleged in paragraph 8 of the Particulars of Claim or at all.
8. It is denied that the Claimant is entitled to interest as claimed in paragraph 9 of the Particulars of Claim.

[Signed by counsel/draftsmen; statement of truth as with statement of case 1]

2. Defence to (5) above — incorporation of exclusion clause — denial of liability for breach of the implied terms as to fitness and quality

IN THE CENTRAL LONDON COUNTY COURT   Claim number

BETWEEN:

CHARLES NEWMAN   Claimant

and

BLACK CAB COMPANY LIMITED   Defendant

DEFENCE

1. Paragraphs 1 to 6 of the Particulars of Claim are admitted.
2. Clause 12 of the written agreement dated the 20th January 2000 provided that:

> 'The Seller shall not be responsible or in any way liable for breach of any implied term or duty at law requiring that the goods mentioned overleaf shall be of satisfactory or merchantable quality or otherwise fit for their purpose or intended use. Further, the Seller shall not be liable for any loss or cost incurred by the Buyer in connection with the goods whether incurred directly or consequently upon their use or otherwise'.

3. The term mentioned in paragraph 2 above is in all the premises reasonable.
4. It is admitted that the taxi was not fit for its purpose or of satisfactory quality as alleged in paragraphs 7 and 8 of the Particulars of Claim. By virtue of the clause stated in paragraph 2 above it is denied that this was in breach of the agreement.
5. Paragraph 9 of the Particulars of Claim is denied. It is admitted that the Claimant purported to reject the taxi but it is denied that he was entitled to do so.
6. Paragraph 10 of the Particulars of Claim is denied. It is admitted that the Defendant has refused to take back the taxi but it is denied that in the premises this was wrongful.
7. Paragraph 11 of the Particulars of Claim is admitted.
8. Paragraph 12 is denied. Any loss which the Claimant may have suffered is not the result of any breach of contract on the part of the Defendant.

[Signed by counsel/draftsmen; statement of truth as with statement of case 1]

3. Defence to (5) above — inspection of the goods

IN THE CENTRAL LONDON COUNTY COURT Claim number

BETWEEN:

CHARLES NEWMAN Claimant

and

BLACK CAB COMPANY LIMITED Defendant

DEFENCE

1. Paragraphs 1 to 6 of the Particulars of Claim are admitted.
2. Immediately prior to the sale the Claimant examined the vehicle for over an hour. Any and all defects listed were clearly visible and such defects were or should have been revealed by that examination.
3. By reason of the Claimant's examination it is denied that any defects within the vehicle form the subject matter of a breach of the implied term listed at paragraph 7 of the Particulars of Claim.
4. Further any defects with the taxi were of a minor nature and pursuant to Section 15A of the Sale of Goods Act 1979 the Defendant contends that it would be unreasonable for the Claimant to reject the taxi by reason of such breaches.
5. Paragraph 8 of the Particulars of Claim is denied. It is admitted that the Claimant purported to reject the taxi on the 5th April 2000, but it is denied that the Claimant was entitled to reject the taxi.
6. Paragraph 9 of the Particulars of Claim is denied. It is admitted that the Defendant has refused to re-take the taxi, but it is denied that it was wrongful.
7. Paragraph 10 of the Particulars of Claim is admitted.
8. Paragraph 11 of the Particulars of Claim is denied. If, which is denied, any defects did form a breach of the term referred to in paragraph 3 of the Particulars of Claim, it is contended that any defects within the taxi were not such as to render the taxi unusable. Any loss of earnings on the part of the Claimant were accordingly not caused by any breach on the part of the Defendant. Alternatively, the Claimant has failed to mitigate his loss by failing to seek alternative employment.

[Signed by counsel/draftsmen; statement of truth as with statement of case 1]

Reply to seller's defence

1. Reply to (2) above — exclusion clause ineffective under UCTA — buyer not a consumer but clause unreasonable

IN THE CENTRAL LONDON COUNTY COURT Claim number

BETWEEN:

CHARLES NEWMAN Claimant

and

BLACK CAB COMPANY LIMITED Defendant

REPLY

1. It is admitted that the Clause stated in paragraph 2 of the Particulars of Claim was a term of the contract.

2. It is admitted that the Claimant dealt otherwise than as a consumer for the purpose of the Unfair Contract Terms Act 1977.
3. Paragraph 3 of the Defence is denied. The Clause stated at paragraph 2 of the Defence was unreasonable within the meaning of Section 11 of the Unfair Contract Terms Act 1977.

PARTICULARS

(a) The Defendant is one of only two manufacturers of Hackney Carriages for use in London;
(b) the Claimant is at a strong disadvantage in terms of its bargaining position given that it would take over six months to obtain a hackney carriage from an alternative source;
(c) etc.;
(d) etc.;
(e) etc.;
(f) Save in so far as it contains admissions or is expressly contended above the Claimant joins issue with each and every allegation in the Defendant's Defence.

[Signed by counsel/draftsmen; statement of truth as with statement of case 1]

C. CONTRACTS FOR SERVICES

Claims by provider of service

1. Claim by builder for the price under a contract of work and materials

IN THE CENTRAL LONDON COUNTY COURT Claim number

BETWEEN:

ROBIN HALSTEAD Claimant

and

JAMES DAVISON Defendant

PARTICULARS OF CLAIM

1. The Claimant is and was at all material times a builder. The Defendant was a customer of the Claimant.
2. By an oral agreement made on or about the 15th January 2000 the Claimant agreed to supply materials and build a retaining wall across the width of the Defendant's rear garden.
3. It was an express term of the agreement that the Defendant would pay £1,000 on the 15th January and a further £1,500 upon completion of the wall.
4. Pursuant to the agreement the Defendant paid the Claimant £1,000 in cash on the 15th January 2000 and between the 22nd January 2000 and the 3rd February 2000 the Claimant built the wall.
5. In breach of the agreement the Defendant has failed to pay the Claimant the sum of £1,500 despite repeated requests to do so.
6. In the premises the sum of £1,500 is due and owing to the Claimant and the Claimant demands it.
7. Further the Claimant claims interest pursuant to Section 69 of the County Courts Act 1984 upon the sum of £1,500 from the 3rd February 2000 to date of judgment or sooner payment at the rate of 8% amounting to £xyz to date and accruing at the rate of £abc per day.

AND the Claimant claims:

(a) The sum of £1,500;

(b) The interest set out above pursuant to Section 69 of the County Courts Act 1984.

[Signed by counsel/draftsmen; statement of truth as with statement of case 1]

2. Claim for price of repairs to car

IN THE CENTRAL LONDON COUNTY COURT — Claim number

BETWEEN:

NICHOLAS SORRELL — Claimant

and

ANTONY MONTGOMMERY — Defendant

PARTICULARS OF CLAIM

1. The Claimant is and was at all material times a motor mechanic. The Defendant was a customer of the Claimant.
2. By an oral agreement made on or about the 10th February 2000 the Claimant agreed to repair the master brake cylinder to the Defendant's Ford Mondeo motor vehicle.
3. It was an express term of the agreement that the Defendant would pay £1,250 within 28 days from completion of the repairs.
4. Pursuant to the agreement the Claimant repaired the Defendant's motor vehicle on the 15th February 2000.
5. In breach of the agreement the Defendant has failed to pay the Claimant the sum of £1,250 despite repeated requests to do so.
6. In the premises the sum of £1,250 is due and owing to the Claimant and the Claimant demands it.
7. Further the Claimant claims interest pursuant to Section 69 of the County Courts Act 1984 upon the sum of £1,250 from the 3rd February 2000 to date of judgment or sooner payment at the rate of 8% amounting to £xyz to date and accruing at the rate of £abc per day.

AND the Claimant claims:

(a) The sum of £1,250;
(b) The interest set out above pursuant to Section 69 of the County Courts Act 1984.

[Signed by counsel/draftsmen; statement of truth as with statement of case 1]

3. Claim for storage charges by warehouseman

IN THE CENTRAL LONDON COUNTY COURT — Claim number

BETWEEN:

SOPHIE BARRETT-BROWN
(t/a SBB REMOVALS AND STORAGE) — Claimant

and

GAVIN HUGHES — Defendant

PARTICULARS OF CLAIM

1. The Claimant operates a firm specialising in the removal and storage of furniture. The Defendant is a customer of the Claimant.
2. On or about the 12th March 2000 the Claimant agreed to pack and remove the contents of the Claimant's house at 123, Bahamas Drive, Charlton, to store the contents for a period of approximately six months and to restore the contents to the Defendant's new house at Mauritious Road, Greenwich upon completion of works at those premises.
3. The Defendant agreed to pay upon invoice by the Claimant £1,000 in respect of each of the removals and a weekly charge of £400 per calendar month for the storage of the goods.
4. Pursuant to the agreement the Claimant packed and collected the Defendant's property on the 13th March and stored the contents at the Claimant's warehouse until requested to deliver the goods to the Defendant's new premises on the 13th September 2000 whereupon the contents were delivered.
5. On the 14th September 2000 the Claimant furnished the Defendant with an invoice in the sum of £3,400, a copy of which is annexed and attached hereto.
6. Despite repeated requests to do so the Defendant has failed or refused to make payment in respect of the contents.
7. In the premises the sum of £3,400 is now due and owing to the Claimant by the Defendant and the Claimant demands it.
8. Further the Claimant claims interest pursuant to Section 69 of the County Courts Act 1984 upon the sum of £3,400 from the 3rd February 2000 to date of judgment or sooner payment at the rate of 8% amounting to £xyz to date and accruing at the rate of £abc per day.

AND the Claimant claims:

(a) The sum of £3,400;
(b) The interest set out above pursuant to Section 69 of the County Courts Act 1984.

[Signed by counsel/draftsmen; statement of truth as with statement of case 1]

Defence by customer under contract for services

1. Defence to (1) above — lack of reasonable skill and care

IN THE CENTRAL LONDON COUNTY COURT Claim number

BETWEEN:

ROBIN HALSTEAD Claimant

and

JAMES DAVISON Defendant

DEFENCE

1. Paragraphs 1 to 4 of the Particulars of Claim are admitted.
2. It was an implied term of the agreement that the Claimant would use reasonable skill and care in the performance of the contract.
3. In breach of the term stated at paragraph 2 above the Claimant failed to use reasonable skill and care in the performance of the contract or any skill or care at all.

PARTICULARS

(a) The wall has been constructed from too few bricks and is consequently too thin to adequately support the pressure from the garden which it is supposed to retain. Accordingly the wall has large cracks appearing throughout it;

(b) the wall is curved and not straight;
(c) the mortar used in the construction of the wall contained too little cement. Accordingly the mortar has not properly bonded and is being washed away by rain;
(d) etc;
(e) etc;
(f) etc.

4. Paragraphs 5 and 6 of the Particulars of Claim are denied.
5. By reason of the matters stated above it is denied that the Claimant is entitled to the relief claimed or to any relief at all.

[Signed by counsel/draftsmen; statement of truth as with statement of case 1]

2. Defence and counter claim to (2) above — lack of reasonable skill and care and damages for personal injury

IN THE CENTRAL LONDON COUNTY COURT Claim number

BETWEEN:

NICHOLAS SORRELL Claimant

and

ANTONY MONTGOMMERY Defendant

DEFENCE

1. Paragraphs 1 to 4 of the Particulars of Claim are admitted.
2. It was an implied term of the agreement that the Claimant would perform the repairs to the vehicle with reasonable skill and care.
3. In breach of the term stated at paragraph 2 the Claimant did not perform the repairs with reasonable skill and care or any skill or care at all.

PARTICULARS

Having replaced the brake fluid master cylinder the Claimant forgot or neglected to tighten the brake fluid drainage nut.

4. The Defendant collected his car on the 16th February 2000 and drove the same to his home where he left the car standing on his driveway overnight. During the night the brake fluid leaked from the brake fluid reservoir and circuit. When the Defendant drove his car from his drive toward the busy road at the front of his house he discovered that the brakes on the car no longer worked at all. Consequently the Defendant was unable to stop the car which was forced into collision with three fast moving cars which were proceeding along the main road.
5. Paragraphs 5, 6 and 7 of the Particulars of Claim are denied. In the premises it is denied that the Claimant is entitled to the relief claimed or to any relief at all.

COUNTERCLAIM

6. The Defendant repeats paragraphs 1, 2, 3 and 4 above.
7. The accident outlined at paragraph 3 above was caused by the Claimant's breach of the term mentioned at paragraph 2 above and/or the Claimant's negligence.
8. It was within the contemplation of the parties at the time of the contract that if the Claimant did not perform the contract with reasonable skill and care that the Defendant would suffer damage to his vehicle and/or injury to himself.

9. By reason of the Claimant's negligence and/or by reason of the breach of the term pleaded at paragraph 2 above the Defendant has suffered loss and damage and sustained pain and suffering.

PARTICULARS OF INJURY

(a) Shock and severe pain;
(b) fracture of the right femur;
(c) bruising and scars to his face.

The Defendant was born on the 12th April 1919 and was 80 years old at the time of the accident. Following the accident he was taken to the Greenwich Hospital's accident and emergency unit. His fractures were manipulated under local anaesthetic and his cuts treated with sutures.

Full particulars of the Defendant's injuries are set out in the report of Mr Really Clever FRCS attached and annexed hereto.

PARTICULARS OF SPECIAL DAMAGE

Pre-accident value of the Defendant's vehicle (now beyond economical repair)	£5,000
Salvage value	£150
Loss	£4,850

9. Further the Claimant claims interest pursuant to Section 69 of the County Courts Act 1984 upon:

- the sum of £4,850 from the 16th February 2000 to date of judgment or sooner payment at the rate of 8% amounting to £xyz to date and accruing at the rate of £abc per day;
- upon such sums as are found to be due to the Defendant by way of damages for pain suffering and loss of amenity at such rate and for such period as the court thinks fit.

AND the Defendant counterclaims:

(a) Damages;
(b) The interest set out above pursuant to Section 69 of the County Courts Act 1984.

[Signed by counsel/draftsmen; statement of truth as with statement of case 1]

3. Defence to (3) above — negligent damage to goods

IN THE CENTRAL LONDON COUNTY COURT Claim number

BETWEEN:

SOPHIE BARRETT-BROWN
(t/a SBB REMOVALS AND STORAGE) Claimant

and

GAVIN HUGHES Defendant

DEFENCE

1. Except that it is denied that the entirety of the Defendant's goods were delivered to him as stated in paragraph 4 of the Particulars of Claim, paragraphs 1 to 6 of the Particulars of Claim are admitted.

2. The Claimant was under a duty to take due care to ensure that the Defendant's goods were stored safely.
3. Further, it was a term of the contract that the Claimant would take reasonable care in storing the goods.
4. In breach of the duty and/or term the Claimant failed to take reasonable care of the Defendant's goods.

PARTICULARS

(a) The Defendant's bedding and linen were stored directly upon a cold and damp concrete floor resulting in their being infected with mildew;
(b) the Defendant's butterfly collection was mishandled during the course of transit or storage resulting in the glass packing cases to the same being broken;
(c) items of the Defendant's furniture were stacked on top of each other with no protective barrier resulting in the same being scratched, cracked and dented;
(d) the Defendant's clothing was never returned to him;
(e) etc.;
(f) etc.;
(g) etc.

5. In the premises it is denied that the Claimant is entitled to the relief claimed at paragraphs 7 and 8 of the Particulars of Claim or to any relief at all.
6. Alternatively, the Defendant seeks to set off any and all sums recovered by way of Counterclaim as set out below in diminution or extinction of any sums found to be due to the Claimant.

COUNTERCLAIM

7. The Defendant repeats paragraphs 1 to 4 above.
8. By reason of the Claimant's failure to take due care of the Defendant's goods and/or by reason of the Claimant's breach of the term set out at paragraph 3 above the Defendant has suffered loss and damage.

PARTICULARS

(a)	Replacement of bedding and linen	£300
(b)	Value of butterfly collection	£800
(c)	Repairs to furniture	£500
(d)	Cost of Defendant's clothing replaced	£12.50
(e)	etc.	
(f)	etc.	
(g)	etc.	

9. Further the Claimant claims interest pursuant to Section 69 of the County Courts Act 1984 upon the sum of £ [total value of repairs/replacements/goods destroyed] from the [date of replacement/repair] to date of judgement or sooner payment at the rate of 8% amounting to £xyz to date and accruing at the rate of £abc per day.

AND the Defendant counterclaims:

(c) The sum of £ [total amount of repairs / replacements];
(d) The interest set out above pursuant to Section 69 of the County Courts Act 1984.

[Signed by counsel/draftsmen; statement of truth as with statement of case 1]

D. CONSUMER CREDIT ACT CASES — CLAIMS BY THE DEBTOR

1. Breach of implied terms as to quality and fitness and misrepresentation — claim against seller and creditor under a debtor-creditor-supplier agreement.

IN THE CENTRAL LONDON COUNTY COURT Claim number

BETWEEN

MADELLAINE COUTTS Claimant

and

SCREW 'EM THEN SUE 'EM FINANCE LIMITED First Defendant

and

SUKHWANT SIDHU Second Defendant

PARTICULARS OF CLAIM

1. On or about 25th April 1999 the Claimant ordered an 'Office Turbo' Computer ('the computer') from the Second Defendant. The purchase was to be financed by credit provided by the First Defendant.
2. By a written agreement dated the 28th May 2000 ('the sale agreement') the Second Defendant agreed to sell the computer to the Claimant and the Claimant agreed that the First Defendant would pay the Second Defendant £3,000 on his behalf.
3. By a written agreement dated the 25th May 2000 ('the credit agreement') the First Defendant agreed to pay the Second Defendant £3,000 on behalf of the Claimant in respect of the purchase of the computer and the Claimant agreed to repay the First Defendant by 36 monthly instalments of £250 commencing 12 months after delivery of the computer.
4. It was an implied term of the sale agreement that the computer would be of satisfactory quality.
5. In breach of the sale agreement the computer was not of satisfactory quality.

PARTICULARS OF BREACH

(a) The computer repeatedly 'crashes' losing data in any programs running at the time of the crash;
(b) the computer fails to reach its benchmark processing speed of 300MHz, but instead only achieves a speed of 100MHz;
(c) the computer mysteriously deletes files when not instructed to do so.

6. By virtue of the breach of contract of the Second Defendant the Claimant was entitled to and did reject the computer by a telephone call of the 15th June 2000.
7. Wrongfully and in breach of contract the Second Defendant has failed to re-take the goods and/or to return any part of the purchase price.
8. Alternatively, by reason of the breach of contract of the Second Defendant the Claimant has suffered loss and damage.

PARTICULARS

As appears from the report of Mr Techy Wizzard dated the 20th June 2000 attached and annexed hereto the computer with all its faults is worth only £200 whereas without such faults it would be worth £3,000.

9. It was a term of the credit agreement that the money be paid direct to the Second Defendant.

10. The credit agreement was made to finance a transaction between the Claimant and the Second Defendant.
11. In the premises the agreement was a restricted use credit agreement within the meaning of Section 11(1)(b) of the Consumer Credit Act 1974.
12. The credit agreement was entered into under pre-existing arrangements between the First Defendant and the Second Defendant.
13. In the premises the agreement was a debtor-creditor-supplier agreement within the meaning of Section 12(1)(b) of the Consumer Credit Act 1974.
14. In the premises and by virtue of Section 75(1) of the Consumer Credit Act 1974 the Claimant has a like claim against the First Defendant in respect of any claim against the Second Defendant, with whom the First Defendant is jointly and severally liable.
15. Further, the Claimant claims interest pursuant to Section 69 of the County Courts Act 1984:

(a) Upon the sum of £3,000 at the rate of 8% from the 15th June 2000 to the date of judgment, amounting to £xyz to date and accruing at the rate of £abc per day.
(b) Upon such sums as are found to be due to him in respect of damages assessed by the Court, at such rate and for such period as the Court thinks fit.

AND the Claimant claims:

(a) The price of the goods, being £2,002;
(b) Alternatively, damages;
(c) The interest set out above pursuant to Section 69 of the County Courts Act 1984.

[Signed by counsel/draftsmen; statement of truth as with statement of case 1]

2. Credit hire — defence to action for hire charges

IN THE CENTRAL LONDON COUNTY COURT Claim number

BETWEEN:

DEAN EMERY Claimant

and

SHARDI SHAMELIA Defendant

DEFENCE

1. For the purposes of this action but for no other purpose it is admitted that the accident between the Claimant and the Defendant which occurred on the 8th October 1999 was caused by the negligent driving of the Defendant. Paragraphs 1, 2 and 3 of the Particulars of Claim are accordingly admitted.
2. Paragraph 4 is denied. As appears below, the agreement by which the Claimant hired a car was a regulated consumer credit agreement and/or a regulated consumer hire agreement within the meaning of the Consumer Credit Act 1974 and is unenforceable by reason of improper execution and failure on the part of the creditor and/or hirer to hold a valid licence to carry out such business.
3. The hire agreement, dated the 12th January 2000 and made between the Claimant and a company known as 'Double Cost Hire Limited', provided that the Claimant would be hired a Mini Metro at a daily rate of £88.50 and that the car would be delivered and collected at a cost of £100 and provided for a collision damage waiver at a price of £5 per day.
4. The Vehicle Hire Agreement was capable of subsisting for a period exceeding 3 months and was a hire agreement made with an individual. The agreement was therefore a

Consumer Hire Agreement within the meaning of Section 15 of the Consumer Credit Act 1974 and was accordingly a regulated agreement.

5. As a regulated agreement the Vehicle Hire Agreement was required to comply with a variety of requirements under the Consumer Credit Act 1974 ('the Act'). The agreement has failed to comply with such requirements, as are set out below, and the agreement is accordingly unenforceable and any sums paid or payable pursuant to the agreement are irrecoverable as a head of loss as against the Defendant.

PARTICULARS OF BREACH OF THE CONSUMER CREDIT ACT — CONSUMER HIRE ELEMENTS

(a) Pursuant to Section 21 of the Act the owner is obliged to hold a licence to carry on consumer hire business, but does not hold such a licence. Pursuant to Section 40 of the Act the agreement is accordingly unenforceable.

(b) Pursuant to Section 61 of the Act the agreement is required to be signed by or on behalf of the owner of the vehicle but is not in fact signed by or on behalf of the owner under the agreement. The agreement is accordingly unenforceable.

6. Further, the agreement is a regulated consumer credit agreement within the meaning of Section 8 of the Consumer Credit Act 1974 ('the Act'). Further, that the agreement has failed to comply with the requirements of the Act and is unenforceable and irrecoverable as a loss as against the Defendant.

7. The agreement is a regulated consumer credit agreement within the meaning of Section 8 of the Act as it provides credit to an individual. It is not an exempt agreement within the meaning of the Consumer Credit (Exempt Agreements) Order 1989 as it does not oblige the debtor to make repayment of the credit within a period of one year and in four instalments or less.

8. Being a regulated consumer credit agreement the agreement is required to comply with various technicalities imposed upon such agreements by the Act but, as appears below, has failed to do so and is consequently unenforceable and irrecoverable as a head of loss as against the Defendant.

PARTICULARS OF BREACH OF THE CONSUMER CREDIT ACT — CREDIT ELEMENTS

(a) Pursuant to Sections 20 and 60 of the Act and the Consumer Credit (Agreements) Regulations 1983 SI 1983/1553, as amended by SI 1984/1600, SI 1985/666 and SI 1988/2047 the agreement is required to be in a particular form and contain certain information as to the amount of credit being advanced. The deficiencies within the credit hire agreement are too numerous too list but include such fundamental matters as failure to specify the amount or total charge for credit.

(b) Pursuant to Section 21 of the Act the creditor and/or hirer is obliged to carry on consumer credit business. Double Cost Hire Limited does not hold such a licence.

(c) The Claimant was introduced to Double Cost Hire Limited by an unlicensed credit-broker within the meaning of Section 145(2) of the Act and the agreement is accordingly unenforceable by virtue of Section 149 of the Act.

9. If, contrary to this defence, the agreement is found to be enforceable as against the Defendant then the Defendant will contend that the Claimant is not entitled to recover the entirety of the cost of hiring the vehicle as the cost is excessive and that the Claimant has failed to mitigate his loss reasonably by entering the hire agreement:

- The cost of hiring the vehicle incorporated the provision of additional benefits conferred upon the Claimant by way of the provision of credit, the collision damage waiver and the assistance of pursuing a claim against the Defendant. Such proportion of the cost of hiring the vehicle as is attributable to such additional benefits is not a loss to the Claimant for which he is entitled to claim. The Defendant will contend that the cost of hiring a replacement vehicle where such additional benefits are not provided (the 'spot hire') rate is appropriate.

- The Defendant will contend that the period of hire was excessive as the vehicle could have been repaired in a shorter time by the Claimant using an alternative repairer.

10. The Defendant made payment in respect of the repairs to the Claimant's vehicle on the 20th September 2000, accordingly the only sums due and payable to the Claimant are in respect of the cost of hiring a replacement vehicle. In the premises the Defendant denies that the Claimant is entitled to the relief as claimed or to any relief at all.

[Signed by counsel/draftsmen; statement of truth as with statement of case 1]

E. CLAIMS AGAINST THIRD PARTIES — WRONGFUL INTERFERENCE WITH GOODS

Claim by the owner of goods

1. Claim by the owner of goods — refusal to deliver up

IN THE CENTRAL LONDON COUNTY COURT Claim number

BETWEEN:

JAMES KIRBY Claimant

and

PATRICIA LLOYD Defendant

PARTICULARS OF CLAIM

1. The Claimant is the owner of a Ford Fiesta car registration number A264 KBW, valued at £8,000.
2. On or about the 1st January 2000 the Claimant's car was stolen from outside the front of his house.
3. On the 1st February 2000 it came to the Claimant's attention that the car was in the possession of the Defendant.
4. On the 1st February and on numerous occasions thereafter the Claimant has demanded that the Defendant gives up the possession of the car, but the Defendant has refused.
5. In the premises the Claimant claims delivery up of the car, alternatively damages in the sum of £8,000.
6. Further, the Claimant claims interest pursuant to Section 69 of the County Courts Act 1984 at the rate of 8% upon the sum of £8,000 amounting to £xyz to date and continuing at the rate of £abc per day.
7. Alternatively, the Claimant claims interest pursuant to Section 69 of the County Courts Act 1984 at such rate and upon such amounts as the Court deems fit.

AND the Claimant claims:

(a) Delivery up of the vehicle;
(b) Alternatively, damages;
(c) The interest set out above pursuant to Section 69 of the County Courts Act 1984.

[Signed by counsel/draftsmen; statement of truth as with statement of case 1]

2. Claim by the owner of goods — conversion by repairer and claim for delivery up against third party

IN THE CENTRAL LONDON COUNTY COURT Claim number

BETWEEN:

ALUN EVANS Claimant

and

JEREMY LYNN First Defendant

and

STEVEN PERIAN Second Defendant

PARTICULARS OF CLAIM

1. The First Defendant is a car mechanic carrying on business at premises known as and situate at 12, Fetter Lane, London. The Claimant is a customer of the Defendant.
2. On the 10th April 2000 the Claimant delivered to the First Defendant his Harley Davison motorcycle, registration number G489 2KBW, valued at £10,000 for the purpose of repair.
3. On the 12th April 2000 the First Defendant sold the Claimant's motorcycle to the Second Defendant for £6,000.
4. On or about the 15th April the Claimant demanded the return of his motorcycle from the Second Defendant, but the Second Defendant has refused.
5. In the premises the Claimant claims against both parties delivery up of the motorcycle, alternatively damages in the sum of £10,000.
6. Further, the Claimant claims interest pursuant to Section 69 of the County Courts Act 1984 at the rate of 8% upon the sum of £10,000 amounting to £xyz to date and continuing at the rate of £ abc per day.
7. Alternatively, the Claimant claims interest pursuant to Section 69 of the County Courts Act 1984 at such rate and upon such amounts as the Court deems fit.

AND the Claimant claims:

(a) Delivery up of the vehicle;
(b) Alternatively, damages;
(c) The interest set out above pursuant to Section 69 of the County Courts Act 1984.

[Signed by counsel/draftsmen; statement of truth as with statement of case 1]

Defences — third party

1. Defence to (2) above — acquisition of good title by virtue of an exception to the *nemo dat* rule — mercantile agent

IN THE CENTRAL LONDON COUNTY COURT Claim number

BETWEEN:

ALUN EVANS Claimant

and

JEREMY LYNN First Defendant

and

STEVEN PERIAN Second Defendant

DEFENCE OF THE SECOND DEFENDANT

1. Except that it is denied that the Claimant is the owner of the said motorcycle as alleged in paragraph 1 of the Particulars of Claim, paragraphs 1 to 4 of the Particulars of Claim are admitted.
2. In the premises it is denied that the Claimant is the owner of the motorcycle. The First Defendant was in the possession of the motorcycle as a mercantile agent with the consent of the Claimant and was purchased by the Second Defendant from the First Defendant in the ordinary course of business, in good faith and without notice of any want of authority on the part of the First Defendant.
3. In the premises the Second Defendant has obtained a good title to the goods.
4. In the premises it is denied that the Claimant is entitled to the relief claimed or to any relief at all.

[Signed by counsel/draftsmen; statement of truth as with statement of case 1]

F. CLAIMS AGAINST THE MANUFACTURER OR SUPPLIER OF GOODS

Claims by the injured party

1. Claim under the Consumer Protection Act for supply of a defective product

IN THE CENTRAL LONDON COUNTY COURT Claim number

BETWEEN:

ABIGAIL DEAN Claimant

and

ANNE DONELON
(t/a DISCOUNT ELECTRICAL SUPPLIES) Defendant

PARTICULARS OF CLAIM

1. The Defendant has at all material times carried on business as a supplier of electrical goods at premises known as and situate at 12, Back Street, London, EC4Y 7DE.
2. On or about the 23rd December 2000 the Claimant's boyfriend, one David Sandeman, purchased from the Defendant a hairdryer for the sum of £5.
3. On the 25th December 2000 Mr Sandeman gave the hairdryer to the Claimant as a Christmas gift.
4. When using the hairdryer for the first time on the 31st December 2000 the hairdryer gave out an intense heat which, upon examination, was found to be 175 degrees centigrade.
5. In the premises the hairdryer contained defects within the meaning of Section 3(1) of the Consumer Protection Act 1987.
6. On the 10th January 2001 the Claimant wrote to the Defendant and requested to know the name of the manufacturer of the hairdryer but to date the Defendant has failed to provide this.
7. In the premises the Defendant is liable to the Claimant in respect of pain, suffering and injury which she has sustained.

PARTICULARS

The Claimant who was born on 10th April 1950 and who was 49 at the date of the accident sustained burns to her head and face. Following the accident she was taken to the Greenwich District Hospital accident and emergency unit, etc. etc.

Further, a report of Mr Burns FRCS is attached and annexed hereto.

8. Further, the Claimant claims interest at such rate and upon such amounts as the Court deems fit.

AND the Claimant claims:

(a) Damages;
(b) The interest set out above pursuant to Section 69 of the County Courts Act 1984.

[Signed by counsel/draftsmen; statement of truth as with statement of case 1]

2. Claim under the Consumer Protection Act for the manufacture of a defective product

IN THE CENTRAL LONDON COUNTY COURT Claim number

BETWEEN:

PETER IRVINE Claimant

and

ELECTRICAL GOODS MANUFACTURER LIMITED Defendant

PARTICULARS OF CLAIM

1. The Defendant has at all material times carried on business as a manufacturer of electrical goods supplied under the trade mark 'Magic'.
2. On or about the 5th January 2000 the Claimant's wife purchased from a shop known as Blackheath Electrical Retail Limited a radio for the sum of £10. The radio was from the Defendant's 'Aqua' range of products as it was designed and advertised as being suitable for use in the bath.
3. On the 10th January 2000 the Claimant's wife gave the radio to the Claimant as a birthday gift.
4. When using the radio for the first time in accordance with the instructions supplied the Claimant attached the radio to the wall of the bathroom using the suction cups provided. After enjoying a bath for ten minutes the suction cups became detached from the bathroom wall causing the radio to fall into the bath, as a result the Claimant was given a series of electrical shocks.
5. In the premises the radio contained defects within the meaning of Section 3(1) of the Consumer Protection Act 1987.
6. In the premises the Defendant is liable to the Claimant in respect of pain, suffering and injury which he has sustained.

PARTICULARS

The Claimant who was born on 5th March 1970 and who was 30 at the date of the accident sustained severe shock and trauma. As a result of the electrical shock his hair has subsequently fallen out etc. etc. etc.
Further, a report of Mr Volt FRCS is attached and annexed hereto.

7. Further, the Claimant claims interest at such rate and upon such amounts as the Court deems fit.

AND the Claimant claims:

(a) Damages;
(b) The interest set out above.

[Signed by counsel/draftsmen; statement of truth as with statement of case 1]

3. Claim under the Consumer Protection Act against a person holding themselves out as the manufacturer of a defective product

<u>IN THE CENTRAL LONDON COUNTY COURT</u> Claim number

BETWEEN:

PETER IRVINE <u>Claimant</u>

and

ELECTRICAL GOODS DISTRIBUTOR LIMITED <u>Defendant</u>

<u>PARTICULARS OF CLAIM</u>

1. The Defendant has at all material times carried on business as a retailer and manufacturer of electrical goods.
2. The Defendant distributes goods under the label 'Top Shelf', some of which it manufactures itself and some of which it has manufactured on its behalf.
3. On or about the 5th January 2000 the Claimant's wife purchased from the Defendant's Charlton shop a radio for the sum of £10. The radio was from the Defendant's 'Aqua' range of products as it was designed and advertised as being suitable for use in the bath. The radio was packaged under the 'Top Shelf' label and was marked with the name of the Defendant. The radio was in fact manufactured by a French firm which the Claimant is unable to fully identify.
4. In the premises the Defendant held itself out as the producer of the radio within the meaning of Section 2(2)(b) of the Consumer Protection Act 1987.
5. On the 10th January 2000 the Claimant's wife gave the radio to the Claimant as a birthday gift.
6. When using the radio for the first time in accordance with the instructions supplied the Claimant attached the radio to the wall of the bathroom using the suction cups provided. After enjoying a bath for ten minutes the suction cups became detached from the bathroom wall causing the radio to fall into the bath, as a result the Claimant was given a series of electrical shocks.
7. In the premises the radio contained defects within the meaning Section 3(1) of the Consumer Protection Act 1987.
8. In the premises the Defendant is liable to the Claimant in respect of pain, suffering and injury which he has suffered.

<u>PARTICULARS</u>

The Claimant who was born on 5th March 1970 and who was 30 at the date of the accident sustained severe shock and trauma. As a result of the electrical shock his hair has subsequently fallen out etc. etc. etc.

Further, a report of Mr Volt FRCS is attached and annexed hereto.

9. Further, the Claimant claims interest at such rate and upon such amounts as the Court deems fit.

AND the Claimant claims:

(c) Damages;
(d) The interest set out above.

[Signed by counsel/draftsmen; statement of truth as with statement of case 1]

Defences

1. Defence to (2) above — counterfeit product

IN THE CENTRAL LONDON COUNTY COURT Claim number

BETWEEN:

PETER IRVINE Claimant

and

ELECTRICAL GOODS MANUFACTURER LIMITED Defendant

DEFENCE

1. Paragraph 1 of the Particulars of Claim is admitted.
2. Paragraph 2 of the Particulars of Claim is denied. It is not admitted where or when the Claimant's wife purchased the radio in question. It is denied that the radio was from the Defendant's 'Aqua' range of products. The radio is similar to a radio from the Defendant's range of products known as 'Aqua' but the particular radio in question is a counterfeit good manufactured by a person or persons unknown.
3. Paragraphs 1, 2 and 3 are not admitted.
4. Paragraphs 6 and 7 are denied. In the premises it is denied that the Claimant is entitled to the relief as claimed or to any relief at all.

[Signed by counsel/draftsmen; statement of truth as with statement of case 1]

2. Defence to (3) above denial that defendant was held out as a producer

IN THE CENTRAL LONDON COUNTY COURT Claim number

BETWEEN:

PETER IRVINE Claimant

and

ELECTRICAL GOODS DISTRIBUTOR LIMITED Defendant

DEFENCE

1. Paragraphs 1, 2 and 3 of the Particulars of Claim are admitted.
2. Paragraph 4 of the Particulars of Claim is denied. The Box, labels on the radio itself, instructions and guarantee provided with the radio were all marked with the statement (in bold print) 'Manufactured on behalf of Electrical Goods Distributor Limited by Disreputable French Firm & Co.'.
3. No admissions are made as to paragraphs 5 to 10 of the Particulars of Claim and the Claimant is put to strict proof of the same.
4. In the premises it is denied that the Claimant is entitled to any relief whereas claimed or at all.

[Signed by counsel/draftsmen; statement of truth as with statement of case 1]

Appendix B
Model contracts

STANDARD CONDITIONS OF SALE

These terms are intended to form the reverse of a model contract of sale to the Seller's design, i.e. these are 'the terms overleaf'

TERMS & CONDITIONS

A. Definitions

In this contract the following terms shall bear the following meaning:

1. 'Seller' shall mean [ABC Supplies Limited of 10 Market Way etc.].
2. 'Buyer' shall mean the name of the person, company or firm as set out overleaf at [box 7].
3. 'Goods' shall mean all the items listed in [box 4] overleaf.
4. 'Price' shall mean the total price of all the goods ordered as set out in [box 3] overleaf together with any delivery charge as specified in [box 12] overleaf exclusive of VAT, as set out in [box 8] overleaf.
5. 'VAT' shall mean the total amount of value added tax due in respect of the price.
6. 'Seller's Price List' shall mean the seller's prevailing price list as displayed at the seller's premises.
7. 'Place of Delivery' shall mean the seller's address as set out in clause A1 above unless a contrary place of delivery has been specified by ticking [box 19] overleaf AND the appropriate charge as set out in the seller's price list has been entered in [box 12] overleaf.
8. 'Delivery Date' shall mean the date specified in [box 17] overleaf.

B. Application of Terms and Conditions

1. These provisions shall apply to all contracts for the sale of goods between the seller and the buyer notwithstanding and to the exclusion of any terms or conditions which the buyer may purport to incorporate under any purchase order, letter of order, confirmation of order or similar document.
2. Any and all future orders shall be deemed to be offers by the buyer to purchase goods pursuant to these terms and conditions unless the seller shall amend these terms and conditions or notify the buyer to the contrary.
3. Any variation to these terms and conditions may only be made by writing by the seller and unless so made shall have no effect.
4. This contract is governed by the law prevailing in England and Wales.

C. Delivery

1. Delivery of the goods shall be at the place of delivery.
2. Delivery shall be made by the seller giving the buyer possession of the goods on the delivery date.
3. The buyer shall make all necessary arrangements to take possession of the goods on the delivery date and at the place of delivery. In the event that the buyer has not made such arrangements delivery may be made by the seller leaving the goods at the place of delivery during the hours of 9 am and 5 pm.
4. The time for delivery shall not be of the essence and in the event that the seller is unable to give the buyer possession of the goods on the delivery date at the place of delivery then this shall form a breach of warranty only and the buyer shall not be entitled to terminate the contract or reject the goods.
5. Any damages awarded under clause C4 above shall be limited to [£10 per day].

D. Payment

1. The buyer will pay to the seller the price together with any and all VAT by no later than the delivery date.
2. Payment may be made by cash, cheque, banker's draft or credit token (within the meaning of the Consumer Credit Act 1974), but in the event that payment is made by cheque then the time for payment as set out in clause D1 above shall be 10 days before the delivery date.
3. The time for payment of the price shall be of the essence.
4. In the event that the buyer fails to make payment in accordance with clause D1 and D2 the buyer shall pay interest on any and all sums outstanding at the rate of [2% above the base rate charged at the time of default by Barclays Bank plc].

E. Acceptance of Goods

1. The buyer shall be deemed to have accepted the goods as if he had expressly written to the seller and stated as such if he fails to notify the seller in writing that he does not accept the goods within 3 days of delivery of the goods.

F. Exclusion and Limitation

1. Unless the buyer deals as a consumer within the meaning of Section 12 of the Unfair Contract Terms Act 1977 then all warranties, terms or conditions which provide that the goods will match any particular description, fitness for purpose or quality whether implied by common law or statute shall be excluded from this contract.
2. The seller shall be under no liability to the buyer for indirect or consequential loss (including loss of profits) sustained by the buyer following breach of this contract by the seller.
3. In any event, the seller's liability to the buyer arising out of any breach by the seller of this contract shall be limited to damages and such damages shall under no circumstances exceed the price.

ADDITIONAL OR ALTERNATIVE CLAUSES

A. Permissible Discrepancy in Quantity

1. The buyer will be bound to take delivery of the goods in accordance with clause C above notwithstanding that the quantity of goods is either [5%] greater or less in quantity than the goods ordered.
2. In the event that the buyer takes delivery in accordance with clause A1 above then the price shall be adjusted accordingly.

B. Permissible Delay in Delivery

1. The buyer will be bound to take delivery of the goods in accordance with clause C1, C3, C4 and C5 above notwithstanding that the seller delivers the goods up to 7 days after the delivery date provided that the seller gives the buyer 24 hours notice of such delay.

C. Rejection of Goods not Conforming to the Contract

1. If the buyer wishes to reject goods which are not in accordance with the contract then he may only do so by giving the seller notice in writing no more than 7 days after delivery of the goods.
2. If the buyer rejects goods in accordance with clause C1 above then the buyer shall nonetheless be obliged to return any goods so rejected to the seller's address during the hours of 9am and 5pm on a normal business day and to pay any carriage costs incurred by doing so.
3. If the buyer purports to reject any goods otherwise than in accordance with clauses C1 and C2 above then any such act shall be ineffective and the seller shall not be bound to re-take possession of the goods and the property in the goods shall remain vested in the buyer.

D. Indemnity in Respect of Sub-sales

1. The seller shall indemnify the buyer in respect of any claims for compensation or the return of the purchase price by the customers of the buyer or any sub-buyer arising by any breach of this contract by the seller.

Appendix C
Statutes and statutory instruments

Statutes

Factors Act 1889
Law Reform (Frustrated Contracts) Act 1943
Hire-Purchase Act 1964
Misrepresentation Act 1967
Unsolicited Goods and Services Act 1971
Supply of Goods (Implied Terms) Act 1973
Consumer Credit Act 1974
Unsolicited Goods and Services (Amendment) Act 1975
Torts (Interference with Goods) Act 1977
Unfair Contract Terms Act 1977
Civil Liability (Contribution) Act 1978
Sale of Goods Act 1979
Sale of Goods and Services Act 1982
Consumer Protection Act 1987
Contracts (Rights of Third Parties) Act 1999

Statutory Instruments

Consumer Credit (Agreements) Regulations 1983, SI 1983/1553
Consumer Credit (Cancellation Notices and Copies of Documents) Regulations 1983, SI 1983/1557
Consumer Credit (Exempt Agreements) Order 1989, SI 1989/869
Package Travel, Package Holidays and Package Tour Regulations 1992, SI 1992/3288
Unfair Terms in Consumer Contracts Regulations 1999, SI 1999/2083

STATUTES

FACTORS ACT 1889
(52 & 53 Vict., c. 45)

An Act to amend and consolidate the Factors Acts. [26th August 1889]

Preliminary

1. Definitions

For the purposes of this Act—

(1) The expression 'mercantile agent' shall mean a mercantile agent having in the customary course of his business as such agent authority either to sell goods or to consign goods for the purpose of sale, or to buy goods, or to raise money on the security of goods:

(2) A person shall be deemed to be in possession of goods or of the documents of title to goods, where the goods or documents are in the actual custody or are held by any other person subject to his control or for him or on his behalf:

(3) The expression 'goods' shall include wares and merchandise:

(4) The expression 'document of title' shall include any bill of lading, dock warrant, warehouse-keeper's certificate, and warrant or order for the delivery of goods, and any other document used in the ordinary course of business as proof of the possession or control of goods, or authorising or purporting to authorise, either by endorsement or by delivery, the possessor of the document to transfer or receive goods thereby represented:

(5) The expression 'pledge' shall include any contract pledging, or giving a lien or security on, goods, whether in consideration of an original advance or of any further or continuing advance or of any pecuniary liability:

(6) The expression 'person' shall include any body of persons corporate or unincorporate.

Dispositions by mercantile agents

2. Powers of mercantile agent with respect to disposition of goods

(1) Where a mercantile agent is, with the consent of the owner, in possession of goods or of the documents of title to goods, any sale, pledge, or other disposition of the goods, made by him when acting in the ordinary course of business of a mercantile agent, shall, subject to the provisions of this Act, be as valid as if he were expressly authorised by the owner of the goods to make the same; provided that the person taking under the disposition acts in good faith, and has not at the time of the disposition notice that the person making the disposition has not authority to make the same.

(2) Where a mercantile agent has, with the consent of the owner, been in possession of goods or of the documents of title to goods, any sale, pledge, or other disposition, which would have been valid if the consent had continued, shall be valid notwithstanding the determination of the consent; provided that the person taking under the disposition has not at the time thereof notice that the consent has been determined.

(3) Where a mercantile agent has obtained possession of any documents of title to goods by reason of his being or having been, with the consent of the owner, in possession of the goods represented thereby, or of any other documents of title to the goods, his possession of the first-mentioned documents shall, for the purposes of this Act, be deemed to be with the consent of the owner.

(4) For the purposes of this Act the consent of the owner shall be presumed in the absence of evidence to the contrary.

3. Effect of pledges of documents of title

A pledge of the documents of title to goods shall be deemed to be a pledge of the goods.

4. Pledge for antecedent debt

Where a mercantile agent pledges goods as security for a debt or liability due from the pledgor to the pledgee before the time of the pledge, the pledgee shall acquire no further right to the goods than could have been enforced by the pledgor at the time of the pledge.

5. Rights acquired by exchange of goods or documents
The consideration necessary for the validity of a sale, pledge, or other disposition of goods, in pursuance of this Act, may be either a payment in cash, or the delivery or transfer of other goods, or of a document of title to goods, or of a negotiable security, or any other valuable consideration; but where goods are pledged by a mercantile agent in consideration of the delivery or transfer of other goods, or of a document of title to goods, or of a negotiable security, the pledgee shall acquire no right or interest in the goods so pledged in excess of the value of the goods, documents, or security when so delivered or transferred in exchange.

6. Agreements through clerks, &c.
For the purposes of this Act an agreement made with a mercantile agent through a clerk or other person authorised in the ordinary course of business to make contracts of sale or pledge on his behalf shall be deemed to be an agreement with the agent.

7. Provisions as to consignors and consignees
(1) Where the owner of goods has given possession of the goods to another person for the purpose of consignment or sale, or has shipped the goods in the name of another person, and the consignee of the goods has not had notice that such person is not the owner of the goods, the consignee shall, in respect of advances made to or for the use of such person, have the same lien on the goods as if such person were the owner of the goods, and may transfer any such lien to another person.
(2) Nothing in this section shall limit or affect the validity of any sale, pledge, or disposition, by a mercantile agent.

Dispositions by sellers and buyers of goods

8. Disposition by seller remaining in possession
Where a person, having sold goods, continues, or is, in possession of the goods or of the documents of title to the goods, the delivery or transfer by that person, or by a mercantile agent acting for him, of the goods or documents of title under any sale, pledge, or other disposition thereof, or under any agreement for sale, pledge, or other disposition thereof, to any person receiving the same in good faith and without notice of the previous sale, shall have the same effect as if the person making the delivery or transfer were expressly authorised by the owner of the goods to make the same.

9. Disposition by buyer obtaining possession
Where a person, having bought or agreed to buy goods, obtains with the consent of the seller possession of the goods or the documents of title to the goods, the delivery or transfer, by that person or by a mercantile agent acting for him, of the goods or documents of title under any sale, pledge, or other disposition thereof, or under any agreement for sale, pledge, or other disposition thereof, to any person receiving the same in good faith and without notice of any lien or other right of the original seller in respect of the goods, shall have the same effect as if the person making the delivery or transfer were a mercantile agent in possession of the goods or documents of title with the consent of the owner.
[For the purposes of this section—
(i) the buyer under a conditional sale agreement shall be deemed not to be a person who has bought or agreed to buy goods, and
(ii) 'conditional sale agreement' means an agreement for the sale of goods which is a consumer credit agreement within the meaning of the Consumer Credit Act 1974 under which the purchase price or part of it is payable in instalments, and the property in the goods is to remain in the seller (notwithstanding that the buyer is to be in possession of the goods) until such conditions as to the payment of instalments or otherwise as may be specified in the agreement are fulfilled.]

10. Effect of transfer of documents on vendor's lien or right of stoppage in transitu
Where a document of title to goods has been lawfully transferred to a person as a buyer or owner of the goods, and that person transfers the document to a person who takes the document in good faith and for valuable consideration, the last-mentioned transfer shall have the same effect for defeating any vendor's lien or right of stoppage in transitu as the transfer of a bill of lading has for defeating the right of stoppage in transitu.

Supplemental

11. Mode of transferring documents
For the purposes of this Act, the transfer of a document may be by endorsement, or, where the document is by custom or by its express terms transferable by delivery or makes the goods deliverable to the bearer, then by delivery.

12. Saving for rights of true owner
(1) Nothing in this Act shall authorise an agent to exceed or depart from his authority as between himself and his principal, or exempt him from any liability, civil or criminal, for so doing.

(2) Nothing in this Act shall prevent the owner of goods from recovering the goods from any agent or his trustee in bankruptcy at any time before the sale or pledge thereof, or shall prevent the owner of goods pledged by an agent from having the right to redeem the goods at any time before the sale thereof, on satisfying the claim for which the goods were pledged, and paying to the agent, if by him required, any money in respect of which the agent would by law be entitled to retain the goods or the documents of title thereto, or any of them, by way of lien as against the owner, or from recovering from any person with whom the goods have been pledged any balance of money remaining in his hands as the produce of the sale of the goods after deducting the amount of his lien.

(3) Nothing in this Act shall prevent the owner of goods sold by an agent from recovering from the buyer the price agreed to be paid for the same, or any part of that price, subject to any right of set off on the part of the buyer against the agent.

13. Saving for common law powers of agent
The provisions of this Act shall be construed in amplification and not in derogation of the powers exercisable by an agent independently of this Act.

[. . .]

16. Extent of Act
This Act shall not extend to Scotland.

17. Short title
This Act may be cited as the Factors Act, 1889.

LAW REFORM (FRUSTRATED CONTRACTS) ACT 1943
(6 & 7 Geo. VI, c. 40)

An Act to amend the law relating to the frustration of contracts. [5th August 1943]

1. Adjustment of rights and liabilities of parties to frustrated contracts
(1) Where a contract governed by English law has become impossible of performance or been otherwise frustrated, and the parties thereto have for that reason been discharged from the further performance of the contract, the following provisions of this section shall, subject to the provisions of section two of this Act, have effect in relation thereto.

(2) All sums paid or payable to any party in pursuance of the contract before the time when the parties were so discharged (in this Act referred to as 'the time of discharge') shall, in the case of sums so paid, be recoverable from him as money received by him for the use of the party by whom the sums were paid, and, in the case of sums so payable, cease to be so payable:

Provided that, if the party to whom the sums were so paid or payable incurred expenses before the time of discharge in, or for the purpose of, the performance of the contract, the court may, if it considers it just to do so having regard to all the circumstances of the case, allow him to retain or, as the case may be, recover the whole or any part of the sums so paid or payable, not being an amount in excess of the expenses so incurred.

(3) Where any party to the contract has, by reason of anything done by any other party thereto in, or for the purpose of, the performance of the contract, obtained a valuable benefit (other than a payment of money to which the last foregoing subsection applies) before the time of discharge there shall be recoverable from him by the said other party such sum (if any), not exceeding the value of the said benefit to the party obtaining it, as the court considers just, having regard to all the circumstances of the case and, in particular,—

(a) the amount of any expenses incurred before the time of discharge by the benefited party in, or for the purpose of, the performance of the contract, including any sums paid or payable by him to any other party in pursuance of the contract and retained or recoverable by that party under the last foregoing subsection, and

(b) the effect, in relation to the said benefit, of the circumstances giving rise to the frustration of the contract.

(4) In estimating, for the purposes of the foregoing provisions of this section, the amount of any expenses incurred by any party to the contract, the court may, without prejudice to the generality of the said provisions, include any sum as appears to be reasonable in respect of overhead expenses and in respect of any work or services performed personally by the said party.

(5) In considering whether any sum ought to be recovered or retained under the foregoing provisions of this section by any party to the contract, the court shall not take into account any sums which have, by reason of the circumstances giving rise to the frustration of the contract, become payable to that party under any contract of insurance unless there was an obligation to insure imposed by an express term of the frustrated contract or by or under any enactment.

(6) Where any person has assumed obligations under the contract in consideration of the conferring of a benefit by any other party to the contract upon any other person, whether a party to the contract or not, the court may, if in all the circumstances of the case it considers it just to do so, treat for the purposes of subsection (3) of this section any benefit so conferred as a benefit obtained by the person who has assumed the obligations as aforesaid.

2. Provision as to application of this Act

(1) This Act shall apply to contracts, whether made before or after the commencement of this Act, as respects which the time of discharge is on or after the first day of July, nineteen hundred and forty-three, but not to contracts as respects which the time of discharge is before the said date.

(2) This Act shall apply to contracts to which the Crown is a party in like manner as to contracts between subjects.

(3) Where any contract to which this Act applies contains any provision which, upon the true construction of the contract, is intended to have effect in the event of circumstances arising which operate, or would but for the said provision operate, to frustrate the contract, or is intended to have effect whether such circumstances arise or not, the court shall give effect to the said provision and shall only give effect to the foregoing section of this Act to such extent, if any, as appears to the court to be consistent with the said provision.

(4) Where it appears to the court that a part of any contract to which this Act applies can be properly severed from the remainder of the contract, being a part wholly performed before the time of discharge, or so performed except for the payment in respect of that part of the contract of sums which are or can be ascertained under the contract, the court shall treat that part of the contract as if it were a separate contract and had not been frustrated and shall treat the foregoing section of this Act as only applicable to the remainder of that contract.

(5) This Act shall not apply—

(a) to any charterparty, except a time charterparty or a charterparty by way of demise, or to any contract (other than a charterparty) for the carriage of goods by sea; or

(b) to any contract of insurance, save as is provided by subsection (5) of the foregoing section; or

(c) to any contract to which [section 7 of the Sale of Goods Act 1979] (which avoids contracts for the sale of specific goods which perish before the risk has passed to the buyer) applies, or to any other contract for the sale, or for the sale and delivery, of specific goods, where the contract is frustrated by reason of the fact that the goods have perished.

3. Short title and interpretation

(1) This Act may be cited as the Law Reform (Frustrated Contracts) Act, 1943.

(2) In this Act the expression 'court' means, in relation to any matter, the court or arbitrator by or before whom the matter falls to be determined.

HIRE-PURCHASE ACT 1964
(1964, c. 53)

An Act to amend the law relating to hire-purchase and credit-sale, and, in relation thereto, to amend the enactments relating to the sale of goods; to make provision with respect to dispositions of motor vehicles which have been let or agreed to be sold by way of hire-purchase or conditional sale; to amend the Advertisements (Hire-Purchase) Act, 1957; and for purposes connected with the matters aforesaid. [16th July 1964]

[PART III
TITLE TO MOTOR VEHICLES ON HIRE-PURCHASE OR CONDITIONAL SALE

27. Protection of purchasers of motor vehicles

(1) This section applies where a motor vehicle has been bailed or (in Scotland) hired under a hire-purchase agreement, or has been agreed to be sold under a conditional sale agreement, and, before the property in the vehicle has become vested in the debtor, he disposes of the vehicle to another person.

(2) Where the disposition referred to in subsection (1) above is to a private purchaser, and he is a purchaser of the motor vehicle in good faith without notice of the hire-purchase or conditional sale agreement (the 'relevant agreement') that disposition shall have effect as if the creditor's title to the vehicle has been vested in the debtor immediately before that disposition.

(3) Where the person to whom the disposition referred to in subsection (1) above is made (the 'original purchaser') is a trade or finance purchaser, then if the person who is the first private purchaser of the motor vehicle after that disposition (the 'first private purchaser') is a purchaser of the vehicle in good faith without notice of the relevant agreement, the disposition of the vehicle to the first private purchaser shall have effect as if the title of the creditor to the vehicle had been vested in the debtor immediately before he disposed of it to the original purchaser.

(4) Where, in a case within subsection (3) above—

(a) the disposition by which the first private purchaser becomes a purchaser of the motor vehicle in good faith without notice of the relevant agreement is itself a bailment or hiring under a hire-purchase agreement, and

(b) the person who is the creditor in relation to that agreement disposes of the vehicle to the first private purchaser, or a person claiming under him, by transferring to him the property in the vehicle in pursuance of a provision in the agreement in that behalf, the disposition referred to in paragraph (b) above (whether or not the person to whom it is made is a purchaser in good faith without notice of the relevant agreement) shall as well as the disposition referred to in paragraph (a) above, have effect as mentioned in subsection (3) above.

(5) The preceding provisions of this section apply—

(a) notwithstanding anything in [section 21 of the Sale of Goods Act 19791 (sale of goods by a person not the owner), but

(b) without prejudice to the provisions of the Factors Acts (as defined by [section 61(1) of the said Act of 1979]) or any other enactment enabling the apparent owner of goods to dispose of them as if he were the true owner.

(6) Nothing in this section shall exonerate the debtor from any liability (whether criminal or civil) to which he would be subject apart from this section; and, in a case where the debtor disposes of the motor vehicle to a trade or finance purchaser, nothing in this section shall exonerate—

(a) that trade or finance purchaser, or

(b) any other trade or finance purchaser who becomes a purchaser of the vehicle and is not a person claiming under the first private purchaser,

from any liability (whether criminal or civil) to which he would be subject apart from this section.

28. Presumptions relating to dealings with motor vehicles

(1) Where in any proceedings (whether criminal or civil) relating to a motor vehicle it is proved—

(a) that the vehicle was bailed or (in Scotland) hired under a hire-purchase agreement, or was agreed to be sold under a conditional sale agreement and

(b) that a person (whether a party to the proceedings or not) became a private purchaser of the vehicle in good faith without notice of the hire-purchase or conditional sale agreement (the 'relevant agreement'), this section shall have effect for the purposes of the operation of section 27 of this Act in relation to those proceedings.

(2) It shall be presumed for those purposes unless the contrary is proved, that the disposition of the vehicle to the person referred to in subsection (1)(b) above (the 'relevant purchaser') was made by the debtor.

(3) If it is proved that that disposition was not made by the debtor, then it shall be presumed for those purposes, unless the contrary is proved—

(a) that the debtor disposed of the vehicle to a private purchaser purchasing in good faith without notice of the relevant agreement, and

(b) that the relevant purchaser is or was a person claiming under the person to whom the debtor so disposed of the vehicle.

(4) If it is proved that the disposition of the vehicle to the relevant purchaser was not made by the debtor, and that the person to whom the debtor disposed of the vehicle (the 'original purchaser') was a trade or finance purchaser, then it shall be presumed for those purposes, unless the contrary is proved,

(a) that the person who, after the disposition of the vehicle to the original purchaser, first became a private purchaser of the vehicle was a purchaser in good faith without notice of the relevant agreement, and

(b) that the relevant purchaser is or was a person claiming under the original purchaser.

(5) Without prejudice to any other method of proof, where in any proceedings a party thereto admits a fact, that fact shall, for the purposes of this section, be taken as against him to be proved in relation to those proceedings.

29. Interpretation of Part III

(1) In this Part of this Act—

'conditional sale agreement' means an agreement for the sale of goods under which the purchase price or part of it is payable by instalments, and the property in the goods is to remain in the seller (notwithstanding that the buyer is to be in possession of the goods) until such conditions as to the payment of instalments or otherwise as may be specified in the agreement are fulfilled;

'creditor' means the person by whom goods are bailed or (in Scotland) hired under a hire-purchase agreement or as the case may be, the seller under a conditional sale agreement, or the person to whom his rights and duties have passed by assignment or operation of law;

'disposition' means any sale or contract of sale (including a conditional sale agreement), any bailment or (in Scotland) hiring under a hire-purchase agreement and any transfer of the property of goods in pursuance of a provision in that behalf contained in a hire-purchase agreement, and includes any transaction purporting to be a disposition (as so defined), and 'dispose of' shall be construed accordingly:

'hire-purchase agreement' means an agreement, other than a conditional sale agreement, under which—

(a) goods are bailed or (in Scotland) hired in return for periodical payments by the person to whom they are bailed or hired, and

(b) the property in the goods will pass to that person if the terms of the agreement are complied with and one or more of the following occurs—

(i) the exercise of an option to purchase by that person,

(ii) the doing of any other specified act by any party to the agreement,

(iii) the happening of any other specified events; and

'motor vehicle' means a mechanically propelled vehicle intended or adapted for use on roads to which the public has access.

(2) In this Part of this Act 'trade or finance purchaser' means a purchaser who, at the time of the disposition made to him, carries on a business which consists, wholly or partly—

(a) of purchasing motor vehicles for the purpose of offering or exposing them for sale, or

(b) of providing finance by purchasing motor vehicles for the purpose of bailing or (in Scotland) hiring them under hire-purchase agreements or agreeing to sell them under conditional sale agreements,

and 'private purchaser' means a purchaser who, at the time of the disposition made to him, does not carry on any such business.

(3) For the purposes of this Part of this Act a person becomes a purchaser of a motor vehicle if, and at the time when, a disposition of the vehicle is made to him; and a person shall be taken to be a purchaser of a motor vehicle without notice of a hire-purchase agreement or conditional sale agreement if, at the time of the disposition made to him, he has no actual notice that the vehicle is or was the subject of any such agreement.

(4) In this Part of this Act the 'debtor' in relation to a motor vehicle which has been bailed or hired under a hire-purchase agreement, or, as the case may be, agreed to be sold under a conditional sale agreement, means the person who at the material time (whether the agreement has before that time been terminated or not) either—

(a) is the person to whom the vehicle is bailed or hired under that agreement, or

(b) is, in relation to the agreement, the buyer,

including a person who at that time is, by virtue of section 130(4) of the Consumer Credit Act 1974 treated as a bailee or (in Scotland) a custodier of the vehicle.

(5) In this Part of this Act any reference to the title of the creditor to a motor vehicle which has been bailed or (in Scotland) hired under a hire-purchase agreement or agreed to be sold under a conditional sale agreement, and is disposed of by the debtor, is a reference to such title (if any) to the vehicle as, immediately before that disposition, was vested in the person who then was the creditor in relation to the agreement.]

MISREPRESENTATION ACT 1967
(1967, c. 7)

An Act to amend the law relating to innocent misrepresentations and to amend sections 11 and 35 of the Sale of Goods Act 1893. [22nd March 1967]

1. Removal of certain bars to rescission for innocent misrepresentation

Where a person has entered into a contract after a misrepresentation has been made to him, and—

(a) the misrepresentation has become a term of the contract, or

(b) the contract has been performed;

or both, then, if otherwise he would be entitled to rescind the contract without alleging fraud, he shall be so entitled, subject to the provisions of this Act, notwithstanding the matters mentioned in paragraphs (a) and (b) of this section.

2. Damages for misrepresentation

(1) Where a person has entered into a contract after a misrepresentation has been made to him by another party thereto and as a result thereof he has suffered loss, then, if the person making the misrepresentation would be liable to damages in respect thereof had the misrepresentation been made fraudulently, that person shall be so liable notwithstanding that the misrepresentation was not made fraudulently, unless he proves that he had reasonable ground to believe and did believe up to the time the contract was made that the facts represented were true.

(2) Where a person has entered into a contract after a misrepresentation has been made to him otherwise than fraudulently, and he would be entitled, by reason of the misrepresentation, to rescind the contract, then, if it is claimed, in any proceedings arising out of the contract, that the contract ought to be or has been rescinded, the court or arbitrator may declare the contract subsisting and award damages in lieu of rescission, if of opinion that it would be equitable to do so having regard to the nature of the misrepresentation and the loss that would be caused by it if the contract were upheld, as well as to the loss that rescission would cause to the other party.

(3) Damages may be awarded against a person under subsection (2) of this section whether or not he is liable to damages under subsection (1) thereof, but where he is so liable any award under the said subsection (2) shall be taken into account in assessing his liability under the said subsection (1).

3. Avoidance of provision excluding liability for misrepresentation

[If a contract contains a term which would exclude or restrict—

(a) any liability to which a party to a contract may be subject by reason of any misrepresentation made by him before the contract was made; or

(b) any remedy available to another party to the contract by reason of such a misrepresentation,

that term shall be of no effect except in so far as it satisfies the requirement of reasonableness as stated in section 11(1) of the Unfair Contract Terms Act 1977; and it is for those claiming that the term satisfies that requirement to show that it does.]

4. Amendments of Sale of Goods Act 1893

. . .

5. Saving for past transactions

Nothing in this Act shall apply in relation to any misrepresentation or contract of sale which is made before the commencement of this Act.

UNSOLICITED GOODS AND SERVICES ACT 1971
(1971, c. 30)

An Act to make provision for the greater protection of persons receiving unsolicited goods, and to amend the law with respect to charges for entries in directories. [12th May 1971]

1. Rights of recipient of unsolicited goods

(1) In the circumstances specified in the following subsection, a person who after the commencement of this Act receives unsolicited goods, may as between himself and the sender, use, deal with or dispose of them as if they were an unconditional gift to him, and any right of the sender to the goods shall be extinguished.

(2) The circumstances referred to in the preceding subsection are that the goods were sent to the recipient with a view to his acquiring them, that the recipient has no reasonable cause to believe that they were sent with a view to their being acquired for the purposes of a trade or business and has neither agreed to acquire nor agreed to return them, and either—

(a) that during the period of six months beginning with the day on which the recipient received the goods the sender did not take possession of them and the recipient did not unreasonably refuse to permit the sender to do so; or

(b) that not less than thirty days before the expiration of the period aforesaid the recipient gave notice to the sender in accordance with the following subsection, and that during the period of thirty days beginning with the day on which the notice was given the sender did not take possession of the goods and the recipient did not unreasonably refuse to permit the sender to do so.

(3) A notice in pursuance of the preceding subsection shall be in writing and shall—

(a) state the recipient's name and address and, if possession of the goods in question may not be taken by the sender at this address, the address at which it may be so taken;

(b) contain a statement, however expressed, that the goods are unsolicited, and may be sent by post.

(4) In this section 'sender', in relation to any goods, includes any person on whose behalf or with whose consent the goods are sent, and any other person claiming through or under the sender or any such person.

2. Demands and threats regarding payment

(1) A person who, not having reasonable cause to believe there is a right to payment, in the course of any trade or business makes a demand for payment, or asserts a present or prospective right to payment, for what he knows are unsolicited goods sent (after the commencement of this Act) to another person with a view to his acquiring them, shall be guilty of an offence and on summary conviction shall be liable to a fine not exceeding £200.

(2) A person who, not having reasonable cause to believe there is a right to payment in the course of any trade or business and with a view to obtaining any payment for what he knows are unsolicited goods sent as aforesaid—

(a) threatens to bring any legal proceedings; or

(b) places or causes to be placed the name of any person on a list of defaulters or debtors or threatens to do so; or

(c) invokes or causes to be invoked any other collection procedure or threatens to do so,

shall be guilty of an offence and shall be liable on summary conviction to a fine not exceeding £400.

3. Directory entries

(1) A person shall not be liable to make any payment, and shall be entitled to recover the payment made by him, by way of charge for including or arranging for the inclusion in a directory of an entry relating to that person or his trade or business, unless there has been signed by him or on his behalf an order complying with this section or a note complying with this section of his agreement to the charge and, in the case of a note of agreement to the charge, before the note was signed, a copy of it was supplied, for retention by him, to him or to a person acting on his behalf.

(2) A person shall be guilty of an offence punishable on summary conviction with a fine not exceeding £400 if, in a case where a payment in respect of a charge would, in the absence of an order or note of agreement to the charge complying with this section, be recoverable from him in accordance with the terms of subsection (1) above, he demands payment, or asserts a present or prospective right to payment, of the charge or any part of it, without knowing or having reasonable cause to believe that the entry to which the charge relates was ordered in accordance with this section or a proper note of agreement has been duly signed.

(3) For the purposes of subsection (1) above, an order for an entry in a directory must be made by means of an order form or other stationery belonging to the person to whom, or to whose trade or business, the entry is to relate and bearing, in print, the name and address (or one or more of the addresses) of that person; and the note required by this section of a person's agreement to a charge must state the amount of the charge immediately above the place for signature, and—

(a) must identify the directory or proposed directory, and give the following particulars of it—

(i) the proposed date of publication of the directory or of the issue in which the entry is to be included and the name and address of the person producing it;

(ii) if the directory or that issue is to be put on sale, the price at which it is to be offered for sale and the minimum number of copies which are to be available for sale;

(iii) if the directory or that issue is to be distributed free of charge (whether or not it is also to be put on sale), the minimum number of copies which are to be so distributed; and

(b) must set out or give reasonable particulars of the entry in respect of which the charge would be payable.

(4) Nothing in this section shall apply to a payment due under a contract entered into before the commencement of this Act, or entered into by the acceptance of an offer made before that commencement.

[3A. Contents and form of notes of agreement, invoices and similar documents

(1) For the purposes of this Act, the Secretary of State may make regulations as to the contents and form of notes of agreement, invoices and similar documents; and, without prejudice to the generality of the foregoing, any such regulations may—

(a) require specified information to be included,

(b) prescribe the manner in which specified information is to be included,

(c) prescribe such other requirements (whether as to presentation, type, size, colour or disposition of lettering, quality or colour of paper or otherwise) as the Secretary of State may consider appropriate for securing that specified information is clearly brought to the attention of the recipient of any note of agreement, invoice or similar document

(d) make different provision for different classes or descriptions of notes of agreement, invoices and similar documents or for the same class or description in different circumstances,

(e) contain such supplementary and incidental provisos as the Secretary of State may consider appropriate.

(2) Any reference in this section to a note of agreement includes any such copy as is mentioned in section 3(1) of this Act.

(3) Regulations under this section shall be made by statutory instrument and shall be subject to annulment in pursuance of a resolution of either House of Parliament.]

4. Unsolicited publications

(1) A person shall be guilty of an offence if he sends or causes to be sent to another person any book, magazine or leaflet (or advertising material for any such publication which he knows or ought reasonably to know is unsolicited and which describes or illustrates human sexual techniques.

(2) A person found guilty of an offence under this section shall be liable on summary conviction to a fine not exceeding £100 for a first offence and to a fine not exceeding £400 for any subsequent offence.

(3) A prosecution for an offence under this section shall not in England and Wales be instituted except by, or with the consent of, the Director of Public Prosecutions.

5. Offences by corporations

(1) Where an offence under this Act which has been committed by a body corporate is proved to have been committed with the consent or connivance of, or to be attributable to any neglect on the part of, any director, manager, secretary, or other similar officer of the body corporate, or of any person who was purporting to act in any such capacity, he as well as the body corporate shall be guilty of that offence and shall be liable to be proceeded against and punished accordingly.

(2) Where the affairs of a body corporate are managed by its members, this section shall apply in relation to the acts or defaults of a member in connection with his functions of management as if he were a director of the body corporate.

6. Interpretation

(1) In this Act, unless the context or subject matter otherwise requires,—

'acquire' includes hire;

'send' includes deliver, and 'sender' shall be construed accordingly;

'unsolicited' means, in relation to goods sent to any person, that they are sent without any prior request made by him or on his behalf.

[(2) For the purposes of this Act any invoice or similar document stating the amount of any payment and not complying with the requirements of regulations under section 3A of this Act applicable thereto shall be regarded as asserting a right to the payment.]

SUPPLY OF GOODS (IMPLIED TERMS) ACT 1973
(1973, c. 13)

An Act to amend the law with respect to the terms to be implied in contracts of sale of goods and hire-purchase agreements and on the exchange of goods for trading stamps, and with respect to the terms of conditional sale agreements; and for connected purposes.

[18th April 1973]

8. Implied terms as title

[(1) In every hire-purchase agreement, other than one to which subsection (2) below applies, there is—

(a) an implied term on the part of the creditor that he will have a right to sell the goods at the time when the property is to pass; and

(b) an implied term that—

(i) the goods are free, and will remain free until the time when the property is to pass, from any charge or encumbrance not disclosed or known to the person to whom the goods are bailed or (in Scotland) hired before the agreement is made, and

(ii) that person will enjoy quiet possession of the goods except so far as it may be disturbed by any person entitled to the benefit of any charge or encumbrance so disclosed or known.

(2) In a hire-purchase agreement, in the case of which there appears from the agreement or is to be inferred from the circumstances of the agreement an intention that the creditor should transfer only such title as he or a third person may have, there is—

(a) an implied term that all charges or encumbrances known to the creditor and not known to the person to whom the goods are bailed or hired have been disclosed to that person before the agreement is made; and

(b) an implied term that neither—

(i) the creditor; nor

(ii) in a case where the parties to the agreement intend that any title which may be transferred shall be only such title as a third person may have, that person; nor

(iii) anyone claiming through or under the creditor or that third person not otherwise than under a charge or encumbrance disclosed or known to the person to whom the goods are bailed or hired, before the agreement is made; will disturb the quiet possession of the person to whom the goods are bailed or hired.

(3) As regards England and Wales and Northern Ireland, the term implied by subsection (1)(a) above is a condition and the terms implied by subsections (1)(b), (2)(a) and (2)(b) above are warranties.]

9. Bailing or hiring by description

[(1) Where under a hire-purchase agreement goods are bailed or (in Scotland) hired by description, there is an implied term that the goods will correspond with the description, and if under the agreement the goods are bailed or hired by reference to a sample as well as a description, it is not sufficient that the bulk of the goods corresponds with the sample if the goods do not also correspond with the description.

(1A) As regards England and Wales and Northern Ireland, the term implied by subsection (1) above is a condition.

(2) Goods shall not be prevented from being bailed or hired by description by reason only that, being exposed for sale, bailment or hire, they are selected by the person to whom they are bailed or hired.]

10. Implied undertakings as to quality or fitness

[(1) Except as provided by this section and section 11 below and subject to the provisions of any other enactment, including any enactment of the Parliament of Northern Ireland or the Northern Ireland Assembly, there is no implied term as to the quality or fitness for any particular purpose of goods bailed or (in Scotland) hired under a hire-purchase agreement.

(2) Where the creditor bails or hires goods under a hire purchase agreement in the course of a business, there is an implied term that the goods supplied under the agreement are of satisfactory quality.

(2A) For the purposes of this Act, goods are of satisfactory quality if they meet the standard that a reasonable person would regard as satisfactory, taking account of any description of the goods, the price (if relevant) and all the other relevant circumstances.

(2B) For the purposes of this Act, the quality of goods includes their state and condition and the following (among others) are in appropriate cases aspects of the quality of goods—

(a) fitness for all the purposes for which goods of the kind in question are commonly supplied,

(b) appearance and finish.

(c) freedom from minor defects,

(d) safety, and

(e) durability.

(2C) The term implied by subsection (2) above does not extend to any matter making the quality of goods unsatisfactory—

(a) which is specifically drawn to the attention of the person to whom the goods are bailed or hired before the agreement is made,

(b) where that person examines the goods before the agreement is made, which that examination ought to reveal, or

(c) where the goods are bailed or hired by reference to a sample, which would have been apparent on a reasonable examination of the sample.

(3) Where the creditor bails or hires goods under a hire-purchase agreement in the course of a business and the person to whom the goods are bailed or hired, expressly or by implication, makes known—

(a) to the creditor in the course of negotiations conducted by the creditor in relation to the making of the hire-purchase agreement, or

(b) to a credit-broker in the course of negotiations conducted by that broker in relation to goods sold by him to the creditor before forming the subject matter of the hire-purchase agreement,

any particular purpose for which the goods are being bailed or hired, there is an implied term that the goods supplied under the agreement are reasonably fit for that purpose, whether or not that is a purpose for which such goods are commonly supplied, except where the circumstances show that the person to whom the goods are bailed or hired does not rely, or that it is unreasonable for him to rely, on the skill or judgment of the creditor or credit-broker.

(4) An implied term as to quality or fitness for a particular purpose may be annexed to a hire-purchase agreement by usage.

(5) The preceding provisions of this section apply to a hire-purchase agreement made by a person who in the course of a business is acting as agent for the creditor as they apply to an agreement made by the creditor in the course of a business, except where the creditor is not bailing or hiring in the course of a business and either the person to whom the goods are bailed or hired knows that fact or reasonable steps are taken to bring it to the notice of that person before the agreement is made.

(6) In subsection (3) above and this subsection—

(a) 'credit-broker' means a person acting in the course of a business of credit brokerage;

(b) 'credit brokerage' means the effecting of introductions of individuals desiring to obtain credit—

(i) to persons carrying on any business so far as it relates to the provision of credit, or

(ii) to other persons engaged in credit brokerage.

(7) As regards England and Wales and Northern Ireland, the terms implied by subsections (2) and (3) above are conditions.]

11. Samples

[(1) Where under a hire-purchase agreement goods are bailed or (in Scotland) hired by reference to a sample, there is an implied term—

(a) that the bulk will correspond with the sample in quality; and

(b) that the person to whom the goods are bailed or hired will have a reasonable opportunity of comparing the bulk with the sample; and

(c) that the goods will be free from any defect, making their quality unsatisfactory, which would not be apparent on reasonable examination of the sample.

(2) As regards England and Wales and Northern Ireland, the term implied by subsection (1) above is a condition.]

[11A. Modification of remedies for breach of statutory condition in non-consumer cases

(1) Where in the case of a hire purchase agreement—

(a) the person to whom goods are bailed would, apart from this subsection, have the right to reject them by reason of a breach on the part of the creditor of a term implied by section 9, 10 or 11(1)(a) or (c) above, but

(b) the breach is so slight that it would be unreasonable for him to reject them,

then, if the person to whom the goods are bailed does not deal as consumer, the breach is not to be treated as a breach of condition but may be treated as a breach of warranty.

(2) This section applies unless a contrary intention appears in, or is to be implied from, the agreement.

(3) It is for the creditor to show—

(a) that a breach fell within subsection (1)(b) above, and
(b) that the person to whom the goods were bailed did not deal as consumer.

(4) The references in this section to dealing as consumer are to be construed in accordance with Part I of the Unfair Contract Terms Act 1977.

(5) This section does not apply to Scotland.]

[12. Exclusion of implied terms

An express term does not negative a term implied by this Act unless inconsistent with it.]

[12A. Remedies for breach of hire-purchase agreements as respects Scotland . . .]

14. Special provisions as to conditional sale agreements

[(1) Section 11(4) of the Sale of Goods Act 1979 (whereby in certain circumstances a breach of a condition in a contract of sale is treated only as a breach of warranty) shall not apply to [a conditional sale agreement where the buyer deals as consumer within Part I of the Unfair Contract Terms Act 1977 . . .

(2) In England and Wales and Northern Ireland a breach of a condition (whether express or implied) to be fulfilled by the seller under any such agreement shall be treated as a breach of warranty, and not as grounds for rejecting the goods and treating the agreement as repudiated, if (but only if) it would have fallen to be so treated had the condition been contained or implied in a corresponding hire-purchase agreement as a condition to be fulfilled by the creditor.]

15. Supplementary

[(1) In sections 8 to 14 above and this section—

'business' includes a profession and the activities of any government department (including a Northern Ireland department), [or local or public authority];

'buyer' and 'seller' includes a person to whom rights and duties under a conditional sale agreement have passed by assignment or operation of law;

'conditional sale agreement' means an agreement for the sale of goods under which the purchase price or part of it is payable by instalments, and the property in the goods is to remain in the seller (notwithstanding that the buyer is to be in possession of the goods) until such conditions as to the payment of instalments or otherwise as may be specified in the agreement are fulfilled;

['consumer sale' has the same meaning as in section 5 5 of the Sale of Goods Act 1979 (as set out in paragraph 11 of Schedule 1 to that Act)];

'creditor' means the person by whom the goods are bailed or (in Scotland) hired under a hire-purchase agreement or the person to whom his rights and duties under the agreement have passed by assignment or operation of law; and

'hire-purchase agreement' means an agreement, other than conditional sale agreement, under which—

(a) goods are bailed or (in Scotland) hired in return for periodical payments by the person to whom they are bailed or hired, and

(b) the property in the goods will pass to that person if the terms of the agreement are complied with and one or more of the following occurs—

(i) the exercise of an option to purchase by that person,
(ii) the doing of any other specified act by any party to the agreement,
(iii) the happening of any other specified event.

(3) In section 14(2) above 'corresponding hire-purchase agreement' means, in relation to a conditional sale agreement, a hire-purchase agreement relating to the same goods as the conditional sale agreement and made between the same parties and at the same time and in the same circumstances and, as nearly as may be, in the same terms as the conditional sale agreement.

(4) Nothing in sections 8 to 13 above shall prejudice the operation of any other enactment including any enactment of the Parliament of Northern Ireland or the Northern Ireland Assembly or any rule of law whereby any term, other than one relating to quality or fitness, is to be implied in any hire-purchase agreement.]

CONSUMER CREDIT ACT 1974
(1974, c. 39)

An Act to establish for the protection of consumers a new system, administered by the Director General of Fair Trading, of licensing and other control of traders concerned with the provision of credit, or the supply of goods on hire or hire-purchase, and their transactions, in place of the present enactments regulating moneylenders, pawnbrokers and hire-purchase traders and their transactions; and for related matters. [31st July 1974]

PART I
DIRECTOR GENERAL OF FAIR TRADING

1. General functions of Director

(1) It is the duty of the Director General of Fair Trading ('the Director')—

(a) to administer the licensing system set up by this Act,

(b) to exercise the adjudicating functions conferred on him by this Act in relation to the issue, renewal, variation, suspension and revocation of licences, and other matters,

(c) generally to superintend the working and enforcement of this Act, and regulations made under it, and

(d) where necessary or expedient, himself to take steps to enforce this Act, and regulations so made.

(2) It is the duty of the Director, so far as appears to him to be practicable and having regard both to the national interest and the interests of persons carrying on businesses to which this Act applies and their customers, to keep under review and from time to time advise the Secretary of State about—

(a) social and commercial developments in the United Kingdom and elsewhere relating to the provision of credit or bailment or (in Scotland) hiring of goods to individuals, and related activities; and

(b) the working and enforcement of this Act and orders and regulations made under it.

2. Powers of Secretary of State

(1) The Secretary of State may by order—

(a) confer on the Director additional functions concerning the provision of credit or bailment or (in Scotland) hiring of goods to individuals, and related activities, and

(b) regulate the carrying out by the Director of his functions under this Act.

(2) The Secretary of State may give general directions indicating considerations to which the Director should have particular regard in carrying out his functions under this Act, and may give specific directions on any matter connected with the carrying out by the Director of those functions.

(3) The Secretary of State, on giving any directions under subsection (2), shall arrange for them to be published in such manner as he thinks most suitable for drawing them to the attention of interested persons.

(4) With the approval of the Secretary of State and the Treasury, the Director may charge, for any service or facility provided by him under this Act, a fee of an amount specified by general notice (the 'specified fee').

(5) Provision may be made under subsection (4) for reduced fees, or no fees at all, to be paid for certain services or facilities by persons of a specified description, and references in this Act to the specified fee shall, in such cases, be construed accordingly.

(6) An order under subsection (1)(a) shall be made by statutory instrument and shall be of no effect unless a draft of the order has been laid before and approved by each House of Parliament.

(7) References in subsection (2) to the functions of the Director under this Act do not include the making of a determination to which section 41 or 150 (appeals from Director to Secretary of State) applies.

4. Dissemination of information and advice

The Director shall arrange for the dissemination, in such form and manner as he considers appropriate, of such information and advice as it may appear to him expedient to give to the public in the United Kingdom about the operation of this Act, the credit facilities available to them, and other matters within the scope of his functions under this Act.

5. Annual and other reports

. . .

6. Form etc. of applications

(1) An application to the Director under this Act is of no effect unless the requirements of this section are satisfied.

(2) The application must be in writing, and in such form, and accompanied by such particulars, as the Director may specify by general notice, and must be accompanied by the specified fee.

(3) After giving preliminary consideration to an application, the Director may by notice require the applicant to furnish him with such further information relevant to the application as may be described in the notice, and may require any information furnished by the applicant (whether at the time of the application or subsequently) to be verified in such manner as the Director may stipulate.

(4) The Director may by notice require the applicant to publish details of his application at a time or times and in a manner specified in the notice.

7. Penalty for false information

A person who, in connection with any application or request to the Director under this Act, or in response to any invitation or requirement of the Director under this Act, knowingly or recklessly gives information to the Director which, in a material particular, is false or misleading, commits an offence.

PART II
CREDIT AGREEMENTS, HIRE AGREEMENTS AND
LINKED TRANSACTIONS

8. Consumer credit agreements

(1) A personal credit agreement is an agreement between an individual ('the debtor') and any other person ('the creditor') by which the creditor provides the debtor with credit of any amount.

(2) A consumer credit agreement is a personal credit agreement by which the creditor provides the debtor with credit not exceeding [£25,000].

(3) A consumer credit agreement is a regulated agreement within the meaning of this Act if it is not an agreement (an 'exempt agreement') specified in or under section 16.

9. Meaning of credit

(1) In this Act 'credit' includes a cash loan, and any other form of financial accommodation.

(2) Where credit is provided otherwise than in sterling it shall be treated for the purposes of this Act as provided in sterling of an equivalent amount.

(3) Without prejudice to the generality of subsection (1), the person by whom goods are bailed or (in Scotland) hired to an individual under a hire-purchase agreement shall be taken to provide him with fixed-sum credit to finance the transaction of an amount equal to the total price of the goods less the aggregate of the deposit (if any) and the total charge for credit.

(4) For the purposes of this Act, an item entering into the total charge for credit shall not be treated as credit even though time is allowed for its payment.

10. Running-account credit and fixed-sum credit

(1) For the purposes of this Act—

(a) running-account credit is a facility under a personal credit agreement whereby the debtor is enabled to receive from time to time (whether in his own person, or by another person) from the creditor or a third party cash, goods and services (or any of them) to an amount or value such that, taking into account payments made by or to the credit of the debtor, the credit limit (if any) is not at any time exceeded; and

(b) fixed-sum credit is any other facility under a personal credit agreement whereby the debtor is enabled to receive credit (whether in one amount or by instalments).

(2) In relation to running-account credit, 'credit limit' means, as respects any period, the maximum debit balance which, under the credit agreement, is allowed to stand on the

account during that period, disregarding any term of the agreement allowing that maximum to be exceeded merely temporarily.

(3) For the purposes of section 8(2), running-account credit shall be taken not to exceed the amount specified in that subsection ('the specified amount') if—

(a) the credit limit does not exceed the specified amount; or

(b) whether or not there is a credit limit, and if there is, notwithstanding that it exceeds the specified amount,—

(i) the debtor is not enabled to draw at any one time an amount which, so far as (having regard to section 9(4)) it represents credit, exceeds the specified amount, or

(ii) the agreement provides that, if the debit balance rises above a given amount (not exceeding the specified amount), the rate of the total charge for credit increases or any other condition favouring the creditor or his associate comes into operation, or

(iii) at the time the agreement is made it is probable, having regard to the terms of the agreement and any other relevant considerations, that the debit balance will not at any time rise above the specified amount.

11. Restricted-use credit and unrestricted-use credit

(1) A restricted-use credit agreement is a regulated consumer credit agreement—

(a) to finance a transaction between the debtor and the creditor, whether forming part of that agreement or not, or

(b) to finance a transaction between the debtor and a person (the 'supplier') other than the creditor, or

(c) to refinance any existing indebtedness of the debtor's, whether to the creditor or another person, and 'restricted-use credit' shall be construed accordingly.

(2) An unrestricted-use credit agreement is a regulated consumer credit agreement not falling within subsection (1), and 'unrestricted-use credit' shall be construed accordingly.

(3) An agreement does not fall within subsection (1) if the credit is in fact provided in such a way as to leave the debtor free to use it as he chooses, even though certain uses would contravene that or any other agreement.

(4) An agreement may fall within subsection (1)(b) although the identity of the supplier is unknown at the time the agreement is made.

12. Debtor-creditor supplier agreements

A debtor-creditor-supplier agreement is a regulated consumer credit agreement being—

(a) a restricted-use credit agreement which falls within section 11(1)(a), or

(b) a restricted-use credit agreement which falls within section 11(1)(b) and is made by the creditor under pre-existing arrangements, or in contemplation of future arrangements, between himself and the supplier, or

(c) an unrestricted-use credit agreement which is made by the creditor under pre-existing arrangements between himself and a person (the 'supplier') other than the debtor in the knowledge that the credit is to be used to finance a transaction between the debtor and the supplier.

13. Debtor-creditor agreements

A debtor-creditor agreement is a regulated consumer credit agreement being—

(a) a restricted-use credit agreement which falls within section 11(1)(b) but is not made by the creditor under pre-existing arrangements, or in contemplation of future arrangements, between himself and the supplier, or

(b) a restricted-use credit agreement which falls within section 11(1)(c), or

(c) an unrestricted-use credit agreement which is not made by the creditor under pre-existing arrangements between himself and a person (the 'supplier') other than the debtor in the knowledge that the credit is to be used to finance a transaction between the debtor and the supplier.

14. Credit-token agreements

(1) A credit-token is a card, check, voucher, coupon, stamp, form, booklet or other document or thing given to an individual by a person carrying on a consumer credit business, who undertakes—

(a) that on the production of it (whether or not some other action is also required) he will supply cash, goods and services (or any of them) on credit, or

(b) that where, on the production of it to a third party (whether or not any other action is also required), the third party supplies cash, goods and services (or any of them), he will pay the third party for them (whether or not deducting any discount or commission), in return for payment to him by the individual.

(2) A credit-token agreement is a regulated agreement for the provision of credit in connection with the use of a credit-token.

(3) Without prejudice to the generality of section 9(1), the person who gives to an individual an undertaking falling within subsection (1)(b) shall be taken to provide him with credit drawn on whenever a third party supplies him with cash, goods or services.

(4) For the purposes of subsection (1), use of an object to operate a machine provided by the person giving the object or a third party shall be treated as the production of the object to him.

15. Consumer hire agreements

(1) A consumer hire agreement is an agreement made by a person with an individual (the 'hirer') for the bailment or (in Scotland) the hiring of goods to the hirer, being an agreement which—

(a) is not a hire-purchase agreement, and

(b) is capable of subsisting for more than three months, and

(c) does not require the hirer to make payments exceeding [£25,000].

(2) A consumer hire agreement is a regulated agreement if it is not an exempt agreement.

16. Exempt agreements

(1) This Act does not regulate a consumer credit agreement where the creditor is a local authority [. . .], or a body specified, or of a description specified, in an order made by the Secretary of State, being—

(a) an insurance company,

(b) a friendly society,

(c) an organisation of employers or organisation of workers,

(d) a charity,

(e) a land improvement company, or

(f) a body corporate named or specifically referred to in any public general Act.

[(ff) a body corporate named or specifically referred to in an order made under—
section 156(4) or 447(2)(a) of the Housing Act 1985,
section 156(4) of that Act as it has effect by virtue of section 17 of the Housing Act 1996 (the right to acquire),
section 223 or 229 of the Housing (Scotland) Act 1987, or
Article 154(1)(a) or 156AA of the Housing (Northern Ireland) Order 1981
or Article 10(6A) of the Housing (Northern Ireland) Order 1983; or

(g) a building society, or

(h) an authorised institution or wholly-owned subsidiary (within the meaning of the Companies Act 1985) of such an institution.]

(2) Subsection (1) applies only where the agreement is—

(a) a debtor-creditor-supplier agreement financing—

(i) the purchase of land, or

(ii) the provision of dwellings on any land, and secured by a land mortgage on that land; or

(b) a debtor-creditor agreement secured by any land mortgage; or

(c) a debtor-creditor-supplier agreement financing a transaction which is a linked transaction in relation to—

(i) an agreement falling within paragraph (a), or

(ii) an agreement failing within paragraph (b) financing—

(aa) the purchase of any land, or

(bb) the provision of dwellings on any land, and secured by a land mortgage on the land referred to in paragraph (a) or, as the case may be, the land referred to in sub-paragraph (ii).

(3) The Secretary of State shall not make, vary or revoke an order—

(a) under subsection (1)(a) without consulting the Minister of the Crown responsible for insurance companies,

(b) under subsection (1)(b) [. . .] without consulting the Chief Registrar of Friendly Societies,

(c) under subsection (1)(d) without consulting the Charity Commissioners, or

(d) under subsection (1)(e), [(f) or (ff)] without consulting any Minister of the Crown with responsibilities concerning the body in question, [or

(e) under subsection (1)(g) without consulting the Building Societies Commission and the Treasury, or

(f) under sub-section (1)(h) without consulting the Treasury and the Financial Services Authority.]

(4) An order under subsection (1) relating to a body may be limited so as to apply only to agreements by that body of a description specified in the order.

(5) The Secretary of State may by order provide that this Act shall not regulate other consumer credit agreements where—

(a) the number of payments to be made by the debtor does not exceed the number specified for that purpose in the order, or

(b) the rate of the total charge for credit does not exceed the rate so specified, or

(c) an agreement has a connection with a country outside the United Kingdom.

(6) The Secretary of State may by order provide that this Act shall not regulate consumer hire agreements of a description specified in the order where—

(a) the owner is a body corporate authorised by or under any enactment to supply electricity, gas or water, and

(b) the subject of the agreement is a meter or metering equipment

[or where the owner is a public telecommunications office specified in the order].

[(6A) This Act does not regulate a consumer credit agreement where the creditor is a housing authority and the agreement is secured by a land mortgage of a dwelling.

(6B) In subsection (6A) 'housing authority' means—

(a) as regards England and Wales, the Housing Corporation, . . . and an authority or body within section 80(1) of the Housing Act 1985 (the landlord condition for secure tenancies), other than a housing association or a housing trust which is a charity;

(b) as regards Scotland, a development corporation established under an order made, or having effect as if made under the New Towns (Scotland) Act 1968, the Scottish Special Housing Association or the Housing Corporation;

(c) as regards Northern Ireland, the Northern Ireland Housing Executive.]

(7) Nothing in this section affects the application of sections 137 to 140 (extortionate credit bargains).

(8) In the application of this section to Scotland subsection (3)(c) shall not have effect.

(9) In the application of this section to Northern Ireland subsection (3) shall have effect as if any reference to a Minister of the Crown were a reference to a Northern Ireland department, any reference to the Chief Registrar of Friendly Societies were a reference to the Registrar of Friendly Societies for Northern Ireland, and any reference to the Charity Commissioners were a reference to the Department of Finance for Northern Ireland.

17. Small agreements

(1) A small agreement is—

(a) a regulated consumer credit agreement for credit not exceeding [£50], other than a hire-purchase or conditional sale agreement; or

(b) a regulated consumer hire agreement which does not require the hirer to make payments exceeding [£50],

being an agreement which is either unsecured or secured by a guarantee or indemnity only (whether or not the guarantee or indemnity is itself secured).

(2) Section 10(3)(a) applies for the purposes of subsection (1) as it applies for the purposes of section 8(2).

(3) Where—

(a) two or more small agreements are made at or about the same time between the same parties, and

(b) it appears probable that they would instead have been made as a single agreement but for the desire to avoid the operation of provisions of this Act which would have applied to that single agreement but, apart from this subsection, are not applicable to the small agreements,

this Act applies to the small agreements as if they were regulated agreements other than small agreements.

(4) If, apart from this subsection, subsection (3) does not apply to any agreements but would apply if, for any party or parties to any of the agreements, there were substituted an associate of that party, or associates of each of those parties, as the case may be, then subsection (3) shall apply to the agreements.

18. Multiple agreements

(1) This section applies to an agreement (a 'multiple agreement') if its terms are such as—

(a) to place a part of it within one category of agreement mentioned in this Act, and another part of it within a different category of agreement so mentioned, or within a category of agreement not so mentioned, or

(b) to place it, or a part of it, within two or more categories of agreement so mentioned.

(2) Where a part of an agreement falls within subsection (1), that part shall be treated for the purposes of this Act as a separate agreement.

(3) Where an agreement falls within subsection (1)(b), it shall be treated as an agreement in each of the categories in question, and this Act shall apply to it accordingly.

(4) Where under subsection (2) a part of a multiple agreement is to be treated as a separate agreement, the multiple agreement shall (with any necessary modifications) be construed accordingly; and any sum payable under the multiple agreement, if not apportioned by the parties, shall for the purposes of proceedings in any court relating to the multiple agreement be apportioned by the court as may be requisite.

(5) In the case of an agreement for running-account credit, a term of the agreement allowing the credit limit to be exceeded merely temporarily shall not be treated as a separate agreement or as providing fixed-sum credit in respect of the excess.

(6) This Act does not apply to a multiple agreement so far as the agreement relates to goods if under the agreement payments are to be made in respect of the goods in the form of rent (other than a rentcharge) issuing out of land.

19. Linked transactions

(1) A transaction entered into by the debtor or hirer, or a relative of his, with any other person ('the other party'), except one for the provision of security, is a linked transaction in relation to an actual or prospective regulated agreement (the 'principal agreement') of which it does not form part if—

(a) the transaction is entered into in compliance with a term of the principal agreement; or

(b) the principal agreement is a debtor-creditor-supplier agreement and the transaction is financed, or to be financed, by the principal agreement; or

(c) the other party is a person mentioned in subsection (2), and a person so mentioned initiated the transaction by suggesting it to the debtor or hirer, or his relative, who enters into it—

(i) to induce the creditor or owner to enter into the principal agreement, or

(ii) for another purpose related to the principal agreement, or

(iii) where the principal agreement is a restricted-use credit agreement, for a purpose related to a transaction financed, or to be financed, by the principal agreement.

(2) The persons referred to in subsection (1)(c) are—

(a) the creditor or owner, or his associate;

(b) a person who, in the negotiation of the transaction, is represented by a credit-broker who is also a negotiator in antecedent negotiations for the principal agreement;

(c) a person who, at the time the transaction is initiated, knows that the principal agreement has been made or contemplates that it might be made.

(3) A linked transaction entered into before the making of the principal agreement has no effect until such time (if any) as that agreement is made.

(4) Regulations may exclude linked transactions of the prescribed description from the operation of subsection (3).

20. Total charge for credit

(1) The Secretary of State shall make regulations containing such provisions as appear to him appropriate for determining the true cost to the debtor of the credit provided or to be provided under an actual or prospective consumer credit agreement (the 'total charge for credit'), and regulations so made shall prescribe—

(a) what items are to be treated as entering into the total charge for credit, and how their amount is to be ascertained;

(b) the method of calculating the rate of the total charge for credit.

(2) Regulations under subsection (1) may provide for the whole or part of the amount payable by the debtor or his relative under any linked transaction to be included in the total charge for credit, whether or not the creditor is a party to the transaction or derives benefit from it.

PART III
LICENSING OF CREDIT AND HIRE BUSINESSES

Licensing principles

21. Businesses needing a licence

(1) Subject to this section, a licence is required to carry on a consumer credit business or consumer hire business.

(2) A local authority does not need a licence to carry on a business.

(3) A body corporate empowered by a public general Act naming it to carry on a business does not need a licence to do so.

22. Standard and group licences

(1) A licence may be—

(a) a standard licence, that is a licence, issued by the Director to a person named in the licence on an application made by him, which, during the prescribed period, covers such activities as are described in the licence, or

(b) a group licence, that is a licence, issued by the Director (whether on the application of any person or of his own motion), which, during such period as the Director thinks fit or, if he thinks fit, indefinitely, covers such persons and activities as are described in the licence.

(2) A licence is not assignable or, subject to section 37, transmissible on death or in any other way.

(3) Except in the case of a partnership or an unincorporated body of persons, a standard licence shall not be issued to more than one person.

(4) A standard licence issued to a partnership or an unincorporated body of persons shall be issued in the name of the partnership or body.

(5) The Director may issue a group licence only if it appears to him that the public interest is better served by doing so than by obliging the persons concerned to apply separately for standard licences.

(6) The persons covered by a group licence may be described by general words, whether or not coupled with the exclusion of named persons, or in any other way the Director thinks fit.

(7) The fact that a person is covered by a group licence in respect of certain activities does not prevent a standard licence being issued to him in respect of those activities or any of them.

(8) A group licence issued on the application of any person shall be issued to that person, and general notice shall be given of the issue of any group licence (whether on application or not).

23. Authorisation of specific activities

(1) Subject to this section, a licence to carry on a business covers all lawful activities done in the course of that business, whether by the licensee or other persons on his behalf.

(2) A licence may limit the activities it covers, whether by authorising the licensee to enter into certain types of agreement only, or in any other way.

(3) A licence covers the canvassing off trade premises of debtor-creditor-supplier agreements or regulated consumer hire agreements only if, and to the extent that, the licence specifically so provides; and such provision shall not be included in a group licence.

(4) Regulations may be made specifying other activities which, if engaged in by or on behalf of the person carrying on a business, require to be covered by an express term in his licence.

24. Control of name of business

A standard licence authorises the licensee to carry on a business under the name or names specified in the licence, but not under any other name.

25. Licensee to be a fit person

(1) A standard licence shall be granted on the application of any person if he satisfies the Director that—

(a) he is a fit person to engage in activities covered by the licence, and

(b) the name or names under which he applies to be licensed is or are not misleading or otherwise undesirable.

(2) In determining whether an applicant for a standard licence is a fit person to engage in any activities, the Director shall have regard to any circumstances appearing to him to be relevant, and in particular any evidence tending to show that the applicant, or any of the applicant's employees, agents or associates (whether past or present) or, where the applicant is a body corporate, any person appearing to the Director to be a controller of the body corporate or an associate of any such person, has—

(a) committed any offence involving fraud or other dishonesty, or violence,

(b) contravened any provision made by or under this Act, or by or under any other enactment regulating the provision of credit to individuals or other transactions with individuals,

(c) practised discrimination on grounds of sex, colour, race or ethnic or national origins in, or in connection with, the carrying on of any business, or

(d) engaged in business practices appearing to the Director to be deceitful or oppressive, or otherwise unfair or improper (whether unlawful or not).

(3) In subsection (2), 'associate', in addition to the persons specified in section 184, includes a business associate.

26. Conduct of business

Regulations may be made as to the conduct by a licensee of his business, and may in particular specify—

(a) the books and other records to be kept by him, and

(b) the information to be furnished by him to persons with whom he does business or seeks to do business, and the way it is to be furnished.

Issue of licences

27. Determination of applications

(1) Unless the Director determines to issue a licence in accordance with an application he shall, before determining the application, by notice—

(a) inform the applicant, giving his reasons, that, as the case may be, he is minded to refuse the application, or to grant it in terms different from those applied for, describing them, and

(b) invite the applicant to submit to the Director representations in support of his application in accordance with section 34.

(2) If the Director grants the application in terms different from those applied for then, whether or not the applicant appeals, the Director shall issue the licence in the terms approved by him unless the applicant by notice informs him that he does not desire a licence in those terms.

28. Exclusion from group licence

Where the Director is minded to issue a group licence (whether on the application of any person or not), and in doing so to exclude any person from the group by name, he shall, before determining the matter,—

(a) give notice of that fact to the person proposed to be excluded, giving his reasons, and
(b) invite that person to submit to the Director representations against his exclusion in accordance with section 34.

Renewal, variation, suspension and revocation of licences

29. Renewal

(1) If the licensee under a standard licence, or the original applicant for, or any licensee under, a group licence of limited duration, wishes the Director to renew the licence, whether on the same terms (except as to expiry) or on varied terms, he must, during the period specified by the Director by general notice or such longer period as the Director may allow, make an application to the Director for its renewal.

(2) The Director may of his own motion renew any group licence.

(3) The preceding provisions of this Part apply to the renewal of a licence as they apply to the issue of a licence, except that section 28 does not apply to a person who was already excluded in the licence up for renewal.

(4) Until the determination of an application under subsection (1) and, where an appeal lies from the determination, until the end of the appeal period, the licence shall continue in force, notwithstanding that apart from this subsection it would expire earlier.

(5) On the refusal of an application under this section, the Director may give directions authorising a licensee to carry into effect agreements made by him before the expiry of the licence.

(6) General notice shall be given of the renewal of a group licence.

30. Variation by request

(1) On an application made by the licensee, the Director may if he thinks fit by notice to the licensee vary a standard licence in accordance with the application.

(2) In the case of a group licence issued on the application of any person, the Director, on an application made by that person, may if he thinks fit by notice to that person vary the terms of the licence in accordance with the application; but the Director shall not vary a group licence under this subsection by excluding a named person, other than the person making the request, unless that named person consents in writing to his exclusion.

(3) In the case of a group licence from which (whether by name or description) a person is excluded, the Director, on an application made by that person, may if he thinks fit, by notice to that person, vary the terms of the licence so as to remove the exclusion.

(4) Unless the Director determines to vary a licence in accordance with an application he shall, before determining the application, by notice—

(a) inform the applicant, giving his reasons, that he is minded to refuse the application, and

(b) invite the applicant to submit to the Director representations in suppprt of his application in accordance with section 34.

(5) General notice shall be given that a variation of a group licence has been made under this section.

31. Compulsory variation

(1) Where at a time during the currency of a licence the Director is of the opinion that, if the licence had expired at that time, he would on an application for its renewal or futher renewal on the same terms (except as to expiry), have been minded to grant the application but on different terms, and that therefore the licence should be varied, he shall proceed as follows.

(2) In the case of a standard licence the Director shall, by notice—

(a) inform the licensee of the variations the Director is minded to make in the terms of the licence, stating his reasons, and

(b) invite him to submit to the Director representations as to the proposed variations in accordance with section 34.

(3) In the case of a group licence the Director shall—

(a) give general notice of the variations he is minded to make in the terms of the licence, stating his reasons, and

(b) in the notice invite any licensee to submit to him representations as to the proposed variations in accordance with section 34.

(4) In the case of a group licence issued on application the Director shall also—

(a) inform the original applicant of the variations the Director is minded to make in the terms of the licence, stating his reasons, and

(b) invite him to submit to the Director representations as to the proposed variations in accordance with section 34.

(5) If the Director is minded to vary a group licence by excluding any person (other than the original applicant) from the group by name the Director shall, in addition, take the like steps under section 28 as are required in the case mentioned in that section.

(6) General notice shall be given that a variation of any group licence has been made under this section.

(7) A variation under this section shall not take effect before the end of the appeal period.

32. Suspension and revocation

(1) Where at a time during the currency of a licence the Director is of the opinion that if the licence had expired at that time he would have been minded not to renew it, and that therefore it should be revoked or suspended, he shall proceed as follows.

(2) In the case of a standard licence the Director shall, by notice—

(a) inform the licensee that, as the case may be, the Director is minded to revoke the licence, or suspend it until a specified date or indefinitely, stating his reasons, and

(b) invite him to submit representations as to the proposed revocation or suspension in accordance with section 34.

(3) In the case of a group licence the Director shall—

(a) give general notice that, as the case may be, he is minded to revoke the licence, or suspend it until a specified date or indefinitely, stating his reasons, and

(b) in the notice invite any licensee to submit to him representations as to the proposed revocation or suspension in accordance with section 34.

(4) In the case of a group licence issued on application the Director shall also—

(a) inform the original applicant that, as the case may be, the Director is minded to revoke the licence, or suspend it until a specified date or indefinitely, stating his reasons, and

(b) invite him to submit representations as to the proposed revocation or suspension in accordance with section 34.

(5) If he revokes or suspends the licence, the Director may give directions authorising a licensee to carry into effect agreements made by him before the revocation or suspension.

(6) General notice shall be given of the revocation or suspension of a group licence.

(7) A revocation or suspension under this section shall not take effect before the end of the appeal period.

(8) Except for the purposes of section 29, a licensee under a suspended licence shall be treated, in respect of the period of suspension, as if the licence had not been issued; and where the suspension is not expressed to end on a specified date it may, if the Director thinks fit, be ended by notice given by him to the licensee or, in the case of a group licence, by general notice.

33. Application to end suspension

(1) On an application made by a licensee the Director may, if he thinks fit, by notice to the licensee end the suspension of a licence, whether the suspension was for a fixed or indefinite period.

(2) Unless the Director determines to end the suspension in accordance with the application he shall, before determining the application, by notice—

(a) inform the applicant, giving his reasons, that he is minded to refuse the application, and

(b) invite the applicant to submit to the Director representations in support of his application in accordance with section 34.

(3) General notice shall be given that a suspension of a group licence has been ended under this section.

(4) In the case of a group licence issued on application

(a) the references in subsection (1) to a licensee include the original applicant;

(b) the Director shall inform the original applicant that a suspension of a group licence has been ended under this section.

Miscellaneous

34. Representations to Director

(1) Where this section applies to an invitation by the Director to any person to submit representations, the Director shall invite that person, within 21 days after the notice containing the invitation is given to him or published, or such longer period as the Director may allow—

(a) to submit his representations in writing to the Director, and

(b) to give notice to the Director, if he thinks fit, that he wishes to make representations orally,

and where notice is given under paragraph (b) the Director shall arrange for the oral representations to be heard.

(2) In reaching his determination the Director shall take into account any representations submitted or made under this section.

(3) The Director shall give notice of his determination to the persons who were required to be invited to submit representations about it or, where the invitation to submit representations was required to be given by general notice, shall give general notice of the determination.

35. The register

(1) The Director shall establish and maintain a register, in which he shall cause to be kept particulars of—

(a) applications not yet determined for the issue, variation or renewal of licences, or for ending the suspension of a licence;

(b) licences which are in force, or have at any time been suspended or revoked, with details of any variation of the terms of a licence;

(c) decisions given by him under this Act, and any appeal from those decisions; and

(d) such other matters (if any) as he thinks fit.

(2) The Director shall give general notice of the various matters required to be entered in the register, and of any change in them made under subsection (1)(d).

(3) Any person shall be entitled on payment of the specified fee—

(a) to inspect the register during ordinary office hours and take copies of any entry, or

(b) to obtain from the Director a copy, certified by the Director to be correct, of any entry in the register.

(4) The Director may, if he thinks fit, determine that the right conferred by subsection (3)(a) shall be exercisable in relation to a copy of the register instead of, or in addition to, the original.

(5) The Director shall give general notice of the place or places where, and times when, the register or a copy of it may be inspected.

36. Duty to notify changes

(1) Within 21 working days after change takes place in any particulars entered in the register in respect of a standard licence or the licensee under section 35(1)(d) (not being a change resulting from action taken by the Director), the licensee shall give the Director notice of the change; and the Director shall cause any necessary amendment to be made in the register.

(2) Within 21 working days after—

(a) any change takes place in the officers of—

(i) a body corporate, or an unincorporated body of persons, which is the licensee under a standard licence, or

(ii) a body corporate which is a controller of a body corporate which is such a Licensee, or

(b) a body corporate which is such a licensee becomes aware that a person has become or ceased to be a controller of the body corporate, or

(c) any change takes place in the members of a partnership which is such a licensee (including a change on the amalgamation of the partnership with another firm, or a change whereby the number of partners is reduced to one), the licensee shall give the Director notice of the change.

(3) Within 14 working days after any change takes place in the officers of a body corporate which is a controller of another body corporate which is a licensee under a standard licence, the controller shall give the licensee notice of the change.

(4) Within 14 working days after a person becomes or ceases to be a controller of a body corporate which is a licensee under a standard licence, that person shall give the licensee notice of the fact.

(5) Where a change in a partnership has the result that the business ceases to be carried on under the name, or any of the names, specified in a standard licence the licence shall cease to have effect.

(6) Where the Director is given notice under sub-section (1) or (2) of any change, and subsection (5) does not apply, the Director may by notice require the licensee to furnish him with such information, verified in such manner, as the Director may stipulate.

37. Death, bankruptcy etc. of licensee

(1) A licence held by one individual terminates if he—

(a) dies, or

(b) is adjudged bankrupt, or

(c) becomes a patient within the meaning of Part VIII of the Mental Health Act 1959.

(2) In relation to a licence held by one individual, or a partnership or other unincorporated body of persons, or a body corporate, regulations may specify other events relating to the licensee on the occurrence of which the licence is to terminate.

(3) Regulations may—

(a) provide for the termination of a licence by subsection (1), or under subsection (2), to be deferred for a period not exceeding 12 months, and

(b) authorise the business of the licensee to be carried on under the licence by some other person during the period of deferment, subject to such conditions as may be prescribed.

(4) This section does not apply to group licences.

38. Application of s. 37 to Scotland and Northern Ireland

. . .

39. Offences against Part III

(1) A person who engages in any activities for which a licence is required when he is not a licensee under a licence covering those activities commits an offence.

(2) A licensee under a standard licence who carries on business under a name not specified in the licence commits an offence.

(3) A person who fails to give the Director or a licensee notice under section 36 within the period required commits an offence.

40. Enforcement of agreements made by unlicensed trader

(1) A regulated agreement, other than a non-commercial agreement, if made when the creditor or owner was unlicensed, is enforceable against the debtor or hirer only where the Director has made an order under this section which applies to the agreement.

(2) Where during any period an unlicensed person (the 'trader') was carrying on a consumer credit business or consumer hire business, he or his successor in title may apply to the Director for an order that regulated agreements made by the trader during that period are to be treated as if he had been licensed.

(3) Unless the Director determines to make an order under subsection (2) in accordance with the application, he shall, before determining the application, by notice—

(a) inform the applicant, giving his reasons, that, as the case may be, he is minded to refuse the application, or to grant it in terms different from those applied for, describing them, and

(b) invite the applicant to submit to the Director representations in support of his application in accordance with section 34.

(4) In determining whether or not to make an order under subsection (2) in respect of any period the Director shall consider, in addition to any other relevant factors—

(a) how far, if at all, debtors or hirers under regulated agreements made by the trader during that period were prejudiced by the trader's conduct,

(b) whether or not the Director would have been likely to grant a licence covering that period on an application by the trader, and

(c) the degree of culpability for the failure to obtain a licence.

(5) If the Director thinks fit, he may in an order under subsection (2)—

(a) limit the order to specified agreements, or agreements of a specified description or made at a specified time;

(b) make the order conditional on the doing of specified acts by the applicant.

41. Appeals to Secretary of State under Part III

(1) If, in the case of a determination by the Director such as is mentioned in column 1 of the table set out at the end of this section, a person mentioned in relation to that determination in column 2 of the table is aggrieved by the determination he may, within the prescribed period, and in the prescribed manner, appeal to the Secretary of State.

(2) Regulations may make provision as to the persons by whom (on behalf of the Secretary of State) appeals under this section are to be heard, the manner in which they are to be conducted, and any other matter connected with such appeals.

(3) On an appeal under this section, the Secretary of State may give such directions for disposing of the appeal as he thinks just, including a direction for the payment of costs by any party to the appeal.

(4) A direction under subsection (3) for payment of costs may be made a rule of the High Court on the application of the party in whose favour it is given.

(5) in Scotland a direction under subsection (3) for payment of expenses may be enforced in like manner as a recorded decree arbitral.

TABLE

Determination	*Appellant*
Refusal to issue, renew or vary licence in accordance with terms of application.	The applicant.
Exclusion of person from group licence.	The person excluded.
Refusal to give directions in respect of a licensee under section 29(5) or 32(5).	The licensee.
Determination	*Appellant*
Compulsory variation, or suspension or revocation, of standard licence.	The licensee.
Compulsory variation, or suspension or revocation, of group licence.	The original applicant or any licensee.
Refusal to end suspension of licence in accordance with terms of application.	The applicant.
Refusal to make order under section 40(2) in accordance with terms of application.	The applicant.

PART IV
SEEKING BUSINESS

Advertising

43. Advertisements to which Part IV applies

(1) This Part applies to any advertisement, published for the purposes of a carried on by the advertiser, indicating that he is willing—

(a) to provide credit, or

(b) to enter into an agreement for the bailment or (in Scotland) the hiring of goods by him.

(2) An advertisement does not fall within subsection (1) if the advertiser does not carry on—

(a) a consumer credit business or consumer hire business, or

(b) a business in the course of which he provides credit to individuals secured on land, or

(c) a business which comprises or relates to unregulated agreements where—

(i) the [law applicable to] the agreement is the law of a country outside the United Kingdom, and

(ii) if the [law applicable to] the agreement were the law of a part of the United Kingdom it would be a regulated agreement.

(3) An advertisement does not fall within subsection (1)(a) if it indicates—

(a) that the credit must exceed [£25,000], and that no security is required, or the security is to consist of property other than land, or

(b) that the credit is available only to a body corporate.

(4) An advertisement does not fall within subsection (1)(b) if it indicates that the advertiser is not willing to enter into a consumer hire agreement.

(5) The Secretary of State may by order provide that this Part shall not apply to other advertisements of a description specified in the order.

44. Form and content of advertisements

(1) The Secretary of State shall make regulations as to the form and content of advertisements to which this Part applies, and the regulations shall contain such provisions as appear to him appropriate with a view to ensuring that, having regard to its subject-matter and the amount of detail included in it, an advertisement conveys a fair and reasonably comprehensive indication of the nature of the credit or hire facilities offered by the advertiser and of their true cost to persons using them.

(2) Regulations under subsection (1) may in particular—

(a) require specified information to be included in the prescribed manner in advertisements, and other specified material to be excluded;

(b) contain requirements to ensure that specified information is clearly brought to the attention of persons to whom advertisements are directed, and that one part of an advertisement is not given insufficient or excessive prominence compared with another.

45. Prohibition of advertisement where goods etc. not sold for cash

If an advertisement to which this Part applies indicates that the advertiser is willing to provide credit under a restricted-use credit agreement relating to goods or services to be supplied by any person, but at the time when the advertisement is published that person is not holding himself out as prepared to sell the goods or provide the services (as the case may be) for cash, the advertiser commits an offence.

46. False or misleading advertisements

(1) If an advertisement to which this Part applies conveys information which in a material respect is false or misleading the advertiser commits an offence.

(2) Information stating or implying an intention on the advertiser's part which he has not got is false.

47. Advertising infringements

(1) Where an advertiser commits an offence against regulations made under section 44 or against section 45 or 46 or would be taken to commit such an offence but for the defence provided by section 168, a like offence is committed by—

(a) the publisher of the advertisement, and

(b) any person who, in the course of a business carried on by him, devised the advertisement, or a part of it relevant to the first-mentioned offence, and

(c) where the advertiser did not procure the publication of the advertisement, the person who did procure it.

(2) In proceedings for an offence under subsection (1)(a) it is a defence for the person charged to prove that—

(a) the advertisement was published in the course of a business carried on by him, and

(b) he received the advertisement in the course of that business, and did not know and had no reason to suspect that its publication would be an offence under this Part.

Canvassing, etc.

48. Definition of canvassing off trade premises (regulated agreements)

(1) An individual (the 'canvasser') canvasses a regulated agreement off trade premises if he solicits the entry (as debtor or hirer) of another individual (the 'consumer') into the agreement by making oral representations to the consumer, or any other individual, during a visit by the canvasser to any place (not excluded by subsection (2)) where the consumer, or that other individual, as the case may be, is, being a visit—

(a) carried out for the purpose of making such oral representations to individuals who are at that place, but

(b) not carried out in response to a request made on a previous occasion.

(2) A place is excluded from subsection (1) if it is a place where a business is carried on (whether on a permanent or temporary basis) by—

(a) the creditor or owner, or

(b) a supplier, or

(c) the canvasser, or the person whose employee or agent the canvasser is, or

(d) the consumer.

49. Prohibition of canvassing debtor-creditor agreements off trade premises

(1) It is an offence to canvass debtor-creditor agreements off trade premises.

(2) It is also an offence to solicit the entry of an individual (as debtor) into a debtor—creditor agreement during a visit carried out in response to a request made on a previous occasion, where—

(a) the request was not in writing signed by or on behalf of the person making it, and

(b) if no request for the visit had been made, the soliciting would have constituted the canvassing of a debtor-creditor agreement off trade premises.

(3) Subsections (1) and (2) do not apply to any soliciting for an agreement enabling the debtor to overdraw on a current account of any description kept with the creditor, where—

(a) the Director has determined that current accounts of that description kept with the creditor are excluded from subsections (1) and (2), and

(b) the debtor already keeps an account with the creditor (whether a current account or not).

(4) A determination under subsection (3)(a)—

(a) may be made subject to such conditions as the Director thinks fit, and

(b) shall be made only where the Director is of opinion that it is not against the interests of debtors.

(5) If soliciting is done in breach of a condition imposed under subsection (4)(a), the determination under subsection (3)(a) does not apply to it.

50. Circulars to minors

(1) A person commits an offence who, with a view to financial gain, sends to a minor any document inviting him to—

(a) borrow money, or

(b) obtain goods on credit or hire, or

(c) obtain services on credit, or

(d) apply for information or advice on borrowing money or otherwise obtaining credit, or hiring goods.

(2) In proceedings under subsection (1) in respect of the sending of a document to a minor, it is a defence for the person charged to prove that he did not know, and had no reasonable cause to suspect, that he was a minor.

(3) Where a document is received by a minor at any school or other educational establishment for minors, a person sending it to him at that establishment knowing or suspecting it to be such an establishment shall be taken to have reasonable cause to suspect that he is a minor.

51. Prohibition of unsolicited credit-tokens

(1) It is an offence to give a person a credit-token if he has not asked for it.

(2) To comply with subsection (1) a request must be contained in a document signed by the person making the request, unless the credit-token agreement is a small debtor-creditor-supplier agreement.

(3) Subsection (1) does not apply to the giving of a credit-token to a person—

(a) for use under a credit-token agreement already made, or

(b) in renewal or replacement of a credit-token previously accepted by him under a credit-token agreement which continues in force, whether or not varied.

Miscellaneous

52. Quotations

(1) Regulations may be made—

(a) as to the form and content of any document (a 'quotation') by which a person who carries on a consumer credit business or consumer hire business, or a business in the course of which he provides credit to individuals secured on land, gives prospective customers information about the terms on which he is prepared to do business;

(b) requiring a person carrying on such a business to provide quotations to such persons and in such circumstances as are prescribed.

(2) Regulations under subsection (1)(a) may in particular contain provisions relating to quotations such as are set out in relation to advertisements in section 44.

53. Duty to display information

Regulations may require a person who carries on a consumer credit business or consumer hire business, or a business in the course of which he provides credit to individuals secured on land, to display in the prescribed manner, at any premises where the business is carried on to which the public have access, prescribed information about the business.

54. Conduct of business regulations

Without prejudice to the generality of section 26, regulations under that section may include provisions further regulating the seeking of business by a licensee who carries on a consumer credit business or a consumer hire business.

PART V
ENTRY INTO CREDIT OR HIRE AGREEMENTS

Preliminary matters

55. Disclosure of information

(1) Regulations may require specified information to be disclosed in the prescribed manner to the debtor or hirer before a regulated agreement is made.

(2) A regulated agreement is not properly executed unless regulations under subsection (1) were complied with before the making of the agreement.

56. Antecedent negotiations

(1) In this Act 'antecedent negotiations' means any negotiations with the debtor or hirer—

(a) conducted by the creditor or owner in relation to the making of any regulated agreement, or

(b) conducted by a credit-broker in relation to goods sold or proposed to be sold by the credit-broker to the creditor before forming the subject-matter of a debtor-creditor-supplier agreement within section 12(a), or

(c) conducted by the supplier in relation to a transaction financed or proposed to be financed by a debtor-creditor-supplier agreement within section 12(b) or (c), and 'negotiator' means the person by whom negotiations are so conducted with the debtor or hirer.

(2) Negotiations with the debtor in a case falling within subsection (1)(b) or (c) shall be deemed to be conducted by the negotiator in the capacity of agent of the creditor as well as in his actual capacity.

(3) An agreement is void if, and to the extent that, it purports in relation to an actual or prospective regulated agreement—

(a) to provide that a person acting as, or on behalf of, a negotiator is to be treated as the agent of the debtor or hirer, or

(b) to relieve a person from liability for acts or omissions of any person acting as, or on behalf of, a negotiator.

(4) For the purposes of this Act, antecedent negotiations shall be taken to begin when the negotiator and the debtor or hirer first enter into communication (including communication by advertisement), and to include any representations made by the negotiator to the debtor or hirer and any other dealings between them.

57. Withdrawal from prospective agreement

(1) The withdrawal of a party from a prospective regulated agreement shall operate to apply this Part to the agreement, any linked transaction and any other thing done in anticipation of the making of the agreement as it would apply if the agreement were made and then cancelled under section 69.

(2) The giving to a party of a written or oral notice which, however expressed, indicates the intention of the other party to withdraw from a prospective regulated agreement operates as a withdrawal from it.

(3) Each of the following shall be deemed to be the agent of the creditor or owner for the purpose of receiving a notice under subsection (2)—

(a) a credit-broker or supplier who is the negotiator in antecedent negotiations, and

(b) any person who, in the course of a business carried on by him, acts on behalf of the debtor or hirer in any negotiations for the agreement.

(4) Where the agreement, if made, would not be a cancellable agreement, subsection (1) shall nevertheless apply as if the contrary were the case.

58. Opportunity for withdrawal from prospective land mortgage

(1) Before sending to the debtor or hirer, for his signature, an unexecuted agreement in a case where the prospective regulated agreement is to be secured on land (the 'mortgaged land'), the creditor or owner shall give the debtor or hirer a copy of the unexecuted agreement which contains a notice in the prescribed form indicating the right of the debtor or hirer to withdraw from the prospective agreement, and how and when the right is exercisable, together with a copy of any other document referred to in the unexecuted agreement.

(2) Subsection (1) does not apply to—

(a) a restricted-use credit agreement to finance the purchase of the mortgaged land, or

(b) an agreement for a bridging loan in connection with the purchase of the mortgaged land or other land.

59. Agreement to enter future agreement void

(1) An agreement is void if, and to the extent that, it purports to bind a person to enter as debtor or hirer into a prospective regulated agreement.

(2) Regulations may exclude from the operation of subsection (1) agreements such as are described in the regulations.

Making the agreement

60. Form and content of agreements

(1) The Secretary of State shall make regulations as to the form and content of documents embodying regulated agreements, and the regulations shall contain such provisions as appear to him appropriate with a view to ensuring that the debtor or hirer is made aware of—

(a) the rights and duties conferred or imposed on him by the agreement,

(b) the amount and rate of the total charge for credit (in the case of a consumer credit agreement),

(c) the protection and remedies available to him under this Act, and

(d) any other matters which, in the opinion of the Secretary of State, it is desirable for him to know about in connection with the agreement.

(2) Regulations under subsection (1) may in particular—

(a) require specified information to be included in the prescribed manner in documents, and other specified material to be excluded;

(b) contain requirements to ensure that specified information is clearly brought to the attention of the debtor or hirer, and that one part of a document is not given insufficient or excessive prominence compared with another.

(3) If, on an application made to the Director by a person carrying on a consumer credit business or a consumer hire business, it appears to the Director impracticable for the applicant to comply with any requirement of regulations under subsection (1) in a particular case, he may, by notice to the applicant direct that the requirement be waived or varied in relation to such agreements, and subject to such conditions (if any), as he may specify, and this Act and the regulations shall have effect accordingly.

(4) The Director shall give a notice under subsection (3) only if he is satisfied that to do so would not prejudice the interests of debtors or hirers'.

61. Signing of agreement

(1) A regulated agreement is not properly executed unless—

(a) a document in the prescribed form itself containing all the prescribed terms and conforming to regulations under section 60(1) is signed in the prescribed manner both by the debtor or hirer and by or on behalf of the creditor or owner, and

(b) the document embodies all the terms of the agreement, other than implied terms, and

(c) the document is, when presented or sent to the debtor or hirer for signature, in such a state that all its terms are readily legible.

(2) In addition, where the agreement is one to which section 58(1) applies, it is not properly executed unless—

(a) the requirements of section 58(1) were complied with, and

(b) the unexecuted agreement was sent, for his signature, to the debtor or hirer by post not less than seven days after a copy of it was given to him under section 58(1), and

(c) during the consideration period, the creditor or owner refrained from approaching the debtor or hirer (whether in person, by telephone or letter, or in any other way) except in response to a specific request made by the debtor or hirer after the beginning of the consideration period, and

(d) no notice of withdrawal by the debtor or hirer was received by the creditor or owner before the sending of the unexecuted agreement.

(3) In subsection (2)(c), 'the consideration period' means the period beginning with the giving of the copy under section 58(1) and ending—

(a) at the expiry of seven days after the day on which the unexecuted agreement is sent, for his signature, to the debtor or hirer, or

(b) on its return by the debtor or hirer after signature by him, whichever first occurs.

(4) Where the debtor or hirer is a partnership or an unincorporated body of persons, subsection (1)(a) shall apply with the substitution for 'by the debtor or hirer' of 'by or on behalf of the debtor or hirer's'.

62. Duty to supply copy of unexecuted agreement

(1) If the unexecuted agreement is presented personally to the debtor or hirer for his signature, but on the occasion when he signs it the document does not become an executed agreement, a copy of it, and of any other document referred to in it, must be there and then delivered to him.

(2) If the unexecuted agreement is sent to the debtor or hirer for his signature, a copy of it, and of any other document referred to in it, must be sent to him at the same time.

(3) A regulated agreement is not properly executed if the requirements of this section are not observed.

63. Duty to supply copy of executed agreement

(1) If the unexecuted agreement is presented personally to the debtor or hirer for his signature, and on the occasion when he signs it the document becomes an executed agreement, a copy of the executed agreement, and of any other document referred to in it, must be there and then delivered to him.

(2) A copy of the executed agreement, and of any other document referred to in it, must be given to the debtor or hirer within the seven days following the making of the agreement unless—

(a) subsection (1) applies, or

(b) the unexecuted agreement was sent to the debtor or hirer for his signature and, on the occasion of his signing it, the document became an executed agreement.

(3) In the case of a cancellable agreement, a copy under subsection (2) must be sent by post.

(4) In the case of a credit-token agreement, a copy under subsection (2) need not be given within the seven days following the making of the agreement if it is given before or at the time when the credit-token is given to the debtor.

(5) A regulated agreement is not properly executed if the requirements of this section are not observed.

64. Duty to give notice of cancellation rights

(1) In the case of a cancellable agreement, a notice in the prescribed form indicating the right of the debtor or hirer to cancel the agreement, how and when that right is

exercisable, and the name and address of a person to whom notice of cancellation may be given,—

(a) must be included in every copy given to the debtor or hirer under section 62 or 63, and

(b) except where section 63(2) applied, must also be sent by post to the debtor or hirer within the seven days following the making of the agreement.

(2) In the case of a credit-token agreement, a notice under subsection (1)(b) need not be sent by post within the seven days following the making of the agreement if either—

(a) it is sent by post to the debtor or hirer before the credit-token is given to him, or

(b) it is sent by post to him together with the credit-token.

(3) Regulations may provide that except where section 63(2) applied a notice sent under subsection (1)(b) shall be accompanied by a further copy of the executed agreement, and of any other document referred to in it.

(4) Regulations may provide that subsection (1)(b) is not to apply in the case of agreements such as are described in the regulations, being agreements made by a particular person, if—

(a) on an application by that person to the Director, the Director has determined that, having regard to—

(i) the manner in which antecedent negotiations for agreements with the applicant of that description are conducted, and

(ii) the information provided to debtors or hirers before such agreements are made, the requirement imposed by subsection (1)(b) can be dispensed with without prejudicing the interests of debtors or hirers, and

(b) any conditions imposed by the Director in making the determination are complied with.

(5) A cancellable agreement is not properly executed if the requirements of this section are not observed.

65. Consequences of improper execution

(1) An improperly-executed regulated agreement is enforceable against the debtor or hirer on an order of the court only.

(2) A retaking of goods or land to which a regulated agreement relates is an enforcement of the agreement.

66. Acceptance of credit-tokens

(1) The debtor shall not be liable under a credit-token agreement for use made of the credit-token by any person unless the debtor had previously accepted the credit-token, or the use constituted an acceptance of it by him.

(2) The debtor accepts a credit-token when—

(a) it is signed, or

(b) a receipt for it is signed, or

(c) it is first used,

either by the debtor himself or by a person who, pursuant to the agreement, is authorised by him to use it.

Cancellation of certain agreements within cooling-off period

67. Cancellable agreements

A regulated agreement may be cancelled by the debtor or hirer in accordance with this Part if the antecedent negotiations included oral representations made when in the presence of the debtor or hirer by an individual acting as, or on behalf of, the negotiator, unless—

(a) the agreement is secured on land, or is a restricted-use credit agreement to finance the purchase of land or is an agreement for a bridging loan in connection with the purchase of land, or

(b) the unexecuted agreement is signed by the debtor or hirer at premises at which any of the following is carrying on any business (whether on a permanent or temporary basis)—

(i) the creditor or owner;

(ii) any party to a linked transaction (other than the debtor or hirer or a relative of his);

(iii) the negotiator in any antecedent negotiations.

68. Cooling-off period

The debtor or hirer may serve notice of cancellation of a cancellable agreement between his signing of the unexecuted agreement and—

(a) the end of the fifth day following the day on which he received a copy under section 63(2) or a notice under section 64(1)(b), or

(b) if (by virtue of regulations made under section 64(4) section 64(1)(b) does not apply, the end of the fourteenth day following the day on which he signed the unexecuted agreement.

69. Notice of cancellation

(1) If within the period specified in section 68 the debtor or hirer under a cancellable agreement serves on—

(a) the creditor or owner, or

(b) the person specified in the notice under section 64(1), or

(c) a person who (whether by virtue of subsection (6) or otherwise) is the agent of the creditor or owner, a notice (a 'notice of cancellation') which, however expressed and whether or not conforming to the notice given under section 64(1), indicates the intention of the debtor or hirer to withdraw from the agreement, the notice shall operate—

(i) to cancel the agreement, and any linked transaction, and

(ii) to withdraw any offer by the debtor or hirer, or his relative, to enter into a linked transaction.

(2) In the case of a debtor-creditor-supplier agreement for restricted-use credit financing—

(a) the doing of work or supply of goods to meet an emergency, or

(b) the supply of goods which, before service of the notice of cancellation, had by the act of the debtor or his relative become incorporated in any land or thing not comprised in the agreement or any linked transaction,

subsection (1) shall apply with the substitution of the following for paragraph (i)—

'(i) to cancel only such provisions of the agreement and any linked transaction as—

(aa) relate to the provision of credit, or

(bb) require the debtor to pay an item in the total charge for credit, or

(cc) subject the debtor to any obligation other than to pay for the doing of the said work, or the supply of the said goods'.

(3) Except so far as is otherwise provided, references in this Act to the cancellation of an agreement or transaction do not include a case within subsection (2).

(4) Except as otherwise provided by or under this Act, an agreement or transaction cancelled under subsection (1) shall be treated as if it had never been entered into.

(5) Regulations may exclude linked transactions of the prescribed description from subsection (1)(i) or (ii).

(6) Each of the following shall be deemed to be the agent of the creditor or owner for the purpose of receiving a notice of cancellation—

(a) a credit-broker or supplier who is the negotiator in antecedent negotiations, and

(b) any person who, in the course of a business carried on by him, acts on behalf of the debtor or hirer in any negotiations for the agreement.

(7) Whether or not it is actually received by him, a notice of cancellation sent by post to a person shall be deemed to be served on him at the time of posting.

70. Cancellation: recovery of money paid by debtor or hirer

(1) On the cancellation of a regulated agreement, and of any linked transaction,—

(a) any sum paid by the debtor or hirer, or his relative, under or in contemplation of the agreement or transaction, including any item in the total charge for credit, shall become repayable, and

(b) any sum, including any item in the total charge for credit, which but for the cancellation is, or would or might become, payable by the debtor or hirer, or his relative, under the agreement or transaction shall cease to be, or shall not become, so payable, and

(c) in the case of a debtor-creditor-supplier agreement falling within section 12(b), any sum paid on the debtor's behalf by the creditor to the supplier shall become repayable to the creditor.

(2) If, under the terms of a cancelled agreement or transaction, the debtor or hirer, or his relative, is in possession of any goods, he shall have a lien on them for any sum repayable to him under subsection (1) in respect of that agreement or transaction, or any other linked transaction.

(3) A sum repayable under subsection (1) is repayable by the person to whom it was originally paid, but in the case of a debtor-creditor-supplier agreement falling within section 12(b) the creditor and the supplier shall be under a joint and several liability to repay sums paid by the debtor, or his relative, under the agreement or under a linked transaction falling within section 19(1)(b) and accordingly, in such a case, the creditor shall be entitled, in accordance with rules of court, to have the supplier made a party to any proceedings brought against the creditor to recover any such sums.

(4) Subject to any agreement between them, the creditor shall be entitied to be indemnified by the supplier for loss suffered by the creditor in satisfying his liability under subsection (3), including costs reasonably incurred by him in defending proceedings instituted by the debtor.

(5) Subsection (1) does not apply to any sum which, if not paid by a debtor, would be payable by virtue of section 71, and applies to a sum paid or payable by a debtor for the issue of a credit-token only where the credit-token has been returned to the creditor or surrendered to a supplier.

(6) If the total charge for credit includes an item in respect of a fee or commission charged by a credit-broker, the amount repayable under subsection (1) in respect of that item shall be the excess over [£5] of the fee or commission.

(7) If the total charge for credit includes any sum payable or paid by the debtor to a credit-broker otherwise than in respect of a fee or commission charged by him, that sum shall for the purposes of subsection (6) be treated as if it were such a fee or commission.

(8) So far only as is necessary to give effect to section 69(2), this section applies to an agreeement or transaction within that subsection as it applies to a cancelled agreement or transaction.

71. Cancellation: repayment of credit

(1) Notwithstanding the cancellation of a regulated consumer credit agreement, other than a debtor-creditor-supplier agreement for restricted-use credit, the agreement shall continue in force so far as it relates to repayment of credit and payment of interest.

(2) If, following the cancellation of a regulated consumer credit agreement, the debtor repays the whole or a portion of the credit—

(a) before the expiry of one month following service of the notice of cancellation, or

(b) in the case of a credit repayable by instalments, before the date on which the first instalment is due,

no interest shall be payable on the amount repaid.

(3) If the whole of a credit repayable by instalments is not repaid on or before the date specified in subsection (2)(b), the debtor shall not be liable to repay any of the credit except on receipt of a request in writing in the prescribed form, signed by or on behalf of the creditor, stating the amounts of the remaining instalments (recalculated by the creditor as nearly as may be in accordance with the agreement and without extending the repayment period), but excluding any sum other than principal and interest.

(4) Repayment of a credit, or payment of interest, under a cancelled agreement shall be treated as duly made if it is made to any person on whom, under section 69, a notice of cancellation could have been served, other than a person referred to in section 69(6)(b).

72. Cancellation: return of goods

(1) This section applies where any agreement or transaction relating to goods, being—

(a) a restricted-use debtor-creditor-supplier agreement, a consumer hire agreement, or a linked transaction to which the debtor or hirer under any regulated agreement is a party, or

(b) a linked transaction to which a relative of the debtor or hirer under any regulated agreement is a party,

is cancelled after the debtor or hirer (in a case within paragraph (a)) or the relative (in a case within paragraph (b)) has acquired possession of the goods by virtue of the agreement or transaction.

(2) In this section—

(a) 'the possessor' means the person who has acquired possession of the goods as mentioned in subsection (1),

(b) 'the other party' means the person from whom the possessor acquired possession, and

(c) 'the pre-cancellation period' means the period beginning when the possessor acquired possession and ending with the cancellation.

(3) The possessor shall be treated as having been under a duty throughout the pre-cancellation period—

(a) to retain possession of the goods, and

(b) to take reasonable care of them.

(4) On the cancellation, the possessor shall be under a duty, subject to any restore the goods to the other party in accordance with this section, and meanwhile to retain possession of the goods and take reasonable care of them.

(5) The possessor shall not be under any duty to deliver the goods except at his own premises and in pursuance of a request in writing signed by or on behalf of the other party and served on the possessor either before, or at the time when, the goods are collected from those premises.

(6) If the possessor—

(a) delivers the goods (whether at his own premises or elsewhere) to any person on whom, under section 69, a notice of cancellation could have been served (other than a person referred to in section 69(6)(b), or

(b) sends the goods at his own expense to such a person, he shall be discharged from any duty to retain the goods or deliver them to any person.

(7) Where the possessor delivers the goods as mentioned in subsection (6)(a), his obligation to take care of the goods shall cease: and if he sends the goods as mentioned in subsection (6)(b), he shall be under a duty to take reasonable care to see that they are received by the other party and not damaged in transit, but in other respects his duty to take care of the goods shall cease.

(8) Where, at any time during the period of 21 days following the cancellation, the possessor receives such a request as is mentioned in subsection (5), and unreasonably refuses or unreasonably fails to comply with it, his duty to take reasonable care of the goods shall continue until he delivers or sends the goods as mentioned in subsection (6), but if within that period he does not receive such a request his duty to take reasonable care of the goods shall cease at the end of that period.

(9) The preceding provisions of this section do not apply to

(a) perishable goods, or

(b) goods which by their nature are consumed by use and which, before the cancellation, were so consumed, or

(c) goods supplied to meet an emergency, or

(d) goods which, before the cancellation, had become incorporated in any land or thing not comprised in the cancelled agreement or a linked transaction.

(10) Where the address of the possessor is specified in the executed agreement, references in this section to his own premises are to that address and no other.

(11) Breach of a duty imposed by this section is actionable as a breach of statutory duty.

73. Cancellation: goods given in part-exchange

(1) This section applies on the cancellation of a regulated agreement where, in antecedent negotiations, the negotiator agreed to take goods in part-exchange (the 'part-exchange goods') and those goods have been delivered to him.

(2) Unless, before the end of the period of ten days beginning with the date of cancellation, the part-exchange goods are returned to the debtor or hirer in a condition substantially as good as when they were delivered to the negotiator, the debtor or hirer shall be entitled to recover from the negotiator a sum equal to the part-exchange allowance (as defined in subsection (7)(b)).

(3) In the case of a debtor-creditor-supplier agreement within section 12(b), the negotiator and the creditor shall be under a joint and several liability to pay to the debtor a sum recoverable under subsection (2).

(4) Subject to any agreement between them, the creditor shall be entitled to be indemnified by the negotiator for loss suffered by the creditor in satisfying his liability under subsection (3), including costs reasonably incurred by him in defending proceedings instituted by the debtor.

(5) During the period of ten days beginning with the date of cancellation, the debtor or hirer, if he is in possession of goods to which the cancelled agreement relates, shall have a lien on them for—

(a) delivery of the part-exchange goods, in a condition substantially as good as when they were delivered to the negotiator, or

(b) a sum equal to the part-exchange allowance;

and if the lien continues to the end of that period it shall thereafter subsist only as a lien for a sum equal to the part-exchange allowance.

(6) Where the debtor or hirer recovers from the negotiator or creditor, or both of them jointly, a sum equal to the part-exchange allowance, then, if the title of the debtor or hirer to the part-exchange goods has not vested in the negotiator, it shall so vest on the recovery of that sum.

(7) For the purposes of this section—

(a) the negotiator shall be treated as having agreed to take goods in part-exchange if, in pursuance of the antecedent negotiations, he either purchased or agreed to purchase those goods or accepted or agreed to accept them as part of the consideration for the cancelled agreement, and

(b) the part-exchange allowance shall be the sum agreed as such in the antecedent negotiations or, if no such agreement was arrived at, such sum as it would have been reasonable to allow in respect of the part-exchange goods if no notice of cancellation had been served.

(8) In an action brought against the creditor for a sum recoverable under subsection (2), he shall be entitled, in accordance with rules of court, to have the negotiator made a party to the proceedings.

Exclusion of certain agreements from Part V

74. Exclusion of certain agreements from Part V

(1) This Part (except section 56) does not apply to—

(a) a non-commercial agreement, or

(b) a debtor-creditor agreement enabling the debtor to overdraw on a current account, or

(c) a debtor-creditor agreement to finance the making of such payments arising on, or connected with, the death of a person as may be prescribed.

(2) This Part (except sections 55 and 56) does not apply to a small debtor-creditor-supplier agreement for restricted-use credit.

[(2A) In the case of an agreement to which the Consumer Protection (Cancellation of Contracts Concluded Away from Business Premises) Regulations 1987 apply the reference in subsection (2) to a small agreement shall be construed as if in section 17(1)(a) and (b) '£35' were substituted for '£50'.]

(3) Subsection (1)(b) or (c) applies only where the Director so determines, and such a determination—

(a) may be made subject to such conditions as the Director thinks fit, and

(b) shall be made only if the Director is of opinion that it is not against the interests of debtors.

[(3A) Notwithstanding anything in subsection (3)(b) above, in relation to a debtor-creditor agreement under which the creditor is the Bank of England or a bank within the meaning of the Bankers' Books Evidence Act 1879, the Director shall make a determination that subsection (1)(b) above applies unless he considers that it would be against the public interest to do so.]

(4) If any term of an agreement falling within subsection [(1)(c)] or (2) is expressed in writing, regulations under section 60(1) shall apply to that term (subject to section 60(3)) as if the agreement were a regulated agreement not falling within subsection [(1)(c)] or (2).

PART VI
MATTERS ARISING DURING CURRENCY OF CREDIT OR HIRE AGREEMENTS

75. Liability of creditor for breaches by supplier

(1) If the debtor under a debtor-creditor-supplier agreement falling within section 12(b) or (c) has, in relation to a transaction financed by the agreement, any claim against the supplier in respect of a misrepresentation or breach of contract, he shall have a like claim against the creditor, who, with the supplier, shall accordingly be jointly and severally liable to the debtor.

(2) Subject to any agreement between them, the creditor shall be entitled to be indemnified by the supplier for loss suffered by the creditor in satisfying his liability under subsection (1), including costs reasonably incurred by him in defending proceedings instituted by the debtor.

(3) Subsection (1) does not apply to a claim—

(a) under a non-commercial agreement, or

(b) so far as the claim relates to any single item to which the supplier has attached a cash price not exceeding [£100] or more than [£30,000].

(4) This section applies notwithstanding that the debtor, in entering into the transaction, exceeded the credit limit or otherwise contravened any term of the agreement.

(5) In an action brought against the creditor under subsection (1) he shall be entitled, in accordance with rules of court, to have the supplier made a party to the proceedings.

76. Duty to give notice before taking certain action

(1) The creditor or owner is not entitled to enforce a term of a regulated agreement by—

(a) demanding earlier payment of any sum, or

(b) recovering possession of any goods or land, or

(c) treating any right conferred on the debtor or hirer by the agreement as terminated, restricted or deferred,

except by or after giving the debtor or hirer not less than seven days' notice of his intention to do so.

(2) Subsection (1) applies only where—

(a) a period for the duration of the agreement is specified in the agreement, and

(b) that period has not ended when the creditor or owner does an act mentioned in subsection (1),

but so applies notwithstanding that, under the agreement, any party is entitled to terminate it before the end of the period so specified.

(3) A notice under subsection (1) is ineffective if not in the prescribed form.

(4) Subsection (1) does not prevent a creditor from treating the right to draw on any credit as restricted or deferred and taking such steps as may be necessary to make the restriction or deferment effective.

(5) Regulations may provide that subsection (1) is not to apply to agreements described by the regulations.

(6) Subsection (1) does not apply to a right of enforcement arising by reason of any breach by the debtor or hirer of the regulated agreement.

77. Duty to give information to debtor under fixed-sum credit agreement

(1) The creditor under a regulated agreement for fixed-sum credit, within the prescribed period after receiving a request in writing to that effect from the debtor and payment of a fee of [£1], shall give the debtor a copy of the executed agreement (if any) and of any other document referred to in it, together with a statement signed by or on behalf of the creditor showing, according to the information to which it is practicable for him to refer,—

(a) the total sum paid under the agreement by the debtor;

(b) the total sum which has become payable under the agreement by the debtor but remains unpaid, and the various amounts comprised in that total sum, with the date when each became due; and

(c) the total sum which is to become payable under the agreement by the debtor, and the various amounts comprised in that total sum, with the date, or mode of determining the date, when each becomes due.

(2) If the creditor possesses insufficient information to enable him to ascertain the amounts and dates mentioned in subsection (1)(c), he shall be taken to comply with that paragraph if his statement under subsection (1) gives the basis on which, under the regulated agreement, they would fall to be ascertained.

(3) Subsection (1) does not apply to—

(a) an agreement under which no sum is, or will or may become, payable by the debtor, or

(b) a request made less than one month after a previous request under that subsection relating to the same agreement was complied with.

(4) If the creditor under an agreement fails to comply with subsection (1)—

(a) he is not entitied, while the default continues, to enforce the agreement; and

(b) if the default continues for one month he commits an offence.

(5) This section does not apply to a non-commercial agreement.

78. Duty to give information to debtor under running-account credit agreement

(1) The creditor under a regulated agreement for running-account credit, within the prescribed period after receiving a request in writing to that effect from the debtor and payment of a fee of [£1], shall give the debtor a copy of the executed agreement (if any) and of any other document referred to in it, together with a statement signed by or on behalf of the creditor showing, according to the information to which it is practicable for him to refer,—

(a) the state of the account, and

(b) the amount, if any, currently payable under the agreement by the debtor to the creditor, and

(c) the amounts and due dates of any payments which, if the debtor does not draw further on the account, will later become payable under the agreement by the debtor to the creditor.

(2) If the creditor possesses insufficient information to enable him to ascertain the amounts and dates mentioned in subsection (1)(c), he shall be taken to comply with that paragraph if his statement under subsection (1) gives the basis on which, under the regulated agreement, they would fall to be ascertained.

(3) Subsection (1) does not apply to—

(a) an agreement under which no sum is, or will or may become, payable by the debtor, or

(b) a request made less than one month after a previous request under that subsection relating to the same agreement was complied with.

(4) Where running-account credit is provided under a regulated agreement, the creditor shall give the debtor statements in the prescribed form, and with the prescribed contents—

(a) showing according to the information to which it is practicable for him to refer, the state of the account at regular intervals of not more than twelve months, and

(b) where the agreement provides, in relation to specified periods, for the making of payments by the debtor, or the charging against him of interest or any other sum, showing according to the information to which it is practicable for him to refer the state of the account at the end of each of those periods during which there is any movement in the account.

(5) A statement under subsection (4) shall be given within the prescribed period after the end of the period to which the statement relates.

(6) If the creditor under an agreement fails to comply with subsection (1)—

(a) he is not entitled, while the default continues, to enforce the agreement; and

(b) if the default continues for one month he commits an offence.

(7) This section does not apply to a non-commercial agreement, and subsections (4) and (5) do not apply to a small agreement.

79. Duty to give hirer information

(1) The owner under a regulated consumer hire agreement, within the prescribed period after receiving a request in writing to that effect from the hirer and payment of a fee of [£1], shall give to the hirer a copy of the executed agreement and of any other document referred to in it, together with a statement signed by or on behalf of the owner showing, according

to the information to which it is practicable for him to refer, the total sum which has become payable under the agreement by the hirer but remains unpaid and the various amounts comprised in that total sum, with the date when each became due.

(2) Subsection (1) does not apply to—

(a) an agreement under which no sum is, or will or may become, payable by the hirer, or

(b) a request made less than one month after a previous request under that subsection relating to the same agreement was complied with.

(3) If the owner under an agreement fails to comply with subsection (1)—

(a) he is not entitled, while the default continues, to enforce the agreement; and

(b) if the default continues for one month he commits an offence.

(4) This section does not apply to a non-commercial agreement.

80. Debtor or hirer to give information about goods

(1) Where a regulated agreement, other than a non-commercial agreement, requires the debtor or hirer to keep goods to which the agreement relates in his possession or control, he shall, within seven working days after he has received a request in writing to that effect from the creditor or owner, tell the creditor or owner where the goods are.

(2) If the debtor or hirer fails to comply with subsection (1), and the default continues for 14 days, he commits an offence.

81. Appropriation of payments

(1) Where a debtor or hirer is liable to make to the same person payments in respect of two or more regulated agreements, he shall be entitled, on making any payment in respect of the agreements which is not sufficient to discharge the total amount then due under all the agreements, to appropriate the sum so paid by him—

(a) in or towards the satisfaction of the sum due under any one of the agreements, or

(b) in or towards the satisfaction of the sums due under any two or more of the agreements in such proportions as he thinks fit.

(2) If the debtor or hirer fails to make any such appropriation where one or more of the agreements is—

(a) a hire-purchase agreement or conditional sale agreement, or

(b) a consumer hire agreement, or

(c) an agreement in relation to which any security is provided,

the payment shall be appropriated towards the satisfaction of the sums due under the several agreements respectively in the proportions which those sums bear to one another.

82. Variation of agreements

(1) Where, under a power contained in a regulated agreement, the creditor or owner varies the agreement, the variation shall not take effect before notice of it is given to the debtor or hirer in the prescribed manner.

(2) Where an agreement (a 'modifying agreement') varies or supplements an earlier agreement, the modifying agreement shall for the purposes of this Act be treated as—

(a) revoking the earlier agreement, and

(b) containing provisions reproducing the combined effect of the two agreements, and obligations outstanding in relation to the earlier agreement shall accordingly be treated as outstanding instead in relation to the modifying agreement.

(3) If the earlier agreement is a regulated agreement but (apart from this subsection) the modifying agreement is not then, unless the modifying agreement is for running-account credit, it shall be treated as a regulated agreement.

(4) If the earlier agreement is a regulated agreement for running-account credit, and by the modifying agreement the creditor allows the credit limit to be exceeded but intends the excess to be merely temporary, Part V (except section 56) shall not apply to the modifying agreement.

(5) If—

(a) the earlier agreement is a cancellable agreement, and

(b) the modifying agreement is made within the period applicable under section 68 to the earlier agreement,

then, whether or not the modifying agreement would, apart from this subsection, be a cancellable agreement, it shall be treated as a cancellable agreement in respect of which a notice may be served under section 68 not later than the end of the period applicable under that section to the earlier agreement.

(6) Except under subsection (5), a modifying agreement shall not be treated as a cancellable agreement.

(7) This section does not apply to a non-commercial agreement.

83. Liability for misuse of credit facilities

(1) The debtor under a regulated consumer credit agreement shall not be liable to the creditor for any loss arising from use of the credit facility by another person not acting, or to be treated as acting, as the debtor's agent.

(2) This section does not apply to a non-commercial agreement, or to any loss in so far as it arises from misuse of an instrument to which section 4 of the Cheques Act 1957 applies.

84. Misuse of credit-tokens

(1) Section 83 does not prevent the debtor under a credit-token agreement from being made liable to the extent of [£50] (or the credit limit if lower) for loss to the creditor arising from use of the credit-token by other persons during a period beginning when the credit-token ceases to be in the possession of any authorised person and ending when the credit-token is once more in the possession of an authorised person.

(2) Section 83 does not prevent the debtor under a credit-token agreement from being made liable to any extent for loss to the creditor from use of the credit-token by a person who acquired possession of it with the debtor's consent.

(3) Subsection (1) and (2) shall not apply to any use of the credit-token after the creditor has been given oral or written notice that it is lost or stolen, or is for any other reason liable to misuse.

(4) Subsections (1) and (2) shall not apply unless there are contained in the credit-token agreement in the prescribed manner particulars of the name, address and telephone number of a person stated to be the person to whom notice is to be given under subsection (3).

(5) Notice under subsection (3) takes effect when received, but where it is given orally, and the agreement so requires, it shall be treated as not taking effect if not confirmed in writing within seven days.

(6) Any sum paid by the debtor for the issue of the credit- token to the extent (if any) that it has not been previously offset by use made of the credit-token, shall be treated as paid towards satisfaction of any liability under subsection (1) or (2).

(7) The debtor, the creditor, and any person authorised by the debtor to use the credit-token, shall be authorised persons for the purposes of subsection (1).

(8) Where two or more credit-tokens are given under one credit-token agreement, the preceding provisions of this section apply to each credit-token separately.

85. Duty on issue of new credit-tokens

(1) Whenever, in connection with a credit-token agreement, a credit-token (other than the first) is given by the creditor to the debtor, the creditor shall give the debtor a copy of the executed agreement (if any) and of any other document referred to in it.

(2) If the creditor fails to comply with this section—

(a) he is not entitied, while the default continues, to enforce the agreement, and

(b) if the default continues for one month he commits an offence.

(3) This section does not apply to a small agreement.

86. Death of debtor or hirer

(1) The creditor or owner under a regulated agreement is not entitied, by reason of the death of the debtor or hirer, to do an act specified in paragraphs (a) to (e) of section 87(1) if at the death the agreement is fully secured.

(2) If at the death of the debtor or hirer a regulated agreement is only partly secured or is unsecured, the creditor or owner is entitled, by reason of the death of the debtor or hirer, to do an act specified in paragraphs (a) to (e) of section 87(1) on an order of the court only.

(3) This section applies in relation to the termination of an agreement only where—

(a) a period for its duration is specified in the agreement, and

(b) that period has not ended when the creditor or owner purports to terminate the agreement, but so applies notwithstanding that, under the agreement, any party is entitled to terminate it before the end of the period so specified.

(4) This section does not prevent the creditor from treating the right to draw on any credit as restricted or deferred, and taking such steps as may be necessary to make the restriction or deferment effective.

(5) This section does not affect the operation of any agreement providing for payment of sums—

(a) due under the regulated agreement, or

(b) becoming due under it on the death of the debtor or hirer,

out of the proceeds of a policy of assurance on his life.

(6) For the purposes of this section an act is done by reason of the death of the debtor or hirer if it is done under a power conferred by the agreement which is—

(a) exercisable on his death, or

(b) exercisable at will and exercised at any time after his death.

PART VII
DEFAULT AND TERMINATION

Default notices

87. Need for default notice

(1) Service of a notice on the debtor or hirer in accordance with section 88 (a 'default notice') is necessary before the creditor or owner can become entitled, by reason of any breach by the debtor or hirer of a regulated agreement,—

(a) to terminate the agreement, or

(b) to demand earlier payment of any sum, or

(c) to recover possession of any goods or land, or

(d) to treat any right conferred on the debtor or hirer by the agreement as terminated, restricted or deferred, or

(e) to enforce any security.

(2) Subsection (1) does not prevent the creditor from treating the right to draw upon any credit as restricted or deferred, and taking such steps as may be necessary to make the restriction or deferment effective.

(3) The doing of an act by which a floating charge becomes fixed is not enforcement of a security.

(4) Regulations may provide that section (1) is not to apply to agreements described by the regulations.

88. Contents and effect of default notice

(1) The default notice must be in the prescribed form and specify—

(a) the nature of the alleged breach;

(b) if the breach is capable of remedy, what action is required to remedy it and the date before which that action is to be taken;

(c) if the breach is not capable of remedy, the sum (if any) required to be paid as compensation for the breach, and the date before which it is to be paid.

(2) A date specified under subsection (1) must not be less than seven days after the date of service of the default notice, and the creditor or owner shall not take action such as is mentioned in section 87(1) before the date so specified or (if no requirement is made under subsection (1)) before those seven days have elapsed.

(3) The default notice must not treat as a breach failure to comply with a provision of the agreement which becomes operative only on breach of some other provision, but if the breach of that other provision is not duly remedied or compensation demanded under subsection (1) is not duly paid, or (where no requirement is made under subsection (1)) if the seven days mentioned in subsection (2) have elapsed, the creditor or owner may treat the failure as a breach and section 87(1) shall not apply to it.

(4) The default notice must contain information in the prescribed terms about the consequences of failure to comply with it.

(5) A default notice making a requirement under subsection (1) may include a provision for the taking of action such as is mentioned in section 87(1) at any time after the restriction

imposed by subsection (2) will cease, together with a statement that the provision will be ineffective if the breach is duly remedied or the compensation duly paid.

89. Compliance with default notice

If before the date specified for that purpose in the default notice the debtor or hirer takes the action specified under section 88(1)(b) or (c) the breach shall be treated as not having occurred.

Further restriction of remedies for default

90. Retaking of protected hire-purchase etc. goods

(1) At any time when—

(a) the debtor is in breach of a regulated hire-purchase or a regulated conditional sale agreement relating to goods, and

(b) the debtor has paid to the creditor one-third or more of the total price of the goods and

(c) the property in the goods remains in the creditor,

the creditor is not entitled to recover possession of the goods from the debtor except on an order of the court.

(2) Where under a hire-purchase or conditional sale agreement the creditor is required to carry out any installation and the agreement specifies, as part of the total price, the amount to be paid in respect of the installation (the 'installation charge') the reference in subsection (1)(b) to one-third of the total price shall be construed as a reference to the aggregate of the installation charge and one-third of the remainder of the total price.

(3) In a case where—

(a) subsection (1)(a) is satisfied, but not subsection (1)(b), and

(b) subsection (1)(b) was satisfied on a previous occasion in relation to an earlier agreement, being a regulated hire-purchase or regulated conditional sale agreement, between the same parties, and relating to any of the goods comprised in the later agreement (whether or not other goods were also included),

subsection (1) shall apply to the later agreement with the omission of paragraph (b).

(4) If the later agreement is a modifying agreement, subsection (3) shall apply with the substitution, for the second reference to the later agreement, of a reference to the modifying agreement.

(5) Subsection (1) shall not apply, or shall cease to apply, to an agreement if the debtor has terminated, or terminates, the agreement.

(6) Where subsection (1) applies to an agreement at the death of the debtor, it shall continue to apply (in relation to the possessor of the goods) until the grant of probate or administration, or (in Scotland) confirmation (on which the personal representative would fall to be treated as the debtor).

(7) Goods falling within this section are in this Act referred to as 'protected goods'.

91. Consequences of breach of s. 90

If goods are recovered by the creditor in contravention of section 90—

(a) the regulated agreement, if not previously terminated, shall terminate, and

(b) the debtor shall be released from all liability under the agreement, and shall be entitled to recover from the creditor all sums paid by the debtor under the agreement.

92. Recovery of possession of goods or land

(1) Except under an order of the court, the creditor or owner shall not be entitled to enter any premises to take possession of goods subject to a regulated hire-purchase agreement, regulated conditional sale agreement or regulated consumer hire agreement.

(2) At any time when the debtor is in breach of a regulated conditional sale agreement relating to land, the creditor is entitled to recover possession of the land from the debtor, or any person claiming under him, on an order of the court only.

(3) An entry in contravention of section (1) or (2) is actionable as a breach of statutory duty.

93. Interest not to be increased on default

The debtor under a regulated consumer credit agreement shall not be obliged to pay interest on sums which, in breach of the agreement, are unpaid by him at a rate—

(a) where the total charge for credit includes an item in respect of interest, exceeding the rate of that interest, or

(b) in any other case, exceeding what would be the rate of the total charge for credit if any items included in the total charge for credit by virtue of section 20(2) were disregarded.

[93A. Summary diligence not competent in Scotland

. . .]

Early payment by debtor

94. Right to complete payments ahead of time

(1) The debtor under a regulated consumer credit agreement is entitled at any time, by notice to the creditor and the payment to the creditor of all amounts payable by the debtor to him under the agreement (less any rebate allowable under section 95), to discharge the debtor's indebtedness under the agreement.

(2) A notice under subsection (1) may embody the exercise by the debtor of any option to purchase goods conferred on him by the agreement, and deal with any other matter arising on, or in relation to, the termination of the agreement.

95. Rebate on early settlement

(1) Regulations may provide for the allowance of a rebate of charges for credit to the debtor under a regulated consumer credit agreement where, under section 94, on refinancing, on breach of the agreement, or for any other reason, his indebtedness is discharged or becomes payable before the time fixed by the agreement, or any sum becomes payable by him before the time so fixed.

(2) Regulations under subsection (1) may provide for calculation of the rebate by reference to any sums paid or payable by the debtor or his relative under or in connection with the agreement (whether to the creditor or some other person), including sums under linked transactions and other items in the total charge for credit.

96. Effect on linked transactions

(1) Where for any reason the indebtedness of the debtor under a regulated consumer credit agreement is discharged before the time fixed by the agreement, he, and any relative of his, shall at the same time be discharged from any liability under a linked transaction, other than a debt which has already become payable.

(2) Subsection (1) does not apply to a linked transaction which is itself an agreement providing the debtor or his relative with credit.

(3) Regulations may exclude linked transactions of the prescribed description from the operation of subsection (1).

97. Duty to give information

(1) The creditor under a regulated consumer credit agreement, within the prescribed period after he has received a request in writing to that effect from the debtor, shall give the debtor a statement in the prescribed form indicating, according to the information to which it is practicable for him to refer, the amount of the payment required to discharge the debtor's indebtedness under the agreement, together with the prescribed particulars showing how the amount is arrived at.

(2) Subsection (1) does not apply to a request made less than one month after a previous request under that subsection relating to the same agreement was complied with.

(3) If the creditor fails to comply with subsection (1)—

(a) he is not entitled, while the default continues, to enforce the agreement; and

(b) if the default continues for one month he commits an offence.

Termination of agreements

98. Duty to give notice of termination (non-default cases)

(1) The creditor or owner is not entitled to terminate a regulated agreement except by or after giving the debtor or hirer not less than seven days' notice of the termination.

(2) Subsection (1) applies only where—

(a) a period for the duration of the agreement is specified in the agreement, and

(b) that period has not ended when the creditor or owner does an act mentioned in subsection (1),

but so applies notwithstanding that, under the agreement, any party is entitled to terminate it before the end of the period so specified.

(3) A notice under subsection (1) is ineffective if not in the prescribed form.

(4) Subsection (1) does not prevent a creditor from treating the right to draw on any credit as restricted or deferred and taking such steps as may be necessary to make the restriction or deferment effective.

(5) Regulations may provide that subsection (1) is not to apply to agreements described by the regulations.

(6) Subsection (1) does not apply to the termination of a regulated agreement by reason of any breach by the debtor or hirer of the agreement.

99. Right to terminate hire-purchase etc. agreements

(1) At any time before the final payment by the debtor under a regulated hire–purchase or regulated conditional sale agreement falls due, the debtor shall be entitled to terminate the agreement by giving notice to any person entitied or authorised to receive the sums payable under the agreement.

(2) Termination of an agreement under subsection (1) does not affect any liability under the agreement which has accrued before the termination.

(3) Subsection (1) does not apply to a conditional sale agreement relating to land after the title to the land has passed to the debtor.

(4) In the case of a conditional sale agreement relating to goods, where the property in the goods, having become vested in the debtor, is transferred to a person who does not become the debtor under the agreement, the debtor shall not thereafter be entitled to terminate the agreement under subsection (1).

(5) Subject to subsection (4), where a debtor under a conditional sale agreement relating to goods terminates the agreement under this section after the property in the goods has become vested in him, the property in the goods shall thereupon vest in the person (the 'previous owner') in whom it was vested immediately before it became vested in the debtor:

Provided that if the previous owner has died, or any other event has occurred whereby that property, if vested in him immediately before that event, would thereupon have vested in some other person, the property shall be treated as having devolved as if it had been vested in the previous owner immediately before his death or immediately before that event, as the case may be.

100. Liability of debtor on termination of hire-purchase etc. agreement

(1) Where a regulated hire-purchase or regulated conditional sale agreement is terminated under section 99 the debtor shall be liable, unless the agreement provides for a smaller payment, or does not provide for any payment, to pay to the creditor the amount (if any) by which one-half of the total price exceeds the aggregate of the sums paid and the sums due in respect of the total price immediately before the termination.

(2) Where under a hire-purchase or conditional sale agreement the creditor is required to carry out any installation and the agreement specifies, as part of the total price, the amount to be paid in respect of the installation (the 'installation charge') the reference in subsection (1) to one-half of the total price shall be construed as a reference to the aggregate of the installation charge and one-half of the remainder of the total price.

(3) If in any action the court is satisfied that a sum less than the amount specified in subsection (1) would be equal to the loss sustained by the creditor in consequence of the termination of the agreement by the debtor, the court may make an order for the payment of that sum in lieu of the amount specified in subsection (1).

(4) If the debtor has contravened an obligation to take reasonable care of the goods or land, the amount arrived at under subsection (1) shall be increased by the sum required to recompense the creditor for that contravention, and subsection (2) shall have effect accordingly.

(5) Where the debtor, on the termination of the agreement, wrongfully retains possession of goods to which the agreement relates, then, in any action brought by the creditor to recover possession of the goods from the debtor, the court, unless it is satisfied that having

regard to the circumstances it would not be just to do so, shall order the goods to be delivered to the creditor without giving the debtor an option to pay the value of the goods.

101. Right to termininate hire agreement

(1) The hirer under a regulated consumer hire agreement is entitled to terminate the agreement by giving notice to any person entitled or authorised to receive the sums payable under the agreement.

(2) Termination of an agreement under subsection (1) does not affect any liability under the agreement which has accrued before the termination.

(3) A notice under subsection (1) shall not expire earlier than eighteen months after the making of the agreement, but apart from that the minimum period of notice to be given under subsection (1), unless the agreement provides for a shorter period, is as follows.

(4) If the agreement provides for the making of payments by the hirer to the owner at equal intervals, the minimum period of notice is the length of one interval or three months, whichever is less.

(5) If the agreement provides for the making of such payments at differing intervals, the minimum period of notice is the length of the shortest interval or three months, whichever is less.

(6) In any other case, the minimum period of notice is three months.

(7) This section does not apply to—

(a) any agreement which provides for the making by the hirer of payments which in total (and without breach of the agreement) exceed [£1,500] in any year, or

(b) any agreement where—

(i) goods are bailed or (in Scotland) hired to the hirer for the purposes of a business carried on by him, or the hirer holds himself out as requiring the goods for those purposes, and

(ii) the goods are selected by the hirer, and acquired by the owner for the purposes of the agreement at the request of the hirer from any person other than the owner's associate, or

(c) any agreement where the hirer requires, or holds himself out as requiring, the goods for the purpose of bailing or hiring them to other persons in the course of a business carried on by him.

(8) If, on an application made to the Director by a person carrying on a consumer hire business, it appears to the Director that it would be in the interest of hirers to do so, he may by notice to the applicant direct that this section shall not apply to consumer hire agreements made by the applicant, and subject to such conditions (if any) as the Director may specify, this Act shall have effect accordingly.

(9) In the case of a modifying agreement, subsection (3) shall apply with the substitution for 'the making of the agreement' of 'the making of the original agreement'.

102. Agency for receiving notice of rescission

(1) Where the debtor or hirer under a regulated agreement claims to have a right to rescind the agreement, each of the following shall be deemed to be the agent of the creditor or owner for the purpose of receiving any notice rescinding the agreement which is served by the debtor or hirer—

(a) a credit-broker or supplier who was the negotiator in antecedent negotiations, and

(b) any person who, in the course of a business carried on by him, acted on behalf of the debtor or hirer in any negotiations for the agreement.

(2) In subsection (1) 'rescind' does not include—

(a) service of a notice of cancellation, or

(b) termination of an agreement under section 99 or 101 or by the exercise of a right or power in that behalf expressly conferred by the agreement.

103. Termination statements

(1) If an individual (the 'customer') serves on any person (the 'trader') a notice—

(a) stating that—

(i) the customer was the debtor or hirer under a regulated agreement described in the notice, and the trader was the creditor or owner under the agreement, and

(ii) the customer has discharged his indebtedness to the trader under the agreement, and

(iii) the agreement has ceased to have any operation; and

(b) requiring the trader to give the customer a notice, signed by or on behalf of the trader, confirming that those statements are correct,

the trader shall, within the prescribed period after receiving the notice, either comply with it or serve on the customer a counter-notice stating that, as the case may be, he disputes the correctness of the notice or asserts that the customer is not indebted to him under the agreement.

(2) Where the trader disputes the correctness of the notice he shall give particulars of the way in which he alleges it to be wrong.

(3) Subsection (1) does not apply in relation to any agreement if the trader has previously complied with that subsection on the service of a notice under it with respect to that agreement.

(4) Subsection (1) does not apply to a non-commercial agreement

(5) If the trader fails to comply with subsection (1), and the default continues for one month, he commits an offence.

104. Goods not to be treated as subject to landlord's hypothec in Scotland

Goods comprised in a hire-purchase agreement or goods comprised in a conditional sale agreement which have not become vested in the debtor shall not be treated in Scotland as subject to the landlord's hypothec—

(a) during the period between the service of a default notice in respect of the goods and the date on which the notice expires or is earlier complied with; or

(b) if the agreement is enforceable on an order of the court only, during the period between the commencement and termination of an action by the creditor to enforce the agreement.

PART VIII
SECURITY

General

105. Form and content of securities

(1) Any security provided in relation to a regulated agreement shall be expressed in writing.

(2) Regulations may prescribe the form and content of documents ('security instruments') to be made in compliance with subsection (1).

(3) Regulations under subsection (2) may in particular—

(a) require specified information to be included in the prescribed manner in documents, and other specified material to be excluded;

(b) contain requirements to ensure that specified information is clearly brought to the attention of the surety, and that one part of a document is not given insufficient or excessive prominence compared with another.

(4) A security instrument is not properly executed unless—

(a) a document in the prescribed form, itself containing all the prescribed terms and conforming to regulations under subsection (2), is signed in the prescribed manner by or on behalf of the surety, and

(b) the document embodies all the terms of the security, other than implied terms, and

(c) the document, when presented or sent for the purpose of being signed by or on behalf of the surety, is in such state that its terms are readily legible, and

(d) when the document is presented or sent for the purpose of being signed by or on behalf of the surety there is also presented or sent a copy of the document.

(5) A security instrument is not properly executed unless—

(a) where the security is provided after, or at the time when, the regulated agreement is made, a copy of the executed agreement, together with a copy of any other document referred to in it, is given to the surety at the time the security is provided, or

(b) where the security is provided before the regulated agreement is made, a copy of the executed agreement, together with a copy of any other document referred to in it, is given to the surety within seven days after the regulated agreement is made.

(6) Subsection (1) does not apply to a security provided by the debtor or hirer.

(7) If—

(a) in contravention of subsection (1) a security is not expressed in writing, or

(b) a security instrument is improperly executed,

the security, so far as provided in relation to a regulated agreement, is enforceable against the surety on an order of the court only.

(8) If an application for an order under subsection (7) is dismissed (except on technical grounds only) section 106 (ineffective securities) shall apply to the security.

(9) Regulations under section 60(1) shall include provision requiring documents embodying regulated agreements also to embody any security provided in relation to a regulated agreement by the debtor or hirer.

106. Ineffective securities

Where, under any provision of this Act, this section is applied to any security provided in relation to a regulated agreement, then, subject to section 177 (saving for registered charges)—

(a) the security, so far as it is so provided, shall be treated as never having effect;

(b) any property lodged with the creditor or owner solely for the purposes of the security as so provided shall be returned by him forthwith;

(c) the creditor or owner shall take any necessary action to remove or cancel an entry in any register, so far as the entry relates to the security as so provided; and

(d) any amount received by the creditor or owner on realisation of the security shall, so far as it is referable to the agreement, be repaid to the surety.

107. Duty to give information to surety under fixed-sum credit agreement

(1) The creditor under a regulated agreement for fixed-sum credit in relation to which security is provided, within the prescribed period after receiving a request in writing to that effect from the surety and payment of a fee of [£1], shall give to the surety (if a different person from the debtor)—

(a) a copy of the executed agreement (if any) and of any other document referred to in it;

(b) a copy of the security instrument (if any); and

(c) a statement signed by or on behalf of the creditor showing, according to the information to which it is practicable for him to refer,—

(i) the total sum paid under the agreement by the debtor,

(ii) the total sum which has become payable under the agreement by the debtor but remains unpaid, and the various amounts comprised in that total sum, with the date when each became due, and

(iii) the total sum which is to become payable under the agreement by the debtor, and the various amounts comprised in that total sum, with the date, or mode of determining the date, when each becomes due.

(2) If the creditor possesses insufficient information to enable him to ascertain the amounts and dates mentioned in subsection (1)(c)(iii), he shall be taken to comply with that sub-paragraph if his statement under subsection (1)(c) gives the basis on which, under the regulated agreement, they would fall to be ascertained.

(3) Subsection (1) does not apply to—

(a) an agreement under which no sum is, or will or may become, payable by the debtor, or

(b) a request made less than one month after a previous request under that subsection relating to the same agreement was complied with.

(4) If the creditor under an agreement fails to comply with subsection (1)—

(a) he is not entitled, while the default continues, to enforce the security, so far as provided in relation to the agreement; and

(b) if the default continues for one month he commits an offence.

(5) This section does not apply to a non-commercial agreement.

108. Duty to give information to surety under running-account credit agreement

(1) The creditor under a regulated agreement for running-account credit in relation to which security is provided, within the prescribed period after receiving a request in writing to that effect from the surety and payment of a fee of [£1], shall give to the surety (if a different person from the debtor)—

(a) a copy of the executed agreement (if any) and of any other document referred to in it;

(b) a copy of the security instrument (if any); and

(c) a statement signed by or on behalf of the creditor showing, according to the information to which it is practicable for him to refer,—

(i) the state of the account, and

(ii) the amount, if any, currently payable under the agreement by the debtor to the creditor, and

(iii) the amounts and due dates of any payments which, if the debtor does not draw further on the account, will later become payable under the agreement by the debtor to the creditor.

(2) If the creditor possesses insufficient information to enable him to ascertain the amounts and dates mentioned in subsection (1)(c)(iii), he shall be taken to comply with that sub-paragraph if his statement under subsection (1)(c) gives the basis on which, under the regulated agreement, they would fall to be ascertained.

(3) Subsection (1) does not apply to—

(a) an agreement under which no sum is, or will or may become, payable by the debtor, or

(b) a request made less than one month after a previous request under that subsection relating to the same agreement was complied with.

(4) If the creditor under an agreement fails to comply with subsection (1)—

(a) he is not entitled, while the default continues, to enforce the security, so far as provided in relation to the agreement; and

(b) if the default continues for one month he commits an offence.

(5) This section does not apply to a non-commercial agreement.

109. Duty to give information to surety under consumer hire agreement

(1) The owner under a regulated consumer hire agreement in relation to which security is provided, within the prescribed period after receiving a request in writing to that effect from the surety and payment of a fee of [£1], shall give to the surety (if a different person from the hirer)—

(a) a copy of the executed agreement and of any other document referred to in it;

(b) a copy of the security instrument (if any); and

(c) a statement signed by or on behalf of the owner showing, according to the information to which it is practicable for him to refer, the total sum which has become payable under the agreement by the hirer but remains unpaid and the various amounts comprised in that total sum, with the date when each became due.

(2) Subsection (1) does not apply to—

(a) an agreement under which no sum is, or will or may become, payable by the hirer, or

(b) a request made less than one month after a previous request under that subsection relating to the same agreement was complied with.

(3) If the owner under an agreement fails to comply with subsection (1)—

(a) he is not entitled, while the default continues, to enforce the security, so far as provided in relation to the agreement; and

(b) if the default continues for one month he commits an offence.

(4) This section does not apply to a non-commercial agreement.

110. Duty to give information to debtor or hirer

(1) The creditor or owner under a regulated agreement, within the prescribed period after receiving a request in writing to that effect from the debtor or hirer and payment of a fee of [£1], shall give the debtor or hirer a copy of any security instrument executed in relation to the agreement after the making of the agreement.

(2) Subsection (1) does not apply to—

(a) a non-commercial agreement, or

(b) an agreement under which no sum is, or will or may become, payable by the debtor or hirer, or

(c) a request made less than one month after a previous request under subsection (1) relating to the same agreement was complied with.

(3) If the creditor or owner under an agreement fails to comply with subsection (1)—

(a) he is not entitled, while the default continues, to enforce the security (so far as provided in relation to the agreement); and

(b) if the default continues for one month he commits an offence.

111. Duty to give surety copy of default etc. notice

(1) When a default notice or a notice under section 76(1) or 98(1) is served on a debtor or hirer, a copy of the notice shall be served by the creditor or owner on any surety (if a different person from the debtor or hirer).

(2) If the creditor or owner fails to comply with subsection (1) in the case of any surety, the security is enforceable against the surety (in respect of the breach or other matter to which the notice relates) on an order of the court only.

112. Realisation of securities

Subject to section 121, regulations may provide for any matters relating to the sale or other realisation, by the creditor or owner, of property over which any right has been provided by way of security in relation to an actual or prospective regulated agreement, other than a non-commercial agreement.

113. Act not to be evaded by use of security

(1) Where a security is provided in relation to an actual or prospective regulated agreement, the security shall not be enforced so as to benefit the creditor or owner, directly or indirectly, to an extent greater (whether as respects the amount of any payment or the time or manner of its being made) than would be the case if the security were not provided and any obligations of the debtor or hirer, or his relative, under or in relation to the agreement were carried out to the extent (if any) to which they would be enforced under this Act.

(2) In accordance with subsection (1), where a regulated agreement is enforceable on an order of the court or the Director only, any security provided in relation to the agreement is enforceable (so far as provided in relation to the agreement) where such an order has been made in relation to the agreement, but not otherwise.

(3) Where—

(a) a regulated agreement is cancelled under section 69(1) or becomes subject to section 69(2), or

(b) a regulated agreement is terminated under section 91, or

(c) in relation to any agreement an application for an order under section 40(2), 65(1), 124(1) or 149(2) is dismissed (except on technical grounds only), or

(d) a declaration is made by the court under section 142(1) (refusal of enforcement order) as respects any regulated agreement,

section 106 shall apply to any security provided in relation to the agreement.

(4) Where subsection (3)(d) applies and the declaration relates to a part only of the regulated agreement, section 106 shall apply to the security only so far as it concerns that part.

(5) In the case of a cancelled agreement, the duty imposed on the debtor or hirer by section 71 or 72 shall not be enforceable before the creditor or owner has discharged any duty imposed on him by section 106 (as applied by subsection (3)(a)).

(6) If the security is provided in relation to a prospective agreement or transaction, the security shall be enforceable in relation to the agreement or transaction only after the time (if any) when the agreement is made; and until that time the person providing the security shall be entitled, by notice to the creditor or owner, to require that section 106 shall thereupon apply to the security.

(7) Where an indemnity [or guarantee] is given in a case where the debtor or hirer is a minor, or [an indemnity is given in a case where he] is otherwise not of full capacity, the reference in subsection (1) to the extent to which his obligations would be enforced shall be read in relation to the indemnity [or guarantee] as a reference to the extent to which [those obligations] would be enforced if he were of full capacity.

(8) Subsections (1) and (3) also apply where a security is provided in relation to an actual or prospective linked transaction, and in that case—

(a) references to the agreement shall be read as references to the linked transaction, and

(b) references to the creditor or owner shall be read as references to any person (other than the debtor or hirer, or his relative) who is a party, or prospective party, to the linked transaction.

Pledges

114. Pawn-receipts

(1) At the time he receives the article, a person who takes any article in pawn under a regulated agreement shall give to the person from whom he receives it a receipt in the prescribed form (a 'pawn-receipt').

(2) A person who takes any article in pawn from an individual whom he knows to be, or who appears to be and is, a minor commits an offence.

(3) This section and sections 115 to 122 do not apply to—

(a) a pledge of documents of title [or of bearer bonds], or

(b) a non-commercial agreement.

115. Penalty for failure to supply copies of pledge agreement, etc.

If the creditor under a regulated agreement to take any article in pawn fails to observe the requirements of section 62 to 64 or 114(1) in relation to the agreement he commits an offence.

116. Redemption period

(1) A pawn is redeemable at any time within six months after it was taken.

(2) Subject to subsection (1), the period within which a pawn is redeemable shall be the same as the period fixed by the parties for the duration of the credit secured by the pledge, or such longer period as they may agree.

(3) If the pawn is not redeemed by the end of the period laid down by subsections (1) and (2) (the 'redemption period'), it nevertheless remains redeemable until it is realised by the pawnee under section 121 except where under section 120(1)(a) the property in it passes to the pawnee.

(4) No special charge shall be made for redemption of a pawn after the end of the redemption period, and charges in respect of the safe keeping of the pawn shall not be at a higher rate after the end of the redemption period than before.

117. Redemption procedure

(1) On surrender of the pawn-receipt, and payment of the amount owing, at any time when the pawn is redeemable, the pawnee shall deliver the pawn to the bearer of the pawn-receipt.

(2) Subsection (1) does not apply if the pawnee knows or has reasonable cause to suspect that the bearer of the pawn-receipt is neither the owner of the pawn nor authorised by the owner to redeem it.

(3) The pawnee is not liable to any person in tort or delict for delivering the pawn where subsection (1) applies, or refusing to deliver it where the person demanding delivery does not comply with subsection (1) or, by reason of subsection (2), subsection (1) does not apply.

118. Loss etc. of pawn-receipt

(1) A person (the 'claimant') who is not in possession of the pawn-receipt but claims to be the owner of the pawn, or to be otherwise entitled or authorised to redeem it, may do so at any time when it is redeemable by tendering to the pawnee in place of the pawn-receipt—

(a) a statutory declaration made by the claimant in the prescribed form, and with the prescribed contents, or

(b) where the pawn is security for fixed-sum credit not exceeding [£75] or running-account credit on which the credit limit does not exceed [£75], and the pawnee agrees, a statement in writing in the prescribed form, and with the prescribed contents, signed by the claimant.

(2) On compliance by the claimant with subsection (1), section 117 shall apply as if the declaration or statement were the pawn-receipt, and the pawn-receipt itself shall become inoperative for the purposes of section 117.

119. Unreasonable refusal to deliver pawn

(1) If a person who has taken a pawn under a regulated agreement refuses without reasonable cause to allow the pawn to be redeemed, he commits an offence.

(2) On the conviction in England and Wales of a pawnee under subsection (1) where the offence does not amount to theft, section 28 (orders for restitution) of the Theft Act 1968, and any provision of the Theft Act 1968 relating to that section, shall apply as if the pawnee had been convicted of stealing the pawn.

(3) On the conviction in Northern Ireland of a pawnee under subsection (1) where the offence does not amount to theft, section 27 (orders for restitution) of the Theft Act (Northern Ireland) 1969, and any provision of the Theft Act (Northern Ireland) 1969 relating to that section, shall apply as if the pawnee had been convicted of stealing the pawn.

120. Consequence of failure to redeem

(1) If at the end of the redemption period the pawn has not been redeemed—

(a) notwithstanding anything in section 113, the property in the pawn passes to the pawnee where the redemption period is six months and the pawn is security for fixed-sum credit not exceeding [£75] or running-account credit on which the credit limit does not exceed [£75]; or

(b) in any other case the pawn becomes realisable by the pawnee.

(2) Where the debtor or hirer is entitled to apply to the court for a time order under section 129, subsection (1) shall apply with the substitution, for 'at the end of the redemption period' of 'after the expiry of five days following the end of the redemption period'.

121. Realisation of pawn

(1) When a pawn has become realisable by him, the pawnee may sell it, after giving to the pawnor (except in such cases as may be prescribed) not less than the prescribed period of notice of the intention to sell, indicating in the notice the asking price and such other particulars as may be prescribed.

(2) Within the prescribed period after the sale takes place, the pawnee shall give the pawnor the prescribed information in writing as to the sale, its proceeds and expenses.

(3) Where the net proceeds of sale are not less than the sum which, if the pawn had been redeemed on the date of the sale, would have been payable for its redemption, the debt secured by the pawn is discharged and any surplus shall be paid by the pawnee to the pawnor.

(4) Where subsection (3) does not apply, the debt shall be treated as from the date of sale as equal to the amount by which the net proceeds of sale fall short of the sum which would have been payable for the redemption of the pawn on that date.

(5) In this section the 'net proceeds of sale' is the amount realised (the 'gross amount') less the expenses (if any) of the sale.

(6) If the pawnor alleges that the gross amount is less than the true market value of the pawn on the date of sale, it is for the pawnee to prove that he and any agents employed by him in the sale used reasonable care to ensure that the true market value was obtained, and if he fails to do so subsections (3) and (4) shall have effect as if the reference in subsection (5) to the gross amount were a reference to the true market value.

(7) If the pawnor alleges that the expenses of the sale were unreasonably high, it is for the pawnee to prove that they were reasonable, and if he fails to do so subsections (3) and (4) shall have effect as if the reference in subsection (5) to expenses were a reference to reasonable expenses.

122. Order in Scotland to deliver pawn

. . .

Negotiable instruments

123. Restrictions on taking and negotiating instruments

(1) A creditor or owner shall not take a negotiable instrument, other than a bank note or cheque, in discharge of any sum payable—

(a) by the debtor or hirer under a regulated agreement, or

(b) by any person as surety in relation to the agreement.

(2) The creditor or owner shall not negotiate a cheque taken by him in discharge of a sum payable as mentioned in subsection (1) except to a banker (within the meaning of the Bills of Exchange Act 1882).

(3) The creditor or owner shall not take a negotiable instrument as security for the discharge of any sum payable as mentioned in subsection (1).

(4) A person takes a negotiable instrument as security for the discharge of a sum if the sum is intended to be paid in some other way, and the negotiable instrument is to be presented for payment only if the sum is not paid in that way.

(5) This section does not apply where the regulated agreement is a non-commercial agreement.

(6) The Secretary of State may by order provide that this section shall not apply where the regulated agreement has a connection with a country outside the United Kingdom.

124. Consequences of breach of s. 123

(1) After any contravention of section 123 has occurred in relation to a sum payable as mentioned in section 123(1)(a), the agreement under which the sum is payable is enforceable against the debtor or hirer on an order of the court only.

(2) After any contravention of section 123 has occurred in relation to a sum payable by any surety, the security is enforceable on an order of the court only.

(3) Where an application for an order under subsection (2) is dismissed (except on technical grounds only) section 106 shall apply to the security.

125. Holders in due course

(1) A person who takes a negotiable instrument in contravention of section 123(1) or (3) is not a holder in due course, and is not entitled to enforce the instrument.

(2) Where a person negotiates a cheque in contravention of section 123(2), his doing so constitutes a defect in his title within the meaning of the Bills of Exchange Act 1882.

(3) If a person mentioned in section 123(1)(a) and (b) ('the protected person') becomes liable to a holder in due course of an instrument taken from the protected person in contravention of section 123(1) or (3), or taken from the protected person and negotiated in contravention of section 123(2), the creditor or owner shall indemnify the protected person in respect of that liability.

(4) Nothing in this Act affects the rights of the holder in due course of any negotiable instrument.

Land mortgages

126. Enforcement of land mortgages

A land mortgage securing a regulated agreement is enforceable (so far as provided in relation to the agreement) on an order of the court only.

PART IX
JUDICIAL CONTROL

Enforcement of certain regulated agreements and securities

127. Enforcement orders in cases of infringement

(1) In the case of an application for an enforcement order under—

(a) section 65(1) (improperly executed agreements), or

(b) section 105(7)(a) or (b) (improperly executed security instruments), or

(c) section 111(2) (failure to serve copy of notice on surety), or

(d) section 124(1) or (2) (taking of negotiable instrument in contravention of section 123),

the court shall dismiss the application if, but (subject to subsections (3) and (4)) only if, it considers it just to do so having regard to—

(i) prejudice caused to any person by the contravention in question, and the degree of culpability for it; and

(ii) the powers conferred on the court by subsection (2) and sections 135 and 136.

(2) If it appears to the court just to do so, it may in an enforcement order reduce or discharge any sum payable by the debtor or hirer, or any surety, so as to compensate him for prejudice suffered as a result of the contravention in question.

(3) The court shall not make an enforcement order under section 65(1) if section 61(1)(a) (signing of agreements) was not complied with unless a document (whether or not in the prescribed form and complying with regulations under section 60(1)) itself containing an the prescribed terms of the agreement was signed by the debtor or hirer (whether or not in the prescribed manner).

(4) The court shall not make an enforcement order under section 65(1) in the case of a cancellable agreement if—

(a) a provision of section 62 or 63 was not complied with, and the creditor or owner did not give a copy of the executed agreement, and of any other document referred to in it, to the debtor or hirer before the commencement of the proceedings in which the order is sought, or

(b) section 64(1) was not complied with.

(5) Where an enforcement order is made in a case to which subsection (3) applies, the order may direct that the regulated agreement is to have effect as if it did not include a term omitted from the document signed by the debtor or hirer.

128. Enforcement orders on death of debtor or hirer

The court shall make an order under section 86(2) if, but only if, the creditor or owner proves that he has been unable to satisfy himself that the present and future obligations of the debtor or hirer under the agreement are likely to be discharged.

Extension of time

129. Time orders

(1) If it appears to the court just to do so—

(a) on an application for an enforcement order; or

(b) on an application made by a debtor or hirer under this paragraph after service on him of—

(i) a default notice, or

(ii) a notice under section 76(1) or 98(1); or

(c) in an action brought by a creditor or owner to enforce a regulated agreement or any security, or recover possession of any goods or land to which a regulated agreement relates,

the court may make an order under this section (a 'time order').

(2) A time order shall provide for one or both of the following, as the court considers just—

(a) the payment by the debtor or hirer or any surety of any sum owed under a regulated agreement or a security by such instalments, payable at such times, as the court having regard to the means of the debtor or hirer and any surety, considers reasonable;

(b) the remedying by the debtor or hirer of any breach of a regulated agreement (other than non-payment of money) within such period as the court may specify.

[(3) Where in Scotland a time to pay direction or a time order has been made in relation to a debt, it shall not thereafter be competent to make a time order in relation to the same debt.]

130. Supplemental provisions about time orders

(1) Where in accordance with rules of court an offer to pay any sum by instalments is made by the debtor or hirer and accepted by the creditor or owner, the court may in accordance with rules of court make a time order under section 129(2)(a) giving effect to the offer without hearing evidence of means.

(2) In the case of a hire-purchase or conditional sale agreement only, a time order under section 129(2)(a) may deal with sums which, although not payable by the debtor at the time the order is made, would if the agreement continued in force become payable under it subsequently.

(3) A time order under section 129(2)(a) shall not be made where the regulated agreement is secured by a pledge if, by virtue of regulations made under section 76(5), 87(4) or 98(5), service of a notice is not necessary for enforcement of the pledge.

(4) Where, following the making of a time order in relation to a regulated hire-purchase or conditional sale agreement or a regulated consumer hire agreement, the debtor or hirer

is in possession of the goods, he shall be treated (except in the case of a debtor to whom the creditor's title has passed) as a bailee or (in Scotland) a custodier of the goods under the terms of the agreement, notwithstanding that the agreement has been terminated.

(5) Without prejudice to anything done by the creditor or owner before the commencement of the period specified in a time order made under section 129(2)(b) ('the relevant period'),—

(a) he shall not while the relevant period subsists take in relation to the agreement any action such as is mentioned in section 87(1);

(b) where—

(i) a provision of the agreement ('the secondary provision') becomes operative only on breach of another provision of the agreement ('the primary provision'), and

(ii) the time order provides for the remedying of such a breach of the primary provision within the relevant period,

he shall not treat the secondary provision as operative before the end of that period;

(c) if while the relevant period subsists the breach to which the order relates is remedied it shall be treated as not having occurred.

(6) On the application of any person affected by a time order, the court may vary or revoke the order.

Protection of property pending proceedings

131. Protection orders

The court, on application of the creditor or owner under a regulated agreement, may make such orders as it thinks just for protecting any property of the creditor or owner, or property subject to any security, from damage or depreciation pending the determination of any proceedings under this Act, including orders restricting or prohibiting use of the property or giving directions as to its custody.

Hire and hire-purchase etc. agreements

132. Financial relief for hirer

(1) Where the owner under a regulated consumer hire agreement recovers possession of goods to which the agreement relates otherwise than by action, the hirer may apply to the court for an order that—

(a) the whole or part of any sum paid by the hirer to the owner in respect of the goods shall be repaid, and

(b) the obligation to pay the whole or part of any sum owed by the hirer to the owner in respect of the goods shall cease,

and if it appears to the court just to do so, having regard to the extent of the enjoyment of the goods by the hirer, the court shall grant the application in full or in part.

(2) Where in proceedings relating to a regulated consumer hire agreement the court makes an order for the delivery to the owner of goods to which the agreement relates the court may include in the order the like provision as may be made in an order under subsection (1).

133. Hire-purchase etc. agreements: special powers of court

(1) If, in relation to a regulated hire-purchase or conditional sale agreement, it appears to the court just to do so—

(a) on an application for an enforcement order or time order; or

(b) in an action brought by the creditor to recover possession of goods to which the agreement relates,

the court may—

(i) make an order (a 'return order') for the return to the creditor of goods to which the agreement relates;

(ii) make an order (a 'transfer order') for the transfer to the debtor of the creditor's title to certain goods to which the agreement relates ('the transferred goods'), and the retum to the creditor of the remainder of the goods.

(2) In determining for the purposes of this section how much of the total price has been paid ('the paid-up sum'), the court may—

(a) treat any sum paid by the debtor, or owed by the creditor, in relation to the goods as part of the paid-up sum;

(b) deduct any sum owed by the debtor in relation to the goods (otherwise than as part of the total price) from the paid-up sum,
and make corresponding reductions in amounts so owed.

(3) Where a transfer order is made, the transferred goods shall be such of the goods to which the agreement relates as the court thinks just; but a transfer order shall be made only where the paid-up sum exceeds the part of the total price referable to the transferred goods by an amount equal to at least one-third of the unpaid balance of the total price.

(4) Notwithstanding the making of a return order or transfer order, the debtor may at any time before the goods enter the possession of the creditor, on payment of the balance of the total price and the fulfilment of any other necessary conditions, claim the goods ordered to be returned to the creditor.

(5) When, in pursuance of a time order or under this section, the total price of goods under a regulated hire-purchase agreement or regulated conditional sale agreement is paid and any other necessary conditions are fulfilled, the creditor's title to the goods vests in the debtor.

(6) If, in contravention of a return order or transfer order, any goods to which the order relates are not returned to the creditor, the court, on the application of the creditor, may—

(a) revoke so much of the order as relates to those goods, and

(b) order the debtor to pay the creditor the unpaid portion of so much of the total price as is referable to those goods.

(7) For the purposes of this section, the part of the total price referable to any goods is the part assigned to those goods by the agreement or (if no such assignment is made) the part determined by the court to be reasonable.

134. Evidence of adverse detention in hire-purchase etc. cases

(1) Where goods are comprised in a regulated hire-purchase agreement, regulated conditional sale agreement or regulated consumer hire agreement, and the creditor or owner—

(a) brings an action or makes an application to enforce a right to recover possession of the goods from the debtor or hirer and

(b) proves that a demand for the delivery of the goods was included in the default notice under section 88(5), or that, after the right to recover possession of the goods accrued but before the action was begun or the application was made, he made a request in writing to the debtor or hirer to surrender the goods,

then, for the purposes of the claim of the creditor or owner to recover possession of the goods, the possession of them by the debtor or hirer shall be deemed to be adverse to the creditor or owner.

(2) In subsection (1) 'the debtor or hirer' includes a person in possession of the goods at any time between the debtor's or hirer's death and the grant of probate or administration, or (in Scotland) confirmation.

(3) Nothing in this section affects a claim for damages for conversion or (in Scotland) for delict.

Supplemental provisions as to orders

135. Power to impose conditions, or suspend operation of order

(1) If it considers it just to do so, the court may in an order made by it in relation to a regulated agreement include provisions—

(a) making the operation of any term of the order conditional on the doing of specified acts by any party to the proceedings;

(b) suspending the operation of any term of the order either—

(i) until such time as the court subsequently directs, or

(ii) untit the occurrence of a specified act or omission.

(2) The court shall not suspend the operation of a term requiring the delivery up of goods by any person unless satisfied that the goods are in his possession or control.

(3) In the case of a consumer hire agreement, the court shall not so use its powers under subsection (1)(b) as to extend the period for which, under the terms of the agreement, the hirer is entitled to possession of the goods to which the agreement relates.

(4) On the application of any person affected by a provision included under subsection (1), the court may vary the provision.

136. Power to vary agreements and securities

(1) The court may in an order made by it under this Act include such provision as it considers just for amending any agreement or security in consequence of a term of the order.

Extortionate credit bargains

137. Extortionate credit bargains

(1) If the court finds a credit bargain extortionate it may reopen the credit agreement so as to do justice between the parties.

(2) In this section and sections 138 to 140,—

(a) 'credit agreement' means any agreement between an individual (the 'debtor') and any other person (the 'creditor') by which the creditor provides the debtor with credit of any amount, and

(b) 'credit bargain'—

(i) where no transaction other than the credit agreement is to be taken into account in computing the total charge for credit, means the credit agreement, or

(ii) where one or more other transactions are to be so taken into account, means the credit agreement and those other transactions, taken together.

138. When bargains are extortionate

(1) A credit bargain is extortionate if it—

(a) requires the debtor or a relative of his to make payments (whether unconditionally, or on certain contingencies) which are grossly exorbitant, or

(b) otherwise grossly contravenes ordinary principles of fair dealing.

(2) In determining whether a credit bargain is extortionate, regard shall be had to such evidence as is adduced concerning—

(a) interest rates prevailing at the time it was made,

(b) the factors mentioned in subsection (3) to (5), and

(c) any other relevant considerations.

(3) Factors applicable under subsection (2) in relation to the debtor include—

(a) his age, experience, business capacity and state of health; and

(b) the degree to which, at the time of making the credit bargain, he was under financial pressure, and the nature of that pressure.

(4) factors applicable under subsection (2) in relation to the creditor include—

(a) the degree of risk accepted by him, having regard to the value of any security provided;

(b) his relationship to the debtor; and

(c) whether or not a colourable cash price was quoted for any goods or services included in the credit bargain.

(5) Factors applicable under subsection (2) in relation to a linked transaction include the question how far the transaction was reasonably required for the protection of debtor or creditor, or was in the interest of the debtor.

139. Reopening of extortionate agreements

(1) A credit agreement may, if the court thinks just, be reopened on the ground that the credit bargain is extortionate—

(a) on an application for the purpose made by the debtor or any surety to the High Court, county court or sheriff court; or

(b) at the instance of the debtor or a surety in any proceedings to which the debtor and creditor are parties, being proceedings to enforce the credit agreement, any security relating to it, or any linked transaction; or

(c) at the instance of the debtor or a surety in other proceedings in any court where the amount paid or payable under the credit agreement is relevant.

(2) In reopening the agreement, the court may, for the purpose of relieving the debtor or a surety from payment of any sum in excess of that fairly due and reasonable, by order—

(a) direct accounts to be taken, or (in Scotland) an accounting to be made, between any persons,

(b) set aside the whole or part of any obligation imposed on the debtor or a surety by the credit bargain or any related agreement,

(c) require the creditor to repay the whole or part of any sum paid under the credit bargain or any related agreement by the debtor or a surety, whether paid to the creditor or any other person,

(d) direct the return to the surety of any property provided for the purposes of the security, or

(e) alter the terms of the credit agreement or any security instrument.

(3) An order may be made under subsection (2) notwithstanding that its effect is to place a burden on the creditor in respect of an advantage unfairly enjoyed by another person who is a party to a linked transaction.

(4) An order under subsection (2) shall not alter the effect of any judgment.

(5) In England and Wales an application under subsection (1)(a) shall be brought only in the county court in the case of—

(a) a regulated agreement, or

(b) an agreement (not being a regulated agreement) under which the creditor provides the debtor with fixed-sum credit not exceeding [the county court limit] or running-account credit on which the credit limit does not exceed [the county court limit].

[(5A) In the preceding subsection 'the county court limit' means the county court limit for the time being specified by an Order in Council under section 145 of the County Courts Act 1984 as the county court limit for the purposes of that subsection.]

(6) In Scotland an application under subsection (1)(a) may be brought in the sheriff court for the district in which the debtor or surety resides or carries on business.

(7) In Northern Ireland an application under subsection (1)(a) may be brought in the county court in the case of—

(a) a regulated agreement, or

(b) an agreement (not being a regulated agreement) under which the creditor provides the debtor with fixed-sum credit not exceeding [£1,000] or running-account credit on which the credit limit does not exceed [£1,000].

140. Interpretation of sections 137 to 139

Where the credit agreement is not a regulated agreement, expressions used in sections 137 to 139 which, apart from this section, apply only to regulated agreements, shall be construed as nearly as may be as if the credit agreement were a regulated agreement.

Miscellaneous

141. Jurisdiction and parties

(1) In England and Wales the county court shall have jurisdiction to hear and determine—

(a) any action by the creditor or owner to enforce a regulated agreement or any security relating to it;

(b) any action to enforce any linked transaction against the debtor or hirer or his relative,

and such an action shall not be brought in any other court.

(2) Where an action or application is brought in the High Court which, by virtue of this Act, ought to have been brought in the county court it shall not be treated as improperly brought, but shall be transferred to the county court.

[(3) In Scotland the sheriff court shall have jurisdiction to hear and determine any action falling within subsection (1) and such an action shall not be brought in any other court.

(3A) Subject to subsection (3B) an action which is brought in the sheriff court by virtue of subsection (3) shall be brought only in one of the following courts, namely—

(a) the court for the place where the debtor or hirer is domiciled (within the meaning of section 41 or 42 of the Civil Jurisdiction and Judgments Act 1982);

(b) the court for the place where the debtor or hirer carries on business; and

(c) where the purpose of the action is to assert, declare or determine proprietary or possessory rights, or rights of security, in or over movable property, or to obtain authority to dispose of movable property, the court for the place where the property is situated.

(3B) Subsection (3A) shall not apply—

(a) where Rule 3 of Schedule 8 to the said Act of 1982 applies; or

(b) where the jurisdiction of another court has been prorogated by an agreement entered into after the dispute has arisen.]

(4) In Northern Ireland the county court shall have jurisdiction to hear and determine any action or application falling within subsection (1).

(5) Except as may be provided by rules of court, all the parties to a regulated agreement, and any surety, shall be made parties to any proceedings relating to the agreement.

142. Power to declare rights of parties

(1) Where under any provision of this Act a thing can be done by a creditor or owner on an enforcement order only, and either—

(a) the court dismisses (except on technical grounds only) an application for an enforcement order, or

(b) where no such application has been made or such an application has been dismissed on technical grounds only an interested party applies to the court for a declaration under this subsection,

the court may if it thinks just make a declaration that the creditor or owner is not entitled to do that thing, and thereafter no application for an enforcement order in respect of it shall be entertained.

(2) Where—

(a) a regulated agreement or linked transaction is cancelled under section 69(1), or becomes subject to section 69(2), or

(b) a regulated agreement is terminated under section 91, and an interested party applies to the court for a declaration under this subsection, the court may make a declaration to that effect.

Northern Ireland

143. Jurisdiction of county court in Northern Ireland

. . .

144. Appeal from county court in Northern Ireland

. . .

PART X
ANCILLARY CREDIT BUSINESSES

Definitions

145. Types of ancillary credit business

(1) An ancillary credit business is any business so far as it comprises or relates to—

(a) credit brokerage,

(b) debt-adjusting,

(c) debt-counselling,

(d) debt-collecting, or

(e) the operation of a credit reference agency.

(2) Subject to section 146(5), credit brokerage is the effecting of introductions—

(a) of individuals desiring to obtain credit—

(i) to persons carrying on businesses to which this sub-paragraph applies, or

(ii) in the case of an individual desiring to obtain credit to finance the acquisition or provision of a dwelling occupied by himself or his relative, to any person carrying on a business in the course of which he provides credit secured on land, or

(b) of individuals desiring to obtain goods on hire to persons carrying on businesses to which this paragraph applies, or

(c) of individuals desiring to obtain credit, or to obtain goods on hire, to other credit-brokers.

(3) Subsection (2)(a)(i) applies to—

(a) a consumer credit business;

(b) a business which comprises or relates to consumer credit agreements being, otherwise than by virtue of section 16(5)(a), exempt agreements;

(c) a business which comprises or relates to unregulated agreements where—

(i) the [law applicable to] the agreement is the law of a country outside the United Kingdom, and

(ii) if the [law applicable to] the agreement were the law of a part of the United Kingdom it would be a regulated consumer credit agreement.

(4) Subsection (2)(b) applies to—

(a) a consumer hire business;

(b) a business which comprises or relates to unregulated agreements where—

(i) the [law applicable to] the agreement is the law of a country outside the United Kingdom, and

(ii) if the [law applicable to] the agreement were the law of a part of the United Kingdom it would be a regulated consumer hire agreement.

(5) Subject to section 146(6), debt-adjusting is, in relation to debts due under consumer credit agreements or consumer hire agreements,—

(a) negotiating with the creditor or owner, on behalf of the debtor or hirer, terms for the discharge of a debt, or

(b) taking over, in return for payments by the debtor or hirer, his obligation to discharge a debt, or

(c) any similar activity concerned with the liquidation of a debt.

(6) Subject to section 146(6), debt-counselling is the giving of advice to debtors or hirers about the liquidation of debts due under consumer credit agreements or consumer hire agreements.

(7) Subject to section 146(6), debt-collecting is the taking of steps to procure payment of debts due under consumer credit agreements or consumer hire agreements.

(8) A credit reference agency is a person carrying on a business comprising the furnishing of persons with information relevant to the financial standing of individuals, being information collected by the agency for that purpose.

146. Exceptions from section 145

(1) A barrister or advocate acting in that capacity is not to be treated as doing so in the course of any ancillary credit business.

(2) A solicitor engaging in contentious business (as defined in [section 87(1) of the Solicitors Act 1974]) is not to be treated as doing so in the course of any ancillary credit business.

(3) A solicitor within the meaning of the Solicitors (Scotland) Act 1933 engaging in business done in or for the purposes of proceedings before a court or before an arbiter is not to be treated as doing so in the course of any ancillary credit business.

(4) A solicitor in Northern Ireland engaging in [contentious business (as defined in Article 3(2) of the Solicitors (Northern Ireland) Order 1976], is not to be treated as doing so in the course of any ancillary credit business.

(5) For the purposes of section 145(2), introductions effected by an individual by canvassing off trade premises either debtor-creditor-supplier agreements falling within section 12(a) or regulated consumer hire agreements shall be disregarded if—

(a) the introductions are not effected by him in the capacity of an employee, and

(b) he does not by any other method effect introductions falling within section 145(2).

(6) It is not debt-adjusting, debt-counselling or debt-collecting for a person to do anything in relation to a debt arising under an agreement if—

(a) he is the creditor or owner under the agreement, otherwise than by virtue of an assignment, or

(b) he is the creditor or owner under the agreement by virtue of an assignment made in connection with the transfer to the assignee of any business other than a debt-collecting business, or

(c) he is the supplier in relation to the agreement, or

(d) he is a credit-broker who has acquired the business of the person who was the supplier in relation to the agreement, or

(e) he is a person prevented by subsection (5) from being treated as a credit-broker, and the agreement was made in consequence of an introduction (whether made by him or another person) which, under subsection (5), is to be disregarded.

Licensing

147. Application of Part III

(1) The provisions of Part III (except section 40) apply to an ancillary credit business as they apply to a consumer credit business.

(2) Without prejudice to the generality of section 26, regulations under that section (as applied by subsection (1)) may include provisions regulating the collection and dissemination of information by credit reference agencies.

148. Agreement for services of unlicensed trader

(1) An agreement for the services of a person carrying on ancillary credit business (the 'trader'), if made when the trader was unlicensed, is enforceable against the other party (the 'customer') only where the Director has made an order under subsection (2) which applies to the agreement.

(2) The trader or his successor in title may apply to the Director for an order that agreements within subsection (1) are to be treated as if made when the trader was licensed.

(3) Unless the Director determines to make an order under subsection (2) in accordance with the application, he shall, before determining the application, by notice—

(a) inform the trader, giving his reasons, that, as the case may be, he is minded to refuse the application, or to grant it in terms different from those applied for, describing them, and

(b) invite the trader to submit to the Director representations in support of his application in accordance with section 34.

(4) In determining whether or not to make an order under subsection (2) in respect of any period the Director shall consider, in addition to any other relevant factors,—

(a) how far, if at all, customers under agreements made by the trader during that period were prejudiced by the trader's conduct,

(b) whether or not the Director would have been likely to grant a licence covering that period on an application by the trader, and

(c) the degree of culpability for the failure to obtain a licence.

(5) If the Director thinks fit, he may in an order under subsection (2)—

(a) limit the order to specified agreements, or agreements of a specified description or made at a specified time;

(b) make the order conditional on the doing of specified acts by the trader.

149. Regulated agreements made on introductions by unlicensed credit-broker

(1) A regulated agreement made by a debtor or hirer who, for the purpose of making that agreement, was introduced to the creditor or owner by an unlicensed credit-broker is enforceable against the debtor or hirer only where—

(a) on the application of the credit-broker, the Director has made an order under section 148(2) in respect of a period including the time when the introduction was made, and the order does not (whether in general terms or specifically) exclude the application of this paragraph to the regulated agreement, or

(b) the Director has made an order under subsection (2) which applies to the agreement.

(2) Where during any period individuals were introduced to a person carrying on a consumer credit business or consumer hire business by an unlicensed credit-broker for the purpose of making regulated agreements with the person carrying on that business, that person or his successor in title may apply to the Director for an order that regulated agreements so made are to be treated as if the credit-broker had been licensed at the time of the introduction.

(3) Unless the Director determines to make an order under subsection (2) in accordance with the application, he shall, before determining the application, by notice—

(a) inform the applicant, giving his reasons, that, as the case may be, he is minded to refuse the application, or to grant it in terms different from those applied for, describing them, and

(b) invite the applicant to submit to the Director representations in support of his application in accordance with section 34.

(4) In determining whether or not to make an order under subsection (2) the Director shall consider, in addition to any other relevant factors—

(a) how far, if at all, debtors or hirers under regulated agreements to which the application relates were prejudiced by the credit-broker's conduct, and

(b) the degree of culpability of the applicant in facilitating the carrying on by the credit-broker of his business when unlicensed.

(5) If the Director thinks fit, he may in an order under subsection (2)—

(a) limit the order to specified agreements, or agreements of a specified description or made at a specified time;

(b) make the order conditional on the doing of specified acts by the applicant.

150. Appeals to the Secretary of State against licensing decisions

Section 41 (as applied by section 147(1)) shall have effect as if the following entry were included in the table set out at the end—

Determination	*Appellant*
Refusal to make order under section 148(2) or 149(2) in accordance with terms of application.	The applicant.

Seeking business

151. Advertisements

(1) Sections 44 to 47 apply to an advertisement published for the purposes of a business of credit brokerage carried on by any person, whether it advertises the services of that person or the services of persons to whom he effects introductions, as they apply to an advertisement to which Part IV applies.

(2) Sections 44, 46 and 47 apply to an advertisement, published for the purposes of a business carried on by the advertiser, indicating that he is willing to advise on debts, or engage in transactions concerned with the liquidation of debts, as they apply to an advertisement to which Part IV applies.

(3) The Secretary of State may by order provide that an advertisement published for the purposes of a business of credit brokerage, debt adjusting or debt counselling shall not fall within subsection (1) or (2) if it is of a description specified in the order.

(4) An advertisement does not fall within subsection (2) if it indicates that the advertiser is not willing to act in relation to consumer credit agreements and consumer hire agreements.

(5) In subsections (1) and (3) 'credit brokerage' includes the effecting of introductions of individuals desiring to obtain credit to any person carrying on a business in the course of which he provides credit secured on land.

152. Application of sections 52 to 54 to credit brokerage etc.

(1) Sections 52 to 54 apply to a business of credit brokerage, debt-adjusting or debt-counselling as they apply to a consumer credit business.

(2) In their application to a business of credit brokerage, sections 52 and 53 shall apply to the giving of quotations and information about the business of any person to whom the credit-broker effects introductions as well as to the giving of quotations and information about his own business.

153. Definition of canvassing off trade premises (agreements for ancillary credit services)

(1) An individual (the 'canvasser') canvasses off trade premises the services of a person carrying on an ancillary credit business if he solicits the entry of another individual (the 'consumer') into an agreement for the provision to the consumer of those services by making oral representations to the consumer, or any other individual, during a visit by the canvasser to any place (not excluded by subsection (2)) where the consumer, or that other individual as the case may be, is, being a visit—

(a) carried out for the purpose of making such oral representations to individuals who are at that place, but

(b) not carried out in response to a request made on a previous occasion.

(2) A place is excluded from subsection (1) if it is a place where (whether on a permanent or temporary basis)—

(a) the ancillary credit business is carried on, or

(b) any business is carried on by the canvasser or the person whose employee or agent the canvasser is, or by the consumer.

154. Prohibition of canvassing certain ancillary credit services off trade premises
It is an offence to canvass off trade premises the services of a person carrying on a business of credit-brokerage, debt-adjusting or debt counselling.

155. Right to recover brokerage fees
(1) The excess over [£5] of a fee or commission for his services charged by a credit-broker to an individual to whom this subsection applies shall cease to be payable or, as the case may be, shall be recoverable by the individual if the introduction does not result in his entering into a relevant agreement within the six months following the introduction (disregarding any agreement which is cancelled under section 69(1) or becomes subject to section 69(2)).

(2) Subsection (1) applies to an individual who sought an introduction for a purpose which would have been fulfilled by his entry into—

(a) a regulated agreement, or

(b) in the case of an individual such as is referred to in section 145(2)(a)(ii), an agreement for credit secured on land, or

(c) an agreement such as is referred to in section 145(3)(b) or (c) or (4)(b).

(3) An agreement is a relevant agreement for the purposes of subsection (1) in relation to an individual if it is an agreement such as is referred to in subsection (2) in relation to that individual.

(4) In the case of an individual desiring to obtain credit under a consumer credit agreement, any sum payable or paid by him to a credit-broker otherwise than as a fee or commission for the credit-broker's services shall for the purposes of subsection (1) be treated as such a fee or commission if it enters, or would enter, into the total charge for credit.

Entry into agreements

156. Entry into agreements
Regulations may make provision, in relation to agreements entered into in the course of a business of credit brokerage, debt-adjusting or debt-counselling, corresponding, with such modifications as the Secretary of State thinks fit, to the provision which is or may be made by or under sections 55, 60, 61, 62, 63, 65, 127, 179 or 180 in relation to agreements to which those sections apply.

Credit reference agencies

157. Duty to disclose name etc. of agency
(1) A creditor, owner or negotiator, within the prescribed period after receiving a request in writing to that effect from the debtor or hirer, shall give him notice of the name and address of any credit reference agency from which the creditor, owner or negotiator has, during the antecedent negotiations, applied for information about his financial standing.

(2) Subsection (1) does not apply to a request received more than 28 days after the termination of the antecedent negotiations, whether on the making of the regulated agreement or otherwise.

(3) If the creditor, owner or negotiator fails to comply with subsection (1) he commits an offence.

158. Duty of agency to disclose filed information
(1) A credit reference agency, within the prescribed period after receiving,—

(a) a request in writing to that effect from any [partnership or other unincorporated body of persons not consisting entirely of bodies corporate] (the 'consumer'), and

(b) such particulars as the agency may reasonably require to enable them to identify the file, and

(c) a fee of [£2],

shall give the consumer a copy of the file relating to [it] kept by the agency.

(2) When giving a copy of the file under subsection (1), the agency shall also give the consumer a statement in the prescribed form of [the consumer's] rights under section 159.

(3) If the agency does not keep a file relating to the consumer it shall give [the consumer] notice of that fact, but need not return any money paid.

(4) If the agency contravenes any provision of this section it commits an offence.

(5) In this Act 'file', in relation to an individual, means all the information about him kept by a credit reference agency, regardless of how the information is stored, and 'copy of the file', as respects information not in plain English, means a transcript reduced into plain English.

159. Correction of wrong information

[(1) Any individual (the 'objector') given—

(a) information under section 7 of the Data Protection Act 1998 by a credit reference agency, or

(b) information under section 158,

who considers that an entry in his file is incorrect, and that if it is not corrected he is likely to be prejudiced, may give notice to the agency requiring it either to remove the entry from the file or amend it.]

(2) Within 28 days after receiving a notice under subsection (1), the agency shall by notice inform the [objector] that it has—

(a) removed the entry from the file, or

(b) amended the entry, or

(c) taken no action,

and if the notice states that the agency has amended the entry it shall include a copy of the file so far as it comprises the amended entry.

(3) Within 28 days after receiving a notice under subsection (2), or where no such notice was given, within 28 days after the expiry of the period mentioned in subsection (2), the [objector] may, unless he has been informed by the agency that it has removed the entry from his file, serve a further notice on the agency requiring it to add to the file an accompanying notice of correction (not exceeding 200 words) drawn up by the [objector], and include a copy of it when furnishing information included in or based on that entry

(4) Within 28 days after receiving a notice under subsection (3), the agency, unless it intends to apply to the [the relevant authority] under subsection (5), shall by notice inform the [objector] that it has received the notice under subsection (3) and intends to comply with it.

(5) If—

(a) the [objector] has not received a notice under subsection (4) within the time required, or

(b) it appears to the agency that it would be improper for it to publish a notice of correction because it is incorrect, or unjustly defames any person, or is frivolous or scandalous, or is for any other reason unsuitable, the [objector] or, as the case may be, the agency may, in the prescribed manner and on payment of the specified fee, apply to the [the relevant authority], who may make such order on the application as he thinks fit.

(6) If a person to whom an order under this section is directed fails to comply with it within the period specified in the order he commits an offence.

[(7) The Data Protection Commissioner may vary or revoke any order made by him under this section.

(8) In this section 'the relevant authority' means

(a) where the objector is a partnership or other unincorporated body of persons, the Director, and

(b) in any other case, the Data Protection Commissioner.]

160. Alternative procedure for business consumers

(1) The Director, on an application made by a credit reference agency, may direct that this section shall apply to the agency if he is satisfied—

(a) that compliance with section 158 in the case of consumers who carry on a business would adversely affect the service provided to its customers by the agency, and

(b) that, having regard to the methods employed by the agency and to any other relevant facts, it is probable that consumers carrying on a business would not be prejudiced by the making of the direction.

(2) Where an agency to which this section applies receives a request, particulars and a fee under section 158(1) from a consumer who carries on a business and section 158(3) does

not apply, the agency, instead of complying with section 158, may elect to deal with the matter under the following subsections.

(3) Instead of giving the consumer a copy of the file, the agency shall within the prescribed period give notice to the consumer that it is proceeding under this section, and by notice give the consumer such information included in or based on entries in the file as the Director may direct, together with a statement in the prescribed form of the consumer's rights under subsections (4) and (5).

(4) If within 28 days after receiving the information given [to the consumer] under subsection (3), or such longer period as the Director may allow, the consumer—

(a) gives notice to the Director that [the consumer] is dissatisfied with the information, and

(b) satisfies the Director that [the consumer] has taken such steps in relation to the agency as may be reasonable with a view to removing the cause of [the consumer's] dissatisfaction, and

(c) pays the Director the specified fee,

the Director may direct the agency to give the Director a copy of the file, and the Director may disclose to the consumer such of the information on the file as the Director thinks fit.

(5) Section 159 applies with any necessary modifications to information given to the consumer under this section as it applies to information given under section 158.

(6) If an agency making an election under subsection (2) fails to comply with subsection (3) or (4) it commits an offence.

[(7) In this section 'consumer' has the same meaning as in section 158.]

PART XI
ENFORCEMENT OF ACT

161. Enforcement authorities

(1) The following authorities ('enforcement authorities') have a duty to enforce this Act and regulations made under it—

(a) the Director,

(b) in Great Britain, the local weights and measures authority,

(c) In Northern Ireland, the Department of Commerce for Northern Ireland.

(2) Where a local weights and measures authority in England or Wales propose to institute proceedings for an offence under this Act (other than an offence under section 162(6), 165(1) or (2) or 174(5)) it shall, as between the authority and the Director, be the duty of the authority to give the Director notice of the intended proceedings, together with a summary of the facts on which the charges are to be founded, and postpone institution of the proceedings until either—

(a) 28 days have expired since that notice was given, or

(b) the Director has notified them of receipt of the notice and summary.

(3) Every local weights and measures authority shall, whenever the Director requires, report to him in such form and with such particulars as he requires on the exercise of their functions under this Act.

[. . .]

162. Powers of entry and inspection

(1) A duly authorised officer of an enforcement authority, at all reasonable hours and on production, if required, of his credentials, may—

(a) in order to ascertain whether a breach of any provision of or under this Act has been committed, inspect any goods and enter any premises (other than premises used only as a dwelling);

(b) if he has reasonable cause to suspect that a breach of any provision of or under this Act has been committed, in order to ascertain whether it has been committed, require any person—

(i) carrying on, or employed in connection with, a business to produce any books or documents relating to it; or

(ii) having control of any information relating to a business recorded otherwise than in a legible form to provide a document containing a legible reproduction of the whole or any part of the information, and take copies of, or of any entry in, the books or documents;

(c) if he has reasonable cause to believe that a breach of any provision of or under this Act has been committed, seize and detain any goods in order to ascertain (by testing or otherwise) whether such a breach has been committed;

(d) seize and detain any goods, books or documents which he has reason to believe may be required as evidence in proceedings for an offence under this Act;

(e) for the purpose of exercising his powers under this subsection to seize goods, books or documents, but only if and to the extent that it is reasonably necessary for securing that the provision of this Act and of any regulations made under it are duly observed, require any person having authority to do so to break open any container and, if that person does not comply, break it open himself.

(2) An officer seizing goods, books or documents in exercise of his powers under this section shall not do so without informing the person he seizes them from.

(3) If a justice of the peace, on sworn information in writing, or, in Scotland, a sheriff or a magistrate or justice of the peace, on evidence on oath,—

(a) is satisfied that there is reasonable ground to believe either—

(i) that any goods, books or documents which a duly authorised officer has power to inspect under this section are on any premises and their inspection is likely to disclose evidence of a breach of any provision of or under this Act; or

(ii) that a breach of any provision of or under this Act has been, is being or is about to be committed on any premises; and

(b) is also satisfied either—

(i) that admission to the premises has been or is likely to be refused and that notice of intention to apply for a warrant under this subsection has been given to the occupier; or

(ii) that an application for admission, or the giving of such a notice, would defeat the object of the entry or that the premises are unoccupied or that the occupier is temporarily absent ad it might defeat the object of the entry to wait for his return.

the justice or, as the case may be, the sheriff or magistrate may by warrant under his hand, which shall continue in force for a period of one month, authorise an officer of an enforcement authority to enter the premises (by force if need be).

(4) An officer entering premises by virtue of this section may take such other persons and equipment with him as he thinks necessary; and on leaving premises entered by virtue of a warrant under subsection (3) shall, if they are unoccupied or the occupier is temporarily absent, leave them as effectively secured against trespassers as he found them.

(5) Regulations may provide that, in cases described by the regulations, an officer of a local weights and measures authority is not to be taken to be duly authorised for the purposes of this section unless he is authorised by the Director.

(6) A person who is not a duly authorised officer of an enforcement authority, but purports to act as such under this section, commits an offence.

(7) Nothing in this section compels a barrister, advocate or solicitor to produce a document containing a privileged communication made by or to him in that capacity or authorises the seizing of any such document in his possession.

163. Compensation for loss

(1) Where, in exercising his powers under section 162, an officer of an enforcement authority seizes and detains goods and their owner suffers loss by reason of—

(a) that seizure, or

(b) the loss, damage or deterioration of the goods during detention,

then, unless the owner is convicted of an offence under this Act committed in relation to the goods, the authority shall compensate him for the loss so suffered.

(2) Any dispute as to the right to or amount of any compensation under subsection (1) shall be determined by arbitration.

164. Power to make test purchases etc.

(1) An enforcement authority may—

(a) make, or authorise any of their officers to make on their behalf, such purchases of goods; and

(b) authorise any of their officers to procure the provision of such services or facilities or to enter into such agreements or other transactions, as may appear to them expedient for determining whether any provisions made by or under this Act are being complied with.

(2) Any act done by an officer authorised to do it under subsection (1) shall be treated for the purposes of this Act as done by him as an individual on his own behalf.

(3) Any goods seized by an officer under this Act may be tested, and in the event of such a test he shall inform the person mentioned in section 162(2) of the test results.

(4) Where any test leads to proceedings under this Act, the enforcement authority shall—

(a) if the goods were purchased, inform the person they were purchased from of the test results, and

(b) allow any person against whom the proceedings are taken to have the goods tested on his behalf if it is reasonably practicable to do so.

165. Obstruction of authorised officers

(1) Any person who—

(a) wilfully obstructs an officer of an enforcement authority acting in pursuance of this Act; or

(b) wilfully fails to comply with any requirement properly made to him by such an officer under section 162; or

(c) without reasonable cause fails to give such an officer (so acting) other assistance or information he may reasonably require in performing his functions under this Act, commits an offence.

(2) If any person, in giving such information as is mentioned in subsection (1)(c), makes any statement which he knows to be false, he commits an offence.

(3) Nothing in this section requires a person to answer any question or give any information if to do so might incriminate that person or (where that person is married) the husband or wife of that person.

166. Notification of convictions and judgments to Director

Where a person is convicted of an offence or has a judgment given against him by or before any court in the United Kingdom and it appears to the court—

(a) having regard to the functions of the Director under this Act, that the conviction or judgment should be brought to the Director's attention, and

(b) that it may not be brought to his attention unless arrangements for that purpose are made by the court,

the court may make such arrangements notwithstanding that the proceedings have been finally disposed of.

167. Penalties

(1) An offence under a provision of this Act specified in column 1 of Schedule 1 is triable in the mode or modes indicated in column 3, and on conviction is punishable as indicated in column 4 (where a period of time indicates the maximum term of imprisonment, and a monetary amount indicates the maximum fine, for the offence in question).

(2) A person who contravenes any regulations made under section 44, 52, 53, or 112, or made under section 26 by virtue of section 54, commits an offence.

168. Defences

(1) In any proceedings for an offence under this Act it is a defence for the person charged to prove—

(a) that his act or omission was due to a mistake, or to reliance on information supplied to him, or to an act or omission by another person, or to an accident or some other cause beyond his control, and

(b) that he took all reasonable precautions and exercised all due diligence to avoid such an act or omission by himself or any person under his control.

(2) If in any case the defence provided by subsection (1) involves the allegation that the act or omission was due to an act or omission by another person or to reliance on information supplied by another person, the person charged shall not, without leave of the court, be entitled to rely on that defence unless, within a period ending seven clear days before the hearing, he has served on the prosecutor a notice giving such information

identifying or assisting in the identification of that other person as was then in his possession.

169. Offences by bodies corporate

Where at any time a body corporate commits an offence under this Act with the consent or connivance of, or because of neglect by, any individual, the individual commits the like offence if at that time—

(a) he is a director, manager, secretary or similar officer of the body corporate, or

(b) he is purporting to act as such an officer, or

(c) the body corporate is managed by its members of whom he is one.

170. No further sanctions for breach of Act

(1) A breach of any requirement made (otherwise than by any court) by or under this Act shall incur no civil or criminal sanction as being such a breach, except to the extent (if any) expressly provided by or under this Act.

(2) In exercising his functions under this Act the Director may take account of any matter appearing to him to constitute a breach of a requirement made by or under this Act, whether or not any sanction for that breach is provided by or under this Act and, if it is so provided, whether or not proceedings have been brought in respect of the breach.

(3) Subsection (1) does not prevent the grant of an injunction, or the making of an order of certiorari, mandamus or prohibition or as respects Scotland the grant of an interdict or of an order under section 91 of the Court of Session Act 1868 (order for specific performance of statutory duty).

171. Onus of proof in various proceedings

(1) If an agreement contains a term signifying that in the opinion of the parties section 10(3)(b)(iii) does not apply to the agreement, it shall be taken not to apply unless the contrary is proved.

(2) It shall be assumed in any proceedings, unless the contrary is proved, that when a person initiated a transaction as mentioned in section 19(1)(c) he knew the principal agreement had been made, or contemplated that it might be made.

(3) Regulations under section 44 or 52 may make provision as to the onus of proof in any proceedings to enforce the regulations.

(4) In proceedings brought by the creditor under a credit-token agreement—

(a) it is for the creditor to prove that the credit-token was lawfully supplied to the debtor, and was accepted by him, and

(b) if the debtor alleges that any use made of the credit-token was not authorised by him, it is for the creditor to prove either—

(i) that the use was so authorised, or

(ii) that the use occurred before the creditor had been given notice under section 84(3).

(5) In proceedings under section 50(1) in respect of a document received by a minor at any school or other educational establishment for minors, it is for the person sending it to him at that establishment to prove that he did not know or suspect it to be such an establishment.

(6) In proceedings under section 119(1) it is for the pawnee to prove that he had reasonable cause to refuse to allow the pawn to be redeemed.

(7) If in proceedings referred to in section 139(1), the debtor or any surety alleges that the credit bargain is extortionate it is for the creditor to prove the contrary.

172. Statements by creditor or owner to be binding

(1) A statement by a creditor or owner is binding on him if given under—

section 77(1),
section 78(1),
section 79(1),
section 97(1),
section 107(1)(c),
section 108(1)(c), or
section 109(1)(c).

(2) Where a trader—

(a) gives a customer a notice in compliance with section 103(1)(b), or

(b) gives a customer a notice under section 103(1) asserting that the customer is not indebted to him under an agreement,

the notice is binding on the trader.

(3) Where in proceedings before any court—

(a) it is sought to reply on a statement or notice given as mentioned in subsection (1) or (2), and

(b) the statement or notice is shown to be incorrect, the court may direct such relief (if any) to be given to the creditor or owner from the operation of subsection (1) or (2) as appears to the court to be just.

173. Contracting-out forbidden

(1) A term contained in a regulated agreement or linked transaction, or in any other agreement relating to an actual or prospective regulated agreement or linked transaction, is void if, and to the extent that, it is inconsistent with a provision for the protection of the debtor or hirer or his relative or any surety contained in this Act or in any regulation made under this Act.

(2) Where a provision specifies the duty or liability of the debtor or hirer or his relative or any surety in certain circumstances, a term is inconsistent with that provision if it purports to impose, directly or indirectly, an additional duty or liability on him in those circumstances.

(3) Notwithstanding subsection (1), a provision of this Act under which a thing may be done in relation to any person on an order of the court or the Director only shall not be taken to prevent its being done at any time with that person's consent given at that time, but the refusal of such consent shall not give rise to any liability.

PART XII
SUPPLEMENTAL

174. Restrictions on disclosure of information

(1) No information obtained under or by virtue of this Act about any individual shall be disclosed without his consent.

(2) No information obtained under or by virtue of this Act about any business shall be disclosed except, so long as the business continues to be carried on, with the consent of the person for the time being carrying it on.

(3) Subsections (1) and (2) do not apply to any disclosure of information made—

(a) for the purpose of facilitating the performance of any functions, under this Act, the Trade Descriptions Act 1968 or Part II or Ill or section 125 (annual and other reports of Director) of the Fair Trading Act 1973 [or the Estate Agents Act 1979 or the Competition Act 1980 or the Telecommunications Act 1984 or the Gas Act 1986 or the Airports Act 1986 or the Consumer Protection Act 1987 or Part II of the Consumer Protection (Northern Ireland) Order 1987 or the Control of Misleading Advertisements Regulations 1988 or the Courts and Legal Services Act 1990 or the Railways Act 1993 or the Coal Industry Act 1994 or the Water Act 1989 or the Water Industry Act 1991 or any of the other consolidation Acts (within the meaning of section 206 of that Act of 1991) or the Electricity Act 1989 or the Electricity (Northern Ireland) Order 1992], of the Secretary of State, any other Minister, [the Director General of Telecommunications, the Director General of Gas Supply, the Civil Aviation Authority the Director General of Water Services, the Director General of Electricity Supply or the Director General of Electricity Supply for Northern Ireland, the Rail Regulator the Authorised Conveyancing Practitioners Board or; the Coal Authority] any enforcement authority or any Northern Ireland department, or

(b) in connection with the investigation of any criminal offence or for the purposes of any criminal proceedings, or

(c) for the purposes of any civil proceedings brought under or by virtue of this Act or under Part III of the Fair Trading Act 1973 [or under the Control of Misleading Advertisements Regulations 1988].

[(3A) Subsections (1) and (2) do not apply to any disclosure of information by the Director to the Financial Services Authority for the purpose of enabling or assisting the

Authority to discharge its functions under the Banking Act 1987 or the Director to discharge his functions under this Act.]

(4) Nothing in subsection (1) and (2) shall be construed—

(a) as limiting the particulars which may be entered in the register; or register.

(5) Any person who discloses information in contravention of this section commits an offence.

175. Duty of persons deemed to be agents

Where under this Act a person is deemed to receive a notice or payment as agent of the creditor or owner under regulated agreement, he shall be deemed to be under a contractual duty to the creditor or owner to transmit the notice, or remit the payment, to him forthwith.

176. Service of documents

(1) A document to be served under this Act by one person ('the server') on another person ('the subject') is to be treated as properly served on the subject if dealt with as mentioned in the following subsections.

(2) The document may be delivered or sent by post to the subject, or addressed to him by name and left at his proper address.

(3) For the purposes of this Act, a document sent by post to, or left at, the address last known to the server as the address of a person shall be treated as sent by post to, or left at, his proper address.

(4) Where the document is to be served on the subject as being the person having any interest in land, and it is not practicable after reasonable inquiry to ascertain the subject's name or address, the document may be served by—

(a) addressing it to the subject by the description of the person having that interest in the land (naming it), and

(b) delivering the document to some responsible person on the land or affixing it, or a copy of it, in a conspicuous position on the land.

(5) Where a document to be served on the subject as being a debtor, hirer or surety, or as having any other capacity relevant for the purposes of this Act, is served at any time on another person who—

(a) is the person last known to the server as having that capacity, but

(b) before that time had ceased to have it, the document shall be treated as having been served at that time on the subject.

(6) Anything done to a document in relation to a person who (whether to the knowledge of the server or not) has died shall be treated for the purposes of subsection (5) as service of the document on that person if it would have been so treated had he not died.

[(7) The following enactments shall not be construed as authorising service on the Public Trustee (in England and Wales) or the Probate Judge (in Northern Ireland) of any document which is to be served under this Act—

section 9 of the Administration of Estates Act 1925;

section 3 of the Administration of Estates Act (Northern Ireland) 1955.]

(8) References in the preceding subsections to the serving of a document on a person include the giving of the document to that person.

177. Saving for registered charges

(1) Nothing in this Act affects the rights of a proprietor of a registered charge (within the meaning of the Land Registration Act 1925), who—

(a) became the proprietor under a transfer for valuable consideration without notice of any defect in the title arising (apart from this section) by virtue of this Act, or

(b) derives title from such a proprietor.

(2) Nothing in this Act affects the operation of section 104 of the Law of Property Act 1925 (protection of purchaser where mortgagee exercises power of sale).

(3) Subsection (1) does not apply to a proprietor carrying on a business of debt-collecting.

(4) Where, by virtue of subsection (1), a land mortgage is enforced which apart from this section would be treated as never having effect, the original creditor or owner shall be liable to indemnify the debtor or hirer against any loss thereby suffered by him.

(5) In the application of this section to Scotland for subsections (1) to (3) there shall be substituted the following subsections—

'(1) Nothing in this Act affects the rights of a creditor in a heritable security who—

(a) became the creditor under a transfer for value without notice of any defect in the title arising (apart from this section) by virtue of this Act; or

(b) derives title from such a creditor.

(2) Nothing in this Act affects the operation of section 41 of the Conveyancing (Scotland) Act 1924 (protection of purchasers), or of that section as applied to standard securities by section 32 of the Conveyancing and Feudal Reform (Scotland) Act 1970.

(3) Subsection (1) does not apply to a creditor carrying on a business of debt-collecting.'.

(6) In the application of this section to Northern Ireland—

(a) any reference to the proprietor of a registered charge (within the meaning of the Land Registration Act 1925) shall be construed as a reference to the registered owner of a charge under the Local Registration of Title (Ireland) Act 1891 or Part IV of the Land Registration Act (Northern Ireland) 1970, and

(b) for the reference to section 104 of the Law Property Act 1925 there shall be substituted a reference to section 21 of the Conveyancing and Law Property Act 1881 and section 5 of the Conveyancing Act 1911.

178. Local Acts

The Secretary of State or the Department of Commerce for Northern Ireland may by order make such amendments or repeals of any provision of any local Act as appears to the Secretary of State or, as the case may be, the Department, necessary or expedient in consequence of the replacement by this Act of the enactments relating to pawnbrokers and moneylenders.

Regulations, orders, etc.

179. Power to prescribe form etc. of secondary documents

(1) Regulations may be made as to the form and content of credit-cards, trading-checks, receipts, vouchers and other documents or things issued by creditors, owners or suppliers under or in connection with regulated agreements or by other persons in connection with linked transactions, and may in particular—

(a) require specified information to be included in the prescribed manner in documents, and other specified material to be excluded;

(b) contain requirements to ensure that specified information is clearly brought to the attention of the debtor or hirer, or his relative, and that one part of a document is not given insufficient or excessive prominence compared with another.

(2) If a person issues any document or thing in contravention of regulations under subsection (1) then, as from the time of the contravention but without prejudice to anything done before it, this Act shall apply as if the regulated agreement had been improperly executed by reason of a contravention of regulations under section 60(1).

180. Power to prescribe form etc. of copies

(1) Regulations may be made as to the form and content of documents to be issued as copies of any executed agreement, security instrument or other document referred to in this Act, and may in particular—

(a) require specified information to be included in the prescribed manner in any copy, and contain requirements to ensure that such information is clearly brought to the attention of a reader of the copy;

(b) authorise the omission from a copy of certain material contained in the original, or the inclusion of such material in condensed form.

(2) A duty imposed by any provision of this Act (except section 35) to supply a copy of any document—

(a) is not safisfied unless the copy supplied is in the prescribed form and conforms to the prescribed requirements;

(b) is not infringed by the omission of any material, or its inclusion in condensed form, if that is authorised by regulations;

and references in this Act to copies shall be construed accordingly.

(3) Regulations may provide that a duty imposed by this Act to supply a copy of a document referred to in an unexecuted agreement or an executed agreement shall not apply to documents of a kind specified in the regulations.

181. Power to alter monetary limits etc.

(1) The Secretary of State may by order made by statutory instrument amend, or further amend, any of the following provisions of this Act so as to reduce or increase a sum mentioned in that provision, namely, sections 8(2), 15(1)(c), 17(1), 43(3)(a), 70(6), 75(3)(b), 77(1), 78(1), 79(1), 84(1), 101(7)(a), 107(1), 108(1), 109(1), 110(1), 118(1)(b), 120(1)(a), 139(5) and (7), 155(1) and 158(1).

(2) An order under subsection (1) amending section 8(2), 15(1)(c), 17(1), 43(3)(a), 75(3)(b) or 139(5) or (7) shall be of no effect unless a draft of the order has been laid before and approved by each House of Parliament.

182. Regulations and orders

(1) Any power of the Secretary of State to make regulations or orders under this Act, except the power conferred by sections 2(1)(a), 181 and 192 shall be exercisable by statutory instrument subject to annulment in pursuance of a resolution of either House of Parliament.

(2) Where a power to make regulations or orders is exercisable by the Secretary of State by virtue of this Act, regulations or orders made in the exercise of that power may—

(a) make different provision in relation to different cases or classes of case, and

(b) exclude certain cases or classes of case, and

(c) contain such transitional provision as the Secretary of State thinks fit.

(3) Regulations may provide that specified expressions, when used as described by the regulations, are to be given the prescribed meaning, notwithstanding that another meaning is intended by the person using them.

(4) Any power conferred on the Secretary of State by this Act to make orders includes power to vary or revoke an order so made.

183. Determinations etc. by Director

The Director may vary or revoke any determination or direction made or given by him under this Act (other than Part III, or Part III as applied by section 147).

Interpretation

184. Associates

(1) A person is an associate of an individual if that person is the individual's husband or wife, or is a relative, or the husband or wife of a relative, of the individual or of the individual's husband or wife.

(2) A person is an associate of any person with whom he is in partnership, and of the husband or wife or a relative of any individual with whom he is in partnership.

(3) A body corporate is an associate of another body corporate—

(a) if the same person is a controller of both, or a person is a controller of one and persons who are his associates, or he and persons who are his associates, are controllers of the other; or

(b) if a group of two or more persons is controller of each company, and the groups either consist of the same persons or could be regarded as consisting of the same persons by treating (in one or more cases) a member of either group as replaced by a person of whom he is an associate.

(4) A body corporate is an associate of another person if that person is a controller of it or if that person and persons who are his associates together are controllers of it.

(5) In this section 'relative' means brother, sister, uncle, aunt, nephew, niece, lineal ancestor or lineal descendant, and references to a husband or wife include a former husband or wife and a reputed husband or wife; and for the purposes of this subsection a relationship shall be established as if any illegitimate child, step-child or adopted child of a person had been a child born to him in wedlock.

185. Agreement with more than one debtor or hirer

(1) Where an actual or prospective regulated agreement has two or more debtors or hirers (not being a partnership or an unincorporated body of persons)—

(a) anything required by or under this Act to be done to or in relation to the debtor or hirer shall be done to or in relation to each of them; and

(b) anything done under this Act by or on behalf of one of them shall have effect as if done by or on behalf of all of them.

(2) Notwithstanding subsection (1)(a), where running-account credit is provided to two or more debtors jointly, any of them may by a notice signed by him (a 'dispensing notice') authorise the creditor not to comply in his case with section 78(4) (giving of periodical statement of account); and the dispensing notice shall have effect accordingly until revoked by a further notice given by the debtor to the creditor;

Provided that:

(a) a dispensing notice shall not take effect if previous dispensing notices are operative in the case of the other debtor, or each of the other debtors, as the case may be;

(b) any dispensing notices operative in relation to an agreement shall cease to have effect if any of the debtors dies;

[(c) a dispensing notice which is operative in relation to an agreement shall be operative also in relation to any subsequent agreement which, in relation to the earlier agreement, is a modifying agreement.]

(3) Subsection (1)(b) does not apply for the purposes of section 61(1)(a) or 127(3).

(4) Where a regulated agreement has two or more debtors or hirers (not being a partnership or an unincorporated body of persons), section 86 applies to the death of any of them.

(5) An agreement for the provision of credit, or the bailment or (in Scotland) the hiring of goods, to two or more persons jointly where—

(a) one or more of those persons is an individual, and

(b) one or more of them is a body corporate,

is a consumer credit agreement or consumer hire agreement if it would have been one had they all been individuals; and the body corporate or bodies corporate shall accordingly be included among the debtors or hirers under the agreement.

(6) Where subsection (5) applies, references in this Act to the signing of any document by the debtor or hirer shall be construed in relation to a body corporate as referring to a signing on behalf of the body corporate.

186. Agreement with more than one creditor or owner

Where an actual or prospective regulated agreement has two or more creditors or owners, anything required by or under this Act to be done to, or in relation to, or by, the creditor or owner shall be effective if done to, or in relation to, or by, any one of them.

187. Arrangements between creditor and supplier

(1) A consumer credit agreement shall be treated as entered into under pre-existing arrangements between a creditor and a supplier if it is entered into in accordance with, or in furtherance of, arrangements previously made between persons mentioned in subsection (4)(a), (b) or (c).

(2) A consumer credit agreement shall be treated as entered into in contemplation of future arrangements between a creditor and a supplier if it is entered into in the expectation that arrangements will subsequently be made between persons mentioned in subsection (4)(a), (b) or (c) for the supply of cash, goods and services (or any of them) to be financed by the consumer credit agreement.

(3) Arrangements shall be disregarded for the purposes of subsection (1) or (2) if—

(a) they are arrangements for the making, in specified circumstances, of payments to the supplier by the creditor, and

(b) the creditor holds himself out as willing to make, in such circumstances, payments of the kind to suppliers generally.

[(3A) Arrangements shall also be disregarded for the purposes of subsections (1) and (2) if they are arrangements for the electronic transfer of funds from a current account at a bank within the meaning of the Bankers' Book Evidence Act 1879.]

(4) The persons referred to in subsections (1) and (2) are—

(a) the creditor and the supplier;

(b) one of them and an associate of the other's;

(c) an associate of one and an associate of the other's.

(5) Where the creditor is an associate of the supplier's, the consumer credit agreement shall be treated, unless the contrary is proved, as entered into under pre-existing arrangements between the creditor and the supplier.

188. Examples of use of new terminology

(1) Schedule 2 shall have effect for illustrating the use of terminology employed in this Act.

(2) The examples given in Schedule 2 are not exhaustive.

(3) In the case of conflict between Schedule 2 and any other provision of this Act, that other provision shall prevail.

(4) The Secretary of State may by order amend Schedule 2 by adding further examples or in any other way.

189. Definitions

(1) In this Act, unless the context otherwise requires—

'advertisement' includes every form of advertising, whether in a publication, by television or radio, by display of notices, signs, labels, showcards or goods, by distribution of samples, circulars, catalogues, price lists or other material, by exhibition of pictures, models or films, or in any other way, and references to the publishing of advertisements shall be construed accordingly;

'advertiser' in relation to an advertisement, means any person indicated by the advertisement as willing to enter into transactions to which the advertisement relates;

'ancillary credit business' has the meaning given by section 145(1),

'antecedent negotiations' has the meaning given by section 56;

'appeal period' means the period beginning on the first day on which an appeal to the Secretary of State may be brought and ending on the last day on which it may be brought or, if it is brought, ending on its final determination, or abandonment;

'assignment', in relation to Scotland, means assignation;

'associate' shall be construed in accordance with section 184;

['authorised institution' means an institution authorised under the Banking Act 1987;]

'bill of sale' has the meaning given by section 4 of the Bills of Sale Act 1878 or, for Northern Ireland, by section 4 of the Bills of Sale (Ireland) Act 1879;

['building society' means a building society within the meaning of the Building Societies Act 1986;]

'business' includes profession or trade, and references to a business apply subject to subsection (2);

'cancellable agreement' means a regulated agreement which, by virtue of section 67, may be cancelled by the debtor or hirer;

'canvass' shall be construed in accordance with sections 48 and 153;

'cash' includes money in any form;

'charity' means as respects England and Wales a charity registered under [the Charities Act 1993] or an exempt charity (within the meaning of that Act), and as respects Scotland and Northern Ireland an institution or other organisation established for charitable purposes only ('organisation' including any persons administering a trust and 'charitable' being construed in the same way as if it were contained in the Income Tax Acts);

'conditional sale agreement' means an agreement for the sale of goods or land under which the purchase price or part of it is payable by instalments, and the property in the goods or land is to remain in the seller (notwithstanding that the buyer is to be in possession of the goods or land) until such conditions as to the payment of instalments or otherwise as may be specified in the agreement are fulfilled;

'consumer credit agreement' has the meaning given by section 8, and includes a consumer credit agreement which is cancelled under section 69(1), or becomes subject to section 69(2), so far as the agreement remains in force;

'consumer credit business' means any business so far as it comprises or relates to the provision of credit under regulated consumer credit agreements;

'consumer hire agreement' has the meaning given by section 15;
'consumer hire business' means any business so far as it comprises or relates to the bailment or (in Scotland) the hiring of goods under regulated consumer hire agreements;
'controller', in relation to a body corporate, means a person—

(a) in accordance with whose directions or instructions the directors of the body corporate or of another body corporate which is its controller (or any of them) are accustomed to act, or

(b) who, either alone or with any associate or associates, is entitled to exercise, or control the exercise of, one third or more of the voting power at any general meeting of the body corporate or of another body corporate which is its controller;

'copy' shall be construed in accordance with section 180;
'costs', in relation to Scotland, means expenses;
'court' means in relation to England and Wales the county court, in relation to Scotland the sheriff court and in relation to Northern Ireland the High Court or the county court;
'credit' shall be construed in accordance with section 9; 'credit-broker' means a person carrying on a business of credit-brokerage;
'credit-brokerage' has the meaning given by section 145(2);
'credit limit' has the meaning given by section 10(2);
'creditor' means the person providing credit under a consumer credit agreement or the person to whom his rights and duties under the agreement have passed by assignment or operation of law, and in relation to a prospective consumer agreement, includes the prospective creditor;
'credit reference agency' has the meaning given by section 145(8);
'credit-sale agreement' means an agreement for the sale of goods, under which the purchase price or part of it is payable by instalments, but which is not a conditional sale agreement;
'credit-token' has the meaning given by section 14(1);
'credit-token agreement' means a regulated agreement for the provision of credit in connection with the use of a credit-token;
'debt-adjusting' has the meaning given by section 145(5);
'debt-collecting' has the meaning given by section 145(7);
'debt-counselling' has the meaning given by section 145(6);
'debtor' means the individual receiving credit under a consumer credit agreement or the person to whom his rights and duties under the agreement have passed by assignment or operation of law, and in relation to a prospective consumer credit agreement includes the prospective debtor;
'debtor-creditor agreement' has the meaning given by section 13;
'debtor-creditor-supplier agreement' has the meaning given by section 12;
'default notice' has the meaning given by section 87(1);
'deposit' means any sum payable by a debtor or hirer by way of deposit or downpayment, or credited or to be credited to him on account of any deposit or downpayment, whether the sum is to be or has been paid to the creditor or owner or any other person, or is to be or has been discharged by a payment of money or a transfer or delivery of goods or by any other means;
'Director' means the Director General of Fair Trading;
'electric line' has the meaning given by [the Electricity Act 1989] or, for Northern Ireland the Electricity Supply (Northern Ireland) Order 1972;
'embodies' and related words shall be construed in accordance with subsection (4);
'enforcement authority' has the meaning given by section 161(1);
'enforcement order' means an order under section 65(1), 105(7)(a) or (b), 111(2) or 124(1) or (2);
'executed agreement' means a document, signed by or on behalf of the parties, embodying the terms of a regulated agreement, or such of them as have been reduced to writing;

'exempt agreement' means an agreement specified in or under section 16;
'finance' means to finance wholly or partly, and 'financed' and 'refinanced' shall be construed accordingly;
'file' and 'copy of the file' have the meanings given by section 158(5);
'fixed-sum credit' has the meaning given by section 10(1)(b);
'friendly society' means a society registered under the 'Friendly Societies Acts 1896 to 1971 [. . .];
'future arrangements' shall be construed in accordance with section 187;
'general notice' means a notice published by the Director at a time and in a manner appearing to him suitable for securing that the notice is seen within a reasonable time by persons likely to be affected by it;
'give' means deliver or send by post to;
'goods' has the meaning given by [section 61(1) of the Sale of Goods Act 1979];
group licence' has the meaning given by section 22(1)(b);
'High Court' means Her Majesty's High Court of Justice, or the Court of Session in Scotland or the High Court of Justice in Northern Ireland;
'hire-purchase agreement' means an agreement, other than a conditional sale agreement, under which—

(a) goods are bailed or (in Scotland) hired in return for periodical payments by the person to whom they are bailed or hired, and

(b) the property in the goods will pass to that person if the terms of the agreement are complied with and one or more of the following occurs—

(i) the exercise of an option to purchase by that person,
(ii) the doing of any other specified act by any party to the agreement,
(iii) the happening of any other specified event;

'hirer' means the individual to whom goods are bailed or (in Scotland) hired under a consumer hire agreement, or the person to whom his rights and duties under the agreement have passed by assignment or operation of law, and in relation to a prospective consumer hire agreement includes the prospective hirer;
'individual' includes a partnership or other unincorporated body of persons not consisting entirely of bodies corporate;
'installation' means—

(a) the installing of any electric line or any gas or water pipe,

(b) the fixing of goods to the premises where they are to be used, and the alteration of premises to enable goods to be used on them,

(c) where it is reasonably necessary that goods should be constructed or erected on the premises where they are to be used, any work carried out for the purpose of constructing or erecting them on those premises;

'insurance company' has the meaning given by [section 96(1) of the Insurance Companies Act 19821, but does not include a friendly society or an organisation of workers or organisation of employers;
'judgment' includes an order or decree made by any court;
'land' includes an interest in land, and in relation to Scotland includes heritable subjects of whatever description;
'land improvement company' means an improvement company as defined by section 7 of the improvement of Land Act 1899;
'land mortgage' includes any security charged on land;
'licence' means a licence under Part III (including that Part as applied to ancillary credit businesses by section 147);
'licensed', in relation to any act, means authorised by a licence to do the act or cause or permit another person to do it;
'licensee', in the case of a group licence, includes any person covered by the licence;
'linked transaction' has the meaning given by section 19(1);
'local authority', in relation to England and Wales, means the Greater London Council, a county council, a London borough council, a district council, the Common Council of the City of London, or the Council of the Isles of Scilly, and in relation to Scotland, means a [council constituted under section 2 of the Local Government

etc. (Scotland) Act 1994], and, in relation to Northern Ireland, means a district council;
'modifying agreement' has the meaning given by section 82(2);
'mortgage', in relation to Scotland, includes any heritable security;
'multiple agreement' has the meaning given by section 18(1);
'negotiator' has the meaning given by section 56(1);
'non-commercial agreement' means a consumer credit agreement or a consumer hire agreement not made by the creditor or owner in the course of a business carried on by him;
'notice' means notice in writing;
'notice of cancellation' has the meaning given by section 69(1);
'owner' means a person who bails or (in Scotland) hires out goods under a consumer hire agreement or the person to whom his rights and duties under the agreement have passed by assignment or operation of law, and in relation to a prospective consumer hire agreement, includes the prospective bailor or person from whom the goods are to be hired;
'pawn' means any article subject to a pledge;
'pawn-receipt' has the meaning given by section 114;
'pawnee' and 'pawnor' include any person to whom the rights and duties of the original pawnee or the original pawnor, as the case may be, have passed by assignment or operation of law;
'payment' includes tender;
'personal credit agreement' has the meaning given by section 8(1);
'pledge' means the pawnee's rights over an article taken in pawn;
'prescribed' means prescribed by regulations made by the Secretary of State;
'pre-existing arrangements' shall be construed in accordance with section 187;
'principal agreement' has the meaning given by section 19(1);
'protected goods' has the meaning given by section 90(7);
'quotation' has the meaning given by section 52(1)(a);
'redemption period' has the meaning given by section 116(3);
'register' means the register kept by the Director under section 35;
'regulated agreement' means a consumer credit agreement, or consumer hire agreement, other than an exempt agreement, and 'regulated' and 'unregulated' shall be construed accordingly;
'regulations' means regulations made by the Secretary of State;
'relative', except in section 184, means a person who is an associate by virtue of section 184(1);
'representation' includes any condition or warranty, and any other statement or undertaking, whether oral or in writing;
'restricted-use credit agreement' and 'restricted-use credit' have the meanings given by section 11(1);
'rules of court', in relation to Northern Ireland means, in relation to the High Court, rules made under section 7 of the Northern Ireland Act 1962, and, in relation to any other court, rules made by the authority having for the time being power to make rules regulating the practice and procedure in that court;
'running-account credit' shall be construed in accordance with section 10;
'security', in relation to an actual or prospective consumer credit agreement or consumer hire agreement, or any linked transaction, means a mortgage, charge, pledge, bond, debenture, indemnity, guarantee, bill, note or other right provided by the debtor or hirer, or at his request (express or implied), to secure the carrying out of the obligations of the debtor or hirer under the agreement;
'security instrument' has the meaning given by section 105(2);
'serve on' means deliver or send by post to;
'signed' shall be construed in accordance with subsection (3);
'small agreement' has the meaning given by section 17(1), and 'small' in relation to an agreement within any category shall be construed accordingly;
'specified fee' shall be construed in accordance with section 2(4) and (5);

'standard licence' has the meaning given by section 22(1)(a);
'supplier' has the meaning given by section 11(1)(b) or 12(c) or 13(c) or, in relation to an agreement failing within section 11(1)(a), means the creditor, and includes a person to whom the rights and duties of a supplier (as so defined) have passed by assignment or operation of law, or (in relation to a prospective agreement) the prospective supplier;
'surety' means the person by whom any security is provided, or the person to whom his rights and duties in relation to the security have passed by assignment or operation of law;
'technical grounds' shall be construed in accordance with subsection (5);
'time order' has the meaning given by section 129(1);
'total charge for credit' means a sum calculated in accordance with regulations under section 20(1);
'total price' means the total sum payable by the debtor under a hire-purchase agreement or a conditional sale agreement, including any sum payable on the exercise of an option to purchase, but excluding any sum payable as a penalty or as compensation or damages for a breach of the agreement;
'unexecuted agreement' means a document embodying the terms of a prospective regulated agreement, or such of them as it is intended to reduce to writing;
'unlicensed' means without a licence, but applies only in relation to acts for which a licence is required;
'unrestricted-use credit agreement' and 'unrestricted-use credit' have the meanings given by section 11(2);
'working day' means any day other than—
(a) Saturday or Sunday,
(b) Christmas Day or Good Friday,
(c) a bank holiday within the meaning given by section 1 of the Banking and Financial Dealings Act 1971.

(2) A person is not to be treated as carrying on a particular type of business merely because occasionally he enters into transactions belonging to a business of that type.

(3) Any provision of this Act requiring a document to be signed is complied with by a body corporate if the document is sealed by that body.

This subsection does not apply to Scotland.

(4) A document embodies a provision if the provision is set out either in the document itself or in another document referred to in it.

(5) An application dismissed by the court or the Director shall, if the court or the Director (as the case may be) so certifies, be taken to be dismissed on technical grounds only.

(6) Except in so far as the context otherwise requires, any reference in this Act to an enactment shall be construed as a reference to that enactment as amended by or under any other enactment, including this Act.

(7) In this Act, except where otherwise indicated—

(a) a reference to a numbered Part, section or Schedule is a reference to the Part or section of, or the Schedule to, this Act so numbered, and

(b) a reference in a section to a numbered subsection is a reference to the subsection of that section so numbered, and

(c) a reference in a section, subsection or Schedule to a numbered paragraph is a reference to the paragraph of that section, subsection or Schedule so numbered.

190. Financial provisions

(1) There shall be defrayed out of money provided by Parliament—

(a) all expenses incurred by the Secretary of State in consequence of the provisions of this Act;

(b) any expenses incurred in consequence of those provisions by any other Minister of the Crown or Government department;

(c) any increase attributable to this Act in the sums payable out of money so provided under the Superannuation Act 1972 or the Fair Trading Act 1973.

(2) Any fees received by the Director under this Act shall be paid into the Consolidated Fund.

191. Special provisions as to Northern Ireland

. . .

192. Transitional and commencement provisions, amendments and repeals

(1) The provisions of Schedule 3 shall have effect for the purposes of this Act.

(2) The appointment of a day for the purposes of any provision of Schedule 3 shall be effected by an order of the Secretary of State made by statutory instrument; and any such order shall include a provision amending Schedule 3 so as to insert an express reference to the day appointed.

(3) Subject to subsection (4)—

(a) the enactments specified in Schedule 4 shall have effect subject to the amendments specified in that Schedule (being minor amendments or amendments consequential on the preceding provisions of this Act), and

(b) the enactments specified in Schedule 5 are hereby repealed to the extent shown in column 3 of that Schedule.

(4) The Secretary of State shall by order made by statutory instrument provide for the coming into operation of the amendments contained in Schedule 4 and the repeals contained in Schedule 5, and those amendments and repeals shall have effect only as provided by an order so made.

193. Short title and extent

(1) This Act may be cited as the Consumer Credit Act 1974.

(2) This Act extends to Northern Ireland.

Section 167

SCHEDULE 1
PROSECUTION AND PUNISHMENT OF OFFENCES

1 *Section*	2 *Offence*	3 *Mode of prosecution*	4 *Imprisonment or fine*
7	. . . Knowingly or recklessly giving false information to Director.	(a) Summarily. (b) On indictment.	[The prescribed sum.] 2 years or a fine or both.
39(1)	. . . Engaging in activities requiring a licence when not a licensee.	(a) Summarily. (b) On indictment.	[The prescribed sum.] 2 years or a fine or both.
39(2)	. . . Carrying on a business under a name not specified in licence.	(a) Summarily. (b) On indictment.	[The prescribed sum.] 2 years or a fine or both.
39(3)	. . . Failure to notify changes in registered particulars.	(a) Summarily. (b) On indictment.	[The prescribed sum.] 2 years or a fine or both.
45	. . . Advertising credit where goods etc. not available for cash.	(a) Summarily. (b) On indictment.	[The prescribed sum.] 2 years or a fine or both.
46(1)	. . . False or misleading advertisements.	(a) Summarily. (b) On indictment.	[The prescribed sum.] 2 years or a fine or both.
47(1)	. . . Advertising infringements.	(a) Summarily. (b) On indictment.	[The prescribed sum.] 2 years or a fine or both.
49(1)	. . . Canvassing debtor-creditor agreements off trade premises.	(a) Summarily. (b) On indictment.	[The prescribed sum.] 1 year or a fine or both.
49(2)	. . . Soliciting debtor-creditor agreements during visits made in response to previous oral requests.	(a) Summarily. (b) On indictment.	[The prescribed sum.] 1 year or a fine or both.
50(1)	. . . Sending circulars to minors.	(a) Summarily. (b) On indictment.	[The prescribed sum.] 1 year or a fine or both.
51(1)	. . . Supplying unsolicited credit-tokens.	(a) Summarily. (b) On indictment.	[The prescribed sum.] 2 years or a fine or both.
77(4)	. . . Failure of creditor under fixed-sum credit agreement to supply copies of documents etc.	Summarily.	[Level 4 on the standard scale.]
78(6)	. . . Failure of creditor under running-account credit agreement to supply copies of documents etc.	Summarily.	[Level 4 on the standard scale.]
79(3)	. . . Failure of owner under consumer hire agreement to supply copies of documents etc.	Summarily.	[Level 4 on the standard scale.]
80(2)	. . . Failure to tell creditor or owner whereabouts of goods.	Summarily.	[Level 3 on the standard scale.]

1 *Section*	2 *Offence*	3 *Mode of prosecution*	4 *Imprisonment or fine*
85(2) . . .	Failure of creditor to supply copy of credit-token agreement.	Summarily.	[Level 4 on the standard scale.]
97(3) . . .	Failure to supply debtor with statement of amount required to discharge agreement.	Summarily.	[Level 3 on the standard scale.]
103(5) . . .	Failure to deliver notice relating to discharge of agreements.	Summarily.	[Level 3 on the standard scale.]
107(4) . . .	Failure of creditor to give information to surety under fixed-sum credit agreement.	Summarily.	[Level 4 on the standard scale.]
108(4) . . .	Failure of creditor to give information to surety under running-account credit agreement.	Summarily.	[Level 4 on the standard scale.]
109(3) . . .	Failure of owner to give information to surety under consumer hire agreement.	Summarily.	[Level 4 on the standard scale.]
110(3) . . .	Failure of creditor or owner to supply a copy of any security instrument to debtor or hirer.	Summarily.	[Level 4 on the standard scale.]
114(2) . . .	Taking pledges from minors.	(a) Summarily. (b) On indictment.	[The prescribed sum.] 1 year or a fine or both.
115 . . .	Failure to supply copies of a pledge agreement or pawn-receipt.	Summarily.	[Level 4 on the standard scale.]
119(1) . . .	Unreasonable refusal to allow pawn to be redeemed.	Summarily.	[Level 4 on the standard scale.]
154 . . .	Canvassing ancillary credit services off trade premises.	(a) Summarily. (b) On indictment.	[The prescribed sum.] 1 year or a fine or both.
157(3) . . .	Refusal to give name etc. of credit reference agency.	Summarily.	[Level 4 on the standard scale.]
158(4) . . .	Failure of credit reference agency to disclose filed information.	Summarily.	[Level 4 on the standard scale.]
159(6) . . .	Failure of credit reference agency to correct information.	Summarily.	[Level 4 on the standard scale.]
160(6) . . .	Failure of credit reference agency to comply with section 160(3) or (4).	Summarily.	[Level 4 on the standard scale.]
162(6) . . .	Impersonation of enforcement authority officers.	(a) Summarily. (b) On indictment.	[The prescribed sum.] 1 year or a fine or both.
165(1) . . .	Obstruction of enforcement authority officers.	Summarily.	[Level 4 on the standard scale.]
165(2) . . .	Giving false information to enforcement authority officers.	(a) Summarily. (b) On indictment.	[The prescribed sum.] 2 years or a fine or both.
167(2) . . .	Contravention of regulations under section 44, 52, 53, 54, or 112.	(a) Summarily. (b) On indictment.	[The prescribed sum.] 2 years or a fine or both.
174(5) . . .	Wrongful disclosure of information.	(a) Summarily. (b) On indictment.	[The prescribed sum.] 2 years or a fine or both.

Section 188(1)

SCHEDULE 2
EXAMPLES OF USE OF NEW TERMINOLOGY

PART I
LIST OF TERMS

Term	*Defined in section*	*Illustrated by examples(s)*
Advertisement	189(1)	2
Advertiser	189(1)	2
Antecedent negotiations	56	1, 2, 3, 4
Cancellable agreement	67	4
Consumer credit agreement	8	5, 6, 7, 15, 19, 21
Consumer hire agreement	15	20, 24
Credit	9	16, 19, 21
Credit-broker	189(1)	2
Credit limit	10(2)	6, 7, 19, 22, 23
Creditor	189(1)	1, 2, 3, 4
Credit-sale agreement	189(1)	5
Credit-token	14	3, 14, 16
Credit-token agreement	14	3, 14, 16, 22
Debtor-creditor agreement	13	8, 16, 17, 18
Debtor-creditor-supplier agreement	12	8, 16
Fixed-sum credit	10	9, 10, 17, 23
Hire-purchase agreement	189(1)	10
Individual	189(1)	19, 24
Linked transaction	19	11
Modifying agreement	82(2)	24
Multiple agreement	18	16, 18
Negotiator	56(1)	1, 2, 3, 4
Personal credit agreement	8(1)	19
Pre-existing arrangements	187	8, 21
Restricted-use credit	11	10, 12, 13, 14, 16
Running-account credit	10	15, 16, 18, 23
Small agreement	17	16, 17, 22
Supplier	189(1)	3, 14
Total charge for credit	20	5, 10
Total price	189(1)	10
Unrestricted-use credit	11	8, 12, 16, 17, 18

PART II
EXAMPLES

Example 1

Facts Correspondence passes between an employee of a money-lending company (writing on behalf of the company) and an individual about the terms on which the company would grant him a loan under a regulated agreement.

Analysis The correspondence constitutes antecedent negotiations falling within section 56(1)(a), the moneylending company being both creditor and negotiator.

Example 2

Facts Representations are made about goods in a poster displayed by a shopkeeper near the goods, the goods being selected by a customer who has read the poster and then sold by the shopkeeper to a finance company introduced by him (with whom he has a business relationship). The goods are disposed of by the finance company to the customer under a regulated hire-purchase agreement.

Analysis The representations in the poster constitute antecedent negotiations falling within section 56(1)(b), the shopkeeper being the credit-broker and negotiator and the finance company being the creditor. The poster is an advertisement and the shopkeeper is the advertiser.

Example 3

Facts Discussions take place between a shopkeeper and a customer about goods the customer wishes to buy using a credit-card issued by the D Bank under a regulated agreement.

Analysis The discussions constitute antecedent negotiations falling within section 56(1)(c), the shopkeeper being the supplier and negotiator and the D Bank the creditor. The credit-card is a credit-token as defined in section 14(1), and the regulated agreement under which it was issued is a credit-token agreement as defined in section 14(2).

Example 4

Facts Discussions take place and correspondence passes between a secondhand car dealer and a customer about a car, which is then sold by the dealer to the customer under a regulated conditional sale agreement. Subsequently, on a revocation of that agreement by consent, the car is resold by the dealer to a finance company introduced by him (with whom he has a business relationship), who in turn dispose of it to the same customer under a regulated hire-purchase agreement.

Analysis The discussions and correspondence constitute antecedent negotiations in relation both to the conditional sale agreement and the hire-purchase agreement. They fall under section 56(1)(a) in relation to the conditional sale agreement, the dealer being the creditor and the negotiator. In relation to the hire-purchase agreement they fall within section 56(1)(b), the dealer continuing to be treated as the negotiator but the finance company now being the creditor. Both agreements are cancellable if the discussions took place when the individual conducting the negotiations (whether the 'negotiator' or his employee or agent) was in the presence of the debtor, unless the unexecuted agreement was signed by the debtor at trade premises (as defined in section 67(b)). If the discussions all took place by telephone however, or the unexecuted agreement was signed by the debtor on trade premises (as so defined) the agreements are not cancellable.

Example 5

Facts E agrees to sell to F (an individual) an item of furniture in return for 24 monthly instalments of £10 payable in arrear. The property in the goods passes to F immediately.

Analysis This is a credit-sale agreement (see definition of 'credit-sale agreement' in section 189(1)). The credit provided amounts to £240 less the amount which, according to regulations made under section 20(1), constitutes the total charge for credit. (This amount is required to be deducted by section 9(4).) Accordingly the agreement falls within section 8(2) and is a consumer credit agreement.

Example 6

Facts The G Bank grants H (an individual) an unlimited over-draft, with an increased rate of interest on so much of any debit balance as exceeds £2,000.

Analysis Although the overdraft purports to be unlimited, the stipulation for increased interest above £2,000 brings the agreement within section 10(3)(b)(ii) and it is a consumer credit agreement.

Example 7

Facts J is an individual who owns a small shop which usually carries a stock worth about £1,000. K makes a stocking agreement under which he undertakes to provide on short-term credit the stock needed from time to time by J without any specified limit.

Analysis Although the agreement appears to provide unlimited credit, it is probable, having regard to the stock usually carried by J, that his indebtedness to K will not at any time rise above £5,000. Accordingly the agreement falls within section 10(3)(b)(iii) and is a consumer credit agreement.

Example 8

Facts U, a moneylender, lends £500 to V (an individual) knowing he intends to use it to buy office equipment from W. W introduced V to U, it being his practice to introduce customers needing finance to him. Sometimes U gives W a commission for this and sometimes not. U pays the £500 direct to V.

Analysis Although this appears to fall under section 11(1)(b), it is excluded by section 11(3) and is therefore (by section 11(2)) an unrestricted-use credit agreement. Whether it is a debtor-creditor agreement (by section 13(c)) or a debtor-creditor-supplier agreement (by section 12(c)) depends on whether the previous dealings between U and W amount to 'pre-existing arrangements', that is whether the agreement can be taken to have been entered into 'in accordance with, or in furtherance of' arrangements previously made between U and W, as laid down in section 187(1).

Example 9

Facts A agrees to lend B (an individual) £4,500 in nine monthly instalments of £500.

Analysis This is a cash loan and is a form of credit (see section 9 and definition of 'cash' in section 189(1)). Accordingly it falls within section 10(1)(b) and is fixed-sum credit amounting to £4,500.

Example 10

Facts C (in England) agrees to bail goods to D (an individual) in return for periodical payments. The agreement provides for the property in the goods to pass to D on payment of a total of £7,500 and the exercise by D of an option to purchase. The sum of £7,500 includes a down-payment of £1,000. It also includes an amount which, according to regulations made under section 20(1), constitutes a total charge for credit of £1,500.

Analysis This is a hire-purchase agreement with a deposit of £1,000 and a total price of £7,500 (see definitions of 'hire-purchase agreement', 'deposit' and 'total price' in section 189(1)). By section 9(3), it is taken to provide credit amounting to £7,500 — (£1,500 + £1,000), which equals £5,000. Under section 8(2), the agreement is therefore a consumer credit agreement, and under sections 9(3) and 11(l) it is a restricted-use credit agreement for fixed-sum credit. A similar result would follow if the agreement by C had been a hiring agreement in Scotland.

Example 11

Facts X (an individual) borrows £500 from Y (Finance). As a condition of the granting of the loan X is required—

(a) to execute a second mortgage on his house in favour of Y (Finance), and

(b) to take out a policy of insurance on his life with Y (Insurances).

In accordance with the loan agreement, the policy is charged to Y (Finance) as collateral security for the loan. The two companies are associates within the meaning of section 184(3).

Analysis The second mortgage is a transaction for the provision of security and accordingly does not fall within section 19(1), but the taking out of the insurance policy is a linked transaction falling within section 19(1)(a). The charging of the policy is a separate transaction (made between different parties) for the provision of security and again is excluded from section 19(1). The only linked transaction is therefore the taking out of the insurance policy. If X had not been required by the loan agreement to take out the policy, but it had been done at the suggestion of Y (Finance) to induce them to enter into the loan agreement, it would have been a linked transaction under section 19(1)(c)(i) by virtue of section 19(2)(a).

Example 12

Facts The N Bank agrees to lend 0 (an individual) £2,000 to buy a car from P. To make sure the loan is used as intended, the N Bank stipulates that the money must be paid by it direct to P.

Analysis The agreement is a consumer credit agreement by virtue of section 8(2). Since it falls within section 11(1)(b), it is a restricted-use credit agreement, P being the supplier. If the N Bank had not stipulated for direct payment to the supplier, section 11(3) would have operated and made the agreement into one for unrestricted-use credit.

Example 13

Facts Q, a debt-adjuster, agrees to pay off debts owed by R (an individual) to various moneylenders. For this purpose the agreement provides for the making of a loan by Q to R in return for R's agreeing to repay the loan by instalments with interest. The loan money is not paid over to R but retained by Q and used to pay off the money lenders.

Analysis This is an agreement to refinance existing indebtedness of the debtor's, and if the loan by Q does not exceed £5,000 is a restricted-use credit agreement falling within section 11(1)(c).

Example 14

Facts On payment of £1, S issues to T (an individual) a trading check under which T can spend up to £20 at any shop which has agreed, or in future agrees, to accept S's trading checks.

Analysis The trading check is a credit-token falling within section 14(1)(b). The credit-token agreement is a restricted-use credit agreement within section 11(1)(b), any shop in which the credit-token is used being the 'supplier'. The fact that further shops may be added after the issue of the credit-token is irrelevant in view of section 11(4).

Example 15

Facts A retailer L agrees with M (an individual) to open an account in M's name and, in return for M's promise to pay a specified minimum sum into the account each month and to pay a monthly charge for credit, agrees to allow to be debited to the account, in respect of purchases made by M from L, such sums as will not increase the debit balance at any time beyond the credit limit, defined in the agreement as a given multiple of the specified minimum sum.

Analysis This agreement provides credit falling within the definition of running- account credit in section 10(1)(a). Provided the credit limit is not over £5,000, the agreement falls within section 8(2) and is a consumer credit agreement for running- account credit.

Example 16

Facts Under an unsecured agreement, A (Credit), an associate of the A Bank, issues to B (an individual) a credit-card for use in obtaining cash on credit from A (Credit), to be paid by branches of the A Bank (acting as agent of A (Credit)), or goods or cash from suppliers or banks who have agreed to honour credit-cards issued by A (Credit). The credit limit is £30.

Analysis This is a credit-token agreement falling within section 14(1)(a) and (b). It is a regulated consumer credit agreement for running-account credit. Since the credit limit does not exceed £30, the agreement is a small agreement. So far as the agreement relates to goods it is a debtor-creditor-supplier agreement within section 12(b), since it provides restricted-use credit under section 11(1)(b). So far as it relates to cash it is a debtor-creditor agreement within section 13(c) and the credit it provides is unrestricted-use credit. This is therefore a multiple agreement. In that the whole agreement falls within several of the categories of agreement mentioned in this Act, it is, by section 18(3), to be treated as an agreement in each of those categories. So far as it is a debtor-creditor-supplier agreement providing restricted-use credit it is, by section 18(2), to be treated as a separate agreement; and similarly so far as it is a debtor-creditor agreement providing unrestricted-use credit. (See also Example 22.)

Example 17

Facts The manager of the C Bank agrees orally with D (an individual) to open a current account in D's name. Nothing is said about overdraft facilities. After maintaining the account in credit for some weeks, D draws a cheque in favour of E for an amount exceeding D's credit balance by £20. E presents the cheque and the Bank pay it.

Analysis In drawing the cheque D, by implication, requests the Bank to grant him an overdraft of £20 on its usual terms as to interest and other charges. In deciding to honour the cheque, the Bank by implication accept the offer. This constitutes a regulated small consumer credit agreement for unrestricted-use, fixed sum credit. It is a debtor-creditor agreement, and falls within section 74(1)(b) if covered by a determination under section 74(3). (Compare Example 18.)

Example 18

Facts F (an individual) has had a current account with the G Bank for many years. Although usually in credit, the account has been allowed by the Bank to become overdrawn from time to time. The maximum such overdraft has been is about £1,000. No explicit agreement has ever been made about overdraft facilities. Now, with a credit balance of £500, F draws a cheque for £1,300.

Analysis It might well be held that the agreement with F (express or implied) under which the Bank operate his account includes an implied term giving him the right to overdraft facilities up to say £1,000. If so, the agreement is a regulated consumer credit agreement for unrestricted-use, running-account credit. It is a debtor-creditor agreement, and falls within section 74(1)(b) if covered by a direction under section 74(3). It is also a multiple agreement, part of which (i.e. the part not dealing with the overdraft), as referred to in section 18(1)(a), falls within a category of agreement not mentioned in this Act. (Compare Example 17.)

Example 19

Facts H (a finance house) agrees with J (a partnership of individuals) to open an unsecured loan account in J's name on which the debit balance is not to exceed £7,500 (having regard to payments into the account made from time to time by J). Interest is to be payable in advance on this sum, with provision for yearly adjustments. H is entitled to debit the account with interest, a 'setting-up' charge, and other charges. Before J has an opportunity to draw on the account it is initially debited with £2,250 for advance interest and other charges.

Analysis This is a personal running-account credit agreement (see sections 8(1) and 10(1)(a), and definition of 'individual' in section 189(1)). By section 10(2) the credit limit is £7,000. By section 9(4) however the initial debit of £2,250, and any other charges later debited to the account by H, are not to be treated as credit even though time is allowed for their payment. Effect is given to this by section 10(3). Although the credit limit of £7,000 exceeds the amount (£5,000) specified in section 8(2) as the maximum for a consumer credit agreement, so that the agreement is not within section 10(3)(a), it is caught by section 10(3)(b)(i). At the beginning J can effectively draw (as credit) no more than £4,750, so the agreement is a consumer credit agreement.

Example 20

Facts K (in England) agrees with L (an individual) to bail goods to L for a period of three years certain at £2,200 a year, payable quarterly. The agreement contains no provision for the passing of the property in the goods to L.

Analysis This is not a hire-purchase agreement (see paragraph (b) of the definition of that term in section 189(1)), and is capable of subsisting for more than three months. Paragraphs (a) and (b) of section 15(1) are therefore satisfied, but paragraph (c) is not. The payments by L must exceed £5,000 if he conforms to the agreement. It is true that under section 101 L has a right to terminate the agreement on giving K three month's notice expiring not earlier than eighteen months after the making of the agreement, but that section applies only where the agreement is a regulated consumer hire agreement apart from the section (see subsection (1)). So the agreement is not a consumer hire agreement, though it would be if the hire charge were say £1,500 a year, or there were a 'break' clause in it operable by either party before the hire charges exceeded £5,000. A similar result would follow if the agreement by K had been a hiring agreement in Scotland.

Example 21

Facts The P Bank decides to issue cheque cards to its customers under a scheme whereby the bank undertakes to honour cheques of up to £30 in every case where the payee has taken the cheque in reliance on the cheque card, whether the customer has funds in his account or not. The P Bank writes to the major retailers advising them of this scheme and also publicises it by advertising. The Bank issues a cheque card to Q (an individual), who uses it to pay by cheque for goods costing £20 bought by Q from R, a major retailer. At the time, Q has £500 in his account at the P Bank.

Analysis The agreement under which the cheque card is issued to Q is a consumer credit agreement even though at all relevant times Q has more than £30 in his account. This is because Q is free to draw out his whole balance and then use the cheque card, in which case the Bank has bound itself to honour the cheque. In other words the cheque card agreement provides Q with credit, whether he avails himself of it or not. Since the amount of the credit is not subject to any express limit, the cheque card can be used any number of times. It may be presumed however that section 10(3)(b)(iii) will apply. The agreement is an unrestricted-use debtor-creditor agreement (by section 13(c)). Although the P Bank wrote to R informing R of the P Bank's willingness to honour any cheque taken by R in reliance on a cheque card, this does not constitute pre-existing arrangements as mentioned in section 13(c) because section 187(3) operates to prevent it. The agreement is not a credit-token agreement within section 14(1)(b) because payment by the P Bank to R, would be a payment of the cheque and not a payment for the goods.

Example 22

Facts The facts are as in Example 16. On one occasion B uses the credit-card in a way which increases his debit balance with A (Credit) to £40. A (Credit) writes to B agreeing to allow the excess on that occasion only, but stating that it must be paid off within one month.

Analysis In exceeding his credit limit B, by implication, requests A (Credit) to allow him a temporary excess (compare Example 17). A (Credit) is thus faced by B's action with the choice of treating it as a breach of contract or granting his implied request. He does the latter. If he had done the former, B would be treated as taking credit to which he was not entitled (see section 14(3)) and, subject to the terms of his contract with A (Credit), would be liable to damages for breach of contract. As it is, the agreement to allow the excess varies the original credit-token agreement by adding a new term. Under section 10(2), the new term is to be disregarded in arriving at the credit limit, so that the credit-token agreement at no time ceases to be a small agreement. By section 82(2) the later agreement is deemed to revoke the original agreement and contain provisions reproducing the combined effect of the two agreements. By section 82(4), this later agreement is exempted from Part V (except section 56).

Example 23

Facts Under an oral agreement made on 10th January, X (an individual) has an overdraft on his current account at the Y bank with a credit limit of £100. On 15th February, when his overdraft stands at £90, X draws a cheque for £25. It is the first time that X has exceeded his credit limit, and on 16th February the bank honours the cheque.

Analysis The agreement of 10th January is a consumer credit agreement for running-account credit. The agreement of 15th-16th February varies the earlier agreement by adding a term allowing the credit limit to be exceeded merely temporarily. By section 82(2) the later agreement is deemed to revoke the earlier agreement and reproduce the combined effect of the two agreements. By section 82(4), Part V of this Act (except section 56) does not apply to the later agreement. By section 18(5), a term allowing a merely temporary excess over the credit limit is not to be treated as a separate agreement, or as providing fixed-sum credit. The whole of the £115 owed to the bank by X on 16th February is therefore running-account credit.

Example 24

Facts On 1st March 1975 Z (in England) enters into an agreement with A (an unincorporated body of persons) to bail to A equipment consisting of two components (component P and component Q). The agreement is not a hire-purchase agreement and is for a fixed term of 3 years, so paragraphs (a) and (b) of section 15(1) are both satisfied. The rental is payable monthly at a rate of £2,400 a year, but the agreement provides that this is to be reduced to £1,200 a year for the remainder of the agreement if at any time during its currency A returns component Q to the owner Z. On 5th May 1976 A is incorporated as A Ltd., taking over A's assets and liabilities. On 1st March 1977, A Ltd. returns component Q. On 1st January 1978, Z and A Ltd. agree to extend the earlier agreement by one year, increasing the rental for the final year by £250 to £1,450.

Analysis When entered into on 1st March 1975, the agreement is a consumer hire agreement. A falls within the definition of 'individual' in section 189(1) and if A returns component Q before 1st May 1976 the total rental will not exceed £5,000 (see section 15(1)(c)). When this date is passed without component Q having been returned it is obvious that the total rental must now exceed £5,000. Does this mean that the agreement then ceases to be a consumer hire agreement? The answer is no, because there has been no change in the terms of the agreement, and without such a change the agreement cannot move from one category to the other. Similarly, the fact that A's rights and duties under the agreement pass to a body corporate on 5th May 1976 does not cause the agreement to cease to be a consumer hire agreement (see definition of 'hirer' in section 189(1)).

The effect of the modifying agreement of 1st January 1978 is governed by section 82(2), which requires it to be treated as containing provisions reproducing the combined effect of the two actual agreements, that is to say as providing that—

(a) obligations outstanding on 1st January 1978 are to be treated as outstanding under the modifying agreement;

(b) the modifying agreement applies at the old rate of hire for the months of January and February 1978, and

(c) for the year beginning 1st March 1978 A Ltd. will be the bailee of component P at a rental of £1,450.

The total rental under the modifying agreement is &1,850. Accordingly the modifying agreement is a regulated agreement. Even if the total rental under the modifying agreement exceeded £5,000 it would still be regulated because of the provisions of section 82(3).

[*Scheds. 3 (transitional and commencement provisions), 4 (minor and consequential amendments) and 5 (repeals) are omitted.*]

UNSOLICITED GOODS AND SERVICES (AMENDMENT) ACT 1975
(1975, c. 13)

An Act to amend the Unsolicited Goods and Services Act 1971, to enable the Secretary of State to make regulations with respect to the contents and forms of notes of agreement, invoices and similar documents and to provide for conviction on indictment in relation to an offence under section 3(2) of the said Act; and for connected matters. [20th March 1975]

2. Amendments consequential on section 1

(1) In section 3(3) of the Act of 1971 for the words from 'must state' to the end there shall be substituted the words 'shall comply with the requirements of regulations under section 3A of this Act applicable thereto'.

3. Provision for offence under section 3(2) of the Act of 1971 to be prosecuted on indictment

(1) An offence under section 3(2) of the Act of 1971 may be prosecuted on indictment; and a person convicted on indictment of an offence under that section shall be liable to a fine.

(2) This section applied only to offences committed after the coming into operation of this section.

4. Short title, citation, commencement, transitional provisions and extent

(2) Sections 1 and 3 of this Act and this section shall come into operation on the passing of this Act but any regulations made by virtue of the said section 1 shall not come into operation before the date appointed by order under subsection (3) below for the coming into operation of section 2 of this Act.

(3) Section 2 of this Act shall come into operation on such dates as the Secretary of State may by order made by statutory instrument appoint; and different dates may be appointed by order under this subsection for different provisions of that section.

TORTS (INTERFERENCE WITH GOODS) ACT 1977
(1977, c. 32)

An Act to amend the law concerning conversion and other torts affecting goods.
[22nd July 1977]

1. Definition of 'wrongful interference with goods'

In this Act 'wrongful interference', or 'wrongful interference with goods', means—

(a) conversion of goods (also called trover),

(b) trespass to goods,

(c) negligence so far as it results in damage to goods or to an interest in goods,

(d) subject to section 2, any other tort so far as it results in damage to goods or to an interest in goods

[and references in this Act (however worded) to proceedings for wrongful interference or to a claim or right to claim for wrongful interference shall include references to proceedings by virtue of Part I of the Consumer Protection Act 1987 (product liability) in respect of any damage to goods and to the interest in goods or, as the case may be, to a claim or right to claim by virtue of that Part in respect of any such damage].

2. Abolition of detinue

(1) Detinue is abolished.

(2) An action lies in conversion for loss or destruction of goods which a bailee has allowed to happen in breach of his duty to his bailor (that is to say it lies in a case which is not otherwise conversion, but would have been detinue before detinue was abolished).

3. Forms of judgment where goods are detained

(1) In proceedings for wrongful interference against a person who is in possession or in control of the goods relief may be given in accordance with this section, so far as appropriate.

(2) The relief is—

(a) an order for delivery of goods, and for payment of any consequential damages, or

(b) an order for delivery of the goods, but giving the defendant the alternative of paying damages by reference to the value of the goods, together in either alternative with payment of any consequential damages, or

(c) damages.

(3) Subject to rules of court—

(a) relief shall be given under only one of paragraphs (a), (b) and (c) of subsection (2),

(b) relief under paragraph (a) of subsection (2) is at the discretion of the court, and the claimant may choose between the others.

(4) If it is shown to the satisfaction of the court that an order under subsection (2)(a) had not been complied with, the court may—

(a) revoke the order, or the relevant part of it, and

(b) make an order for payment of damages by reference to the value of the goods.

(5) Where an order is made under subsection (2)(b) the defendant may satisfy the order by returning the goods at any time before execution of judgment, but without prejudice to liability to pay any consequential damages.

(6) An order for delivery of the goods under subsection (2)(a) or (b) may impose such conditions as may be determined by the court, or pursuant to rules of court, and in particular, where damages by reference to the value of the goods would not be the whole of the value of the goods, may require an allowance to be made by the claimant to reflect the difference.

For example, a bailor's action against the bailee may be one in which the measure of damages is not the full value of the goods, and then the court may order delivery of the goods, but require the bailor to pay the bailee a sum reflecting the difference.

(7) Where under subsection (1) or subsection (2) of section 6 an allowance is to be made in respect of an improvement of the goods, and an order is made under subsection (2)(a) or (b), the court may assess the allowance to be made in respect of the improvement, and by the order require, as a condition for delivery of the goods, that allowance to be made by the claimant.

(8) This section is without prejudice—

(a) to the remedies afforded by section 133 of the Consumer Credit Act, or . . .

(c) to any jurisdiction to afford ancillary or incidental relief.

4. Interlocutory relief where goods are detained

(1) In this section 'proceedings' means proceedings for wrongful interference.

(2) On the application of any person in accordance with rules of court, the High Court shall, in such circumstances as may be specified in the rules, have power to make an order providing for the delivery up of any goods which are or may become subject matter of subsequent proceedings in the court, or as to which any question may arise in proceedings.

(3) Delivery shall be, as the order may provide, to the claimant or to a person appointed by the court for the purpose, and shall be on such terms and conditions as may be specified in the order.

5. Extinction of title on satisfaction of claim for damages

(1) Where damages for wrongful interference are, or would fall to be, assessed on the footing that the claimant is being compensated—

(a) for the whole of his interest in the goods, or

(b) for the whole of his interest in the goods subject to a reduction for contributory negligence,

payment of the assessed damages (under all heads), or as the case may be settlement of a claim for damages for the wrong (under all heads), extinguishes the claimant's title to that interest.

(2) In subsection (1) the reference to the settlement of the claim includes—

(a) where the claim is made in court proceedings, and the defendant has paid a sum into court to meet the whole claim, the taking of that sum by the claimant, and

(b) where the claim is made in court proceedings, and the proceedings are settled or compromised, the payment of what is due in accordance with the settlement or compromise, and

(c) where the claim is made out of court and is settled or compromised, the payment of what is due in accordance with the settlement or compromise.

(3) It is hereby declared that subsection (1) does not apply where damages are assessed on the footing that the claimant is being compensated for the whole of his interest in the goods, but the damages paid are limited to some lesser amount by virtue of any enactment or rule of law.

(4) Where under section 7(3) the claimant accounts over to another person (the 'third party') so as to compensate (under all heads) the third party for the whole of his interest in the goods, the third party's title to that interest is extinguished.

(5) This section has effect subject to any agreement varying the respective rights of the parties to the agreement, and where the claim is made in court proceedings has effect subject to any court.

6. Allowance for improvement of the goods

(1) If in proceedings for wrongful interference against a person (the 'improver') who has improved the goods, it is shown that the improver acted in the mistaken but honest belief that he had a good title to them, an allowance shall be made for the extent to which, at the time as at which the goods fall to be valued in assessing damages, the value of the goods is attributable to the improvement.

(2) If, in proceedings for wrongful interference against a person ('the purchaser') who has purported to purchase the goods—

(a) from the improver, or

(b) where after such a purported sale the goods passed by a further purported sale on one or more occasions, on any such occasion,

it is shown that the purchaser acted in good faith, an allowance shall be made on the principle set out in subsection (1).

For example, where a person in good faith buys a stolen car from the improver and is sued in conversion by the true owner the damages may be reduced to reflect the improvement, but if the person who bought the stolen car from the improver sues the improver for failure of consideration, and the improver acted in good faith, subsection (3) below will ordinarily make a comparable reduction in the damages he recovers from the improver.

(3) If in a case within subsection (2) the person purporting to sell the goods acted in good faith, then in proceedings by the purchaser for recovery of the purchase price because of failure of consideration, or in any other proceedings founded on that failure of consideration, an allowance shall, where appropriate, be made on the principle set out in subsection (1).

(4) This section applies, with the necessary modifications, to a purported bailment or other disposition of goods as it applies to a purported sale of goods.

7. Double liability

(1) In this section 'double liability' means the double liability of the wrongdoer which can arise—

(a) where one of two or more rights of action for wrongful interference is founded on a possessory title, or

(b) where the measure of damages in an action for wrongful interference founded on a proprietary title is or includes the entire value of the goods, although the interest is one of two or more interests in the goods.

(2) In proceedings to which any two or more claimants are parties, the relief shall be such as to avoid double liability of the wrongdoer as between those claimants.

(3) On satisfaction, in whole or in part, of any claim for an amount exceeding that recoverable if subsection (2) applied, the claimant is liable to account over to the other person having a right to claim to such extent as will avoid double liability.

(4) Where, as the result of enforcement of a double liability, any claimant is unjustly enriched to an extent, he shall be liable to reimburse the wrongdoer to that extent.

For example, if a converter of goods pays damages first to a finder of the goods, and then to the true owner, the finder is unjustly enriched unless he accounts over to the true owner under subsection (3); and then the true owner is unjustly enriched and becomes liable to reimburse the converter of the goods.

8. Competing rights to the goods

(1) The defendant in an action for wrongful interference shall be entitled to show, in accordance with rules of court, that a third party has a better right than the plaintiff as respects all or any part of the interest claimed by the plaintiff, or in right of which he sues, and any rule of law (sometimes called jus tertii) to the contrary is abolished.

(2) Rules of court relating to proceedings for wrongful interference may—

(a) require the plaintiff to give particulars of his title,

(b) require the plaintiff to identify any person who, to his knowledge, has or claims any interest in the goods,

(c) authorise the defendant to apply for directions as to whether any person should be joined with a view to establishing whether he has a better right than the plaintiff, or has a claim of a result of which the defendant might be doubly liable,

(d) where a party fails to appear on an application within paragraph (c), or to comply with any direction given by the court on such an application, authorise the court to deprive him of any right of action against the defendant for the wrong either unconditionally, or subject to such terms or conditions as may be specified.

(3) Subsection (2) is without prejudice to any power of making rules of court.

9. Concurrent actions

. . .

10. Co-owners

(1) Co-ownership is no defence to an action founded on conversion or trespass to goods where the defendant without the authority of the other co-owner—

(a) destroys the goods, or disposes of the goods in a way giving a good title to the entire property in the goods, or otherwise does anything equivalent to the destruction of the other's interest in the goods, or

(b) purports to dispose of the goods in a way which would give a good title to the entire property in the goods if he was acting with the authority of all co-owners of the goods.

(2) Subsection (1) shall not affect the law concerning execution or enforcement of judgments, or concerning any form of distress.

(3) Subsection (1)(a) is by the way of restatement of existing law so far as it relates to conversion.

11. Minor amendments

(1) Contributory negligence is no defence in proceedings founded on conversion, or on intentional trespass to goods.

(2) Receipt of goods by way of pledge is conversion if the delivery of the goods is conversion.

(3) Denial of title is not of itself conversion.

12. Bailee's power of sale

(1) This section applies to goods in the possession or under the control of a bailee where—

(a) the bailor is in breach of an obligation to take delivery of the goods or, if the terms of the bailment so provide, to give directions as to their delivery, or

(b) the bailee could impose such an obligation by giving notice to the bailor, but is unable to trace or communicate with the bailor, or

(c) the bailee can reasonably expect to be relieved of any duty to safeguard the goods on giving notice to the bailor, but is unable to trace or communicate with the bailor.

(2) In the cases of Part I of Schedule 1 to this Act a bailee may, for the purposes of subsection (1), impose an obligation on the bailor to take delivery of the goods, or as the case may be to give directions as to their delivery, and in those cases the said Part I sets out the method of notification.

(3) If the bailee—

(a) has in accordance with Part II of Schedule 1 to this Act given notice to the bailor of his intention to sell the goods under this subsection, or

(b) has failed to trace or communicate with the bailor with a view to giving him such a notice, after having taken reasonable steps for the purpose, and is reasonably satisfied that the bailor owns the goods, he shall be entitled, as against the bailor, to sell the goods.

(4) Where subsection (3) applies but the bailor did not in fact own the goods, a sale under this section, or under section 13, shall not give a good title as against the owner, or as against a person claiming under the owner.

(5) A bailee exercising his powers under subsection (3) shall be liable to account to the bailor for the proceeds of sale, less any cost of sale, and—

(a) the account shall be taken on the footing that the bailee should have adopted the best method of sale reasonably available in the circumstances, and

(b) where subsection (3)(a) applies, any sum payable in respect of the goods by the bailor to the bailee which accrued due before the bailee gave notice of intention to sell the goods shall be deductible from the proceeds of sale.

(6) A sale duly made under this section gives a good title to the purchaser as against the bailor.

(7) In this section, section 13, and Schedule 1 to the Act,

(a) 'bailor' and 'bailee' include their respective successors in title, and

(b) references to what is payable, paid or due to the bailee in respect of the goods include references to what would be payable by the bailor to the bailee as a condition of delivery of the goods at the relevant time.

(8) This section, and Schedule 1 to this Act, have effect subject to the terms of the bailment.

(9) this section shall not apply where the goods were bailed before the commencement of this Act.

13. Sale authorised by the court

(1) If a bailee of the goods to which section 12 applies satisfies the court that he is entitied to see the goods under section 12, or that he would be so entitied if he had given any notice required in accordance with Schedule 1 to this Act, the court—

(a) may authorise the sale of the goods subject to such terms and conditions, if any, as may be specified in the order and,

(b) may authorise the bailee to deduct from the proceeds of sale any costs of sale and any amount due from the bailor to the bailee in respect of the goods, and

(c) may direct the payment into court of the net proceeds of sale, less any amount deducted under paragraph (b), to be held to the credit of the bailor.

(2) A decision of the court authorising a sale under this section shall, subject to any right of appeal, be conclusive, as against the bailor, of the bailee's entitlement to sell the goods, and gives a good title to the purchaser as against the bailor.

(3) In this section 'the court' means the High Court or a county court, and a county court shall have jurisdiction in the proceedings if the value of the goods does not exceed the county court limit.

14. Interpretation

(1) In this Act, unless the context otherwise requires—

. . .

'goods' includes all chattels personal other than things in action and money . . . .

15. . . .

16. Extent and application to the Crown

(3) This Act shall bind the Crown, but as regards the Crown's liability in tort shall not bind the Crown further than the Crown is made liable in tort by the Crown Proceedings Act 1947.

SCHEDULES

Section 12 SCHEDULE 1

UNCOLLECTED GOODS

PART I

POWER TO IMPOSE OBLIGATION TO COLLECT GOODS

1. (1) For the purposes of section 12(1) a bailee may, in the circumstances specified in this Part of this Schedule, by notice given to the bailor impose on him an obligation to take delivery of the goods.

(2) The notice shall be in writing, and may be given either—

(a) by delivering it to the bailor, or

(b) by leaving it at his proper address, or

(c) by post.

(3) The notice shall—

(a) specify the name and address of the bailee, and give sufficient particulars of the goods and the address or place where they are held, and

(b) state that the goods are ready for delivery to the bailor, or where combined with a notice terminating the contract of bailment, will be ready for delivery when the contract is terminated, and

(c) specify the amount, if any, which is payable by the bailor to the bailee in respect of the goods and which became due before the giving of the notice.

(4) Where the notice is sent by post it may be combined with a notice under Part II of this Schedule if the notice is sent by post in a way complying with paragraph 6(4).

(5) References in this Part of this Schedule to taking delivery of the goods include, where the terms of the bailment admit, references to giving directions as to their delivery.

(6) This Part of this Schedule is without prejudice to the provisions of any contract requiring the bailor to take delivery of the goods.

Goods accepted for repair or other treatment

2. If a bailee has accepted goods for repair or other treatment on the terms (expressed or implied) that they will be re-delivered to the bailor when the repair or other treatment has been carried out, the notice may be given at any time after the repair or other treatment has been carried out.

Goods accepted for valuation or appraisal

3. If a bailee has accepted goods in order to value or appraise them, the notice may be given at any time after the bailee has carried out the valuation or appraisal.

Storage, warehousing, etc.

4. (1) If a bailee is in possession of goods which he has held as custodian, and his obligation as custodian has come to an end, the notice may be given at any time after the ending of the obligation, or may be combined with any notice terminating his obligation as custodian.

(2) This paragraph shall not apply to goods held by a person as mercantile agent, that is to say by a person having in the customary course of his business as a mercantile agent authority either to sell goods or to consign goods for the purpose of sale, or to buy goods, or to raise money on the security of goods.

Supplemental

5. Paragraphs 2, 3 and 4 apply whether or not the bailor has paid any amount due to the bailee in respect of the goods, and whether or not the bailment is for reward, or in the course of business, or gratuitous.

PART II
NOTICE OF INTENTION TO SELL GOODS

6. (1) A notice under section 12(3) shall—
(a) specify the name and address of the bailee, and give sufficient particulars of the goods and the address or place where they are held, and
(b) specify the date on or after which the bailee proposes to sell the goods, and
(c) specify the amount, if any, which is payable by the bailor to the bailee in respect of the goods, and which became due before giving of the notice.
(2) The period between giving of the notice and the date specified in the notice as that on or after which the bailee proposes to exercise the power of sale shall be such as will afford the bailor a reasonable opportunity of taking delivery of the goods.
(3) If any amount is payable in respect of the goods by the bailor to the bailee, and become due before giving of the notice, the said period shall be not less than three months.
(4) The notice shall be in writing and shall be sent by post in a registered letter, or by the recorded delivery service.
7. (1) The bailee shall not give a notice under section 12(3), or exercise his right to sen the goods pursuant to such a notice, at a time when he has notice that, because of a dispute concerning the goods, the bailor is questioning or refusing to pay all or any part of what the bailee claims to be due to him in respect of the goods.
(2) This paragraph shall be left out of account in determining under section 13(1) whether a bailee of goods is entitled to see the goods under section 12, or would be so entitied if he had given any notice required in accordance with this Schedule.

UNFAIR CONTRACT TERMS ACT 1977
(1977, c. 50)

An act to impose further limits on the extent to which under the law of England and Wales and Northern Ireland civil liability for breach of contract, or for negligence or other breach of duty, can be avoided by means of contract terms and otherwise, and under the law of Scotland civil liability can be avoided by means of contract terms. [26th October 1977]

PART I

1. Scope of Part I

(1) For the purposes of this Part of this Act, 'negligence' means the breach—
(a) of any obligation, arising from the express or implied terms of a contract, to take reasonable care or exercise reasonable skill in the performance of the contract;
(b) of any common law duty to take reasonable care or exercise reasonable skill (but not any stricter duty);
(c) of the common duty of care imposed by the Occupiers' Liability Act 1957 or the Occupier's Liability Act (Northern Ireland) 1957.
(2) This Part of the Act is subject to Part III; and in relation to contracts, the operation of sections 2 to 4 and 7 is subject to the exceptions made by Schedule I.
(3) In the case of both contract and tort, sections 2 to 7 apply (except where the contrary is stated in section 6(4)) only to business liability, that is liability to breach of obligations or duties arising—
(a) from things done or to be done by a person in the course of a business (whether his own business or another's); or
(b) from the occupation of premises used for business purposes of the occupier; and references to liability are to be read accordingly [but liability of an occupier of premises for breach of an obligation or duty towards a person obtaining access to the premises for

recreational or educational purposes, being liability for loss or damage suffered by reason of the dangerous state of the premises, is not a business liability of the occupier unless granting that person such access for the purposes concerned falls within the business purposes of the occupier].

(4) In relation to any breach of duty or obligation, it is immaterial for any purpose of this Part of this Act whether the breach was inadvertent or intentional, or whether liability for it arises directly or vicariously.

2. Negligence liability

(1) A person cannot by reference to any contract term or to a notice given to persons generally or to particular persons exclude or restrict his liability for death or personal injury resulting from negligence.

(2) In the case of other loss or damage, a person cannot so exclude or restrict his liability for negligence except in so far as the term or notice satisfies the requirement of reasonableness.

(3) Where a contract term or notice purports to exclude or restrict liability for negligence a person's agreement to or awareness of it is not of itself to be taken as indicating his voluntary acceptance of any risk.

3. Liability arising in contract

(1) This section applies as between contracting parties where one of them deals as consumer or on the other's written standard terms of business.

(2) As against that party, the other cannot by reference to any contract term—

(a) when himself in breach of contract, exclude or restrict any liability of his in respect of the breach; or

(b) claim to be entitled—

(i) to render a contractual performance substantially different from that which was reasonably expected of him, or

(ii) in respect of the whole of any part of his contractual obligation, to render no performance at all,

except in so far as (in any of the cases mentioned above in this subsection) the contract term satisfies the requirement of reasonableness.

4. Unreasonable indemnity clauses

(1) A person dealing as consumer cannot by reference to any contract term be made to indemnify another person (whether a party to the contract or not) in respect of liability that may be incurred by the other for negligence or breach of contract, except in so far as the contract term satisfies the requirement of reasonableness.

(2) This section applies whether the liability in question—

(a) is directly that of the person to be indemnified or is incurred by him vicariously;

(b) is to the person dealing as consumer or to someone else.

5. 'Guarantee' of consumer goods

(1) In the case of goods of a type ordinarily supplied for private use of consumption, where loss or damage—

(a) arises from the goods proving defective while in consumer use; and

(b) results from the negligence of a person concerned in the manufacture or distribution of the goods,

liability for the loss or damage cannot be excluded or restricted by reference to any contract term or notice contained in or operating by reference to a guarantee of the goods.

(2) For these purposes—

(a) goods are to be regarded as 'in consumer use' when a person is using them, or has them in his possession for use, otherwise than exclusively for the purposes of a business; and

(b) anything in writing is a guarantee if it contains or purports to contain some promise or assurance (however worded or presented) that defects will be made good by complete or partial replacement, or by repair, monetary compensation or otherwise.

(3) This section does not apply as between the parties to a contract under or in pursuance of which possession or ownership of the goods passed.

6. Sale and hire-purchase

(1) Liability for breach of the obligations arising from—

(a) [section 12 of the Sale of Goods Act 1979] (seller's implied undertakings as to title, etc.);

(b) section 8 of the Supply of Goods (Implied Terms) Act 1973 (the corresponding thing in relation to hire-purchase),

cannot be excluded or restricted by reference to any contract term.

(2) As against a person dealing as consumer, liability for breach of the obligations arising from—

(a) [section 13, 14 or 15 of the [1979] Act] (seller's implied undertakings as to conformity of goods with description or sample, or as to their quality of fitness for a particular purpose);

(b) section 9, 10 or 11 of the 1973 Act (the corresponding things in relation to hire-purchase),

cannot be excluded or restricted by reference to any contract term.

(3) As against a person dealing otherwise than as consumer, the liability specified in subsection (2) above can be excluded or restricted by reference to a contract term, but only in so far as the term satisfies the requirement of reasonableness.

(4) The liabilities referred to in this section are not only the business liabilities defined by section 1(3), but include those arising under any contract of sale of goods or hire-purchase agreement.

7. Miscellaneous contracts under which goods pass

(1) Where the possession or ownership of goods passes under or in pursuance of a contract not governed by the law of sale of goods or hire-purchase, subsections (2) to (4) below apply as regards the effect (if any) to be given to contract terms excluding or restricting liability for breach of obligation arising by implication of law from the nature of the contract.

(2) As against a person dealing as consumer, liability in respect of the goods' correspondence with description or sample, or their quality or fitness for any particular purpose, cannot be excluded or restricted by reference to any such term.

(3) As against a person dealing otherwise than as consumer, that liability can be excluded or restricted by reference to such a term, but only in so far as the term satisfies the requirement of reasonableness.

[(3A) Liability for breach of the obligations arising under section 2 of the Supply of Goods and Services Act 1982 (implied terms about title etc. in certain contracts for the transfer of the property in goods) cannot be excluded or restricted by reference to any such term.]

(4) Liability in respect of—

(a) the right to transfer ownership of the goods, or give possession; or

(b) the assurance of quiet possession to a person taking goods in pursuance of the contract,

cannot [(in a case to which subsection (3A) above does not apply)] be excluded or restricted by reference to any such term except in so far as the term satisfies the requirement of reasonableness.

(c) This section does not apply in the case of goods passing on a redemption of trading stamps within the Trading Stamps Act 1964 or the Tradings Stamps Act (Northern Ireland) 1965.

9. Effect of breach

(1) Where for reliance upon it a contract term has to satisfy the requirement of reasonableness, it may be found to do so-and be given effect accordingly notwithstanding that the contract has been terminated either by breach or by a party electing to treat it as repudiated.

(2) Where on a breach the contract is nevertheless affirmed by a party entitled to treat it as repudiated, this does not of itself exclude the requirement of reasonableness in relation to any contract term.

10. Evasion by means of secondary contract

A person is not bound by any contract term prejudicing or taking away rights of his which arise under, or in connection with the performance of, another contract, so far as those rights extend to the enforcement of another's liability which this Part of this Act prevents that other from excluding or restricting.

11. The 'reasonableness' test

(1) In relation to a contract term, the requirement of reasonableness for the purposes of this Part of this Act, section 3 of the Misrepresentation Act 1967 and section 3 of the Misrepresentation Act (Northern Ireland) 1967 is that the term shall have been a fair and reasonable one to be included having regard to the circumstances which were, or ought reasonably to have been, known to or in the contemplation of the parties when the contract was made.

(2) In determining for the purposes of section 6 or 7 above whether a contract term satisfies the requirement of reasonableness, regard shall be had in particular to the matters specified in Schedule 2 to this Act; but this subsection does not prevent the court or arbitrator from holding, in accordance with any rule of law, that a term which purports to exclude or restrict any relevant liability is not a term of the contract.

(3) In relation to a notice (not being a notice having contractual effect), the requirement of reasonableness under this Act is that it should be fair and reasonable to allow reliance on it, having regard to all the circumstances obtaining when the liability arose or (but for the notice) would have arisen.

(4) Where by reference to a contract term or notice a person seeks to restrict liability to a specified sum of money, and the question arises (under this or any other Act) whether the term or notice satisfies the requirement of reasonableness, regard shall be had in particular (but without prejudice to subsection (2) above in the case of contract terms) to—

(a) the resources which he could expect to be available to him for the purpose of meeting the liability should it arise; and

(b) how far it was open to him to cover himself by insurance.

(5) It is for those claiming that a contract term or notice satisfies the requirement of reasonableness to show that it does.

12. 'Dealing as consumer'

(1) A party to contract 'deals as consumer' in relation to another party if—

(a) he neither makes the contract in the course of a business nor holds himself out as doing so; and

(b) the other party does make the contract in the course of a business; and

(c) in the case of a contract governed by the law of sale of goods or hire-purchase, or by section 7 of this Act, the goods passing under or in pursuance of the contract are of a type ordinarily supplied for private use or consumption.

(2) But on a sale by auction or by competitive tender the buyer is not in any circumstances to be regarded as dealing as consumer.

(3) Subject to this, it is for those claiming that a party does not deal as consumer to show that he does not.

13. Varieties of exemption clause

(1) To the extent that this Part of this Act prevents the exclusion or restriction of any liability it also prevents—

(a) making the liability or its enforcement subject to restrictive or onerous conditions;

(b) excluding or restricting any right or remedy in respect of the liability, or subjecting a person to any prejudice in consequence of his pursuing any such right or remedy;

(c) excluding or restricting rules of evidence or procedure;

and (to that extent) sections 2 and 5 to 7 also prevent excluding or restricting liability by reference to terms and notices which exclude or restrict the relevant obligation or duty.

(2) But an agreement in writing to submit present or future differences to arbitration is not to be treated under this Part of this Act as excluding or restricting any liability.

14. Interpretation of Part I

In this Part of the Act—

'business' includes a profession and the activities of any government department or local or public authority;

'goods' has the same meaning as in [the Sales of Goods Act 1979];
'hire-purchase agreement' has the same meaning as in the Consumer Credit Act 1974;
'negligence' has the meaning given by section 1(1);
'notice' includes an announcement, whether or not in writing, and any other communication or pretended communication; and
'personal injury' includes any disease and any impairment of physical or mental condition.

PART II

15. Scope of Part II

(1) This Part of this Act [. . .] is subject to Part III of this Act and does not affect the validity of any discharge or indemnity given by a person in consideration of the receipt by him of compensation in settlement of any claim which he has.

(2) Subject to subsection (3) below, sections 16 to 18 of this Act apply to any contract only to the extent that the contract—

(a) relates to the transfer of the ownership or possession of goods from one person to another (with or without work having been done on them);

(b) constitutes a contract of service or apprenticeship;

(c) relates to services of whatever kind, including (without prejudice to the foregoing generality) carriage, deposit and pledge, care and custody, mandate, agency, loan and services relating to the use of land;

(d) relates to the liability of an occupier of land to persons entering upon or using that land;

(e) relates to a grant of any right or permission to enter upon or use land not amounting to an estate or interest in the land.

(3) Notwithstanding anything in subsection (2) above, sections 16 to 18—

(a) do not apply to any contract to the extent that the contract—

(i) is a contract of insurance (including a contract to pay an annuity on human life);

(ii) relates to the formation, constitution or dissolution of any body corporate or unincorporated association or partnership;

(b) apply to—

a contract of marine salvage or towage;
a charter party of a ship or hovercraft;
a contract for the carriage of goods by ship or hovercraft; or
a contract to which subsection (4) below relates,

only to the extent that—

(i) both parties deal or hold themselves out as dealing in the course of a business (and then only in so far as the contract purports to exclude or restrict liability for breach of duty in respect of death or personal injury); or

(ii) the contract is a consumer contract (and then only in favour of the consumer).

(4) This subsection relates to a contract in pursuance of which goods are carried by ship or hovercraft and which either—

(a) specifies ship or hovercraft as the means of carriage over part of the journey to be covered; or

(b) makes no provision as to the means of carriage and does not exclude ship or hovercraft as that means,

in so far as the contract operates for and in relation to the carriage of the goods by that means.

16. Liability for breach of duty

(1) [Subject to subsection (1A) below,] Where a term of a contract [, or a provision of a notice given to persons generally or to particular persons,] purports to exclude or restrict liability for breach of duty arising in the course of any business or from the occupation of any premises used for business purposes of the occupier, that term [or provision]—

(a) shall be void in any case where such exclusion or restriction is in respect of death or personal injury;

(b) shall, in any other case, have no effect if it was not fair and reasonable to incorporate the term in the contract [or, as the case may be, if it is not fair and reasonable to allow reliance on the provision].

[(1A) Nothing in paragraph (b) of subsection (1) above shall be taken as implying that a provision of a notice has effect in circumstances where, apart from that paragraph, it would not have effect.]

(2) Subsection (1)(a) above does not affect the validity of any discharge and indemnity given by a person, on or in connection with an award to him of compensation for pneumoconiosis attributable to employment in the coal industry, in respect of any further claim arising from his contracting that disease.

(3) Where under subsection (1) above a term of a contract [or a provision of a notice] is void or has no effect, the fact that a person agreed to, or was aware of, the term [or provision] shall not of itself be sufficient evidence that he knowingly and voluntarily assumed any risk.

17. Control of unreasonable exemptions in consumer or standard form contracts

(1) Any term of a contract which is a consumer contract or a standard form contract shall have no effect for the purpose of enabling a party to the contract—

(a) who is in breach of a contractual obligation, to exclude or restrict any liability of his to the consumer or customer in respect of the breach;

(b) in respect of a contractual obligation, to render no performance, or to render a performance substantially different from that which the consumer or customer reasonably expected from the contract;

if it was not fair and reasonable to incorporate the term in the contract.

(2) In this section 'customer' means a party to a standard form contract who deals on the basis of written standard terms of business of the other party to the contract who himself deals in the course of a business.

18. Unreasonable indemnity clauses in consumer contracts

(1) Any term of a contract which is a consumer contract shall have no effect for the purpose of making the consumer indemnify another person (whether a party to the contract or not) in respect of liability which that other person may incur as a result of breach of duty or breach of contract, if it was not fair and reasonable to incorporate the term in the contract.

(2) In this section 'liability' means liability arising in the course of any business or from the occupation of any premises used for business purposes of the occupier.

19. 'Guarantee' of consumer goods

(1) This section applies to a guarantee—

(a) in relation to goods which are of a type ordinarily supplied for private use or consumption; and

(b) which is not a guarantee given by one party to the other party to a contract under or in pursuance of which the ownership or possession of the goods to which the guarantee relates is transferred.

(2) A term of a guarantee to which this section applies shall be void in so far as it purports to exclude or restrict liability for loss or damage (including death or personal injury)—

(a) arising from the goods proving defective while—

(i) in use otherwise than exclusively for the purposes of a business; or

(ii) in the possession of a person for such use; and

(b) resulting from the breach of duty of a person concerned in the manufacture or distribution of the goods.

(3) For the purposes of this section, any document is a guarantee if it contains or purports to contain some promise or assurance (however worded or presented) that defects will be made good by complete or partial replacement, or by repair, monetary compensation or otherwise.

20. Obligations implied by law in sale and hire-purchase contracts

(1) Any term of a contract which purports to exclude or restrict liability for breach of the obligations arising from—

(a) section 12 of the Sale of Goods Act [1979] (seller's implied undertakings as to title etc.);

(b) section 8 of the Supply of Goods (Implied Terms) Act 1973 (implied terms as to title in hire-purchase agreements),
shall be void.

(2) Any term of a contract which purports to exclude or restrict liability for breach of the obligations arising from—

(a) section 13, 14 or 15 of the said Act of [1979] (seller's implied undertakings as to conformity of goods with description or sample, or as to their quality or fitness for a particular purpose);

(b) section 9, 10 or 11 of the said Act of 1973 (the corresponding provisions in relation to hire-purchase),
shall—

(i) in the case of a consumer contract, be void against the consumer;

(ii) in any other case, have no effect if it was not fair and reasonable to incorporate the term in the contract.

21. Obligations implied by law in other contracts for the supply of goods

(1) Any term of a contract to which this section applies purporting to exclude or restrict liability for breach of an obligation—

(a) such as is referred to in subsection (3)(a) below—

(i) in the case of a consumer contract, shall be void against the consumer, and

(ii) in any other case, shall have no effect if it was not fair and reasonable to incorporate the term in the contract;

(b) such as is referred to in subsection (3)(b) below, shall have no effect if it was not fair and reasonable to incorporate the term in the contract.

(2) This section applies to any contract to the extent that it relates to any such matter as is referred to in section 15(2)(a) of this Act, but does not apply to—

(a) a contract of sale of goods or a hire-purchase agreement; or

(b) a charterparty of a ship or hovercraft unless it is a consumer contract (and then only in favour of the consumer).

(3) An obligation referred to in this subsection is an obligation incurred under a contract in the course of a business and arising by implication of law from the nature of the contract which relates—

(a) to the correspondence of goods with description or sample, or to the quality or fitness of goods for any particular purpose; or

(b) to any right to transfer ownership or possession of goods, or to the enjoyment of quiet possession of goods.

[(3A) Notwithstanding anything in the foregoing provisions of this section, any term of a contract which purports to exclude or restrict liability for breach of the obligations arising under section 11B of the Supply of Goods and Services Act 1982 (implied terms about title, freedom from encumbrances and quiet possession in certain contracts for the transfer of property in goods) shall be void.]

(4) Nothing in this section applies to the supply of goods on a redemption of trading stamps within the Trading Stamps Act 1964.

22. Consequence of breach

For the avoidance of doubt, where any provision of this Part of this Act requires that the incorporation of a term in a contract must be fair and reasonable for that term to have effect—

(a) if that requirement is satisfied, the term may be given effect to notwithstanding that the contract has been terminated in consequence of breach of that contract;

(b) for the term to be given effect to, that requirement must be satisfied even where a party who is entitled to rescind the contract elects not to rescind it.

23. Evasion by means of secondary contract

Any term of any contract shall be void which purports to exclude or restrict, or has the effect of excluding or restricting—

(a) the exercise, by a party to any other contract, of any right or remedy which arises in respect of that other contract in consequence of breach of duty, or of obligation, liability for which could not by virtue of the provisions of this Part of this Act be excluded or restricted by a term of that other contract;

(b) the application of the provisions of this Part of this Act in respect of that or any other contract.

24. The 'reasonableness' test

(1) In determining for the purposes of this Part of this Act whether it was fair and reasonable to incorporate a term in a contract, regard shall be had only to the circumstances which were, or ought reasonably to have been, known to or in the contemplation of the parties to the contract at the time the contract was made.

(2) In determining for the purposes of section 20 or 21 of this Act whether it was fair and reasonable to incorporate a term in a contract, regard shall be had in particular to the matters specified in Schedule 2 to this Act; but this sub-section shall not prevent a court or arbiter from holding in accordance with any rule of law, that a term which purports to exclude or restrict any relevant liability is not a term of the contract.

[(2A) In determining for the purposes of this Part of this Act whether it is fair and reasonable to allow reliance on a provision of a notice (not being a notice having contractual effect), regard shall be had to all the circumstances obtaining when the liability arose or (but for the provision) would have arisen.]

(3) Where a term in a contract [or a provision of a notice] purports to restrict liability to a specified sum of money, and the question arises for the purposes of this Part of this Act whether it was fair and reasonable to incorporate the term in the contract [or whether it is fair and reasonable to allow reliance on the provision], then, without prejudice to subsection (2) above [in the case of a term in a contract], regard shall be had in particular to—

(a) the resources which the party seeking to rely on that term [or provision] could expect to be available to him for the purpose of meeting the liability should it arise;

(b) how far it was open to that party to cover himself by insurance.

(4) The onus of proving that it was fair and reasonable to incorporate a term in a contract [or that it is fair and reasonable to allow reliance on a provision of a notice] shall lie on the party so contending.

25. Interpretation of Part II

(1) In this Part of this Act—

'breach of duty' means the breach—

(a) of any obligation, arising from the express or implied terms of a contract, to take reasonable care or exercise reasonable skill in the performance of the contract;

(b) of any common law duty to take reasonable care or exercise reasonable skill;

(c) of the duty of reasonable care imposed by section 2(1) of the Occupiers' Liability (Scotland) Act 1960;

'business' includes a profession and the activities of any government department or local or public authority;

'consumer' has the meaning assigned to that expression in the definition in this section of 'consumer contract';

'consumer contract' means a contract (not being a contract of sale by auction or competitive tender) in which—

(a) one party to the contract deals, and the other party to the contract ('the consumer') does not deal or hold himself out as dealing, in the course of a business, and

(b) in the case of a contract such as is mentioned in section 15(2)(a) of this Act, the goods are of a type ordinarily supplied for private use or consumption;

and for the purposes of this Part of this Act the onus of proving that a contract is not to be regarded as a consumer contract shall lie on the party so contending;

'goods' has the same meaning as in the Sale of Goods Act [1979];

'hire-purchase agreement' has the same meaning as in section 189(1) of the Consumer Credit Act 1974;

['notice' includes an announcement, whether or not in writing, and any other communication or pretended communication;]

'personal injury' includes any disease and any impairment of physical or mental condition.

(2) In relation to any breach of duty or obligation, it is immaterial for any purpose of this Part of this Act whether the act or omission giving rise to that breach was inadvertent or intentional or whether liability for it arises directly or vicariously.

(3) In this Part of this Act, any reference to excluding or restricting any liability includes—

(a) making the liability or its enforcement subject to any restrictive or onerous conditions;

(b) excluding or restricting any right or remedy in respect of the liability, or subjecting a person to any prejudice in consequence of his pursuing any such right or remedy;

(c) excluding or restricting any rule of evidence or procedure;

[. . .]

(5) In section 15 and 16 and 19 to 21 of this Act, any reference to excluding or restricting liability for breach of any obligation or duty shall include a reference to excluding or restricting the obligation or duty itself.

PART III

26. International supply contracts

(1) The limits imposed by this Act on the extent to which a person may exclude or restrict liability by reference to a contract term do not apply to liability arising under such a contract as is described in subsection (3) below.

(2) The terms of such a contract are not subject to any requirement of reasonableness under section 3 or 4: and nothing in Part II of this Act should require the incorporation of the terms of such a contract to be fair and reasonable for them to have effect.

(3) Subject to subsection (4), that description of contract is one whose characteristics are the following—

(a) either it is a contract of sale of goods or it is one under or in pursuance of which the possession of ownership of goods passes, and

(b) it is made by parties whose places of business (or, if they have none, habitual residences) are in the territories of different States (the Channel Islands and the Isle of Man being treated for this purpose as different States from the United Kingdom).

(4) A contract falls within subsection (3) above only if either—

(a) the goods in question are, at the time of the conclusion of the contract, in the course of carriage, or will be carried, from the territory of one State to the territory of another; or

(b) the acts constituting the offer and acceptance have been done in the territories of different States; or

(c) the contract provides for the goods to be delivered to the territory of a state other than that within whose territory those acts were done.

27. Choice of law clauses

(1) Where the [law applicable to] a contract is the law of any part of the United Kingdom only by choice of the parties (and apart from that choice would be the law of some country outside the United Kingdom) sections 2 to 7 and 16 to 21 of this Act do not operate as part [of the law applicable to the contract].

(2) This Act has effect notwithstanding any contract term which applies or purports to apply the law of some country outside the United Kingdom, where (either or both)—

(a) the term appears to the court, or arbitrator or arbiter to have been imposed wholly or mainly for the purpose of enabling the party imposing it to evade the operation of this Act; or

(b) in the making of the contract one of the parties dealt as consumer, and he was then habitually resident in the United Kingdom, and the essential steps necessary for the making of the contract were taken there, whether by him or by others on his behalf.

28. . . .

29. Saving for other relevant legislation

(1) Nothing in this Act removes or restricts the effect of, or prevents reliance upon, any contractual provision which—

(a) is authorised or required by the express terms or necessary implication of an enactment; or

(b) being made with a view to compliance with an international agreement to which the United Kingdom is a party, does not operate more restrictively than is contemplated by the agreement.

(2) A contract terms is to be taken—

(a) for the purposes of Part I of this Act, as satisfying the requirement of reasonableness . . .

if it is incorporated or approved by, or incorporated pursuant to a decision or ruling of, a competent authority acting in the exercise of any statutory jurisdiction or function and is not a term in a contract to which the competent authority is itself a party.

(3) In this section—

'competent authority' means any court, arbitrator or arbiter, government department or public authority;

'enactment' means any legislation (including subordinate legislation) of the United Kingdom or Northern Ireland and any instrument having effect by virtue of such legislation; and

statutory' means conferred by an enactment.

SCHEDULES

Section 1(2)

SCHEDULE 1

SCOPE OF SECTIONS 2 TO 4 AND 7

1. Sections 2 to 4 of this Act do not extend to—

(a) any contract of insurance (including a contract to pay an annuity on human life);

(b) any contract so far as it relates to the creation or transfer of an interest in land, or to the termination of such an interest, whether by extinction, merger, surrender, forfeiture or otherwise;

(c) any contract so far as it relates to the creation or transfer of a right or interest in any patent, trade mark, copyright, registered design, technical or commercial information or other intellectual property, or relates to the termination of any such right or interest;

(d) any contract so far as it relates—

(i) to the formation or dissolution of a company (which means any body corporate or unincorporated association and includes a partnership), or

(ii) to its constitution or the rights or obligations of its corporators or members;

(e) any contract so far as it relates to the creation or transfer of securities or of any right or interest in securities.

2. Section 2(1) extends to—

(a) any contract of marine salvage or towage;

(b) any charterparty of a ship or hovercraft; and

(c) any contract for the carriage of goods by ship or hovercraft;

but subject to this sections 2 to 4 and 7 do not extend to any such contract except in favour of a person dealing as a consumer.

3. Where goods are carried by ship or hovercraft in pursuance of a contract which either—

(a) specifies that as the means of carriage over part of the journey to be covered, or

(b) makes no provision as to the means of carriage and does not exclude that means,

then sections 2(2), 3 and 4 do not, except in favour of a person dealing as consumer, extend to the contract as it operates for and in relation to the carriage of the goods by that means.

4. Section 2(1) and (2) do not extend to a contract of employment, except in favour of the employee.

5. Section 2(1) does not affect the validity of any discharge and indemnity given by a person, on or in connection with an award to him of compensation for pneumoconiosis attributable to employment in the coal industry, in respect of any further claim arising from his contracting the disease.

Sections 11(2) and 24(2)

SCHEDULE 2

'GUIDELINES' FOR APPLICATION OF REASONABLENESS TEST

The matters to which regard is to be had in particular for the purposes of sections 6(3), 7(3) and (4), 20 and 21 are any of the following which appear to be relevant—

(a) the strength of the bargaining positions of the parties relative to each other, taking into account (among other things) alternative means by which the customer's requirements could have been met;

(b) whether the customer received an inducement to agree to the term, or in accepting it had an opportunity of entering into a similar contract with other persons, but without having to accept a similar term;

(c) whether the customer knew or ought reasonably to have known of the existence and extent of the term (having regard, among other things, to any custom of the trade and any previous course of dealing between the parties);

(d) where the term excludes or restricts any relevant liability if some condition is not complied with, whether it was reasonable at the time of the contract to expect that compliance with that condition would be practicable;

(e) whether the goods were manufactured, processed or adapted to the special order of the customer.

CIVIL LIABILITY (CONTRIBUTION) ACT 1978
(1978, c. 47)

An Act to make new provision for contribution between persons who are jointly or severally, or both jointly and severally, liable for the same damage and in certain other similar cases where two or mare persons have paid or may be required to pay compensation for the same damage; and to amend the law relating to proceedings against persons jointly liable for the same debt or jointly or severally, or both jointly or severally, liable for the same damage.

[31st July 1978]

1. Entitlement to contribution

(1) Subject to the following provisions of this section, any person liable in respect of any damage suffered by another person may recover contribution from any other person liable in respect of the same damage (whether jointly with him or otherwise).

(2) A person shall be entitled to recover contribution by virtue of subsection (1) above notwithstanding that he has ceased to be liable in respect of the damage in question since the time when the damage occurred, provided that he was so liable immediately before he made or was ordered or agreed to make the payment in respect of which the contribution is sought.

(3) A person shall be liable to make contribution by virtue of subsection (1) above notwithstanding that he has ceased to be liable in respect of the damage in question since the time when the damage occurred, unless he ceased to be liable by virtue of the expiry of a period of limitation or prescription which extinguished the right on which the claim against him in respect of the damage was based.

(4) A person who has made or agreed to make any payment in bona fide settlement or compromise of any claim made against him in respect of any damage (including a payment into court which as been accepted) shall be entitled to recover contribution in accordance with this section without regard to whether or not he himself is or ever was liable in respect of the damage, provided, however, that he would have been liable assuming that the factual basis of the claim against him could be established.

(5) A judgment given in any action brought in any part of the United Kingdom by or on behalf of the person who suffered the damage in question against any person from whom contribution is sought under this section shall be conclusive in the proceedings for contribution as to any issue determined by that judgment in favour of the person from whom the contribution is sought.

(6) References in this section to a person's liability in respect of any damage are references to any such liability which has been or could be established in an action brought against him in England and Wales by or on behalf of the person who suffered the damage; but it is immaterial whether any issue arising in any such action was or would be determined (in accordance with the rules of private international law) by reference to the law of a country outside England and Wales.

2. Assessment of contribution

(1) Subject to subsection (3) below, in any proceedings for contribution under section 1 above the amount of the contribution recoverable from any person shall be such as may be found by the court to be just and equitable having regard to the extent of that person's responsibility for the damage in question.

(2) Subject to subsection (3) below, the court shall have power in any such proceedings to exempt any person from liability to make contribution or to direct that the contribution to be recovered from any person shall amount to a complete indemnity.

(3) Where the amount of the damages which have or might have been awarded in respect of the damage in question in any action brought in England and Wales by or on behalf of the person who suffered it against the person from whom the contribution is sought was or would have been subject to—

(a) any limit imposed by or under any enactment or by any agreement made before the damage occurred;

(b) any reduction by virtue of section 1 of the Law Reform (Contributory Negligence) Act 1945 or section 5 of the Fatal Accidents Act 1976; or

(c) any corresponding limit or reduction under the law of a country outside England and Wales;

the person from whom the contribution is sought shall not by virtue of any contribution awarded under section 1 above be required to pay in respect of the damage a greater amount than the amount of those damages as so limited or reduced.

3. Proceedings against persons jointly liable for the same debt or damage

Judgment recovered against any person liable in respect of any debt or damage shall not be a bar to an action, or to the continuance of an action, against any person who is (apart from any such bar) jointly liable with him in respect of the same debt or damage.

4. Successive actions against persons liable (jointly or otherwise) for the same damage

If more than one action is bought in respect of any damage by or on behalf of the person by whom it was suffered against persons liable in respect of the damage (whether jointly or otherwise) the plaintiff shall not be entitied to costs in any of those actions, other than that in which judgment is first given, unless the court is of the opinion that there was reasonable ground for bringing the action.

5. Application to the Crown

Without prejudice to section 4(1) of the Crown Proceedings Act 1947 (indemnity and contribution), this Act shall bind the Crown, but nothing in this Act shall be construed as in any way affecting Her Majesty in Her private capacity (including in right of Her Duchy of Lancaster) or the Duchy of Cornwall.

6. Interpretation

(1) A person is liable in respect of any damage for the purposes of this Act if the person who suffered it (or anyone representing his estate or dependants) is entitled to recover compensation from him in respect of that damage (whatever the legal basis of his liability, whether tort, breach of contract, breach of trust or otherwise).

(2) References in this Act to an action brought by or on behalf of the person who suffered any damage include references to an action brought for the benefit of his estate or dependents.

(3) In this Act 'dependants' has the same meaning as in the Fatal Accidents Act 1976.

(4) In this Act, except in section 1(5) above, 'action' means an action brought in England and Wales.

7. Savings

. . .

(3) The right to recover contribution in accordance with section 1 above supersedes any right, other than an express contractual right, to recover contribution (as distinct from indemnity) otherwise than under this Act in corresponding circumstances; but nothing in this Act shall affect—

(a) any express or implied contractual or other right to indemnity; or

(b) any express contractual provision regulating or excluding contribution; which would be enforceable apart from this Act (or render enforceable any agreement for indemnity or contribution which would not be enforceable apart from this Act).

SALE OF GOODS ACT 1979
(1979, c. 54)

An Act to consolidate the law relating to the sale of goods. [6th December 1979]

PART I
CONTRACTS TO WHICH ACT APPLIES

1. Contracts to which Act applies

(1) This Act applies to contracts of sale of goods made on or after (but not to those made before) 1 January 1894.

(2) In relation to contracts made on certain dates, this Act applies subject to the modification of certain of its sections as mentioned in Schedule 1 below.

(3) Any such modification is indicated in the section concerned by a reference to Schedule 1 below.

(4) Accordingly, where a section does not contain such a reference, this Act applies in relation to the contract concerned without such modification of the section.

PART II
FORMATION OF THE CONTRACT

Contract of sale

2. Contract of sale

(1) A contract of sale of goods is a contract by which the seller transfers or agrees to transfer the property in goods to the buyer for a money consideration, called the price.

(2) There may a contract of sale between one part owner and another.

(3) A contract of sale may be absolute or conditional.

(4) Where under a contract of sale the property in the goods is transferred from the seller to the buyer the contact is called a sale.

(5) Where under a contract of sale the transfer of the property in the goods is to take place at a future time or subject to some condition later to be fulfilled the contract is called an agreement to sell.

(6) An agreement to sell becomes a sale when the time elapses or the conditions are fulfilled subject to which the property in the goods is to be transferred.

3. Capacity to buy and sell

(1) Capacity to buy and sell is regulated by the general law concerning capacity to contract and to transfer and acquire property.

(2) Where necessaries are sold and delivered to a minor or to a person who by reason of mental incapacity or drunkenness is incompetent to contract, he must pay a reasonable price for them.

(3) In subsection (2) above 'necessaries' means goods suitable to the condition in life of the minor or other person concerned and to his actual requirements at the time of the sale and delivery.

[The words 'to a minor or' in s. 3(2) and 'minor or other' in s. 3(3) were repealed, for Scotland only, by the Age of Legal Capacity (Scotland) Act 1991, s. 10, Sched. 2.]

Formalities of contract

4. How contract of sale is made

(1) Subject to this and any other Act, a contract of sale may be made in writing (either with or without seal), or by word of mouth, or partly in writing and partly by word of mouth, or may be implied from the conduct of the parties.

(2) Nothing in this section affects the law relating to corporations.

Subject matter of contract

5. Existing or future goods

(1) The goods which form the subject of a contract of sale may be either existing goods, owned or possessed by the seller, or goods to be manufactured or acquired by him after the making of the contract of sale, in this Act called future goods.

(2) There may be a contract for the sale of goods the acquisition of which by the seller depends on a contingency which may or may not happen.

(3) Where by a contract of sale the seller purports to effect a present sale of future goods, the contract operates as an agreement to sell the goods.

6. Goods which have perished

Where there is a contract for the sale of specific goods, and the goods without the knowledge of the seller have perished at the time when a contract is made, the contract is void.

7. Goods perishing before sale but after agreement to sell

Where there is an agreement to sell specific goods and subsequently the goods, without any fault on the part of the seller or buyer, perish before the risk passes to the buyer, the agreement is avoided.

The price

8. Ascertainment of price

(1) The price in a contract of sale may be fixed by the contract, or may be left to be fixed in a manner agreed by the contract, or may be determined by the course of dealing between the parties.

(2) Where the price is not determined as mentioned in subsection (1) above the buyer must pay a reasonable price.

(3) What is a reasonable price is a question of fact dependent on the circumstances of each particular case.

9. Agreement to sell at valuation

(1) Where there is an agreement to sell goods on the terms that the price is to be fixed by the valuation of a third party, and he cannot or does not make the valuation, the agreement is avoided; but if the goods or any part of them have been delivered to and appropriated by the buyer he must pay a reasonable price for them.

(2) Where the third party is prevented from making the valuation by the fault of the seller or buyer, the party not at fault may maintain an action for damages against the party at fault.

[*Implied terms etc.*]

10. Stipulations about time

(1) Unless a different intention appears from the terms of the contract, stipulations as to time of payment are not of the essence of a contract of sale.

(2) Whether any other stipulation as to time is or is not of the essence of the contract depends on the terms of the contract.

(3) In a contract of sale 'month' prima facie means calendar month.

11. When condition to be treated as warranty

[(1) This section does not apply to Scotland.]

(2) Where a contract of sale is subject to a condition to be fulfilled by the seller, the buyer may waive the condition, or may elect to treat the breach of the condition as a breach of warranty and not as a ground for treating the contract as repudiated.

(3) Whether a stipulation in a contract of sale is a condition, the breach of which may give rise to a right to treat the contract as repudiated, or a warranty, the breach of which may give rise to a claim for damages but not to a right to reject the goods and treat the contract as repudiated, depends in each case on the construction of the contract; and a stipulation may be a condition, though called a warranty in the contract.

(4) [Subject to section 35A below] Where a contract of sale is not severable and the buyer has accepted the goods or part of them, the breach of a condition to be fulfilled by the seller can only be treated as a breach of warranty, and not as a ground for rejecting the goods and treating the contract as repudiated, unless there is an express or implied term of the contract to that effect.

(6) Nothing in this section affects a condition or warranty whose fulfilment is excused by law by reason of impossibility or otherwise.

(7) Paragraph 2 of Schedule 1 below applies in relation to a contract made before 22 April 1967 or (in the application of this Act to Northern Ireland) 28 July 1967.

12. Implied terms about title, etc.

(1) In a contract of sale, other than one to which subsection (3) below applies, there is an implied [term] on the part of the seller that in the case of a sale he has a right to sell the goods, and in the case of an agreement to sell he will have such a right at the time when the property is to pass.

(2) In a contract of sale, other than one to which subsection (3) below applies, there is also an implied [term] that—

(a) the goods are free, and will remain free until the time when the property is to pass, from any charge or encumbrance not disclosed or known to the buyer before the contract is made, and

(b) the buyer will enjoy quiet possession of the goods except so far as it may be disturbed by the owner or other person entitled to the benefit of any charge or encumbrance so disclosed or known.

(3) This subsection applies to a contract of sale in the case of which there appears from the contract or is to be inferred from its circumstances an intention that the seller should transfer only such title as he or a third person may have.

(4) In a contract to which subsection (3) above applies there is an implied [term] that all charges or encumbrances known to the seller and not known to the buyer have been disclosed to the buyer before the contract is made.

(5) In a contract to which subsection (3) above applies there is also an implied [term] that none of the following will disturb the buyer's quiet possession of the goods, namely—

(a) the seller;

(b) in a case where the parties to the contract intend that the seller should transfer only such title as a third person may have, that person;

(c) anyone claiming through or under the seller or that third person otherwise than under a charge or encumbrance disclosed or known to the buyer before the contract is made.

[(5A) As regards England and Wales and Northern Ireland, the term implied by subsection (1) above is a condition and the terms implied by subsections (2), (4) and (5) above are warranties.]

(6) Paragraph 3 of Schedule 1 below applies in relation to a contract made before 18 May 1973.

13. Sale by description

(1) Where there is a contract for the sale of goods by description, there is an implied [term] that the goods will correspond with the description.

[(1A) As regards England and Wales and Northern Ireland, the term implied by subsection (1) above is a condition.]

(2) If the sale is by sample as well as by description it is not sufficient that the bulk of the goods corresponds with the sample if the goods do not also correspond with the description.

(3) A sale of goods is not prevented from being a sale by description by reason only that, being exposed for sale or hire, they are selected by the buyer.

(4) Paragraph 4 of Schedule 1 below applies in relation to a contract made before 18 May 1973.

14. Implied terms about quality or fitness

(1) Except as provided by this section and section 15 below and subject to any other enactment, there is no implied [term] about the quality or fitness for any particular purpose of goods supplied under a contract of sale.

[(2) Where the seller sells goods in the course of a business, there is an implied term that the goods supplied under the contract are of satisfactory quality.

(2A) For the purposes of this Act, goods are of satisfactory quality if they meet the standard that a reasonable person would regard as satisfactory, taking account of any description of the goods, the price (if relevant) and all the other relevant circumstances.

(2B) For the purposes of this Act, the quality of goods includes their state and condition and the following (among others) are in appropriate cases aspects of the quality of goods—

(a) fitness for all the purposes for which goods of the kind in question are commonly supplied,

(b) appearance and finish,
(c) freedom from minor defects,
(d) safety, and
(e) durability.

(2C) The term implied by subsection (2) above does not extend to any matter making the quality of goods unsatisfactory—

(a) which is specifically drawn to the buyer's attention before the contract is made,

(b) where the buyer examines the goods before the contract is made, which that examination ought to reveal, or

(c) in the case of a contract for sale by sample, which would have been apparent on a reasonable examination of the sample.]

(3) Where the seller sells goods in the course of a business and the buyer, expressly or by implication, makes known—

(a) to the seller, or

(b) where the purchase price of part of it is payable by instalments and the goods were previously sold by a credit-broker to the seller, to that credit-broker, any particular purpose for which the goods are being bought,

there is an implied [term] that the goods supplied under the contract are reasonably fit for that purpose, whether or not that is a purpose for which such goods are commonly supplied, except where the circumstances show that the buyer does not rely, or that it is unreasonable for him to rely, on the skill or judgment of the seller or credit-broker.

(4) An implied [term] about quality or fitness for a particular purpose may be annexed to a contract of sale by usage.

(5) The preceding provisions of this section apply to a sale by a person who in the course of a business is acting as agent for another as they apply to a sale by a principal in the course of a business, except where that other is not selling in the course of a business and either the buyer knows that fact or reasonable steps are taken to bring it to the notice of the buyer before the contract is made.

[(6) As regards England and Wales and Northern Ireland, the terms implied by subsections (2) and (3) above are conditions.]

(7) Paragraph 5 of Schedule 1 below applies in relation to a contract made on or after 18 May 1973 and before the appointed day, and paragraph 6 in relation to one made before 18 May 1973.

(8) In subsection (7) above and paragraph 5 of Schedule 1 below references to the appointed day are to the day appointed for the purposes of those provisions by an order of the Secretary of State made by statutory instrument.

Sale by sample

15. Sale by sample

(1) A contract of sale is a contract for sale by sample where there is an express or implied term to that effect in the contract.

(2) In the case of a contract for sale by sample there is an implied [term]—

(a) that the bulk will correspond with the sample in quality;

[. . .]

(c) that the goods will be free from any defect, making their quality unsatisfactory, which would not be apparent on reasonable examination of the sample.

[(3) As regards England and Wales and Northern Ireland, the term implied by subsection (2) above is a condition.]

(4) Paragraph 7 of Schedule 1 below applies in relation to a contract made before 18 May 1973.

Miscellaneous

[15A. Modification of remedies for breach of condition in non-consumer cases

(1) Where in the case of a contract of sale—

(a) the buyer would, apart from this subsection, have the right to reject goods by reason of a breach on the part of the seller of a term implied by section 13, 14 or 15 above, but

(b) the breach is so slight that it would be unreasonable for him to reject them, then, if the buyer does not deal as consumer, the breach is not to be treated as a breach of condition but may be treated as a breach of warranty.

(2) This section applies unless a contrary intention appears in, or is to be implied from, the contract.

(3) It is for the seller to show that a breach fell within subsection (1)(b) above.

(4) This section does not apply to Scotland.]

[15B. Remedies for breach of contract as respects Scotland

(1) Where in a contract of sale the seller is in breach of any term of the contract (express or implied), the buyer shall be entitled—

(a) to claim damages, and

(b) if the breach is material, to reject any goods delivered under the contract and treat it as repudiated.

(2) Where a contract of sale is a consumer contract, then, for the purposes of subsection (1)(b) above, breach by the seller of any term (express or implied)—

(a) as to the quality of the goods or their fitness for a purpose,

(b) if the goods are, or are to be, sold by description, that the goods will correspond with the description,

(c) if the goods are, or are to be, sold by reference to a sample, that the bulk will correspond with the sample in quality,

shall be deemed to be a material breach.

(3) This section applies to Scotland only.]

PART III
EFFECTS OF THE CONTRACT

Transfer of property as between seller and buyer

16. Goods must be ascertained

[Subject to section 20A below] Where there is a contract for the sale of unascertained goods no property in the goods is transferred to the buyer unless and until the goods are ascertained.

17. Property passes when intended to pass

(1) Where there is a contract for the sale of specific or ascertained goods the property in them is transferred to the buyer at such time as the parties to the contract intend it to be transferred.

(2) For the purpose of ascertaining the intention of the parties regard shall be had to the terms of the contract, the conduct of the parties and the circumstances of the case.

18. Rules for ascertaining intention

Unless a different intention appears, the following are rules for ascertaining the intention of the parties as to the time at which the property in the goods is to pass to the buyer.

Rule 1.—Where there is an unconditional contract for the sale of specific goods in a deliverable state the property in the goods passes to the buyer when the contract is made, and it is immaterial whether the time of payment or the time of delivery, or both, be postponed.

Rule 2.—Where there is a contract for the sale of specific goods and the seller is bound to do something to the goods for the purpose of putting them into a deliverable state, the property does not pass until the thing is done and the buyer has notice that it has been done.

Rule 3.—Where there is a contract for the sale of specific goods in a deliverable state but the seller is bound to weigh, measure, test, or do some other act or thing with reference to the goods for the purpose of ascertaining the price, the property does not pass until the act or thing is done and the buyer has notice that it has been done.

Rule 4.—When goods are delivered to the buyer on approval or on sale or return or other similar terms the property in the goods passes to the buyer:—

(a) when he signifies his approval or acceptance to the seller or does any other act adopting the transaction;

(b) if he does not signify his approval or acceptance to the seller but retains the goods without giving notice of rejection, then, if a time has been fixed for the return of the goods, on the expiration of that time, and, if no time has been fixed, on the expiration of a reasonable time.

Rule 5.—(1) Where there is a contract for the sale of unascertained or future goods by description, and goods of that description and in a deliverable state are unconditionally appropriated to the contract, either by the seller with the assent of the buyer or by the buyer with the assent of the seller, the property in the goods then passes to the buyer; and the assent may be express or implied, and may be given either before of after the appropriation is made.

(2) Where, in pursuance of the contract, the seller delivers the goods to the buyer or to a carrier or other bailee or custodier (whether named by the buyer or not) for the purpose of transmission to the buyer, and does not reserve the right of disposal, he is to be taken to have unconditionally appropriated the goods to the contract.

[(3) Where there is a contract for the sale of a specified quantity of unascertained goods in a deliverable state forming part of a bulk which is identified either in the contract or by subsequent agreement between the parties and the bulk is reduced to (or to less than) that quantity, then, if the buyer under that contract is the only buyer to whom goods are then due out of the bulk—

(a) the remaining goods are to be taken as appropriated to that contract at the time when the bulk is so reduced; and

(b) the property in those goods then passes to that buyer.

(4) Paragraph (3) above applies also (with the necessary modifications) where a bulk is reduced to (or to less than) the aggregate of the quantities due to a single buyer under separate contracts relating to that bulk and he is the only buyer to whom goods are then due out of that bulk.]

19. Reservation of right of disposal

(1) Where there is a contract for the sale of specific goods or where goods are subsequently appropriated to the contract, the seller may, by the terms of the contract or appropriation, reserve the right of disposal of the goods until certain conditions are fulfilled; and in such a case, notwithstanding the delivery of the goods to the buyer, or to a carrier or other bailee or custodier for the purpose of transmission to the buyer, the property in the goods does not pass to the buyer until the conditions imposed by the seller are fulfilled.

(2) Where goods are shipped, and by the bill of lading the goods are deliverable to the order of the seller or his agent, the seller is prima facie to be taken to reserve the right of disposal.

(3) Where the seller of goods draws on the buyer for the price, and transmits the bill of exchange and bill of lading to the buyer together to secure acceptance or payment of the bill of exchange, the buyer is bound to return the bill of lading if he does not honour the bill of exchange, and if he wrongfully retains the bill of lading the property in the goods does not pass to him.

20. Risk prima facie passes with property

(1) Unless otherwise agreed, the goods remain at the seller's risk until the property in them is transferred to the buyer, but when the property in them is transferred to the buyer the goods are at the buyer's risk whether delivery has been made or not.

(2) But where delivery has been delayed through the fault of either buyer or seller the goods are at the risk of the party at fault as regards any loss which might not have occurred but for such fault.

(3) Nothing in this section affects the duties or liabilities of either seller or buyer as a bailee or custodier of the goods of the other party.

[20A. Undivided shares in goods forming part of a bulk

(1) This section applies to a contract for the sale of a specified quantity of unascertained goods if the following conditions are met—

(a) the goods or some of them form part of a bulk which is identified either in the contract or by subsequent agreement between the parties; and

(b) the buyer has paid the price for some or all of the goods which are the subject of the contract and which form part of the bulk.

(2) Where this section applies, then (unless the parties agree otherwise), as soon as the conditions specified in paragraphs (a) and (b) of subsection (1) above are met or at such later time as the parties may agree—

(a) property in an undivided share in the bulk is transferred to the buyer; and

(b) the buyer becomes an owner in common of the bulk.

(3) Subject to subsection (4) below, for the purposes of this section, the undivided share of a buyer in a bulk at any time shall be such share as the quantity of goods paid for and due to the buyer out of the bulk bears to the quantity of goods in the bulk at that time.

(4) Where the aggregate of the undivided shares of buyers in a bulk determined under subsection (3) above would at any time exceed the whole of the bulk at that time, the undivided share in the bulk of each buyer shall be reduced proportionately so that the aggregate of the undivided shares is equal to the whole bulk.

(5) Where a buyer has paid the price for only some of the goods due to him out of a bulk, any delivery to the buyer out of the bulk shall, for the purposes of this section, be ascribed in the first place to the goods in respect of which payment has been made.

(6) For the purpose of this section payment of part of the price for any goods shall be treated as payment for a corresponding part of the goods.]

[20B. Deemed consent by co-owner to dealings in bulk goods

(1) A person who has become an owner in common of a bulk by virtue of section 20A above shall be deemed to have consented to—

(a) any delivery of goods out of the bulk to any other owner in common of the bulk, being goods which are due to him under his contract;

(b) any removal, dealing with, delivery or disposal of goods in the bulk by any other person who is an owner in common of the bulk in so far as the goods fall within that co-owner's undivided share in the bulk at the time of the removal, dealing, delivery or disposal.

(2) No cause of action shall accrue to anyone against a person by reason of that person having acted in accordance with paragraph (a) or (b) of subsection (1) above in reliance on any consent deemed to have been given under that subsection.

(3) Nothing in this section or section 20A above shall—

(a) impose an obligation on a buyer of goods out of a bulk to compensate any other buyer of goods out of that bulk for any shortfall in the goods received by that other buyer;

(b) affects any contractual arrangement between buyers of goods out of a bulk for adjustments between themselves; or

(c) affect the rights of any buyer under his contract.]

Transfer of title

21. Sale by person not the owner

(1) Subject to this Act, where goods are sold by a person who is not their owner, and who does not sell them under the authority or with the consent of the owner, the buyer acquires no better title to the goods than the seller had, unless the owner of the goods is by his conduct precluded from denying the seller's authority to sell.

(2) Nothing in this Act affects—

(a) the provisions of the Factors Acts or any enactment enabling the apparent owner of goods to dispose of them as if he were their true owner;

(b) the validity of any contract of sale under any special common law or statutory power of sale or under the order of a court of competent jurisdiction.

22. Market overt

[. . .]

(2) This section does not apply to Scotland.

(3) Paragraph 8 of Schedule 1 below applies in relation to a contract under which goods were sold before 1 January 1968 or (in the application of this Act to Northern Ireland) 29 August 1967.

23. Sale under voidable title

When the seller of goods has a voidable title to them, but his title has not been avoided at the time of the sale, the buyer acquires a good title to the goods, provided he buys them in good faith and without notice of the seller's defect of title.

24. Seller in possession after sale

Where a person having sold goods continues or is in possession of the goods, or of the documents of title to the goods, the delivery or transfer by that person, or by a mercantile agent acting for him, of the goods or documents of title under any sale, pledge, or other disposition thereof, to any person receiving the same in good faith and without notice of the previous sale, has the same effect as if the person making the delivery or transfer were expressly authorised by the owner of the goods to make the same.

25. Buyer in possession after sale

(1) Where a person having bought or agreed to buy goods obtains, with the consent of the seller, possession of the goods or the documents of title to the goods, the delivery or transfer by that person, or by a mercantile agent acting for him, of the goods or documents of title, under any sale, pledge, or other disposition thereof, to any person receiving the same in good faith and without notice of any lien or other right of the original seller in respect of the goods, has the same effect as if the person making the delivery or transfer were a mercantile agent in possession of the goods or documents of title with the consent of the owner.

(2) For the purposes of subsection (1) above—

(a) the buyer under a conditional sale agreement is to be taken not to be a person who has bought or agreed to buy goods, and

(b) 'conditional sale agreement' means an agreement for the sale of goods which is a consumer credit agreement within the meaning of the Consumer Credit Act 1974 under which the purchase price or part of it is payable by instalments, and the property in the goods is to remain in the seller (notwithstanding that the buyer is to be in possession of the goods) until such conditions as to the payment of instalments or otherwise as may be specified in the agreement are fulfilled.

(3) Paragraph 9 of Schedule 1 below applies in relation to a contract under which a person buys or agrees to buy goods and which is made before the appointed day.

(4) In subsection (3) above and paragraph 9 of Schedule 1 below references to the appointed day are to the day appointed for the purposes of those provisions by an order of the Secretary of State made by statutory instrument.

26. Supplementary to sections 24 and 25

In sections 24 and 25 above 'mercantile agent' means a mercantile agent having in the customary course of his business as such agent authority either—

(a) to sell goods, or
(b) to consign goods for the purpose of sale, or
(c) to buy goods, or
(d) to raise money on the security of goods.

PART IV
PERFORMANCE OF THE CONTRACT

27. Duties of seller and buyer

It is the duty of the seller to deliver the goods, and of the buyer to accept and pay for them, in accordance with the terms of the contract of sale.

28. Payment and delivery are concurrent conditions

Unless otherwise agreed, delivery of the goods and payment of the price are concurrent conditions, that is to say, the seller must be ready and willing to give possession of the goods to the buyer in exchange for the price and the buyer must be ready and willing to pay the price in exchange for possession of the goods.

29. Rules about delivery

(1) Whether it is for the buyer to take possession of the goods or for the seller to send them to the buyer is a question depending in each case on the contract, express or implied, between the parties.

(2) Apart from any such contract, express or implied, the place of delivery is the seller's place of business if he has one, and if not, his residence; except that, if the contract is for

the sale of specific goods, which to the knowledge of the parties when the contract is made are in some other place, then that place is the place of delivery.

(3) Where under the contract of sale the seller is bound to send the goods to the buyer, but no time for sending them is fixed, the seller is bound to send them within a reasonable time.

(4) Where the goods at the time of sale are in the possession of a third person, there is no delivery by seller to buyer unless and until the third person acknowledges to the buyer that he holds the goods on his behalf; but nothing in this section affects the operation of the issue or transfer of any document of title to goods.

(5) Demand or tender of delivery may be treated as ineffectual unless made at a reasonable hour; and what is a reasonable hour is a question of fact.

(6) Unless otherwise agreed, the expenses of and incidental to putting the goods into a deliverable state must be borne by the seller.

30. Delivery of wrong quantity

(1) Where the seller delivers to the buyer a quantity of goods less than he contracted to sell, the buyer may reject them, but if the buyer accepts the goods so delivered he must pay for them at the contract rate.

(2) Where the seller delivers to the buyer a quantity of goods larger than he contracted to sell, the buyer may accept the goods included in the contract and reject the rest, or he may reject the whole.

[(2A) A buyer who does not deal as consumer may not—

(a) where the seller delivers a quantity of goods less than he contracted to sell, reject the goods under subsection (1) above, or

(b) where the seller delivers a quantity of goods larger than he contracted to sell, reject the whole under subsection (2) above,

if the shortfall or, as the case may be, excess is so slight that it would be unreasonable for him to do so.

(2B) It is for the seller to show that a shortfall or excess fell within subsection (2A) above.

(2C) Subsections (2A) and (2B) above do not apply to Scotland.

(2D) Where the seller delivers a quantity of goods—

(a) less than he contracted to sell, the buyer shall not be entitled to reject the goods under subsection (1) above,

(b) larger than he contracted to sell, the buyer shall not be entitled to reject the whole under subsection (2) above,

unless the shortfall or excess is material.

(2E) Subsection (2D) above applies to Scotland only.]

(3) Where the seller delivers to the buyer a quantity of goods larger than he contracted to sell and the buyer accepts the whole of the goods so delivered he must pay for them at the contract rate.

(5) This section is subject to any usage of trade, special agreement, or course of dealing between the parties.

31. Instalment deliveries

(1) Unless otherwise agreed, the buyer of goods is not bound to accept delivery of them by instalments.

(2) Where there is a contract for the sale of goods to be delivered by stated instalments, which are to be separately paid for, and the seller makes defective deliveries in respect of one or more instalments, or the buyer neglects or refuses to take delivery of or pay for one or more instalments, it is a question in each case depending on the terms of the contract and the circumstances of the case whether the breach of contract is a repudiation of the whole contract or whether it is a severable breach giving rise to a claim for compensation but not to a right to treat the whole contract as repudiated.

32. Delivery to carrier

(1) Where, in pursuance of a contract of sale, the seller is authorised or required to send the goods to the buyer, delivery of the goods to a carrier (whether named by the buyer or not) for the purpose of transmission to the buyer is prima facie deemed to be delivery of the goods to the buyer.

(2) Unless otherwise authorised by the buyer, the seller must make such contact with the carrier on behalf of the buyer as may be reasonable having regard to the nature of the goods and the other circumstances of the case; and if the seller omits to do so, and the goods are lost or damaged in course of transit, the buyer may decline to treat the delivery to the carrier as a delivery to himself or may hold the seller responsible in damages.

(3) Unless otherwise agreed, where goods are sent by the seller to the buyer by a route involving sea transit, under circumstances in which it is usual to insure, the seller must give such notice to the buyer as may enable him to insure them during their sea transit, and if the seller fails to do so, the goods are at his risk during such sea transit.

33. Risk where goods are delivered at distant place

Where the seller of goods agrees to deliver them at his own risk at a place other than that where they are when sold, the buyer must nevertheless (unless otherwise agreed) take any risk of deterioration in the goods necessarily incident to the course of transit.

34. Buyer's right of examining the goods

[Unless otherwise agreed, when the seller tenders delivery of goods to the buyer, he is bound on request to afford the buyer a reasonable opportunity of examining the goods for the purpose of ascertaining whether they are in conformity with the contract [and, in the case of a contract for sale by sample, of comparing the bulk with the sample.]

35. Acceptance

(1) The buyer is deemed to have accepted the goods [subject to subsection (2) below—

(a) when he intimates to the seller that he has accepted them, or

(b) when the goods have been delivered to him and he does any act in relation to them which is inconsistent with the ownership of the seller.

(2) Where goods are delivered to the buyer, and he has not previously examined them, he is not deemed to have accepted them under subsection (1) above until he has had a reasonable opportunity of examining them for the purpose—

(a) of ascertaining whether they are in conformity with the contract, and

(b) in the case of a contract for sale by sample, of comparing the bulk with the sample.

(3) Where the buyer deals as consumer or (in Scotland) the contract of sale is a consumer contract, the buyer cannot lose his right to rely on subsection (2) above by agreement, waiver or otherwise.

(4) The buyer is also deemed to have accepted the goods when after the lapse of a reasonable time he retains the goods without intimating to the seller that he has rejected them.

(5) The questions that are material in determining for the purposes of subsection (4) above whether a reasonable time has elapsed include whether the buyer has had a reasonable opportunity of examining the goods for the purpose mentioned in subsection (2) above.

(6) The buyer is not by virtue of this section deemed to have accepted the goods merely because—

(a) he asks for, or agrees to, their repair by or under an arrangement with the seller, or

(b) the goods are delivered to another under a sub-sale or other disposition.

(7) Where the contract is for the sale of goods making one or more commercial units, a buyer accepting any goods included in a unit is deemed to have accepted all the goods making the unit; and in this subsection 'commercial unit' means a unit division of which would materially impair the value of the goods or the character of the unit.

(8)] Paragraph 10 of Schedule 1 below applies in relation to a contract made before 22 April 1967 or (in the application of this Act to Northern Ireland) 28 July 1967.

[35A. Right of partial rejection

(1) If the buyer—

(a) has the right to reject the goods by reason of a breach on the part of the seller that affects some or all of them, but

(b) accepts some of the goods, including, where there are any goods unaffected by the breach, all such goods,

he does not by accepting them lose his right to reject the rest.

(2) In the case of a buyer having the right to reject an instalment of goods, subsection (1) above applies as if references to the goods were references to the goods comprised in the instalment.

(3) For the purposes of subsection (1) above, goods are affected by a breach if by reason of the breach they are not in conformity with the contract.

(4) This section applies unless a contrary intention appears in, or is to be implied from, the contract.]

36. Buyer not bound to return rejected goods

Unless otherwise agreed, where goods are delivered to the buyer, and he refuses to accept them, having the right to do so, he is not bound to return them to the seller, but it is sufficient if he intimates to the seller that he refuses to accept them.

37. Buyer's liability for not taking delivery of goods

(1) When the seller is ready and willing to deliver the goods, and requests the buyer to take delivery, and the buyer does not within a reasonable time after such request take delivery of the goods, he is liable to the seller for any loss occasioned by his neglect or refusal to take delivery, and also for a reasonable charge for the care and custody of the goods.

(2) Nothing in this section affects the rights of the seller where the neglect or refusal of the buyer to take delivery amounts to a repudiation of the contract.

PART V
RIGHTS OF UNPAID SELLER AGAINST THE GOODS

Preliminary

38. Unpaid seller defined

(1) The seller of goods is an unpaid seller within the meaning of this Act—

(a) when the whole of the price has not been paid or tendered;

(b) when a bill of exchange or other negotiable instrument has been received as conditional payment, and the condition on which it was received has not been fulfilled by reason of the dishonour of the instrument or otherwise.

(2) In this Part of this Act 'seller' includes any person who is in the position of a seller, as, for instance, an agent of the seller to whom the bill of lading has been indorsed, or a consignor or agent who has himself paid (or is directly responsible for) the price.

39. Unpaid seller's rights

(1) Subject to this and any other Act, notwithstanding that the property in the goods may have passed to the buyer, the unpaid seller of goods, as such, has by implication of law—

(a) a lien on the goods or right to retain them for the price while he is in possession of them;

(b) in the case of the insolvency of the buyer, a right of stopping the goods in transit after he has parted with the possession of them;

(c) a right of re-sale as limited by this Act.

(2) Where the property in goods has not passed to the buyer, the unpaid seller has (in addition to his other remedies) a right of withholding delivery similar to and coextensive with his rights of lien or retention and stoppage in transit where the property has passed to the buyer.

Unpaid seller's lien

41. Seller's lien

(1) Subject to this Act, the unpaid seller of goods who is in possession of them is entitled to retain possession of them until payment or tender of the price in the following cases:—

(a) where the goods have been sold without any stipulation as to credit;

(b) where the goods have been sold on credit but the term of credit has expired;

(c) where the buyer becomes insolvent.

(2) The seller may exercise his lien or right of retention notwithstanding that he is in possession of the goods as agent or bailee or custodier for the buyer.

42. Part delivery
Where an unpaid seller has made part delivery of the goods, he may exercise his lien or right of retention on the remainder, unless such part delivery has been made under such circumstances as to show an agreement to waive the lien or right of retention.

43. Termination of lien
(1) The unpaid seller of goods loses his lien or right of retention in respect of them—
(a) when he delivers the goods to a carrier or other bailee or custodier for the purpose of transmission to the buyer without reserving the right of disposal of the goods;
(b) when the buyer or his agent lawfully obtains possession of the goods;
(c) by waiver of the lien or right of retention.
(2) An unpaid seller of goods who has a lien or right of retention in respect of them does not lose his lien or right of retention by reason only that he has obtained judgment or decree for the price of the goods.

Stoppage in transit

44. Right of stoppage in transit
Subject to this Act, when the buyer of goods becomes insolvent the unpaid seller who has parted with the possession of the goods has the right of stopping them in transit, that is to say, he may resume possession of the goods as long as they are in course of transit, and may retain them until payment or tender of the price.

45. Duration of transit
(1) Goods are deemed to be in course of transit from the time when they are delivered to a carrier or other bailee or custodier for the purpose of transmission to the buyer, until the buyer or his agent in that behalf takes delivery of them from the carrier or other bailee or custodier.
(2) If the buyer or his agent in that behalf obtains delivery of the goods before their arrival at the appointed destination, the transit is at an end.
(3) If, after the arrival of the goods at the appointed destination, the carrier or other bailee or custodier acknowledges to the buyer or his agent that he holds the goods on his behalf and continues in possession of them as bailee or custodier for the buyer or his agent, the transit is at an end, and it is immaterial that a further destination for the goods may have been indicated by the buyer.
(4) If the goods are rejected by the buyer, and the carrier or other bailee or custodier continues in possession of them, the transit is not deemed to be at an end, even if the seller has refused to receive them back.
(5) When goods are delivered to a ship chartered by the buyer it is a question depending on the circumstances of the particular case whether they are in the possession of the master as a carrier or as agent to the buyer.
(6) Where the carrier or other bailee or custodier wrongfully refuses to deliver the goods to the buyer or his agent in that behalf, the transit is deemed to be at an end.
(7) Where part delivery of the goods has been made to the buyer or his agent in that behalf, the remainder of the goods may be stopped in transit, unless such part delivery has been made under such circumstances as to show an agreement to give up possession of the whole of the goods.

46. How stoppage in transit is effected
(1) The unpaid seller may exercise his right of stoppage in transit either by taking actual possession of the goods or by giving notice of his claim to the carrier or other bailee or custodier in whose possession the goods are.
(2) The notice may be given either to the person in actual possession of the goods or to his principal.
(3) If given to the principal, the notice is ineffective unless given at such time and under such circumstances that the principal, by the exercise of reasonable diligence, may communicate it to his servant or agent in time to prevent a delivery to the buyer.
(4) When notice of stoppage in transit is given by the seller to the carrier or other bailee or custodier in possession of the goods, he must re-deliver the goods to, or according to the directions of, the seller; and the expenses of the re-delivery must be borne by the seller.

Re-sale etc. by buyer

47. Effect of sub-sale etc. by buyer

(1) Subject to this Act, the unpaid seller's right of lien or retention or stoppage in transit is not affected by any sale or other disposition of the goods which the buyer may have made, unless the seller has assented to it.

(2) Where a document of title to goods has been lawfully transferred to any person as buyer or owner of the goods, and that person transfers the document to a person who takes it in good faith and for valuable consideration, then—

(a) if the last-mentioned transfer was by way of sale the unpaid seller's right of lien or retention or stoppage in transit is defeated; and

(b) if the last-mentioned transfer was made by way of pledge or other disposition for value, the unpaid seller's right of lien or retention of stoppage in transit can only be exercised subject to the rights of the transferee.

Rescission: and re-sale by seller

48. Rescission: and re-sale by seller

(1) Subject to this section, a contract of sale is not rescinded by the mere exercise by an unpaid seller of his right of lien or retention or stoppage in transit.

(2) Where an unpaid seller who has exercised his right of lien or retention or stoppage in transit re-sells the goods, the buyer acquires a good title to them as against the original buyer.

(3) Where the goods are of a perishable nature, or where the unpaid seller gives notice to the buyer of his intention to re-sell, and the buyer does not within a reasonable time pay or tender the price, the unpaid seller may re-sell the goods and recover from the original buyer damages for any loss occasioned by his breach of contract.

(4) Where the seller expressly reserves the right of re-sale in case the buyer should make default, and on the buyer making default re-sells the goods, the original contract of sale is rescinded but without prejudice to any claim the seller may have for damages.

PART VI
ACTIONS FOR BREACH OF THE CONTRACT

Seller's remedies

49. Action for price

(1) Where, under a contract of sale, the property in the goods has passed to the buyer and he wrongfully neglects or refuses to pay for the goods according to the terms of the contract, the seller may maintain an action against him for the price of the goods.

(2) Where, under a contract of sale, the price is payable on a day certain irrespective of delivery and the buyer wrongfully neglects or refuses to pay such price, the seller may maintain an action for the price, although the property in goods has not passed and the goods have not been appropriated to the contract.

(3) Nothing in this section prejudices the right of the seller in Scotland to recover interest on the price from the date of tender of the goods, or from the date on which the price was payable, as the case may be.

50. Damages for non-acceptance

(1) Where the buyer wrongfully neglects or refuses to accept and pay for the goods, the seller may maintain an action against him for damages for non-acceptance.

(2) The measure of damages is the estimated loss directly and naturally resulting in the ordinary course of events, from the buyer's breach of contract.

(3) Where there is an available market for the goods in question the measure of damages is prima facie to be ascertained by the difference between the contract price and the market or current price at the time or times when the goods ought to have been accepted or (if no time was fixed for acceptance) at the time of the refusal to accept.

Buyer's remedies

51. Damages for non-delivery

(1) Where the seller wrongfully neglects or refuses to deliver the goods to the buyer, the buyer may maintain an action against the seller for damages for non-delivery.

(2) The measure of damages is the estimated loss directly and naturally resulting, in the ordinary course of events, from the seller's breach of contract.

(3) Where there is an available market for the goods in question the measure of damages is prima facie to be ascertained by the difference between the contract price and the market or current price of the goods at the time or times when they ought to have been delivered or (if no time was fixed) at the time of the refusal to deliver.

52. Specific performance

(1) If any action for breach of contract to deliver specific or ascertained goods the court may, if it thinks fit, on the plaintiff s application, by its judgment or decree direct that the contract shall be performed specifically, without giving the defendant the option of retaining the goods on payment of damages.

(2) The plaintiff s application may be made at any time before judgment or decree.

(3) The judgment or decree may be unconditional, or on such terms and conditions as to damages, payment of the price and otherwise as seem just to the court.

(4) The provisions of this section shall be deemed to be supplementary to, and not in derogation of, the right of specific implement in Scotland.

53. Remedy for breach of warranty

(1) Where there is a breach of warranty by the seller, or where the buyer elects (or is compelled) to treat any breach of a condition on the part of the seller as a breach of warranty, the buyer is not by reason only of such breach of warranty entitled to reject the goods; but he may—

(a) set up against the seller the breach of warranty in diminution of extinction of the price, or

(b) maintain an action against the seller for damages for the breach of warranty.

(2) The measure of damages for breach of warranty is the estimated loss directly and naturally resulting, in the ordinary course of events, from the breach of warranty.

(3) In the case of breach of warranty of quality such loss is prima facie the difference between the value of the goods at the time of delivery to the buyer and the value they would have had if they had fulfilled the warranty.

(4) The fact that the buyer has set up the breach of warranty in diminution or extinction of the price does not prevent him from maintaining an action for the same breach of warranty if he has suffered further damage.

[(5) This section does not apply to Scotland.]

[53A. Measure of damages as respects Scotland

(1) The measure of damages for the seller's breach of contract is the estimated loss directly and naturally resulting, in the ordinary course of events, from the breach.

(2) Where the seller's breach consists of the delivery of goods which are not of the quality required by the contract and the buyer retains the goods, such loss as aforesaid is prima facie the difference between the value of the goods at the time of delivery to the buyer and the value they would have had if they had fulfilled the contract.

(3) This section applies to Scotland only.]

Interest, etc.

54. Interest, etc.

Nothing in this Act affects the right of the buyer or the seller to recover interest or special damages in any case where by law interest or special damages may be recoverable, or to recover money paid where the consideration for the payment of it has failed.

PART VII
SUPPLEMENTARY

55. Exclusion of implied terms

(1) Where a right duty or liability would arise under a contract of sale of goods by implication of law, it may (subject to the Unfair Contract Terms Act 1977) be negatived or varied by express agreement, or by the course of dealing between the parties, or by such usage as binds both parties to the contract.

(2) An express [term] does not negative a [term] implied by this Act unless inconsistent with it.

(3) Paragraph 11 of Schedule 1 below applies in relation to a contract made on or after 18 May 1973 and before 1 February 1978, and paragraph 12 in relation to one made before 18 May 1973.

56. Conflict of laws

Paragraph 13 of Schedule 1 below applies in relation to a contract made on or after 18 May 1973 and before 1 February 1978, so as to make provision about conflict of laws in relation to such a contract.

57. Auction sales

(1) Where goods are put up for sale by auction in lots, each lot is prima facie deemed to be the subject of a separate contract of sale.

(2) A sale by auction is complete when the auctioneer announces its completion by the fall of the hammer, or in other customary manner; and until the announcement is made any bidder may retract his bid.

(3) A sale by auction may be notified to be subject to a reserve or upset price, and a right to bid may also be reserved expressly by or on behalf of the seller.

(4) Where a sale by auction is not notified to be subject to a right to bid by or on behalf of the seller, it is not lawful for the seller to bid himself or to employ any person to bid at the sale, or for the auctioneer knowingly to take any bid from the seller or any such person.

(5) A sale contravening subsection (4) above may be treated as fraudulent by the buyer.

(6) Where, in respect of a sale by auction, a right to bid is expressly reserved (but not otherwise) the seller or any one person on his behalf may bid at the auction.

58. Payment into court in Scotland

In Scotland where a buyer has elected to accept goods which he might have rejected, and to treat a breach of contract as only giving rise to a claim for damages, he may, in an action by the seller for the price, be required, in the discretion of the court before which the action depends, to consign or pay into court the price of the goods, or part of the price, or to give other reasonable security for its due payment.

59. Reasonable time a question of fact

Where a reference is made in this Act to a reasonable time the question what is a reasonable time is a question of fact.

60. Rights etc. enforceable by action

Where a right, duty or liability is declared by this Act, it may (unless otherwise provided by this Act) be enforced by action.

61. Interpretation

(1) In this Act, unless the context or subject matter otherwise requires,—

'action' includes counterclaim and set-off, and in Scotland condescendence and claim and compensation;

['bulk' means a mass or collection of goods of the same kind which—

(a) is contained in a defined space or area; and

(b) is such that any goods in the bulk are interchangeable with any other goods therein of the same number or quantity;]

'business' includes a profession and the activities of any government department (including a Northern Ireland department) or local or public authority;

'buyer' means a person who buys or agrees to buy goods;

['consumer contract' has the same meaning as in section 25(1) of the Unfair Contract Terms Act 1977; and for the purposes of this Act the onus of proving that a contract is not to be regarded as a consumer contract shall lie on the seller]

'contract of sale' includes an agreement to sell as well as a sale,

'credit-broker' means a person acting in the course of a business of credit brokerage carried on by him, that is a business of effecting introductions of individuals desiring to obtain credit—

(a) to persons carrying on any business so far as it relates to the provision of credit, or

(b) to other persons engaged in credit brokerage;

'defendant' includes in Scotland defender, respondent, and claimant in a multiplepoinding;

'delivery' means voluntary transfer of possession from one person to another; [except that in relation to sections 20A and 20B above it includes such appropriation of goods to the contract as results in property in the goods being transferred to the buyer;]

'document of title to goods' has the same meaning as it has in the Factors Acts;

'Factors Acts' means the Factors Act 1889, the Factors (Scotland) Act 1890, and any enactment amending or substituted for the same;

'fault' means wrongful act or default;

'future goods' means goods to be manufactured or acquired by the seller after the making of the contract of sale;

'goods' includes all personal chattels other than things in action and money, and in Scotland all corporeal moveables except money; and in particular 'goods' includes emblements, industrial growing crops, and things attached to or forming part of the land which are agreed to be severed before sale or under the contract of sale; [and includes an undivided share in goods;]

'plaintiff' includes pursuer, complainer, claimant in a multiplepoinding and defendant or defender counter-claiming;

'property' means the general property in goods, and not merely a special property;

'sale' includes a bargain and sale as well as a sale and delivery;

'seller' means a person who sells or agrees to sell goods;

'specific goods' means goods identified and agreed on at the time a contract of sale is made; [and includes an undivided share, specified as a fraction or percentage, of goods identified and agreed on as aforesaid;]

'warranty' (as regards England and Wales and Northern Ireland) means an agreement with reference to goods which are the subject of a contract of sale, but collateral to the main purpose of such contract, the breach of which gives rise to a claim for damages, but not to a right to reject the goods and treat the contract as repudiated.

(3) A thing is deemed to be done in good faith within the meaning of this Act when it is in fact done honestly, whether it is done negligently or not.

(4) A person is deemed to be insolvent within the meaning of this Act if he has either ceased to pay his debts in the ordinary course of business or he cannot pay his debts as they become due, [. . .]

(5) Goods are in a deliverable state within the meaning of this Act when they are in such a state that the buyer would under the contract be bound to take delivery of them.

[(5A) References in this Act to dealing as consumer are to be construed in accordance with Part I of the Unfair Contract Terms Act 1977; and, for the purposes of this Act, it is for a seller claiming that the buyer does not deal as consumer to show that he does not.]

(6) As regards the definition of 'business' in subsection (1) above, paragraph 14 of Schedule 1 below applies in relation to a contract made on or after 18 May 1973 and before 1 February 1978, and paragraph 15 in relation to one made before 18 May 1973.

62. Savings: rules of law etc.

(1) The rules in bankruptcy relating to contracts of sale apply to those contracts, notwithstanding anything in this Act.

(2) The rules of the common law, including the law merchant, except in so far as they are inconsistent with the provisions of this Act, and in particular the rules relating to the law of principal and agent and the effect of fraud, misrepresentation, duress or coercion, mistake, or other invalidating cause, apply to contracts for the sale of goods.

(3) Nothing in this Act or the Sale of Goods Act 1893 affects the enactments relating to bills of sale, or any enactment relating to the sale of goods which is not expressly repealed or amended by this Act or that.

(4) The provisions of this Act about contracts of sale do not apply to a transaction in the form of a contract of sale which is intended to operate by way of mortgage, pledge, charge, or other security.

(5) Nothing in this Act prejudices or affects the landlord's right of hypothec or sequestration for rent in Scotland.

63. Consequential amendments, repeals and savings

. . .

64. Short title and commencement

(1) This Act may be cited as the Sale of Goods Act 1979.

(2) This act comes into force on 1 January 1980.

SUPPLY OF GOODS AND SERVICES ACT 1982
(1982, c. 29)

An Act to amend the law with respect to the terms to be implied in certain contracts for the transfer of property in goods, in certain contracts for the hire of goods and in certain contracts for the supply of a service; and for connected purposes. [13th July 1982]

PART I
SUPPLY OF GOODS

Contracts for the transfer of property in goods

1. The contracts concerned

(1) In this Act [in its application to England and Wales and Northern Ireland] a 'contract for the transfer of goods' means a contract under which one person transfers or agrees to transfer to another the property in goods, other than an excepted contract.

(2) For the purposes of this section an excepted contract means any of the following:—

(a) a contract of sale of goods;

(b) a hire-purchase agreement;

(c) a contract under which the property in goods is (or is to be) transferred in exchange for trading stamps on their redemption;

(d) a transfer or agreement to transfer which is made by deed and for which there is no consideration other than the presumed consideration imported by the deed;

(e) a contract intended to operate by way of mortgage, pledge, charge or other security.

(3) For the purposes of this Act [in its application to England and Wales and Northern Ireland] a contract is a contract for the transfer of goods whether or not services are also provided or to be provided under the contract, and (subject to subsection (2) above) whatever is the nature of the consideration for the transfer or agreement to transfer.

2. Implied terms about title, etc.

(1) In a contract for the transfer of goods, other than one to which subsection (3) below applies, there is an implied condition on the part of the transferor that in the case of a transfer of the property in the goods he has a right to transfer the property and in the case of an agreement to transfer the property in the goods he will have such a right at the time when the property is to be transferred.

(2) In a contract for the transfer of goods, other than one to which subsection (3) below applies, there is also an implied warranty that—

(a) the goods are free, and will remain free until the time when the property is to be transferred, from any charge or encumbrance not disclosed or known to the transferee before the contract is made, and

(b) the transferee will enjoy quiet possession of the goods except so far as it may be disturbed by the owner or other person entitled to the benefit of any charge or encumbrance so disclosed or known.

(3) This subsection applies to a contract for the transfer of goods in the case of which there appears from the contract or is to be inferred from its circumstances an intention that the transferor should transfer only such title as he or a third person may have.

(4) In a contract to which subsection (3) above applies there is an implied warranty that all charges or encumbrances known to the transferor and not known to the transferee have been disclosed to the transferee before the contract is made.

(5) In a contract to which subsection (3) above applies, there is also an implied warranty that none of the following will disturb the transferee's quiet possession of the goods, namely—

(a) the transferor;

(b) in a case where the parties to the contract intend that the transferor should transfer only such title as a third person may have, that person;

(c) anyone claiming through or under the transferor or that third person otherwise than under a charge or encumbrance disclosed or known to the transferee before the contract is made.

3. Implied terms where transfer is by description

(1) This section applies where, under a contract for the transfer of goods, the transferor transfers or agrees to transfer the property in the goods by description.

(2) In such case there is an implied condition that the goods will correspond with the description.

(3) If the transferor transfers or agrees to transfer the property in the goods by sample as well as by description it is not sufficient that the bulk of the goods corresponds with the sample if the goods do not also correspond with the description.

(4) A contract is not prevented from falling within subsection (1) above by reason only that, being exposed for supply, the goods are selected by the transferee.

4. Implied terms about quality or fitness

(1) Except as provided by this section and section 5 below and subject to the provision of any other enactment, there is no implied condition or warranty about the quality or fitness for any particular purpose of goods supplied under a contract for the transfer of goods.

[(2) Where, under such a contract, the transferor transfers the property in goods in the course of a business, there is an implied condition that the goods supplied under the contract are of satisfactory quality.

(2A) For the purposes of this section and section 5 below, goods are of satisfactory quality if they meet the standard that a reasonable person would regard as satisfactory, taking account of any description of the goods, the price (if relevant) and all the other relevant circumstances.]

[(3) The condition implied by subsection (2) above does not extend to any matter making the quality of goods unsatisfactory—

(a) which is specifically drawn to the transferee's attention before the contract is made,

(b) where the transferee examines the goods before the contract is made, which that examination ought to reveal, or

(c) where the property in the goods is transferred by reference to a sample, which would have been apparent on a reasonable examination of the sample.]

(4) Subsection (5) below applies where, under a contract for the transfer of goods, the transferor transfers the property in goods in the course of a business and the transferee, expressly or by implication, makes known—

(a) to the transferor, or

(b) where the consideration or part of the consideration for the transfer is a sum payable by instalments and the goods were previously sold by a credit-broker to the transferor, to that credit-broker,

any particular purpose for which the goods are being acquired.

(5) In that case there is (subject to subsection (6) below) an implied condition that the goods supplied under the contract are reasonably fit for that purpose, whether or not that is a purpose for which such goods are commonly supplied.

(6) Subsection (5) above does not apply where the circumstances show that the transferee does not rely, or that it is unreasonable for him to rely, on the skill or judgment of the transferor or credit-broker.

(7) An implied condition or warranty about quality or fitness for a particular purpose may be annexed by usage to a contract for the transfer of goods.

(8) The preceding provisions of this section apply to a transfer by a person who in the course of a business is acting as agent for another as they apply to a transfer by a principal in the course of a business, except where that other is not transferring in the course of a business and either the transferee knows that fact or reasonable steps are taken to bring it to the transferee's notice before the contract concerned is made.

5. Implied terms where transfer is by sample

(1) This section applies where, under a contract for the transfer of goods, the transferor transfers or agrees to transfer the property in the goods by reference to a sample.

(2) In such a case there is an implied condition—

(a) that the bulk will correspond with the sample in quality; and

(b) that the transferee will have a reasonable opportunity of comparing the bulk with the sample; and

(c) that the goods will be free from any defect, [making their quality unsatisfactory], which would not be apparent on reasonable examination of the sample.

(4) For the purposes of this section a transferor transfers or agrees to transfer the property in goods by reference to a sample where there is an express or implied term to that effect in the contract concerned.

[5A. Modification of remedies for breach of statutory condition in non-consumer cases

(1) Where in the case of a contract for the transfer of goods—

(a) the transferee would, apart from this subsection, have the right to treat the contract as repudiated by reason of a breach on the part of the transferor of a term implied by section 3, 4 or 5(2)(a) or (c) above, but

(b) the breach is so slight that it would be unreasonable for him to do so,

then, if the transferee does not deal as consumer, the breach is not to be treated as a breach of condition but may be treated as a breach of warranty.

(2) This section applies unless a contrary intention appears in, or is to be implied from, the contract.

(3) It is for the transferor to show that a breach fell within subsection (1)(b) above.]

Contracts for the hire of goods

6. The contracts concerned

(1) In this Act [in its application to England and Wales and Northern Ireland] a 'contract for the hire of goods' means a contract under which one person bails or agrees to bail goods to another by way of hire, other than an excepted contract.

(2) For the purposes of this section an excepted contract means any of the following—

(a) a hire-purchase agreement;

(b) a contract under which goods are (or are to be) bailed in exchange for trading stamps on their redemption.

(3) For the purposes of this Act [in its application to England and Wales and Northern Ireland] a contract is a contract for the hire of goods whether or not services are also provided or to be provided under the contract, and (subject to subsection (2) above) whatever is the nature of the consideration for the bailment or agreement to bail by way of hire.

7. Implied terms about right to transfer possession, etc.

(1) In a contract for the hire of goods there is an implied condition on the part of the bailor that in the case of a bailment he has a right to transfer possession of the goods by way of hire for the period of the bailment and in the case of an agreement to bail he will have such a right at the time of the bailment.

(2) In a contract for the hire of goods there is also an implied warranty that the bailee will enjoy quiet possession of the goods for the period of the bailment except so far as the possession may be disturbed by the owner or other person entitled to the benefit of any charge or encumbrance disclosed or known to the bailee before the contract is made.

(3) The preceding provisions of this section do not affect the right of the bailor to repossess the goods under an express or implied term of contract.

8. Implied terms where hire is by description

(1) This section applies where, under a contract for the hire of goods, the bailor bails or agrees to bail the goods by description.

(2) In such a case there is an implied condition that the goods will correspond with the description.

(3) If under the contract the bailor bails or agrees to bail the goods by reference to a sample as well as a description it is not sufficient that the bulk of the goods corresponds with the sample if the goods do not also correspond with the description.

(4) A contract is not prevented from falling within subsection (1) above by reason only that, being exposed for supply, the goods are selected by the bailee.

9. Implied terms about quality or fitness

(1) Except as provided by this section and section 10 below and subject to the provisions of any other enactment, there is no implied condition or warranty about the quality or fitness for any particular purpose of goods bailed under a contract for the hire of goods.

[(2) Where, under such a contract, the bailor bails goods in the course of a business, there is an implied condition that the goods supplied under the contract are of satisfactory quality.

(2A) For the purposes of this section and section 10 below, goods are of satisfactory quality if they meet the standard that a reasonable person would regard as satisfactory, taking account of any description of the goods, the consideration for the bailment (if relevant) and all the other relevant circumstances.

(3) The condition implied by subsection (2) above does not extend to any matter making the quality of goods unsatisfactory—

(a) which is specifically drawn to the bailee's attention before the contract is made,

(b) where the bailee examines the goods before the contract is made, which that examination ought to reveal, or

(c) where the goods are bailed by reference to a sample, which would have been apparent on a reasonable examination of the sample.]

(4) Subsection (5) below applies where, under a contract for the hire of goods, the bailor bails goods in the course of a business and the bailee, expressly or by implication, makes known—

(a) to the bailor in the course of negotiations conducted by him in relation to the making of the contract, or

(b) to a credit-broker in the course of negotiations conducted by that broker in relation to goods sold by him to the bailor before forming the subject matter of the contract,

any particular purpose for which the goods are being bailed.

(5) In that case there is (subject to subsection (6) below) an implied condition that the goods supplied under the contract are reasonably fit for that purpose, whether or not that is a purpose for which such goods are commonly supplied.

(6) Subsection (5) above does not apply where the circumstances show that the bailee does not rely, or that it is unreasonable for him to rely, on the skill or judgment of the bailor or credit-broker.

(7) An implied condition or warranty about quality or fitness for a particular purpose may be annexed by usage to a contract for the hire of goods.

(8) The preceding provisions of this section apply to a bailment by a person who in the course of a business is acting as agent for another as they apply to a bailment by a principal in the course of a business, except where that other is not bailing in the course of a business and either the bailee knows that fact or reasonable steps are taken to bring it to the bailee's notice before the contract concerned is made.

10. Implied terms where hire is by sample

(1) This section applies where, under a contract for the hire of goods, the bailor bails or agrees to bail the goods by reference to a sample.

(2) In such a case there is an implied condition—

(a) that the bulk will correspond with the sample in quality; and

(b) that the bailee will have a reasonable opportunity of comparing the bulk with the sample; and

(c) that the goods will be free from any defect, [making their quality unsatisfactory], which would not be apparent on reasonable examination of the sample.

(4) For the purposes of this section a bailor bails or agrees to bail goods by reference to a sample where there is an express or implied term to that effect in the contract concerned.

[10A. Modification of remedies for breach of statutory condition in non-consumer cases

(1) Where in the case of a contract for the hire of goods—

(a) the bailee would, apart from this subsection, have the right to treat the contract as repudiated by reason of a breach on the part of the bailor of a term implied by section 8, 9 or 10(2)(a) or (c) above, but

(b) the breach is so slight that it would be unreasonable for him to do so,

then, if the bailee does not deal as consumer, the breach is not to be treated as a breach of condition but may be treated as a breach of warranty.

(2) This section applies unless a contrary intention appears in, or is to be implied from, the contract.

(3) It is for the bailor to show that a breach fell within subsection (1)(b) above.]

Exclusion of implied terms, etc.

11. Exclusion of implied terms, etc.

(1) Where a right, duty or liability would arise under a contract for the transfer of goods or a contract for the hire of goods by implication of law, it may (subject to subsection (2) below and the 1977 Act) be negatived or varied by express agreement, or by the course of dealing between the parties, or by such usage as binds both parties to the contract.

(2) An express condition or warranty does not negative a condition or warranty implied by the preceding provisions of this Act unless inconsistent with it.

(3) Nothing in the preceding provisions of this Act prejudices the operation of any other enactment or any rule of law whereby any condition or warranty (other than one relating to quality or fitness) is to be implied in a contract for the transfer of goods or a contract for hire of goods.

[PART IA

SUPPLY OF GOODS AS RESPECTS SCOTLAND

Contracts for the transfer of property in goods

11A. The contracts concerned

(1) In this Act in its application to Scotland a 'contract for the transfer of goods' means a contract under which one person transfers or agrees to transfer to another the property in goods, other than an excepted contract.

(2) For the purposes of this section an excepted contract means any of the following—

(a) a contract of sale of goods;

(b) a hire-purchase agreement;

(c) a contract under which the property in goods is (or is to be) transferred in exchange for trading stamps on their redemption;

(d) a transfer or agreement to transfer for which there is no consideration;

(e) a contract intended to operate by way of mortgage, pledge, charge or other security.

(3) For the purposes of this Act in its application to Scotland a contract is a contract for the transfer of goods whether or not services are also provided or to be provided under the contract, and (subject to subsection (2) above) whatever is the nature of the consideration for the transfer or agreement to transfer.

11B. Implied terms about title, etc.

(1) In a contract for the transfer of goods, other than one to which subsection (3) below applies, there is an implied term on the part of the transferor that in the case of a transfer of the property in the goods he has a right to transfer the property and in the case of an agreement to transfer the property in the goods he will have such a right at the time when the property is to be transferred.

(2) In a contract for the transfer of goods, other than one to which subsection (3) below applies, there is also an implied term that—

(a) the goods are free, and will remain free until the time when the property is to be transferred, from any charge or encumbrance not disclosed or known to the transferee before the contract is made, and

(b) the transferee will enjoy quiet possession of the goods except so far as it may be disturbed by the owner or other person entitled to the benefit of any charge or encumbrance so disclosed or known.

(3) This subsection applies to a contract for the transfer of goods in the case of which there appears from the contract or is to be inferred from its circumstances an intention that the transferor should transfer only such title as he or a third person may have.

(4) In a contract to which subsection (3) above applies there is an implied term that all charges or encumbrances known to the transferor and not known to the transferee have been disclosed to the transferee before the contract is made.

(5) In a contract to which subsection (3) above applies there is also an implied term that none of the following will disturb the transferee's quiet possession of the goods, namely—

(a) the transferor;

(b) in a case where the parties to the contract intend that the transferor should transfer only such title as a third person may have, that person;

(c) anyone claiming through or under the transferor or that third person otherwise than under a charge or encumbrance disclosed or known to the transferee before the contract is made.

11C. Implied terms where transfer is by description

(1) This section applies where, under a contract for the transfer of goods, the transferor transfers or agrees to transfer the property in the goods by description.

(2) In such a case there is an implied term that the goods will correspond with the description.

(3) If the transferor transfers or agrees to transfer the property in the goods by reference to a sample as well as by description it is not sufficient that the bulk of the goods corresponds with the sample if the goods do not also correspond with the description.

(4) A contract is not prevented from falling within subsection (1) above by reason only that, being exposed for supply, the goods are selected by the transferee.

11D. Implied terms about quality or fitness

(1) Except as provided by this section and section 11E below and subject to the provisions of any other enactment, there is no implied term about the quality or fitness for any particular purpose of goods supplied under a contract for the transfer of goods.

(2) Where, under such a contract, the transferor transfers the property in goods in the course of a business, there is an implied term that the goods supplied under the contract are of satisfactory quality.

(3) For the purposes of this section and section 11E below, goods are of satisfactory quality if they meet the standard that a reasonable person would regard as satisfactory, taking account of any description of the goods, the price (if relevant) and all the other relevant circumstances.

(4) The term implied by subsection (2) above does not extend to any matter making the quality of goods unsatisfactory—

(a) which is specifically drawn to the transferee's attention before the contract is made,

(b) where the transferee examines the goods before the contract is made, which that examination ought to reveal, or

(c) where the property in the goods is, or is to be, transferred by reference to a sample, which would have been apparent on a reasonable examination of the sample.

(5) Subsection (6) below applies where, under a contract for the transfer of goods, the transferor transfers the property in goods in the course of a business and the transferee, expressly or by implication, makes known—

(a) to the transferor, or

(b) where the consideration or part of the consideration for the transfer is a sum payable by instalments and the goods were previously sold by a credit-broker to the transferor, to that credit-broker,

any particular purpose for which the goods are being acquired.

(6) In that case there is (subject to subsection (7) below) an implied term that the goods supplied under the contract are reasonably fit for the purpose, whether or not that is a purpose for which such goods are commonly supplied.

(7) Subsection (6) above does not apply where the circumstances show that the transferee does not rely or that it is unreasonable for him to rely, on the skill or judgment of the transferor or credit-broker.

(8) An implied term about quality or fitness for a particular purpose may be annexed by usage to a contract for the transfer of goods.

(9) The preceding provisions of this section apply to a transfer by a person who in the course of a business is acting as agent for another as they apply to a transfer by a principal in the course of a business, except where that other is not transferring in the course of a business and either the transferee knows that fact or reasonable steps are taken to bring it to the transferee's notice before the contract concerned is made.

11E. Implied terms where transfer is by sample

(1) This section applies where, under a contract for the transfer of goods, the transferor transfers or agrees to transfer the property in the goods by reference to a sample.

(2) In such a case there is an implied term—

(a) that the bulk will correspond with the sample in quality;

(b) that the transferee will have a reasonable opportunity of comparing the bulk with the sample; and

(c) that the goods will be free from any defect, making their quality unsatisfactory, which would not be apparent on reasonable examination of the sample.

(3) For the purposes of this section a transferor transfers or agrees to transfer the property in goods by reference to a sample where there is an express or implied term to that effect in the contract concerned.

11F. Remedies for breach of contract

(1) Where in a contract for the transfer of goods a transferor is in breach of any term of the contract (express or implied), the other party to the contract (in this section referred to as 'the transferee') shall be entitled—

(a) to claim damages; and

(b) if the breach is material, to reject any goods delivered under the contract and treat it as repudiated.

(2) Where a contract for the transfer of goods is a consumer contract and the transferee is the consumer, then, for the purposes of subsection (1)(b) above, breach by the transferor of any term (express or implied)—

(a) as to the quality of the goods or their fitness for a purpose;

(b) if the goods are, or are to be, transferred by description, that the goods will correspond with the description;

(c) if the goods are, or are to be, transferred by reference to a sample, that the bulk will correspond with the sample in quality,

shall be deemed to be a material breach.

(3) In subsection (2) above, 'consumer contract' has the same meaning as in section 25(1) of the 1977 Act; and for the purposes of that subsection the onus of proving that a contract is not to be regarded as a consumer contract shall lie on the transferor.

Contracts for the hire of goods

11G. The contracts concerned

(1) In this Act in its application to Scotland a 'contract for the hire of goods' means a contract under which one person ('the supplier') hires or agrees to hire goods to another, other than an excepted contract.

(2) For the purposes of this section, an excepted contract means any of the following—

(a) a hire-purchase agreement;

(b) a contract under which goods are (or are to be) hired in exchange for trading stamps on their redemption.

(3) For the purposes of this Act in its application to Scotland a contract is a contract for the hire of goods whether or not services are also provided or to be provided under the contract, and (subject to subsection (2) above) whatever is the nature of the consideration for the hire or agreement to hire.

11H. Implied terms about right to transfer possession etc.

(1) In a contract for the hire of goods there is an implied term on the part of the supplier that—

(a) in the case of a hire, he has a right to transfer possession of the goods by way of hire for the period of the hire; and

(b) in the case of an agreement to hire, he will have such a right at the time of commencement of the period of the hire.

(2) In a contract for the hire of goods there is also an implied term that the person to whom the goods are hired will enjoy quiet possession of the goods for the period of the hire except so far as the possession may be disturbed by the owner or other person entitled to the benefit of any charge or encumbrance disclosed or known to the person to whom the goods are hired before the contract is made.

(3) The preceding provisions of this section do not affect the right of the supplier to repossess the goods under an express or implied term of the contract.

11I. Implied terms where hire is by description

(1) This section applies where, under a contract for the hire of goods, the supplier hires or agrees to hire the goods by description.

(2) In such a case there is an implied term that the goods will correspond with the description.

(3) If under the contract the supplier hires or agrees to hire the goods by reference to a sample as well as by description it is not sufficient that the bulk of the goods corresponds with the sample if the goods do not also correspond with the description.

(4) A contract is not prevented from falling within subsection (1) above by reason only that, being exposed for supply, the goods are selected by the person to whom the goods are hired.

11J. Implied terms about quality or fitness

(1) Except as provided by this section and section 11K below and subject to the provisions of any other enactment, there is no implied term about the quality or fitness for any particular purpose of goods hired under a contract for the hire of goods.

(2) Where, under such a contract, the supplier hires goods in the course of a business, there is an implied term that the goods supplied under the contract are of satisfactory quality.

(3) For the purposes of this section and section 11K below, goods are of satisfactory quality if they meet the standard that a reasonable person would regard as satisfactory, taking account of any description of the goods, the consideration for the hire (if relevant) and all the other relevant circumstances.

(4) The term implied by subsection (2) above does not extend to any matter making the quality of goods unsatisfactory—

(a) which is specifically drawn to the attention of the person to whom the goods are hired before the contract is made, or

(b) where that person examines the goods before the contract is made, which that examination ought to reveal; or

(c) where the goods are hired by reference to a sample, which would have been apparent on reasonable examination of the sample.

(5) Subsection (6) below applies where, under a contract for the hire of goods, the supplier hires goods in the course of a business and the person to whom the goods are hired, expressly or by implication, makes known—

(a) to the supplier in the course of negotiations conducted by him in relation to the making of the contract; or

(b) to a credit-broker in the course of negotiations conducted by that broker in relation to goods sold by him to the supplier before forming the subject matter of the contract, any particular purpose for which the goods are being hired.

(6) In that case there is (subject to subsection (7) below) an implied term that the goods supplied under the contract are reasonably fit for that purpose, whether or not that is a purpose for which such goods are commonly supplied.

(7) Subsection (6) above does not apply where the circumstances show that the person to whom the goods are hired does not rely, or that it is unreasonable for him to rely, on the skill or judgment of the hirer or credit-broker.

(8) An implied term about quality or fitness for a particular purpose may be annexed by usage to a contract for the hire of goods.

(9) The preceding provisions of this section apply to a hire by a person who in the course of a business is acting as agent for another as they apply to a hire by a principal in the course of a business, except where that other is not hiring in the course of a business and either the person to whom the goods are hired knows that fact or reasonable steps are taken to bring it to that person's notice before the contract concerned is made.

11K. Implied terms where hire is by sample

(1) This section applies where, under a contract of the hire of goods, the supplier hires or agrees to hire the goods by reference to a sample.

(2) In such a case there is an implied term—

(a) that the bulk will correspond with the sample in quality; and

(b) that the person to whom the goods are hired will have a reasonable opportunity of comparing the bulk with the sample; and

(c) that the goods will be free from any defect, making their quality unsatisfactory, which would not be apparent on reasonable examination of the sample.

(3) For the purposes of this section a supplier hires or agrees to hire goods by reference to a sample where there is an express or implied term to that effect in the contract concerned.

Exclusion of implied terms, etc.

11L. Exclusion of implied terms etc.

(1) Where a right, duty or liability would arise under a contract for the transfer of goods or a contract for the hire of goods by implication of law, it may (subject to subsection (2) below and the 1977 Act) be negatived or varied by express agreement, or by the course of dealing between the parties, or by such usage as binds both parties to the contract.

(2) An express term does not negative a term implied by the preceding provisions of this Part of this Act unless inconsistent with it.

(3) Nothing in the preceding provisions of this Part of this Act prejudices the operation of any other enactment or any rule of law whereby any term (other than one relating to quality or fitness) is to be implied in a contract for the transfer of goods or a contract for the hire of goods.]

PART II
SUPPLY OF SERVICES

12. The contracts concerned

(1) In this Act a 'contract for the supply of a service' means, subject to subsection (2) below a contract under which a person ('the supplier') agrees to carry out a service.

(2) For the purposes of this Act, a contract of service or apprenticeship is not a contract for the supply of a service.

(3) Subject to subsection (2) above, a contract is a contract for the supply of a service for the purposes of this Act whether or not goods are also—

(a) transferred or to be transferred, or

(b) bailed or to be bailed by way of hire,

under the contract, and whatever is the nature of the consideration for which the service is to be carried out.

(4) The Secretary of State may by order provide that one or more of sections 13 to 15 below shall not apply to services of a description specified in the order, and such an order may make different provision for different circumstances.

(5) The power to make an order under subsection (4) above shall be exercisable by statutory instrument subject to annulment in pursuance of a resolution of either House of Parliament.

13. Implied term about care and skill

In a contract for the supply of a service where the supplier is acting in the course of a business, there is an implied term that the supplier will carry out the service with reasonable care and skill.

14. Implied term about time of performance

(1) Where, under a contract for the supply of a service by a supplier acting in the course of a business, the time for the service to be carried out is not fixed by the contract, left to

be fixed in a manner agreed by the contract or determined by the course of dealing between the parties, there is an implied term that the supplier will carry out the service within a reasonable time.

(2) What is a reasonable time is a question of fact.

15. Implied term about consideration

(1) Where, under a contract for the supply of a service, the consideration for the service is not determined by the contract, left to be determined in a manner agreed by the contract or determined by the course of dealing between the parties, there is an implied term that the party contracting with the supplier will pay a reasonable charge.

(2) What is a reasonable charge is a question of fact.

16. Exclusion of implied terms, etc.

(1) Where a right, duty or liability would arise under contract for the supply of a service by virtue of this Part of this Act, it may (subject to subsection (2) below and the 1977 Act) be negatived or varied by express agreement, or by the course of dealing between the parties, or by such usage as binds both parties to the contract.

(2) An express term does not negative a term implied by this Part of this Act unless inconsistent with it.

(3) Nothing in this Part of this Act prejudices—

(a) any rule of law which imposes on the supplier a duty stricter than that imposed by section 13 or 14 above; or

(b) subject to paragraph (a) above, any rule of law whereby any term not inconsistent with this Part of this Act is to be implied in a contract for the supply of a service.

(4) This Part of this Act has effect to any other enactment which defines or restricts the rights, duties or liabilities arising in connection with a service of any description.

PART III
SUPPLEMENTARY

18. Interpretation: general

(1) In the preceding provisions of this Act and this section—

'bailee', in relation to a contract for the hire of goods means (depending on the context) a person to whom the goods are bailed under a contract, or a person to whom they are to be so bailed, or a person to whom the rights under the contract of either of those persons have passed;

'bailor', in relation to a contract for the hire of goods, means (depending on the context) a person who bails the goods under the contract, or a person who agrees to do so, or a person to whom the duties under the contract of either of those persons have passed;

'business' includes a profession and the activities of any government department or local or public authority;

'credit-broker' means a person acting in the course of a business of credit brokerage carried on by him;

'credit brokerage' means the effecting of introductions—

(a) of individuals desiring to obtain credit to persons carrying on any business so far as it relates to the provision of credit; or

(b) of individuals desiring to obtain goods on hire to persons carrying on a business which comprises or relates to the bailment [or as regards Scotland the hire] of goods under a contract for the hire of goods; or

(c) of individuals desiring to obtain credit, or to obtain goods on hire, to other credit-brokers;

'enactment' means any legislation (including subordinate legislation) of the United Kingdom or Northern Ireland;

'goods' [includes all personal chattels, other than things in action and money, and as regards Scotland all corporeal moveables; and in particular 'goods' includes] emblements, industrial growing crops, and things attached to or forming part of the land which are agreed to be severed before the transfer [bailment or hire] concerned or under the contract concerned [. . .];

'hire-purchase agreement' has the same meaning as in the 1974 Act;
'property', in relation to goods, means the general property in them and not merely a special property;
'redemption', in relation to trading stamps, has the same meaning as in the Trading Stamps Act 1964 or, as respects Northern Ireland, the Trading Stamps Act (Northern Ireland) 1965;
'trading stamps' has the same meaning as in the said Act of 1964 or, as respects Northern Ireland, the said Act of 1965;
'transferee', in relation to a contract for the transfer of goods, means (depending on the context) a person to whom the property in the goods is transferred under the contract, or a person to whom the property is to be so transferred, or a person to whom the rights under the contract of either of those persons have passed;
'transferor', in relation to a contract for the transfer of goods, means (depending on the context) a person who transfers the property in the goods under the contract, or a person who agrees to do so, or a person to whom the duties under the contract of either of those persons have passed.

(2) In subsection (1) above, in the definitions of bailee, bailor, transferee and transferor, a reference to rights or duties passing is to their passing by assignment, [assignation] operation of law or otherwise.

[(3) For the purposes of this Act, the quality of goods includes their state and condition and the following (among others) are in appropriate cases aspects of the quality of goods—

(a) fitness for all the purposes for which goods of the kind in question are commonly supplied,
(b) appearance and finish,
(c) freedom from minor defects,
(d) safety, and
(e) durability.

(4) References in this Act to dealing as consumer are to be construed in accordance with Part I of the Unfair Contract Terms Act 1977; and, for the purposes of this Act, it is for the transferor or bailor claiming that the transferee or bailee does not deal as consumer to show that he does not.]

19. Interpretation: references to Acts

In this Act—

'the 1973 Act' means the Supply of Goods (Implied Terms) Act 1973;
'the 1974 Act' means the Consumer Credit Act 1974;
'the 1977 Act' means the Unfair Contract Terms Act 1977; and
'the 1979 Act' means the Sale of Goods Act 1979.

20. Citation, transitional provisions, commencement and extent

(1) This Act may be cited as the Supply of Goods and Services Act 1982.

. . .

CONSUMER PROTECTION ACT 1987
(1987, c. 43)

An Act to make provision with respect to the liability of persons for damage caused by defective products; to consolidate with amendments the Consumer Safety Act 1978 and the Consumer Safety (Amendment) Act 1986; to make provision with respect to the giving of price indications; to amend Part I of the Health and Safety at Work etc. Act 1974 and sections 31 and 80 of the Explosives Act 1875; to repeal the Trade Descriptions Act 1972 and the Fabrics (Misdescription) Act 1913; and for connected purposes. [15th May 1987]

PART I
PRODUCT LIABILITY

1. Purpose and construction of Part I

(1) This Part shall have effect for the purpose of making such provision as is necessary in order to comply with the product liability Directive and shall be construed accordingly.

(2) In this Part, except in so far as the context otherwise requires—
'agricultural produce' means any produce of the soil, of stock-farming or of fisheries;
'dependant' and 'relative' have the same meaning as they have in, respectively, the Fatal Accidents Act 1976 and the Damages (Scotland) Act 1976;
'producer', in relation to a product, means—
(a) the person who manufactured it;
(b) in the case of a substance which has not been manufactured but has been won or abstracted, the person who won or abstracted it;
(c) in the case of a product which has not been manufactured, won or abstracted but essential characteristics of which are attributable to an industrial or other process having been carried out (for example, in relation to agricultural produce), the person who carried out that process;
'product, means any goods or electricity and (subject to subsection (3) below) includes a product which is comprised in another product, whether by virtue of being a component part or raw material or otherwise; and
' the product liability Directive' means the Directive of the Council of the European Communities, dated 25th July 1985, (No.85/374/EEC) on the approximation of the laws, regulations and administrative provisions of the member States concerning liability for defective products.

(3) For the purposes of this Part a person who supplies any product in which products are comprised, whether by virtue of being component parts or raw materials or otherwise, shall not be treated by reason only of his supply of that product as supplying any of the products so comprised.

2. Liability for defective products

(1) Subject to the following provisions of this Part, where any damage is caused wholly or partly by a defect in a product, every person to whom subsection (2) below applies shall be liable for the damage.

(2) This subsection applies to—
(a) the producer of the product;
(b) any person who, by putting his name on the product or using a trade mark or other distinguishing mark in relation to the product, has held himself out to be the producer of the product;
(c) any person who has imported the product into a member State from a place outside the member States in order, in the course of any business of his, to supply it to another.

(3) Subject as aforesaid, where any damage is caused wholly or partly by a defect in a product, any person who supplied the product (whether to the person who suffered the damage, to the producer of any product in which the product in question is comprised or to any other person) shall be liable for the damage if—
(a) the person who suffered the damage requests the supplier to identify one or more of the persons (whether still in existence or not) to whom subsection (2) above applies in relation to the product;
(b) that request is made within a reasonable period after the damage occurs and at a time when it is not reasonably practicable for the person making the request to identify all those persons; and
(c) the supplier fails, within a reasonable period after receiving the request, either to comply with the request or to identify the person who supplied the product to him.

(4) Neither subsection (2) nor subsection (3) above shall apply to a person in respect of any defect in any game or agricultural produce if the only supply of the game or produce by that person to another was at a time when it had not undergone an industrial process.

(5) Where two or more persons are liable by virtue of this Part for the same damage, their liability shall be joint and several.

(6) This section shall be without prejudice to any liability arising otherwise than by virtue of this Part.

3. Meaning of 'defect'

(1) Subject to the following provisions of the section, there is a defect in a product for the purposes of this Part if the safety of the product is not such as persons generally are

entitled to expect; and for those purposes 'safety', in relation to a product, shall include safety with respect to products comprised in that product and safety in the context of risks of damage to property, as well as in the context of risks of death or personal injury.

(2) In determining for the purposes of subsection (1) above what persons generally are entitled to expect in relation to a product all the circumstances shall be taken into account, including—

(a) the manner in which, and purposes for which, the product has been marketed, its get-up, the use of any mark in relation to the product and any instructions for, or warnings with respect to, doing or refraining from doing anything with or in relation to the product;

(b) what might reasonably be expected to be done with or in relation to the product; and

(c) the time when the product was supplied by its producer to another;

and nothing in this section shall require a defect to be inferred from the fact alone that the safety of a product which is supplied after that time is greater than the safety of the product in question.

4. Defences

(1) In any civil proceedings by virtue of this Part against any person ('the person proceeded against') in respect of a defect in a product it shall be a defence for him to show—

(a) that the defect is attributable to compliance with any requirement imposed by or under any enactment or with any Community obligation; or

(b) that the person proceeded against did not at any time supply the product to another; or

(c) that the following conditions are satisfied, that is to say—

(i) that the only supply of the product to another by the person proceeded against was otherwise than in the course of a business of that person's; and

(ii) that section 2(2) above does not apply to that person or applies to him by virtue only of things done otherwise than with a view to profit; or

(d) that the defect did not exist in the product at the relevant time; or

(e) that the state of scientific and technical knowledge at the relevant time was not such that a producer of products of the same description as the product in question might be expected to have discovered the defect if it had existed in his products while they were under his control; or

(f) that the defect—

(i) constituted a defect in a product ('the subsequent product') in which the product in question had been comprised; and

(ii) was wholly attributable to the design of the subsequent product or to compliance by the producer of the product in question with instructions given by the producer of the subsequent product.

(2) In this section 'the relevant time', in relation to electricity, means the time at which it was generated, being a time before it was transmitted or distributed, and in relation to any other product, means—

(a) if the person proceeded against is a person to whom subsection (2) of section 2 above applies in relation to the product, the time when he supplied the product to another;

(b) if that subsection does not apply to that person in relation to the product, the time when the product was last supplied by a person to whom that subsection does apply in relation to the product.

5. Damage giving rise to liability

(1) Subject to the following provisions of this section, in this Part 'damages' means death or personal injury or any loss of or damage to any property (including land).

(2) A person shall not be liable under section 2 above in respect of any defect in a product for the loss of or any damage to the product itself or for the loss of or any damage to the whole or any part of any product which has been supplied with the product in question comprised in it.

(3) A person shall not be liable under section 2 above for any loss of or damage to any property which, at the time it is lost or damaged, is not—

(a) of a description of property ordinarily intended for private use, occupation or consumption; and

(b) intended by the person suffering the loss or damage mainly for his own private use, occupation or consumption.

(4) No damages shall be awarded to any person by virtue of this Part in respect of any loss of or damage to any property if the amount which would fall to be so awarded to that person, apart from this subsection and any liability for interest, does not exceed £275.

(5) In determining for the purposes of this Part who has suffered any loss of or damage to property and when any such loss or damage occurred, the loss or damage shall be regarded as having occurred at the earliest time at which a person with an interest in the property had knowledge of the material facts about the loss or damage.

(6) For the purposes of subsection (5) above the material facts about any loss of or damage to any property are such facts about the loss or damage as would lead a reasonable person with an interest in the property to consider the loss or damage sufficiently serious to justify his instituting proceedings for damages against a defendant who did not dispute liability and was able to satisfy a judgment.

(7) For the purposes of subsection (5) above a person's knowledge includes knowledge which he might reasonably have been expected to acquire—

(a) from facts observable or ascertainable by him; or

(b) from facts ascertainable by him with help of appropriate expert advice which it is reasonable for him to seek;

but a person shall not be taken by virtue of this subsection to have knowledge of a fact ascertainable by him only with the help of expert advice unless he has failed to take all reasonable steps to obtain (and, where appropriate, to act on) that advice.

(8) Subsections (5) to (7) above shall not extend to Scotland.

6. Application of certain enactments etc.

(1) Any damage for which a person is liable under section 2 above shall be deemed to have been caused—

(a) for the purposes of the Fatal Accidents Act 1976, by that person's wrongful act, neglect or default;

(b) for the purposes of section 3 of the Law Reform (Miscellaneous Provisions) (Scotland) Act 1940 (contribution among joint wrongdoers), by that person's wrongful act or negligent act or omission;

(c) for the purposes of section 1 of the Damages (Scotland) Act 1976 (rights of relatives of a deceased), by that person's act or omission, and

(d) for the purposes of Part II of the Administration of Justice Act 1982 (damages for personal injuries, etc. — Scotland), by an act or omission giving rise to liability in that person to pay damages.

(2) Where—

(a) a person's death is caused wholly or partly by a defect in a product, or a person dies after suffering damage which has been so caused;

(b) a request such as mentioned in paragraph (a) of subsection (3) of section 2 above is made to a supplier of the product by that person's personal representatives or, in the case of a person whose death is caused wholly or partly by the defect, by any dependant or relative of that person; and

(c) the conditions specified in paragraphs (b) and (c) of that subsection are satisfied in relation to that request,

this Part shall have effect for the purposes of the Law Reform (Miscellaneous Provisions) Act 1934, the Fatal Accidents Acts 1976 and the Damages (Scotland) Act 1976 as if liability of the supplier to that person under that subsection did not depend on that person having requested the supplier to identify certain persons or on the said conditions having been satisfied in relation to a request made by that person.

(3) Section 1 of the Congenital Disabilities (Civil Liability) Act 1976 shall have effect for the purposes of this Part as if—

(a) a person were answerable to a child in respect of an occurrence caused wholly or partly by a defect in a product if he is or has been liable under section 2 above in respect of any effect of the occurrence on a parent of the child, or would be so liable if the occurrence caused a parent of the child to suffer damage;

(b) the provisions of this Part relating to liability under section 2 above applied in relation to liability by virtue of paragraph (a) above under the said section 1; and

(c) subsection (6) of the said section 1 (exclusion of liability) were omitted.

(4) Where any damage is caused partly by a defect in a product and partly by the fault of the person suffering the damage, the Law Reform (Contributory Negligence) Act 1945 and section 5 of the Fatal Accidents Act 1976 (contributory negligence) shall have effect as if the defect were the fault of every person liable by virtue of this Part for the damage caused by the defect.

(5) In subsection (4) above 'fault' has the same meaning as in the said Act of 1945.

(6) Schedule 1 to this Act shall have effect for the purpose of amending the Limitation Act 1980 and the Prescription and Limitation (Scotland) Act 1973 in their application in relation to the bringing of actions by virtue of this Part.

(7) It is hereby declared that liability by virtue of this Part is to be treated as liability in tort for the purposes of any enactment conferring jurisdiction on any court with respect to any matter.

(8) Nothing in this Part shall prejudice the operation of section 12 of the Nuclear Installations Act 1965 (rights to compensation for certain breaches of duties confined to rights under that Act).

7. Prohibition on exclusions from liability

The liability of a person by virtue of this Part to person who has suffered damage caused wholly or partly by a defect in a product, or to a dependant or relative of such a person, shall not be limited or excluded by any contract term, by any notice or by any other provision.

8. Power to modify Part I

(1) Her Majesty may by Order in Council make such modifications of this Part and of any other enactment (including an enactment contained in the following Parts of this Act, or in an Act passed after this Act) as appear to Her Majesty in Council to be necessary or expedient in consequence of any modification of the product liability Directive which is made at any time after the passing of this Act.

(2) An Order in Council under subsection (1) above shall not be submitted to Her Majesty in Council unless a draft of the Order has been laid before, and approved by a resolution of, each House of Parliament.

9. Application of Part I to Crown

(1) Subject to subsection (2) below, this Part shall bind the Crown.

(2) The Crown shall not, as regards the Crown's liability by virtue of this Part, be bound by this Part further than the Crown is made liable in tort or in reparation under the Crown Proceedings Act 1947, as that Act has effect from time to time.

PART II
CONSUMER SAFETY

10. The general safety requirement

(1) A person shall be guilty of an offence if he—

(a) supplies any consumer goods which fail to comply with the general safety requirement;

(b) offers or agrees to supply any such goods; or

(c) exposes or possesses any such goods for supply.

(2) For the purpose of this section consumer goods fail to comply with the general safety requirement if they are not reasonably safe having regard to all the circumstances, including—

(a) the manner in which, and purposes for which, the goods are being or would be marketed, the get-up of the goods, the use of any mark in relation to the goods and any instructions or warnings which are given with respect to the keeping, use or consumption of the goods;

(b) any standards of safety published by any person either for goods of a description which applies to the goods in question or for matters relating to goods of that description; and

(c) the existence of any means by which it would have been reasonable (taking into account the cost, likelihood and extent of any improvement) for the goods to have been made safer.

(3) For the purposes of this section consumer goods shall not be regarded as failing to comply with the general safety requirement in respect of—

(a) anything which is shown to be attributable to compliance with any requirement imposed by or under any enactment or with any Community obligation;

(b) any failure to do more in relation to any matter than is required by—

(i) any safety regulations imposing requirements with respect to that matter;

(iii) any provision of any enactment or subordinate legislation imposing such requirements with respect to that matter as are designated for the purposes of this subsection by any such regulations.

(4) In any proceedings against any person for an offence under this section in respect of any goods it shall be a defence for that person to show—

(a) that he reasonably believed that the goods would not be used or consumed in the United Kingdom; or

(b) that the following conditions are satisfied, that is to say—

(i) that he supplied the goods, offered or agreed to supply them or, as the case may be, exposed or possessed them for supply in the course of carrying on a retail business; and

(ii) that, at the time he supplied the goods or offered or agreed to supply them or exposed or possessed them for supply, he neither knew nor had reasonable grounds for believing that the goods failed to comply with the general safety requirement; or

(c) that the terms on which he supplied the goods or agreed or offered to supply them or, in the case of goods which he exposed or possessed for supply, the terms on which he intended to supply them—

(i) indicated that the goods were not supplied or to be supplied as new goods; and

(ii) provided for, or contemplated, the acquisition of an interest in the goods by the persons supplied or to be supplied.

(5) For the purposes of subsection (4)(b) above goods are supplied in the course of carrying on a retail business; if—

(a) whether or not they are themselves acquired for a person's private use or consumption, they are supplied in the course of carrying on a business of making a supply of consumer goods available to persons who generally acquire them for private use or consumption; and

(b) the descriptions of goods the supply of which is made available in the course of that business do not, to a significant extent, include manufactured or imported goods which have not previously been supplied in the United Kingdom.

(6) A person guilty of an offence under this section shall be liable on summary conviction to imprisonment for a term not exceeding six months or to a fine not exceeding level 5 on the standard scale or to both.

(7) In this section 'consumer goods' means any goods which are ordinarily intended for private use or consumption, not being—

(a) growing crops or things comprised in land by virtue of being attached to it;

(b) water, food, feeding stuff or fertiliser;

(c) gas which is, is to be or has been supplied by a person authorised to supply it by or under [section 7A of the Gas Act 1986 (licensing of gas suppliers and gas shippers) or paragraph 5 of Schedule 2A to that Act (supply to very large customers an exception to prohibition on unlicensed activities)];

(d) aircraft (other than hang-gliders) or motor vehicles;

(e) controlled drugs or licensed medicinal products;

(f) tobacco.

11. Safety regulations

(1) The Secretary of State may by regulations under this section ('safety regulations') make such provision as he considers appropriate for the purposes of section 10(3) above and for the purpose of securing—

(a) that goods to which this section applies are safe;

(b) that goods to which this section applies which are unsafe, or would be unsafe in the hands of persons of a particular description, are not made available to persons generally or, as the case may be, to persons of that description, and

(c) that appropriate information is, and inappropriate information is not, provided in relation to goods to which this section applies.

(2) Without prejudice to the generality of subsection (1) above, safety regulations may contain provision—

(a) with respect to the composition or contents, design, construction, finish or packing of goods to which this section applies, with respect to standards for such goods and with respect to other matters relating to such goods;

(b) with respect to the giving, refusal, alteration or cancellation of approvals of such goods, of descriptions of such goods or of standards for such goods;

(c) with respect to the conditions that may be attached to any approval given under the regulations;

(d) for requiring such fees as may be determined by or under the regulations to be paid on the giving or alteration of any approval under the regulations and on the making of an application for such an approval or alteration;

(e) with respect to appeals against refusals, alterations and cancellations of approvals given under the regulations and against the conditions contained in such approvals;

(f) for requiring goods to which this section applies to be approved under the regulations or to conform to the requirements of the regulations or to descriptions or standards specified in or approved by or under the regulations;

(g) with respect to the testing or inspection of goods to which this section applies (including provision for determining the standards to be applied in carrying out any test or inspection);

(h) with respect to the way of dealing with goods of which some or all do not satisfy a test required by or under the regulations or a standard connected with a procedure so required;

(i) for requiring a mark, warning or instruction or any other information relating to goods to be put on or to accompany the goods or to be used or provided in some other manner in relation to the goods, and for securing that inappropriate information is not given in relation to goods either by means of misleading marks or otherwise;

(j) for prohibiting persons from supplying, or from offering to supply, agreeing to supply, exposing for supply or possessing for supply, goods to which this section applies and component parts and raw materials for such goods;

(k) for requiring information to be given to any such person as may be determined by or under the regulations for the purpose of enabling that person to exercise any function conferred on him by the regulations.

(3) Without prejudice as aforesaid, safety regulations may contain provision—

(a) for requiring persons on whom functions are conferred by or under section 27 below to have regard, in exercising their functions so far as relating to any provision of safety regulations, to matters specified in a direction issued by the Secretary of State with respect to that provision;

(b) for securing that a person shall not be guilty of an offence under section 12 below unless it is shown that the goods in question do not conform to a particular standard;

(c) for securing that proceedings for such an offence are not brought in England and Wales except by or with the consent of the Secretary of State or the Director of Public Prosecutions;

(d) for securing that proceedings for such an offence are not brought in Northern Ireland except by or with consent of the Secretary of State or the Director of Public Prosecutions for Northern Ireland;

(e) for enabling a magistrate's court in England and Wales or Northern Ireland to try an information or, in Northern Ireland, a complaint in respect of such an offence if the information was laid or the complaint made within twelve months from the time when the offence was committed;

(f) for enabling summary proceedings for such an offence to be brought in Scotland at any time within twelve months from the time when the offence was committed; and

(g) for determining the persons by whom, and the manner in which, anything required to be done by or under the regulations is to be done.

(4) Safety regulations shall not provide for any contravention of the regulations to be an offence.

(5) Where the Secretary of State proposes to make safety regulations it shall be his duty before he makes them—

(a) to consult such organisations as appear to him to be representative of interests substantially affected by the proposal;

(b) to consult such other persons as he considers appropriate; and

(c) in the case of proposed regulations relating to goods suitable for use at work to consult the Health and Safety Commission in relation to the application of the proposed regulations to Great Britain;

but the preceding provisions of this subsection shall not apply in the case of regulations which provide for the regulations to cease to have effect at the end of a period of not more than twelve months beginning with the day on which they come into force and which contain a statement that it appears to the Secretary of State that the need to protect the public requires that the regulations should be made without delay.

(6) The power to make safety regulations shall be exercisable by statutory instrument subject to annulment in pursuance of a resolution of either House of Parliament and shall include power—

(a) to make different provision for different cases; and

(b) to make such supplemental, consequential and transitional provision as the Secretary of State considers appropriate.

(7) This section applies to any goods other than—

(a) growing crops and things comprised in land by virtue of being attached to it;

(b) water, food, feeding stuff and fertiliser;

(c) gas which is, is to be or has been supplied by a person authorised to supply it by or under [section 7A of the Gas Act 1986 (licensing of gas suppliers and gas shippers) or paragraph 5 of Schedule 2A to that Act (supply to very large customers an exception to prohibition on unlicensed activities)];

(d) controlled drugs and licensed medicinal products.

12. Offences against the safety regulations

(1) Where safety regulations prohibit a person from supplying or offering or agreeing to supply any goods or from exposing or possessing any goods for supply that person shall be guilty of an offence if he contravenes the prohibition.

(2) Where safety regulations require a person who makes or processes any goods in the course of carrying on a business—

(a) to carry out a particular test or use a particular procedure in connection with the making or processing of the goods with a view to ascertaining whether the goods satisfy any requirements of such regulations; or

(b) to deal or not to deal in a particular way with a quantity of the goods of which the whole or part does not satisfy such a test or does not satisfy standards connected with such a procedure,

that person shall be guilty of an offence if he does not comply with the requirement.

(3) If a person contravenes a provision of safety regulations which prohibits or requires the provision, by means of a mark or otherwise, of information of a particular kind in relation to goods, he shall be guilty of an offence.

(4) Where safety regulations require any person to give information to another for the purpose of enabling that other to exercise any function, that person shall be guilty of an offence if—

(a) he fails without reasonable cause to comply with the requirement; or

(b) in giving the information which is required of him—

(i) he makes any statement which he knows is false in a material particular; or

(ii) he recklessly makes any statement which is false in a material particular.

(5) A person guilty of an offence under this section shall be liable on summary conviction to imprisonment for a term not exceeding six months or to a fine not exceeding level 5 on the standard scale or to both.

13. Prohibition notices and notices to warn

(1) The Secretary of State may—

(a) serve on any person a notice ('a prohibition notice') prohibiting that person, except with the consent of the Secretary of State, from supplying, or from offering to supply, agreeing to supply or possessing for supply, any relevant goods which the Secretary of State considers are unsafe and which are described in the notice;

(b) serve on any person a notice ('a notice to warn') requiring that person at his own expense to publish, in a form and manner and on occasions specified in the notice, a warning about any relevant goods which the Secretary of State considers are unsafe, which that person supplies or has supplied and which are described in the notice.

(2) Schedule 2 to this Act shall have effect with respect to prohibition notices and notices to warn, and the Secretary of State may by regulations make provision specifying the manner in which information is to be given to any person under that Schedule.

(3) A consent given by the Secretary of State for the purposes of a prohibition notice may impose such conditions on the doing of anything for which the consent is required as the Secretary of State considers appropriate.

(4) A person who contravenes a prohibition notice or a notice to warn shall be guilty of an offence and liable on summary conviction to imprisonment for a term not exceeding six months or to a fine not exceeding level 5 on the standard scale or to both.

(5) The power to make regulations under subsection (2) above shall be exercisable by statutory instrument subject to annulment in pursuance of a resolution of either House of Parliament and shall include power—

(a) to make different provision for different cases; and

(b) to make such supplemental, consequential and transitional provision as the Secretary of State considers appropriate.

(6) In this section 'relevant goods' means—

(a) in relation to a prohibition notice, any goods to which section 11 above applies; and

(b) in relation to a notice to warn, any goods to which that section applies or any growing crops or things comprised in land by virtue of being attached to it.

14. Suspension notices

(1) Where an enforcement authority has reasonable grounds for suspecting that any safety provision has been contravened in relation to any goods, the authority may serve a notice ('suspension notice') prohibiting the person on whom it is served, for such period ending not more than six months after the date of the notice as is specified therein, from doing any of the following things without the consent of the authority, that is to say, supplying the goods, offering to supply them, agreeing to supply them or exposing them for supply.

(2) A suspension notice served by an enforcement authority in respect of any goods shall—

(a) describe the goods in a manner sufficient to identify them;

(b) set out the grounds on which the authority suspects that a safety provision has been contravened in relation to the goods, and

(c) state that, and the manner in which, the person on whom the notice is served may appeal against the notice under section 15 below.

(3) A suspension notice served by an enforcement authority for the purpose of prohibiting a person for any period from doing the things mentioned in subsection (1) above in relation to any goods may also require that person to keep the authority informed of the whereabouts throughout that period of any of those goods in which he has an interest.

(4) Where a suspension notice has been served on any person in respect of any goods, no further such notice shall be served on that person in respect of the same goods unless—

(a) proceedings against that person for an offence in respect of a contravention in relation to the goods of a safety provision (not being an offence under this section); or

(b) proceedings for the forfeiture of the goods under section 16 or 17 below, are pending at the end of the period specified in the first-mentioned notice.

(5) A consent given by an enforcement authority for the purposes of subsection (1) above may impose such conditions on the doing of anything for which the consent is required as the authority considers appropriate.

(6) Any person who contravenes a suspension notice shall be guilty of an offence and liable on summary conviction to imprisonment for a term not exceeding six months or to a fine not exceeding level 5 on the standard scale or to both.

(7) Where an enforcement authority serves a suspension notice in respect of any goods, the authority shall be liable to pay compensation to any person having an interest in the goods in respect of any loss or damage caused by reason of the service of the notice if—

(a) there has been no contravention in relation to the goods of any safety provision; and

(b) the exercise of the power is not attributable to any neglect or default by that person.

(8) Any disputed question as to the right to or the amount of any compensation payable under this section shall be determined by arbitration or, in Scotland, by a single arbiter appointed, failing agreement between the parties, by the sheriff.

15. Appeals against suspension notices

(1) Any person having an interest in any goods in respect of which a suspension notice is for the time being in force may apply for an order setting aside the notice.

(2) An application under this section may be made—

(a) to any magistrates' court in which proceedings have been brought in England and Wales or Northern Ireland—

(i) for an offence in respect of a contravention in relation to the goods of any safety provision; or

(ii) for the forfeiture of the goods under section 16 below;

(b) where no such proceedings have been so brought, by way of complaint to a magistrates' court; or

(c) in Scotland, by summary application to the sheriff.

(3) On an application under this section to a magistrates' court in England and Wales or Northern Ireland the court shall make an order setting aside the suspension notice only if the court is satisfied that there has been no contravention in relation to the goods of any safety provision.

(4) On an application under this section to the sheriff he shall make an order setting aside the suspension notice only if he is safisfied that at the date of making the order—

(a) proceedings for an offence in respect of a contravention in relation to the goods of any safety provision; or

(b) proceedings for the forfeiture of the goods under section 17 below, have not been brought or, having been brought, have been concluded.

(5) Any person aggrieved by an order made under this section by a magistrates' court in England and Wales or Northern Ireland, or by a decision of such a court not to make such an order, may appeal against that order or decision—

(a) in England and Wales, to the Crown Court;

(b) in Northern Ireland, to the county court;

and an order so made may contain such provision as appears to the court to be appropriate for delaying the coming into force of the order pending the making and determination of any appeal (including any application under section Ill of the Magistrates' Courts Act 1980 or Article 146 of the Magistrates' Courts (Northern Ireland) Order 1981 (statement of case)).

16. Forfeiture: England and Wales and Northern Ireland

(1) An enforcement authority in England and Wales or Northern Ireland may apply under this section for an order for the forfeiture of any goods on the grounds that there has been a contravention in relation to the goods of a safety provision.

(2) An application under this section may be made—

(a) where proceedings have been brought in a magistrates' court for an offence in respect of a contravention in relation to some or all of the goods of any safety provision, to that court;

(b) where an application with respect to some or all of the goods has been made to a magistrates' court under section 15 above or section 33 below, to that court; and

(c) where no application for the forfeiture of the goods has been made under paragraph (a) or (b) above, by way of complaint to a magistrates' court.

(3) On an application under this section the court shall make an order for the forfeiture of any goods only if it is satisfied that there has been a contravention in relation to the goods of a safety provision.

(4) For the avoidance of doubt it is declared that a court may infer for the purposes of this section that there has been a contravention in relation to any goods of a safety provision if it is satisfied that any such provision has been contravened in relation to goods which are representative of those goods (whether by reason of being of the same design or part of the same consignment or batch or otherwise).

(5) Any person aggrieved by an order made under this section by a magistrates' court, or by a decision of such a court not to make such an order, may appeal against that order or decision—

(a) in England and Wales, to the Crown Court;

(b) in Northern Ireland, to the county court;

and an order so made may contain such provision as appears to the court to be appropriate for delaying the coming into force of the order pending the making and determination of any appeal (including any application under section III of the Magistrates' Courts Act 1980 or Article 146 of the Magistrates' Courts (Northern Ireland) Order 1981 (statement of case)).

(6) Subject to subsection (7) below, where any goods are forfeited under this section they shall be destroyed in accordance with such directions as the court may give.

(7) On making an order under this section a magistrates' court may, if it considers it appropriate to do so, direct that the goods to which the order relates shall (instead of being destroyed) be released, to such person as the court may specify, on condition that that person—

(a) does not supply those goods to any person otherwise than as mentioned in section 46(7)(a) or (b) below, and

(b) complies with any order to pay costs or expenses (including any order under section 35 below) which has been made against that person in the proceedings for the order for forfeiture.

17. Forfeiture: Scotland

(1) In Scotland a sheriff may make an order for forfeiture of any goods in relation to which there has been a contravention of a safety provision—

(a) on an application by the procurator-fiscal made in the manner specified in section 310 of the Criminal Procedure (Scotland) Act 1975; or

(b) where a person is convicted of any offence in respect of any such contravention, in addition to any other penalty which the sheriff may impose.

(2) The procurator-fiscal making an application under subsection (1)(a) above shall serve on any person appearing to him to be the owner of, or otherwise to have an interest in, the goods to which the application relates a copy of the application, together with a notice giving him the opportunity to appear at the hearing of the application to show cause why the goods should not be forfeited.

(3) Service under subsection (2) above shall be carried out, and such service may be proved, in the manner specified for citation of an accused in summary proceedings under the Criminal Procedure (Scotland) Act 1975.

(4) Any person upon whom notice is served under subsection (2) above and any other person claiming to be the owner of, or otherwise to have an interest in, goods to which an application under this section relates shall be entitled to appear at the hearing of the application to show cause why the goods should not be forfeited.

(5) The sheriff shall not make an order following an application under subsection (1)(a) above—

(a) if any person on whom notice is served under subsection (2) above does not appear, unless service of the notice on that person is proved; or

(b) if no notice under subsection (2) above has been served, unless the court is satisfied that in the circumstances it was reasonable not to serve notice on any person.

(6) The sheriff shall make an order under this section only if he is satisfied that there has been a contravention in relation to those goods of a safety provision.

(7) For the avoidance of doubt it is declared that the sheriff may infer for the purposes of this section that there has been a contravention in relation to any goods of a safety

provision if he is satisfied that any such provision has been contravened in relation to any goods which are representative of those goods (whether by reason of being of the same design or part of the same consignment or batch or otherwise).

(8) Where an order for the forfeiture of any goods is made following an application by the procurator-fiscal under subsection (1)(a) above, any person who appeared, or was entitled to appear, to show cause why goods should not be forfeited may, within twenty-one days of the making of the order, appeal to the High Court by Bill of Suspension on the ground of an alleged miscarriage of justice; [and section 182(5)(a) to (e) of the Criminal Procedure (Scotland) Act 1995 shall apply to an appeal under this subsection as it applies to a stated case under Part X of that Act].

(9) An order following an application under subsection (1)(a) above shall not take effect—

(a) until the end of the period of twenty-one days beginning with the day after the day on which the order is made; or

(b) if an appeal is made under subsection (8) above within that period, until the appeal is determined or abandoned.

(10) An order under subsection (1)(b) above shall not take effect—

(a) until the end of the period within which an appeal against the order could be brought under the Criminal Procedure (Scotland) Act 1975; or

(b) if an appeal is made within that period, until the appeal is determined or abandoned.

(11) Subject to subsection (12) below, goods forfeited under this section shall be destroyed in accordance with such directions as the sheriff may give.

(12) If he thinks fit the sheriff may direct that the goods be released, to such person as he may specify, on condition that that person does not supply those goods to any other person otherwise than as mentioned in section 46(7)(a) or (b) below.

18. Power to obtain information

(1) If the Secretary of State considers that, for the purpose of deciding whether—

(a) to make, vary or revoke any safety regulations; or

(b) to serve, vary or revoke a prohibition notice; or

(c) to serve or revoke a notice to warn,

he requires information which another person is likely to be able to furnish, the Secretary of State may serve on the other person a notice under this section.

(2) A notice served on any person under this section may require that person—

(a) to furnish to the Secretary of State, within a period specified in the notice, such information as is so specified;

(b) to produce such records as are specified in the notice at a time and place so specified and to permit a person appointed by the Secretary of State for the purpose to take copies of the records at that time and place.

(3) A person shall be guilty of an offence if he—

(a) fails, without reasonable cause, to comply with a notice served on him under this section; or

(b) in purporting to comply with a requirement which by virtue of paragraph (a) of subsection (2) above is contained in such a notice—

(i) furnishes information which he knows is false in a material particular; or

(ii) recklessly furnishes information which is false in a material particular.

(4) A person guilty of an offence under subsection (3) above shall—

(a) in the case of an offence under paragraph (a) of that subsection, be liable on summary conviction to a fine not exceeding level 5 on the standard scale; and

(b) in the case of an offence under paragraph (b) of that subsection be liable—

(i) on conviction on indictment, to a fine,

(ii) on summary conviction, to a fine not exceeding the statutory maximum.

19. Interpretation of Part II

(1) In this Part—

'controlled drug' means a controlled drug within the meaning of the Misuse of Drugs Act 1971;

'feeding stuff' and 'fertiliser' have the same meaning as in Part IV of the Agriculture Act 1970;

'food' does not include anything containing tobacco but, subject to that, has the same meaning as in the [Food Safety Act 1990] or, in relation to Northern Ireland, the same meaning as in the Food and Drugs Act (Northern Ireland) 1958;

'licensed medicinal product' means—

(a) any medicinal product within the meaning of the Medicines Act 1968 in respect of which a product licence within the meaning of that Act is for the time being in force; or

(b) any other article or substance in respect of which any such licence is for the time being in force in pursuance of an order under section 104 or 105 of that Act (application of Act to other articles and substances);

'safe', in relation to any goods, means such that there is no risk, or no risk apart from one reduced to a minimum, that any of the following will (whether immediately or after a definite or indefinite period) cause the death of, or any personal injury to, any person whatsoever, that is to say—

(a) the goods;

(b) the keeping, use or consumption of the goods;

(c) the assembly of any of the goods which are, or are to be supplied unassembled;

(d) any emission or leakage from the goods or, as a result of the keeping, use or consumption of the goods, from anything else; or

(e) reliance on the accuracy of any measurement, calculation or other reading made by or by means of the goods,

and 'safer' and 'unsafe' shall be construed accordingly;

'tobacco' includes any tobacco product within the meaning of the Tobacco Products Duty Act 1979 and any article or substance containing tobacco and intended for oral or nasal use.

(2) In the definition of 'safe' in subsection (1) above, references to the keeping, use or consumption of any goods are references to—

(a) the keeping, use or consumption of the goods by the persons by whom, and in all or any of the ways or circumstances in which, they might reasonably be expected to be kept, used or consumed; and

(b) the keeping, use or consumption of the goods either alone or in conjunction with other goods in conjunction with which they might reasonably be expected to be kept, used or consumed.

PART III
MISLEADING PRICE INDICATIONS

20. Offence of giving misleading indication

(1) Subject to the following provisions of this Part, a person shall be guilty of an offence if, in the course of any business of his, he gives (by any means whatever) to any consumers an indication which is misleading as to the price at which any goods, services, accommodation or facilities are available (whether generally or from particular persons).

(2) Subject as aforesaid, a person shall be guilty of an offence if—

(a) in the course of any business of his, he has given an indication to any consumers which, after it was given, has become misleading as mentioned in subsection (1) above; and

(b) some or all of those consumers might reasonably be expected to rely on the indication at a time after it has become misleading; and

(c) he fails to take all such steps as are reasonable to prevent those consumers from relying on the indication.

(3) For the purposes of this section it shall be immaterial—

(a) whether the person who gives or gave the indication is or was acting on his own behalf or on behalf of another;

(b) whether or not that person is the person, or included among the persons, from whom the goods, services, accommodation or facilities are available; and

(c) whether the indication is or has become misleading in relation to all the consumers to whom it is or was given or only in relation to some of them.

(4) A person guilty of an offence under subsection (1) or (2) above shall be liable—

(a) on conviction on indictment, to a fine;
(b) on summary conviction, to a fine not exceeding the statutory maximum.

(5) No prosecution for an offence under subsection (1) or (2) above shall be brought after whichever is the earlier of the following, that is to say—

(a) the end of the period of three years beginning with the day on which the offence was committed; and

(b) the end of the period of one year beginning with the day on which the person bringing the prosecution discovered that the offence had been committed.

(6) In this Part—

'consumer'—

(a) in relation to any goods, means any person who might wish to be supplied with the goods for his own private use or consumption;

(b) in relation to any services or facilities, means any person who might wish to be provided with the services or facilities otherwise than for the purposes of any business of his; and

(c) in relation to any accommodation, means any person who might wish to occupy the accommodation otherwise than for the purposes of any business of his;

'price', in relation to any goods, services, accommodation or facilities, means—

(a) the aggregate of the sums required to be paid by a consumer for or otherwise in respect of the supply of the goods or the provision of the services, accommodation or facilities; or

(b) except in section 21 below, any method which will be or has been applied for the purpose of determining that aggregate.

21. Meaning of 'misleading'

(1) For the purposes of section 20 above an indication given to any consumers is misleading as to a price if what is conveyed by the indication, or what those consumers might reasonably be expected to infer from the indication or any omission from it, includes any of the following, that is to say—

(a) that the price is less than in fact it is;

(b) that the applicability of the price does not depend on facts or circumstances on which its applicability does in fact depend;

(c) that the price covers matters in respect of which an additional charge is in fact made;

(d) that a person who in fact has no such expectation—

(i) expects the price to be increased or reduced (whether or not at a particular time or by a particular amount); or

(ii) expects the price, or the price as increased or reduced, to be maintained (whether or not for a particular period); or

(e) that the facts or circumstances by reference to which the consumers might reasonably be expected to judge the validity of any relevant comparison made or implied by the indication are not what in fact they are.

(2) For the purpose of section 20 above, an indication given to any consumers is misleading as to a method of determining a price if what is conveyed by the indication, or what those consumers might reasonably be expected to infer from the indication or any omission from it, includes any of the following, that is to say—

(a) that the method is not what in fact it is;

(b) that the applicability of the method does not depend on facts or circumstances on which its applicability does in fact depend;

(c) that the method takes into account matters in respect of which an additional charge will in fact be made;

(d) that a person who in fact has no such expectation—

(i) expects the method to be altered (whether or not at a particular time or in a particular respect); or

(ii) expects the method, or that method as altered, to remain unaltered (whether or not for a particular period); or

(e) that the facts or circumstances by reference to which the consumers might reasonably be expected to judge the validity of any relevant comparison made or implied by the indication are not what in fact they are.

(3) For the purposes of subsection (1)(e) and (2)(e) above a comparison is a relevant comparison in relation to a price or method of determining a price if it is made between that price or that method, or any price which has been or may be determined by that method, and

(a) any price or value which is stated or implied to be, to have been or to be likely to be attributed to the goods, services, accommodation or facilities in question or to any other goods, services, accommodation or facilities; or

(b) any method, or other method, which is stated or implied to be, to have been or to be likely to be applied or applicable for the determination of the price or value of the goods, services, accommodation or facilities in question or of the price or value of any other goods, services, accommodation or facilities.

22. Application to provision of services and facilities

(1) Subject to the following provisions of this section, references in this Part to services or facilities are references to any services or facilities whatever including, in particular—

(a) the provision of credit or of banking or insurance services and the provision of facilities incidental to the provision of such services;

(b) the purchase or sale of foreign currency;

(c) the supply of electricity;

(d) the provision of a place, other than on a highway, for the parking of a motor vehicle;

(e) the making of arrangements for a person to put or keep a caravan on any land other than arrangements by virtue of which that person may occupy the caravan as his only or main residence.

(2) References in this Part to services shall not include references to services provided to an employer under a contract of employment.

(3) References in this Part to services or facilities shall not include references to services or facilities which are provided by an authorised person or appointed representative in the course of the carrying on of an investment business.

(4) In relation to a service consisting in the purchase or sale of foreign currency, references in this Part to the method by which the price of the service is determined shall include references to the rate of exchange.

(5) In this section—

'appointed representative', 'authorised person' and 'investment business' have the same meanings as in the Financial Services Act 1986;

'caravan' has the meaning as in the Caravan Sites and Control of Development Act 1960;

'contract of employment' and 'employer' have the same meanings as in [the Employment Rights Act 1996];

'credit' has the same meaning as in the Consumer Credit Act 1974.

23. Application to provision of accommodation etc.

(1) Subject to subsection (2) below, references in this Part to accommodation or facilities being available shall not include references to accommodation or facilities being available to be provided by means of the creation or disposal of an interest in land except where—

(a) the person who is to create or dispose of the interest will do so in the course of any business of his; and

(b) the interest to be created or disposed of is a relevant interest in a new dwelling and is to be created or disposed of for the purpose of enabling that dwelling to be occupied as a residence, or one of the residences, of the person acquiring the interest.

(2) Subsection (1) above shall not prevent the application of any provision of this Part in relation to—

(a) the supply of any goods as part of the same transaction as any creation or disposal of an interest in land; or

(b) the provision of any services or facilities for the purpose of, or in connection with, any transaction for the creation or disposal of such an interest.

(3) In this section—

'new dwelling' means any building or part of a building in Great Britain which—

(a) has been constructed or adapted to be occupied as a residence; and

(b) has not previously been so occupied or has been so occupied only with other premises or as more than one residence,

and includes any yard, garden, out-houses or appurtenances which belong to that building or part or are to be enjoyed with it;

'relevant interest'—

(a) in relation to a new dwelling in England and Wales, means the freehold estate in the dwelling or a leasehold interest in the dwelling for a term of years absolute of more than twenty-one years, not being a term of which twenty-one years or less remains unexpired;

(b) in relation to a new dwelling in Scotland, means the dominium utile of the land comprising the dwelling, or a leasehold interest in the dwelling where twenty-one years or more remains unexpired.

24. Defences

(1) In any proceedings against a person for an offence under subsection (1) or (2) of section 20 above in respect of any indication it shall be a defence for that person to show that his acts or omissions were authorised for the purposes of this subsection by regulations made under section 26 below.

(2) In proceedings against a person for an offence under subsection (1) or (2) of section 20 above in respect of an indication published in a book, newspaper, magazine [or film or in a programme included in a programme service (within the meaning of the Broadcasting Act 1990),] it shall be a defence for that person to show that the indication was not contained in an advertisement.

(3) In proceedings against a person for an offence under subsection (1) or (2) of section 20 above in respect of an indication published in an advertisement it shall be a defence for that person to show that—

(a) he is a person who carries on a business of publishing or arranging for the publication of advertisements;

(b) he received the advertisement for publication in the ordinary course of that business; and

(c) at the time of publication he did not know and had no grounds for suspecting that the publication would involve the commission of the offence.

(4) In any proceedings against a person for an offence under subsection (1) of section 20 above in respect of any indication, it shall be a defence for that person to show that—

(a) the indication did not relate to the availability from him of any goods, services, accommodation or facilities;

(b) a price had been recommended to every person from whom the goods, services, accommodation or facilities were indicated as being available;

(c) the indication related to that price and was misleading as to that price only by reason of a failure by any person to follow the recommendation; and

(d) it was reasonable for the person who gave the indication to assume that the recommendation was for the most part being followed.

(5) The provisions of this section are without prejudice to the provisions of section 39 below.

(6) In this section—

'advertisement' includes a catalogue, a circular and a price list.

25. Code of practice

(1) The Secretary of State may, after consulting the Director General of Fair Trading and such other persons as the Secretary of State considers it appropriate to consult, by order approve any code of practice issued (whether by the Secretary of State or another person) for the purpose of—

(a) giving practical guidance with respect to any of the requirements of section 20 above; and

(b) promoting what appear to the Secretary of State to be desirable practices as to the circumstances and manner in which any person gives an indication as to the price at which any goods, services, accommodation or facilities are available or indicates any other matter in respect of which any such indication may be misleading.

(2) A contravention of a code of practice approved under this section shall not of itself give rise to any criminal or civil liability, but in any proceedings against any person for an offence under section 20(1) or (2) above—

(a) any contravention by that person of such a code may be relied on in relation to any matter for the purpose of establishing that that person committed the offence or of negativing any defence; and

(b) compliance by that person with such a code may be relied on in relation to any matter for the purpose of showing that the commission of the offence by that person has not been established or that that person has a defence.

(3) Where the Secretary of State approves a code of practice under this section he may, after such consultation as is mentioned in subsection (1) above, at any time by order—

(a) approve any modification of the code; or

(b) withdraw his approval;

and references in subsection (2) above to a code of practice approved under this section shall be construed accordingly.

(4) The power to make an order under this section shall be exercisable by statutory instrument subject to annulment in pursuance of a resolution of either House of Parliament.

26. Power to make regulations

(1) The Secretary of State may, after consulting the Director General of Fair Trading and such other persons as the Secretary of State considers it appropriate to consult, by regulations make provision—

(a) for the purpose of regulating the circumstances and manner in which any person—

(i) gives any indication as to the price at which any goods, services, accommodation or facilities will be or are available or have been supplied or provided; or

(ii) indicates any other matter in respect of which any such indication may be misleading;

(b) for the purpose of facilitating the enforcement of the provisions of section 20 above or of any regulations made under this section.

(2) The Secretary of State shall not make regulations by virtue of subsection (1)(a) above except in relation to—

(a) indications given by persons in the course of business; and

(b) such indications given otherwise than in the course of business as—

(i) are given by or on behalf of persons by whom accommodation is provided to others by means of leases or licences; and

(ii) relate goods, services or facilities supplied or provided to those others in connection with the provision of the accommodation.

(3) Without prejudice to the generality of subsection (1) above, regulations under this section may—

(a) prohibit an indication as to a price from referring to such matters as may be prescribed by the regulations;

(b) require an indication as to a price or other matter to be accompanied or supplemented by such explanation or such additional information as may be prescribed by the regulations;

(c) require information or explanations with respect to a price or other matter to be given to an officer of an enforcement authority and to authorise such an officer to require such information or explanations to be given;

(d) require any information or explanation provided for the purposes of any regulations made by virtue of paragraph (b) or (c) above to be accurate;

(e) prohibit the inclusion in indications as to a price or other matter of statements that the indications are not to be relied upon;

(f) provide that expressions used in any indication as to a price or other matter shall be construed in a particular way for the purposes of this Part;

(g) provide that a contravention of any provision of the regulations shall constitute a criminal offence punishable—

(i) on conviction on indictment, by a fine;

(ii) on summary conviction, by a fine not exceeding the statutory maximum;

(h) apply any provision of this Act which relates to a criminal offence created by virtue of paragraph (g) above.

(4) The power to make regulations under this section shall be exercisable by statutory instrument subject to annulment in pursuance of a resolution of either House of Parliament and shall include power—

(a) to make different provision for different cases; and

(b) to make such supplemental, consequential and transitional provision as the Secretary of State considers appropriate.

(5) In this section 'lease' includes a sub-lease and an agreement for a lease and a statutory tenancy (within the meaning of the Landlord and Tenant Act 1985 or the Rent (Scotland) Act 1984).

PART IV
ENFORCEMENT OF PARTS II AND III

27. Enforcement

(1) Subject to the following provisions of this section—

(a) it shall be the duty of every weights and measures authority in Great Britain to enforce within their area the safety provisions and the provisions made by or under Part III of this Act; and

(b) it shall be the duty of every district council in Northern Ireland to enforce within their area the safety provisions.

(2) The Secretary of State may by regulations—

(a) wholly or partly transfer any duty imposed by subsection (1) above on a weights and measures authority or a district council in Northern Ireland to such other person who has agreed to the transfer as is specified in the regulations;

(b) relieve such an authority or council of any such duty so far as it is exercisable in relation to such goods as may be described in the regulations.

(3) The power to make regulations under subsection (2) above shall be exercisable by statutory instrument subject to annulment in pursuance of a resolution of either House of Parliament and shall include power—

(a) to make different provision for different cases; and

(b) to make such supplemental, consequential and transitional provision as the Secretary of State considers appropriate.

(4) Nothing in this section shall authorise any weights and measures authority, or any person whom functions are conferred by regulations under subsection (2) above, to bring proceedings in Scotland for an offence.

28. Test purchases

(1) An enforcement authority shall have power, for the purpose of ascertaining whether any safety provision or any provision made by or under Part III of this Act has been contravened in relation to any goods, services, accommodation or facilities—

(a) to make, or to authorise an officer of the authority to make, any purchase of any goods; or

(b) to secure, or to authorise an officer of the authority to secure, the provision of any services, accommodation or facilities.

(2) Where—

(a) any goods purchased under this section by or on behalf of an enforcement authority are submitted to a test; and

(b) the test leads to—

(i) the bringing of proceedings for an offence in respect of a contravention in relation to the goods of any safety provision or of any provision made by or under Part III of this Act or for the forfeiture of the goods under section 16 or 17 above; or

(ii) the serving of a suspension notice in respect of any goods; and

(c) the authority is requested to do so and it is practicable for the authority to comply with the request,

the authority shall allow the person from whom the goods were purchased or any person who is a party to the proceedings or has an interest in any goods to which the notice relates to have the goods tested.

(3) The Secretary of State may by regulations provide that any test of goods under this section by or on behalf of an enforcement authority shall—

(a) be carried out at the expense of the authority in a manner and by a person prescribed by or determined under the regulations; or

(b) be carried out either as mentioned in paragraph (a) above or by the authority in a manner prescribed by the regulations.

(4) The power to make regulations under subsection (3) above shall be exercisable by statutory instrument subject to annulment in pursuance of a resolution of either House of Parliament and shall include power—

(a) to make different provision for different cases; and

(b) to make such supplemental, consequential and transitional provision as the Secretary of State considers appropriate.

(5) Nothing in this section shall authorise the acquisition by or on behalf of an enforcement authority of any interest in land.

29. Powers of search etc.

(1) Subject to the following provisions of this Part, a duly authorised officer of an enforcement authority may at any reasonable hour and on production, if required, of his credentials exercise any of the powers conferred by the following provisions of this section.

(2) The officer may, for the purpose of ascertaining whether there has been any contravention of any safety provision or of any provision made by or under Part III of this Act, inspect any goods and enter any premises other than premises occupied only as a person's residence.

(3) The officer may, for the purpose of ascertaining whether there has been any contravention of any safety provision, examine any procedure (including any arrangements for carrying out a test) connected with the production of any goods.

(4) If the officer has reasonable grounds for suspecting that any goods are manufactured or imported goods which have not been supplied in the United Kingdom since they were manufactured or imported he may—

(a) for the purpose of ascertaining whether there has been any contravention of any safety provision in relation to the goods, require any person carrying on a business, or employed in connection with a business, to produce any records relating to the business;

(b) for the purpose of ascertaining (by testing or otherwise) whether there has been any such contravention, seize and detain the goods;

(c) take copies of, or of any entry in, any records produced by virtue of paragraph (a) above.

(5) If the officer has reasonable grounds for suspecting that there has been a contravention in relation to any goods of any safety provision or of any provision made by or under Part III of this Act, he may—

(a) for the purpose of ascertaining whether there has been any such contravention, require any person carrying on a business, or employed in connection with a business, to produce any records relating to the business;

(b) for the purpose of ascertaining (by testing or otherwise) whether there has been any such contravention, seize and detain the goods;

(c) take copies of, or of any entry in, any records produced by virtue of paragraph (a) above.

(6) The officer may seize and detain—

(a) any goods or records which he has reasonable grounds for believing may be required as evidence in proceedings for an offence in respect of a contravention of any safety provision or of any provision made by or under Part III of this Act;

(b) any goods which he has reasonable grounds for suspecting may be liable to be forfeited under section 16 or 17 above.

(7) If and to the extent that it is reasonably necessary to do so to prevent a contravention of any safety provision or of any provision made by or under Part III of this Act, the officer may, for the purpose of exercising his power under subsection (4), (5) or

(6) above to seize any goods or records—

(a) require any person having authority to do so to open any container or to open any vending machine; and

(b) himself open or break open any such container or machine where a requirement made under paragraph (a) above in relation to the container or machine has not been complied with.

30. Provisions supplemental to s. 29

(1) An officer seizing any goods or records under section 29 above shall inform the following persons that the goods or records have been so seized, that is to say—

(a) the person from whom they are seized; and

(b) in the case of imported goods seized on any premises under the control of the Commissioners of Customs and Excise, the importer of those goods (within the meaning of the Customs and Excise Management Act 1979).

(2) If a justice of the peace—

(a) is satisfied by any written information on oath that there are reasonable grounds for believing either—

(i) that any goods or records which any officer has power to inspect under section 29 above are on any premises and that their inspection is likely to disclose evidence that there has been a contravention of any safety provision or of any provision made by or under Part III of this Act; or

(ii) that such a contravention has taken place, is taking place or is about to take place on any premises; and

(b) is also satisfied by any such information either—

(i) that admission to the premises has been or is likely to be refused and that notice of intention to apply for a warrant under this section has been given to the occupier; or

(ii) that an application for admission, or the giving of such a notice, would defeat the object of entry or that the premises are unoccupied or that the occupier is temporarily absent and it might defeat the object of the entry to await his return, the justice may by warrant under his hand, which shall continue in force for a period of one month, authorise any officer of an enforcement authority to enter the premises, if need be by force.

(3) An officer entering any premises by virtue of section 29 above or a warrant under subsection (2) above may take with him such other persons and such equipment as may appear to him necessary.

(4) On leaving any premises which a person is authorised to enter by a warrant under subsection (2) above, that person shall, if the premises are unoccupied or the occupier is temporarily absent, leave the premises as effectively secured against trespassers as he found them.

(5) If any person who is not an officer of an enforcement authority purports to act as such under section 29 above of this section he shall be guilty of an offence and liable on summary conviction to a fine not exceeding level 5 on the standard scale.

(6) Where any goods seized by an officer under section 29 above are submitted to a test, the officer shall inform the persons mentioned in subsection (1) above of the result of the test and, if—

(a) proceedings are brought for an offence in respect of a contravention in relation to the goods of any safety provision or of any provision made by or under Part III of this Act or for the forfeiture of the goods under section 16 or 17 above, or a suspension notice is served in respect of any goods; and

(b) the officer is requested to do so and it is practicable to comply with the request, the officer shall allow any person who is a party to the proceedings or, as the case may be, has an interest in the goods to which the notice relates to have the goods tested.

(7) The Secretary of State may by regulations provide that any test of goods seized under section 29 above by an officer of an enforcement authority shall—

(a) be carried out at the expense of the authority in a manner and by a person prescribed by or determined under the regulations; or

(b) be carried out either as mentioned in paragraph (a) above or by the authority in a manner prescribed by the regulations.

(8) The power to make regulations under subsection (7) above shall be exercisable by statutory instrument subject to annulment in pursuance of a resolution of either House of Parliament and shall include power—

(a) to make different provision for different cases; and

(b) to make such supplemental, consequential and transitional provisions as the Secretary of State considers appropriate.

(9) In the application of this section to Scotland, the reference in subsection (2) above to a justice of the peace shall include a reference to a sheriff and the references to written information on oath shall be construed as references to evidence on oath.

(10) In the application of this section to Northern Ireland, the references in subsection (2) above to any information on oath shall be construed as references to any complaint on oath.

31. Power of customs officer to detain goods

(1) A customs officer may, for the purpose of facilitating the exercise by an enforcement authority or officer of such an authority of any functions conferred on the authority or officer by or under Part II of this Act, or by or under this Part in its application for the purposes of the safety provisions, seize any imported goods and detain them for not more than two working days.

(2) Anything seized and detained under this section shall be dealt with during the period of its detention in such manner as the Commissioners of Customs and Excise may direct.

(3) In subsection (1) above the reference to two working days is a reference to a period of forty-eight hours calculated from the time when the goods in question are seized but disregarding so much of any period as falls on a Saturday or Sunday or on Christmas Day, Good Friday or a day which is a bank holiday under the Banking and Financial Dealings Act 1971 in the part of the United Kingdom where the goods are seized.

(4) In this section and section 32 below 'customs officer' means any officer within the meaning of the Customs and Excise Management Act 1979.

32. Obstruction of authorised officer

(1) Any person who

(a) intentionally obstructs any officer of an enforcement authority who is acting in pursuance of any provision of this Part or any customs officer who is so acting; or

(b) intentionally fails to comply with any requirements made of him by any officer of an enforcement authority under any provision of this Part, or

(c) without reasonable cause fails to give any officer of an enforcement authority who is so acting any other assistance or information which the officer may reasonably require of him for the purposes of the exercise of the officer's functions under any provision of this Part,

shall be guilty of an offence and liable on summary conviction to a fine not exceeding level 5 on the standard scale.

(2) A person shall be guilty of an offence if, in giving any information which is required of him by virtue of subsection (1)(c) above—

(a) he makes any statement which he knows is false in a material particular, or

(b) he recklessly makes a statement which is false in a material particular.

(3) A person guilty of an offence under subsection (2) above shall be liable—

(a) on conviction on indictment to a fine;

(b) on summary conviction, to a fine not exceeding the statutory maximum.

33. Appeals against detention of goods

(1) Any person having an interest in any goods which are for the time being detained under any provision of this Part by an enforcement authority or by an officer of such an authority may apply for an order requiring the goods to be released to him or to another person.

(2) An application under this section may be made—

(a) to any magistrates' court in which proceedings have been brought in England and Wales or Northern Ireland—

(i) for an offence in respect of a contravention in relation to the goods of any safety provision or of any provision made by or under Part III of this Act; or

(ii) for the forfeiture of the goods under section 16 above;

(b) where no such proceedings have been so brought, by way of complaint to a magistrates' court; or

(c) makes an order under section 16 or 17 above for the forfeiture of any goods.

(2) The court may (in addition to any other order it may make as to costs or expenses) order the person convicted or, as the case may be, any person having an interest in the goods to reimburse an enforcement authority for any expenditure which has been or may be incurred by that authority—

(a) in connection with any seizure or detention of the goods by or on behalf of the authority; or

(b) in connection with any compliance by the authority with directions given by the court for the purposes of any order for the forfeiture of the goods.

PART V
MISCELLANEOUS AND SUPPLEMENTAL

36. Amendments of Part I of the Health and Safety at Work etc. Act 1974

. . .

37. Power of Commissioners of Customs and Excise to disclose information

(1) If they think it appropriate to do so for the purpose of facilitating the exercise by any person to whom subsection (2) below applies of any function conferred on that person by or under Part II of this Act, or by or under Part IV of this Act in its application for the purposes of the safety provisions, the Commissioners of Customs and Excise may authorise the disclosure to that person of any information obtained for the purposes of the exercise by the Commissioners of their functions in relation to imported goods.

(2) This subsection applies to an enforcement authority and to any officer of an enforcement authority.

(3) A disclosure of information made to any person under subsection (1) above shall be made in such manner as may be directed by the Commissioners of Customs and Excise and may be through such persons acting on behalf of that person as may be so directed.

(4) Information may be disclosed to a person under subsection (1) above whether or not the disclosure of the information has been requested by or on behalf of that person.

38. Restrictions on disclosure of information

(1) Subject to the following provisions of this section, a person shall be guilty of an offence if he discloses any information—

(a) which was obtained by him in consequence of its being given to any person in compliance with any requirement imposed by safety regulations or regulations under section 26 above;

(b) which consists in a secret manufacturing process or a trade secret and was obtained by him in consequence of the inclusion of the information—

(i) in written or oral representations made for the purposes of Part I or II of Schedule 2 to this Act; or

(ii) in a statement of a witness in connection with any such oral representations;

(c) which was obtained by him in consequence of the exercise by the Secretary of State of the power conferred by section 18 above;

(d) which was obtained by him in consequence of the exercise by any person of any power conferred by Part IV of this Act; or

(e) which was disclosed to or through him under section 37 above.

(2) Subsection (1) above shall not apply to a disclosure of information if the information is publicised information or the disclosure is made—

(a) for the purpose of facilitating the exercise of a relevant person's functions under this Act or any enactment or subordinate legislation mentioned in subsection (3) below;

(b) for the purposes of compliance with a Community obligation; or

(c) in connection with the investigation of any criminal offence or for the purposes of any civil or criminal proceedings.

(3) The enactments and subordinate legislation referred to in subsection (2)(a) above are—

(a) the Trade Descriptions Act 1968;

(b) Parts II and III and section 125 of the Fair Trading Act 1973;

(c) the relevant statutory provisions within the meaning of Part I of the Health and Safety at Work Act 1974 or within the meaning of the Health and Safety at Work (Northern Ireland) Order 1978;

(d) the Consumer Credit Act 1974;

[. . .]

(g) the Estate Agents Act 1979;

(h) the Competition Act 1980;

(i) the Telecommunications Act 1984;

(j) the Airports Act 1986;

(k) the Gas Act 1986;

(l) any subordinate legislation made (whether before or after the passing of this Act) for the purpose of securing compliance with the Directive of the Council of the European Communities, dated 10th September 1984 (No.84/450/EEC) on the approximation of the laws, regulations and administrative provisions of the member States concerning misleading advertising.

[(m) the Electricity Act 1989.]

[(n) the Electricity (Northern Ireland) Order 1992]

[(o) the Railways Act 1993]

[(p) the Competition Act 1998.]

(4) In subsection (2)(a) above the reference to a person's functions shall include a reference to any function of making, amending or revoking any regulations or order.

(5) A person guilty of an offence under this section shall be liable—

(a) on summary conviction, to a fine not exceeding the statutory maximum.

(b) on conviction on indictment, to imprisonment for a term not exceeding two years or to a fine or to both.

(6) In this section—

'publicised information' means any information which has been disclosed in any civil or criminal proceedings or is or has been required to be contained in a warning published in pursuance of a notice to warn; and

'relevant person' means any of the following, that is to say—

(a) a Minister of the Crown, Government department or Northern Ireland department;

(b) the [Competition] Commission, the Director General of Fair Trading, the Director General of Telecommunications or the Director General of Gas Supply [or the Director General of Electricity Supply or the Director General of Electricity Supply for Northern Ireland or the Rail Regulator];

(c) the Civil Aviation Authority;

(d) any weights and measures authority, any district council in Northern Ireland or any person on whom functions are conferred by regulations under section 27(2) above;

(e) any person who is an enforcing authority for the purposes of Part I of the Health and Safety at Work etc. Act 1974 or for the purposes of Part II of the Health and Safety at Work (Northern Ireland) Order 1978.

39. Defence of due diligence

(1) Subject to the following provisions of this section, in proceedings against any person for an offence to which this section applies it shall be a defence for that person to show that he took all reasonable steps and exercised all due diligence to avoid committing the offence.

(2) Where in any proceedings against any person for such an offence the defence provided by subsection (1) above involves an allegation that the commission of the offence was due—

(a) to the act or default of another; or

(b) to reliance on information given by another,

that person shall not, without the leave of the court, be entitled to rely on the defence unless, not less than seven clear days before the hearing of the proceedings, he has served a notice under subsection (3) below on the person bringing the proceedings.

(3) A notice under this subsection shall give such information identifying or assisting in the identification of the person who committed the act or default or gave the information as is in the possession of the person serving the notice at the time he serves it.

(4) It is hereby declared that a person shall not be entitled to rely on the defence provided by subsection (1) above by reason of his reliance on information supplied by

another, unless he shows that it was reasonable in all the circumstances for him to have relied on the information, having regard in particular—

(a) to the steps which he took, and those which might reasonably have been taken, for the purpose of verifying the information, and

(b) to whether he had any reason to disbelieve the information.

(5) This section shall apply to an offence under section 10, 12(1), (2) or (3), 13(4), 14(6) or 20(1) above.

40. Liability of persons other than principal offender

(1) Where the commission by any person of an offence to which section 39 above applies is due to an act or default committed by some other person in the course of any business of his, the other person shall be guilty of the offence and may be proceeded against and punished by virtue of this subsection whether or not proceedings are taken against the first-mentioned person.

(2) Where a body corporate is guilty of an offence under this Act (including where it is so guilty by virtue of subsection (1) above) in respect of any act or default which is shown to have been committed with the consent or connivance of, or to be attributable to any neglect on the part of, any director, manager, secretary or other similar officer of the body corporate or any person who was purporting to act in any such capacity he, as well as the body corporate, shall be guilty of that offence and shall be liable to be proceeded against and punished accordingly.

(3) Where the affairs of a body corporate are managed by its members, subsection (2) above shall apply in relation to the acts and defaults of a member in connection with his functions of management as if he were a director of the body corporate.

41. Civil proceedings

(1) An obligation imposed by safety regulations shall be a duty owed to any person who may be affected by a contravention of the obligation and, subject to any provisions to the contrary in the regulations and to the defences and other incidents applying to actions for breach of statutory duty, a contravention of any such obligation shall be actionable accordingly.

(2) This Act shall not be construed as conferring any other right of action in civil proceedings, apart from the right conferred by virtue of Part I of this Act, in respect of any loss or damage suffered in consequence of a contravention of a safety provision or of a provision made by or under Part III of this Act.

(3) Subject to any provision to the contrary in the agreement itself, an agreement shall not be void or unenforceable by reason only of a contravention of a safety provision or of a provision made by or under Part III of this Act.

(4) Liability by virtue of subsection (1) above shall not be limited or excluded by any contract term, by any notice or (subject to the power contained in subsection (1) above to limit or exclude it in safety regulations) by any other provision.

(5) Nothing in subsection (1) above shall prejudice the operation of section 12 of the Nuclear Installations Act 1965 (rights to compensation for certain breaches of duties confined to rights under that Act).

(6) In this section 'damage' includes personal injury and death.

42. Reports etc.

(1) It shall be the duty of the Secretary of State at least once in every five years to lay before each House of Parliament a report on the exercise during the period to which the report relates of the functions which under Part II of this Act, or under Part IV of this Act in its application for the purposes of the safety provisions, are exercisable by the Secretary of State, weights and measures authorities, district councils in Northern Ireland and persons on whom functions are conferred by regulations made under section 27(2) above.

(2) The Secretary of State may from time to time prepare and lay before each House of Parliament such other reports on the exercise of those functions as he considers appropriate.

(3) Every weights and measures authority, every district council in Northern Ireland and every person on whom functions are conferred by regulations under subsection (2) of section 27 above shall, whenever the Secretary of State so directs, make a report to the Secretary of State on the exercise of the functions exercisable by that authority or council under that section or by that person by virtue of any such regulations.

(4) A report under subsection (3) above shall be in such form and shall contain such particulars as are specified in the direction of the Secretary of State.

(5) The first report under subsection (1) above shall be laid before each House of Parliament not more than five years after the laying of the last report under section 8(2) of the Consumer Safety Act 1978.

43. Financial provisions

(1) There shall be paid out of money provided by Parliament—

(a) any expenses incurred or compensation payable by a Minister of the Crown or Government department in consequence of any provision of this Act; and

(b) any increase attributable to this Act in the sums payable out of money so provided under any other Act.

(2) Any sums received by a Minister of the Crown or Government department by virtue of this Act shall be paid into the Consolidated Fund.

44. Service of documents etc.

(1) Any documents required or authorised by virtue of this Act to be served on a person may be so served—

(a) by delivering it to him or by leaving it at his proper address or by sending it by post to him at that address; or

(b) if the person is a body corporate, by serving it in accordance with paragraph (a) above on the secretary or clerk of that body; or

(c) if the person is a partnership, by serving it in accordance with that paragraph on a partner or on a person having control or management of the partnership business.

(2) For the purposes of subsection (1) above, and for the purposes of section 7 of the Interpretation Act 1978 (which relates to the service of documents by post) in its application to that subsection, the proper address of any person on whom a document is to be served by virtue of this Act shall be his last known address except that—

(a) in the case of service on a body corporate or its secretary or clerk, it shall be the address of the registered or principal office of the body corporate;

(b) in the case of service on a partnership or a partner or a person having the control or management of a partnership business, it shall be the principal office of the partnership;

and for the purposes of this subsection the principal office of a company registered outside the United Kingdom or of a partnership carrying on business outside the United Kingdom is its principal office within the United Kingdom.

(3) The Secretary of State may by regulations make provision for the manner in which any information is to be given to any person under any provision of Part IV of this Act.

(4) Without prejudice to the generality of subsection (3) above regulations made by the Secretary of State may prescribe the person, or manner of determining the person, who is to be treated for the purposes of section 28(2) or 30 above as the person from whom goods were purchased or seized where the goods were purchased or seized from a vending machine.

(5) The power to make regulations under subsection (3) or (4) above shall be exercisable by statutory instrument subject to annulment in pursuance of a resolution of either House of Parliament and shall include power—

(a) to make different provision for different cases; and

(b) to make such supplemental, consequential and transitional provision as the Secretary of State considers appropriate.

45. Interpretation

(1) In this Act, expect in so far as the context otherwise requires—

'aircraft' includes gliders, balloons and hovercraft;

'business' includes a trade or profession and the activities of a professional or trade association or of a local authority or other public authority;

'conditional sale agreement', 'credit-sale agreement' and 'hire-purchase agreement' have the same meanings as in the Consumer Credit Act 1974 but as if in the definitions in that Act 'goods' had the same meaning as in this Act;

'contravention' includes a failure to comply and cognate expressions shall be construed accordingly;

'enforcement authority' means the Secretary of State, any other Minister of the Crown in charge of a Government department, any such department and any authority, council or other person on whom functions under this Act are conferred by or under section 27 above;
'gas' has the same meaning as in Part I of the Gas Act 1986;
'goods' includes substances, growing crops and things comprised in land by virtue of being attached to it and any ship, aircraft or vehicle;
'information' includes accounts, estimates and returns;
'magistrates' court', in relation to Northern Ireland, means a court of summary jurisdiction;
'modifications' includes additions, alterations and omissions, and cognate expressions shall be construed accordingly;
'motor vehicle' has the same meaning as in the Road Traffic Act 1972;
'notice' means a notice in writing;
'notice to warn' means a notice under section 13(1)(b) above;
'officer', in relation to an enforcement authority, means a person authorised in writing to assist the authority in carrying out its functions under or for the purposes of the enforcement of any of the safety provisions or of any of the provisions made by or under Part III of this Act;
'personal injury' includes any disease and any other impairment of a person's physical or mental condition;
'premises' includes any place and any ship, aircraft or vehicle;
'prohibition notice' means a notice under section 13(1)(a) above;
'records' includes any books or documents and any records in non-documentary form;
'safety provision' means the general safety requirement in section 10 above or any provision of safety regulations, a prohibition notice or a suspension notice;
'safety regulations' means regulations under section 11 above;
'ship' includes any boat and any other description of vessel used in navigation;
'subordinate legislation' has the same meaning as in the Interpretation Act 1978;
'substance' means any natural or artificial substance, whether in solid, liquid or gaseous form or in the form of a vapour, and includes substances that are comprised in or mixed with other goods;
'supply' and cognate expressions shall be construed in accordance with section 46 below;
'suspension notice' means a notice under section 14 above.

(2) Except in so far as the context otherwise requires, references in this Act to a contravention of a safety provision shall, in relation to any goods, include references to anything which would constitute such a contravention if the goods were supplied to any person.

(3) References in this Act to any goods in relation to which any safety provision has been or may have been contravened shall include references to any goods which it is not reasonably practicable to separate from any such goods.

(4) Section 68(2) of the Trade Marks Act 1938 (construction of references to use of a mark) shall apply for the purposes of this Act as it applies for the purposes of that Act.

(5) In Scotland, any reference in this Act to things comprised in land by virtue of being attached to it is a reference to moveables which have become heritable by accession to heritable property.

46. Meaning of 'supply'

(1) Subject to the following provisions of this section, references in this Act to supplying goods shall be construed as references to doing any of the following, whether as principal or agent, that is to say—

(a) selling, hiring out or lending the goods;

(b) entering into a hire-purchase agreement to furnish the goods;

(c) the performance of any contract for work and materials to furnish the goods;

(d) providing the goods in exchange for any consideration (including trading stamps) other than money;

(e) providing the goods in or in connection with the performance of any statutory function; or

(f) giving the goods as a prize or otherwise making a gift of the goods;

and, in relation to gas or water, those references shall be construed as including references to providing the service by which the gas or water is made available for use.

(2) For the purposes of any reference in this Act to supplying goods, where a person ('the ostensible supplier') supplies goods to another person ('the customer') under a hire-purchase agreement, conditional sale agreement or credit-sale agreement or under an agreement for the hiring of goods (other than a hire-purchase agreement) and the ostensible supplier—

(a) carries on the business of financing the provision of goods for others by means of such agreements; and

(b) in the course of that business acquired his interest in the goods supplied to the customer as a means of financing the provision of them for the customer by a further person ('the effective supplier'),

the effective supplier and not the ostensible supplier shall be treated as supplying the goods to the customer.

(3) Subject to subsection (4) below, the performance of any contract by the erection of any building or structure on any land or by the carrying out of any other building works shall be treated for the purposes of this Act as a supply of goods in so far as, but only in so far as, it involves the provision of any goods to any person by means of their incorporation into the building, structure or works.

(4) Except for the purposes of, and in relation to, notices to warn or any provision made by or under Part III of this Act, references in this Act to supplying goods shall not include references to supplying goods comprised in land where the supply is effected by the creation or disposal of an interest in the land.

(5) Except in Part I of this Act references in this Act to a person's supplying goods shall be confined to references to that person's supplying goods in the course of a business of his, but for the purposes of this subsection it shall be immaterial whether the business is a business of dealing in the goods.

(6) For the purposes of subsection (5) above goods shall not be treated as supplied in the course of a business if they are supplied, in pursuance of an obligation arising under or in connection with the insurance of the goods, to the person with whom they were insured.

(7) Except for the purposes of, and in relation to, prohibition notices or suspension notices, references in Parts II to IV of this Act to supplying goods shall not include—

(a) references to supplying goods where the person supplied carries on a business of buying goods of the same description as those goods and repairing or reconditioning them,

(b) references to supplying goods by a sale of articles as scrap (that is to say, for the value of materials included in the articles rather that for the value of the articles themselves).

(8) Where any goods have at any time been supplied by being hired out or lent to any person, neither a continuation or renewal of the hire or loan (whether on the same or different terms) nor any transaction for the transfer after that time of any interest in the goods to the person to whom they were hired or lent shall be treated for the purposes of this Act as a further supply of the goods to that person.

(9) A ship, aircraft or motor vehicle shall not be treated for the purposes of this Act as supplied to any person by reason only that services consisting in the carriage of goods or passengers in that ship, aircraft or vehicle, or in its use for any other purpose, are provided to that person in pursuance of an agreement relating to the use of the ship, aircraft or vehicle for a particular period or for particular voyages, flights or journeys.

47. Savings for certain privileges

(1) Nothing in this Act shall be taken as requiring any person to produce any records if he would be entitled to refuse to produce those records in any proceedings in any court on the ground that they are the subject of legal professional privilege or, in Scotland, that they contain a confidential communication made by or to an advocate or solicitor in that capacity, or as authorising any person to take possession of any records which are in the possession of a person who would be so entitled.

(2) Nothing in this Act shall be construed as requiring a person to answer any question or give any information if to do so would incriminate that person or that person's spouse.

48. Minor and consequential amendments and repeals

. . .

49. Northern Ireland

(1) This Act shall extend to Northern Ireland with the exception of—

(a) the provisions of Parts I and III;

(b) any provision amending or repealing an enactment which does not so extend; and

(c) any other provision so far as it has effect for the purposes of, or in relation to, a provision falling within paragraph (a) or (b) above.

. . .

50. Short title, commencement and transitional provision

(1) This Act may be cited as the Consumer Protection Act 1987.

(2) This Act shall come into force on such day as the Secretary of State may by order made by statutory instrument appoint, and different days may be so appointed for different provisions or for different purposes.

(3) The Secretary of State shall not make an order under subsection (2) above bringing into force the repeal of the Trade Descriptions Act 1972, a repeal of any provision of that Act or a repeal of that Act or of any provision of it for any purposes, unless a draft of the order has been laid before, and approved by a resolution of, each House of Parliament.

(4) An order under subsection (2) above bringing a provision into force may contain such transitional provision in connection with the coming into force of that provision as the Secretary of State considers appropriate.

(5) Without prejudice to the generality of the power conferred by subsection (4) above, the Secretary of State may by order provide for any regulations made under the Consumer Protection Act 1961 or the Consumer Protection Act (Northern Ireland) 1965 to have effect as if made under section 11 above and for any regulations to have effect with such modifications as he considers appropriate for that purpose.

(6) The power of the Secretary of State by order to make such provision as is mentioned in subsection (5) above, shall, in so far as it is not exercised by an order under subsection (2) above, be exercisable by statutory instrument subject to annulment in pursuance of a resolution of either House of Parliament.

(7) Nothing in this Act or in any order under subsection (2) above shall make any person liable by virtue of Part I of this Act for any damage caused wholly or partly by a defect in a product which was supplied to any person by its producer before the coming into force of Part I of this Act.

(8) Expressions used in subsection (7) above and in Part I of this Act have the same meaning in that subsection as in that Part.

SCHEDULES

Section 13

SCHEDULE 2
PROHIBITION NOTICES AND NOTICES TO WARN

PART I
PROHIBITION NOTICES

1. A prohibition notice in respect of any goods shall—

(a) state that the Secretary of State considers that the goods are unsafe;

(b) set out the reasons why the Secretary of State considers that the goods are unsafe;

(c) specify the day on which the notice is to come into force; and

(d) state that the trader may at any time make representations in writing to the Secretary of State for the purpose of establishing that the goods are safe.

2.—(1) If representations in writing about a prohibition notice are made by the trader to the Secretary of State, it shall be the duty of the Secretary of State to consider whether to revoke the notice and—

(a) if he decides to revoke it, to do so;

(b) in any other case, to appoint a person to consider those representations, any further representations made (whether in writing or orally) by the trader about the notice and the statements of any witnesses examined under this Part of this Schedule.

(2) Where the Secretary of State has appointed a person to consider representations about a prohibition notice, he shall serve a notification on the trader which—

(a) states that the trader may make oral representations to the appointed person for the purpose of establishing that the goods to which the notice relates are safe; and

(b) specifies the place and time at which the oral representations may be made.

(3) The time specified in a notification served under sub-paragraph (2) above shall not be before the end of the period of twenty-one days beginning with the day on which the notification is served, unless the trader otherwise agrees.

(4) A person on whom a notification has been served under sub-paragraph (2) above or his representative may, at the place and time specified in the notification—

(a) make oral representations to the appointed person for the purpose of establishing that the goods in question are safe; and

(b) call and examine witnesses in connection with representations.

3.—(1) Where representations in writing about a prohibition notice are made by the trader to the Secretary of State at any time after a person has been appointed to consider representations about that notice, then, whether or not the appointed person has made a report to the Secretary of State, the following provisions of this paragraph shall apply instead of paragraph 2 above.

(2) The Secretary of State shall, before the end of the period of one month beginning with the day on which he receives the representations, serve a notification on the trader which states—

(a) that the Secretary of State has decided to revoke the notice, has decided to vary it or, as the case may be, has decided neither to revoke nor to vary it; or

(b) that, a person having been appointed to consider representations about the notice, the trader may, at a place and time specified in the notification, make oral representations to the appointed person for the purpose of establishing that the goods to which the notice relates are safe.

(3) The time specified in a notification served for the purposes of sub-paragraph (2)(b) above shall not be before the end of the period of twenty-one days beginning with the day on which the notification is served, unless the trader otherwise agrees or the time is the time already specified for the purposes of paragraph 2(2)(b) above.

(4) A person on whom a notification has been served for the purposes of sub-paragraph (2)(b) above or his representative may, at the place and time specified in the notification—

(a) make oral representations to the appointed person for the purpose of establishing that the goods in question are safe; and

(b) call and examine witnesses in connection with the representations.

4.—(1) Where a person is appointed to consider representations about a prohibition notice, it shall be his duty to consider—

(a) any written representations made by the trader about the notice, other than those in respect of which a notification is served under paragraph 3(2)(a) above;

(b) any oral representations made under paragraph 2(4) or 3(4) above; and

(c) any statements made by witnesses in connection with the oral representations, and after considering any matters under this paragraph, to make a report (including recommendations) to the Secretary of State about the matters considered by him and the notice.

(2) It shall be the duty of the Secretary of State to consider any report made to him under sub-paragraph (1) above and, after considering the report, to inform the trader of his decision with respect to the prohibition notice to which the report relates.

5.—(1) The Secretary of State may revoke or vary a prohibition notice by serving on the trader a notification stating that the notice is revoked or, as the case may be, is varied as specified in the notification.

(2) The Secretary of State shall not vary a prohibition notice so as to make the effect of the notice more restrictive for the trader.

(3) Without prejudice to the power conferred by section 13(2) of this Act, the service of a notification under sub-paragraph (1) above shall be sufficient to satisfy the requirement of paragraph 4(2) above that the trader shall be informed of the Secretary of State's decision.

PART II
NOTICES TO WARN

6.—(1) If the Secretary of State proposes to serve a notice to warn on any person in respect of any goods, the Secretary of State, before he serves the notice shall serve on that person a notification which—

(a) contains a draft of the proposed notice;

(b) states that the Secretary of State proposes to serve a notice in the form of the draft on that person;

(c) states that the Secretary of State considers that the goods described in the draft are unsafe;

(d) sets out the reasons why the Secretary of State considers that those goods are unsafe; and

(e) states that that person may make representations to the Secretary of State for the purpose of establishing that the goods are safe if, before the end of the period of fourteen days beginning with the day on which the notification is served, he informs the Secretary of State—

(i) of his intention to make representations; and

(ii) whether the representations will be made only in writing or both in writing and orally.

(2) Where the Secretary of State has served a notification containing a draft of a proposed notice to warn on any person, he shall not serve a notice to warn on that person in respect of the goods to which the proposed notice relates unless—

(a) the period of fourteen days beginning with the day on which the notification was served expires without the Secretary of State being informed as mentioned in subparagraph (1)(e) above;

(b) the period of twenty-eight days beginning with that day expires without any written representations being made by that person to the Secretary of State about the proposed notice; or

(c) the Secretary of State has considered a report about the proposed notice by a person appointed under paragraph 7(1) below.

7.—(1) Where a person on whom a notification containing a draft of a proposed notice to warn has been served—

(a) informs the Secretary of State as mentioned in paragraph 6(1)(e) above before the end of the period of fourteen days beginning with the day on which the notification was served; and

(b) makes written representations to the Secretary of State about the proposed notice before the end of the period of twenty-eight days beginning with that day, the Secretary of State shall appoint a person to consider those representations, any further representations made by that person about the draft notice and the statements of any witnesses examined under this Part of this Schedule.

(2) Where—

(a) the Secretary of State has appointed a person to consider representations about a proposed notice to warn; and

(b) the person whose representations are to be considered has informed the Secretary of State for the purposes of paragraph 6(1)(e) above that the representations he intends to make will include oral representations,

the Secretary of State shall inform the person intending to make the representations of the place and time at which oral representations may be made to the appointed person.

(3) Where a person on whom a notification containing a draft of a proposed notice to warn has been served is informed of a time for the purposes of sub-paragraph (2) above, that time shall not be—

(a) before the end of the period of twenty-eight days beginning with the day on which the notification was served; or

(b) before the end of the period of seven days beginning with the day on which that person is informed of the time.

(4) A person who has been informed of a place and time for the purposes of subparagraph (2) above or his representative may, at that place and time—

(a) make oral representations to the appointed person for the purpose of establishing that the goods to which the proposed notice relates are safe; and

(b) call and examine witnesses in connection with the representations.

8.—(1) Where a person is appointed to consider representations about a proposed notice to warn, it shall be his duty to consider—

(a) any written representations made by the person on whom it is proposed to serve the notice; and

(b) in a case where a place and time has been appointed under paragraph 7(2) above for oral representations to be made by that person or his representative, any representations so made and any statements made by witnesses in connection with those representations, and, after considering those matters to make a report (including recommendations) to the Secretary of State about the matters considered by him and the proposal to serve the notice.

(2) It shall be the duty of the Secretary of State to consider any report made to him under sub-paragraph (1) above, and after considering the report, to inform the person on whom it was proposed that a notice to warn should be served of his decision with respect to the proposal.

(3) If at any time after serving a notification on a person under paragraph 6 above the Secretary of State decides not to serve on that person either the proposed notice to warn or that notice with modifications, the Secretary of State shall inform that person of the decision, and nothing done for the purposes of any of the preceding provisions of this Part of this Schedule before that person was so informed shall—

(a) entitle the Secretary of State subsequently to serve the proposed notice or the notice with modifications; or

(b) require the Secretary of State, or any person appointed to consider representations about the proposed notice, subsequently to do anything in respect of, or in consequence of, any such representations.

(4) Where a notification containing a draft of a proposed notice to warn is served on a person in respect of any goods, a notice to warn served on him in consequence of a decision made under sub-paragraph (2) above shall either be in the form of the draft or shall be less onerous than the draft.

(9) The Secretary of State may revoke a notice to warn by serving on the person on whom the notice was served a notification stating that the notice is revoked.

PART III
GENERAL

10.—(1) Where in a notification served on any person under this Schedule the Secretary of State has appointed a time for the making of oral representations or the examination of witnesses, he may, by giving that person such notification as the Secretary of State considers appropriate, change that time to a later time or appoint further times at which further representations may be made or the examination of witnesses may be continued; and paragraphs 2(4), 3(4) and 7(4) above shall have effect accordingly.

(2) For the purposes of this Schedule the Secretary of State may appoint a person (instead of the appointed person) to consider any representations or statements, if the person originally appointed, or last appointed under this sub-paragraph, to consider those representations or statements has died or appears to the Secretary of State to be otherwise unable to act.

11. In this Schedule—

'the appointed person' in relation to a prohibition notice or a proposal to serve a notice to warn, means the person for the time being appointed under this Schedule to consider representations about the notice or, as the case may be, about the proposed notice;

'notification' means a notification in writing;

'trader', in relation to a prohibition notice, means the person on whom the notice is or was served.

CONTRACTS (RIGHTS OF THIRD PARTIES) ACT 1999
(1999, c. 31)

An Act to make provision for the enforcement of contractual terms by third parties.

[11th November 1999]

1. Right of third party to enforce contractual term

(1) Subject to the provisions of this Act, a person who is not a party to a contract (a 'third party') may in his own right enforce a term of the contract if—

(a) the contract expressly provides that he may, or

(b) subject to subsection (2), the term purports to confer a benefit on him.

(2) Subsection (1)(b) does not apply if on a proper construction of the contract it appears that the parties did not intend the term to be enforceable by the third party.

(3) The third party must be expressly identified in the contract by name, as a member of a class or as answering a particular description but need not be in existence when the contract is entered into.

(4) This section does not confer a right on a third party to enforce a term of a contract otherwise than subject to and in accordance with any other relevant terms of the contract.

(5) For the purpose of exercising his right to enforce a term of the contract, there shall be available to the third party any remedy that would have been available to him in an action for breach of contract if he had been a party to the contract (and the rules relating to damages, injunctions, specific performance and other relief shall apply accordingly).

(6) Where a term of a contract excludes or limits liability in relation to any matter references in this Act to the third party enforcing the term shall be construed as references to his availing himself of the exclusion or limitation.

(7) In this Act, in relation to a term of a contract which is enforceable by a third party—

'the promisor' means the party to the contract against whom the term is enforceable by the third party, and

'the promisee' means the party to the contract by whom the term is enforceable against the promisor.

2. Variation and rescission of contract

(1) Subject to the provisions of this section, where a third party has a right under section 1 to enforce a term of the contract, the parties to the contract may not, by agreement, rescind the contract, or vary it in such a way as to extinguish or alter his entitlement under that right, without his consent if—

(a) the third party has communicated his assent to the term to the promisor,

(b) the promisor is aware that the third party has relied on the term, or

(c) the promisor can reasonably be expected to have foreseen that the third party would rely on the term and the third party has in fact relied on it.

(2) The assent referred to in subsection (1)(a)—

(a) may be by words or conduct, and

(b) if sent to the promisor by post or other means, shall not be regarded as communicated to the promisor until received by him.

(3) Subsection (1) is subject to any express term of the contract under which—

(a) the parties to the contract may by agreement rescind or vary the contract without the consent of the third party, or

(b) the consent of the third party is required in circumstances specified in the contract instead of those set out in subsection (1)(a) to (c).

(4) Where the consent of a third party is required under subsection (1) or (3), the court or arbitral tribunal may, on the application of the parties to the contract, dispense with his consent if satisfied—

(a) that his consent cannot be obtained because his whereabouts cannot reasonably be ascertained, or

(b) that he is mentally incapable of giving his consent.

(5) The court or arbitral tribunal may, on the application of the parties to a contract, dispense with any consent that may be required under subsection (1)(c) if satisfied that it cannot reasonably be ascertained whether or not the third party has in fact relied on the term.

(6) If the court or arbitral tribunal dispenses with a third party's consent, it may impose such conditions as it thinks fit, including a condition requiring the payment of compensation to the third party.

(7) The jurisdiction conferred on the court by subsections (4) to (6) is exercisable by both the High Court and a county court.

3. Defences etc. available to promisor

(1) Subsections (2) to (5) apply where, in reliance on section 1, proceedings for the enforcement of a term of a contract are brought by a third party.

(2) The promisor shall have available to him by way of defence or set-off any matter that—

(a) arises from or in connection with the contract and is relevant to the term, and

(b) would have been available to him by way of defence or set-off if the proceedings had been brought by the promisee.

(3) The promisor shall also have available to him by way of defence or set-off any matter if—

(a) an express term of the contract provides for it to be available to him in proceedings brought by the third party, and

(b) it would have been available to him by way of defence or set-off if the proceedings had been brought by the promisee.

(4) The promisor shall also have available to him—

(a) by way of defence or set-off any matter, and

(b) by way of counterclaim any matter not arising from the contract,

that would have been available to him by way of defence or set-off or, as the case may be, by way of counterclaim against the third party if the third party had been a party to the contract.

(5) Subsections (2) and (4) are subject to any express term of the contract as to the matters that are not to be available to the promisor by way of defence, set-off or counterclaim.

(6) Where in any proceedings brought against him a third party seeks in reliance on section 1 to enforce a term of a contract (including, in particular, a term purporting to exclude or limit liability), he may not do so if he could not have done so (whether by reason of any particular circumstances relating to him or otherwise) had he been a party to the contract.

4. Enforcement of contract by promisee

Section 1 does not affect any right of the promisee to enforce any term of the contract.

5. Protection of promisor from double liability

Where under section 1 a term of a contract is enforceable by a third party, and the promisee has recovered from the promisor a sum in respect of—

(a) the third party's loss in respect of the term, or

(b) the expense to the promisee of making good to the third party the default of the promisor,

then, in any proceedings brought in reliance on that section by the third party, the court or arbitral tribunal shall reduce any award to the third party to such extent as it thinks appropriate to take account of the sum recovered by the promisee.

6. Exceptions

(1) Section 1 confers no rights on a third party in the case of a contract on a bill of exchange, promissory note or other negotiable instrument.

(2) Section 1 confers no rights on a third party in the case of any contract binding on a company and its members under section 14 of the Companies Act 1985.

(3) Section 1 confers no right on a third party to enforce—

(a) any term of a contract of employment against an employee,

(b) any term of a worker's contract against a worker (including a home worker), or

(c) any term of a relevant contract against an agency worker.

(4) In subsection (3)—

(a) 'contract of employment', 'employee', 'worker's contract', and 'worker' have the meaning given by section 54 of the National Minimum Wage Act 1998,

(b) 'home worker' has the meaning given by section 35(2) of that Act,

(c) 'agency worker' has the same meaning as in section 34(1) of that Act, and

(d) 'relevant contract' means a contract entered into, in a case where section 34 of that Act applies, by the agency worker as respects work falling within subsection (1)(a) of that section.

(5) Section 1 confers no rights on a third party in the case of—

(a) a contract for the carriage of goods by sea, or

(b) a contract for the carriage of goods by rail or road, or for the carriage of cargo by air, which is subject to the rules of the appropriate international transport convention,

except that a third party may in reliance on that section avail himself of an exclusion or limitation of liability in such a contract.

(6) In subsection (5) 'contract for the carriage of goods by sea' means a contract of carriage—

(a) contained in or evidenced by a bill of lading, sea waybill or a corresponding electronic transaction, or

(b) under or for the purposes of which there is given an undertaking which is contained in a ship's delivery order or a corresponding electronic transaction.

(7) For the purposes of subsection (6)—

(a) 'bill of lading', 'sea waybill' and 'ship's delivery order' have the same meaning as in the Carriage of Goods by Sea Act 1992, and

(b) a corresponding electronic transaction is a transaction within section 1(5) of that Act which corresponds to the issue, indorsement, delivery or transfer of a bill of lading, sea waybill or ship's delivery order.

(8) In subsection (5) 'the appropriate international transport convention' means—

(a) in relation to a contract for the carriage of goods by rail, the Convention which has the force of law in the United Kingdom under section 1 of the International Transport Conventions Act 1983,

(b) in relation to a contract for the carriage of goods by road, the Convention which has the force of law in the United Kingdom under section 1 of the Carriage of Goods by Road Act 1965, and

(c) in relation to a contract for the carriage of cargo by air—

(i) the Convention which has the force of law in the United Kingdom under section 1 of the Carriage by Air Act 1961, or

(ii) the Convention which has the force of law under section 1 of the Carriage by Air (Supplementary Provisions) Act 1962, or

(iii) either of the amended Conventions set out in Part B of Schedule 2 or 3 to the Carriage by Air Acts (Application of Provisions) Order 1967.

7. Supplementary provisions relating to third party

(1) Section 1 does not affect any right or remedy of a third party that exists or is available apart from this Act.

(2) Section 2(2) of the Unfair Contract Terms Act 1977 (restriction on exclusion etc. of liability for negligence) shall not apply where the negligence consists of the breach of an obligation arising from a term of a contract and the person seeking to enforce it is a third party acting in reliance on section 1.

(3) In sections 5 and 8 of the Limitation Act 1980 the references to an action founded on a simple contract and an action upon a specialty shall respectively include references to an action brought in reliance on section 1 relating to a simple contract and an action brought in reliance on that section relating to a specialty.

(4) A third party shall not, by virtue of section 1(5) or 3(4) or (6), be treated as a party to the contract for the purposes of any other Act (or any instrument made under any other Act).

8. Arbitration provisions

(1) Where—

(a) a right under section 1 to enforce a term ('the substantive term') is subject to a term providing for the submission of disputes to arbitration ('the arbitration agreement'), and

(b) the arbitration agreement is an agreement in writing for the purposes of Part I of the Arbitration Act 1996,

the third party shall be treated for the purposes of that Act as a party to the arbitration agreement as regards disputes between himself and the promisor relating to the enforcement of the substantive term by the third party.

(2) Where—

(a) a third party has a right under section 1 to enforce a term providing for one or more descriptions of dispute between the third party and the promisor to be submitted to arbitration ('the arbitration agreement'),

(b) the arbitration agreement is an agreement in writing for the purposes of Part I of the Arbitration Act 1996, and

(c) the third party does not fall to be treated under subsection (1) as a party to the arbitration agreement,

the third party shall, if he exercises the right, be treated for the purposes of that Act as a party to the arbitration agreement in relation to the matter with respect to which the right is exercised, and be treated as having been so immediately before the exercise of the right.

9. Northern Ireland

(1) In its application to Northern Ireland, this Act has effect with the modifications specified in subsections (2) and (3).

(2) In section 6(2), for 'section 14 of the Companies Act 1985' there is substituted 'Article 25 of the Companies (Northern Ireland) Order 1986'.

(3) In section 7, for subsection (3) there is substituted—

'(3) In Articles 4(a) and 15 of the Limitation (Northern Ireland) Order 1989, the references to an action founded on a simple contract and an action upon an instrument under seal shall respectively include references to an action brought in reliance on section 1 relating to a simple contract and an action brought in reliance on that section relating to a contract under seal.'.

. . .

10. Short title, commencement and extent

. . .

(2) This Act comes into force on the day on which it is passed but, subject to subsection (3), does not apply in relation to a contract entered into before the end of the period of six months beginning with that day.

(3) The restriction in subsection (2) does not apply in relation to a contract which—

(a) is entered into on or after the day on which this Act is passed, and

(b) expressly provides for the application of this Act.

(4) This Act extends as follows—

(a) section 9 extends to Northern Ireland only;

(b) the remaining provisions extend to England and Wales and Northern Ireland only.

EXPLANATORY NOTES

1. These explanatory notes have been prepared by the Lord Chancellor's Department in order to assist the reader in understanding the Act. They do not form part of the Act and have not been endorsed by Parliament.

Section 3: Defences etc. available to promisor

15. *Section 3* enables the promisor, in a claim by the third party, to rely on any defence or set-off arising out of the contract and relevant to the term being enforced, which would have been available to him had the claim been by the promisee. He may also rely on any defence or set-off, or make any counterclaim, where this would have been possible had the third party been a party to the contract.

16. *Subsection (2)* can be illustrated as follows—

(I) a third party can no more enforce a void, discharged or unenforceable contract than a promisee could;

(II) P1 (the promisor) and P2 (the promisee) contract that P2 will sell goods to P1, who will pay the contract price to P3 (the third party). In breach of contract, P2 delivers goods that are not of the standard contracted for. In an action for the price by P3 (just as in an action for the price by P2) P1 is entitled to reduce or extinguish the price by reason of the damages for breach of contract.

17. *Subsection (3)* can be illustrated as follows—

P1 and P2 contract that P1 will pay P3 if P2 transfers his car to P1. P2 owes P1 money under a wholly unrelated contract. P1 and P2 agree to an express term in the contract which provides that P1 can raise against a claim by P3 any matter which would have given P1 a defence or set-off to a claim by P2.

18. *Subsection (4)* makes it clear that the promisor also has available any defence or set-off, and any counterclaim not arising from the contract, which is specific to the third party. It can be illustrated as follows—

(I) P1 contracts with P2 to pay P3 £1000. P3 already owes P1 £600. P1 has a set-off to P3's claim so that P1 is only bound to pay P3 £400.

(II) P3 induced P1 to enter into the contract with P2 by misrepresentation, but P2 has no actual or constructive notice of that misrepresentation. P1 may have a defence (or a counterclaim for damages) against P3 which would not have been available had the action been brought by P2.

19. *Subsection (5)* makes subsections (2) and (4) subject to any express term of the contract which narrows the defences or set-offs available under section 3(2) or narrows the defences, set-offs or counterclaims available under section 3(4). For example—

(I) in relation to subsection (2), P2 agrees with P1 to purchase a painting, the painting to be delivered to P3, who is expressly given a right to enforce the delivery obligation. P2 owes P1 considerable sums for other art works purchased. P2 wishes to ensure that P3's right is not affected. P1 and P2 expressly agree that P1 may not raise against P3 defences and set-offs that would have been available to P1 in an action by P2.

(II) in relation to subsection (4), P1 agrees with P2 to pay £5000 to P3 if P2 will transfer a number of cases of wine to P1. P3 is in dispute with P1 over a prior contract and P1 alleges that P3 owes P1 money. P2 is concerned that P1 may seek to withhold part of the £5000 payable to P3 by raising a set-off or counterclaim against P3 in relation to the prior contract. Consequently P1 and P2 include an express term that P1 may raise no defences, set-offs or counterclaims of any nature whatever against a claim by P3 to enforce P1's obligation to pay the £5000.

20. *Subsection (6)* ensures that an analogous approach to that set out in subsections (2) to (5) applies where the proceedings are brought against the third party and he seeks to avail himself of, for example, an exclusion section.

STATUTORY INSTRUMENTS

CONSUMER CREDIT (AGREEMENTS) REGULATIONS 1983 (SI 1983, No. 1553)

1. Citation, commencement and interpretation

(1) These Regulations may be cited as the Consumer Credit (Agreements) Regulations 1983 and shall come into operation on 19 May 1985.

(2) In these Regulations, unless the context otherwise requires—

'the Act' means the Consumer Credit Act 1974;

'advance payment' includes any deposit and in relation to a regulated consumer credit agreement includes also any part-exchange allowance in respect of any goods agreed in antecedent negotiations to be taken by the creditor in part-exchange but does not include a repayment of credit or any insurance premium or any amount entering into the total charge for credit;

'the APR' means the annual percentage rate of charge for credit determined in accordance with the Total Charge for Credit Regulations and Schedule 7 to these Regulations and, in the case of modifying agreements, Regulation 7 of, and Part I of Schedule 8 to, these Regulations;

'cancellable agreement' includes an agreement which is a modifying agreement treated under section 82(5) of the Act as a cancellable agreement;

'cash price' in relation to any goods, services, land or other things means the price or charge at which the goods, services, land or other things may be purchased by, or supplied to, the debtor for cash;

['contract of insurance' has the same meaning as it has in the Insurance Companies Act 1982;]

'earlier credit agreement' means an earlier agreement for the provision of credit;

'earlier hire agreement' means an earlier agreement for the bailment or the hiring of goods;

['guarantee of goods' means anything in writing which contains or purports to contain some promise or assurance (however worded or presented) that defects in goods will be made good by complete or partial replacement, or by repair, monetary compensation or otherwise;]

'hire payment' means any payment to be made by the hirer in relation to any period in consideration of the bailment or hiring to him of goods under a regulated consumer hire agreement;

'lettering' includes figures and symbols;

'modified agreement' means an earlier agreement as varied or supplemented by a modifying agreement, which is treated as—

(a) revoking the earlier agreement, and

(b) containing provisions reproducing the combined effect of the two agreements;

'the relevant date' shall be determined in accordance with the Total Charge for Credit Regulations and, in the case of modifying agreements, Regulation 7(7) below;

'total charge for credit' shall be determined in accordance with the Total Charge for Credit Regulations and, in the case of modifying agreements, Regulation 7 of, and Part I of Schedule 8 to, these Regulations; and

'the Total Charge for Credit Regulations' means the Consumer Credit (Total Charge for Credit) Regulations 1980.

(3) In these Regulations, any reference to a repayment is a reference to—

(a) a repayment of the whole or any part of the credit;

(b) a payment of the whole or any part of the total charge for credit; or

(c) a combination of such repayments and payments.

2. Form and content of regulated consumer credit agreements

(1) Subject to [paragraphs (2) and (7A)] below, documents embodying regulated consumer credit agreements (other than modifying agreements) shall contain the information set out in Column 2 of Schedule 1 to these Regulations in so far as it relates to the type of agreement referred to in Column 1.

(2) Where any information about financial and related particulars set out in paragraphs 9 to 11 of Schedule 1 to these Regulations cannot be exactly ascertained by the creditor, estimated information based on such assumptions as the creditor may reasonably make in all the circumstances of the case and an indication of the assumptions made shall be included in documents embodying regulated consumer credit agreements.

(3) [Subject to paragraph (7A) below,] documents embodying regulated consumer credit agreements [other than agreements of the description specified in the Schedule to the Consumer Credit (Notices of Cancellation Rights) (Exemption) Regulations in relation to which there are no charges forming part of the total charge for credit] shall contain statements of the protection and remedies available to debtors under the Act, in the Form numbered in Column 1 of Part I of Schedule 2 to these Regulations and set out in Column 3, in so far as they relate to the type of agreement referred to in Column 2.

(4) Subject to paragraph (5) below, the information about financial and related particulars set out in paragraphs 3 to 19 of Schedule 1 to these Regulations, and also the statements of the protection and remedies available to debtors under the Act specified in Forms 5, [7 and 9] of Part I of Schedule 2, shall be shown together as a whole in documents embodying regulated consumer credit agreements and not interspersed with other information apart from subtotals of total amounts and cross-references to terms of the agreement:

Provided that the said statements specified in Forms 5, [7 and 9] of Part I of Schedule 2 need not be shown together as a whole with the said information about financial and related particulars, if a reference to those statements is shown together with the said information about financial and related particulars.

(5) In the case of documents embodying restricted-use debtor-creditor-supplier agreements for fixed-sum credit to finance a transaction comprising the acquisition of goods, services, land or other things specified in the agreement or identified and agreed on at the time the agreement is made and relating to more than one description of goods, services, land or other things, the cash prices, and the total cash price, referred to in paragraph 4 of Schedule 1 to these Regulations may be shown in a schedule to such document together with each description of the goods, services, land or other things, provided that the total cash price and a reference to the schedule to such document are shown together with the remaining financial and related particulars specified in paragraphs 5 to 19 of Schedule 1.

(6) The APR referred to in paragraphs 15 to 17 of Schedule 1 to these Regulations shall in documents embodying regulated consumer credit agreements [other than agreements of

the description specified in the Schedule to the Consumer Credit (Notice of Cancellation Rights) (Exemption) Regulations in relation to which there are no charges forming part of the total charge for credit]—

(a) be denoted as 'APR' or 'annual percentage rate' or 'annual percentage rate of the total charge for credit'; and

(b) be afforded no less prominence than any of the other financial and related particulars referred to in paragraphs 3 to 19 of Schedule 1 and the statements specified in Forms 5 to 10 of Part I of Schedule 2.

(7) [Subject to paragraph (7A) below,] documents embodying regulated consumer credit agreements [other than agreements of the description specified in the Schedule to the Consumer Credit (Notice of Cancellation Rights) (Exemption) Regulations in relation to which there are no charges forming part of the total charge for credit] shall contain a signature box in the Form numbered in Column 1 of Part I of Schedule 5 to these Regulations and set out in Column 3 in so far as it relates to the type of agreement referred to in Column 2 and shall, if the agreement is one to which section 58(1) of the Act applies, is a cancellable agreement or is an agreement under which a person takes any article in pawn and under which the pawn-receipt is not separate from the document embodying the agreement, contain a separate box immediately above, below or adjacent to the signature box in which shall be included the appropriate statements specified in Forms 1 to 4 of Part I, and in Part II, of Schedule 2.

(7A) Documents embodying a debtor-creditor-supplier agreement falling within section 12(a) of the Act or a debtor-creditor agreement (in this paragraph in either case referred to as 'the principal agreement') and also embodying, or containing the option of, a debtor-creditor-supplier agreement falling within section 12(b) of the Act (in this paragraph referred to as 'the subsidiary agreement') where the subsidiary agreement is to finance a premium under either or both of—

(a) a contract of insurance to provide a sum payable in the event of one or more of the following—

(i) accident;

(ii) sickness;

(iii) unemployment;

(iv) death only,

of a debtor before the credit under the principal agreement and the subsidiary agreement has been repaid, where the sum payable does not exceed the amount sufficient to defray the sums payable to the creditor in respect of that credit and of the total charge for credit and where the policy monies payable under the contract of insurance are to be used for a repayment under the principal agreement and the subsidiary agreement;

(b) any other contract in so far as it relates to a guarantee of goods,

may contain instead of the headings, statements of the protection and remedies available to debtors under the Act and signature boxes that would otherwise apply—

(aa) a heading and signature box in so far as they relate to the principal agreement;

(bb) a statement in Form 12 of Part I of Schedule 2 to these Regulations; and

(cc) other statements (other than in Form 14 of Part I of Schedule 2) of the protection and remedies available to debtors under the Act in so far as they relate to the principal agreement.

(8) Documents embodying regulated consumer credit agreements shall embody any security provided in relation to the regulated agreement by the debtor.

3. Form and content of regulated consumer hire agreements

(1) Subject to paragraph (2) below, documents embodying regulated consumer hire agreements (other than modifying agreements) shall contain the information set out in Column 2 of Schedule 3 to these Regulations in so far as it relates to the type of agreement referred to in Column 1.

(2) Where any information about financial and related particulars set out in paragraphs 5 and 6 of Schedule 3 to these Regulations cannot be exactly ascertained by the owner, estimated information based on such assumptions as the owner may reasonably make in all the circumstances of the case and an indication of the assumptions made shall be included in documents embodying regulated consumer hire agreements.

(3) Documents embodying regulated consumer hire agreements shall contain statements of the protection and remedies available to hirers under the Act, in the Form numbered in Column 1 of Schedule 4 to these Regulations and set out in Column 3, in so far as they relate to the type of agreement referred to in Column 2.

(4) Subject to paragraph (5) below, the information about financial and related particulars set out in paragraphs 3 to 8 of Schedule 3 to these Regulations shall be shown together as a whole in documents embodying regulated consumer hire agreements and not interspersed with other information apart from subtotals of total amounts and cross-references to terms of the agreement.

(5) In the case of documents embodying consumer hire agreements relating to more than one description of goods to be bailed or hired under the agreement, the list or other description of the goods referred to in paragraph 3 of Schedule 3 to these Regulations may be shown in a schedule to such document, provided that a reference to the schedule to such document is shown together with the remaining financial and related particulars specified in paragraphs 4 to 8 of Schedule 3.

(6) Documents embodying regulated consumer hire agreements shall contain a signature box in the Form numbered in Column 1 of Part II of Schedule 5 to these Regulations and set out in Column 3, in so far as it relates to the type of agreement referred to in Column 2 and shall, if the agreement is one to which section 58(1) of the Act applies or is a cancellable agreement, contain a separate box immediately above, below or adjacent to the signature box in which shall be included the appropriate statements specified in Forms 1 to 3 of Schedule 4.

(7) Documents embodying regulated consumer hire agreements shall embody any security provided in relation to the regulated agreement by the hirer.

4. Pawn-receipts

Where a pawn-receipt is given under section 114(1) of the Act, by a person who takes any article in pawn under a regulated consumer credit agreement or a modifying agreement varying or supplementing an earlier credit agreement which is, or is treated under section 82(3) of the Act as, a regulated agreement, and where the pawn-receipt is not separate from any document embodying such an agreement, it shall—

(a) contain the information set out in paragraphs 1, 2 and 20 of Schedule 1 to these Regulations, or, in the case of a modifying agreement varying or supplementing an earlier credit agreement, in paragraphs 1, 2 and 20 of Part I of Schedule 8; and

(b) contain a notice in the Form numbered 16 in Column 1 of Part II of Schedule 2 to these Regulations and set out in Column 3.

5. Statutory Forms

(1) The wording of any Form specified in Schedules 2, 4 and 5 to these Regulations shall be reproduced in documents embodying regulated agreements without any alteration or addition, except that—

(a) the words 'the creditor' or 'the owner' may be replaced by the name of the creditor or owner, by the expression by which the creditor or owner is referred to in the agreement or by an appropriate pronoun, and any consequential changes to pronouns and verbs or other consequential grammatical changes may be made:

(b) the word 'DEBTOR' may be replaced by 'BORROWER' or 'CUSTOMER' and the word 'Debtor(s)' may be replaced by 'Borrower(s)' or 'Customer(s)'; and

(c) every Form shall be completed in accordance with any footnote.

(2) Any such footnote shall not be treated as part of any Form specified in the said Schedules and may be reproduced in addition to any such Form.

(3) Where any such footnote requires any words to be omitted, those words shall be omitted or deleted.

(4) Where words are shown in capital letters in any Form specified in Schedule 2, 4 or 5 to these Regulations and are reproduced in documents embodying regulated agreements, they shall be afforded more prominence (whether by capital letters, underlining, large or bold print or otherwise) than any other lettering in that Form except lettering inserted in accordance with paragraph (1)(c) above and no less prominence than that given to any other information in the document apart from the heading to the document, the APR, trade names, names of parties to the agreement or lettering in the document inserted in handwriting.

6. Signing of agreement

(1) The terms specified in Column 2 of Schedule 6 to these Regulations in relation to the type of regulated agreement referred to in Column 1 (and no other terms) are hereby prescribed for the purposes of section 61(1)(a) of the Act (the terms which must be contained in a document if a regulated agreement is not to be improperly executed) and of section 127(3) (the terms which must be contained in a document before any enforcement order can be made under section 65(1), if section 61(1)(a) was not complied with).

(2) The lettering of the terms of the agreement included in the document referred to in section 61(1)(a) of the Act, containing all the prescribed terms of the regulated agreement, and of the information contained in that document for the purpose of conforming to these Regulations shall, apart from any signature, be easily legible and of a colour which is readily distinguishable from the colour of the paper.

(3) The signature of the said document shall be made in the following manner—

(a) by the debtor or hirer, or by or on behalf of the debtor or hirer in the case of a partnership or an unincorporated body of persons, in the space in the document indicated for the purpose, and, subject to sub-paragraph (c) below, the date of the signature shall be inserted in the space in the document indicated for the purpose;

(b) by the creditor or owner, or by a person on his behalf, outside any signature box in which the debtor or hirer may sign and, subject to sub-paragraph (c) below, the date of the signature shall be inserted outside any such signature box;

(c) in the case of a regulated agreement which is not a cancellable agreement, the date on which the unexecuted agreement becomes an executed agreement may be inserted in the document and in such a case any other date specified in paragraphs (a) and (b) above need not be inserted; and

(d) nothing in this Regulation shall prohibit the inclusion in the said document, near to any such signature, of the signature by any witness outside any signature box in which the debtor or hirer may sign.

(4) In Scotland any provision in paragraph (3) above requiring the said document to be signed shall be complied with by a body corporate if the document is properly executed in accordance with the law of Scotland.

7. Modifying agreements which are, or are treated as, regulated agreements

(1) The provisions of these Regulations shall apply to modifying agreements which vary or supplement earlier credit agreements or earlier hire agreements and which are, or are treated under section 82(3) of the Act as, regulated agreements, subject as hereinafter mentioned.

(2) Subject to paragraphs (3) and (12) below, documents embodying modifying agreements varying or supplementing earlier credit agreements shall contain the information set out in Column 2 of Part I of Schedule 8 to these Regulations in so far as it relates to the type of modifying agreement referred to in Column 1.

(3) Where any information about financial and related particulars set out in paragraphs 8 to 10 of Part I of Schedule 8 to these Regulations cannot be exactly ascertained by the creditor, estimated information based on such assumptions as the creditor may reasonably make in all the circumstances of the case and an indication of the assumptions made shall be included in documents embodying modifying agreements varying or supplementing earlier credit agreements.

(4) Subject to paragraph (5) below, the information about financial and related particulars set out in paragraphs 3 to 19 of Part I of Schedule 8 to these Regulations shall be shown together as a whole in documents embodying modifying agreements varying or supplementing earlier credit agreements in relation to the credit to be provided under the modified agreement and not interspersed with other information apart from subtotals of total amounts and cross-references to terms of the modifying agreement.

(5) In the case of documents embodying agreements varying or supplementing earlier restricted-use debtor-creditor-supplier agreements for fixed-sum credit which were to finance a transaction comprising the acquisition of goods, services, land or other things specified in the earlier agreement or identified and agreed on at the time the earlier agreement was made and relating to more than one description of goods, services, land or other things, the cash prices, and the total cash price, referred to in paragraph 3 of Part I of

Schedule 8 to these Regulations may be shown in a schedule to such document together with each description of the goods, services, land or other things, provided that the total cash price and a reference to the schedule to such document are shown together with the remaining financial and related particulars specified in paragraphs 4 to 19 of Part I of Schedule 8.

(6) The APR referred to in paragraphs 14 to 17 of Part I of Schedule 8 to these Regulations shall in documents embodying modifying agreements varying or supplementing earlier credit agreements—

(a) be denoted as 'APR' or 'annual percentage rate' or 'annual percentage rate of the total charge for credit'; and

(b) be afforded no less prominence than any of the other financial and related particulars referred to in paragraphs 3 to 19 of Part I of Schedule 8 and the statements specified in Forms 5 to 10 of Part I of Schedule 2.

(7) For the purposes of Part I of Schedule 8 to these Regulations, in calculating—

(a) the amount of repayments or of any capital outstanding under an earlier agreement;

(b) the total charge for credit (or any items included in it) in relation to the credit to be provided under the modified agreement; or

(c) the APR in relation to the modified agreement,

the relevant date shall be determined by reference to the date of the modifying agreement.

(8) For the purposes of Part I of Schedule 8 to these Regulations, the total cash price under the modified agreement shall be taken to be the total of—

(a) the total amount of the capital outstanding under the earlier agreement on the relevant date within the meaning of paragraph 5 of Part I of Schedule 8; and

(b) the cash price in relation to each list or other description of any additional goods, services, land or other things the acquisition of which is to be financed by credit under the modifying agreement.

(9) Subject to paragraphs (10), (12) and (15) below, documents embodying modifying agreements varying or supplementing earlier hire agreements shall contain the information set out in Column 2 to Part II of Schedule 8 to these Regulations in so far as it relates to the type of modifying agreement referred to in Column 1.

(10) Where the information about financial and related particulars set out in paragraphs 5 and 6 of Part II of Schedule 8 to these Regulations cannot be exactly ascertained by the owner, estimated information based on such assumptions as the owner may reasonably make in all the circumstances of the case and an indication of the assumptions made shall be included in documents embodying modifying agreements varying or supplementing earlier hire agreements.

(11) The information about financial and related particulars set out in paragraphs 3 to 8 of Part II of Schedule 8 to these Regulations shall be shown together as a whole in documents embodying modifying agreements varying or supplementing earlier hire agreements in relation to the goods to be bailed or hired under the modified agreement and not interspersed with other information apart from subtotals of total amounts and cross-references to terms of the modifying agreement.

(12) Where any information about financial and related particulars set out in paragraphs 3 to 19 of Schedule 1 to these Regulations and paragraphs 3 to 8 of Schedule 3 is contained in any document embodying an earlier agreement, nothing in the preceding provisions of this Regulation shall require the information to be contained in any document embodying a modifying agreement varying or supplementing an earlier agreement except as mentioned in Schedule 8 if the information is not varied or supplemented by the modifying agreement and the document contains a statement to this effect.

(13) Documents embodying modifying agreements shall identify clearly the terms and financial and related particulars of earlier agreements varied or supplemented by modifying agreements.

(14) In the application of Regulation 6(1) above and Schedule 6 to these Regulations to modifying agreements, which are, or are treated under section 82(3) of the Act as, regulated agreements—

(a) for any reference to the type of agreement referred to in Column 1 of Schedule 6 there shall be substituted a reference to modifying agreements which vary or supplement the type of agreement referred to in Column 1 of Schedule 6;

(b) any reference in Column 2 of Schedule 6 to an agreement, or a term, shall be a reference to a modified agreement, or a term of a modified agreement, as the case may be; and

(c) any term referred to in Column 2 of Schedule 6 in relation to the type of modifying agreement referred to in sub-paragraph (a) above shall not be a prescribed term for the purposes of sections 61(1)(a) and 127(3) of the Act, if the term was a term of the earlier agreement and has not been varied or supplemented by the modifying agreement.

(15) Where a modifying agreement varies or supplements an earlier hire agreement and the modified agreement is, or is treated as, a restricted-use debtor-creditor-supplier agreement, the provisions of this Regulation shall apply to any document embodying the modifying agreement as though it varied or supplemented an earlier restricted-use debtor-creditor-supplier agreement, except that its heading shall be 'Agreement modifying a Hire Agreement and regulated by the Consumer Credit Act 1974'.

8. Application of Regulations

(1) Subject to paragraph (2) below, Regulations 1 to 3 and 5 to 7 shall apply to regulated agreements, and modifying agreements treated under section 82(3) of the Act as regulated agreements, made on or after 19 May 1985.

(2) In the case of a modifying agreement of a type specified in paragraphs 3 to 19 of Part I and 3 to 8 of Part II of Schedule 8 to these Regulations made on or after 19 May 1985 which varies or supplements an earlier credit agreement or an earlier hire agreement made before that date, nothing in these Regulations shall require the information about financial and related particulars specified in those paragraphs to be contained in any document embodying the modifying agreement if no term of the earlier agreement relating to such financial and related particulars has been varied or supplemented by the modifying agreement.

(3) Nothing in these Regulations applies to a regulated agreement which purports to bind a person to enter as debtor or hirer into a prospective regulated agreement and which is excluded from the operation of section 59(1) of the Act by the Consumer Credit (Agreements to enter Prospective Agreements) (Exemptions) Regulations 1983.

Regulation 2(1) SCHEDULE I

INFORMATION TO BE CONTAINED IN DOCUMENTS EMBODYING REGULATED CONSUMER CREDIT AGREEMENTS OTHER THAN MODIFYING AGREEMENTS

Type of agreement (1)	*Information* (2)
	Nature of agreement
1. All types.	(1) A heading in one of the following forms of words shown prominently on the first page of the document: (a) 'Hire-Purchase Agreement regulated by the Consumer Credit Act 1974'; (b) 'Conditional Sale Agreement regulated by the Consumer Credit Act 1974'; or (c) 'Credit Agreement regulated by the Consumer Credit Act 1974', as the case may require. (2) Where the document and a pawn-receipt are combined, the words ', and Pawn-Receipt,' shall be inserted in the heading after the word 'Agreement'. (3) Where the document embodies an agreement of which at least one part is a credit agreement not regulated by the Act,

Type of agreement (1)	*Information* (2)
	the word 'partly' shall be inserted before 'regulated' unless the regulated and unregulated parts of the agreement are clearly separate.

Parties to agreement

2. All types.	(1) The name and a postal address of the creditor. (2) The name and a postal address of the debtor.

FINANCIAL AND RELATED PARTICULARS

Description of goods, services, land etc

3. Restricted-use debtor-creditor-supplier agreements for fixed-sum credit to finance a transaction comprising the acquisition of goods, services, land or other things specified in the agreement or identified and agreed on at the time the agreement is made.	A list or other description of the goods, services or other things and, in the case of land, a general description of the land, the acquisition of which is to be financed by credit under the agreement.

Cash price

4. Agreements falling within paragraph 3.	The cash price in relation to each list or other description of goods, services, land or other things, to be shown under paragraph 3 above, and the total cash price.

Advance payments

5. All types in relation to which any advance payment it to be made by the debtor (whether under the agreement or as a condition precedent to the making of the agreement) before he is provided with credit under the agreement or, as the case may be, before he enters into the agreement.	The amount of the advance payments to be made by the debtor and, in the case of a cancellable agreement, the nature of such payments.

Amount of credit

6. Agreements falling within paragraph 3 except agreements under which both: (a) the total amount payable by the debtor is not greater than the total cash price referred to in paragraph 4; and (b) there is no advance payment falling within paragraph 5.	The amount of the credit to be provided under the agreement, namely the difference between the total cash price to be shown under paragraph 4 above and the total of any advance payments to be shown under paragraph 5 above.
7. Agreements for fixed-sum credit not falling within paragraph 3.	The amount of the credit to be provided under the agreement.

Credit limit

8. Agreements for running-account credit.	The credit limit expressed as— (a) a sum of money; (b) a statement that the credit limit will be determined by the creditor from time to time under the agreement and that notice of it will be given by him to the debtor;

Type of agreement (1)	*Information* (2)
	(c) a sum of money together with a statement that the creditor may vary the credit limit to such sum as he may from time to time determine under the agreement and that notice of it will be given by him to the debtor; or (d) in a case not falling within head (a), (b) or (c) above, either a statement indicating the manner in which the credit limit will be determined and that notice of it will be given by the creditor to the debtor or a statement indicating that there is no credit limit.
Total charge for credit, rate of interest, etc	
9. Agreements for fixed-sum credit except agreements— (a) which do not specify either the intervals between repayments or the amounts of repayments or both the intervals and the amounts; (b) under which the total amount payable by the debtor to discharge his indebtedness in respect of the amount of credit provided may vary according to any formula specified in the agreement having effect by reference to movements in the level of any index or to any other factor; (c) which provide for a variation of, or permit the creditor to vary, (whether or not by reference to any index) the amount or rate of any item included in the total charge for credit after the relevant date; and (d) under which the total amount payable by the debtor is not greater than the total cash price referred to in paragraph 4.	The total charge for credit (with or without a list of its constituent parts).
10. Agreements for: (a) running-account credit; and (b) fixed-sum credit falling within the exceptions in paragraphs 9(a) to (c).	(1) The rate of any interest on the credit to be provided under the agreement. (2) The total amount of other charges included in the total charge for credit in relation to the credit to be provided under the agreement, except that, where any such charge cannot be stated as an amount, the rate of the charge or the formula in accordance with which it may be calculated and the total amount of the other such charges shall be shown separately.
Total amount payable	
11. Agreements falling within paragraph 9.	The total amount payable, being the total of any amounts to be shown under paragraphs 5, 6 or 7, and 9 above.

Type of agreement (1)	*Information* (2)
	Timing of repayments
12. All types.	The timing of repayments to be made under the agreement expressed by reference to one or more of the following— (a) the dates on which each repayment is to be made; (b) the frequency and number of the repayments and the date of the first repayment or a statement indicating the manner in which that date will be determined; (c) a statement indicating the manner in which the dates of the repayments will be determined.
	Amounts of repayments
13. All types except those falling within paragraph 14.	The amount of each repayment to be made under the agreement expressed as— (a) a sum of money; (b) a specified proportion of a specified amount (including the amount outstanding from time to time); (c) a combination of heads (a) and (b) above; or (d) in a case where the amount of any repayment cannot be expressed in accordance with head (a), (b) or (c) above, a statement indicating the manner in which the amount will be determined.
14. Agreements where— (i) the credit to be provided is repayable by two or more instalments; and (ii) the interest on the credit is of a type to which section 26 of, and Schedule 7 to, the Finance Act 1982 apply.	The amount of each repayment to be made under the agreement (with or without the equivalent repayment after deduction of tax in accordance with section 26 of, and Schedule 7 to the Finance Act 1982), expressed as— (a) a sum of money; (b) a specified proportion of a specified amount (including the amount outstanding from time to time); (c) a combination of heads (a) and (b) above; or (d) in a case where the amount of any repayment cannot be expressed in accordance with head (a), (b) or (c) above, a statement indicating the manner in which the amount will be determined; Provided that, where the amounts to be paid by the debtor after deduction of tax in accordance with section 26 of, and Schedule 7 to, the Finance Act 1982 are the same, the requirements of this paragraph may be satisfied by a statement indicating the lowest and highest amounts of the repayments to be made under the agreement before deduction of tax.

Type of agreement (1)	*Information* (2)
	APR
15. All types except those referred to in paragraph 16.	The APR in relation to the agreement or a statement indicating that the total amount payable under the agreement is not greater than the total cash price of the goods, services, land or other things, the acquisition of which is to be financed by credit under the agreement.
16. Debtor-creditor-supplier agreements for running-account credit under which: (a) the debtor agrees to pay the creditor an amount specified in the agreement on specified occasions; (b) there is a credit limit; and (c) charges for credit are either— (i) a fixed amount in respect of each transaction, or (ii) calculated as a proportion of the price payable under a transaction financed by the credit.	(1) The APR in relation to the agreement calculated on the assumptions specified in sub-paragraphs (2) and (3) below. (2) The first assumption referred to in sub-paragraph (1) above is the assumption that— (a) the debtor is provided with an amount of credit at the date of the making of the agreement which, taken with the amount of the charge for that credit ascertained at that date, is equal to the credit limit; and (b) the debtor repays the sum of the amounts referred to in head (a) above by payments of the amounts specified in the agreement on the occasions specified in the agreement and makes no other payment and obtains no further credit in relation to the account. (3) The second assumption referred to in sub-paragraph (1) above is the like assumption as in sub-paragraph (2) above save that the sum of the amounts referred to in head (a) thereof shall be taken to be one third of the credit limit.
17. Agreements where the APR is based on a total charge for credit which is calculated to take account of relief available under section 19 of the Income and Corporation Taxes Act 1970 and Schedule 4 to the Finance Act 1976.	A statement indicating that it has been assumed in the calculation of the APR in relation to the agreement that relief may be available under section 19 of the Income and Corporation Taxes Act 1970 and Schedule 4 to the Finance Act 1976 in respect of premiums under certain policies of insurance without any deduction under section 21 of the said Act of 1970.
	Variable rates or items
18. Agreements under which the rate or amount of any item included in the total charge for credit will or may be varied (other than a variation in consequence of an event which is certain to occur).	A statement indicating that in calculating the APR no account has been taken of any variation which may occur under the agreement of the rate or amount of any item entering into that calculation.
19. Agreements falling within paragraph 18.	A statement indicating the circumstances in which any variation referred to in paragraph 18 above may occur and, where that information is ascertainable at the time at

Type of agreement (1)	*Information* (2)
	which the document referred to in section 61(1) of the Act is presented or sent to the debtor for signature, the time at which any such variation may occur.
19A. Agreements to which regulation 15A of the total Charge for Credit Regulations applies.	The initial standard variable rate within the meaning of regulation 15A(2) of the Total Charge for Credit Regulations together with a statement explaining: (a) what rate that is; and (b) that it has been taken into account in calculating the APR
OTHER INFORMATION	
Security provided by the debtor	
20. Agreements, to which section 114 of the Act applies, under which a person takes any article in pawn and where no separate pawn-receipt is given.	A statement indicating that an article has been taken in pawn under the agreement and a description of the article sufficient to identify it.
21. All types except those referred to in paragraph 20 in relation to which any security is to be provided by the debtor to secure the carrying out of the obligations of the debtor under the agreement.	A description of the security to be provided by the debtor in relation to the agreement sufficient to identify it and— (a) a general description of any stocks and shares (including any right to become a stockholder or shareholder) to which it relates; and (b) in any other case a description of the subject matter to which it relates.
Charges on default	
22. All types including provisions for charges on default.	An indication of any charges payable under the agreement to the creditor upon failure by the debtor or a relative of his to do or refrain from doing anything which he is required to do or refrain from doing, as the case may be.

Regulation 2(3) SCHEDULE 2

PART I

FORMS OF STATEMENT OF PROTECTION AND REMEDIES AVAILABLE UNDER THE CONSUMER CREDIT ACT 1974 TO DEBTORS UNDER REGULATED CONSUMER CREDIT AGREEMENTS

Form no (1)	*Type of agreement* (2)	*Form of statement* (3)
1	Agreements to which section 58(1) of the Act applies.	YOUR RIGHTS Under the Consumer Credit Act 1974, the creditor should have given you a copy of this agreement at least seven days ago to allow you time to consider whether to go ahead. If he did not, the agreement cannot be enforced without a court order.

Form no (1)	*Type of agreement* (2)	*Form of statement* (3)
2	Cancellable agreements to which section 68(b) of the Act applies.	YOUR RIGHT TO CANCEL You have a right to cancel this agreement for FOURTEEN DAYS starting with the day after you signed it. You can do this by sending or taking a WRITTEN notice of cancellation to [1]. If you intend to cancel, you should not use any goods you already have under the agreement and you should keep them safe. You can wait for them to be collected from you and you need not hand them over unless you have received a written request. [If you wish, however, you may return the goods yourself.] [You are warned that it would be dangerous and could be in contravention of Health and Safety legislation for you to attempt to disconnect and return the goods yourself.][2] Notes: 1 Creditor or agent to insert the name and address of person to whom notice may be given or an indication of the person to whom notice may be given with a clear reference to the place in the document embodying the agreement where his name and address appear. 2 Creditor or agent to include the words in the first set of square brackets unless the words in the second set of square brackets are applicable i.e. in a case where the subject matter of the agreement is a liquefied petroleum gas vessel of greater than 150 litres water capacity.
3	Cancellable agreements not included in paragraph 2 or 4.	YOUR RIGHT TO CANCEL Once you have signed this agreement, you will have for a short time a right to cancel [it] [that part of this agreement which is related by the Consumer Credit Act 1974][1]. Exact details of how and when you can do this will be sent to you by post by the creditor.

Form no (1)	*Type of agreement* (2)	*Form of statement* (3)
		Note: 1 Creditor to omit passage in square brackets which does not apply to the agreement.
4	Modifying agreements treated under section 82(5) of the Act as cancellable agreements.	YOUR RIGHT TO CANCEL This agreement modifies an earlier agreement. Once you have signed it, your right to cancel [that part of][1] the earlier agreement [which was regulated by the Consumer Credit Act 1974][1] will be widened to cover the [regulated[1]] agreement as modified. The cancellation period itself will be unchanged. Details of how you can cancel are given in your copy of this agreement. Note: 1 Creditor to omit passages in square brackets except in the case of an agreement of which at least one part is a credit agreement not regulated by the Act.
5	Hire-purchase and conditional sale agreements relating to goods, not included in paragraph 6.	TERMINATION: YOUR RIGHTS You have a right to end this agreement. If you wish to do so, you should write to the person authorised to receive your payments. The creditor will then be entitled to the return of the goods and to [the installation charge plus half the rest of the total amount payable under this agreement, that is] [half the total amount payable under this agreement, that is][1] £x^2. If you have already paid at least this amount plus any overdue instalments, you will not have to pay any more, provided you have taken reasonable care of the goods. Notes: 1 Creditor to insert the appropriate passage in square brackets where the amount calculated in accordance with the provisions of section 100 of the Act applies. If the agreement provides for a sum below the minimum prescribed in the Act, both passages in square brackets are to be omitted. 2 Creditor to insert the amount calculated in accordance with the provisions of section 100 of the Act or such lesser sum as the agreement may provide.

Form no (1)	*Type of agreement* (2)	*Form of statement* (3)
6	Agreements modifying hire-purchase and conditional sale agreements relating to goods.	TERMINATION: YOUR RIGHTS You have a right to end this agreement. If you wish to do so, you should write to the person authorised to receive your payments. The creditor will then be entitled to the return of the goods and to [the installation charge plus half the rest of the total amount payable under your earlier agreement as modified by this agreement, that is] [half the total amount payable under your earlier agreement as modified by this agreement, that is][1] £x[2]. If you have already paid at least this amount plus any overdue instalments, you will not have to pay any more, provided you have taken reasonable care of the goods. Notes: 1 Creditor to insert the appropriate passage in square brackets where the amount calculated in accordance with the provisions of section 100 of the Act applies. If the modified agreement provides for a sum below the minimum prescribed in the Act, both passages in square brackets are to be omitted. 2 Creditor to insert the amount calculated in accordance with the provisions of section 100 of the Act or such lesser sum as the modified agreement may provide.
7	Conditional sale agreements relating to land, not included in paragraph 8.	TERMINATION: YOUR RIGHTS Until the title to the land has passed to you, you have a right to end this agreement. If you wish to do so, you should write to the person authorised to receive your payments. The creditor will then be entitled to the return of the land and to [half the total amount payable under this agreement, that is][1] £x[2]. If you have already paid at least this amount plus any overdue instalments, you will not have to pay any more, provided you have taken reasonable care of the land. Notes: 1 Creditor to insert the passage in square brackets where the amount calculated in accordance with the provisions of section 100 of the Act

Form no (1)	*Type of agreement* (2)	*Form of statement* (3)
		applies. If the agreement provides for a sum below the minimum prescribed in the Act, the passage in square brackets is to be omitted. 2 Creditor to insert the amount calculated in accordance with the provisions of section 100 of the Act or such lesser sum as the agreement may provide.
8	Agreements modifying conditional sale agreements relating to land.	TERMINATION: YOUR RIGHTS Until the title to the land has passed to you, you have a right to end this agreement. If you wish to do so, you should write to the person authorised to receive your payments. The creditor will then be entitled to the return of the land and to [half the total amount payable under your earlier agreement as modified by this agreement, that is][1] £x^2. If you have already paid at least this amount plus any overdue instalments, you will not have to pay any more, provided you have taken reasonable care of the land. Notes: 1 Creditor to insert the passage in square brackets where the amount calculated in accordance with the provisions of section 100 of the Act applies. If the modified agreement provides for a sum below the minimum prescribed in the Act, the passage in square brackets is to be omitted. 2 Creditor to insert the amount calculated in accordance with the provisions of section 100 of the Act or such lesser sum as the modified agreement may provide.
9	Hire-purchase and conditional sale agreements relating to goods, not included in paragraph 10.	REPOSSESSION: YOUR RIGHTS If you fail to keep to your side of this agreement but you have paid at least [the installation charge plus one third of the rest of the total amount payable under this agreement, that is] [one third of the total amount payable under this agreement, that is][1] £y^2, the creditor may not take back the goods against your wishes unless he gets a court order. (In Scotland, he may need to get a court order at any time.) If he does take them without your consent or a

Form no (1)	Type of agreement (2)	Form of statement (3)
		court order, you have the right to get back all the money you have paid under the agreement. Notes: 1 Creditor to insert the appropriate passage in square brackets. 2 Creditor to insert the amount calculated in accordance with the provisions of section 90 of the Act.
10	Agreements modifying hire-purchase and conditional sale agreements relating to goods.	REPOSSESSION: YOUR RIGHTS If you fail to keep to your side of this agreement [but you have paid at least £*y*,[1]][2] the creditor may not take back the goods against your wishes unless he gets a court order. [(In Scotland, he may need to get a court order at any time.)][2] If he does take them without your consent or a court order, you have the right to get back all the money you have paid under the agreement. Notes: 1 Creditor to insert the amount calculated in accordance with the provisions of section 90 of the Act. 2 Creditor to omit both passages in square brackets in the case of a modifying agreement where the goods are protected at the time the modifying agreement is made.
11	Agreements, to which section 114 of the Act applies, under which a person takes any article in pawn.	IMPORTANT — YOU SHOULD READ THIS CAREFULLY YOUR RIGHTS The Consumer Credit Act 1974 covers this agreement and lays down certain requirements for your protection which must be satisfied when the agreement is made. If they are not, the creditor cannot enforce the agreement against you without a court order. The Act also gives you a number of rights and, in particular, you should read the NOTICE TO DEBTOR [in this agreement][1] [in your pawn-receipt][2]. If you would like to know more about the protection and remedies provided under the Act, you should contact either your local Trading Standards Department or your nearest Citizens Advice Bureau.

Form no (1)	*Type of agreement* (2)	*Form of statement* (3)
		Notes: 1 Phrase in square brackets to be included by creditor in agreements where any document embodying the agreement is not separate from the pawn-receipt. Creditor to omit 'in your pawn-receipt'. 2 Phrase in square brackets to be included by creditor in agreements where a separate pawn-receipt is given to the debtor. Creditor to Omit 'in this agreement'.
12	Debtor-creditor-supplier agreements falling within section 12(b) and (c) of the Act, and multiple agreements not falling within paragraph 13 of which at least one part is a debtor-creditor-supplier agreement falling within section 12(b) or (c) of the Act.	IMPORTANT — YOU SHOULD READ THIS CAREFULLY YOUR RIGHTS The Consumer Credit Act 1974 covers this agreement and lays down certain requirements for your protection which must be satisfied when the agreement is made. If they are not, the creditor cannot enforce the agreement against you without a court order. The Act also gives you a number of rights. You have a right to settle this agreement at any time by giving notice in writing and paying off all amounts payable under the agreement [which may be reduced by a rebate][1]. If you have obtained unsatisfactory goods or services under a transaction financed by this agreement [, apart from any purchased out of a cash loan,][2] you may have a right to sue the supplier, the creditor or both. Similarly, if the contract is not fulfilled, perhaps because the supplier has gone out of business, you may still be able to sue the creditor. If you would like to know more about the protection and remedies provided under the Act, you should contact either your local Trading Standards Department or your nearest Citizens Advice Bureau. Notes: 1 Creditor to insert phrase in square brackets in any agreement where rebate is payable under the agreement or the Consumer Credit (Rebate on Early Settlement) Regulations 1983. 2 Creditor to insert phrase in square brackets in any multiple agreement, of which at least one part is a

Form no (1)	Type of agreement (2)	Form of statement (3)
		debtor-creditor-supplier agreement falling within section 12(b) or (c) of the Act and at least one part is a debtor-creditor agreement falling within section 13(c) of the Act.
13	Multiple agreements of which at least one part is a credit agreement not regulated by the Act.	IMPORTANT — YOU SHOULD READ THIS CAREFULLY YOUR RIGHTS That part of this agreement which deals with [ ][1] is a regulated agreement for the purposes of the Consumer Credit Act 1974. As a result, certain requirements for your protection must be satisfied when it is made. If they are not, the creditor cannot enforce it against you without a court order. The Act also gives you a number of rights. You have a right to settle the regulated agreement at any time by giving notice in writing and paying off all amounts payable under the regulated agreement [which may be reduced by a rebate][2]. If you would like to know more about the protection and remedies provided under the Act, you should contact either your local Trading Standards Department or your nearest Citizens Advice Bureau. Notes: 1 Creditor to insert description of regulated agreement for example, 'the cash advance facility'. 2 Creditor to insert phrase in square brackets in any agreement where rebate is payable under the agreement or the Consumer Credit (Rebate on Early Settlement) Regulations 1983.
14	All types not included in paragraphs 11, 12 and 13.	IMPORTANT — YOU SHOULD READ THIS CAREFULLY YOUR RIGHTS The Consumer Credit Act 1974 covers this agreement and lays down certain requirements for your protection which must be satisfied when the agreement is made. If they are not, the creditor cannot enforce the agreement against you without a court order. The Act also gives you a number of rights. You have a right to settle this

Form no (1)	*Type of agreement* (2)	*Form of statement* (3)
		agreement at any time by giving notice in writing and paying off all amounts payable under the agreement [which may be reduced by a rebate][1]. If you would like to know more about the protection and remedies provided under the Act, you should contact either your local Trading Standards Department or your nearest Citizens Advice Bureau. Note: 1 Creditor to insert phrase in square brackets in any agreement where rebate is payable under the agreement or the Consumer Credit (Rebate on Early Settlement) Regulations 1983.
15	Credit-token agreements which make debtors liable for loss to the creditor resulting from the misuse of credit-tokens by other persons.	LOSS OR MISUSE OF CREDIT-TOKEN[1] If the credit-token[1] is lost, stolen or misused by someone who obtained it without your consent, you may be liable for up to £[2] of any loss to the creditor. If it is misused with your permission you will probably be liable for ALL losses. You will not be liable for losses to the creditor which take place after you have told him of the theft, etc [provided you confirm any oral message in writing within seven days][3]. [However, the credit-token[1] can also be used under an agreement to which this protection does not apply. As a result, there may be circumstances under which the creditor could enforce full liability against you.][4] Notes: 1 Creditor may insert specific designation or trade name of credit-token for example, credit card instead of 'credit-token'. 2 Creditor to insert the extent of the liability laid down in section 84(1) of the Act or the credit limit if lower or such lower figure as he may decide. 3 Creditor to omit phrase in square brackets if written confirmation is not required under the credit-token agreement. 4 Creditor to omit passage in square brackets if inapplicable.

Regulation 4

PART II

NOTICE TO BE CONTAINED IN DOCUMENTS EMBODYING A COMBINED CONSUMER CREDIT AGREEMENT AND PAWN-RECEIPT

Form No (1)	*Type of agreement* (2)	*Form of statement* (3)
16	Agreements, to which section 114 of the Act applies, under which a person takes any article in pawn and where any document embodying the agreement is not separate from the pawn-receipt.	NOTICE TO DEBTOR IMPORTANT — YOU SHOULD READ THIS CAREFULLY Right to Redeem Articles If you give in this agreement (which is also your pawn-receipt) and pay the amount owing, you may redeem the article(s) taken in pawn at any time within six months of the date of this agreement or any longer time agreed between you and the creditor ('the redemption period'). IF YOU DO NOT REDEEM THE ARTICLE(S) ON OR BEFORE [1] YOU MAY LOSE YOUR RIGHT TO REDEEM IT (THEM). Loss of Receipt If you lose your receipt you may provide in its place either a statutory declaration or, if the credit (or credit limit) is not more than £[2] and the creditor agrees, a signed statement. The creditor can supply the form to use. He may make a charge for it. Unredeemed Articles An article not redeemed within the redemption period becomes the creditor's property, if the credit (or credit limit) is not more than £[3] and the redemption period is six months. In any other circumstances it may be sold by the creditor, but it goes on being redeemable until it is sold. Interest is payable until the actual date of redemption. Where the credit (or credit limit) is more than £[4] the creditor must give you 14 days' notice of his intention to sell. When an article has been sold you will receive information about the sale. If the proceeds (less expenses) are more than the amount that would have been payable to redeem the article on the date of the sale you will be entitled to receive the surplus. If they are less than that amount you will owe the creditor the shortfall.

Form No (1)	*Type of agreement* (2)	*Form of statement* (3)
		Your goods will not be insured by the creditor while they are in pawn.[5] Notes: 1 Creditor to insert the date of the end of the redemption period. 2 Creditor to insert the amount specified in section 118(1)(b) of the Act. 3 Creditor to insert the amount specified in section 120(1)(a) of the Act. 4 Creditor to insert the amount specified in the Consumer Credit (Realisation of Pawn) Regulations 1983. 5 Creditor to omit this paragraph if applicable.

Regulation 3(1)

SCHEDULE 3

INFORMATION TO BE CONTAINED IN DOCUMENTS EMBODYING REGULATED CONSUMER HIRE AGREEMENTS OTHER THAN MODIFYING AGREEMENTS

Type of agreement (1)	*Information* (2)
	Nature of agreement
1. All types.	A heading in the following form of words shown prominently on the first page of the document— 'Hire Agreement regulated by the Consumer Credit Act 1974'.
	Parties to agreement
2. All types.	(1) The name and a postal address of the owner. (2) The name and a postal address of the hirer.
	FINANCIAL AND RELATED PARTICULARS
	Description of goods
3. All types.	A list or other description of the goods to be bailed or hired under the agreement.
	Advance payments
4. All types in relation to which any advance payment is to be made by the hirer (whether under the agreement or as a condition precedent to the making of the agreement) before he is to take possession of the goods to be bailed or hired under the agreement or, as the case may be, before he enters into the agreement.	The amount of the advance payments to be made by the hirer and, in the case of a cancellable agreement, the nature of such payments.

Type of agreement (1)	*Information* (2)
	Hire payments
5. All types.	(1) The amount of each hire payment, other than an advance payment to be shown under paragraph 4 above. (2) The timing of such payments to be made under the agreement expressed by reference to one or more of the following— (a) the dates on which each payment is to be made; (b) the frequency and number of the payments and the date of the first payment or a statement indicating the manner in which that date will be determined; (c) a statement indicating the manner in which the dates of the payments will be determined.
	Other payments
6. All types including provisions for payments other than advance payments and hire payments.	(1) The amount (or a statement indicating the manner in which the amount will be determined) of each of the following descriptions of payments (not being an advance payment to be shown under paragraph 4 above or a hire payment to be shown under paragraph 5) to be made under the agreement by, or on behalf of, the hirer, or a relative of his, to the owner, that is to say— (a) any payment under arrangements for the installation, care, maintenance or protection of any goods; (b) any premium under a contract of insurance; or (c) any payment payable on termination of the agreement (other than a payment on default to be shown under paragraph 10 below). (2) The timing of such payments expressed by reference to one or more of the following: (a) the dates on which each payment is to be made; (b) the frequency and number of the payments and the date of the first payment or a statement indicating the manner or in which that date will be determined; (c) a statement indicating the manner in which the dates of the payments will be determined. (3) References in this paragraph to the owner include references to his near relative, his partner and a member of a group of which he is a member, to any

Type of agreement (1)	*Information* (2)
	person nominated by him or by any such person in relation to the arrangements, the contract of insurance or the termination of the agreement, and to a near relative of his partner; and 'near relative' means, in relation to any person, the husband, wife, father, mother, brother, sister, son or daughter of that person and 'group' means the person (including a company) having control of a company together with all the companies directly or indirectly controlled by him.
Variable payments	
7. All types including provisions for variation of hire or other payments, where the amount of any such payment following any variation cannot be ascertained at the time of the making of the agreement.	(1) Subject to sub-paragraph (2) below, a statement indicating the circumstances in which any hire payment to be shown under paragraph 5 above or any other payment to be shown under paragraph 6 may be varied under the agreement and, where that information is ascertainable at the time at which the document referred to in section 61(1) of the Act is presented or sent to the hirer for signature, the time at which any such variation may occur. (2) Sub-paragraph (1) above does not apply to a variation under the agreement which takes account only of a change in value added tax. (3) References in sub-paragraph (2) above to a change in value added tax include references to a change to or from no tax being charged.
Duration of hire	
8. All types including a provision that goods are to be bailed or hired for a fixed period or a minimum period.	A statement indicating that goods are to be bailed or hired under the agreement for a fixed period or a minimum period, as the case may be, and the duration of that period.
OTHER INFORMATION	
Security provided by the hirer	
9. All types in relation to which any security is to be provided by the hirer to secure the carrying out of the obligations of the hirer under the agreement.	A description of the security to be provided by the hirer in relation to the agreement sufficient to identify it and a description of the subject matter to which it relates.
10. All types including provisions for charges on default.	An indication of any charges payable under the agreement to the owner upon failure by the hirer or a relative of his to do or refrain from doing anything which he is required to do or refrain from doing, as the case may be.

Regulation 3(3)

SCHEDULE 4

FORMS OF STATEMENT OF PROTECTION AND REMEDIES AVAILABLE UNDER THE CONSUMER CREDIT ACT 1974 TO HIRERS UNDER REGULATED CONSUMER HIRE AGREEMENTS

Form No (1)	*Type of agreement* (2)	*Form of statement* (3)
1	Agreements to which section 58(1) of the Act applies.	YOUR RIGHTS Under the Consumer Credit Act 1974, the owner should have given you a copy of this agreement at least seven days ago to allow you time to consider whether to go ahead. If he did not, the agreement cannot be enforced without a court order.
2	All cancellable agreements not included in paragraph 3.	YOUR RIGHT TO CANCEL Once you have signed this agreement, you will have for a short time a right to cancel it. Exact details of how and when you can do this will be sent to you by post by the owner.
3	Modifying agreements treated under section 82(5) of the Act as cancellable agreements.	YOUR RIGHT TO CANCEL This agreement modifies an earlier agreement. Once you have signed it, your right to cancel the earlier agreement will be widened to cover the agreement as modified. The cancellation period itself will be unchanged. Details of how you can cancel are given in your copy of this agreement.
4	Agreements which the hirer is entitled to terminate by notice under section 101(1) of the Act and which provide for the bailment or hiring of goods for at least 18 months after the making of the agreement.	IMPORTANT — YOU SHOULD READ THIS CAREFULLY YOUR RIGHTS The Consumer Credit Act 1974 covers this agreement and lays down certain requirements for your protection which must be satisfied when the agreement is made. If they are not, the owner cannot enforce the agreement against you without a court order. The Act also gives you a number of rights. Among these is the right to end the agreement by writing to the person authorised to receive your payments and giving at least [1] notice. The agreement must be allowed to run for at least 18 months [from the date of the original agreement][2] though this may include the period of notice. You will

Form No (1)	*Type of agreement* (2)	*Form of statement* (3)
		have to make all the payments including any arrears until the time the agreement comes to an end. If you would like to know more about the protection and remedies provided under the Act, you should contact either your local Trading Standards Department or your nearest Citizens Advice Bureau. Notes: 1 Owner to insert minimum period of notice as determined by section 101. 2 Owner to omit passage in square brackets except where this notice appears in a modifying agreement.
5	Agreements not included in paragraph 4.	IMPORTANT — YOU SHOULD READ THIS CAREFULLY YOUR RIGHTS The Consumer Credit Act 1974 covers this agreement and lays down certain requirements for your protection which must be satisfied when the agreement is made. If they are not, the owner cannot enforce the agreement against you without a court order. If you would like to know more about the protection and remedies provided under the Act, you should contact either your local Trading Standards Department or your nearest Citizens Advice Bureau.

Regulation 2(7)

SCHEDULE 5

FORMS OF SIGNATURE BOX

PART I

REGULATED CONSUMER CREDIT AGREEMENTS

Form No (1)	*Type of agreement* (2)	*Form of signature box* (3)
1	Hire-purchase agreements.	This is a Hire-Purchase Agreement regulated by the Consumer Credit Act 1974. Sign it only if you want to be legally bound by its terms. Signature(s) of Debtor(s) Date(s) of signature(s)[1] The goods will not become your property until you have made all the payments. You must not sell them before then.

Form No (1)	*Type of agreement* (2)	*Form of signature box* (3)
		Note: 1 Creditor may omit 'Date(s) of signature(s)' where, by virtue of Regulation 6(3)(c), the date is not required.
2	Conditional sale agreements relating to land.	This is a Conditional Sale Agreement regulated by the Consumer Credit Act 1974. Sign it only if you want to be legally bound by its terms. Signature(s) of Debtor(s) Date(s) of signature(s)[1] The land will not become your property until you have made [2] payments. You must not sell it before then. Notes: 1 Creditor may omit 'Date(s) of signature(s)' where, by virtue of Regulation 6(3)(c), the date is not required. 2 Creditor to insert 'all the' or the number of payments as appropriate.
3	Conditional sale agreements relating to goods.	This is a Conditional Sale Agreement regulated by the Consumer Credit Act 1974. Sign it only if you want to be legally bound by its terms. Signature(s) of Debtor(s) Date(s) of signature(s)[1] The goods will not become your property until you have made [2] payments. You must not sell them before then. Notes: 1 Creditor may omit 'Date(s) of signature(s)' where, by virtue of Regulation 6(3)(c), the date is not required. 2 Creditor to insert 'all the' or the number of payments as appropriate.
4	Agreements under which a person takes any article in pawn and where the agreement is not separate from the pawn-receipt.	This is a Credit Agreement regulated by the Consumer Credit Act 1974. Sign it only if you want to be legally bound by its terms. Signature(s) of Debtor(s) Date(s) of signature(s)[1] This document is also your PAWN-RECEIPT. Keep it safely.

Form No (1)	*Type of agreement* (2)	*Form of signature box* (3)
		Note: 1 Creditor may omit 'Date(s) of signature(s)' where, by virtue of Regulation 6(3)(c), the date is not required.
5	Multiple agreements of which at least one part is a credit agreement not regulated by the Act.	This is a Credit Agreement partly regulated by the Consumer Credit Act 1974. Sign it only if you want to be legally bound by its terms. Signature(s) of Debtor(s) Date(s) of signature(s)[1] Note: 1 Creditor may omit 'Date(s) of signature(s)' where, by virtue of Regulation 6(3)(c), the date is not required.
6	Agreements not included in paragraphs 1–5 or 7–8.	This is a Credit Agreement regulated by the Consumer Credit Act 1974. Sign it only if you want to be legally bound by its terms. Signature(s) of Debtor(s) Date(s) of signature(s)[1] Note: 1 Creditor may omit 'Date(s) of signature(s)' where, by virtue of Regulation 6(3)(c), the date is not required.
7	Modifying agreements varying or supplementing earlier multiple agreements of which at least one part was a credit agreement not regulated by the Act and where at least one part of the modified agreement is not regulated.	This Agreement varies and/or supplements a Credit Agreement and is partly regulated by the Consumer Credit Act 1974. Sign it only if you want to be legally bound by the new terms. Signature(s) of Debtor(s) Date(s) of signature(s)[1] Note: 1 Creditor may omit 'Date(s) of signature(s)' where, by virtue of Regulation 6(3)(c), the date is not required.
8	Modifying agreements other than those included in paragraph 7.	This Agreement varies and/or supplements a [1] Agreement regulated by the Consumer Credit Act 1974. Sign it only if you want to be legally bound by the new terms. Signature(s) of Debtor(s) Date(s) of signature(s)[2]

Form No (1)	*Type of agreement* (2)	*Form of signature box* (3)
		Notes: 1 Creditor to insert 'Hire-Purchase' or 'Conditional Sale' or 'Credit' as appropriate. 2 Creditor may omit 'Date(s) of signature(s)' where by virtue of Regulation 6(3)(c), the date is not required.

Regulation 3(6)

PART II
REGULATED CONSUMER HIRE AGREEMENTS

Form No (1)	*Type of agreement* (2)	*Form of statement* (3)
9	All types not included in paragraph 10.	This is a Hire Agreement regulated by the Consumer Credit Act 1974. Sign it only if you want to be legally bound by its terms. Signature(s) of Hirer(s) Date(s) of signature(s)[1] Under this agreement the goods do not become your property and you must not sell them. Note: 1 Owner may omit 'Date(s) of signature(s)' where, by virtue of Regulation 6(3)(c), the date is not required.
10	Modifying agreements.	This Agreement varies and/or supplements a Hire Agreement regulated by the Consumer Credit Act 1974. Sign it only if you want to be legally bound by the new terms. Signature(s) of Hirer(s) Date(s) of signature(s)[1] Note: 1 Owner may omit 'Date(s) of signature(s)' where, by virtue of Regulation 6(3)(c), the date is not required.

Regulation 6(1)

SCHEDULE 6

PRESCRIBED TERMS FOR THE PURPOSES OF SECTIONS 61(1)(a) AND 127(3) OF THE CONSUMER CREDIT ACT 1974

Type of agreement (1)	*Prescribed terms* (2)
	Amount of credit
1. Restricted-use debtor-creditor-supplier agreements for fixed-sum credit— (a) to finance a transaction comprising the acquisition of goods, services, land or other things specified in the agreement or identified and agreed on at the time the agreement is made; (b) under which the total amount payable by the debtor is not greater than the total cash price; and (c) under which there is no advance payment.	A term stating the amount of the credit, which may be expressed as the total cash price of the goods, services, land or other things, the acquisition of which is to be financed by credit under the agreement.
2. Agreements for fixed-sum credit not falling within paragraph 1.	A term stating the amount of the credit.
	Credit limit
3. Agreement for running-account credit.	A term stating the credit limit or the manner in which it will be determined or that there is no credit limit.
	Rate of interest
4. Agreements for: (a) running-account credit; and (b) fixed-sum credit falling within the exceptions in paragraph 9(a) to (c) of Schedule 1 to these Regulations.	A term stating the rate of any interest on the credit to be provided under the agreement.
	Repayments
5. Consumer credit agreements.	A term stating how the debtor is to discharge his obligations under the agreement to make the repayments, which may be expressed by reference to a combination of any of the following— (a) number of repayments; (b) amount of repayments; (c) frequency and timing of repayments; (d) dates of repayments; (e) the manner in which any of the above may be determined; or in any other way, and any power of the creditor to vary what is payable.
6. Consumer hire agreements.	A term stating how the hirer is to discharge his obligations under the agreement to pay the hire payments, which may be expressed by reference to a combination of any of the following— (a) number of payments;

Type of agreement (1)	*Prescribed terms* (2)
	(b) amount of payments; (c) frequency and timing of payments; (d) dates of payments; (e) the manner in which any of the above may be determined; or in any other way, and any power of the owner to vary what is payable.

Regulation 1(2) SCHEDULE 7

PROVISIONS RELATING TO DISCLOSURE OF THE APR

1. Permissible tolerances in disclosure of the APR

For the purposes of these Regulations, it shall be sufficient compliance with the requirements to show the APR if there is included in the document—

(a) a rate which exceeds the APR by not more than one; or

(b) a rate which falls short of the APR by not more than 0·1; or

(c) in a case to which any of paragraphs 2 to 5 below applies, a rate determined in accordance with the paragraph or such of them as apply to that case.

[**2. Tolerance where repayments are nearly equal**

In the case of an agreement under which all repayments but one are equal and that one repayment does not differ from any repayment by more whole pence than there are repayments, there may be included in the document a rate found under Regulation 7 of the Total Charge for Credit Regulations as if that one repayment were equal to the other repayments.

3. Tolerance where intervals between relevant date and first repayment is greater than interval between repayments

In the case of an agreement under which—

(a) three or more repayments are to be made at equal intervals; and

(b) the interval between the relevant date and the first repayment is greater than the interval between the repayments,

there may be included in the document a rate found under Regulation 7 of the Total Charge for Credit Regulations as if the interval between the relevant date and the first repayment were shortened so as to be equal to the interval between the repayments.]

4. Tolerance where Consumer credit tables do not exactly apply

(1) In a case where, in relation to any agreement, the charge per pound lent, the flat rate or the period rate of charge, as the case may be, is not exactly represented by an entry in a table contained in the Consumer credit tables, there may be included in the document a rate found by applying the next greater entry appearing in those tables for the purposes of calculating that rate.

(2) In sub-paragraph (1) above 'charge per pound lent', 'flat rate' and 'period rate of charge' have the meanings assigned to them by the relevant Introduction or Instructions contained in the Consumer credit tables and 'Consumer credit tables' means tables contained in Parts 1 to 15 of 'Consumer credit tables' published in 1977 by Her Majesty's Stationery Office as modified by Correction Slips so published in December 1978 (being tables calculated in accordance with the principles set out in the Total Charge for Credit Regulations).

5. Tolerance where period rate of charge is charged

In the case of an agreement to which Regulation 7(1) of the Total Charge for Credit Regulations (agreements under which a period rate of charge is charged) applies, there may be included in the document a rate, being the APR determined as if no account were taken of any amount by which the total amount of the charges included in the total charge for credit in relation to each period is varied so as to bring that amount to the nearest whole penny, one half-penny being for this purpose expressed to the next higher whole penny.

Regulation 7(2)

SCHEDULE 8

REGULATED MODIFYING AGREEMENTS

PART I
INFORMATION TO BE CONTAINED IN DOCUMENTS EMBODYING REGULATED MODIFYING AGREEMENTS VARYING OR SUPPLEMENTING EARLIER CREDIT AGREEMENTS

Type of modifying agreement (1)	*Information* (2)
	Nature of modifying agreement
1. All types.	(1) A heading in one of the following forms of words shown prominently on the first page of the document— (a) 'Agreement modifying a Hire-Purchase Agreement and regulated by the Consumer Credit Act 1974'; (b) 'Agreement modifying a Conditional Sale Agreement and regulated by the Consumer Credit Act 1974'; or (c) 'Agreement modifying a Credit Agreement and regulated by the Consumer Credit Act 1974', as the case may require. (2) Where the document and a pawn-receipt are combined, the words, 'and Pawn-Receipt,' shall be inserted in the heading after the word 'Agreement' in the second place that it occurs. (3) Where the document embodies an agreement of which at least one part is a credit agreement not regulated by the Act, the word 'partly' shall be inserted before 'regulated' unless the regulated and unregulated parts of the agreement are clearly separate.
	Parties to modifying agreement
2. All types.	(1) The name and a postal address of the creditor. (2) The name and a postal address of the debtor.
	FINANCIAL AND RELATED PARTICULARS
	Description of goods, services, land etc and cash price
3. Modifying agreements under which— (a) goods, services, land or other things, the acquisition of which was to be comprised in a transaction to be financed by an earlier restricted-use debtor-creditor-supplier agreement for fixed-sum credit and which were specified in the earlier agreement or identified and agreed on at the time the earlier agreement was made, are varied or supplemented; or	(1) A list or other description of the goods, services or other things and, in the case of land, a general description of the land (whether or not varied or supplemented under the modifying agreement) the acquisition of which is to be financed by credit under the modified agreement and the cash price (whether or not so varied or supplemented) in relation to each such list or other description:

Type of modifying agreement (1)	*Information* (2)
(b) the cash price of goods, services, land or other things, the acquisition of which was to be comprised in a transaction to be financed by an earlier restricted-use debtor-creditor-supplier agreement for fixed-sum credit and which were specified in the earlier agreement or identified and agreed on at the time the earlier agreement was made, is varied but the goods, services, land or other things are not varied or supplemented.	Provided that, where both the description and the cash price of all the goods, services, land or other things the acquisition of which was to be comprised in a transaction to be financed by the earlier agreement are unchanged, the requirements of this paragraph may be satisfied in relation to such goods, services, land or other things by a statement clearly indicating that the descriptions and cash prices in the earlier agreement are unchanged. (2) The total cash price under the modified agreement.
Advance payments	
4. Modifying agreements in relation to which any advance payment is to be made by the debtor additional to any made in relation to an earlier agreement (whether under the modifying agreement or as a condition precedent to the making of that agreement) before he is provided with additional credit under that agreement, or, as the case may be, before he enters into that agreement.	The amount of the additional advance payments to be made by the debtor in relation to the modifying agreement, and, where the modifying agreement is a cancellable agreement, the nature of such payments.
Amount of credit	
5. Modifying agreements under which any charge included in the total charge for credit in relation to an earlier agreement for fixed-sum credit is varied or supplemented or under which the amount of the credit to be provided under such an earlier agreement is varied or supplemented, except— (a) modifying agreements falling within paragraph 3 under which both— (i) the total amount payable by the debtor under the modified agreement is not greater than the total cash price under that agreement; and (ii) there is no advance payment under the modifying agreement; (b) modifying agreements where the earlier agreement is an agreement such as is described in regulation 2(2) of the Consumer Credit (Rebate on Early Settlement) Regulations 1983.	(1) The total amount of the credit to be provided under the modified agreement calculated as follows, namely the total amount of the capital outstanding under the earlier agreement on the relevant date calculated in accordance with sub-paragraph (2) below increased or reduced, as the case may require, by— (a) the amount of any additional credit to be provided under the modifying agreement; or (b) the amount of any reduction of credit to be effected under the modifying agreement. (2) The total amount of the capital outstanding referred to in sub-paragraph (1) above shall be the difference between— (a) the total amount of the repayments outstanding under the earlier agreement at the relevant date (whether or not due at that date); and (b) the total amount of the charges on the credit not yet accrued under the earlier agreement calculated in accordance with sub-paragraph (3) below. (3) The total amount of the charges on the credit not yet accrued referred to in sub-paragraph (2) above shall be the amount

Type of modifying agreement (1)	*Information* (2)
	of a notional rebate calculated in accordance with the Consumer Credit (Rebate on Early Settlement) Regulations 1983 as if early settlement had taken place and as if the settlement date were the relevant date disregarding any deferment of the settlement date under Regulation 5 of those Regulations.
6. Modifying agreements both under which the amount of the credit to be provided under an earlier agreement for fixed-sum credit is varied or supplemented and where the earlier agreement is an agreement such as is described in Regulation 2(2) of the Consumer Credit (Rebate on Early Settlement) Regulations 1983.	The total amount of the credit to be provided under the modified agreement calculated as follows, namely the total of: (a) the balance of the credit outstanding under the earlier agreement at the relevant date; (b) any charges thereon (included in the total charge for credit in relation to the credit to be provided under the earlier agreement) due and unpaid at the relevant date; and (c) the amount of any additional credit to be provided under the modifying agreement.
Credit limit	
7. Modifying agreements under which the provisions relating to any credit limit under an earlier agreement for running-account credit are varied, including a change to or from there being no credit limit.	The varied credit limit under the modified agreement expressed as— (a) a sum of money; (b) a statement that the credit limit will be determined by the creditor from time to time under that agreement and that notice of it will be given by him to the debtor; (c) a sum of money together with a statement that the creditor may vary the credit limit to such sum as he may from time to time determine under that agreement and that notice of it will be given by him to the debtor; or (d) in a case not falling within head (a), (b) or (c) above, either a statement indicating the manner in which the credit limit will be determined and that notice of it will be given by the creditor to the debtor or a statement indicating that there is no credit limit.
Total charge for credit, rate of interest, etc	
8. Modifying agreement under which any charge included in the total charge for credit in relation to an earlier agreement for fixed-sum credit is varied or supplemented, except modifying agreements— (a) which do not specify either the intervals between repayments under the	The total charge for credit (with or without a list of its constituent parts) in relation to the credit to be provided under the modified agreement.

Type of modifying agreement (1)	*Information* (2)
modified agreement or the amounts of repayments or both the intervals and the amounts; (b) under which the total amount payable by the debtor under the modified agreement to discharge his indebtedness in respect of the amount of credit provided may vary according to any formula specified in such agreement having effect by reference to movements in the level of any index or to any other factor; (c) which provide for a variation of, or permit the creditor to vary, (whether or not by reference to any index) the amount or rate of any item included in the total charge for credit in relation to the modified agreement after the relevant date; or (d) under which the total amount payable by the debtor under the modified agreement is not greater than the total cash price under that agreement.	
9. Modifying agreements under which— (a) any charge included in the total charge for credit in relation to an earlier agreement for fixed-sum credit is varied or supplemented and which fall within the exceptions in paragraph 8(a) to (c); or (b) the rate of interest or any other charge included in the total charge for credit in relation to an earlier agreement for running-account credit is varied or supplemented.	(1) The varied or supplemented rate of any interest on the credit to be provided under the modified agreement or a statement that the rate of interest under the earlier agreement is unchanged. (2) The total amount of other charges included in the total charge for credit in relation to the credit to be provided under the modified agreement, except that, where any such charge cannot be stated as an amount, the rate of the charge or the formula in accordance with which it may be calculated and the total amount of the other such charges shall be shown separately.

Total amount payable

10. Modifying agreements falling within paragraph 8.	The total amount payable under the modified agreement, being the total of any amounts to be shown under paragraphs 4, 5 or 6, and 8 above.

Timing of repayment

11. Modifying agreements under which— (i) the amount of the credit to be provided under an earlier agreement for fixed-sum credit is varied or supplemented; (ii) the repayment provisions of an earlier agreement for fixed-sum or for running-account credit are varied or supplemented; or	The timing of repayments to be made under the modified agreement expressed by reference to one or more of the following— (a) the dates on which each repayment is to be made; (b) the frequency and number of the repayments and the date of the first repayment or a statement indicating the

Type of modifying agreement (1)	*Information* (2)
(iii) any charge included in the total charge for credit in relation to an earlier agreement for fixed-sum or for running-account credit is varied or supplemented.	manner in which that date will be determined; (c) a statement indicating the manner in which the dates of the repayments will be determined.
Amount of repayments	
12. Modifying agreements falling within paragraph 11 but not falling within paragraph 13.	The amount of each repayment to be made under the modified agreement expressed as— (a) a sum of money; (b) a specified proportion of a specified amount (including the amount outstanding from time to time); (c) a combination of heads (a) and (b) above; or (d) in a case where the amount of any repayment cannot be expressed in accordance with head (a), (b) or (c) above, a statement indicating the manner in which the amount will be determined.
13. Modifying agreements falling within paragraph 11 where— (i) the credit to be provided under the modified agreement is repayable by two or more instalments; and (ii) the interest on such credit is of a type to which section 26 of, and Schedule 7 to, the Finance Act 1982 apply.	The amount of each repayment to be made under the modified agreement (with or without the equivalent repayment after deduction of tax in accordance with section 26 of, and Schedule 7 to, the Finance Act 1982) expressed as— (a) a sum of money; (b) a specified proportion of a specified amount (including the amount outstanding from time to time); (c) a combination of heads (a) and (b) above; or (d) in a case where the amount of any repayment cannot be expressed in accordance with head (a), (b) or (c) above, a statement indicating the manner in which the amount will be determined: Provided that, where the amounts to be paid by the debtor after deduction of tax in accordance with section 26 of, and Schedule 7 to, the Finance Act 1982 are the same, the requirements of this paragraph may be satisfied by a statement indicating the lowest and highest amounts of the repayments to be made under the modified agreement before deduction of tax.
APR	
14. Modifying agreements under which— (a) the amount of the credit to be provided under an earlier agreement for fixed-sum credit is varied or supplemented;	The APR in relation to the modified agreement or a statement indicating that the total amount payable under the modified agreement is not greater than the total cash

Type of modifying agreement (1)	*Information* (2)
(b) the repayment provisions of such an agreement are varied or supplemented; or (c) any charge included in the total charge for credit in relation to such an agreement is varied or supplemented.	price of the goods, services, land or other things, the acquisition of which is to be financed by credit under that agreement.
15. Modifying agreements not falling within paragraph 16 under which— (a) the provisions relating to any credit limit under an earlier agreement for running-account credit are varied, including a change to or from there being no credit limit; (b) the repayment provisions of such an agreement are varied or supplemented; or (c) any charge included in the total charge for credit in relation to such an agreement is varied or supplemented.	The APR in relation to the modified agreement.
16. (a) Modifying agreements under which— (i) the provisions relating to the credit limit under an earlier debtor-creditor-supplier agreement for running-account credit which fulfils all the criteria in sub-paragraph (b) below are varied; (ii) the repayment provisions of such an agreement are varied or supplemented; or (iii) any charge included in the total charge for credit in relation to such an agreement is varied or supplemented. (b) The criteria referred to in sub-paragraph (a) above are that— (i) the debtor agrees to pay the creditor an amount specified in the agreement on specified occasions; (ii) there is a credit limit; and (iii) charges for credit are either— (aa) a fixed amount in respect of each transaction; or (bb) calculated as a proportion of the price payable under a transaction financed by the credit.	(1) The APR in relation to the modified agreement calculated on the assumptions specified in sub-paragraphs (2) and (3) below. (2) The first assumption referred to in sub-paragraph (1) above is the assumption that— (a) the debtor is provided with an amount of credit at the date of the making of the modifying agreement which, taken with the amount of the charge for that credit ascertained at that date under the provisions of the modified agreement, is equal to the credit limit under the modified agreement; and (b) the debtor repays the sum of the amounts referred to in head (a) above by payments of the amounts specified in the modified agreement on the occasions specified in that agreement and makes no other payment and obtains no further credit in relation to the account. (3) The second assumption referred to in sub-paragraph (1) above is the like assumption as in sub-paragraph (2) above save that the sum of the amounts referred to in head (a) thereof shall be taken to be one third of the credit limit under the modified agreement.
17. Modifying agreements which are required under paragraph 14, 15 or 16 to disclose an APR in relation to the modified agreements and where the APR is based on a total charge for credit which is calculated to take account of relief available under	A statement indicating that it has been assumed in the calculation of the APR in relation to the modified agreement that relief may be available under section 19 of the Income and Corporation Taxes Act 1970 and Schedule 4 to the Finance Act 1976 in

Type of modifying agreement (1)	*Information* (2)
section 19 of the Income and Corporation Taxes Act 1970 and Schedule 4 to the Finance Act 1976.	respect of premiums under certain policies of insurance without any deduction under section 21 of the said Act of 1970.
Variable rates or items	
18. Modifying agreements which are required under paragraph 14, 15 or 16 to disclose an APR in relation to the modified agreement and under which the rate or amount of any item included in the total charge for credit in relation to the modified agreement will or may be varied (other than a variation in consequence of an event which is certain to occur).	A statement indicating that in calculating the APR in relation to the credit to be provided under the modified agreement no account has been taken of any variation which may occur under that agreement of the rate or amount of any item entering into that calculation.
19. Modifying agreements falling within paragraph 18.	A statement indicating the circumstances in which any variation referred to in paragraph 18 above may occur and, where that information is ascertainable at the time at which the document referred to in section 61(1) of the Act is presented or sent to the debtor for signature, the time at which any such variation may occur.
19A. Modifying agreements which are required under paragraph 14, 15 or 16 to disclose an APR in relation to the modified agreement and under which the provisions of an earlier agreement are varied or supplemented with the result that the modified agreement is an agreement to which regulation 15A of the Total Charge for Credit Regulations applies.	The initial standard variable rate (within the meaning of regulation 15A(2) of the Total Charge for Credit Regulations) in relation to the modified agreement, together with a statement explaining— (a) what the rate is; and (b) that is has been taken into account in calculating the APR in relation to the modified agreement.
OTHER INFORMATION	
Security provided by the debtor	
20. Modifying agreements (to which section 114 of the Act applies) under which an article taken in pawn by any person under an earlier agreement is varied or supplemented and where no separate pawn-receipt is given.	A statement indicating that an article has been taken in pawn under the modified agreement and a description of the article, unless unchanged from that in the earlier agreement, sufficient to identify it.
21. Modifying agreements (except those referred to in paragraph 20) under which— (a) any provisions for security provided by the debtor in relation to an earlier agreement to secure the carrying out of the obligations of the debtor under the earlier agreement are varied (including a variation to or from there being no security provided by the debtor); or (b) new or additional security is to be provided by the debtor.	A description of the new, additional or varied security to be provided by the debtor in relation to the modified agreement and of the subject matter to which it relates, sufficient to identify the new, additional or varied security, or a statement indicating that the debtor is no longer providing any security in relation to that agreement.

Type of modifying agreement (1)	*Information* (2)
Charges on default	
22. Modifying agreements under which any provisions for charges on default under an earlier agreement are varied, including a variation to or from there being no such charges.	An indication of any charges payable under the modified agreement to the creditor upon failure by the debtor or a relative of his to do or refrain from doing anything which he is required to do or refrain from doing, as the case may be, or a statement indicating that no such charges are payable under that agreement.

Regulation 7(9)

PART II
INFORMATION TO BE CONTAINED IN DOCUMENTS EMBODYING REGULATED MODIFYING AGREEMENTS VARYING OR SUPPLEMENTING EARLIER HIRE AGREEMENTS

Type of modifying agreement (1)	*Information* (2)
1. All types.	A heading in the following form of words shown prominently on the first page of the document— 'Agreement modifying a Hire Agreement [and] regulated by the Consumer Credit Act 1974'.
Parties to modifying agreement	
2. All types.	(1) The name and a postal address of the owner. (2) The name and a postal address of the hirer.
FINANCIAL AND RELATED PARTICULARS	
Description of goods	
3. Modifying agreements under which— (a) goods to be bailed or hired under an earlier agreement are varied or supplemented; or (b) any provision of an earlier agreement relating to advance, hire or other payments is varied but the goods to be bailed or hired under the earlier agreement are not varied or supplemented.	A list or other description of the goods to be bailed or hired under the modified agreement (whether or not varied or supplemented under the modifying agreement): Provided that, where the description of all the goods to be bailed or hired under the earlier agreement is unchanged, the requirements of this paragraph may be satisfied in relation to such goods by a statement clearly indicating that the descriptions in the earlier agreement are unchanged.
Advance payments	
4. Modifying agreements in relation to which any advance payment is to be made by the hirer additional to any made in relation to an earlier agreement (whether under the modifying agreement or as a condition precedent to the making of that agreement) before he is to take possession	The amount of the additional advance payments to be made by the hirer in relation to the modifying agreement, and, where the modifying agreement is a cancellable agreement, the nature of such payments.

Type of modifying agreement (1)	*Information* (2)
of any additional goods to be bailed or hired under that agreement or, as the case may be, before he enters into that agreement.	
Hire payments	
5. Modifying agreements under which any provisions of an earlier agreement relating to hire payments, other than advance payments, are varied or supplemented.	(1) The amount of each hire payment (other than an advance payment) to be made by the hirer under the modified agreement in relation to any period on or after the date of the modifying agreement. (2) The timing of such payments expressed by reference to one or more of the following— (a) the dates on which each payment is to be made; (b) the frequency and number of the payments and the date of the first payment or a statement indicating the manner in which that date will be determined; (c) a statement indicating the manner in which the dates of the payments will be determined.
Other payments	
6. Modifying agreements under which any provisions of an earlier agreement relating to payments other than advance payments and hire payments are varied or supplemented, including a change to or from there being no such other payments.	(1) The amount (or a statement indicating the manner in which the amount will be determined) of each of the following descriptions of payments (not being an advance payment or a hire payment) to be made under the modified agreement by, or on behalf of, the hirer, or a relative of his, to the owner in relation to any period on or after the date of the modifying agreement, that is to say— (a) any payment under arrangements for the installation, care, maintenance or protection of any goods; (b) any premium under a contract of insurance; or (c) any payment payable on termination of the modified agreement (other than a payment on default to be shown under paragraph 10 below). (2) The timing of such payments to be made under the modified agreement expressed by reference to one or more of the following— (a) the dates on which each payment is to be made; (b) the frequency and number of the payments and the date of the first payment or a statement indicating the manner in which that date will be determined; or (c) a statement indicating the manner in which the dates of the payments will be determined.

Type of modifying agreement (1)	*Information* (2)
	(3) References in this paragraph to the owner include references to his near relative, his partner and a member of a group of which he is a member, to any person nominated by him or by any such person in relation to the arrangements, the contract of insurance or the termination of the modified agreement, and to a near relative of his partner; and 'near relative' means, in relation to any person, the husband, wife, father, mother, brother, sister, son or daughter of that person and 'group' means the person (including a company) having control of a company together with all the companies directly or indirectly controlled by him.
Variable payments	
7. Modifying agreements including provisions for variation of hire or other payments, where the amount of any such payment following any variation cannot be ascertained at the time of the making of the modifying agreement.	(1) Subject to sub-paragraph (2) below, a statement indicating the circumstances in which any hire payment to be shown under paragraph 5 above or any other payment to be shown under paragraph 6 may be varied under the modified agreement and, where that information is ascertainable at the time at which the document referred to in section 61(1) of the Act is presented or sent to the hirer for signature, the time at which any such variation may occur. (2) Sub-paragraph (1) above does not apply to a variation under the modified agreement which takes account only of a change in value added tax. (3) References in sub-paragraph (2) above to a change in value added tax include references to a change to or from no tax being charged.
Duration of hire	
8. Modifying agreements under which— (a) additional goods are to be bailed or hired for a fixed period or a minimum period; or (b) any provisions of an earlier agreement that goods are to be bailed or hired for a fixed period or a minimum period are varied, including a variation to or from there being no such fixed or minimum period.	A statement indicating that goods are to be bailed or hired under the modified agreement for a fixed period or a minimum period, as the case may be, and the duration of that period.
OTHER INFORMATION	
Security provided by the hirer	
9. Modifying agreements under which— (a) any provisions for security by the hirer in relation to an earlier agreement to	A description of the new, additional or varied security to be provided by the hirer in relation to the modified agreement and of

Type of modifying agreement (1)	*Information* (2)
secure the carrying out of the obligations of the hirer under the earlier agreement are varied (including a variation to or from there being no security provided by the hirer); or (b) new or additional security is to be provided by the hirer.	the subject matter to which it relates, sufficient to identify the new, additional or varied security, or a statement indicating that the hirer is no longer providing any security in relation to that agreement.
Charges on default	
10. Modifying agreements under which any provisions for charges on default under an earlier agreement are varied, including a variation to or from there being no such charges.	An indication of any charges payable under the modified agreement to the owner upon failure by the hirer or a relative of his to do or refrain from doing anything which he is required to do or refrain from doing, as the case may be, or a statement indicating that no such charges are payable under that agreement.

CONSUMER CREDIT (CANCELLATION NOTICES AND COPIES OF DOCUMENTS) REGULATIONS 1983 (SI 1983, No. 1557)

1. Citation, commencement and interpretation

(1) These Regulations may be cited as the Consumer Credit (Cancellation Notices and Copies of Documents) Regulations 1983 and shall come into operation on 19 May 1985.

(2) In these Regulations—

'the Act' means the Consumer Credit Act 1974;

'Agreements Regulations' means the Consumer Credit (Agreements) Regulations 1983 and any reference to any provision of those Regulations includes in the case of modifying agreements which are, or are treated as, regulated agreements a reference to Regulation 7 of, and the appropriate paragraph of Schedule 8 to, those Regulations;

'cancellable agreement' includes an agreement which is a modifying agreement treated under section 82(5) of the Act as a cancellable agreement; and

'lettering' includes figures and symbols.

2. Legibility of notices and copy documents and wording of prescribed Forms

(1) The lettering in every notice in a Form prescribed by these Regulations and in every copy of an executed agreement, security instrument or other document referred to in the Act and delivered or sent to a debtor, hirer or surety under any provision of the Act shall, apart from any signature, be easily legible and of a colour which is readily distinguishable from the colour of the paper.

(2) The wording of any Form prescribed by these Regulations shall be reproduced in copies of unexecuted or executed agreements or in Notices of Cancellation Rights sent by post under section 64(1)(b) or (2) of the Act without any alteration or addition, except that—

(a) the creditor or owner may enter the name and address of the debtor or hirer in any Cancellation Form prescribed by these Regulations; and

(b) every Form shall be completed in accordance with any footnote.

(3) Any such footnote shall not be treated as part of any Form prescribed by these Regulations and may be reproduced in addition to any such Form.

(4) Where any such footnote requires any words to be omitted, those words shall be omitted or deleted.

(5) Where words are shown in capital letters in any Form prescribed in Parts I to IV of the Schedule to these Regulations and are reproduced in copies of unexecuted or executed agreements they shall be afforded more prominence (whether by capital letters, underlining,

large or bold print or otherwise) than any other lettering in that Form except lettering inserted in accordance with paragraph (2) above and no less prominence than that given to any other information in the copy apart from the heading to the agreement or copy, the annual percentage rate of charge for credit, trade names, names of parties to the agreement or lettering in the document inserted in handwriting.

(6) Where words are shown in capital letters in any Form prescribed in Part VI of the Schedule to these Regulations and are reproduced in Notices of Cancellation Rights sent by post under section 64(1)(b) or (2) of the Act they shall be afforded more prominence (whether by capital letters, underlining, large or bold print or otherwise) than any other lettering in that Form except lettering inserted in accordance with paragraph (2) above.

3. General requirements as to form and content of copy documents

(1) Subject to the following provisions of these Regulations, every copy of an executed agreement, security instrument or other document referred to in the Act and delivered or sent to a debtor, hirer or surety under any provision of the Act shall be a true copy thereof.

(2) There may be omitted from any such copy—

(a) any information included in an executed agreement, security instrument or other document relating to the debtor, hirer or surety or included for the use of the creditor or owner only which is not required to be included therein by the Act or any Regulations thereunder as to the form and content of the document of which it is a copy;

(b) any signature box, signature or date of signature (other than, in the case of a copy of a cancellable executed agreement delivered to the debtor under section 63(1) of the Act, the date of signature by the debtor of an agreement to which section 68(b) of the Act applies);

(c) in the case of any copy of an unexecuted agreement delivered or sent to the debtor or hirer under section 62 of that Act, the name and address of the debtor or hirer; and

[(d) in the case of any copy of an executed agreement given to the debtor under section 77(1) of the Act for fixed-sum credit, or under section 78(1) for running-account credit, under which a person takes any article in pawn, any description of the article taken in pawn.]

4. Copies of unexecuted agreements given under section 58(1) of the Act

Where the agreement is one to which section 58(1) of the Act applies, every copy of the unexecuted agreement given to a debtor or hirer under section 58(1) of the Act shall include—

(a) a heading which shall be in the Form numbered 1 in Column 1 of Part I of the Schedule to these Regulations and set out in Column 3 shown prominently on the first page of the copy, instead of any heading referred to in Regulation 2(1) and 3(1) of, and paragraph 1 of Schedules 1 and 3 to, the Agreements Regulations; and

(b) a box containing only a notice indicating the right of the debtor or hirer to withdraw from the prospective agreement, and how and when the right is exercisable, in the Form numbered 2 in Column 1 of Part I of the Schedule to these Regulations and set out in Column 3, instead of any statement of the rights of the debtor or hirer referred to in Regulations 2(3) and 3(3) of, and Form 1 of Schedules 2 and 4 to, the Agreements Regulations.

5. Copies of cancellable unexecuted and executed agreements

(1) Every copy of a cancellable unexecuted agreement delivered or sent to a debtor or hirer under section 62 of the Act or of a cancellable executed agreement delivered to him under section 63(1) of the Act shall include a box containing only a notice indicating the right of the debtor or hirer to cancel the agreement, and how and when that right is exercisable, in the Form numbered in Column 1 in Part II of the Schedule to these Regulations and set out in Column 3 appropriate to the type of agreement referred to in Column 2, instead of any statement of the rights of the debtor or hirer referred to in Regulations 2(3) and 3(3) of, and Forms 2 to 4 of Schedule 2 and Forms 2 and 3 of Schedule 4 to, the Agreements Regulations.

(2) Every copy of a cancellable executed agreement sent by post to the debtor or hirer under section 63(2) of the Act within the seven days following the making of the agreement or under section 63(4) shall include—

(a) a box containing only a notice indicating the right of the debtor or hirer to cancel the agreement, and how and when that right is exercisable, in the Form numbered in Column 1 in Part III of the Schedule to these Regulations and set out in Column 3 appropriate to the type of agreement referred to in Column 2, instead of any statement of the rights of the debtor or hirer referred to in Regulations 2(3) and 3(3) of, and Forms 2 to 4 of Schedule 2 and Forms 2 and 3 of Schedule 4 to, the Agreements Regulations; and

(b) a Cancellation Form which shall be in the Form specified in Part IV of the Schedule.

(3) Where a notice indicating the right of the debtor or hirer to cancel a cancellable unexecuted or executed agreement does not appear prominently on the first page of any copy of such an agreement delivered or sent to the debtor or hirer under section 62 or 63 of the Act, the copy shall include on its first page a box containing only the statement in the Form specified in Part V of the Schedule to these Regulations.

[(4) In the case of—

(a) an unexecuted agreement a copy of which is required to be delivered or sent to a debtor or hirer under section 62 of the Act;

(b) an executed agreement a copy of which is required to be delivered to a debtor or hirer under section 63(1); or

(c) an executed agreement a copy of which is required to be given to a debtor or hirer under section 63(2) or (4), and

which is not a cancellable agreement within the meaning of the Act and these Regulations but which may be cancellable by the debtor or hirer in accordance with terms of the agreement conferring upon him similar rights as if the agreement were such a cancellable agreement, the agreement may be treated for the purposes of this Regulation as if it were a cancellable agreement within the meaning of the Act and of these Regulations, and Regulation 2 shall then apply as if the agreement were such a cancellable agreement.]

6. Notices of cancellation rights sent by post under section 64(1)(b) or (2) of the Act

Any notice which indicates the right of the debtor or hirer to cancel a cancellable agreement, and how and when that right is exercisable, and which is sent by post to the debtor or hirer under section 64(1)(b) of the Act within the seven days following the making of the agreement or under section 64(2), shall be—

(a) in the Form numbered in Column 1 in Part VI of the Schedule to these Regulations and set out in Column 3 appropriate to the type of agreement referred to in Column 2; and

(b) on a single sheet of paper, and

(i) if the notice is entirely on one side of the paper, the Cancellation Form forming part of that notice shall be on that side; or

(ii) if the notice is continued on the back of the paper, the symbol and word '/over' shall be shown below that part of the text which appears on the front of the paper.

7. Copies of agreements or security instruments where the agreement or security instrument has been varied

(1) Where an agreement has been varied in accordance with section 82(1) of the Act, every copy of the executed agreement given to a debtor, hirer or surety under any provision of the Act other than section 85(1) shall include either—

(a) an easily legible copy of the latest notice of variation given in accordance with section 82(1) of the Act relating to each discrete term of the agreement which has been varied; or

(b) an easily legible statement of the terms of the agreement as varied in accordance with section 82(1) of the Act.

(2) Where a security provided in relation to a regulated agreement has been varied, every copy of the security instrument relating to it given to a debtor, hirer or surety under any provision of the Act shall include either—

(a) an easily legible copy of any document varying the security; or

(b) an easily legible statement of the terms of the security as varied.

8. Copies of credit-token agreements where the agreement contains a power of variation

Every copy of an executed credit-token agreement given to the debtor under section 85(1) of the Act where the agreement may be varied under a power contained in it shall comprise an easily legible statement of the current terms of the agreement (whether or not varied in accordance with section 82(1) of the Act).

9. Copies of old agreements and security instruments where the agreement or security instrument has been lost etc.

Any copy of an executed agreement made before 19 May 1985 or of a security instrument relating to security provided before that date which is given to the debtor, hirer or surety under any provision of the Act on or after that date may comprise an easily legible statement of the current terms of the agreement or security as the case may be insofar as they are known to the creditor or owner where, due to an accident or some other cause beyond his control, the creditor or owner does not have in his possession the executed agreement or security instrument or any copy thereof.

10. Surety's copy of enforcement, default and termination notices

Every copy of a default notice or a notice under section 76(1) or 98(1) of the Act served on any surety under section 111(1) of the Act shall contain a prominent heading in one of the following forms of words—

'Surety's copy of notice served on debtor' or

'Surety's copy of notice served on hirer',

as the case may require.

11. Duty to supply copies of documents not to apply to certain kinds of documents

A duty imposed by the Act to supply a copy of a document referred to in an unexecuted agreement or an executed agreement shall not apply to a document of any of the following kinds—

(a) a document obtained by the debtor or hirer from a person other than the creditor or owner and supplied by the debtor or hirer to the creditor or owner;

[(aa) in the case of an agreement of the description specified in the Schedule to the Consumer Credit (Notice of Cancellation Rights) (Exemption) Regulations 1983 and terms of which are contained in a catalogue which is at all reasonable times during the agreement readily available for inspection by the debtor, a copy of the catalogue in question;]

(b) a document, not being a security, which constitutes, evidences or relates to title to property of any kind or relates to the rights or duties of the debtor or hirer in respect of such property;

(c) a document kept, or to be kept, by the debtor or hirer under the terms of, or in consequence of, the agreement;

(d) an official or certified copy of any entry in a register maintained by, or on behalf of, a government department or other body charged with a public administrative or statutory function and open to public inspection (whether in the United Kingdom or elsewhere);

(e) an enactment, other than Schedule 3 to the Conveyancing and Feudal Reform (Scotland) Act 1970;

(f) a document, other than an enactment, published by, or on behalf of, a government department or other body charged with a public administrative or statutory function (whether in the United Kingdom or elsewhere);

(g) in the case of a modifying agreement, a document embodying the terms of the earlier agreement other than a document a copy of which is required to be given under section 77(1), 78(1), 79(1), 85(1), 105(5), 107(1), 108(1) or 109(1) of the Act; or

[(h) in the case of an unexecuted agreement where the prospective regulated agreement or regulated agreement as the case may be is to be or is secured on land, any document referred to in the unexecuted or executed agreement as the case may be in a case where the debtor or hirer has earlier been supplied with a copy of that document in an identical form by virtue of any requirement of the Act.]

Regulation 4

SCHEDULE

PART I

Form of heading to be included in copies of unexecuted agreements where the prospective regulated agreement is to be secured on land given to the debtor or hirer under section 58(1) of the Act

Form no (1)	*Type of agreement* (2)	*Form* (3)
1	An agreement to which section 58(1) of the Act applies.	Copy of proposed [credit] [hire][1] agreement containing notice of your right to withdraw. Do NOT sign or return this copy Note: 1 Creditor or owner to omit word in square brackets not applicable.

Form of notice of right to withdraw to be included in copies of unexecuted agreements where the prospective regulated agreement is to be secured on land, given to the debtor or hirer under section 58(1) of the Act

Form no (1)	*Type of agreement* (2)	*Form* (3)
2	An agreement of the kind to which Form 1 applies.	YOUR RIGHT TO WITHDRAW This is a copy of your proposed [credit] [hire][1] agreement which is to be secured on land. It has been given to you now so that you may have at least a week to consider its terms before the actual agreement is sent to you for signature. You should read it carefully. If you do not understand it, you may need to seek professional advice. If you do not wish to go ahead with it, you need not do so. If you decide NOT to go ahead with the agreement you should inform [2] or, if you prefer, any supplier or broker involved in the negotiations. You can do this in writing or orally for example by telephone. If the agreement arrives for signature and you have decided NOT to go ahead. DO NOT SIGN IT. Then you will not be legally bound by the agreement.

Form no (1)	*Type of agreement* (2)	*Form* (3)
		[Note: Your notice of withdrawal will not affect [your contract for life assurance] [your contract for insurance] [your contract of guarantee] [your contract to open a current account] [your contract to open a deposit account].][1] [The place where your financial obligations consequent upon withdrawal from this agreement are shown is [3].][4]][1]
		Notes: 1 Creditor or owner to omit words in square brackets where not applicable. 2 Creditor or owner to insert the words 'the creditor' or 'the owner' as the case may require or the expression by which the creditor or owner is referred to in the copy of the unexecuted agreement, or an appropriate pronoun. 3 Creditor or owner to insert a clear reference to the place where these obligations appear. 4 Creditor or owner may include words in square brackets where applicable.

Regulation 5(1)

PART II

Forms of notice of cancellation rights to be included in copies of cancellable unexecuted or executed agreements given to the debtor or hirer under section 62 or 63(1) of the Act

Form no (1)	*Type of agreement* (2)	*Form* (3)
3	A regulated consumer credit agreement to which section 68(b) of the Act applies.	YOUR RIGHT TO CANCEL You have a right to cancel this agreement for FOURTEEN DAYS starting with the day after you signed it. You can do this by sending or taking a WRITTEN notice of cancellation to [1]. If you intend to cancel, you should not use any goods you already have under the agreement and you should keep them safe. You can wait for them to be collected from you and you need not hand them over unless you receive a written request. [If you wish, however, you may return

Form no (1)	*Type of agreement* (2)	*Form* (3)
		the goods yourself.][2] [You are warned that it would be dangerous and could be in contravention of Health and Safety legislation for you to attempt to disconnect and return the goods yourself.][2] Notes: 1 Creditor or agent to insert name and address of person to whom notice may be given, or an indication of the person to whom notice may be given with a clear reference to the place in the document where his name and address appear. 2 Creditor or agent to include the words in the first set of square brackets unless the words in the second set of square brackets are applicable, i.e. in a case where the subject matter of the agreement is a liquefied petroleum gas vessel of greater than 150 litres water capacity.
4	A regulated hire-purchase agreement, conditional sale agreement or consumer hire agreement (other than one to which Form 3 applies or, in the case of a modifying agreement, one to which Form 9 applies).	YOUR RIGHT TO CANCEL Once you have signed, you will have for a short time a right to cancel this agreement. You can do this by sending or taking a WRITTEN notice of cancellation to[1]. If you cancel this agreement, any money you have paid [, goods given in part-exchange (or their value) and property given as security][2] must be returned to you. You will not have to make any further payment. If you have any goods under the agreement, you should not use them and should keep them safe. (Legal action may be taken against you if you do not take proper care of them.) You can wait for them to be collected from you and you need not hand them over unless you receive a written request. [If you wish, however, you may return the goods yourself.][3] [You are warned that it would be dangerous and could be contravention of Health and Safety legislation for you to attempt to disconnect and return the goods yourself.][3]

Form no (1)	*Type of agreement* (2)	*Form* (3)
		Note: Your notice of cancellation will not affect [your contract for life assurance] [your contract for insurance] [your contract of guarantee] [your contract to open a current account] [your contract to open a deposit account].[4] [The place where your financial obligations consequent upon cancellation of this agreement are shown is[5].][6] Notes: 1 Creditor or owner to insert name and address of person to whom notice may be given, or an indication of the person to whom notice may be given with a clear reference to the place in the document where his name and address appear. 2 Creditor or owner may omit words in square brackets where not applicable. 3 Creditor or owner to include the words in the first set of square brackets unless the words in the second set of square brackets are applicable, i.e. in a case where the subject matter of the agreement is a liquefied petroleum gas vessel of greater than 150 litres water capacity. 4 Creditor or owner to omit words in square brackets where not applicable. 5 Creditor or owner to insert a clear reference to the place where these obligations appear. 6 Creditor or owner may include words in square brackets where applicable.
5	A debtor-creditor-supplier agreement falling within section 12(a) or (b) of the Act (other than one to which Form 3 or 4 applies or, in the case of a modifying agreement, one to which Form 9 applies).	YOUR RIGHT TO CANCEL Once you have signed, you will have for a short time a right to cancel this agreement. You can do this by sending or taking a WRITTEN notice of cancellation to [1]. If you cancel this agreement, any money you have paid [, goods given in part-exchange (or their value) and property given as security][2] must be returned to you. You will not have to make any further payment.

Form no (1)	*Type of agreement* (2)	*Form* (3)
		[If you already have any goods under the agreement, you should not use them and should keep them safe. (Legal action may be taken against you if you do not take proper care of them.) You can wait for them to be collected from you and you need not hand them over unless you receive a written request. [If you wish, however, you may return the goods yourself.][3] [You are warned that it would be dangerous and could be in contravention of Health and Safety legislation for you to attempt to disconnect and return the goods yourself.][3]][2] [You will not, however, be required to hand back any goods supplied to meet an emergency or which have already been incorporated, for example in your home. But you will still be liable to pay for emergency goods or services or for any goods which have been incorporated by you or one of your relatives.][2] [Note. Your notice of cancellation will not affect [your contract for life assurance] [your contract for insurance] [your contract of guarantee] [your contract to open a current account] [your contract to open a deposit account].[4] [The place where your financial obligations consequent upon cancellation of this agreement are shown is [5].][6]][4]
		Notes: 1 Creditor to insert name and address of person to whom notice may be given, or an indication of the person to whom notice may be given with a clear reference to the place in the document where his name and address appear. 2 Creditor may omit words in square brackets where not applicable. 3 Creditor to include the words in the first set of square brackets unless the words in the second set of square brackets are applicable, i.e. in a case where the subject matter of the agreement is a liquefied petroleum gas

Form no (1)	*Type of agreement* (2)	*Form* (3)
		vessel of greater than 150 litres water capacity. 4 Creditor to omit words in square brackets where not applicable. 5 Creditor to insert a clear reference to the place where these obligations appear. 6 Creditor may include words in square brackets where applicable.
6	A regulated consumer credit agreement (other than one to which Form 3, 4 or 5 applies or which is a multiple agreement of the kind to which Form 7 or 8 applies or, in the case of a modifying agreement, one to which Form 9 applies).	YOUR RIGHT TO CANCEL Once you have signed, you will have for a short time a right to cancel this agreement. You can do this by sending or taking a WRITTEN notice of cancellation to [1]. If you cancel this agreement, any money you have paid [and any property given as security][2] must be returned to you. You will still have to repay any money lent to you. But if you repay all of it before your first instalment is due — or, if you are not paying by instalments, within one month after cancellation — you will not have to pay interest or other charges. [Note: Your notice of cancellation will not affect [your contract for life assurance] [your contract for insurance] [your contract of guarantee] [your contract to open a current account] [your contract to open a deposit account].[3] [The place where your financial obligations consequent upon cancellation of this agreement are shown is [4].][5]][3]. Notes: 1 Creditor to insert name and address of person to whom notice may be given, or an indication of the person to whom notice may be given with a clear reference to the place in the document where his name and address appear. 2 Creditor may omit words in square brackets where not applicable. 3 Creditor to omit words in square brackets where not applicable. 4 Creditor to insert a clear reference to the place where these obligations appear.

Form no (1)	*Type of agreement* (2)	*Form* (3)
		5 Creditor may include words in square brackets where applicable.
7	A multiple agreement which places at least one part within one category of agreement to which either Form 4 or 5 applies and at least one part within one category of agreement to which Form 6 applies (other than one to which Form 8 applies).	YOUR RIGHT TO CANCEL Once you have signed, you will have for a short time a right to cancel this agreement. You can do this by sending or taking a WRITTEN notice of cancellation to [1]. If you cancel this agreement, any money you have paid [, goods given in part-exchange (or their value) and property given as security][2] must be returned to you. You will still have to repay any money lent to you. But if you repay all of it before your first instalment is due — or, if you are not paying by instalments, within one month after cancellation — you will not have to pay interest or other charges. [Any goods which you already have under the agreement, apart from any purchased out of a cash loan, will have to be returned. Such goods should not be used and should be kept safe. (Legal action may be taken against you if you do not take proper care of them.) You can wait for them to be collected from you and you need not hand them over unless you receive a written request. [If you wish, however, you may return the goods yourself.][3] [You are warned that it would be dangerous and could be in contravention of Health and Safety legislation for you to attempt to disconnect and return the goods yourself.][3]][2] [You will not, however, be required to hand back any goods supplied to meet an emergency or which have already been incorporated, for example in your home. But you will still be liable to pay for emergency goods or services or for any goods which have been incorporated by you or one of your relatives.][4] [Note: Your notice of cancellation will not affect [your contract for life assurance] [your contract for

Form no (1)	*Type of agreement* (2)	*Form* (3)
		insurance] [your contract of guarantee] [your contract to open a current account] [your contract to open a deposit account].[5] [The place where your financial obligations consequent upon cancellation of this agreement are shown is [6],][7]][5]
		Notes: 1 Creditor or owner to insert name and address of person to whom notice maybe given, or an indication of the person to whom notice may be given with a clear reference to the place in the document where his name and address appear. 2 Creditor or owner may omit words in square brackets where not applicable. 3 Creditor or owner to include the words in the first set of square brackets unless the words in the second set of square brackets are applicable, i.e. in a case where the subject matter of the agreement is a liquefied petroleum gas vessel of greater than 150 litres water capacity. 4 Paragraph in square brackets applies only where the notice relates to a multiple agreement of which at least one part is a debtor-creditor-supplier agreement falling within section 12(a) or (b) of the Act, not being a hire-purchase or conditional sale agreement. Creditor may omit this paragraph if inapplicable. 5 Creditor or owner to omit words in square brackets where not applicable. 6 Creditor or owner to insert a clear reference to the place where these obligations appear. 7 Creditor or owner may include words in square brackets where applicable.
8	A multiple agreement of which at least one part is a debtor-creditor agreement and at least one part is a credit agreement not regulated by the Act.	YOUR RIGHT TO CANCEL Once you have signed, you will have for a short time a right to cancel that part of this agreement which is regulated by the Consumer Credit Act 1974. You can do this by

Form no (1)	Type of agreement (2)	Form (3)
		sending or taking a WRITTEN notice of cancellation to [1]. If you cancel, any money you have paid in connection with the regulated agreement [and any property given as security in relation to that agreement][2] must be returned to you. You will still have to repay any money lent to you. But if you repay all of it before your first instalment is due — or, if you are not paying by instalments, within one month after cancellation — you will not have to pay interest or other charges. [Note: Your notice of cancellation will not affect [your contract for life assurance] [your contract for insurance] [your contract of guarantee] [your contract to open a current account] [your contract to open a deposit account].[3] [The place where your financial obligations consequent upon cancellation of this agreement are shown is [4].][5]][3]
		Notes: 1 Creditor to insert name and address of person to whom notice may be given, or an indication of the person to whom notice may be given with a clear reference to the place in the document where his name and address appear. 2 Creditor may omit words in square brackets where not applicable. 3 Creditor to omit words in square brackets where not applicable. 4 Creditor to insert a clear reference to the place where these obligations appear. 5 Creditor may include words in square brackets where applicable.
9	A modifying agreement treated under section 82(5) of the Act as a cancellable agreement.	YOUR RIGHT TO CANCEL This agreement modifies an earlier agreement. Once you have signed it, your right to cancel [that part of][1] the earlier agreement [which was regulated by the Consumer Credit Act 1974][1] will be widened to cover the [regulated][1] agreement as

Form no (1)	*Type of agreement* (2)	*Form* (3)
		modified. The cancellation period itself is unchanged. A [copy of the earlier agreement containing a][2] notice of your cancellation rights may have already been sent to you giving you details of when that period expires. If you wish to cancel the [regulated][1] agreement as modified, you can do this by sending or taking a WRITTEN notice of cancellation to [3].
		Notes: 1 Creditor or owner to omit passages in square brackets except in the case of a multiple agreement of which at least one part is a credit agreement not regulated by the Act. 2 Creditor or owner to omit words in square brackets where not applicable. 3 Creditor or owner to insert name and address of person to whom notice may be given, or an indication of the person to whom notice may be given with a clear reference to the place in the document where his name and address appear.

Regulation 5(2)(a) PART III

Forms of notice of cancellation rights to be included in copies of cancellable executed agreements sent by post to the debtor or hirer under section 63(2) or (4) of the Act

Form no (1)	*Type of agreement* (2)	*Form* (3)
10	A regulated hire-purchase agreement, conditional sale agreement or consumer hire agreement (other than, in the case of a modifying agreement, one to which Form 15 applies).	YOUR RIGHT TO CANCEL You have a right to cancel this agreement. You can do this by sending or taking a WRITTEN notice of cancellation to [1]. You have FIVE DAYS starting with the day after you received this copy. You can use the form provided. If you cancel this agreement, any money you have paid [, goods given in part-exchange (or their value) and property given as security][2] must be returned to you. You will not have to make any further payment.

Form no (1)	*Type of agreement* (2)	*Form* (3)
		[If you already have any goods under the agreement, you should not use them and should keep them safe. (Legal action may be taken against you if you do not take proper care of them.) You can wait for them to be collected from you and you need not hand them over unless you receive a written request. [If you wish, however, you may return the goods yourself.][3] [You are warned that it would be dangerous and could be in contravention of Health and Safety legislation for you to attempt to disconnect and return the goods yourself.][3]][2] [Note: Your notice of cancellation will not affect [your contract for life assurance] [your contract for insurance] [your contract of guarantee] [your contract to open a current account] [your contract to open a deposit account].[4] [The place where your financial obligations consequent upon cancellation of this agreement are shown is [5].][6]][4]
		Notes: 1 Creditor or owner to insert name and address of person to whom notice may be given, or an indication of the person to whom notice may be given with a clear reference to the place in the document where his name and address appear. 2 Creditor or owner to omit words in square brackets where not applicable. 3 Creditor or owner to include the words in the first set of square brackets unless the words in the second set of square brackets are applicable, i.e. in a case where the subject matter of the agreement is a liquefied petroleum gas vessel of greater than 150 litres water capacity. 4 Creditor or owner to omit words in square brackets where not applicable. 5 Creditor or owner to insert a clear reference to the place where these obligations appear. 6 Creditor or owner may include words in square brackets where applicable.

Form no (1)	*Type of agreement* (2)	*Form* (3)
11	A debtor-creditor-supplier agreement falling within section 12(a) or (b) of the Act (other than one to which Form 10 applies or, in the case of a modifying agreement, one to which Form 15 applies).	YOUR RIGHT TO CANCEL You have a right to cancel this agreement. You can do this by sending or taking a WRITTEN notice of cancellation to [1]. You have FIVE DAYS starting with the day after you received this copy. You can use the form provided. If you cancel this agreement, any money you have paid [, goods given in part-exchange (or their value) and property given as security][2] must be returned to you. You will not have to make any further payment. [If you already have any goods under the agreement, you should not use them and should keep them safe. (Legal action may be taken against you if you do not take proper care of them.) You can wait for them to be collected from you and you need not hand them over unless you receive a written request. (If you wish, however, you may return the goods yourself.][3] [You are warned that it would be dangerous and could be in contravention of Health and Safety legislation for you to attempt to disconnect and return the goods yourself.][3]][2] [You will not, however, be required to hand back any goods supplied to meet an emergency or which have already been incorporated, for example in your home. But you will still be liable to pay for emergency goods or services or for any goods which have been incorporated by you or one of your relatives.][2] [Note: Your notice of cancellation will not affect [your contract for life assurance] [your contract for insurance] [your contract of guarantee] [your contract to open a current account] [your contract to open a deposit account].[4] [The place where your financial obligations consequent upon cancellation of this agreement are shown is [5].][6]][4]

Form no (1)	*Type of agreement* (2)	*Form* (3)
		Notes: 1 Creditor to insert name and address of person to whom notice may be given, or an indication of the person to whom notice may be given with a clear reference to the place in the document where his name and address appear. 2 Creditor may omit words in square brackets where not applicable. 3 Creditor to include the words in the first set of square brackets unless the words in the second set of square brackets are applicable, i.e. in a case where the subject matter of the agreement is a liquefied petroleum gas vessel of greater than 150 litres water capacity. 4 Creditor to omit words in square brackets where not applicable. 5 Creditor to insert a clear reference to the place where these obligations appear. 6 Creditor may include words in square brackets where applicable.
12	A regulated consumer credit agreement (other than one to which Form 10 or 11 applies or which is a multiple agreement of the kind to which Form 14 or 15 applies or, in the case of a modifying agreement, one to which Form 15 applies).	YOUR RIGHT TO CANCEL You have a right to cancel this agreement. You can do this by sending or taking a WRITTEN notice of cancellation to [1]. You have FIVE DAYS starting with the day after you received this copy. You can use the form provided. If you cancel this agreement, any money you have paid [and any property given as security][2] must be returned to you. You will still have to repay any money lent to you. But if you repay all of it before your first instalment is due — or, if you are not paying by instalments, within one month after cancellation — you will not have to pay interest or other charges. [Note: Your notice of cancellation will not affect [your contract for life assurance] [your contract for insurance] [your contract of guarantee] [your contract to open a current account] [your contract to open a deposit account].[3] [The place where your financial obligations

Form no (1)	Type of agreement (2)	Form (3)
		consequent upon cancellation of this agreement are shown is [4].][5]][3]
		Notes: 1 Creditor to insert name and address of person to whom notice may be given, or an indication of the person to whom notice may be given with a clear reference to the place in the document where his name and address appear. 2 Creditor may omit words in square brackets where not applicable. 3 Creditor to omit words in square brackets where not applicable. 4 Creditor to insert a clear reference to the place where these obligations appear. 5 Creditor may include words in square brackets where applicable.
13	A multiple agreement which places at least one part within one category of agreement to which either Form 10 or 11 applies and at least one part within one category of agreement to which Form 12 applies (other than one to which Form 14 applies).	YOUR RIGHT TO CANCEL You have a right to cancel this agreement. You can do this by sending or taking a WRITTEN notice of cancellation to [1]. You have FIVE DAYS starting with the day after you received this copy. You can use the form provided. If you cancel this agreement, any money you have paid [, goods given in part-exchange (or their value) and property given as security][2] must be returned to you. You will still have to repay any money lent to you. But if you repay all of it before your first instalment is due — or, if you are not paying by instalments, within one month after cancellation — you will not have to pay interest or other charges. [Any goods which you already have under the agreement, apart from any purchased out of a cash loan, will have to be returned. Such goods should not be used and should be kept safe. (Legal action may be taken against you if you do not take proper care of them.) You can wait for them to be collected from you and you need not hand them over unless you receive a

Form no (1)	*Type of agreement* (2)	*Form* (3)
		written request. [If you wish, however, you may return the goods yourself.][3] [You are warned that it would be dangerous and could be in contravention of Health and Safety legislation for you to attempt to disconnect and return the goods yourself.][3]][2] [You will not, however, be required to hand back any goods supplied to meet an emergency or which have already been incorporated, for example in your home. But you will still be liable to pay for emergency goods or services or for any goods which have been incorporated by you or one of your relatives.][4] [Note: Your notice of cancellation will not affect [your contract for life assurance] [your contract for insurance] [your contract of guarantee] [your contract to open a current account] [your contract to open a deposit account].[5] [The place where your financial obligations consequent upon cancellation of this agreement are shown is [6].][7]][5]
		Notes: 1 Creditor or owner to insert name and address of person to whom notice may be given, or an indication of the person to whom notice may be given with a clear reference to the place in the document where his name and address appear. 2 Creditor or owner may omit words in square brackets where not applicable. 3 Creditor or owner to include the words in the first set of square brackets unless the words in the second set of square brackets are applicable, i.e. in a case where the subject matter of the agreement is a liquefied petroleum gas vessel of greater than 150 litres water capacity. 4 Paragraph in square brackets applies only where the notice relates to a multiple agreement of which at least one part is a debtor-creditor-supplier

Form no (1)	*Type of agreement* (2)	*Form* (3)
		agreement falling within section 12(a) or (b) of the Act, not being a hire-purchase or conditional sale agreement. Creditor may omit this paragraph if inapplicable. 5 Creditor or owner to omit words in square brackets where not applicable. 6 Creditor or owner to insert a clear reference to the place where these obligations appear. 7 Creditor or owner may include words in square brackets where applicable.
14	A multiple agreement of which at least one part is a debtor-creditor agreement and at least one part is a credit agreement not regulated by the Act.	YOUR RIGHT TO CANCEL You have a right to cancel that part of this agreement which is regulated by the Consumer Credit Act 1974. You can do this by sending or taking a WRITTEN notice of cancellation to [1]. You have FIVE DAYS starting with the day after you received this copy. You can use the form provided. If you cancel, any money you have paid in connection with the regulated agreement [and any property given as security in relation to that agreement][2] must be returned to you. You will still have to repay any money lent to you. But if you repay all of it before your first instalment is due — or, if you are not paying by instalments, within one month after cancellation — you will not have to pay interest or other charges. [Note: Your notice of cancellation will not affect [your contract for life assurance] [your contract for insurance] [your contract of guarantee] [your contract to open a current account] [your contract to open a deposit account].[3] [The place where your financial obligations consequent upon cancellation of this agreement are shown is [4].][5]][3] Notes: 1 Creditor to insert name and address of person to whom notice may be given, or an indication of the person to

Form no (1)	*Type of agreement* (2)	*Form* (3)
		whom notice may be given with a clear reference to the place in the document where his name and address appear. 2 Creditor may omit words in square brackets where not applicable. 3 Creditor to omit words in square brackets where not applicable. 4 Creditor to insert a clear reference to the place where these obligations appear. 5 Creditor may include words in square brackets where applicable.
15	A modifying agreement treated under section 82(5) of the Act as a cancellable agreement.	YOUR RIGHT TO CANCEL This agreement modifies an earlier agreement. Your right to cancel [that part of][1] the earlier agreement [which was regulated by the Consumer Credit Act 1974][1] has been widened to cover the [regulated][1] agreement as modified. The cancellation period itself is unchanged. A [copy of the earlier agreement containing a][2] notice of your cancellation rights may have already been sent to you giving you details of when that period expires. If you wish to cancel the [regulated][1] agreement as modified, you can do this by sending or taking a WRITTEN notice of cancellation to [3]. You can use the form provided. Notes: 1 Creditor or owner to omit passages in square brackets except in the case of a multiple agreement of which at least one part is a credit agreement not regulated by the Act. 2 Creditor or owner to omit words in square brackets where not applicable. 3 Creditor or owner to insert name and address of person to whom notice may be given, or an indication of the person to whom notice may be given with a clear reference to the place in the document where his name and address appear.

Regulation 5(2)(b) PART IV

Cancellation form to be included in copy cancellable executed agreements sent by post to the debtor or hirer under section 63(2) or (4) of the Act

Form no (1)	*Type of agreement* (2)	*Form* (3)
16	A cancellable agreement in respect of which a copy is sent by post to the debtor or hirer under section 63(2) or (4) of the Act.	CANCELLATION FORM (Complete and return this form ONLY IF YOU WISH TO CANCEL THE [REGULATED PART OF THE][1] AGREEMENT.) To: [2] I/We* hereby give notice that I/we* wish to [exercise my/our* right to][1] cancel [that part of][1] agreement [3] [which is regulated by the Consumer Credit Act 1974][1]. Signed Date *Delete as appropriate Notes: 1 Creditor or owner to omit passages in square brackets except in the case of a multiple agreement of which at least one part is a credit agreement not regulated by the Act. 2 Creditor or owner to insert name and address of person to whom notice may be given. 3 Creditor or owner to insert reference number, code or other identification details.

Regulation 5(3) PART V

Form of statement to be included in copy cancellable agreements given to the debtor or hirer under section 62 or 63 of the Act, where a notice of cancellation rights does not appear prominently on the first page of the copy

Form no (1)	*Type of agreement* (2)	*Form* (3)
17	A cancellable agreement in respect of which a copy must be given to the debtor or hirer under section 62 or 63 of the Act, where the cancellation notice prescribed in Part II or III of this Schedule is not shown prominently on the first page of the copy.	This is a copy of your agreement for you to keep. It includes a notice about your cancellation rights which you should read.

Regulation 6 PART VI

Forms of notice of cancellation rights to be sent by post to the debtor or hirer under section 64(1)(b) or (2) of the Act

Form no (1)	*Type of agreement* (2)	*Form* (3)
18	A regulated hire-purchase agreement, conditional sale agreement or consumer hire agreement (other than, in the case of a modifying agreement, one to which Form 23 applies).	IMPORTANT — YOU SHOULD READ THIS CAREFULLY STATUTORY NOTICE RELATING TO A REGULATED [HIRE-PURCHASE] [CONDITIONAL SALE] [CONSUMER HIRE][1] AGREEMENT YOUR RIGHT TO CANCEL You recently made a [hire-purchase] [conditional sale] [consumer hire][1] agreement [2] with [3]. You have a right to cancel it if you wish. You can do this by sending or taking a WRITTEN notice of cancellation to [4]. You have FIVE DAYS starting with the day after you received this notice. You can use the form provided. If you cancel the agreement, any money you have paid [, goods given in part-exchange (or their value) and property given as security][5] must be returned to you. You will not have to make any further payment. [If you already have any goods under the agreement, you should not use them and should keep them safe. (Legal action may be taken against you if you do not take proper care of them.) You can wait for them to be collected from you and you need not hand them over unless you receive a written request. [If you wish, however, you may return the goods yourself.][6] [You are warned that it would be dangerous and could be in contravention of Health and Safety legislation for you to attempt to disconnect and return the goods yourself.][6]][5] [Note: Your notice of cancellation will not affect [your contract for life assurance] [your contract for insurance] [your contract of guarantee] [your contract to open a current account] [your contract to open a deposit account].[1] [The place where your financial obligations consequent upon cancellation of this agreement are shown is [7].][8]][1]

Form no (1)	*Type of agreement* (2)	*Form* (3)
		CANCELLATION FORM (Complete, detach and return this form ONLY IF YOU WISH TO CANCEL THE AGREEMENT.) To: [4] I/We* hereby give notice that I/we* wish to cancel agreement Signed Date *Delete as appropriate Notes: 1 Creditor or owner to omit words in square brackets where not applicable. 2 Creditor or owner to insert reference number, code or other identification details. 3 Creditor or owner to enter his name. 4 Creditor or owner to insert name and address of person to whom notice may be given. 5 Creditor or owner may omit words in square brackets where not applicable. 6 Creditor or owner to include the words in the first set of square brackets unless the words in the second set of square brackets are applicable, i.e. in a case where the subject matter of the agreement is a liquefied petroleum gas vessel of greater than 150 litres water capacity. 7 Creditor or owner to insert a clear reference to the place where these obligations appear. 8 Creditor or owner may include words in square brackets where applicable.
19	A debtor-creditor-supplier agreement falling within section 12(a) or (b) of the Act (other than one to which Form 18 applies or, in the case of a modifying agreement, one to which Form 23 applies).	IMPORTANT — YOU SHOULD READ THIS CAREFULLY STATUTORY NOTICE RELATING TO A REGULATED CONSUMER CREDIT AGREEMENT YOUR RIGHT TO CANCEL You recently made a credit agreement [1] with [2]. You have a right to cancel it if you wish. You can do this by sending or taking a WRITTEN notice of cancellation to [3]. You have FIVE DAYS starting with the day after you received this notice. You can use the form provided.

Form no (1)	*Type of agreement* (2)	*Form* (3)
		If you cancel the agreement, any money you have paid [, goods given in part-exchange (or their value) and property given as security][4] must be returned to you. You will not have to make any further payment. [If you already have any goods under the agreement, you should not use them and should keep them safe. (Legal action may be taken against you if you do not take proper care of them.) You can wait for them to be collected from you and you need not hand them over unless you receive a written request. [If you wish, however, you may return the goods yourself.][5] [You are warned that it would be dangerous and could be in contravention of Health and Safety legislation for you to attempt to disconnect and return the goods yourself.][5]][4] [You will not, however, be required to hand back any goods supplied to meet an emergency or which have already been incorporated, for example in your home. But you will still be liable to pay for emergency goods or services or for any goods which have been incorporated by you or one of your relatives.][1] [Note: Your notice of cancellation will not affect [your contract for life assurance] [your contract for insurance] [your contract of guarantee] [your contract to open a current account] [consequent upon cancellation your contract to open a deposit account].[6] [The place where your financial obligations of this agreement are shown is [7].][8]][6] CANCELLATION FORM (Complete, detach and return this form ONLY IF YOU WISH TO CANCEL THE AGREEMENT.) To: [3] I/We* hereby give notice that I/we* wish to cancel agreement [1]. Signed Date *Delete as appropriate

Form no (1)	*Type of agreement* (2)	*Form* (3)
		Notes: 1 Creditor to insert reference number, code or other identification details. 2 Creditor to enter his name. 3 Creditor to insert name and address of person to whom notice may be given. 4 Creditor may omit words in square brackets where not applicable. 5 Creditor to include the words in the first set of square brackets unless the words in the second set of square brackets are applicable, i.e. in a case where the subject matter of the agreement is a liquefied petroleum gas vessel of greater than 150 litres water capacity. 6 Creditor to omit words in square brackets where not applicable. 7 Creditor to insert a clear reference to the place where these obligations appear. 8 Creditor may include words in square brackets where applicable.
20	A regulated consumer credit agreement (other than one to which Form 18 or 19 applies or which is a multiple agreement of the kind to which Form 21 or 22 applies or, in the case of a modifying agreement, one to which Form 23 applies).	IMPORTANT — YOU SHOULD READ THIS CAREFULLY STATUTORY NOTICE RELATING TO A REGULATED CONSUMER CREDIT AGREEMENT YOUR RIGHT TO CANCEL You recently made a credit agreement [1] with [2]. You have a right to cancel it if you wish. You can do this by sending or taking a WRITTEN notice of cancellation to [3]. You have FIVE DAYS starting with the day after you received this notice. You can use the form provided. If you cancel the agreement, any money you have paid [and any property given as security][4] must be returned to you. You will still have to repay any money lent to you. But if you repay all of it before your first instalment is due — or, if you are not paying by instalments, within one month after cancellation — you will not have to pay interest or other charges. [Note: Your notice of cancellation will not affect [your contract for life assurance] [your contract for insurance] [your contract of guarantee] [your

Form no (1)	*Type of agreement* (2)	*Form* (3)
		contract to open a current account] [your contract to open a deposit account[5]]. [The place where your financial obligations consequent upon cancellation of this agreement are shown is [6].][7]][5]
		CANCELLATION FORM (Complete, detach and return this form ONLY IF YOU WISH TO CANCEL THE AGREEMENT.) To: [3] I/We* hereby give notice that I/we* wish to cancel agreement [1] Signed Date *Delete as appropriate
		Notes: 1 Creditor to insert reference number, code or other identification details. 2 Creditor to enter his name. 3 Creditor to insert name and address of person to whom notice may be given. 4 Creditor may omit words in square brackets where not applicable. 5 Creditor to omit words in square brackets where not applicable. 6 Creditor to insert a clear reference to the place where these obligations appear. 7 Creditor may include words in square brackets where applicable.
21	A multiple agreement which places at least one part within one category of agreement to which either Form 18 or 19 applies and at least one part within one category of agreement to which Form 20 applies (other than one to which Form 22 applies).	IMPORTANT — YOU SHOULD READ THIS CAREFULLY STATUTORY NOTICE RELATING TO A REGULATED CONSUMER [CREDIT] [HIRE][1] AGREEMENT YOUR RIGHT TO CANCEL You recently made a [credit] [hire][1] agreement [2] with [3]. You have a right to cancel it if you wish. You can do this by sending or taking a WRITTEN notice of cancellation to [4]. You have FIVE DAYS starting with the day after you received this notice. You can use the form provided. If you cancel the agreement, any money you have paid [, goods given in part-exchange (or their value) and property given as

Form no (1)	*Type of agreement* (2)	*Form* (3)
		security[5]] must be returned to you. You will still have to repay any money lent to you. But if you repay all of it before your first instalment is due — or, if you are not paying by instalments, within one month after cancellation — you will not have to pay interest or other charges. [Any goods which you already have under the agreement, apart from any purchased out of a cash loan, will have to be returned. Such goods should not be used and should be kept safe. (Legal action may be taken against you if you do not take proper care of them.) You can wait for them to be collected from you and you need not hand them over unless you receive a written request. [If you wish, however, you may return the goods yourself[6].] [You are warned that it would be dangerous and could be in contravention of Health and Safety legislation for you to attempt to disconnect and return the goods yourself[6].][5]] [You will not, however, be required to hand back any goods supplied to meet an emergency or which have already been incorporated, for example in your home. But you will still be liable to pay for emergency goods or services or for any goods which have been incorporated by you or one of your relatives.][7] [Note: Your notice of cancellation will not affect [your contract for life assurance] [your contract for insurance] [your contract of guarantee] [your contract to open a current account] [your contract to open a deposit account].[1] [The place where your financial obligations consequent upon cancellation of this agreement are shown is [8].][9]][1]

Form no (1)	*Type of agreement* (2)	*Form* (3)
		CANCELLATION FORM (Complete, detach and return this form ONLY IF YOU WISH TO CANCEL THE AGREEMENT.) To: [4] I/WE* hereby give notice that I/we* wish to cancel agreement [2]. Signed Date * Delete as appropriate
		Notes: 1 Creditor or owner to omit words in square brackets where not applicable. 2 Creditor or owner to insert reference number, code or other identification details. 3 Creditor or owner to enter his name. 4 Creditor or owner to insert name and address of person to whom notice may be given. 5 Creditor or owner may omit words in square brackets where not applicable. 6 Creditor or owner to include the words in the first set of square brackets unless the words in the second set of square brackets are applicable, i.e. in a case where the subject matter of the agreement is a liquefied petroleum gas vessel of greater than 150 litres water capacity. 7 Paragraph in square brackets applies only where the notice relates to a multiple agreement of which at least one part is a debtor-creditor-supplier agreement falling within section 12(a) or (b) of the Act, not being a hire-purchase or conditional sale agreement. Creditor may omit this paragraph if inapplicable. 8 Creditor to insert a clear reference to the place where these obligations appear. 9 Creditor may include words in square brackets where applicable.

Form no (1)	*Type of agreement* (2)	*Form* (3)
22	A multiple agreement of which at least one part is a debtor-creditor agreement and at least one part is a credit agreement not regulated by the Act.	IMPORTANT — YOU SHOULD READ THIS CAREFULLY STATUTORY NOTICE RELATING TO A PARTLY REGULATED CONSUMER CREDIT AGREEMENT YOUR RIGHT TO CANCEL You recently made a credit agreement [1] with [2]. If you wish, you can cancel that part of the agreement which is regulated by the Consumer Credit Act 1974. You can do this by sending or taking a WRITTEN notice of cancellation to [3]. You have FIVE DAYS starting with the day after you received this notice. You can use the form provided. If you cancel, any money you have paid in connection with the regulated agreement [and any property given as security in relation to that agreement][4] must be returned to you. You will still have to repay any money lent to you. But if you repay all of it before your first instalment is due — or, if you are not paying by instalments, within one month after cancellation — you will not have to pay interest or other charges. [Note: Your notice of cancellation will not affect [your contract for life assurance] [your contract for insurance] [your contract of guarantee] [your contract to open a current account] [your contract to open a deposit account].[5] [The place where your financial obligations consequent upon cancellation of this agreement are shown is [6].][7]][5]
		CANCELLATION FORM (Complete, detach and return this form ONLY IF YOU WISH TO CANCEL THE REGULATED PART OF THE AGREEMENT.) To: [3] I/We* hereby give notice that I/we* wish to exercise my/our* right to cancel that part of agreement [1] which is regulated by the Consumer Credit Act 1974. Signed Date * Delete as appropriate

Form no (1)	*Type of agreement* (2)	*Form* (3)
		Notes: 1 Creditor to insert reference number, code or other identification details. 2 Creditor to enter his name. 3 Creditor to insert name and address of person to whom notice may be given. 4 Creditor may omit words in square brackets where not applicable. 5 Creditor to omit words in square brackets where not applicable. 6 Creditor to insert a clear reference to the place where these obligations appear. 7 Creditor may include words in square brackets where applicable.
23	A modifying agreement treated under section 82(5) of the Act as a cancellable agreement.	IMPORTANT — YOU SHOULD READ THIS CAREFULLY STATUTORY NOTICE RELATING TO A [PARTLY][1] REGULATED CONSUMER [CREDIT] [HIRE][2] AGREEMENT YOUR RIGHT TO CANCEL You recently made an agreement [3] with [4] which modified an earlier [credit] [hire][2] agreement. Your right to cancel [that part of][1] the earlier agreement [which was regulated by the Consumer Credit Act 1974][1] has been widened to cover the [regulated][1] agreement as modified. The cancellation period itself is unchanged. A [copy of the earlier agreement containing a][2] notice of your cancellation rights may have already been sent to you giving details of when that period expires. If you wish to cancel the [regulated][1] agreement as modified, you can do this by sending or taking a WRITTEN notice of cancellation to [5]. You can use the form provided. CANCELLATION FORM (Complete, detach and return this form ONLY IF YOU WISH TO CANCEL THE [REGULATED PART OF THE][1] AGREEMENT.)

Form no (1)	Type of agreement (2)	Form (3)
		To: 5 I/We* hereby give notice that I/we* wish to [exercise my/our* right to][1] cancel [that part of][1] agreement 3 [which is regulated by the Consumer Credit Act 1974][1]. Signed Date * Delete as appropriate Notes: 1 Creditor or owner to omit passages in square brackets except in the case of a multiple agreement of which at least one part is a credit agreement not regulated by the Act. 2 Creditor or owner to omit words in square brackets where not applicable. 3 Creditor or owner to insert reference number, code or other identification details. 4 Creditor or owner to enter his name. 5 Creditor or owner to insert name and address of person to whom notice maybe given.

CONSUMER CREDIT (EXEMPT AGREEMENTS) ORDER 1989 (SI 1989, No. 869)

1. Citation, commencement, interpretation and revocation

(2) In this Order—

'the Act' means the Consumer Credit Act 1974;

'business premises' means premises for occupation for the purposes of a business (including any activity carried on by a body of persons, whether corporate or unincorporate) or for those and other purposes;

and references to the total charge for credit and the rate thereof are respectively references to the total charge for credit and the rate thereof calculated in accordance with the Consumer Credit (Total Charge for Credit) Regulations 1980.

2. Exemption of certain consumer credit agreements secured on land

(1) The Act shall not regulate a consumer credit agreement which falls within section 16(2) of the Act, being an agreement to which this paragraph applies.

(2) Where the creditor is a body specified in Part 1 of Schedule 1 to this Order, or a building society authorised under the Building Societies Act 1986, or an authorised institution under the Banking Act 1987 or a wholly-owned subsidiary of such an institution, paragraph (1) above applies only to—

(a) a debtor-creditor-supplier agreement falling within section 16(2)(a) or (c) of the Act;

(b) a debtor-creditor agreement secured by any land mortgage to finance—

(i) the purchase of land; or

(ii) the provision of dwellings or business premises on any land; or

(iii) subject to paragraph (3) below, the alteration, enlarging, repair or improvement of a dwelling or business premises on any land;

(c) a debtor-creditor agreement secured by any land mortgage to refinance any existing indebtedness of the debtor, whether to the creditor or another person, under any agreement by which the debtor was provided with credit for any of the purposes specified in heads (i) to (iii) of sub-paragraph (b) above.

(3) Head (iii) of sub-paragraph (b) of paragraph (2) above applies only—

(i) where the creditor is the creditor under—

(a) an agreement (whenever made) by which the debtor is provided with credit for any of the purposes specified in head (i) and head (ii) of that sub-paragraph; or

(b) an agreement (whenever made) refinancing an agreement under which the debtor is provided with credit for any of the said purposes,

being, in either case, an agreement relating to the land referred to in the said head (iii) and secured by a land mortgage on that land; or

(ii) where a debtor-creditor agreement to finance the alteration, enlarging, repair or improvement of a dwelling, secured by a land mortgage on that dwelling, is made as a result of any such services as are described in [section 4(3)(e) of the Housing Associations Act 1985] which are certified as having been provided by—

(a) a local authority;

(b) a housing association within the meaning of section 1 of the Housing Associations Act 1985 or [Article 3 of the Housing (Northern Ireland) Order 1992];

(c) a body established by such a housing association for the purpose of providing such services as are described in the said [section 4(3)(e)];

(d) a charity;

(e) the National Home Improvement Council; [. . .]

(f) the Northern Ireland Housing Executive [; or

(g) a body, or a body of any description, that has been approved by the Secretary of State under section 169(4)(c) of the Local Government and Housing Act 1989 or the Department of the Environment for Northern Ireland under article 103(4)(c) of the Housing (Northern Ireland) Order 1992].

(4) Where the creditor is a body specified in Part II of Schedule 1 to this Order, paragraph (1) above applies only to an agreement of a description specified in that Part in relation to that body and made pursuant to an enactment or for a purpose so specified.

(5) Where the creditor is a body specified in Part III of Schedule 1 to this Order, paragraph (1) above applies only to an agreement of a description falling within Article 2(2)(a) to (c) above, being an agreement advancing money on the security of a dwelling-house.

3. Exemption of certain consumer credit agreements by reference to the number of payments to be made by the debtor

(1) The Act shall not regulate a consumer credit agreement which is an agreement of one of the following descriptions, that is to say—

(a) a debtor-creditor-supplier agreement being either—

(i) an agreement for fixed-sum credit under which the total number of payments to be made by the debtor does not exceed four, and those payments are required to be made within a period not exceeding 12 months beginning with the date of the agreement; or

(ii) an agreement for running-account credit which provides for the making of payments by the debtor in relation to specified periods and requires that the number of payments to be made by the debtor in repayment of the whole amount of the credit provided in each such period shall not exceed one;

not being, in either case, an agreement of a description specified in pararaph (2) below; and in this sub-paragraph, 'payment' means a payment comprising an amount in respect of credit with or without any other amount;

(b) a debtor-creditor-supplier agreement financing the purchase of land being an agreement under which the number of payments to be made by the debtor does not exceed four; and in this sub-paragraph, 'payment' means a payment comprising or including an amount in respect of credit or the total charge for credit (if any);

(c) a debtor-creditor-supplier agreement for fixed-sum credit to finance a premium under a contract of insurance relating to any land or to anything thereon where—

(i) the creditor is the creditor under an agreement secured by a land mortgage on that land which either is an exempt agreement by virtue of section 16(1) of the Act or of article 2 above, or is a personal credit agreement which would be an exempt agreement by virtue of either of those provisions if the credit provided were not to exceed £15,000;

(ii) the amount of the credit is to be repaid within the period to which the premium relates, not being a period exceeding 12 months; and

(iii) there is no charge forming part of the total charge for credit under the agreement other than interest at a rate not exceeding the rate of interest from time to time payable under the agreement mentioned in head (i) above,

and the number of payments to be made by the debtor does not exceed twelve;

and in this sub-paragraph 'payment' has the same meaning as it has in paragraph (1)(b) above; and

(d) a debtor-creditor-supplier agreement for fixed-sum credit where—

(i) the creditor is the creditor under an agreement secured by a land mortgage on any land which either is an exempt agreement by virtue of section 16(1) of the Act or of article 2 above, or is a personal credit agreement which would be an exempt agreement by virtue of either of those provisions if the credit provided were not to exceed £15,000;

(ii) the agreement is to finance a premium under a contract of life insurance which provides, in the event of the death before the credit under the agreement referred to in head (i) above has been repaid of the person on whose life the contract is effected, for payment of a sum not exceeding the amount sufficient to defray the sums which, immediately after that credit has been advanced, would be payable to the creditor in respect of that credit and of the total charge for that credit; and

(iii) there is no charge forming part of the total charge for credit under the agreement other than interest at a rate not exceeding the rate of interest from time to time payable under the agreement referred to in head (i) above,

and the number of payments to be made by the debtor does not exceed twelve;

and in this sub-paragraph, 'payment' has the same meaning as it has in sub-paragraph (1)(b) above.

(2) The descriptions of agreement referred to in sub-paragraph (a) of paragraph (1) above and to which accordingly that sub-paragraph does not apply are—

(a) agreements financing the purchase of land;

(b) agreements which are conditional sale agreements or hire-purchase agreements; and

(c) agreements secured by a pledge (other than a pledge of documents of title or of bearer bonds).

[4. Exemption of certain consumer credit agreements by reference to the rate of the total charge for credit

(1) The Act shall not regulate—

(a) a debtor-creditor agreement where the creditor is a credit union and the rate of the total charge for credit does not exceed 12.7 per cent;

(b) (subject to paragraph (2) below) a debtor-creditor agreement—

(i) which is an agreement of a type offered to a particular class, or particular classes, of individuals and not offered to the public generally; and

(ii) under the terms of which the only charge included in the total charge for credit is interest which cannot at any time exceed the sum of one per cent and the highest of the base rates published by the banks named in paragraph (3) below, being the latest rates in operation on the date 28 days before any such time; or

(c) (subject to paragraph (2) below) a debtor-creditor agreement—

(i) which is an agreement of a type offered to a particular class, or particular classes, of individuals and not offered to the public generally;

(ii) under which there can be no increase after the relevant date in the rate or amount of any item which is included in the total charge for credit or which would be included but for regulation 14 of the Total Charge for Credit Regulations; and

(iii) in respect of which the rate of the total charge for credit does not exceed the sum of one per cent and the highest of the base rates published by the banks named in paragraph (3) below, being the latest rates in operation on the date 28 days before the date on which the agreement is made.

(2) Paragraph (1)(b) and (c) above does not apply to an agreement under which the total amount to be repaid by the debtor to discharge his indebtedness in respect of the amount of credit provided may vary according to a formula which is specified in the agreement and which has effect by reference to movements in the level of any index or to any other factor.

(3) The banks referred to in paragraph (1)(b) and (c) above are—

Bank of England
Bank of Scotland
Barclays Bank PLC
Clydesdale Bank PLC
Co-operative Bank Public Limited Company
Coutts & Co
Lloyds TSB Bank plc
Midland Bank Public Limited Company
National Westminster Bank Public Limited Company
The Royal Bank of Scotland p.l.c.

(4) In this article—

'credit union' means—

(a) a society registered under the Industrial and Provident Societies Act 1965 by virtue of section 1 of the Credit Unions Act 1979; or

(b) a society registered under the Credit Unions (Northern Ireland) Order 1985 or a society registered under the Industrial and Provident Societies Act (Northern Ireland) 1969 as a credit union;

'interest' means interest at a rate determined in accordance with the formula set out in regulation 7(1) of the Total Charge for Credit Regulations, and in that formula as applied by paragraph (1)(b) above;

'period rate of charge' has the meaning given in regulation 7(2) of those Regulations;

'the relevant date' has the meaning given in regulation 1(2) of the Total Charge for Credit Regulations; and

'the Total Charge for Credit Regulations' means the Consumer Credit (Total Charge for Credit) Regulations 1980.]

5. Exemption of certain consumer credit agreements having a connection with a country outside the United Kingdom

The Act shall not regulate a consumer credit agreement made—

(a) in connection with trade in goods or services between the United Kingdom and a country outside the United Kingdom or within a country or between countries outside the United Kingdom, being an agreement under which credit is provided to the debtor in the course of a business carried on by him; or

(b) between a creditor listed in Part IV of Schedule 1 to this Order and a debtor who is—

(i) a member of any of the armed forces of the United States of America;

(ii) an employee not habitually resident in the United Kingdom of any of those forces; or

(iii) any such member's or employee's wife or husband or any other person (whether or not a child of his) whom he wholly or partly maintains and treats as a child of the family.

6. Exemption of certain consumer hire agreements

The Act shall not regulate a consumer hire agreement where the owner is a body corporate authorised by or under any enactment to supply [gas] electricity or water and the subject of the agreement is a meter or metering equipment used or to be used in connection with the supply of [gas] electricity or water, as the case may be.

PACKAGE TRAVEL, PACKAGE HOLIDAYS AND PACKAGE TOURS REGULATIONS 1992 (SI 1992, No. 3288)

2. Interpretation

(1) In these Regulations —

'brochure' means any brochure in which packages are offered for sale;

'contract' means the agreement linking the consumer to the organiser or to the retailer, or to both, as the case may be;

'the Directive' means Council Directive 90/314/EEC on package travel, package holidays and package tours;
'offer' includes an invitation to treat whether by means of advertising or otherwise, and cognate expressions shall be construed accordingly;
'organiser' means the person who, otherwise than occasionally, organises packages and sells or offers them for sale, whether directly or through a retailer;
'the other party to the contract' means the party, other than the consumer, to the contract, that is, the organiser or the retailer, or both, as the case may be;
'package' means the pre-arranged combination of at least two of the following components when sold or offered for sale at an inclusive price and when the service covers a period of more than twenty-four hours or includes overnight accommodation—

(a) transport;
(b) accommodation;
(c) other tourist services not ancillary to transport or accommodation and accounting for a significant proportion of the package,

and

(i) the submission of separate accounts for different components shall not cause the arrangements to be other than a package;
(ii) the fact that a combination is arranged at the request of the consumer and in accordance with his specific instructions (whether modified or not) shall not of itself cause it to be treated as other than pre-arranged;

and
'retailer' means the person who sells or offers for sale the package put together by the organiser.

(2) In the definition of 'contract' in paragraph (1) above, 'consumer' means the person who takes or agrees to take the package ('the principal contractor') and elsewhere in these Regulations 'consumer' means, as the context requires, the principal contractor, any person on whose behalf the principal contractor agrees to purchase the package ('the other beneficiaries') or any person to whom the principal contractor or any of the other beneficiaries transfers the package ('the transferee').

3. Application of Regulations

(1) These Regulations apply to packages sold or offered for sale in the territory of the United Kingdom.

4. Descriptive matter relating to packages must not be misleading

(1) No organiser or retailer shall supply to a consumer any descriptive matter concerning a package, the price of a package or any other conditions applying to the contract which contains any misleading information.

(2) If an organiser or retailer is in breach of paragraph (1) he shall be liable to compensate the consumer for any loss which the consumer suffers in consequence.

5. Requirements as to brochures

(1) Subject to paragraph (4) below, no organiser shall make available a brochure to a possible consumer unless it indicates in a legible, comprehensive and accurate manner the price and adequate information about the matters specified in Schedule 1 to these Regulations in respect of the packages offered for sale in the brochure to the extent that those matters are relevant to the packages so offered.

(2) Subject to paragraph (4) below, no retailer shall make available to a possible consumer a brochure which he knows or has reasonable cause to believe does not comply with the requirements of paragraph (1).

(3) An organiser who contravenes paragraph (1) of this regulation and a retailer who contravenes paragraph (2) thereof shall be guilty of an offence and liable—

(a) on summary conviction, to a fine not exceeding level 5 on the standard scale; and
(b) on conviction on indictment, to a fine.

(4) Where a brochure was first made available to consumers generally before 31st December 1992 no liability shall arise under this regulation in respect of an identical brochure being made available to a consumer at any time.

6. Circumstances in which particulars in brochure are to be binding

(1) Subject to paragraphs (2) and (3) of this regulation, the particulars in the brochure (whether or not they are required by regulation 5(1) above to be included in the brochure) shall constitute implied warranties (or, as regards Scotland, implied terms) for the purposes of any contract to which the particulars relate.

(2) Paragraph (1) of this regulation does not apply —

(a) in relation to information required to be included by virtue of paragraph 9 of Schedule 1 to these Regulations; or

(b) where the brochure contains an express statement that changes may be made in the particulars contained in it before a contract is concluded and changes in the particulars so contained are clearly communicated to the consumer before a contract is concluded.

(3) Paragraph (1) of this regulation does not apply when the consumer and the other party to the contract agree after the contract has been made that the particulars in the brochure, or some of those particulars, should not form part of the contract.

7. Information to be provided before contract is concluded

(1) Before a contract is concluded, the other party to the contract shall provide the intending consumer with the information specified in paragraph (2) below in writing or in some other appropriate form.

(2) The information referred to in paragraph (1) is—

(a) general information about passport and visa requirements which apply to [nationals of the member State or States concerned] who purchase the package in question, including information about the length of time it is likely to take to obtain the appropriate passports and visas;

(b) information about health formalities required for the journey and the stay; and

(c) the arrangements for security for the money paid over and (where applicable) for the repatriation of the consumer in the event of insolvency.

(3) If the intending consumer is not provided with the information required by paragraph (1) in accordance with that paragraph the other party to the contract shall be guilty of an offence and liable—

(a) on summary conviction, to a fine not exceeding level 5 on the standard scale; and

(b) on conviction on indictment, to a fine.

8. Information to be provided in good time

(1) The other party to the contract shall in good time before the start of the journey provide the consumer with the information specified in paragraph (2) below in writing or in some other appropriate form.

(2) The information referred to in paragraph (1) is the following—

(a) the times and places of intermediate stops and transport connections and particulars of the place to be occupied by the traveller (for example, cabin or berth on ship, sleeper compartment on train);

(b) the name, address and telephone number —

(i) of the representative of the other party to the contract in the locality where the consumer is to stay,

or, if there is no such representative,

(ii) of an agency in that locality on whose assistance a consumer in difficulty would be able to call,

or, if there is no such representative or agency, a telephone number or other information which will enable the consumer to contact the other party to the contract during the stay; and

(c) in the case of a journey or stay abroad by a child under the age of 16 on the day when the journey or stay is due to start, information enabling direct contact to be made with the child or the person responsible at the place where he is to stay; and

(d) except where the consumer is required as a term of the contract to take out an insurance policy in order to cover the cost of cancellation by the consumer or the cost of assistance, including repatriation, in the event of accident or illness, information about an insurance policy which the consumer may, if he wishes, take out in respect of the risk of those costs being incurred.

(3) If the consumer is not provided with the information required by paragraph (1) in accordance with that paragraph the other party to the contract shall be guilty of an offence and liable—

(a) on summary conviction, to a fine not exceeding level 5 on the standard scale; and

(b) on conviction on indictment, to a fine.

9. Contents and form of contract

(1) The other party to the contract shall ensure that—

(a) depending on the nature of the package being purchased, the contract contains at least the elements specified in Schedule 2 to these Regulations;

(b) subject to paragraph (2) below, all the terms of the contract are set out in writing or such other form as is comprehensible and accessible to the consumer and are communicated to the consumer before the contract is made; and

(c) a written copy of these terms is supplied to the consumer.

(2) Paragraph (1)(b) above does not apply when the interval between the time when the consumer approaches the other party to the contract with a view to entering into a contract and the time of departure under the proposed contract is so short that it is impracticable to comply with the sub-paragraph.

(3) It is an implied condition (or, as regards Scotland, an implied term) of the contract that the other party to the contract complies with the provisions of paragraph (1).

10. Transfer of bookings

(1) In every contract there is an implied term that where the consumer is prevented from proceeding with the package the consumer may transfer his booking to a person who satisfies all the conditions applicable to the package, provided that the consumer gives reasonable notice to the other party to the contract of his intention to transfer before the date when departure is due to take place.

(2) Where a transfer is made in accordance with the implied term set out in paragraph (1) above, the transferor and the transferee shall be jointly and severally liable to the other party to the contract for payment of the price of the package (or, if part of the price has been paid, for payment of the balance) and for any additional costs arising from such transfer.

11. Price revision

(1) Any term in a contract to the effect that the prices laid down in the contract may be revised shall be void and of no effect unless the contract provides for the possibility of upward or downward revision and satisfies the conditions laid down in paragraph (2) below.

(2) The conditions mentioned in paragraph (1) are that —

(a) the contract states precisely how the revised price is to be calculated;

(b) the contract provides that price revisions are to be made solely to allow for variations in—

(i) transportation costs, including the cost of fuel,

(ii) dues, taxes or fees chargeable for services such as landing taxes or embarkation or disembarkation fees at ports and airports, or

(iii) the exchange rates applied to the particular package; and

(3) Notwithstanding any terms of a contract,

(i) no price increase may be made in a specified period which may not be less than 30 days before the departure date stipulated; and

(ii) as against an individual consumer liable under the contract, no price increase may be made in respect of variations which would produce an increase of less than 2 per cent, or such greater percentage as the contract may specify, ('non-eligible variations') and that the non-eligible variations shall be left out of account in the calculation.

12. Significant alterations to essential terms

In every contract there are implied terms to the effect that —

(a) where the organiser is constrained before the departure to alter significantly an essential term of the contract, such as the price (so far as regulation 11 permits him to do so), he will notify the consumer as quickly as possible in order to enable him to take appropriate decisions and in particular to withdraw from the contract without penalty or to accept a rider to the contract specifying the alterations made and their impact on the price; and

(b) the consumer will inform the organiser or the retailer of his decision as soon as possible.

13. Withdrawal by consumer pursuant to regulation 12 and cancellation by organiser

(1) The terms set out in paragraphs (2) and (3) below are implied in every contract and apply where the consumer withdraws from the contract pursuant to the term in it implied by virtue of regulation 12(a), or where the organiser, for any reason other than the fault of the consumer, cancels the package before the agreed date of departure.

(2) The consumer is entitled —

(a) to take a substitute package of equivalent or superior quality if the other party to the contract is able to offer him such a substitute; or

(b) to take a substitute package of lower quality if the other party to the contract is able to offer him one and to recover from the organiser the difference in price between the price of the package purchased and that of the substitute package; or

(c) to have repaid to him as soon as possible all the monies paid by him under the contract.

(3) The consumer is entitled, if appropriate, to be compensated by the organiser for non-performance of the contract except where —

(a) the package is cancelled because the number of persons who agree to take it is less than the minimum number required and the consumer is informed of the cancellation, in writing, within the period indicated in the description of the package; or

(b) the package is cancelled by reason of unusual and unforeseeable circumstances beyond the control of the party by whom this exception is pleaded, the consequences of which could not have been avoided even if all due care had been exercised.

(4) Overbooking shall not be regarded as a circumstance falling within the provisions of sub-paragraph (b) of paragraph (3) above.

14. Significant proportion of services not provided

(1) The terms set out in paragraphs (2) and (3) below are implied in every contract and apply where, after departure, a significant proportion of the services contracted for is not provided or the organiser becomes aware that he will be unable to procure a significant proportion of the services to be provided.

(2) The organiser will make suitable alternative arrangements, at no extra cost to the consumer, for the continuation of the package and will, where appropriate, compensate the consumer for the difference between the services to be supplied under the contract and those supplied.

(3) If it is impossible to make arrangements as described in paragraph (2), or these are not accepted by the consumer for good reasons, the organiser will, where appropriate, provide the consumer with equivalent transport back to the place of departure or to another place to which the consumer has agreed and will, where appropriate, compensate the consumer.

15. Liability of other party to the contract for proper performance of obligations under contract

(1) The other party to the contract is liable to the consumer for the proper performance of the obligations under the contract, irrespective of whether such obligations are to be performed by that other party or by other suppliers of services but this shall not affect any remedy or right of action which that other party may have against those other suppliers of services.

(2) The other party to the contract is liable to the consumer for any damage caused to him by the failure to perform the contract or the improper performance of the contract unless the failure or the improper performance is due neither to any fault of that other party nor to that of another supplier of services, because —

(a) the failures which occur in the performance of the contract are attributable to the consumer;

(b) such failures are attributable to a third party unconnected with the provision of the services contracted for, and are unforeseeable or unavoidable; or

(c) such failures are due to —

(i) unusual and unforeseeable circumstances beyond the control of the party by whom this exception is pleaded, the consequences of which could not have been avoided even if all due care had been exercised; or

(ii) an event which the other party to the contract or the supplier of services, even with all due care, could not foresee or forestall.

(3) In the case of damage arising from the non-performance or improper performance of the services involved in the package, the contract may provide for compensation to be limited in accordance with the international conventions which govern such services.

(4) In the case of damage other than personal injury resulting from the non-performance or improper performance of the services involved in the package, the contract may include a term limiting the amount of compensation which will be paid to the consumer, provided that the limitation is not unreasonable.

(5) Without prejudice to paragraph (3) and paragraph (4) above, liability under paragraphs (1) and (2) above cannot be excluded by any contractual term.

(6) The terms set out in paragraphs (7) and (8) below are implied in every contract.

(7) In the circumstances described in paragraph (2)(b) and (c) of this regulation, the other party to the contract will give prompt assistance to a consumer in difficulty.

(8) If the consumer complains about a defect in the performance of the contract, the other party to the contract, or his local representative, if there is one, will make prompt efforts to find appropriate solutions.

(9) The contract must clearly and explicitly oblige the consumer to communicate at the earliest opportunity, in writing or any other appropriate form, to the supplier of the services concerned and to the other party to the contract any failure which he perceives at the place where the services concerned are supplied.

23. Enforcement

Schedule 3 to these Regulations (which makes provision about the enforcement of regulations 5, 7, 8, 16 and 22 of these Regulations) shall have effect.

24. Due diligence defence

(1) Subject to the following provisions of this regulation, in proceedings against any person for an offence under regulation 5, 7, 8, 16 or 22 of these Regulations, it shall be a defence for that person to show that he took all reasonable steps and exercised all due diligence to avoid committing the offence.

(2) Where in any proceedings against any person for such an offence the defence provided by paragraph (1) above involves an allegation that the commission of the offence was due —

(a) to the act or default of another; or

(b) to reliance on information given by another,

that person shall not, without the leave of the court, be entitled to rely on the defence unless, not less than seven clear days before the hearing of the proceedings, or, in Scotland, the trial diet, he has served a notice under paragraph (3) below on the person bringing the proceedings.

(3) A notice under this paragraph shall give such information identifying or assisting in the identification of the person who committed the act or default or gave the information as is in the possession of the person serving the notice at the time he serves it.

(4) It is hereby declared that a person shall not be entitled to rely on the defence provided by paragraph (1) above by reason of his reliance on information supplied by another, unless he shows that it was reasonable in all the circumstances for him to have relied on the information, having regard in particular —

(a) to the steps which he took, and those which might reasonably have been taken, for the purpose of verifying the information; and

(b) to whether he had any reason to disbelieve the information.

25. Liability of persons other than principal offender

(1) Where the commission by any person of an offence under regulations 5, 7, 8, 16 or 22 of these Regulations is due to an act or default committed by some other person in the

course of any business of his, the other person shall be guilty of the offence and may be proceeded against and punished by virtue of this paragraph whether or not proceedings are taken against the first-mentioned person.

(2) Where a body corporate is guilty of an offence under any of the provisions mentioned in paragraph (1) above (including where it is so guilty by virtue of the said paragraph (1)) in respect of any act or default which is shown to have been committed with the consent or connivance of, or to be attributable to any neglect on the part of, any director, manager, secretary or other similar officer of the body corporate or any person who was purporting to act in any such capacity he, as well as the body corporate, shall be guilty of that offence and shall be liable to be proceeded against and punished accordingly.

(3) Where the affairs of a body corporate are managed by its members, paragraph (2) above shall apply in relation to the acts and defaults of a member in connection with his functions of management as if he were a director of the body corporate.

(5) On proceedings for an offence under regulation 5 by virtue of paragraph (1) above committed by the making available of a brochure it shall be a defence for the person charged to prove that he is a person whose business it is to publish or arrange for the publication of brochures and that he received the brochure for publication in the ordinary course of business and did not know and had no reason to suspect that its publication would amount to an offence under these Regulations.

26. Prosecution time limit

(1) No proceedings for an offence under regulation 5, 7, 8, 16 or 22 of these Regulations or under paragraphs 5(3), 6 or 7 of Schedule 3 thereto shall be commenced after —

(a) the end of the period of three years beginning within the date of the commission of the offence; or

(b) the end of the period of one year beginning with the date of the discovery of the offence by the prosecutor,

whichever is the earlier.

(2) For the purposes of this regulation a certificate signed by or on behalf of the prosecutor and stating the date on which the offence was discovered by him shall be conclusive evidence of that fact; and a certificate stating that matter and purporting to be so signed shall be treated as so signed unless the contrary is proved.

27. Saving for civil consequences

No contract shall be void or unenforceable, and no right of action in civil proceedings in respect of any loss shall arise, by reason only of the commission of an offence under regulations 5, 7, 8, 16 or 22 of these Regulations.

28. Terms implied in contract

Where it is provided in these Regulations that a term (whether so described or whether described as a condition or warranty) is implied in the contract it is so implied irrespective of the law which governs the contract.

Regulation 5 SCHEDULE 1

INFORMATION TO BE INCLUDED (IN ADDITION TO THE PRICE) IN BROCHURES WHERE RELEVANT TO PACKAGES OFFERED

1. The destination and the means, characteristics and categories of transport used.
2. The type of accommodation, its location, category or degree of comfort and its main features and, where the accommodation is to be provided in a member State, its approval or tourist classification under the rules of that member State.
3. The meals which are included in the package.
4. The itinerary.
5. General information about passport and visa requirements which apply for [nationals of the member State or States in which the brochure is made available] and health formalities required for the journey and the stay.
6. Either the monetary amount or the percentage of the price which is to be paid on account and the timetable for payment of the balance.

7. Whether a minimum number of persons is required for the package to take place and, if so, the deadline for informing the consumer in the event of cancellation.
8. The arrangements (if any) which apply if consumers are delayed at the outward or homeward points of departure.
9. The arrangements for security for money paid over and for the repatriation of the consumer in the event of insolvency.

Regulation 9

SCHEDULE 2
ELEMENTS TO BE INCLUDED IN THE CONTRACT IF RELEVANT TO THE PARTICULAR PACKAGE

1. The travel destination(s) and, where periods of stay are involved, the relevant periods, with dates.
2. The means, characteristics and categories of transport to be used and the dates, times and points of departure and return.
3. Where the package includes accommodation, its location, its tourist category or degree of comfort, its main features and, where the accommodation is to be provided in a member State, its compliance with the rules of that member State.
4. The meals which are included in the package.
5. Whether a minimum number of persons is required for the package to take place and, if so, the deadline for informing the consumer in the event of cancellation.
6. The itinerary.
7. Visits, excursions or other services which are included in the total price agreed for the package.
8. The name and address of the organiser, the retailer and, where appropriate, the insurer.
9. The price of the package, if the price may be revised in accordance with the term which may be included in the contract under regulation 11, an indication of the possibility of such price revisions, and an indication of any dues, taxes or fees chargeable for certain services (landing, embarkation or disembarkation fees at ports and airports and tourist taxes) where such costs are not included in the package.
10. The payment schedule and method of payment.
11. Special requirements which the consumer has communicated to the organiser or retailer when making the booking and which both have accepted.
12. The periods within which the consumer must make any complaint about the failure to perform or the inadequate performance of the contract.

Regulation 23

SCHEDULE 3
ENFORCEMENT

1. Enforcement authority

(1) Every local weights and measures authority in Great Britain shall be an enforcement authority for the purposes of regulations 5, 7, 8, 16 and 22 of these Regulations ('the relevant regulations'), and it shall be the duty of each such authority to enforce those provisions within their area.

2. Prosecutions

(1) Where an enforcement authority in England or Wales proposes to institute proceedings for an offence under any of the relevant regulations, it shall as between the enforcement authority and the Director General of Fair Trading be the duty of the enforcement authority to give to the Director General of Fair Trading notice of the intended proceedings, together with a summary of the facts on which the charges are to be founded, and to postpone institution of the proceedings until either —

(a) twenty-eight days have elapsed since the giving of that notice; or

(b) the Director General of Fair Trading has notified the enforcement authority that he has received the notice and the summary of the facts.

(2) Nothing in paragraph 1 above shall authorise a local weights and measures authority to bring proceedings in Scotland for an offence.

UNFAIR TERMS IN CONSUMER CONTRACTS REGULATIONS 1999 (SI 1999, No. 2083)

3. Interpretation

(1) In these Regulations—

'the Community' means the European Community;

'consumer' means any natural person who, in contracts covered by these Regulations, is acting for purposes which are outside his trade, business or profession;

'court' in relation to England and Wales and Northern Ireland means a county court or the High Court, and in relation to Scotland, the Sheriff or the Court of Session;

'Director' means the Director General of Fair Trading;

'EEA Agreement' means the Agreement on the European Economic Area signed at Oporto on 2nd May 1992 as adjusted by the protocol signed at Brussels on 17th March 1993;

'Member State' means a State which is a contracting party to the EEA Agreement;

'notified' means notified in writing;

'qualifying body' means a person specified in Schedule 1;

'seller or supplier' means any natural or legal person who, in contracts covered by these Regulations, is acting for purposes relating to his trade, business or profession, whether publicly owned or privately owned;

'unfair terms' means the contractual terms referred to in regulation 5.

(2) In the application of these Regulations to Scotland for references to an 'injunction' or an 'interim injunction' there shall be substituted references to an 'interdict' or 'interim interdict' respectively.

4. Terms to which these Regulations apply

(1) These Regulations apply in relation to unfair terms in contracts concluded between a seller or a supplier and a consumer.

(2) These Regulations do not apply to contractual terms which reflect—

(a) mandatory statutory or regulatory provisions (including such provisions under the law of any Member State or in Community legislation having effect in the United Kingdom without further enactment);

(b) the provisions or principles of international conventions to which the Member States or the Community are party.

5. Unfair terms

(1) A contractual term which has not been individually negotiated shall be regarded as unfair if, contrary to the requirement of good faith, it causes a significant imbalance in the parties' rights and obligations arising under the contract, to the detriment of the consumer.

(2) A term shall always be regarded as not having been individually negotiated where it has been drafted in advance and the consumer has therefore not been able to influence the substance of the term.

(3) Notwithstanding that a specific term or certain aspects of it in a contract has been individually negotiated, these Regulations shall apply to the rest of a contract if an overall assessment of it indicates that it is a pre-formulated standard contract.

(4) It shall be for any seller or supplier who claims that a term was individually negotiated to show that it was.

(5) Schedule 2 to these Regulations contains an indicative and non-exhaustive list of the terms which may be regarded as unfair.

6. Assessment of unfair terms

(1) Without prejudice to regulation 12, the unfairness of a contractual term shall be assessed, taking into account the nature of the goods or services for which the contract was concluded and by referring, at the time of conclusion of the contract, to all the circumstances attending the conclusion of the contract and to all the other terms of the contract or of another contract on which it is dependent.

(2) In so far as it is in plain intelligible language, the assessment of fairness of a term shall not relate—

(a) to the definition of the main subject matter of the contract, or

(b) to the adequacy of the price or remuneration, as against the goods or services supplied in exchange.

7. Written contracts

(1) A seller or supplier shall ensure that any written term of a contract is expressed in plain, intelligible language.

(2) If there is doubt about the meaning of a written term, the interpretation which is most favourable to the consumer shall prevail but this rule shall not apply in proceedings brought under regulation 12.

8. Effect of unfair term

(1) An unfair term in a contract concluded with a consumer by a seller or supplier shall not be binding on the consumer.

(2) The contract shall continue to bind the parties if it is capable of continuing in existence without the unfair term.

9. Choice of law clauses

These Regulations shall apply notwithstanding any contract term which applies or purports to apply the law of a non-Member State, if the contract has a close connection with the territory of the Member States.

10. Complaints — consideration by Director

(1) It shall be the duty of the Director to consider any complaint made to him that any contract term drawn up for general use is unfair, unless—

(a) the complaint appears to the Director to be frivolous or vexatious; or

(b) a qualifying body has notified the Director that it agrees to consider the complaint.

(2) The Director shall give reasons for his decision to apply or not to apply, as the case may be, for an injunction under regulation 12 in relation to any complaint which these Regulations require him to consider.

(3) In deciding whether or not to apply for an injunction in respect of a term which the Director considers to be unfair, he may, if he considers it appropriate to do so, have regard to any undertakings given to him by or on behalf of any person as to the continued use of such a term in contracts concluded with consumers.

11. Complaints — consideration by qualifying bodies

(1) If a qualifying body specified in Part One of Schedule 1 notifies the Director that it agrees to consider a complaint that any contract term drawn up for general use is unfair, it shall be under a duty to consider that complaint.

(2) Regulation 10(2) and (3) shall apply to a qualifying body which is under a duty to consider a complaint as they apply to the Director.

12. Injunctions to prevent continued use of unfair terms

(1) The Director or, subject to paragraph (2), any qualifying body may apply for an injunction (including an interim injunction) against any person appearing to the Director or that body to be using, or recommending use of, an unfair term drawn up for general use in contracts concluded with consumers.

(2) A qualifying body may apply for an injunction only where—

(a) it has notified the Director of its intention to apply at least fourteen days before the date on which the application is made, beginning with the date on which the notification was given; or

(b) the Director consents to the application being made within a shorter period.

(3) The court on an application under this regulation may grant an injunction on such terms as it thinks fit.

(4) An injunction may relate not only to use of a particular contract term drawn up for general use but to any similar term, or a term having like effect, used or recommended for use by any person.

13. Powers of the Director and qualifying bodies to obtain documents and information

(1) The Director may exercise the power conferred by this regulation for the purpose of—

(a) facilitating his consideration of a complaint that a contract term drawn up for general use is unfair; or

(b) ascertaining whether a person has complied with an undertaking or court order as to the continued use, or recommendation for use, of a term in contracts concluded with consumers.

(2) A qualifying body specified in Part One of Schedule 1 may exercise the power conferred by this regulation for the purpose of—

(a) facilitating its consideration of a complaint that a contract term drawn up for general use is unfair; or

(b) ascertaining whether a person has complied with—

(i) an undertaking given to it or to the court following an application by that body, or

(ii) a court order made on an application by that body,

as to the continued use, or recommendation for use, of a term in contracts concluded with consumers.

(3) The Director may require any person to supply to him, and a qualifying body specified in Part One of Schedule 1 may require any person to supply to it—

(a) a copy of any document which that person has used or recommended for use, at the time the notice referred to in paragraph (4) below is given, as a pre-formulated standard contract in dealings with consumers;

(b) information about the use, or recommendation for use, by that person of that document or any other such document in dealings with consumers.

(4) The power conferred by this regulation is to be exercised by a notice in writing which may—

(a) specify the way in which and the time within which it is to be complied with; and

(b) be varied or revoked by a subsequent notice.

(5) Nothing in this regulation compels a person to supply any document or information which he would be entitled to refuse to produce or give in civil proceedings before the court.

(6) If a person makes default in complying with a notice under this regulation, the court may, on the application of the Director or of the qualifying body, make such order as the court thinks fit for requiring the default to be made good, and any such order may provide that all the costs or expenses of and incidental to the application shall be borne by the person in default or by any officers of a company or other association who are responsible for its default.

14. Notification of undertakings and orders to Director

A qualifying body shall notify the Director—

(a) of any undertaking given to it by or on behalf of any person as to the continued use of a term which that body considers to be unfair in contracts concluded with consumers;

(b) of the outcome of any application made by it under regulation 12, and of the terms of any undertaking given to, or order made by, the court;

(c) of the outcome of any application made by it to enforce a previous order of the court.

15. Publication, information and advice

(1) The Director shall arrange for the publication in such form and manner as he considers appropriate, of—

(a) details of any undertaking or order notified to him under regulation 14;

(b) details of any undertaking given to him by or on behalf of any person as to the continued use of a term which the Director considers to be unfair in contracts concluded with consumers;

(c) details of any application made by him under regulation 12, and of the terms of any undertaking given to, or order made by, the court;

(d) details of any application made by the Director to enforce a previous order of the court.

(2) The Director shall inform any person on request whether a particular term to which these Regulations apply has been—

(a) the subject of an undertaking given to the Director or notified to him by a qualifying body; or

(b) the subject of an order of the court made upon application by him or notified to him by a qualifying body;
and shall give that person details of the undertaking or a copy of the order, as the case may be, together with a copy of any amendments which the person giving the undertaking has agreed to make to the term in question.

(3) The Director may arrange for the dissemination in such form and manner as he considers appropriate of such information and advice concerning the operation of these Regulations as may appear to him to be expedient to give to the public and to all persons likely to be affected by these Regulations.

Regulation 3

SCHEDULE 1
QUALIFYING BODIES
PART ONE

1. The Data Protection Registrar.
2. The Director General of Electricity Supply.
3. The Director General of Gas Supply.
4. The Director General of Electricity Supply for Northern Ireland.
5. The Director General of Gas for Northern Ireland.
6. The Director General of Telecommunications.
7. The Director General of Water Services.
8. The Rail Regulator.
9. Every weights and measures authority in Great Britain.
10. The Department of Economic Development in Northern Ireland.

PART TWO

11. Consumers' Association.

Regulation 5(5)

SCHEDULE 2
INDICATIVE AND NON-EXHAUSTIVE LIST OF TERMS WHICH MAY BE REGARDED AS UNFAIR

1. Terms which have the object or effect of—

(a) excluding or limiting the legal liability of a seller or supplier in the event of the death of a consumer or personal injury to the latter resulting from an act or omission of that seller or supplier;

(b) inappropriately excluding or limiting the legal rights of the consumer vis-à-vis the seller or supplier or another party in the event of total or partial non-performance or inadequate performance by the seller or supplier of any of the contractual obligations, including the option of offsetting a debt owed to the seller or supplier against any claim which the consumer may have against him;

(c) making an agreement binding on the consumer whereas provision of services by the seller or supplier is subject to a condition whose realisation depends on his own will alone;

(d) permitting the seller or supplier to retain sums paid by the consumer where the latter decides not to conclude or perform the contract, without providing for the consumer to receive compensation of an equivalent amount from the seller or supplier where the latter is the party cancelling the contract;

(e) requiring any consumer who fails to fulfil his obligation to pay a disproportionately high sum in compensation;

(f) authorising the seller or supplier to dissolve the contract on a discretionary basis where the same facility is not granted to the consumer, or permitting the seller or supplier to retain the sums paid for services not yet supplied by him where it is the seller or supplier himself who dissolves the contract;

(g) enabling the seller or supplier to terminate a contract of indeterminate duration without reasonable notice except where there are serious grounds for doing so;

(h) automatically extending a contract of fixed duration where the consumer does not indicate otherwise, when the deadline fixed for the consumer to express his desire not to extend the contract is unreasonably early;

(i) irrevocably binding the consumer to terms with which he had no real opportunity of becoming acquainted before the conclusion of the contract;

(j) enabling the seller or supplier to alter the terms of the contract unilaterally without a valid reason which is specified in the contract;

(k) enabling the seller or supplier to alter unilaterally without a valid reason any characteristics of the product or service to be provided;

(l) providing for the price of goods to be determined at the time of delivery or allowing a seller of goods or supplier of services to increase their price without in both cases giving the consumer the corresponding right to cancel the contract if the final price is too high in relation to the price agreed when the contract was concluded;

(m) giving the seller or supplier the right to determine whether the goods or services supplied are in conformity with the contract, or giving him the exclusive right to interpret any term of the contract;

(n) limiting the seller's or supplier's obligation to respect commitments undertaken by his agents or making his commitments subject to compliance with a particular formality;

(o) obliging the consumer to fulfil all his obligations where the seller or supplier does not perform his;

(p) giving the seller or supplier the possibility of transferring his rights and obligations under the contract, where this may serve to reduce the guarantees for the consumer, without the latter's agreement;

(q) excluding or hindering the consumer's right to take legal action or exercise any other legal remedy, particularly by requiring the consumer to take disputes exclusively to arbitration not covered by legal provisions, unduly restricting the evidence available to him or imposing on him a burden of proof which, according to the applicable law, should lie with another party to the contract.

2. Scope of paragraphs 1(g), (j) and (l)—

(a) Paragraph 1(g) is without hindrance to terms by which a supplier of financial services reserves the right to terminate unilaterally a contract of indeterminate duration without notice where there is a valid reason provided that the supplier is required to inform the other contracting party or parties thereof immediately.

(b) Paragraph 1(j) is without hindrance to terms under which a supplier of financial services reserves the right to alter the rate of interest payable by the consumer or due to the latter, or the amount of other charges for financial services without notice where there is a valid reason, provided that the supplier is required to inform the other contracting party or parties thereof at the earliest opportunity and that the latter are free to dissolve the contract immediately.

Paragraph 1(j) is also without hindrance to terms under which a seller or supplier reserves the right to alter unilaterally the conditions of a contract of indeterminate duration, provided that he is required to inform the consumer with reasonable notice and that the consumer is free to dissolve the contract.

(c) Paragraphs 1(g), (j) and (l) do not apply to:

— transactions in transferable securities, financial instruments and other products or services where the price is linked to fluctuations in a stock exchange quotation or index or a financial market rate that the seller or supplier does not control; — contracts for the purchase or sale of foreign currency, traveller's cheques or international money orders denominated in foreign currency;

(d) Paragraph 1(l) is without hindrance to price indexation clauses, where lawful, provided that the method by which prices vary is explicitly described.

Index